MARKETING

Foundations and Applications

CAROLYN F. SIEGEL
Eastern Kentucky University

GLENCOE
McGraw-Hill

New York, New York   Columbus, Ohio   Woodland Hills, California   Peoria, Illinois

Send all inquiries to:
Glencoe/McGraw-Hill
936 Eastwind Drive
Westerville, OH 43081

    Library of Congress Cataloging-in-Publication Data
Siegel, Carolyn F.
    Marketing : foundations and applications / Carolyn F. Siegel.
       p.   cm.
    ISBN 0-256-16298-0
    1. Marketing.   I. Title.
    HF5415.S467   1996
    658.8—dc20   95–4179

Printed in the United States of America.
3 4 5 6 7 8 9   073   03 02 01 00 99 98

Preface

WHY STUDY MARKETING?

As consumers in the most competitive market in the world, you already have a firsthand knowledge of marketing activities. When you turn on the television, open a magazine or newspaper, or walk through cities and towns, you are exposed to marketing campaigns aimed at informing you—the consumer—of a wide array of products, services, and careers. As a consumer, an understanding of marketing lets you see beyond the range of available products and services to the factors that determine which products are marketed and why and when they are marketed. As a consumer and perhaps a future marketer, an understanding of the marketing process, encompassing the stages of the planning process, the interrelated factors of the marketplace, and an insight into consumer buying behavior, is an invaluable career tool that will give you an advantage in jobs involving marketing activities. A solid foundation in marketing offers long-term rewards for everyone.

Marketing generates excitement—few people feel neutral about it. Marketing has been praised for contributing to a high standard of living and criticized for encouraging overconsumerism. Marketing has evolved from simple one-on-one bartering between buyer and seller to a highly sophisticated field that deeply influences our lives. Marketing is both a science and an art, based on a factual knowledge of product and the marketplace as well as an intuitive knowledge of human nature. Marketing is a richly challenging area of study. My goal in *Marketing: Foundations and Applications* is to share my enthusiasm for marketing and, in the process, guide students to become better businesspeople who can more effectively use marketing to benefit individual consumers as well as society at large.

STREAMLINED COVERAGE

Marketing: Foundations and Applications provides a comprehensive examination of the foundations of contemporary marketing in an organized, understandable, and engaging fashion. This streamlined text is briefer than many introductory marketing texts, yet marketing content has not been sacrificed—all key topics are covered in depth. The book's 15 chapters are grouped into four parts. Part 1, "Introduction: Marketplace, Decision Making and Consumers," presents the underlying concepts of marketing. Chapter 1 provides an overview of marketing, Chapter 2 focuses on making marketing decisions, and Chapter 3 examines the targets of those decisions, both personal use and business/organization consumers.

In Part 2 "Market Analysis—A Broader Perspective," Chapter 4 considers contemporary issues of importance to marketers, including ethics, societal responsibilities, regulation, and green marketing. Chapter 5 introduces the topics of cultural diversity and international marketing, making the point that as the United States becomes more diverse, an understanding of different cultures will assume greater importance in both domestic and international marketing. (Note that the issues of diversity and globalization are woven through the entire text, as they are central to contemporary marketing philosophy.) Marketing skills and technologies are discussed in Chapter 6, particularly noting technologies used in segmentation, targeting and positioning, marketing communication, and marketing decision systems.

Part 3 "The Marketing Mix," covers the Four Ps. Chapters 7 and 8 are devoted to understanding the product, developing new products, and responding to the market. Chapter 9 takes a close look at price, Chapters 10 and 11 are devoted to place (distribution), and Chapters 12 and 13 examine promotion (including advertising, personal selling, and publicity).

Chapters 14 and 15 make up Part 4, "Extending Marketing." These chapters cover the marketing of services not-for-profit marketing, and managing marketing.

Finally, three Appendixes offer valuable student resources. Appendix A, "Writing a Small Business Marketing Plan," details the necessary steps in creating an effective marketing plan geared toward small businesses. Appendix B, "Using Mathematics in Marketing Decisions," covers basic marketing math. Appendix C, "An Introduction to Marketing Careers," describes marketing-related jobs and prepares students to create a personal marketing plan.

A SYSTEMATIC APPROACH

Each chapter in *Marketing: Foundations and Applications* is organized around a numbered system of interrelated chapter objectives, major headings, "Check Your Understanding" questions, and summaries.

This unique system guides students through each chapter logically and systematically. Numbered chapter objectives are keyed to major areas of coverage in each chapter. "Check Your Understanding" questions at the end of each section check on comprehension of each objective, and keyed Review of Chapter Objectives points at the end of each chapter ensure that students have successfully met the chapter objectives. Chapter objective key points are also used to organize the *Instructor's Resource Manual* and the student *Study Guide*. Students will find this integrated approach an excellent learning tool, because it provides focus and direction for independent reading and study. Instructors can use the integrated system as a framework for building lectures, organizing marketing application activities, and developing classroom discussions.

AN INTERACTIVE AND INTEGRATED APPROACH

The many boxed features and application-oriented exercises throughout *Marketing: Foundations and Applications* are designed to keep students interested and involved—keys to focused learning.

Marketing Applications Application exercises in each chapter, designed for group and individual work, are activities that complement the text and apply concepts to realistic marketing situations. Among the activities students are asked to engage in are writing a mission statement, researching sources of international marketing information, becoming a sophisticated comparison shopper, and brainstorming about marketing plans.

What Do You Think Thought-provoking vignettes of contemporary marketing problems are presented in each chapter for students to consider and discuss. These focus on controversial marketing issues that stimulate both debate and critical thinking. Topics include the marketing of harmful products, the relationship between trade and human rights, and paying consumers to listen to advertising delivered over the phone.

Mini-Cases Examples of contemporary real-life marketing activities are presented in two case studies per chapter. These focus on a wide range of issues that marketers face domestically and internationally. Questions are provided for each mini-case.

International Marketing Reports These boxes explore the types and extent of marketing done in and for other countries. Integrating this theme into every chapter underlines the importance of taking a global perspective.

Marketing on the Internet   The rapid commercialization of the Internet is a source of growing interest to marketers. *Marketing on the Internet* is a unique special feature of this book and appears in each chapter to explore the many fascinating aspects of this emerging and dynamic electronic environment. Some people believe that marketing and the Internet were made for one another; *Marketing on the Internet* examines the possibilities.

Consumer Insight   These features in each chapter discuss the role of consumers as a target of marketing as well as a force to which marketers must respond and react when developing marketing plans and strategies.

Career Watch   These profiles provide a glimpse into the working lives of marketers in a range of businesses, from the automobile industry to the fashion world, the sports industry, and food services. These boxes give students insight into the many ways in which marketing skills are important in a wide variety of career fields.

Key Terms/Discussion Questions   These end-of-chapter features keep students focused on key concepts and themes in each chapter. Key terms are also called out in the margin where they appear in the chapter and are defined in a text glossary. Objective and essay discussion questions are included to be used for homework or as a basis of class discussion.

SUPPORT FOR INSTRUCTORS AND STUDENTS

Instructor's Resource Manual   The *Instructor's Resource Manual* that accompanies *Marketing: Foundations and Applications* contains a lecture outline for each chapter keyed to the text's numbered chapter objective system, teaching suggestions, sample syllabi, suggestions for the use of marketing applications, additional exercises and cases beyond the student text including Internet exercises, advice about the use of supplemental materials, suggested answers for text discussion questions, cases, applications, and activities, and recommendations on the use of the student *Study Guide.*

Test Bank   A test bank is also available with a comprehensive set of test items and answers for each text chapter. (This also comes in computerized form.)

Student Study Guide   Each chapter in the student *Study Guide* is keyed to the corresponding text chapter and includes a chapter outline with sections keyed to the numbered learning objective system. Chapters include definitions of key terms, objective and essay study questions, and a new mini-case with questions. "Marketing Yourself" exercises help students prepare for a job search in marketing careers.

ACKNOWLEDGEMENTS

The completion of a project of this complexity is due in great measure to the encouragement, firm guidance, and hard work of the gifted people at Mirror Press, David Helmstadter, Carla Tishler, and Nancy Seglin, and at Richard D. Irwin, notably Amy Lund. Their expertise, good judgment, and patience are deeply appreciated. My loving family—Malcolm, Erik, and Mark—have endured an absentee wife and mom for many long months with unwavering love and support. Thanks also to my students who, over the years, have stimulated me to find better ways of teaching marketing. I hope that by reading this book you come to share my fascination with this dynamic activity we call *marketing*.

Many people contribute to the development of a book. In particular, the following marketing professionals and marketers are thanked for their considerable assistance in reviewing *Marketing: Foundations and Applications*.

Larry Basham, Kentucky College of Business, Louisville, KY; Subodh Bhat, San Francisco State University, San Francisco, CA; Waleck Dalpour, University of Maine, Farmington, ME; John Todd III, Miami-Jacobs College, Dayton, OH; Ted Valvoda, Lakeland Community College, Mentor, OH; Charles Vitaska, Metropolitan State University, Denver, CO; Randy Wade, Rogue Community College, Grant's Pass, OR; Jim Malone, University of Massachusetts, Amherst, MA; Peter McClure, University of Massachusetts, Boston, MA; Alexander Mosely, Miami Dade Community College, Miami, FL; Frank Pribyl, Western State College of Colorado, Gunnison, CO; John Reino, Greenfield Community College, Greenfield, MA; Ronald Taylor, Mississippi State University, Starkville, MS; Carolyn Tripp, University of Tennessee–Martin, Martin, TN; David Wheeler, Suffolk University, Boston, MA; Carla Dando, National College, Rapid City, SD; Robin Delaney, The Hickey School, St. Louis, MO; Dean Headley, Wichita State University, Wichita, KS; Richard Koch, National College, Albuquerque, NM; Tom Maguire, Bryant & Stratton, Albany, NY; North Smith, Rutledge College, Fayetteville, NC; Roni Miller, Fashion Institute of Design and Marketing, Sylmar, CA.

Brief Contents

*Introduction:
Marketplace,
Decision
Making, and
Consumers*

*Market
Analysis—A
Broader
Perspective*

*The Marketing
Mix*

P A R T 4

Extending Marketing

Contents

PART

2

*Market
Analysis—A
Broader
Perspective*

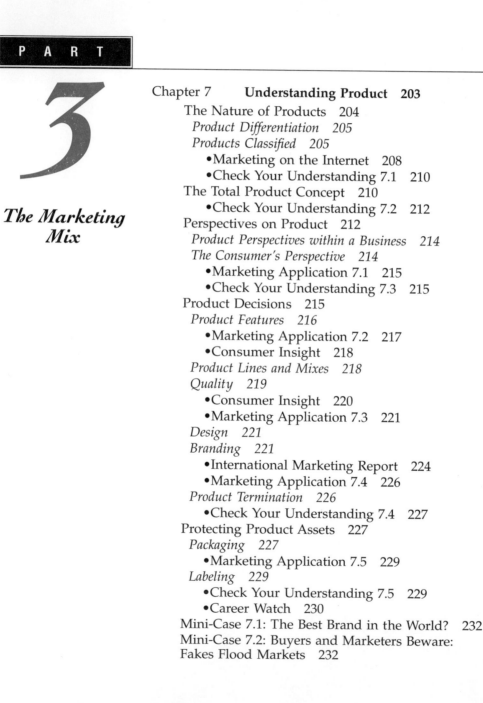

*The Marketing
Mix*

P A R T

4

*Extending
Marketing*

Introduction: Marketplace, Decision Making, and Consumers

An Introduction to Marketing

Chapter Objectives

After studying Chapter 1 you should be able to

1. Define *marketing* and explain its origins and contemporary meanings.
2. Identify the key foundation concepts of marketing.
3. Explain why it is important to study marketing.
4. Discuss why and how marketing is still evolving.
5. Describe how marketers use the marketing mix variables to satisfy consumers and achieve organizational goals.

*M*arketing is one of the broadest areas of study in the business fields. It is a dynamic process that touches us from birth to death. We are all familiar with marketing from our personal experiences and observations as consumers in the most advanced consumer-oriented society in the world. Our complex contemporary marketing system of buyers and sellers demands that businesses effectively compete in the marketplace—if they do not, they will not survive. They must effectively manage their resources (people, money, technology, and materials) and efficiently use marketing tools in order to be able to make attractive offers that satisfy and, hopefully, delight their target markets. While you read Chapter 1 and begin to draw conclusions about marketing as it contributes to our society, consider this question: What would *your* life be like if there were no marketing?

A Trip to the
Food-&-More Store

Sara and Jay, a young married couple, are talking as they push a shopping cart half-filled with groceries down the aisle of their favorite grocery store. Both are sipping cups of fresh hot coffee provided free by the store manager, while background music plays on the store's stereo system.

As they enter aisle nine, laundry products, their eyes are drawn to the bright red instant coupon machines (see Photo 1.1) that stick out from the detergent shelves, flapping cents-off coupons that beckon them as they pass by. Sara turns toward a mass of brightly colored detergent boxes. She takes a box from the shelf and says, "Let's get this one. The package is recycled and it's an ultra, which means it's concentrated and biodegradable; more friendly to the environment." Jay agrees and they move on to aisle 10, eggs and refrigerated dairy products. As they approach the egg display, Sara searches her coupon organizer for the 55-cent Egg Beaters coupon she clipped from the morning's newspaper. Coupon in hand, she takes a carton of Egg Beaters from the shelf and places it in the cart.

Their choices made, the couple moves on to aisle 11, continuing the same orderly progression of being informed and making decisions until all of their shopping is completed. Maneuvering their filled shopping cart into a checkout line, they pay for their purchases with a national credit card issued by a bank in a city over 2,000 miles from their home.[1]

Sara and Jay are satisfied with their trip to the grocery store. After all, they found everything they wanted on the well-stocked shelves, saved money by using cents-off coupons, enjoyed a free cup of fresh coffee, paid for their purchases by credit card, and had their bagged groceries brought to their car by a careful and courteous store employee.

What we take for granted in the way we shop, where we shop, and the products we shop for reflects the breadth of contemporary marketing activities. Marketing strives to facilitate exchanges between buyers and sellers in the marketplace and, in the process, makes a significant contribution to the high standard of living enjoyed by the majority of consumers in the United States.

Photo 1.1

Instant coupon machines offer instant access to savings and an incentive to buy NOW.

Marketing Application 1.1

Shopping for groceries is a necessary task for most Americans, yet it is often not a particularly pleasant one. This troubles marketers, because satisfying customers is a goal that guides marketing activities. Marketers seek **consumer insight,** understanding the consumer's perspective about marketplace activities, in order to be able to develop better strategies for delivering customer satisfaction.

This is a good point to begin developing your own consumer insight skills. Divide an 8½- by 11-inch sheet of paper into three equal lengthwise columns. Label the left column "Likes," the middle column "Dislikes," and the right column "Solutions." In the "Likes" column, list everything you like about the grocery store where you routinely shop. In the "Dislikes" column, list everything you dislike. (Note: If you are not familiar with a grocery store, use another type of store instead.)

Now, take the marketer's role and consider each "Dislike" as a problem that can be solved. For each "Dislike," identify a possible solution and make a note of it in the "Solutions" column. To illustrate how consumers differ, compare your list with those of others in your class. How alike are the lists? What conclusions can you draw from this activity about obstacles to developing consumer insights? ■

WHAT IS MARKETING?

Marketing is not a particularly easy thing to define.[2] Far too often, you'll hear someone say, "Marketing? Why, it's just selling!" This is a narrow view of what is actually a broad and expanding set of activities. The American Marketing Association (AMA), an international association of individuals who practice, study, and teach marketing, characterizes marketing this way:

> **Marketing** is the process of planning and executing the conception, pricing, promotion and distribution of ideas, goods and services to create exchanges that satisfy individual and organizational objectives.[3]

The AMA is describing what most of us were already doing at a fairly early age. If, as a teenager, you baby-sat or mowed lawns, you were marketing your talent and time in exchange for something you valued—spending money. Later, you may have worked for McDonald's or as a grocery bagger, participating in customer service activities and receiving a paycheck for your efforts. If you ran for class office at school or sent a résumé to a prospective employer, you were marketing yourself. You formed insights about marketing activities, even if you weren't aware of them. For example, try answering the following questions about price, product, and place:

- Is three dollars a reasonable amount of money to spend on a stick of ordinary chewing gum?

Objective 1 Define *marketing* and explain its origins and contemporary meanings.

consumer insight
Understanding the consumer's perspective about marketplace activities.

marketing The process of planning and executing the conception, pricing, promotion, and distribution of ideas, goods, and services to create exchanges that satisfy individual and organizational objectives.

- Who is more likely to survive a head-on automobile crash at 65 miles per hour, the driver of a car equipped with a driver-side air bag and an antilock braking system or a driver whose car is not similarly equipped?
- Where would you shop for low-price, everyday household items if you were a cost-conscious consumer: at a discount store or a full-service department store?

Obviously, no stick of ordinary chewing gum is worth three dollars. Likewise, in most situations, having air bags and an antilock braking system is safer than not having them. Finally, a discount store is more likely to have everyday household items at a lower price than a full-service department store. We know this because the human mind is like a sponge, absorbing information gained from our own and others' experiences and from advertisements, salespeople, magazine articles, and television programs. We sort, process, categorize, and store this information until it is needed to help us make decisions in the marketplace.

The goal of this book is to build on your personal knowledge to develop a more sophisticated and professional understanding of marketing. Let's begin by examining the definition of marketing in greater detail and identifying some foundation concepts that underlie it.

Origins of Marketing

If you were visiting one of the older cities of Europe and traveled to the city center, you would probably find evidence that the center was once the site of a bustling open-air market, where people brought their goods to barter and sell. There are still open-air markets in many places in Europe and around the world, where people gather to buy or barter for fresh eggs, cheeses, chickens, flowers, cloth, and all types of goods, such as the pottery shown in Photo 1.2. The open-air market was probably the starting point for the development of the term *marketing,* which meant bringing your goods to a market.

Contemporary Usage

Today, when we speak of marketing we include the activities of for-profit businesses, government, not-for-profit organizations, institutions, and individuals. We market many different things in addition to goods, including ideas, causes, places, services, performances, groups, and people. Marketing targets are our present and potential customers. These may include personal use consumers, like Sara and Jay, as well as other businesses and organizations who purchase products for resale, as inputs to production, or to run their own operations.

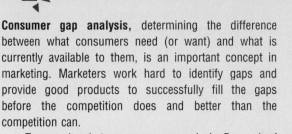

Marketing Application 1.2

Consumer gap analysis, determining the difference between what consumers need (or want) and what is currently available to them, is an important concept in marketing. Marketers work hard to identify gaps and provide good products to successfully fill the gaps before the competition does and better than the competition can.

Try your hand at consumer gap analysis. For each of the following products, identify the gap (or gaps) the product filled at the time it was introduced:

- Automobile.
- Automated teller machine.
- Fat-free bakery goods.

From your own experience, identify a gap that you wish a product would be developed to fill. Do you think this gap is felt by other consumers? Does it represent a feasible marketing opportunity? What obstacles might prevent this product from being marketed? Bring your gap analysis to class for discussion. ■

Photo 1.2

A Chinese open-air market that offers goods.

Marketers try to identify gaps in the marketplace that represent consumers' unfilled needs and wants. Then, marketers develop products to satisfy those needs and wants and make those products available when, where, how, and at a price consumers are willing to pay. Marketing activities create value. **Value** is defined by consumers and is the worth added to products through marketing activities designed to satisfy, and thus build customer loyalty so they will make many repeat purchases.

consumer gap analysis
Determining the difference between what consumers need (or want) and what is currently available to them.

value The consumer's definition of the worth added to products through marketing activities.

Consumer Insight

How many consumers are there? Figure 1.1 shows projected populations and projected annual population growth for the year 2000 for the world, the United States, its North American Free Trade Agreement (NAFTA) partners Canada and Mexico, our major international competitors the European Union and Japan, and China. The combined Year 2000 projected population for the NAFTA nations is over 400 million people, far less than China's current population of over one billion. Many marketers believe China will be the most fought-over consumer market in the 21st century, as the Chinese people's standard of living rises along with their purchasing power (resources available for consumption purposes) and interest (desire to consume). ■

Figure 1.1

Consumer Insight: Population

	Projected Year 2000 Population (in millions)	Projected Annual Population Growth
World	5,500	2.0%
United States	270	0.8
Canada	30	1.1
Mexico	110	2.2
European Union	350	0.3
Japan	130	0.4
China	1,300	1.6

marketers The people and organizations that perform the various marketing functions.

Marketers are the people and organizations that perform various marketing functions (see Figure 1.2). Marketers connect a business and its target customers in exchanges. Not all marketing activities are like personal selling, which requires direct contact with customers. Many marketers never personally interact with customers, yet their work requires that they use information about customers' needs, wants, and behaviors to develop insights for making effective marketing decisions. In making a purchase, customers surrender information about their needs, wants, and behaviors. Marketers collect and study this information and information from many other different sources and use it to make strategic and tactical decisions designed to facilitate subsequent exchanges. Increasingly, marketing information is captured electronically by scanners and processed by computers.

Marketing is closely linked with other disciplines. Marketers use information and skills gained both from marketing studies and studies in the social sciences and other areas of business. Likewise, in businesses that have adopted the marketing concept philosophy, marketing links operational areas by joining them together in a common philosophy of doing business. This concept proposes that

MARKETING FUNCTIONS	
Function	**Activities Related to . . .**
Exchange	Buying, selling, and leasing products; communicating information about products; negotiating product exchanges.
Physical Distribution	Transporting and storing products.
Servicing	Information gathering, marketing research; financing the activities; standardizing and grading products; assuming risks involved in the processing of products and their transfer from seller to buyer.

Figure 1.2

Marketing Functions

Marketing functions are the activities that must be performed by individuals and organizations during the process of providing products for exchange. The functions are often grouped by similar activities.

all operational areas place consumer satisfaction first—that satisfying consumers *is* the reason for the business.

In a marketing system, sellers bring offers to the marketplace (see Figure 1.3) often with the assistance of wholesalers and retailers. Offers may take the form of tangible goods (shoes); services (haircuts); ideas (stop drunk driving); places (Walt Disney World); people (a candidate for mayor); causes (American Cancer Society); performances (the Nutcracker ballet); experiences (swimming with dolphins); or organizations (U.S. Army). In return, buyers offer something of value to sellers, usually cash or credit, but sometimes labor or even other products.

What consumers value (and sellers are motivated to offer) is influenced by cultural factors, including the accepted standards of a society, its cultural norms, and group values. Consumers are directly influenced by their families and friends, and what they see on

Figure 1.3 Marketing in a Social System

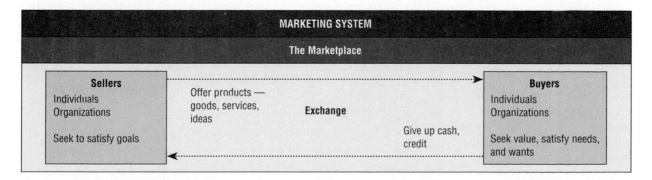

television, read in newspapers, and learn in school. Through marketing exchanges, consumers seek to satisfy their needs and wants; sellers seek to satisfy organizational goals.

Check Your Understanding *1.1*	1. In your own words, what is marketing? 2. Explain how sending a résumé to a prospective employer is marketing. Who is the buyer? Who is the seller? 3. Does marketing occur when seven families on your street get together to have a garage sale? Explain.

FOUNDATION CONCEPTS

Objective 2 Identify the key foundation concepts of marketing.

Every area of study, whether it is psychology, biology, engineering, or marketing, has its own foundation concepts that help define the discipline, direct research efforts, and guide practical applications. Let's examine the foundation concepts in marketing: exchange, products, sellers, buyers, and satisfaction.

Exchange

exchange A voluntary trading of items of value between parties.

In our opening story, Sara and Jay are involved in trading something of value (their money) for products in the Food-&-More Store. **Exchange** means a voluntary trading of things of value between parties, with the expectation that the parties will be better off after the trade than they were before it.[4] Two children trading baseball cards are involved in exchange, as is a computer manufacturer buying microprocessing chips. Sometimes exchange may occur directly between buyer and seller. A direct exchange occurs when Sara orders an exercise machine for Jay by telephone straight from the manufacturer. Most personal use consumers like Sara and Jay make purchases from retailers (e.g., the grocery store) who buy products from wholesalers and manufacturers for resale. Such purchases represent indirect exchanges between the ultimate buyer and the producer, whose products are brought to the marketplace by others.

Five conditions must be met for exchange to occur. If any one is not met, exchange is blocked:

1. At least two parties must be voluntarily involved—a buyer and a seller.
2. Each must have something of value to offer to the other.
3. Buyers and sellers must be able to communicate in order to establish terms for the exchange.

4. The parties must be willing to trade.
5. Both buyer and seller must have the authority to trade, make the purchase, or offer.

Even when all these conditions for exchange are met, circumstances may still prevent the exchange from being completed. For example, when an ice storm caused widespread power outages in northern Florida over Christmas 1989, all of the conditions for exchange were met, yet buyers and sellers were unable to complete their transactions because electric cash registers couldn't operate without power. A powerful and unexpected intervening variable (the weather) blocked what should have been viable exchanges.

Products

The American Marketing Association's definition of marketing identifies "ideas, goods and services" as products offered by sellers to buyers. **Products** are the things of value that the seller brings to the exchange and the buyer needs and/or wants.

> **products** The items of value that the seller brings to the exchange and the buyer needs and/or wants.

Marketers seek to create **utility,** the benefit or value buyers receive from exchange. In economic terms, the sole reason for exchange is to create utility. Four types of utility are of particular concern to marketing:

> **utility** The benefit or value that buyers receive from the exchange.

1. *Place*—Convenient locations where products are exchanged.
2. *Time*—The availability of products when needed.
3. *Possession*—The actual transfer of ownership to consumers.
4. *Form*—The benefits consumers realize from the characteristics of the product (as in its shape, color, size, smell, or taste).

Marketers have the greatest control over place, time, and possession utilities. Marketers do not control product, but they often have significant input into product design and production because of the knowledge they can contribute about consumers' needs, wants, and behaviors.

Sellers

A **market,** in economic terms, consists of sellers and buyers. A **marketplace** is where exchanges are negotiated and made. Except for a monopoly, a market has many sellers, often competing head-to-head with other sellers targeting comparable products to the same buyers. In the carbonated nonalcoholic beverage market there are two giant sellers, Coca-Cola and PepsiCo, offering relatively inexpensive

> **market** Buyers and sellers.
> **marketplace** Where exchanges are negotiated and made.

substitute products to hundreds of millions of buyers around the world. Seller rivalries are also very common in other industries, as shown in a comparative advertisement for automobiles (Photo 1.3).

Sellers seek to gain market advantage over the competition and sustain it. There are many ways to achieve a competitive advantage and no single right way that fits all situations.

Business sellers range in size from multinational global giants like Procter & Gamble to small, independent, owner-owned and operated businesses like your local dry cleaner, florist, or restaurant. Sellers also can be governments and not-for-profit organizations like museums, universities, and charities. Other sellers are places and persons. Even nonprofit sellers participate in exchange (although they lack the profit motive).

Buyers

Like sellers, buyers also come in many forms and sizes, including individuals, households, businesses, and organizations. For our purposes, potential buyers are categorized broadly as either personal use consumers or business/organization consumers. Consumers who are specifically targeted for marketing efforts are current or potential customers.

Buyers have considerable leverage in the marketplace because they can vote with their pocketbooks to favor one seller over another. Because one condition for exchange is the voluntary participation of buyers and sellers, free exchange means freedom of choice. Remember—in the final analysis the assumption is that both the buyer and the seller will be better off as a result of their exchange, so there is plenty of room for negotiation as both seek an advantage.

Photo 1.3

Audi targets its advertisements against rivals in the same target market.

Normally, sellers outnumber buyers. However, when demand exceeds supply, buyers compete among themselves for sellers' products. Some expensive restaurants limit dinner reservations in order to artificially restrict supply, thereby creating an exclusive image and encouraging buyers to compete for reservations. Demand may exceed supply when natural supply interruptions are caused by weather and crop failures, or when production is interrupted or falls short because of management's miscalculations or production problems. **Demarketing** is the term used to describe a situation when consumer demand is greater than product supply and the marketer must act to dampen demand temporarily or permanently, often through price, place, or promotion activities. Nabisco's SnackWell's Devil's Food Cookie Cakes were demarketed when consumer demand nationwide still exceeded supply a year after the product's launch. Nabisco's fat-free, cholesterol-free chocolate cake and marshmallow cookie is a dieter's delight that tastes good. Although consumers were frenzied to get the cookie, stores couldn't keep the cookies stocked. Because Nabisco was caught off guard by the extent of the demand, the company had to ration or suspend shipments to many parts of the country. Nabisco lost sales and apologized to consumers in a national television commercial, promising to bake and distribute more cookies as soon as possible.[5] The company tried to divert demand by urging consumers to try other cookies in the SnackWell line.

demarketing A situation in which consumer demand is greater than product supply and the marketer must act to temporarily or permanently dampen demand.

Satisfaction

Picture yourself running a 10K race under a blistering sun on a 90° day. As you near the finish line, your body is crying out for liquids. You may need liquids to replenish yourself, but you *want* a specially formulated branded sports beverage like Gatorade. A **need** represents a state of tension caused by a deprivation, in this case of fluids. A **want** is a desire or preference that represents a socially molded need. Other runners also need liquids, but instead of Gatorade they may prefer "designer" waters such as Evian or Perrier. In reality, if runners' needs are powerful enough, they will drink whatever refreshing liquid is offered and disregard product or brand preference. When you are deprived of something, such as liquids during a race, your frustration level increases and you are motivated to act to remove the frustration and achieve satisfaction. How you satisfy that need is socially influenced, often through marketing activities that promote a particular brand or product.

need A state of tension caused by a deprivation.

want A desire or preference that represents a socially molded need.

A widely used concept of shared human needs was first proposed in the 1940s by Professor Abraham Maslow, a psychologist. He arranged needs hierarchically on the assumption that biogenic,

Marketing Application 1.3

Marketing is traditionally directed toward stimulating consumer demand, not dampening it. However, there are times when demarketing is called for in order to regulate demand that exceeds product supply. Try your hand at developing a demarketing strategy. Assume the role of a marketing consultant to Bridge State Park. You have been told that the park opens May 1 and closes October 1. During the peak visitor months of June, July, and August, the number of tourists wanting to use the facility is so great that it is unsafe for visitors and destructive to the park's vegetation. Currently, a one-dollar fee is charged each car (regardless of the number of occupants) entering the park during the months it is open. How can the park dampen excessive consumer demand during the peak summer months without permanently alienating the public? Bring your demarketing strategies to class for discussion. ■

physiological needs for such essentials as food and water must be satisfied before a person can begin to think about higher-level psychological needs for such things as social belonging and achievement.[6] Needs are powerful motivators of human behavior. Marketers must understand human needs in order to be able to successfully develop need-satisfying products and want-activating promotions. Figure 1.4 presents Maslow's hierarchy of human needs, along with some advertising slogans designed to appeal to them.

Figure 1.4

Maslow's Hierarchy of
Human Needs "Translated"
by Advertising.

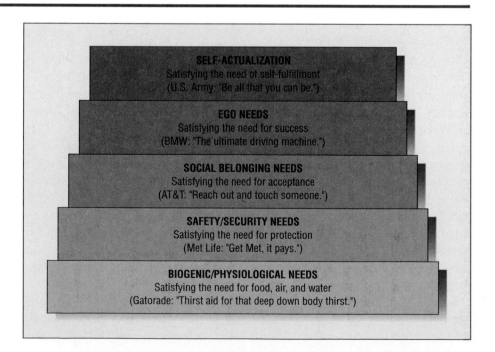

SELF-ACTUALIZATION
Satisfying the need of self-fulfillment
(U.S. Army: "Be all that you can be.")

EGO NEEDS
Satisfying the need for success
(BMW: "The ultimate driving machine.")

SOCIAL BELONGING NEEDS
Satisfying the need for acceptance
(AT&T: "Reach out and touch someone.")

SAFETY/SECURITY NEEDS
Satisfying the need for protection
(Met Life: "Get Met, it pays.")

BIOGENIC/PHYSIOLOGICAL NEEDS
Satisfying the need for food, air, and water
(Gatorade: "Thirst aid for that deep down body thirst.")

Consumer Satisfaction

Consumer satisfaction is very important to marketers. Many businesses pride themselves on having adopted the marketing concept philosophy of doing business, which stresses consumer satisfaction. Such things as a quality product, fair price, good service, and convenience can satisfy customers and increase the probability of repeat purchases.[7] Yet, there are significant problems associated with trying to measure satisfaction, let alone deliver it. It is not always clear what satisfies consumers, and often consumers themselves don't know or won't tell. Although price is the key consideration for buyers in some situations, high quality may prevail in other situations. This situational influence complicates our understanding of what satisfies consumers and under what circumstances it does so. Marketers know it is harder to find a new customer than keep an old one, yet keeping an old customer happy is a considerable challenge for even the most astute business.

---

1. What are the foundation concepts of marketing?
2. Explain the concept of exchange.
3. Why is satisfaction such an important concept in marketing?

Check Your Understanding
1.2

WHY STUDY MARKETING?

There are many good reasons why it is important for you to study marketing. The following section will help you understand these reasons and, hopefully, encourage you to set a personal goal to learn as much as you can about marketing in class and afterward through your life experiences.

Objective 3 Explain why it is important to study marketing.

Marketing in Our Daily Lives

The United States of America is the most attractive consumer market in the world. Consumer spending by over 262 million Americans accounts for more than two-thirds of the United States's economic activity. American consumers are touched by marketing every day, because they are the hotly contested targets of marketers' efforts. Marketing communications are pervasive, appearing on television, in stores, on blimps in the sky, at sporting events, and even on clothing. Marketers study consumer purchasing behaviors and preferences and observe consumers as they make purchases. Because it

Marketing Application 1.4

Businesses often hire marketing experts to help them gather information about customer satisfaction. Perhaps you have participated in such an activity by filling out a customer satisfaction survey. Assume that you have been hired as a marketing consultant by a small business to develop a written survey that will determine customer satisfaction with the business. To help focus your thoughts, select as your imagined employer any small business where you frequently shop. This can be a franchise of a national chain (like a McDonald's) or a locally owned and operated business. Begin your customer satisfaction survey with a brief set of instructions on how customers should complete the survey. Then write 5 to 10 customer satisfaction questions. Bring your survey and a short explanation of how, when, where, and to whom you would administer the survey to class for discussion. ∎

is virtually impossible to avoid being the target of marketing activities, it is in your own best interest to learn everything you can about marketing. By becoming better informed about how marketing works, you can become a more careful, competent, and satisfied consumer.

Consumer Responsibilities

When Sara and Jay found everything they wanted on the well-stocked shelves of the Food-&-More Store, they didn't consider what it cost to stock those shelves, produce the many alternative brands, transport the products, or advertise them. It is estimated that for every dollar spent on a purchase, marketing activities account for more than 50 cents. Critics suggest that the expense of marketing is too great. They blame marketing for inciting consumers to indulge in excessive numbers of exchanges and to be overly demanding in their expectations for satisfaction. As a consumer, you have a voice in the debates over the issues of marketing expense, materialism, conspicuous consumption, and the quality of life as they relate to marketplace choices.

Self-interest, as well as concern for the welfare of those who are less fortunate or not competent to make wise choices, should motivate consumers to watch over sellers to guard against ethical shortcomings. Consumers can form powerful citizen groups to affect changes in the marketplace. For example, consumer efforts motivated some tuna fish processors to stop using drift nets that trapped and killed dolphins (see Photo 1.4), prompted McDonald's to speed its return to paper packaging, and inspired legislators to pass laws restricting advertising to children.

Photo 1.4

Marketers are aware of issues that touch the public's emotions and influence purchasing, as shown by the "dolphin safe" logo on this product.

Marketing Careers

It is estimated that between 25 and 50 percent of the United States's workforce is directly or indirectly involved in marketing activities. This includes 19.6 million people working in retailing, the 6.2 million in wholesaling, and the 5.6 million in transportation.[8] Considering the dynamic nature of marketing and the diverse areas in which marketing activities take place, it's reasonable to expect that you may find a marketing career to appeal to your special interests. Marketing promotions and particularly advertising will appeal to people with creative skills. Transportation logistics, marketing models, and marketing decision support systems will challenge the mathematically inclined. Consumer behavior will intrigue people-watchers. International marketing may beckon students seeking foreign business experience. If your interest is more general, look carefully at *all* areas of marketing.

The outlook is good for marketing job growth through the beginning of the next century. According to the U.S. Department of Labor, job growth in marketing and sales is expected to increase 20.6 percent between 1992 and 2005.[9] This reflects several converging factors, including projections for a growing economy, competition within such recently deregulated industries as banking and communications, growing foreign competition in the United States's domestic market and abroad, and increased marketing by hospitals, schools, and governments. Many jobs will be in smaller businesses, which are credited with creating many jobs.

Consumer Insight

Smaller businesses in many parts of the world, including fully industrialized nations, are regarded as important stimuli for economic growth. In regions ranging from Eastern and Western Europe to China, Latin America, and the United States, smaller businesses are creating jobs and fueling innovation and change. They range from low-tech businesses in food services and trade contracting to high-tech businesses in computers, data processing, scientific equipment manufacturing, and medical products. More women and minorities are both working in and owning smaller businesses. Continued good job growth is predicted for small and mid-size businesses in the United States. Many recent graduates find jobs in smaller businesses, where employees throughout the business, regardless of their job titles, are often called on to perform marketing activities. Fewer than 10 percent of the 4.6 million jobs created from 1989 to 1994 were in Fortune 500 companies. ■

J. A. Byrne, "Enterprise," *Business Week/Enterprise 1993*, 1993, pp. 12–18; R. Piirto, "Women, Minorities Own More Small Businesses," *The Wall Street Journal*, August 12, 1992, p. B1; H. Gleckman, "Small Is Powerful: Meet the Giant-Killers," *Business Week/Enterprise 1993*, 1993, pp. 68–73; D. Warner, "Small Businesses Growing in Number, Creating Jobs," *Nation's Business*, 83, no. 2 (1995), p. 6.

Importance to Business

Marketing is a key factor in determining whether or not a business or organization will be successful. In the United States, many markets are mature and saturated, which means that growth opportunities are becoming limited. Even in mature markets, however, market share can be captured from competitors through the astute use of the **marketing mix variables (Four Ps)**—product, price, place (distribution), and promotion. (These are discussed at length in Chapters 7 through 13.) Therefore, many businesses are becoming more marketing-oriented. Marketing has been called the competitive advantage of the 1990s.

marketing mix variables (Four Ps) The Four Ps: product, price, place, and promotion.

Among the operational areas of business, only marketing is directly responsible for generating revenue. The importance of marketing to business is reflected in the number of chief executive officers who advance to these positions after spending their careers in marketing. In colleges and universities, marketing plays an increasingly vital role in generating student enrollments. In health care facilities, marketing attracts patients as well as attending clinicians. In these and similar cases, marketing activities are critical to organizational success, if not survival.

Finally, there is a very powerful argument for learning as much about marketing as possible, even if you have no intention of ever working in the field. If you are going to become an accountant, a financial officer, a production manager, or take some other business-related position, chances are at some point you will work with someone who is in marketing. An understanding of the background perspectives of people trained in business areas other than your own can help establish a more productive work environment. In businesses operating under the marketing concept philosophy, knowledge of marketing can also provide insights on how to do your own job more effectively.

Marketing and Global Competitiveness

The United States consumer marketplace remains a competitive battlefield for both domestic and foreign businesses. In order to grow, many American businesses must look abroad to create markets and become global competitors. For example, Coca-Cola's international soft drink sales increased 28.7 percent between 1989 and 1990, to $10.2 billion, while its domestic sales for the period grew by less than half that amount.[10] Coca-Cola is not alone in reporting international sales greater than those in the domestic U.S. market. Although Coke is perhaps the world's first and most successful global product (see Photo 1.5), there are many other world-class American businesses, including Procter & Gamble, IBM, Ford Motor Co., H. J. Heinz, Kodak, KFC, Tambrands, and Nike (which in 1991 had a remarkable 20.7 percent world market share in athletic footwear).[11] These businesses and others make skillful use of marketing to achieve international success.

Check Your Understanding
1.3

1. Of the reasons given for studying marketing, identify the ones that are most important to you.
2. How can marketing contribute to a standard of living?
3. How is your daily life affected by marketing?

Photo 1.5

International labels (from top left clockwise) in Arabic, Polish, Hebrew, Chinese, Thai, Japanese, and French show the worldwide appeal of Coca-Cola.

THE EVOLUTION OF MARKETING

Objective 4 Discuss why and how marketing is still evolving.

Marketing is a dynamic process that continues to evolve as society, technologies, and markets change. Contemporary marketing is evolving rapidly as marketers learn how to use new information technologies to reach consumers more efficiently and effectively. Figure 1.5 organizes marketing historically into two broad overlapping time periods. The first period was the Individual Era, in which the focus was first on exchange between individuals and, later, between individuals and small businesses. During the second period, the Industrial Revolution led to the establishment of larger businesses and the Organization Era. The times on the time line in Figure 1.5 are not exact, because it is rarely possible to pinpoint with certainty when activities and dominant philosophies shift.

The Individual Era

During the first period, from the earliest North American settlements in the 1600s through the late 1700s, exchange was primarily between individuals, and production and marketing as we know them were mostly local in scope and associated with small, single-product-line businesses. We enter the time line during the settlement period, before the United States existed as a nation. Some organized

Figure 1.5   The Continuing Evolution of Marketing

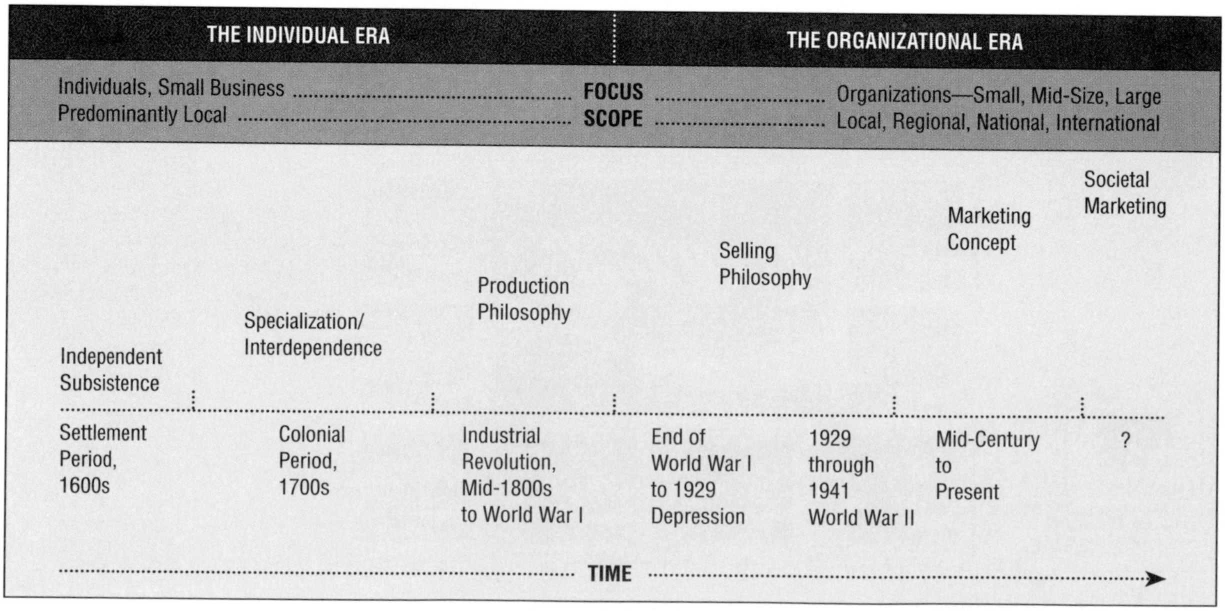

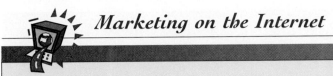 *Marketing on the Internet*

Marketing on-line on the Internet has become a hot topic these days. Many marketers believe that marketing and the Internet were made for one another. Some see it as an incredible opportunity to reach business and personal use consumers directly through their office or home computers in the ultimate application of niche marketing (highly targeted marketing designed to reach small numbers of very select consumers); others see it as a trendy novelty.

What is the Internet? It is a large number of computer networks in the United States and around the world that are linked at incredible speeds through physical connections (computers, modems, and telephones). With the right hardware and software, Internet users can send and receive text messages, images, sounds, and video. By linking your office or home computer to the Internet, you can set up an electronic mailbox (e-mail), browse the products of virtual merchants in electronic shopping malls, search for an advertising agency and view samples of their work, perform a reference search in books and journals, tour an art gallery, download software, listen to a compact disc, play games, "talk" on screen in real time to people with similar interests, make airline reservations, and, in some parts of the country, order a pizza from your local Pizza Hut!

The convergence of the telephone, computer, and television is already radically changing the way many people work, shop, and play. In each of the following chapters, we will explore some of the exciting things happening in *Marketing on the Internet.* ■

K. Shermach, "Business Marketers Are Heavy Users of Interactive Catalogs," *Marketing News* 29, no. 2 (January 16, 1995), p. 15; Associated Press, "Infohome Could Become a Reality within Five Years," *Marketing News* 29, no. 4 (February 13, 1995), p. 11; V. Clift, "On-Line Marketing: Hot Opportunity or a Trendy Novelty?" *Marketing News* 28, no. 22 (October 24, 1994) pp. 13, 43; B. Lamons, "Interactive Reveille Sounds for Agencies," *Marketing News* 20, no. 22 (October 24, 1994), p. 12; P. Huber, "Madison Avenue Meets the Net," *Forbes* 154, no. 14 (December 19, 1994), p. 306.

trading existed, but economic activity was mainly individual and family subsistence was predominately based on farming and hunting. The earliest settlers were both producer and consumer; a surplus was not traded, only stored for future consumption. People were self-sufficient, and markets and marketing as we know them in a contemporary sense did not exist.

Trading emerged in a decentralized fashion as individuals began to specialize in tasks, thereby achieving a division of labor. This was a more efficient means of ensuring survival, even as it meant greater dependence between people. Decentralized trading occurred without intermediaries; individuals traded one on one, bartering for goods and services.

In the next phase of the Individual Era, during the Colonial period, centralized markets developed with intermediaries facilitating trade between sellers and buyers in towns and villages. Many small businesses flourished—for example, silversmiths, coopers, and shopkeepers. Often, intermediaries took possession of goods or handled them on a consignment basis, receiving payment when the goods were sold. Clothing, farm implements, and household items were made to order to fit specific customer needs. Barter was common. Small factories developed; often, they were water powered or relied on hand labor.

International Marketing Report

Three centuries after the Colonial period, barter continues to flourish, even in technologically advanced countries. Businesses specialize in mediating barter trades between other businesses, as shown in Photo 1.6. A modern version of barter—countertrade—occurs when a business operating in a country that lacks hard currency or has a nonconvertible currency arranges to pay for purchased goods with other goods. This modern international barter system is illustrated by PepsiCo's $3 billion deal with the former Soviet Union. Pepsi bartered its bottled cola product along with the technology of producing it, for Stolichnaya vodka and ocean-going freighters and tankers. The former Soviet Union had a nonconvertible currency; therefore, accepting vodka in payment was Pepsi's only option for winning a contract there. Countertrade is growing as nations find themselves strapped for hard currency. It now represents as much as 40 percent of the world's trade. ■

C. Miller, "Worldwide Money Crunch Fuels More International Barter," *Marketing News* 26, no. 5 (March 2, 1992), p. 5; M. J. McCarthy, "PepsiCo Signs a 10-Year Trade Accord with Moscow That Includes Soviet Ships," *The Wall Street Journal,* April 10, 1990, p. A8.

Photo 1.6

Barter, one of the oldest forms of exchange, is growing in popularity, even among businesses in industrialized countries.

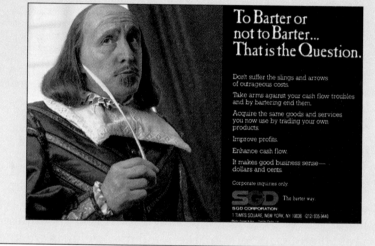

The Organizational Era

The Individual Era gave way to the Organizational Era as the Industrial Revolution gained steam. The Industrial Revolution began in England in the 18th century and diffused to Europe and America in two waves. The first wave introduced railroads, the steam engine, and water-powered mills. Roughly 100 years later, the second wave brought electricity, the internal combustion engine, and manufactured chemicals. A third industrial revolution is currently underway in the computer, semiconductor, robotic, and biotechnology industries, this one being led by the United States.[12]

The 19th century was marked by the emergence of large organizations with multiple businesses and product lines undertaking mass production and mass marketing locally, regionally, nationally, and, eventually, internationally. This era gave rise to marketing as we know it today.

With industrialization, businesses expanded, adopted new production systems, and added product lines, organizational layers, and complexity. As shown on the time line, the focus shifted from individual sellers to organizational producers, like the Ford Motor Co. Many of these businesses were becoming highly sophisticated in mass producing standardized goods, and they assumed that any product surplus would sell without much marketing effort because consumer demand was greater than product supply. Thus, the period of the 1870s through the late 1920s is often referred to as the **production period.** The primary, but not the only, operating philosophy of businesses was to increase output and improve production efficiency, processes, products, and distribution. All manner of inventions changed the way products were made and distributed, from moving assembly lines to electric motors, automobiles, railroads, and wireless communication devices. Because consumer demand exceeded product supply, businesses showed more concern for improving their skills in mass production and distribution than for satisfying consumers. For example, in 1913 Henry Ford introduced the assembly line and standardized parts to the production of automobiles, yet he still offered automobiles only in black, regardless of consumers' color preferences.

production period The late 1870s through the late 1920s.

Not all businesses were solely production-oriented during this time; many consumer-focused companies flourished. However, production and products were the dominant focal points as technologies were mastered that both allowed a constant stream of new products to reach the market and reflected the great strides made in production efficiencies.

By the 1920s, product supply had become more abundant than consumer demand. The production period philosophy began to give way to the **selling period,** which became dominant during the time from the Great Depression to the mid-20th century.

selling period The Great Depression to the mid-20th century.

During the Great Depression, which lasted worldwide from the stock market crash in October 1929 through the 1930s, goods were available but unemployment and a generally bleak economy stifled demand. Also during the period from the early 1900s through World War II, the United States experienced successive waves of consumer discontent. These consumerism movements were directed toward correcting businesses' disregard for consumer health, safety, and welfare.

The Marketing Concept World War II, the defining event of the 20th century, has also been called "mass production's crowning moment."[13] During the war, production shifted to provide huge quantities of war materials, not personal use consumer goods. However, after the war servicemen returned to the United States, eager to spend their accumulated savings, start families, and buy homes and consumer products. Businesses responded by producing an abundance of products that consumers wanted—automobiles, refrigerators, televisions, furniture, and houses. It was a period of unprecedented growth and optimism that gave rise to the **marketing concept period.** During the latter half of the 20th century, when supply once again grew larger than demand and domestic and international competition intensified, the marketing concept became the operating philosophy for consumer-oriented companies like General Electric, Coca-Cola, and Procter & Gamble, as well as many others. The marketing concept period is shown on the time line in Figure 1.5 and its philosophy outlined in Figure 1.6.

The **marketing concept** is an operating philosophy that has customer satisfaction at its core and requires that not only marketing, but all business operational areas, cooperate to satisfy consumers and achieve organizational goals. Consumer research is conducted on a regular, ongoing basis to keep the business informed about consumers and changes in the marketplace, and customer service activities are stressed.[14] As a guide to strategic planning, the marketing concept philosophy requires a long-run strategic perspective. The organization also seeks to achieve its own goals, whether for profit, efficiency, survival, or not-for-profit service delivery.

marketing concept period The latter half of the 20th century.

marketing concept An operating philosophy that has customer satisfaction at its core and requires that not only marketing, but all business operational areas, cooperate to satisfy consumers and achieve business goals.

Figure 1.6

The Marketing Concept Philosophy: Key Interlocking Elements

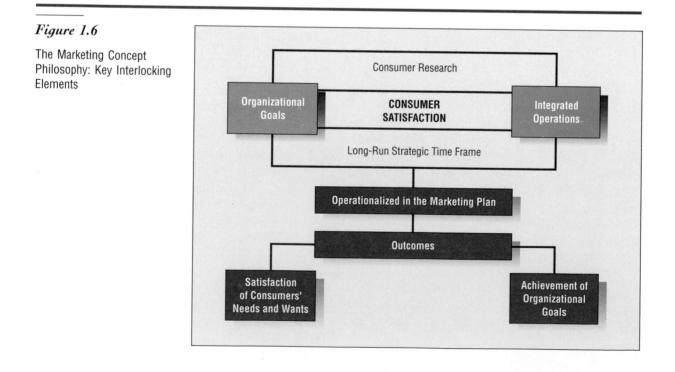

Photo 1.7

Satisfying individual needs is crucial for businesses and personal use consumers.

What do consumers need and want? That's not an easy question to answer, nor can it be answered for all consumers, all the time. Many consumers are price-conscious, and prices must be discounted to satisfy them. Other consumers place a premium on higher-quality products or products that offer more service or save time. Growing numbers of consumers choose products and services that are environmentally friendly. The same consumer who is quality-conscious in one purchase situation may be environmentally or price-conscious in another. The challenge for any business is to determine what is necessary to satisfy its target customers, and then deliver it. The difficulty of this task helps explain why so many businesses fail at successfully implementing the marketing concept.

The Societal Marketing Concept   Are consumers always right? Should products be offered even if they may have long-term harmful effects on both consumers and society? These difficult questions are increasingly being debated. The **societal marketing concept** follows the basic form of the marketing concept, but in an expanded framework. The concept includes the good of society as a goal and requires that the businesses satisfy both consumers and society.

Because of the complex problems facing society, it is becoming more difficult for businesses to ignore the consequences of their actions, particularly because so many of their employees, customers, and shareholders express societal concerns. There also is a risk of government intervention if businesses ignore the issue of the societal good.

societal marketing concept
The marketing concept that includes the good of society as a goal and requires that the business satisfy both consumers and society.

1. Explain the focus and scope of the Individual and Organizational Eras of marketing.
2. What is the marketing concept? Give an example of a company that you believe is operating under this philosophy; explain your answer.
3. Should businesses adopt the societal marketing concept?

MARKETERS AND THEIR TOOLS

Objective 5 Describe how marketers use marketing mix variables to satisfy consumers and achieve organizational goals.

Certain to make the list of the most widely reported marketing events of 1993 is the 29-cent Elvis stamp (see Photo 1.8). The U.S. Postal Service (USPS) finally delivered what ardent Elvis Presley fans have been requesting almost from the day he died: A stamp carrying Elvis's picture. The USPS asked consumers to vote for their choice of an "old, plump" or "young, sexy" Elvis to grace the stamp. This move has been described either as an effort to avoid consumer dissatisfaction by making sure Elvis was portrayed to his fans' liking or as a spectacularly successful example of marketing promotion. Over 800,000 consumers expressed a picture preference by returning their vote via postcard to the USPS. The postcard was free, but voters had to pay the postage. The Elvis stamp is a hot seller, not only for use as postage, but also for collectors and die-hard Elvis fans who have no intention of ever using the stamp. Over a half billion Elvis stamps were printed in advance of the January 8, 1993, issue date.[15]

Photo 1.8

The Elvis Presley stamp quickly generated over $20 million in revenue after it was released in 1993. This popular stamp is even appearing on articles of clothing.

Marketing Application 1.5

Select a brand that you've used in the past six months that either satisfied or dissatisfied you. Find the customer service address on the product package or call the 1-800 toll-free telephone number and ask for a mailing address. Write a letter to the company that reflects your experiences with the product. *Be honest in your communication,* whether it is praise for the product or a complaint. As soon as you get a response from the company, bring it to class along with a short written analysis of whether you believe the company has adopted the marketing concept philosophy, based on this interaction. Use caution, however, in assuming that a single interaction is a sufficient basis for a broad generalization. ■

Many different kinds of individuals, businesses, and organizations engage in marketing, just like the USPS. This section briefly discusses the Four Ps of the marketing mix—the variables under the marketer's control that are used to bring offers to the marketplace and satisfy consumers. These variables—product, price, place (distribution), and promotion—will be considered at length in Chapters 7 through 13.

The Four Ps: The Marketing Mix Variables

The Four Ps are the marketing mix variables of product, price, place (also called *distribution*), and promotion. The Four Ps together are the tactical marketing tools controlled by the marketer and used to direct the tactical offer toward the **target market,** groups of consumers who are current or potential customers. The Four Ps are shown in Figure 1.7.

target market Groups of consumers who are current or potential customers.

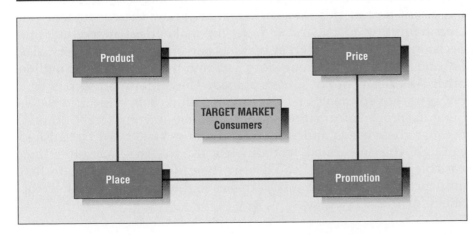

Figure 1.7

The Four Ps of Marketing: The Marketing Mix Variables

Product, price, place (distribution), and promotion are the marketing mix variables tools that marketers use to achieve their goals. They are more controllable than variables in the environment, such as competition, the economy, government, technology, and society. (Environmental factors will be discussed in Chapter 2.)

product The offer made in the marketplace, including packaging, warranties and guarantees, associated services, installations, and maintenance.

price The amount charged for the product that generates revenues to cover costs and return a profit.

place Refers to where, when, and how the product is made available to consumers.

promotion Activities—including advertising, personal selling, sales promotions, and public relations—used by marketers to communicate with consumers.

Product, the offer made in the marketplace, has features that benefit consumers through form utility. Product includes packaging, warranties and guarantees, associated services, installations, and maintenance. The USPS's product, a first-class stamp, is a near monopoly for letters. The stamp's features can be modified, principally through the use of different images or pictures, colors, sizes, or adhesives. Possessing a stamp means a consumer can use it to dispatch mail, add it to a collection, or hold it for investment purposes.

Price is the amount charged for the product, and should generate revenues that cover costs and return a profit. The marketer often has considerable flexibility in setting and changing prices. Likewise, buyers have considerable latitude in deciding whether or not to accept the seller's price, because typically there are many substitutes or alternatives available, often at a better price. Face-value stamp prices are set by the USPS governors. However, philatelists (stamp hobbyists) are often willing to pay far more than face value for a stamp because of its physical condition or rarity.

Place or distribution refers to where, when, and how the product is made available to consumers. Stamps are available at the post office, by mail order, in vending machines, at retail stores like supermarkets, at kiosks, and in offices through meter machines. Place is under the marketer's control and is used to satisfy consumer preferences for convenience through place and time utilities.

Promotion is how marketers communicate with consumers, and includes such activities as advertising, personal selling, sales promotions, and public relations. The goal of promotion is to persuade, inform, remind, and sometimes even entertain consumers. The USPS was very skillful in promoting the Elvis stamp through general interest news stories, television commercials, and mailings to stamp collectors.

The marketing mix variables are the tactical tools that marketers use to achieve their strategic goals. Target market selection is an important part of this process; you must know the consumers you are attempting to satisfy in order to make wise marketing mix decisions. The target market may be personal use consumers, like Jay and Sara in our opening story, you and me, and over 262 million other Americans or consumers abroad. The target market may be a business, government, or other organization. It is critical to determine as much information as possible about your target market, because their needs and wants are the ones that must be satisfied through the integrated, coordinated use of the marketing mix variables. In Chapter 2, you'll learn how decisions are made that influence the marketing mix variables as they are used to develop offers for the marketplace.

Career Watch

Jan Thompson is a seasoned marketing veteran. She has worked her way up from being a distribution manager for Chrysler in Los Angeles to writing the marketing plan for Lexus (Toyota's luxury car), to vice president for sales operations for Mazda Motor Corporation of America, becoming one of the highest-ranking women in the automotive industry. She is credited with advocating the successful use of the personal appeal slogan "It Just Feels Right." Women are her special interest, for she recognizes the importance of women as both primary purchasers and influencers of purchase decisions. In 1994, she left Mazda to join Wilson Sporting Goods Company as head of their U.S. Golf Division. ■

L. Armstrong, "Woman Power at Mazda," *Business Week,* September 21, 1992, p. 84; K. Rottenberger-Murtha, "Driving Force: Jan Thompson, One of the Highest-Ranking Women in the Automotive Industry Is Racing to Improve Mazda's Sales Strategy," *Sales & Marketing Management,* November 1993, pp. 76–81; M. Rechtin, "Mazda's Thompson Trades Cars for Golf," *Automotive News,* July 18, 1994, p. 8.

Photo 1.9

Mazda, "It Just Feels Right," according to Jan Thompson (shown in the right-hand photo) formerly of Mazda Motor, Inc.

Review of Chapter Objectives

1. *Define marketing and explain its origins and contemporary meanings.* According to the American Marketing Association, "Marketing is the process of planning and executing the conception, pricing, promotion and distribution of ideas, goods and services to create exchanges that satisfy individual and organizational objectives." Marketing originated when people began bringing their products to markets in order to make exchanges with others. Contemporary marketing uses sophisticated tools to facilitate exchanges between sellers and buyers, but the fundamental principle of exchange endures.

2. *Identify the key foundation concepts of marketing.* The key foundation concepts that underlie marketing are exchange, products, buyers, sellers, and satisfaction.

3. *Explain why it is important to study marketing.* The study of marketing is important for several reasons. Marketing affects our daily lives. Because it is a force in society, we have responsibilities as citizen consumers to be wise consumers and ensure that marketing power is not abused. Marketing offers many attractive career paths. Marketing is important to businesses and organizations and essential to global competitiveness.

4. *Discuss why and how marketing is still evolving.* Marketing has evolved from an individual-centered to an organization-centered process as society, technologies, and markets have evolved. Production and product were the primary concerns during the Industrial Revolution, when sellers were perfecting their production technologies and consumer demand was greater than product supply. This shifted to a selling orientation when supply began to outpace demand. World War II brought many changes as production shifted to wartime products and demand for consumer products exceeded supply. However, at the war's end, consumer demand fueled a period of great growth and optimism. This also marked the eve of the dominance of the marketing concept philosophy. The marketing concept is an integrated, coordinated philosophy of management that is long range, consumer oriented, and based on research to determine consumer needs and wants, yet also directed to achieve organizational goals. Although not all firms and organizations have adopted this concept, it is the dominant business operating philosophy in our modern consumer society. The societal marketing concept philosophy extends the marketing concept to ensure that market offers are not harmful to society.

5. *Describe how marketers use the marketing mix variables to satisfy consumers and achieve organizational goals.* The Four Ps of product, price, place (distribution), and promotion are marketing mix variables that are more under the marketer's control than are other external environmental elements. They are used together as tactical tools to develop integrated marketing strategies for providing products that satisfy consumers.

Key Terms

After studying Chapter 1, you should be able to define each of the following key terms and use them in describing marketing activities.

Marketing, page 7
Consumer Insight, page 7
Consumer Gap Analysis, page 9
Value, page 9
Marketers, page 10
Exchange, page 12
Products, page 13
Utility, page 13
Market, page 13
Marketplace, page 13
Demarketing, page 15

Need, page 15
Want, page 15
Marketing Mix Variables (Four Ps), page 20
Production Period, page 25
Selling Period, page 25
Marketing Concept Period, page 26
Marketing Concept, page 26
Societal Marketing Concept, page 27
Target Market, page 29
Product, page 30
Price, page 30
Place, page 30
Promotion, page 30

Discussion Questions

1. What is being exchanged between each of the following pairs of sellers and buyers?
   a. Schools–students.
   b. American Cancer Society–contributors.
   c. Presidential candidate–voters.
   d. Mothers Against Drunk Driving (MADD)–general driving public.
   e. Local government garbage disposal service–citizens.

2. "Marketing is responsible for our materialistic society." Comment on this statement. Do you agree or disagree?

3. Do each of the following perform marketing activities? If so, what is the goal of their marketing effort?
   a. Arthur Andersen (accounting firm).
   b. American Express (bank card).
   c. Good Samaritan Hospital (not-for-profit public hospital).
   d. U.S. Army (volunteer government unit).
   e. Toyota U.S.A. Motor Manufacturing Company (automobile company).

4. Is the societal marketing concept realistic for a business to adopt? Why or why not?

5. Explain why consumer insights are important to marketers.

6. What types of utility are created by each of the following?
   a. Blockbuster Video.
   b. Mr. Suds' automated, drive-through car wash.
   c. BancTwo automated teller machine.

7. Explain which is more difficult to market—an idea or a place.

8. Describe the foundation concepts of marketing.

9. If you were a marketing teacher, how would you explain to your class the importance of studying marketing?

10. Describe how marketing has evolved in the United States. Do you think it will continue to evolve?

What Do You Think?

Smoking is a highly controversial subject in the United States and other countries around the world. Although some anti-smoking consumer groups and legislators call for a ban on all tobacco marketing in the United States, other government officials are helping tobacco producers find foreign markets for their products. Domestic tobacco consumption has been dropping 2 to 3 percent annually for the past several decades, while tobacco use continues to accelerate abroad, particularly in East Europe and Asia. In Japan, tobacco companies from the United States control almost 20 percent of the cigarette market, which is made up of an estimated 60 percent of Japanese men and 13 percent of Japanese women. In the United States, cigarette packages are legally required to carry such explicit labels as "Smoking causes lung cancer, heart disease, emphysema, and may complicate pregnancy." Japanese cigarette labels are more reserved. One reads "It is possible that tobacco may hurt your health, so don't smoke too much." In other countries, there are no warning labels. Is there a conflict between the marketing concept's focus on delivering consumer satisfaction and the marketing of products that are potentially harmful to consumers? Whose marketing standards should be followed, those of the seller's country or the buyer's? What do you think?

Sources: J. Guyon, "Tobacco Companies Race for Advantage in Eastern Europe While Critics Fume," *The Wall Street Journal,* December 28, 1992, pp. B1, 4; W. Konrad, "RJR Can't Seem to Find a Spot in the Shade," *Business Week,* July 20, 1992, pp. 70–71; J. S. Stroud, "Stakes High for U.S. Tobacco," *Lexington Herald-Leader,* December 29, 1992, pp. A1, 6; M. Mintz, "The Tobacco Pushers' Marketing Smokescreen," *Business and Society Review,* Fall 1991, pp. 49–54; W. Beaver, "The Marlboro Man Rides into the Eastern Bloc," *Business and Society Review,* Winter 1994, pp. 19–23.

Mini-Case 1.1

"Pig's Eye" Beats Out "Landmark" as Customers' Favorite

Minnesota Brewing Company (MBC) began operations in fall 1991 after buying a 140-year-old brewery from G. Heileman Brewing Company in St. Paul, Minnesota. The market MBC inherited was loyal and blue collar. The purchase was supported by the community, because it meant that 110 laid-off brewery workers were reemployed, and the state provided loans of almost $1 million to the company for saving a landmark brewery.

Getting in on the excitement, the city newspaper ran a contest to get readers to name the company's new flagship brew. Over 2,600 people entered, and the name "Pig's Eye Pilsner" received 21.5 percent of the vote. The name came from the nickname Pig's Eye, which was given to a local, mid-19th century bootlegger Pierre Parrant.

MBC made a number of costly marketing mistakes in its first year of operations. Instead of using "Pig's Eye," the company selected a more dignified name, "Landmark," even though that name received only 4 percent of the votes in the newspaper contest. MBC changed the product from the light brew favored by their loyal market to a heavier, European lager preferred by the company's managers. Promotions promised a different taste from what was actually delivered. Finally, the beer was priced as a premium beer, much higher than the major labels, when the market wanted an inexpensive beer. Sales in Minnesota during the first year were one-third of what was needed to break even.

Case Questions

1. Is MBC using the marketing concept philosophy? Explain your answer.

2. Evaluate the mistakes made by MBC for each of the marketing mix variables (product, price, place, promotion).

3. How can MBC fix its mistakes? What changes should it make?

Source: B. Marsh, "Brewery Learns Expensive Lesson: Know Thy Market," *The Wall Street Journal*, December 28, 1992, p. B2.

Mini-Case 1.2

Twentysomethings: The Consumers That Marketers Almost Forgot

The over 76 million American baby boomers, consumers born between 1946 and 1964, have long been the favorite of marketers because of their liberal spending habits and the similarities of their attitudes and lifestyles, which make them attractive targets. Relatively neglected, by comparison, are the 47 million Americans who are 20 to 29 years of age and from the generation born immediately following the baby boomers. Labeled twentysomethings, generation X, gen Xers, baby busters, and slackers, this is the MTV generation known for their channel surfing and eclectic tastes in clothing and music. Some critics label them angry, cynical, dissatisfied, and hopeless. Defenders respond that they are bright, brash, intelligent, have a keen and sometimes bizarre sense of humor, don't take themselves or anyone else too seriously, and really aren't that different from the baby boomers—only younger. Marketers are having difficulty communicating with them because of their diversity and resistance to marketing efforts. They have been called "the generation that hates to be marketed to." However, this age group has over $125 billion in annual spending power, so marketing efforts targeted at twentysomethings are bound to intensify. The question is, who is right—are twentysomethings antimarketing or just not well understood?

Case Questions

1. Mazda ran a very conservative advertising campaign directed at baby boomers and used cues like a woman wearing pearls and classical music in the background. How might Mazda change their advertising for generation X targets?

2. How can marketers find out what the generation X market is really all about? What would it take to develop consumer insight about the twentysomethings?

Sources: P. Goodman, "Marketing to Age Groups Is All in the Mind-Set," *Marketing News* 27, no. 25 (December 6, 1993), p. 4; D. Lavin, "Chrysler Directs Neon Campaign at Generation X," *The Wall Street Journal,* August 27, 1993, pp. B1, 8; C. Miller, "X Marks the Lucrative Spot, but Some Advertisers Can't Hit Target," *Marketing News* 27, no. 16 (August 2, 1993), pp. 1, 14; C. Miller, "Xers Know They're a Target Market, and They Hate That," *Marketing News* 27, no. 25 (December 6, 1993), pp. 2, 15; R. Morin, "Much Ado About Twentysomethings," *Washington Post National Weekly Edition* 11, no. 14 (January 31–February 6, 1994), p. 37.

Chapter 1 Notes

1. C. Goerne, "Buying Groceries on Credit: Growing Numbers of Shoppers Prefer to Pay with Plastic," *Marketing News* 26, no. 20 (September 1992), pp. 1, 11; V. Reitman, "Turning Coupon Flood into Guided Trickle," *The Wall Street Journal,* June 3, 1992, p. B1; "Computer Kiosks Move Beyond Information to Products," *Marketing News* 27, no. 20 (September 27, 1993), p. 2.

2. S. D. Hunt, *Modern Marketing Theory: Critical Issues in the Philosophy of Marketing Science* (Cincinnati, OH: South-Western Publishing Co., 1991); R. S. Tedlow, *New and Improved: The Story of Mass Marketing in America* (New York: Basic Books, 1990), p. 5.

3. "AMA Board Approves New Marketing Definition," *Marketing News* 19, no. 5 (March 1, 1985), p. 1.

4. F. S. Houston and J. B. Gassenheimer, "Marketing and Exchange," *Journal of Marketing,* October 1987, pp. 3–18; R. P. Bagozzi, "Marketing as Exchange," *Journal of Marketing,* October 1975, pp. 32–39.

5. K. Deveny, "Man Walked on the Moon but Man Can't Make Enough Devil's Food Cookie Cakes," *The Wall Street Journal,* September 28, 1993, pp. B1, 3; W. Royal, "SnackWell's: Yes, We Have No Cookie Cakes," *Sales & Marketing Management,* September 1994, pp. 80, 81.

6. A. H. Maslow, "A Theory of Human Motivation," *Psychological Review* 50 (1943), pp. 189–99.

7. L. G. Gulledge, "Simplify Complexity of Satisfying Customers," *Marketing News* 25, no. 1 (January 8, 1990), pp. 6–7; L. Loro, "The Customer Is Always Right: Satisfaction Research Booms," *Advertising Age* 63 (February 10, 1992), p. 25; C. Power, W. Konrad, A. Z. Cuneo, and J. B. Treece, "Value Marketing: Quality, Service, and Fair Pricing Are the Keys to Selling in the '90s," *Business Week,* November 11, 1991, pp. 132–40, 190; B. Farber and J. Wycoff, "Customer Service: Evolution and Revolution," *Sales & Marketing Management,* May 1991, pp. 44–48, 50–51.

8. U.S. Bureau of the Census, *Statistical Abstracts* (Washington, DC: U.S. Government Printing Office, 1994), Table no. 844.

9. M. Campanelli, "Job Hunting," *Sales & Marketing Management,* January 1995, p. 57.

10. "Advertising Age's 100 Leading National Advertisers," *Advertising Age* 62 (September 25, 1991), p. 23.

11. J. E. Goodman, "Go for Global Profits with America's Best-Known Brands," *Money,* August 1991, pp. 43–44, 49; T. W. Ferguson, "Nike Seems to Be Doing It Right (and Left)," *The Wall Street Journal,* July 14, 1992, p. A15; E. R. Koepfler, "Strategic Options for Global Marketing Players," *Journal of Business Strategies,* July/August 1989, pp. 46–50.

12. C. Farrell, "A Wellspring of Innovation," *Business Week/ Enterprise 1993,* 1993, pp. 57–62.

13. Ibid., p. 61.

14. J. Carlson, *Moments of Truth* (New York: HarperBusiness, 1987); J. C. Szabo, "Service = Survival," *Nation's Business,* March 1989, pp. 16–19, 22, 24; S. Phillips, A. Dunkin, J. B. Treece, and K. H. Hammonds, "King Customer: At Companies That Listen Hard and Respond Fast," *Business Week,* March 12, 1990, pp. 88–91, 94.

15. L. Wiener, A. K. Smith, M. Mannix, and D. Podolsky, "All the King's Stamps," *U.S. News & World Report* 114, no. 1 (January 11, 1993), p. 67; C. Miller, "U.S. Postal Service Discovers the Merits of Marketing," *Marketing News* 27, no. 3 (February 1, 1993), pp. 9, 18; D. Saks, "Elvis in the Spotlight," *The American Philatelist* 107, no. 3 (March, 1993), pp. 196–97.

Making Marketing Decisions—Developing Marketing Plans

Chapter Objectives

After studying Chapter 2 you should be able to

1. Describe the characteristics of marketing decisions.
2. Explain the importance of planning and describe the building blocks of plans.
3. Describe how plans are developed.
4. Discuss marketing planning at the business level.
5. Distinguish between the different environments that affect marketing decisions and plans.

*F*amed business scholar Peter F. Drucker has observed that "doing the right thing is more important than doing things right."[1] The right thing in marketing means making decisions that result in getting the right product to the right consumers at the right time, place, and price with the right promotions. If this were easy to do, far fewer businesses would fail in today's marketplace. Successful marketers consistently make the right decisions. They skillfully perform marketing activities designed to satisfy consumers and achieve organizational goals. They know how to solve consumers' problems, monitor important changes in their environments, cope with uncertainty, and plan for the future. As you read this chapter, consider this question: Why is making the *right* marketing decision sometimes so difficult?

<table>
<tr><td>

*Making the Right
Decisions for the
Food-&-More Store*

</td><td>

In Chapter 1, Sara and Jay had just completed a very successful grocery shopping trip. They regularly shop at the Food-&-More Store because the store stocks the products they want at acceptable prices and offers a pleasing shopping environment not far from their apartment. The store's manager, Ron Garcia, operates with only a 1 percent profit margin, so he knows that keeping consumers satisfied is good business and can determine whether the store survives in its highly competitive environment. Like most marketing professionals, Ron views his job as being a customer person, responsible for keeping their satisfaction firmly in focus as he makes marketing decisions for the store.

If Ron owned the Food-&-More Store, he would be making marketing decisions solely for himself, his employees, and his customers. However, the Food-&-More Store is only one store in the grocery business unit of a large company, a multibusiness corporation based in another state. The decisions Ron makes for the Food-&-More Store implement higher-level decisions made earlier by a top-level management team at company headquarters. This team represents all of the company's business units, of which the recently acquired grocery unit is only one part. The team meets regularly to develop and update big picture, long-range, companywide plans. Their goal for the grocery business unit is to develop what had been a small, successful regional business into a large national chain during the next five years.

As a result, Ron receives company support to modernize and upgrade his store because an improved store will generate greater revenues—a goal set for it in the company plan. Consequently, consumers like Sara and Jay benefit from the latest technology, enhanced services, and an expanded product selection. These improvements reflect operational level decisions made by Ron about *how* to upgrade the Food-&-More Store, following the company's instructions *to* upgrade. The company bought the grocery business unit because it was beating the competition at satisfying consumers and, given time and added resources, it should become a shining star for the company. Employees at all levels are making marketing work for the company and consumers.

</td></tr>
</table>

MAKING THE RIGHT MARKETING DECISIONS

Objective 1 Describe the characteristics of marketing decisions.

Sara and Jay's expectations for a supermarket are very different from what their parents expected when they were newlyweds 30 years ago. At that time, many grocery stores were small, independent, local businesses that only offered basics like fresh fruits and vegetables, meat, poultry, dairy products, frozen foods, packaged goods, and cleaning supplies. Most stores stayed open about 18 hours a day; few were open on Sundays. Because Sara and Jay are satisfied with what a 1990s supermarket offers, they would be quite dissatisfied if forced to shop in a typical 1960s grocery store. Their satisfaction suggests that the right decisions are being made for the Food-&-More Store. These decisions ensure that the business adapts in a timely manner to changing consumer expectations, challenges from the competition, and changes in its operating environments. Businesses that fail to adapt are usually discarded by a marketplace that has little tolerance for complacency.

Marketing Application 2.1

How well do the competing grocery stores in your area compare with the Food-&-More Store in satisfying consumers? This can be determined in part by collecting participant observations of local stores. On your next grocery shopping trip, closely observe your own store's features: customer service, technology (e.g., bar code scanners, instant coupon machines), product selection, prices, cleanliness, design (how easy it is to find things), and store location. Grade each feature, from A (excellent) to F (failure). Bring your results to class for discussion. Do differences between stores suggest different approaches to satisfying consumers? Do consumers consider the features to be equally important? If the same store is evaluated by different observers, what might explain variations between their grades? What effect might these variations have on drawing valid conclusions about a store's efforts to satisfy consumers? ■

The Nature of Decisions

Decisions are choices between sets of alternatives. We make decisions all the time. Some are easy to make and may require little additional information or deliberation, like choosing between two diet colas in a vending machine. Other decisions may be difficult and require considerable information, time, and study. This latter type of decision may pose considerable risk if the wrong choice is made, as in selecting a new car or deciding which job offer to accept. Some decisions are made independently; others require consultation and negotiation. Most of our personal decisions directly involve ourselves and our families, our friends, or the social groups to which we belong.

> **decisions** Choices between sets of alternatives.

We make business or professional decisions for our employers or, if we own a business, on behalf of our employees, customers, and stockholders. Making the right decision in a people-centered profession like marketing requires good marketing skills, good information, research, and a thorough understanding of people.

Making the right marketing decision is difficult, because decision making is often hampered by time constraints and imperfect or insufficient information. Because marketers work in volatile environments, decision making is further complicated by competitors' actions and consumer preferences and expectations that can change with lightning speed. Perhaps the one certainty in marketing is that nothing remains certain for long and, if the environment is left unmonitored, today's right decision may become tomorrow's mistake.

International Marketing Report

The recent passage of the North American Free Trade Agreement (NAFTA) has intensified marketing activities by U.S. firms in Mexico. One particularly volatile industry is telephone services. AT&T has joined with Grupo Alfa, a Mexican conglomerate, to offer phone services throughout Mexico in direct competition to Telefonos de Mexico SA. Their $1 billion joint venture is only the tip of the iceberg, because every major U.S. telecommunications company is in the market for part of an ambitious effort to provide telecommunications links throughout North and South America. The AT&T venture initially will target corporate customers, focusing on local and long-distance telephone and data transmittal services, and eventually expand to residential customers. This all fits into AT&T's global plan to become the dominant marketer of telecommunications services worldwide.■

J. J. Keller and C. Torres, "AT&T Corp. and Grupo Alfa Plan Venture," *The Wall Street Journal*, November 10, 1994, p. A3.

Marketing Decisions Are Varied

Marketers make decisions that are as varied as the profession itself. You will recall from Chapter 1 that marketing activities can be categorized within three broad functions—exchange, physical distribution, and servicing. People in various marketing occupations undertake the activities within the functions. These marketers make decisions appropriate to their occupational activities. For example, selling is an exchange function activity that occurs in retail, wholesale, and industrial settings. Marketing decisions in personal selling relate to such issues as sales territories, salesperson compensation and motivation, hiring, and training. On the other hand, inventory control activities in the physical distribution function require decisions about forecasting consumer demand for goods, product stocking and reordering, transportation, and delivery scheduling. Marketing research is a servicing function activity that involves decisions about research techniques, sample selection, and survey administration. Other marketing activities and related decisions are shown in Figure 2.1.

Generally, marketing decisions, regardless of the function or activity involved, vary along a number of dimensions. They vary in *complexity*, from simple decisions to those that are quite complicated. Marketing decisions also vary in *timing*, from decisions that must be made immediately to those that can be deliberated over a lengthy period of time. *Focus* differs in that some decisions are primarily about people, whereas others are about time, materials, money, or technology, independently or collectively. Marketing decisions also vary in their *scope*, from operational-level decisions that are narrowly focused and highly detailed, such as those made by Ron Garcia specifically for the Food-&-More Store that he manages, to

Marketing Function	Activity–Related Occupations	Make Decisions About . . .
Exchange	Advertising account manager	Client relations, accounts
	Advertising copy writer	Advertising message content
	Brand manager	Price, place, promotion
	Manufacturer's representative	Selling products
	Media specialist	Media selection, buying
	Retail buyer	Merchandise selection
	Store manager	Personnel, stock, operations
Physical distribution	Freight forwarder	Transport of goods
	Inventory manager	Storage, handling, inventory
	Operations manager	Warehousing, storing goods
	Traffic manager	Physical movement of goods
Servicing	Financing (brokers)	Credit terms, debts, assets
	Marketing researcher	Surveys, samples, methods
	Risk taking (agents)	Risk, security of goods

Figure 2.1

Marketing Activities and Decisions

Each marketing function involves many different activities that may be performed by people in many different types of marketing jobs. Although marketing decisions vary, they are all ultimately designed to satisfy consumers and achieve organizational goals. For more information on marketing careers, see the study guide.

broad marketing management decisions made by top management in a multibusiness company. Additionally, decisions vary in *risk*, from minimal risk to such significant risk that a mistake can cost people their jobs and affect profitability, consumers, and stockholders for years to come. Photo 2.1 illustrates how a product can be promoted by pointing out its risk-reducing features. Finally, marketing decisions vary by numbers and types of *participants*, whether the decision is made by one or several marketers or by a cross-functional team that includes people from marketing, finance, production, and other departments.

PLANNING

Businesses, organizations, and governments try to reduce the risk and uncertainty of decision making in a variety of ways; one is through planning. **Plans** are coordinated, integrated, systematic sets of decisions that act as blueprints to guide future actions during a specified time period. Marketers plan ahead to take advantage of windows of opportunity as well as to avoid traps that can suck the business into a downward spiral of costly mistakes. **Windows of opportunity** exist when there is a good match between a need or gap in the marketplace and a business's unique competency to fill that gap with consumer-pleasing products. For example, shopping habits are changing rapidly in Japan, and the international division of Toys "Я " Us recognized a window of opportunity where others saw only

Objective 2 Explain the importance of planning and describe the building blocks of plans.

plans Coordinated, integrated, systematic sets of decisions that act as blueprints to guide future actions during a specified time period.

window of opportunity A chance for a business to meet a need or gap in the marketplace.

Photo 2.1

AT&T makes a clear statement about reducing risk.

barriers. Their plans called for a militarylike attack on the market, a massive "hard and fast" invasion, opening 35 American-style toy superstores within two years. Their success is paving the way for other retailers willing to work at cracking the Japanese market.[2]

By the 1960s, planning had become a widely accepted business practice. In succeeding decades, it became a necessity because of increased environmental uncertainties, heightened competition, and the accelerated pace of technological change. For example, the 1970s were years marked by resource shortages, soaring energy costs and, in large businesses, the centralization of decision-making authority and resource control at the companywide, corporate level. The 1980s was a decade of growth, mergers and acquisitions, leveraged buyouts, and overextensions, which contributed to an economic recession in the late 1980s through the early 1990s. The slow economic recovery during the early 1990s was accompanied by corporate downsizing, the elimination of both white- and blue-collar jobs, slow or no growth in large companies, and a rise in the number of smaller businesses. One important outcome of these turbulent years has been the acceptance and use of strategic planning by the Fortune 1000 companies and a newly expanded strategic role for marketing in corporate management and companywide decision making.[3]

planning A process for preparing to make quick, efficient, and effective decisions.

A definition of planning that clearly links it to decision processes was offered by Kirby E. Warren in 1966. He suggested that **planning** is "Essentially a process directed toward making today's decisions with tomorrow in mind; a means of preparing for future decisions so that they may be made rapidly, economically and with as little disruption to the business as possible."[4] This definition is applicable

Figure 2.2 The Planning Process

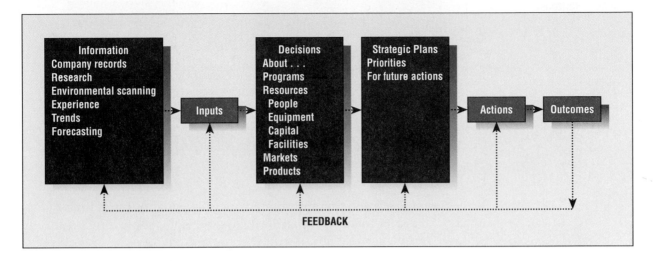

to large and small businesses as well as governments, not-for-profit organizations, and individuals. By planning, we focus on making decisions that will allocate resources (people, money, time, materials, technology) most effectively, position the business to take advantage of windows of opportunity, and prepare it to cope with threats. We commit to a course of action that we expect will allow us to realize our goals. Planning effectiveness depends on making the right decisions based on the careful evaluation of timely, accurate, complete, and useful information. As illustrated in Figure 2.2, information used in the planning process comes from many different sources. Outcomes from executed plans provide fresh information for future decisions as the planning process continually repeats itself.

**Check Your Understanding
2.1**

1. Explain this statement: "Marketing decisions are as varied as the profession itself."
2. What is a window of opportunity? Why are windows of opportunity so important to marketers?
3. Explain why plans are called *blueprints*.

Planning Horizons

Plans are made for various time frames, often called **planning horizons,** which indicate how far ahead into the future the plan will reach and the time that will be allotted to achieve the plan's goals. Figure 2.3 presents the most common planning horizons. As planning

planning horizons Time frames indicating how far into the future the plan will reach and the time allotted to achieve the plan's goals.

Figure 2.3

Planning Horizons

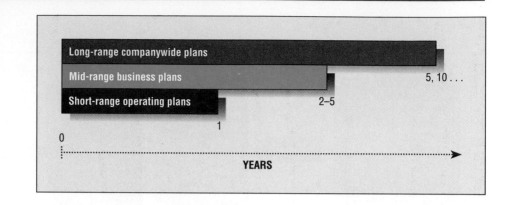

horizons increase, there is greater uncertainty about what may actually happen during the period covered. Few people can accurately forecast events very far ahead; therefore, plans must be revised regularly in order to correct for unexpected events and the acquisition of new information.

Short-range plans tend to be much more detailed and specific than long-range plans. **Short-range plans** are constructed upon problem-solving decisions made on a daily, weekly, monthly, quarterly, or yearly basis. These decisions are specific and detailed, as needed in the present or near future to run a business, an operational area (e.g., marketing, accounting, finance, production, management, human resources), or a specific marketing activity.

A short-range marketing plan requires making decisions about how to use marketing resources effectively (to meet a desired purpose) and efficiently (at an acceptable cost). For example, a small business short-range marketing plan identifies in detail how the marketing mix variables (Four Ps) are to function in the near future. This includes setting goals for what the variables are to accomplish and identifying what actions must be initiated and when they should be initiated. A short-range marketing promotion plan is a blueprint for the promotion activities that will be initiated over the next month, six months, or year. It specifies how much of the annual promotion budget is divided among different promotion activities such as advertising, sales promotions, and personal selling. A short-range advertising plan may identify the exact date to begin increasing the volume of television advertising for a product and may specify the media vehicles (stations) on which the advertisements will run. A short-range sales promotion plan may identify the starting date for a national coupon distribution program to accompany the launch of a new product. Such a plan would specify the issue and expiration dates for cents-off coupons and give details about a contest that would be used to boost sales during a period beginning, say, January 1 and ending June 30.

short-range plans Specific, detailed, problem-solving decisions made to run a business, business area, or marketing activity.

Short-range planning decisions are based on information from such sources as company records, employees' observations, intelligence collected about the competition, primary and secondary research on consumers and markets, and environmental scanning. In businesses that are part of large companies, short-range plans must be consistent with plans made at higher levels. If Ron's short-range plans for the Food-&-More Store were not consistent with the company's plans for all of its grocery stores, confusion and possibly disaster could result.

Annual plans reflect decisions made for an entire year, most commonly beginning January 1 (tax year), but alternatively starting at other times, such as the first day of a federal or state fiscal year. In most businesses, annual marketing plans are integrated with plans for other areas, such as annual production plans and annual financial plans. Such plans identify important benchmarks for achieving businesswide goals, as well as encourage cooperation between units to support one another's activities and discourage damaging internal conflicts over scarce resources. For example, annual new product planning frequently is a team activity that involves marketers contributing knowledge about the best way to market a product, production people providing knowledge of how best to make the product, and finance people offering knowledge about how to raise the money needed to produce and market the product.

annual plans Plans based on decisions made for an entire year, most often beginning January 1 or the first day of a federal or state fiscal year.

Large North American companies often are criticized for caring too much about the short-range bottom line, focusing on short-term profits while neglecting long-range goals. This short-term, bottom-line orientation hinders long-range planning. Fortunately, this orientation appears to be changing.

Mid-range plans are based on decisions made for two to five years into the future. These plans are longer range and less specific than are short-range plans. Mid-range plans also focus on the actions a business or company must take to achieve its goals, but provide fewer details on how to do so. These plans identify which products will be offered and what markets served, as well as how marketing and the other operational areas must cooperate to achieve business- and companywide goals.

mid-range plans Plans based on decisions made for two to five years into the future.

Long-range plans reach ahead for 5, 10, or 25 years, even as far in the future as a half-century or more. Konosuke Matsushita, founder of Panasonic, announced but never revealed the details of a 250-year plan for his company.[5] Most large multibusiness companies plan no more than 10 to 15 years ahead. Long-range plans generally reflect big-picture decisions made for a business or multibusiness company based on trends, forecasts, and a certain amount of conjecture. These plans stress broad actions the organization must take in order to achieve long-range goals. Top executives may develop a number of different scenarios that could occur, given certain conditions. Strategic

long-range plans Plans that reach ahead for 5, 10, 25, 50, or more years.

Marketing Application 2.2

Try your hand at planning. Assume the role of a marketing assistant for a florist who owns and operates three floral stores in your city. The florist has asked you to develop a preliminary annual advertising plan for the stores. The local newspaper will help design the print advertisements, but you need to decide when the ads should run. You must develop a plan that is effective, efficient, and stays within budget; therefore, you cannot advertise heavily with equal intensity year-round. How would you allocate your advertising dollars? Would you advertise at a low level every month and heavily only during certain times? Make your decisions, then write a short statement that outlines your plan over 12 months and explains your decisions. State priorities for times when advertising must be heavy. Bring your planning statement to class for discussion. ■

plans are then written based on the scenarios. Long-range plans are renewed on a regular basis, often yearly, in order to update and refocus them.

Who Plans?

Marketing plans in a multibusiness company are made by people throughout the company, from top management to field salespeople. Obviously, the decisions underlying the plans differ in their complexity, timing, focus, scope, and participants, just as the plans themselves vary in content. Small and mid-size businesses must also make marketing plans, but there are some differences. The smaller the business is, the fewer decision-making levels are involved in planning, and often this means that planning is less formal. Because smaller businesses can exhibit greater flexibility and responsiveness to marketplace events and changing consumer needs, they can change their plans rapidly. Although small businesses have the advantage of flexibility and a more rapid response, they typically lack the marketplace clout of business units backed by large, well-capitalized companies. In some large companies, this clout can overcome, at least temporarily, the bureaucratic handicaps that slow decision making and planning. In some cases, it cannot overcome bureaucratic inertia, as shown in the early 1990s by IBM and Borden.[6] At IBM, central planning became so bureaucratic that it slowed decision making to the extent that profitable opportunities to beat the competition in laptop computers, notebooks, and workstations were lost. Borden's problem was a reliance on centralized decision making, failed marketing plans, and a drift away from the core business definition that undermined the company's ability to make cohesive decisions and plans.

Consumer Insight

Where does a small business go for help in developing a marketing plan? One source of advice is free! There are 56 small business development centers (SBDCs) and over 700 subcenters scattered throughout the United States that provide counseling, training, and research help for small business start-ups. Financial and marketing counseling are the most frequently sought services. SBDCs also help mature small businesses that need refresher courses in marketing. These centers are university-based and receive support from the United States Small Business Administration as well as state governments, private sources, and the sponsoring universities.■

A. Bianchi, "The Best Advice May Still Be Free," *INC.* 15, no. 2 (February 1993), p. 51; J. Saddkerm, "First Steps: More Than Money," *The Wall Street Journal Reports/Small Business,* October 15, 1993, p. R9; "The Needs of Small-Business Owners," *The Lane Report* 8, no. 9 (October 1992), pp. 46–47.

Most business advisors strongly endorse the development of a comprehensive plan as the first step in starting a small business. Indeed, most lenders won't finance a business start-up without first having the opportunity to evaluate a written business plan that includes a detailed marketing plan. The process of bringing people together to develop a plan is beneficial for forging a consensus, articulating the business's mission, and setting goals for the future. Although a written plan is the expected and perhaps most desirable outcome of the planning process, not all businesses write them. Small businesses in particular often do not have written plans because of time constraints and the pressure of running a business with relatively few employees.

Large company planning, whether companywide or for a single business unit, involves many organizational layers and participants (see Figure 2.4) and usually results in written planning documents. This is understandable because planning documents often must be transmitted among people, offices, and management levels as changes are made and a consensus reached. Although a small business can operate with a verbally agreed to plan, large businesses use written plans to avoid misunderstandings and misinterpretations.

Marketing planning in multibusiness companies occurs at all three levels: corporate (companywide), business unit, and operational. Ron Garcia, in the chapter-opening story, is the operational-level retail manager of one store in the grocery business unit of a large multibusiness company. In other companies, operational-level managers may be brand or product managers or managers of marketing activities such as advertising, public relations, marketing research, or personal selling.

Figure 2.4

Decision Processes and
Planning: Under the
Corporate Umbrella

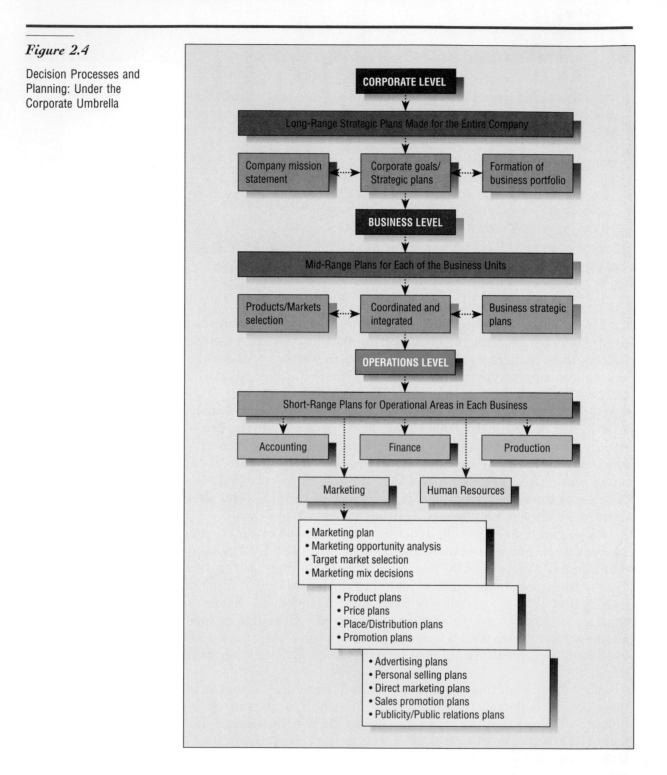

1. Why is planning important to achieving marketing success?
2. Should all organizations plan ahead? Explain your answer.
3. What differences are there among short-range, mid-range, and long-range planning horizons?

The Building Blocks of Plans

Two sets of very important building blocks go into building a plan: goals and objectives, and strategy and tactics. The relationship between them is shown in Figure 2.5. Goals and objectives are the ends that are being sought. Strategies are the larger-scale decisions that identify broadly how objectives and goals are to be achieved. Tactics are highly focused problem-solving decisions that support a strategy.

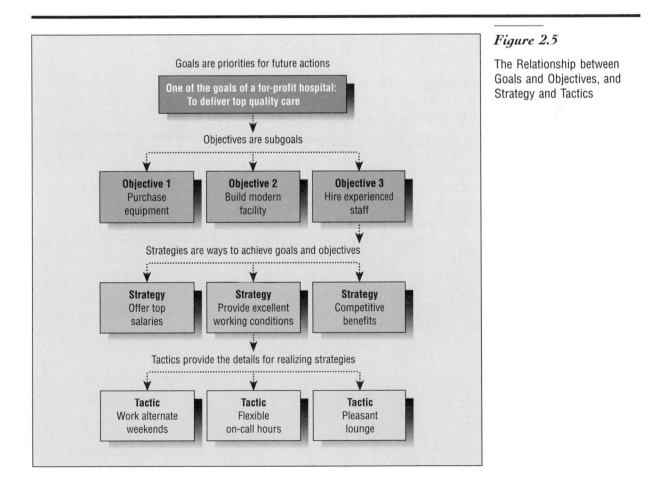

Figure 2.5

The Relationship between Goals and Objectives, and Strategy and Tactics

goals Long-range, general, and relatively unbounded ends to be achieved.

objectives Bounded, shorter-range, specific intermediate stages on the way to achieving goals.

Goals and Objectives   Although some people consider goals and objectives to be synonymous, there are differences between the two. **Goals** are long-range, general, and relatively unbounded ends to be achieved. **Objectives** are more bounded, shorter-range, specific intermediate stages on the way to achieving goals.[7] For example, a business may express a long-range growth goal to be achieved over a five-year period. Objectives are the subgoals that must be achieved in order to reach the point specified in the five-year goal. These may include reaching such short-range objectives as increasing by 20 percent the number of stores in which a product is offered within the first year, broadening the customer base by 10 percent within two years, to include both younger and older customers, and increasing salesperson per capita productivity by 25 percent over three years.

Long-range goals should be stated for all businesses, large and small; however, they are more apt to be found in large businesses. Most often these are growth goals, but a downturn in the economy (e.g., a recession) may cause goals to shift from growth to maintaining the status quo or survival. The result may be tactical responses such as slashing operating costs; downsizing or divesting people, products, or departments; or, within multibusiness companies, selling off business units.

strategy A plan or method that establishes broad directions for future actions.

tactics The specific details on actions needed to advance a strategy.

Strategy and Tactics   Companywide planners in the chapter-opening story made a strategic decision to expand the grocery business nationwide. This strategy eventually resulted in significant changes in the Food-&-More Store that Ron Garcia manages. The expansion strategy directs the company, its businesses, and units like the Food-&-More Store to develop ways to achieve the expansion goal. A **strategy** establishes broad directions for future actions. **Tactics** provide specific details on what must be done to advance the strategy. The upgrading and modernization efforts at the Food-&-More Store were tactics that advanced the corporate expansion strategy designed to achieve growth goals. By adopting an expansion strategy, a company states its long-range priorities to its employees, shareholders, suppliers, customers, and competition. How the expansion is to occur requires making tactical decisions about actions that will be needed to implement the strategy.

Check Your Understanding *2.3*	1. How are goals and objectives related? 2. What is the difference between strategy and tactics? 3. Give examples of how individuals also use strategies and tactics, and goals and objectives, in their daily lives.

DEVELOPING PLANS

The basic premise offered at the beginning of this chapter is that making marketing work means making the right marketing decisions. In a large company, such as the multibusiness corporation that owns the Food-&-More Store, marketing decisions are made at all levels and marketers contribute to these decisions directly and indirectly by participating in the planning process. Steps typically associated with developing companywide plans are:

Objective 3 Explain how plans are developed.

1. Develop a mission statement.
2. Establish priorities—actionable goals and objectives.
3. Develop a strategic plan.
4. Form a business unit portfolio.

The Mission Statement

The first step in companywide planning requires making decisions about the company's present and future direction. The outcomes are expressed in a **mission statement,** a written proclamation that defines the current business and indicates what the company should look like in 5, 10, or more years. An important task facing companywide planners is the development of a mission statement that includes all of its business units. Mission statements typically reflect a company's past achievements, its **distinctive competencies** (what the company and its businesses do best), and the environments in which it operates. In large companies, each strategic business unit also develops a mission statement that reflects the companywide mission but is tailored to the specific industry, products, and markets served by that business. Thus, the grocery business unit that operates the Food-&-More Store has its own mission statement in addition to the broader companywide mission statement. Obviously, the two mission statements must be complementary.

mission statement A written definition of the present state of a business, indicating what the company should look like at a specified time in the future.

distinctive competencies What the company and its businesses do best.

Today, over 50 percent of large businesses in the United States have mission statements, twice the number reported in the late 1980s. Marriott International has mission statements at all levels. In addition to the companywide corporate mission statement, there is a mission statement for its hotel business unit. Each of the hotel business's 250 hotels has its own mission statement, developed cooperatively by top managers and their staff, cooks, desk clerks, housekeepers, and customers.[8]

According to management scholar Peter Drucker, a business should be defined by answering three questions: Who are our customers? What do they buy from us? What are they looking for in our products? By answering these questions and posing them in terms of the future (i.e., Who will be our customers in 10 years? What will they be buying from us? What benefits will our products give them?), the company has taken a step toward establishing strategies for reaching its goals.[9] Using Drucker's model, the mission statement provides a showcase for the company's commitment to the marketing concept and its customers.

Marketers provide important consumer insights into the formulation of the mission statement for companies operating by the marketing concept philosophy. After all, marketing links the company to its environments and has the most intimate knowledge of consumers—their wants, desires, and behaviors—and the competition. Therefore, marketers can provide useful information for decisions about what business to be in both now and in the future, and how to compete in the marketplace.

Developing a mission statement in a small business often involves employees throughout the business. For example, a cross-section of salaried and hourly employees of the Bread Loaf Construction Co. in Middlebury, Vermont, spent two-and-a-half days working together to develop a statement that would reflect their vision for the company over the next 10 years. Although the final result was only three sentences long (Figure 2.6), the words had

Figure 2.6

A mission statement reflects what the business is and what it wants to become in the future.

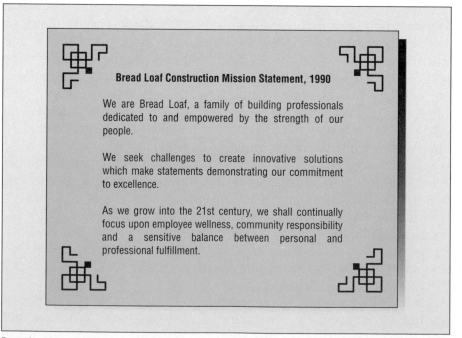

Bread Loaf Construction Mission Statement, 1990

We are Bread Loaf, a family of building professionals dedicated to and empowered by the strength of our people.

We seek challenges to create innovative solutions which make statements demonstrating our commitment to excellence.

As we grow into the 21st century, we shall continually focus upon employee wellness, community responsibility and a sensitive balance between personal and professional fulfillment.

Reproduced by permission of Bread Loaf Construction Company. R. R. 4, Box 1274, Route 7 South, Middlebury, Vermont 05753.

Photo 2.2

Smaller size means more value for consumers staying at Kimco's Prescott Hotel, Triton, and Village Plaza.

personal meaning for the owners and employees, and gave a sense of direction and purpose for the business.[10]

A useful mission statement must be more than empty words. Employees must be able to see mission statements as real and actionable declarations of company priorities, not as "fields of dreams."[11] Getting employees to take the mission statement to heart can be a formidable challenge, particularly if they had no part in its development.

It is seldom easy to write a mission statement. As Theodore Levitt pointed out in a widely quoted article, often a company will define its business too narrowly and thereby miss out on marketing opportunities.[12] Levitt maintained that there really are no growth industries, only growth opportunities that can be achieved by better serving customer needs and accurately defining the business. For example, Kimco Hotel Management Co., a mid-sized hotel chain, has found success in the U.S. hotel industry despite an industrywide slump. Unlike many of its competitors who consider themselves in the entertainment business, Kimco defines its mission more narrowly as being in the sleep business—its goal is to provide business travelers good value at a reasonable price. Kimco hotels (shown in Photo 2.2) have a cozy, clublike atmosphere with fireplaces in the lobby, overstuffed sofas, and average occupancy rates of 75 percent (compared to an industry average of only 60 percent).[13]

Check Your Understanding
2.4

1. What is a mission statement? How does a mission statement affect marketing activities?

2. Peter Drucker believes that a business should be defined by answering three questions. What are these questions?

3. Do nonprofit organizations and governments have mission statements? Should they? Explain your answer.

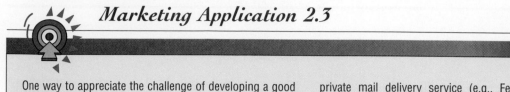

Marketing Application 2.3

One way to appreciate the challenge of developing a good mission statement is to write one. Using what you have learned, write short mission statements (several sentences long) for both the U.S. Postal Service and any private mail delivery service (e.g., Federal Express or United Parcel Service—UPS). How do the statements differ? How are they alike? Bring your statements to class for discussion. ■

Establishing Priorities

Once the mission has been stated, the next step is to establish priorities. These are the goals and objectives that must be achieved in order to carry out a mission statement. Goals and objectives are articulated in a strategic plan, the outcome of the third planning step. Based on the goals stated in a plan for a multibusiness company, business units are formed, bought, or divested in order to configure the company so that it is organized to act on its priorities and goals. A multibusiness company establishes a portfolio of businesses (step 4) by expanding existing businesses, developing or spinning off new businesses, or acquiring other businesses. A small company that is one business (e.g., a business unit in a multibusiness company) performs the same tasks, although usually not as formally as does a multibusiness corporation.

MARKETING PLANNING AT THE BUSINESS LEVEL

Objective 4 Discuss marketing planning at the business level.

Marketing planning in a business unit or in an independent business is designed to provide specific details on how marketing will be used to satisfy consumers and achieve business goals. Marketing managers begin their planning by identifying marketing opportunities. Taking aim at the opportunities, they select appropriate target markets and develop a marketing mix strategy that is stated in a marketing plan. For example, see Appendix A, a marketing plan.

The Situation Analysis

situation analysis An evaluation of a business's internal and external environments.

The first step in marketing planning requires that marketers perform a **situation analysis,** an evaluation of their internal and external environments based on information gathered from such sources as internal business records and field salespeople reports, U.S. government

Marketing on the Internet

The Internet is expanding rapidly as current members extend their presence and new members join. With every passing day, more information becomes available through this vast worldwide system of interlinked computers.

The U.S. government, the largest and most efficient collector of information in the world, is an active Internet participant. A marketer can easily access U.S. government information services on-line from an office or home computer. A simple path is to initiate a search request for "U.S. Federal Government Agencies" using one of the search systems, such as veronica or jughead. A connection to the U.S. Government Home Page (Fedworld) is usually made within seconds of a request, unless a very high volume of traffic lengthens the wait. The home page is a multipage text menu that is a one-stop location for federal government branches with information on-line. All marketers have to do is select the agency or office they want information from, press their computer's enter key (or click on the name with a mouse), then wait for a selection menu. For example, a marketer who needs census information can link directly to the U.S. Bureau of the Census Home Page, then select the Statistical Abstract of the United States from the menu. A marketer seeking information on marketing opportunities abroad can link to the Department of Commerce, then select the National Trade Data Bank or Best Market Reports.

Other frequently used information sites include the Small Business Administration, Environmental Protection Agency, Patent and Trademark Offices, and Federal Register. ■

documents (Department of Commerce, Labor, etc.), trade journals, and original research. The information is analyzed and used to identify trends in the marketplace, evaluate opportunities for the business to use its competencies to meet consumer needs, and identify potential external threats in time for them to be met and averted.

A **SWOT** analysis is a systematic situation analysis that requires evaluating the environments within which the business currently operates. SWOT stands for *s*trengths, *w*eaknesses, *o*pportunities, and *t*hreats. An analysis of a business's internal environment should reveal its strengths as well as its weaknesses. An analysis of the external factors should reveal opportunities and threats. Internal factors usually considered are the business's competencies, core technologies, financial situation, image, and resources (including people, products, equipment, and facilities). Although the evaluation of some of these factors is subjective, the act of engaging in self-examination may be valuable to determine the company's strengths and weaknesses.

Marketers also gather information about the business's external environment, including such business-specific factors as consumers, competitors, and suppliers, as well as broader factors such as the economy, government regulation, and societal changes. A SWOT analysis should enable a business to identify opportunities for matching its core competencies with consumer needs, and ways for

SWOT A systematic situation analysis of a business's strengths, weaknesses, opportunities, and threats.

it to achieve a sustainable competitive advantage over the competition. For example, Smart & Final's 122 West Coast supermarkets responded to a need they found in their external environment for low-priced products to be sold, in bulk, to small businesses and organizations. This niche (single target market segment) has been profitable for the chain and its parent company, a French conglomerate. On the other hand, Mazda Motor Corporation abandoned its long-range plan to introduce a new brand-name automobile, the Amati, into the U.S. luxury-car market because of economic downturns at home and the cost of establishing a new U.S. dealer network.[14] These examples illustrate the importance of environmental scanning and analysis and the kinds of actions that may result.

Target Market Selection

market segmentation   The process of grouping consumers by shared characteristics.

Market segments must be formed before a target market can be selected. **Market segmentation** is the process of grouping consumers by shared characteristics. Many different segmentation schemes are possible. For example, a personal use consumer market can be divided into groups according to age, which may result in the identification of a youth segment (ages 10 to 18), a college segment (ages 19 to 22), a young adult segment (ages 23 to 35), and so forth. Other segments may be formed by grouping consumers along lifestyle characteristics. A business market may be segmented by such characteristics as size or location. Targeting means that marketers decide which segments will be the targets of their marketing efforts.

Photo 2.3

The Amati, a high-end luxury car, had to be held back from production due to a weakened U.S. economy during the late 1980s and early 1990s.

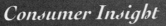

Consumer Insight

Marketers use a number of different tools to identify consumer segments. For over 20 years, Claritas Inc. (based in Virginia) has used ZIP codes to group consumers by common lifestyles as reflected in the houses they buy and where they live. Claritas's PRIZM (potential rating index by ZIP market) program statistically analyzes masses of demographic data to identify 62 different consumer segments that are matched to different ZIP codes where the segments can be found across the country. For example, the segment "cashmere & country clubs" identifies aging baby boomers whose incomes average $70,000. These consumers live the good life in the suburbs, take European holidays, and buy high-end

TVs. On the other hand, "rural industria" identifies young families with incomes slightly under $23,000 who live in middle America, work on farms and in factories, drive pick-up trucks, and enjoy fishing. Marketers for a bank, restaurant chain, or local retail store can identify which consumer segments represent the greatest potential for their product, use PRIZM to match each targeted segment with their ZIP code, and then direct tailored marketing messages to the groups. ∎

C. Del Valle, "They Know Where You Live—and How You Buy," *Business Week*, February 7, 1994, p. 89.

Marketing Mix Strategies

Once target markets are selected, strategic decisions must be made about how to use the marketing mix variables of product, price, place (distribution), and promotion to facilitate exchanges. With some mass market commodity-type products, one marketing mix strategy may fit all. However, it is more likely that different target markets will require a somethat different tailoring of the marketing mix. For example, a local bank marketing its services may target "cashmere & country clubs" and "rural industria" as well as other targets such as "American dreams," "kids & cul-de-sacs," or "executive suites." The bank will highlight different services for the different targets, as well as use different promotions and prices for some of its products. Chapters 7 through 13 examine the marketing mix variables in depth and elaborate on marketing mix decisions.

The Marketing Plan

A **marketing plan** is a blueprint for how the marketing mix variables will be used to satisfy consumers and achieve organizational goals. It specifies marketing strategy, marketing actions, product–market matches, marketing programs, and evaluation and control mechanisms. As the short-range marketing component of a business's long-range strategic plan, it must be integrated and coordinated with plans from the other operational areas, such as finance, production,

marketing plan A blueprint for using the marketing mix variables to satisfy consumers and achieve organizational goals.

and human resources. The marketing plan, as shown in Figure 2.7, is a detailed document usually written to cover a one-year period. It is subdivided into several major parts: situation analysis, statement of marketing objectives, marketing strategies, budget summary, and sometimes an appendix. Like any plan it is only a blueprint, not a substitute for leadership. At any one time, a large business may be operating under several marketing plans, one or more for each brand, product, or activity.

Planning, Implementation, and Control

In large businesses, marketing managers provide the leadership to implement the marketing plan in a marketing program. They institute evaluation procedures to determine whether or not the executed plan is working. Small business marketers also implement marketing

Figure 2.7   Components of a Typical Marketing Plan

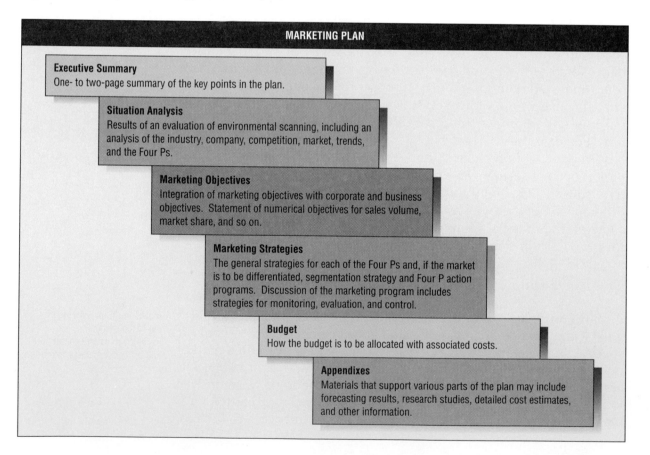

MARKETING PLAN

Executive Summary
One- to two-page summary of the key points in the plan.

Situation Analysis
Results of an evaluation of environmental scanning, including an analysis of the industry, company, competition, market, trends, and the Four Ps.

Marketing Objectives
Integration of marketing objectives with corporate and business objectives. Statement of numerical objectives for sales volume, market share, and so on.

Marketing Strategies
The general strategies for each of the Four Ps and, if the market is to be differentiated, segmentation strategy and Four P action programs. Discussion of the marketing program includes strategies for monitoring, evaluation, and control.

Budget
How the budget is to be allocated with associated costs.

Appendixes
Materials that support various parts of the plan may include forecasting results, research studies, detailed cost estimates, and other information.

plans and controls. The marketing plan and the interrelated marketing management processes of planning, implementation, and control are examined more in Chapter 15 and Appendix A.

MARKETING ENVIRONMENTS

Marketing does not occur in a vacuum—it is at the center of a number of volatile environments that affect all marketing decisions and actions, both directly and indirectly. These environments are internal as well as external.

Objective 5 Distinguish between the different environments that affect marketing decisions and plans.

Internal Environments

In a smaller business, the **internal marketing environment** (shown in Figure 2.8) includes marketing as well as finance, research and development, production, human resources, purchasing, and accounting sections that affect marketing activities. In a business unit of a multibusiness company, the internal environment extends to also include the other businesses in the business portfolio as well as the entire company. Marketing is affected by factors such as the culture established within the business and the company, power and authority, lines of communication, traditional responses to change, and competition for scarce resources. It is essential that marketers recognize how their internal environments influence marketing activities.

internal marketing environment The departments and functions that affect marketing activities within the business.

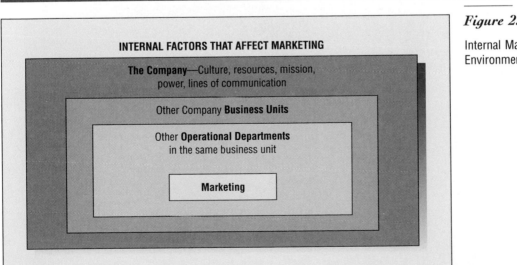

INTERNAL FACTORS THAT AFFECT MARKETING

The Company—Culture, resources, mission, power, lines of communication

Other Company **Business Units**

Other **Operational Departments** in the same business unit

Marketing

Figure 2.8

Internal Marketing Environments

Although marketers like to think of marketing as being the activity that drives the company, not everyone accepts this view. Whenever professionals from different disciplines work together there are bound to be divergent opinions and priorities. Although marketers may seek to promote the marketing concept as the business's operating priority, production may promote a production efficiency priority, human resources may have a staffing priority, and finance and accounting may promote bottom-line effectiveness. The result is that marketing decisions, plans, and programs are affected by internal factors that can act to advance or sometimes compromise marketing success.

External Environments

external marketing environment
All the external factors that directly affect or indirectly impact on marketing success.

The **external marketing environment** can be subdivided into those external factors that most directly affect the business and other, more distant and broader external factors that still can have a considerable impact on marketing success.

Immediate External Environment   As seen in Figure 2.9, many different factors in a business's immediate external environment can influence marketing decisions and activities:

• *Consumers:* The consumers in a business's target market are a critical factor, because they are who a business's marketing efforts

Figure 2.9

External Marketing
Environments

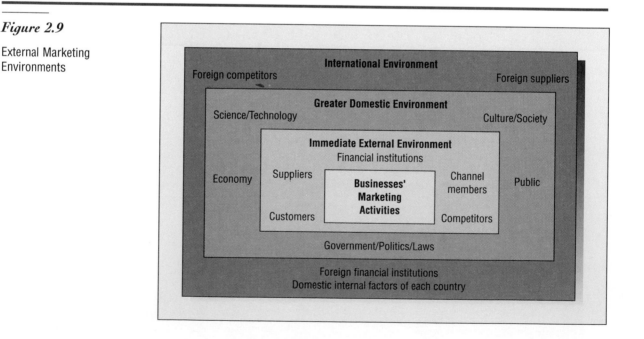

aim to please. Consumers are divided into two types: **Personal use consumers** are people purchasing products for their own or family use, or to give as gifts to others; **business and organization consumers** are people making purchases on behalf of their companies, to use in production processes, for resale, or to operate their business. Such consumers may be from not-for-profit organizations and governments, as well as from for-profit businesses.

- *The competition:* The competition can have powerful effects on one's marketing efforts. This includes competitors with directly similar products and those who produce indirect, substitute products. In the carbonated soft drink category, direct competitors are cola drinks like Coca-Cola and Pepsi Cola. An example of an indirect substitute for a cola drink is a fruit drink or a carbonated flavored water, such as Perrier or La Croix. Competitors must be closely monitored for a number of reasons: Not only do they try to sell their products to your target markets, but they also compete for your suppliers and members of your channel of distribution.

- *Suppliers, distribution channels, financial institutions, interest groups:* Other important influences in the immediate external environment are suppliers (businesses and individuals supplying resources needed in production and operations), channel of distribution members (they move your products from point of production to point of exchange), financial institutions (to provide capital), and public interest groups (who oversee the public impact of your products and marketing efforts). Suppliers can affect the success of the marketing effort because the materials they supply, the prices they charge, and the efficiency of their delivery influence business costs, which, in turn, affect product pricing and consumer acceptance. Likewise, an efficient channel can control costs; an inefficient one can escalate costs and product prices. Even when the channel is owned and operated by the marketer's own business, channel efficiency can be a serious concern.

Greater Domestic Environment Among the broader influences on marketing are:

- *Government, politics, and laws:* Businesses in the United States are regulated by laws, oversight agencies, regulations, organizations, and individuals such as a state's attorney general. Marketers must operate within the limits placed on them by these entities and continually be alert to changes that may directly or indirectly affect marketing activities.

- *Science and technology:* Breakthroughs in microprocessors, robotics, and biotechnology are fueling rapid advances in science and

personal use consumers People purchasing products for their own or family use, or to give as gifts.

business and organization consumers People making purchases on behalf of their companies, to use in production processes, for resale, or to operate a business.

Marketing Application 2.4

Business marketers are not the only ones influenced by environmental factors: Not-for-profit organizations as well as governments and other groups are all affected by both their internal and their external environments. In order to illustrate this, consider a not-for-profit hospital, public transit company, or public library in your area. Identify the internal and external environmental factors that affect this organization's decisions and activities. What internal factors have you identified? Which external factors are most influential? How do these factors compare with those affecting a for-profit business? ■

technology. These changes impact marketing as new products are developed, production efficiencies reduce costs, new product delivery systems emerge, and consumer preferences become technologically more sophisticated.

• *The economy:* When the economy is booming during a growth period, marketing activities flourish, because people with jobs have confidence in the economy and the future. Therefore, they feel less reluctant to make purchases, and markets become active. However, when the economy enters a slowdown or a recession, consumers' confidence and spending decline, which calls for different marketing responses to counter consumer price sensitivity.

• *Culture and society:* Culture and society are not static and, as they change, people's tastes and preferences also shift. Marketing reflects society and also influences it; therefore, constant monitoring is essential to determine when cultural shifts present opportunities or threats.

• *The general public:* Marketing activities are highly visible and often call attention to the marketer as well as to the marketing process. When there is a perception of unethical, irresponsible, or harmful marketing activities, the general public can exert considerable pressure on marketers through letter-writing campaigns, boycotts, and lobbying efforts. The consequences can be costly. It is highly advisable for marketers to act ethically, responsibly, and without causing harm, because it is the right thing to do *and* because it is good business and what the general public expects and demands.

International Environment   Since the end of World War II, marketers must consider more than just domestic environmental influences on their decisions and activities. The period since the end of the war has been marked by two concurrent trends: the growing

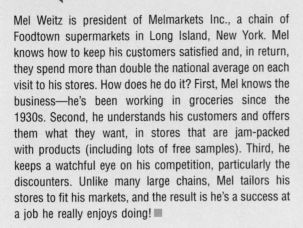

Career Watch

Mel Weitz is president of Melmarkets Inc., a chain of Foodtown supermarkets in Long Island, New York. Mel knows how to keep his customers satisfied and, in return, they spend more than double the national average on each visit to his stores. How does he do it? First, Mel knows the business—he's been working in groceries since the 1930s. Second, he understands his customers and offers them what they want, in stores that are jam-packed with products (including lots of free samples). Third, he keeps a watchful eye on his competition, particularly the discounters. Unlike many large chains, Mel tailors his stores to fit his markets, and the result is he's a success at a job he really enjoys doing! ■

M. Schifrin, "Ah, Smell That Bread," *Forbes* 150, no. 12 (November 23, 1992), pp. 78, 80; S. Weinstein, "Melmarkets' New Look," *Progressive Grocer* 73, no. 12 (December 1994), pp. 67–71.

Photo 2.4

Mel Weitz, President of Melmarkets, Inc.

---

influence of U.S. marketing activities in international locations, and the deep penetration of the U.S. domestic market by international companies and conglomerates. In both cases, to stay competitive the marketer must become knowledgeable about international influences and use this information to remain competitive, both domestically *and* internationally.

In Chapter 3 you will learn about the targets of marketing planning activities—consumers, both personal use consumers and business/organization consumers.

Check Your Understanding
2.5

1. What kinds of marketing decisions are made at the different levels of company, business, and operations?
2. Explain this statement: "Marketing does not occur in a vacuum."
3. What are the internal and external environments that may influence marketing decisions and activities?

Review of Chapter Objectives

1. *Describe the characteristics of marketing decisions.* We all make decisions, both personal and professional, throughout our lives. Business decisions are often particularly risky, because they are made within highly uncertain environments, under time pressures, and with incomplete or insufficient information. Marketing decisions vary by function and marketing activity.

2. *Explain the importance of planning and describe the building blocks of plans.* Plans are blueprints for action, decisions made in the present in order to take advantage of windows of opportunity and avoid mistakes in the future. Short-range plans typically are made for no longer than one year; mid-range plans cover two to five years into the future; and long-range plans are proposed for the coming 10 to 15 years. Top management usually assumes responsibility for long-range, companywide strategic plans; business-level managers construct mid-range business plans; and operations managers write short-range plans for the operational areas, such as marketing, finance, or production. The building blocks of plans are goals and objectives, and strategies and tactics. Goals are long range, general, and relatively unbounded. Objectives are subgoals. Strategies are broader statements of how goals will be achieved. Tactics are the details that specify how strategies will be implemented.

3. *Explain how plans are developed.* Companywide planning tasks call for developing a companywide mission statement, establishing priorities for the future, developing a strategic plan, and, in multibusiness companies, forming the business unit portfolio.

4. *Discuss marketing planning at the business level.* Business units and independent businesses often have their own mission statements. Their marketing plans are specific blueprints for how marketing will satisfy their customers and achieve business goals. Marketing planning at the business level requires performing a situation analysis, segmenting and targeting markets, deciding how the marketing mix variables will be used, and developing a marketing plan. Planning, implementation, and control are interrelated, coordinated marketing management processes.

5. *Distinguish between the different environments that affect marketing decisions and plans.* Marketing decisions, plans, and actions are affected by both internal and external environments. Marketing links the business with its external environments and, particularly, its customers, suppliers, competitors, and channels of distribution.

Key Terms

After studying Chapter 2, you should be able to define each of the following key terms and use them in describing marketing activities.

Decisions, page 39
Plans, page 41
Window of Opportunity, page 41
Planning, page 42
Planning Horizons, page 43
Short-Range Plans, page 44
Annual Plans, page 45
Mid-Range Plans, page 45
Long-Range Plans, page 45
Goals, page 50
Objectives, page 50

Strategy, page 50
Tactics, page 50
Mission Statement, page 51
Distinctive Competencies, page 51
Situation Analysis, page 54
SWOT, page 55
Market Segmentation, page 56
Marketing Plan, page 57
Internal Marketing Environment, page 59
External Marketing Environment, page 60
Personal Use Consumers, page 61
Business and Organization Consumers, page 61

Discussion Questions

1. Marketers make many different kinds of decisions. Describe some of them.

2. Why is it important to do the right thing rather than just do things right?

3. Why do individuals plan for their personal lives? Why do marketers plan?

4. Why is a mission statement important to a business?

5. What is a distinctive competency? List a distinctive competency of each of the following:
   a. Dallas Cowboys Football Team.
   b. The University of California.
   c. The U.S. Army.
   d. Ben and Jerry's Ice Cream Company.

6. What is environmental analysis? Why is it so important?

7. What is the most important outcome for marketing decisions? Why?

8. Why is it important for marketers to carefully identify their target markets?

9. Describe the major parts of a marketing plan. How are these parts related?

10. List some external environmental factors that influence the marketing decisions of each of the following:
    a. McDonald's.
    b. A local bank.
    c. A local police force.

What Do You Think?

Marketing is a boundary-spanning activity, linking the business to its outside environments, including its competition. One of the important jobs that marketers perform for the business is to collect marketing intelligence on the competition. There are a number of ways this can be accomplished, including gathering information from the salesforce and customers, reading trade journals and industry publications, collecting competitors' annual reports and other publications, and asking competitors directly about their market offers. When the product is a tangible good, a product autopsy can be conducted. This requires purchasing the competition's products and taking them apart to determine what makes them tick. This is also called *reverse engineering*, and is very common in high-tech industries such as electronics, automobiles, pharmaceuticals, and foods. What do you think about the practice of product autopsy? Is it a good idea? Why or why not?

Source: S. Greco, M. P. Cronin, and P. Hise, "Scouting Out the Competition," *INC.* (August 1992), p. 79; A. F. Doody and R. Bingaman, *Reinventing the Wheels: Ford's Spectacular Comeback* (Cambridge, MA: Ballinger, 1988); "Dissecting a Product," *Food Product Design* 4, no. 2 (May 1, 1994), p. 52.

Mini-Case 2.1

Small Can Be Beautiful for Niche Marketers

Unless you live in or near Atlanta, it's fair to guess that you've never heard of Larder of Lady Bustle Lemon Sauce. This lemon curd sauce is one in a line of six sauces and condiments produced by Larder of Lady Bustle Ltd., a tiny (1992 sales: $100,000) specialty food manufacturer. The United States is dotted with small, local food manufacturers; over 380 are listed in *Food Finds*, a directory of local food producers. Many more are joining the ranks. The recent recession has created a business boomlet as the newly unemployed or early retirees turn to home-based food production as a low-start-up-cost opportunity to stay home and earn enough to live comfortably, but not lavishly.

Like many other small food businesses, the owners of Larder of Lady Bustle (LLB) have decided to stay small and local. They maintain that the quality of their products will suffer if they grow to the next step, and quality is a major concern for LLB's owners. Their reputation and sales are built on a quality reputation and positive word of mouth. LLB, like most small food businesses, does little advertising. Instead, sales are made at local gourmet food stores and farmer's markets (but not at supermarkets, where slotting allowances—payments to get products on crowded shelves—would be prohibitive).

Small food businesses are niche marketers. They have found profitable small gaps in the marketplace that they are filling with high-quality products. The food giants would find these niches far too small to be profitable, but consumer desires for gourmet cooking and healthy foods are a trend that sustain small niche marketers. As for the brand name Larder of Lady Bustle, the English-born owner thought her products should have a proper Victorian title, hence the tongue-twisting brand name.

Case Questions

1. What do you think is in LLB's mission statement?

2. What environmental factors might influence LLB's business?

3. Do you think that small niche businesses plan? Do they have marketing plans? Explain your answers.

Source: E. Carlson, "Small-Time Food Producers Find Growth Doesn't Pay," *The Wall Street Journal*, January 4, 1993, p. B2

Mini-Case 2.2

Euro Disney: Even a Master Marketer's Plans Can Go Wrong

Euro Disney opened near Paris in 1992, with Walt Disney Co. as a 49 percent owner. In 1993, Disney reported losses of nearly $1 billion on the park. The company claims that the European economy's slump is the reason. Others suggest that Disney made two mistakes in developing its plans: (1) assuming that Disney is always successful, and (2) forgetting that economies don't always grow. European visitors to the park complain about high prices, long lines, and no beer or wine for sale. Disney's response is to make everything, including hotels, more affordable, cut operating costs (mainly by eliminating jobs), and increase promotions.

Case Questions

1. Disney's older parks (in Orlando, Anaheim, and Tokyo) are all very profitable. What effect might their profitability have had on Disney's decisions for Euro Disney?

2. Even a company of Disney's size cannot directly affect the European economy. Does this mean that what a marketer can't control shouldn't be considered in planning?

Sources: L. Gubernick, "Mickey N'est Pas Fini," *Forbes* 153, no. 4 (February 14, 1994), pp. 42–44; J. Solomon, T. Stranger, T. Waldrop, H. Takayama, and A. Underwood, "Mickey's Trip to Trouble," *Newsweek*, February 14, 1994, pp. 34–39.

Chapter 2 Notes

1. B. A. Weitz and R. Wensley, *Strategic Marketing: Planning, Implementation, and Control* (Boston: Kent, 1984), p. 2.

2. G. Eisenstodt, "Bull in the Japan Shop," *Forbes* 153, no. 3 (January 31, 1994), pp. 41–42.

3. S. C. Jain, *Marketing Planning and Strategy*, 3rd ed. (Cincinnati, OH: South-Western Publishing Company, 1990), pp. 4–7.

4. K. E. Warren, *Long Range Planning: The Executive Viewpoint* (Englewood Cliffs, NJ: Prentice Hall, 1966), p. 5; Jain, 1990, *Marketing Planning*.

5. A. B. Fisher, "Is Long-Range Planning Worth It?", *Fortune* 121, no. 9 (April 23, 1990), pp. 281–84.

6. P. B. Carroll, "The Failures of Central Planning at IBM," *The Wall Street Journal*, January 28, 1993, p. A14; E. A. Lesly, "Borden Faces Facts: It's Time to Shed the Flab," *Business Week*, November 9, 1992, p. 44; E. Lesly, "Why Things Are So Sour at Borden," *Business Week*, November 22, 1993, pp. 78–85.

7. J. A. Czepiel, *Competitive Marketing Strategy* (Englewood Cliffs, NJ: Prentice Hall, 1992), p. 10.

8. G. Fuchsberg, " 'Visioning' Missions Becomes Its Own Mission," *The Wall Street Journal*, January 7, 1994, pp. B1, 4.

9. P. F. Drucker, *The Practice of Management* (New York: Harper & Row, 1954), pp. 50–57.

10. T. Lammers, "The Effective and Indispensable Mission Statement," *INC.* 14, no. 8 (August 1992), pp. 75–77.

11. S. F. Stershic, "Mission Statements Can Be a 'Field of Dreams,' " *Marketing News* 27, no. 3 (February 1, 1993), pp. 7, 12.

12. T. Levitt, "Marketing Myopia," *Harvard Business Review* 53 (September–October 1975), pp. 26–44, 173–81.

13. D. Machan, "We Sell Sleep," *Forbes* 150, no. 6 (September 14, 1992), pp. 421–22; M. Rowe, "Beverly Thrills," *Lodging Hospitality* 49, no. 11 (October 1993), pp. 52–54.

14. J. H. Taylor, "Niche Guys Finish First," *Forbes* 150, no. 10 (October 26, 1992), pp. 128, 132; L. Armstrong and K. L. Miller, "The Luxury Mazda Just Couldn't Afford," *Business Week*, November 9, 1992, p. 46.

Segmenting the Market: Consumer Buying Decisions

Chapter Objectives

After studying Chapter 3 you should be able to

1. Describe the two segments of consumers: business/organization and personal use.
2. Identify the characteristics of consumer purchase decisions.
3. Describe influences on business/organization consumers.
4. Recognize external influences on personal use consumers.
5. Recognize internal influences on personal use consumers.

---

*C*onsumers are the targets of marketing activities, and marketers must understand them in order to be able to bring about mutually beneficial exchanges. Consumer targets are of two types: (1) individuals purchasing products for personal use, or (2) people obtaining products for their business or organization to use in production, in operations, or for resale. The goal of this chapter is to lay the foundation for understanding the characteristics of personal use and business/organization consumers, the influences on their purchase decisions, and how those decisions are made. As you read the chapter and become more knowledgeable about consumer behavior, consider this question: Why is it that, despite all our knowledge about consumers, they still are often a puzzle to marketers?

Marketers Must Know
Their Customers

When Sara and Jay go shopping at the Food-&-More Store, they are personal use consumers, which means that the products they purchase are for their own use, to operate their household, or for family or friends. Sara, Jay, and hundreds of millions of other personal use consumers are targets of marketing activities. Marketers use the marketing mix variables (product, price, place/distribution, promotion) to try to influence consumer decisions about products and brands, which stores to patronize, when to shop, how much to buy, and whether to pay by credit, cash, or barter.

Ron Garcia, the Food-&-More Store's manager, is also a marketing target. Because space in every retail grocery store is limited, manufacturers and wholesalers constantly target Ron and other retail store managers to get shelf space for new products and acquire additional or more desirable space for existing products. A business/organization consumer like Ron obtains products to operate a business, to use in producing other products, or for resale. At other times, he obtains products for his personal use.

THE CONSUMER MIX: TWO MARKET SEGMENTS

Objective 1   Describe the two segments of consumers.

The United States is a very complex market, with millions of sellers and buyers simultaneously trying to make satisfactory exchanges. Some sellers view it as a mass market and direct only one marketing mix to all consumers. They either assume that consumers are enough alike that one offer will produce satisfactory marketing results, or consider the cost of targeting different consumer segments greater than the anticipated benefit. Other sellers modify their marketing mixes, tailoring them to satisfy different consumer targets.

Business/Organization Consumers

Business/organization consumers are classified into 1 of 11 major groups via a standard industrial classification (SIC) code number established by the Department of Commerce, Bureau of the Census. The SIC categories represent:

> *The industrial market* of manufacturers like General Motors, General Electric, Motorola, Procter & Gamble, and IBM, as well as farmers, electric utilities, building contractors, transportation companies, and such services as banks, insurance companies, and real estate agencies.
>
> *The reseller market* of wholesalers and retailers, intermediaries like Sam's Club, Home Depot, and department stores that add value to products by further processing them, breaking them into desired quantities, or selling completely finished products such as toys, refrigerators, or clothing.
>
> *The government market* of local, state, and the federal governments.

Marketing on the Internet

Buyers and sellers, personal use consumers, and business and organization consumers alike are meeting in computer space on the Internet to exchange information and make transactions. Two frequently asked questions are "How may Internet users are there?" and "How much buying and selling is going on?" Although answers to these questions change by the minute, several attempts have been made to gauge the extent of the Internet's growth and commercial activity. It is estimated that the Internet is approximately doubling in size every year. The entire Matrix (which includes the consumer Internet and core Internet) was estimated to be 27.5 million users as of October 1994. It is estimated that half the Fortune 1000 companies have an Internet address.

In 1993, business-to-business sales from about 200 to 300 Internet catalogs were judged to be $20 to $30 billion. Growing numbers of business and personal use consumers are browsing through virtual shopping centers and visiting home pages provided by such companies as AT&T, IBM, JCPenney, Hyatt, Volvo, and Toyota. Accurate sales figures, however, are not readily available. The only thing that's certain about Internet numbers is that they will rise dramatically in the coming years. ■

J. S. Quarterman, "Preliminary Partial Results of the Second TIC/MIDS Internet Demographic Survey," *Matrix News,* December 1994, mids@tic.com, http://www.tic.com; C. Lazzareschi, "Wired: Businesses Create Cyberspace Land Rush on the Internet," *Los Angeles Times* 112 (August 22, 1993), p. D1; J. Pitkow and M. Recker, "Results from the First World-Wide Web User Survey," *Computer Networks and ISDN Systems* 27, no. 2 (November 1994), pp. 243–55; C. A. Duffy, "Notable Numbers from the Road," *PC Week* 11, no. 3 (January 24, 1994), p. N1; C. Miller, "Marketers Find It's Hip to Be on the Internet," *Marketing News* 29, no. 5 (February 27, 1995), pp. 1–2; K. Shermach, "Business Marketers Are Heavy Users of Interactive Catalogs," *Marketing News* 29, no. 2 (January 16, 1995), p. 15.

The nonclassified institutional market of universities, hospitals and health centers, professional and charitable organizations, and other not-for-profit entities.

Personal Use Consumers

There are many more personal use consumers than business/organization consumers. A mass marketer may target millions of personal use consumers in the United States at the same time. Many business or organization marketers have target markets of fewer than a hundred other businesses or, if the market is really large, several thousand.

By the year 2000, the population of the United States is expected to reach over 276 million people,[1] the number of personal use consumers in the domestic market. Although marketers often refer to a mass market, the United States is actually quite diverse, reflecting differences in ethnic backgrounds, ages, religious preferences, educational levels, incomes, professions, lifestyles, and living arrangements. Despite this diversity, mass marketing continues to work profitably for many products and marketers. **Target marketing,** selecting well-defined groups of potential customers and tailoring a marketing mix to their needs and preferences, is a necessity for other

target marketing Selecting well-defined groups of potential customers and tailoring a marketing mix to their needs and preferences.

Consumer Insight

When most of us hear the term *consumer,* we usually think of personal use consumers like ourselves and less frequently consider business/organization consumers. However, businesses and organizations are equally important as consumers. A **business** is a for-profit organization under a single management that may or may not have multiple physical locations where business is conducted. An **organization** is a not-for-profit entity, such as a government, educational institution, cultural organization, zoo, health or medical association, religious group, athletic association, chamber of commerce, club, or professional membership group. In the United States there are an estimated 6.2 million industrial establishments; over 2.5 million wholesalers and retailers; a government market of one federal government, 50 state governments, and more than 86,000 local governments; and over 22,000 national nonprofit associations. Consumer insights about *both* types of consumers appear throughout this book in order to broaden your knowledge and emphasize the importance of consumers to marketing. ■

United States Department of Commerce, Bureau of the Census, *Statistical Abstract of the United States* (Washington, D.C.: U.S. Government Printing Office), January 1994, pp. 546, 794, 797, 844.

---

business A for-profit organization under a single management.

organization A not-for-profit entity or a government, educational institution, or cultural or religious association.

marketers and products. Targeting is part of the three-step process of segmentation, targeting, and positioning that will be discussed in greater detail in Chapter 6.

Market segmentation requires sorting large groups of consumers into segments—smaller groups of consumers who are similar to one another and different from other consumer groups along some prespecified dimensions. In order to be usable, segments must be similar enough (homogeneous) so that they respond alike to product offers, different enough (heterogeneous) from other groups so that they are clearly identifiable, large enough so that they are profitable to reach, and reachable so that they can be influenced by marketing efforts. Figure 3.1 identifies commonly used segmentation variables or bases. Marketers often combine several variables to better segment consumers; for example, by *demographic* variables like age and sex, *geographic* variables like region of the country, *psychographic* variables like activities and lifestyles, and *behavior* variables (whether consumers are purchasers or nonpurchasers of certain products).

A marketer selects targets from among the segments. For example, a marketer of women's jogging shoes targets consumers *demographically* as women, age 25 to 45 years, with annual incomes from $25,000 to $45,000; *geographically* as living in the midwestern and southeastern United States, in cities with populations of 125,000 or more; *psychographically* as living an active life that includes jogging; and *behaviorally* as brand loyal to top brands of jogging shoes, seeking support and fit from these shoes, not interested in style, and only moderately concerned with price.

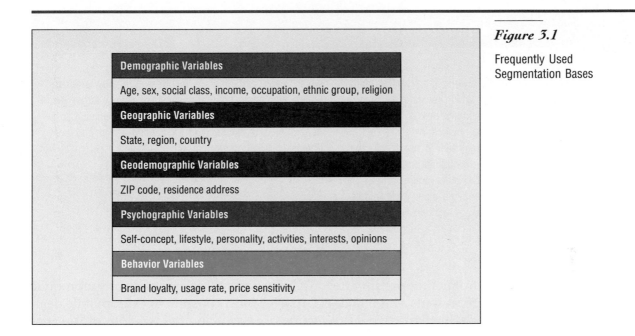

Figure 3.1

Frequently Used
Segmentation Bases

Finally, marketers seek to achieve preferential **positioning** for their brands or products, that is, how the consumer mentally views the product in relation to others. Advertising is an effective tool for helping consumers develop a mental position for national brands because it can show the brand in use.

positioning Consumer perception of a product in relation to others.

Satisfying Consumers

Consumer satisfaction is an important concept in contemporary marketing; it means narrowing the gap between what the consumer expects and values and what the marketer delivers. Some people believe marketers must go beyond satisfaction and delight consumers.[2] This means listening to consumers more carefully and frequently, being more creative in attending to consumer needs and wants, empowering employees to take the initiative to correct mistakes or make amends when something goes wrong, and instilling a service culture in the business. Saturn Corporation is trying to accomplish the latter by positioning itself as a different car and a different car company that takes care of its customers (see Photo 3.1).

Marketers can anticipate situations in which consumers may become dissatisfied, and thus counteract them. For example, marketers know that consumers often experience dissatisfaction after they've made a high-price, high-risk purchase decision. Postpurchase dissatisfaction, also called *buyer's remorse* or **cognitive dissonance,**

consumer satisfaction
Correspondence between what the consumer expects and what the marketer delivers.

cognitive dissonance
Postpurchase dissatisfaction.

Consumer Insight

A concept gaining popularity among marketers is multi-generational target marketing, which means marketing to a broader age base of consumers across generations instead of marketing to small niches or slices of the market. Support for this strategy lies in two trends that represent a convergence of psychological outlook and behaviors across generations. Young adults (18 to 29 years old) are thinking and behaving older while middle-age adults (45 to 60+) are thinking and behaving younger, which leads marketers of health and beauty products, liquor, and home entertainment products to target their products to a broader, multigenerational market. Cross-generational marketing can be a very useful and cost-effective marketing strategy. ■

S. Elliott, "Mass-Marketing to a Nation That Thinks Middle-Aged," *New York Times*, Prentice Hall Supplement (June 11, 1992), p. 6.

frequently occurs after a new car purchase because an automobile represents a high financial risk for most consumers. Automobile dealers have discovered the value of reinforcing the wisdom of the consumer's purchase decision by making personal calls on consumers immediately after the purchase to reassure them that their choice was a wise one. Saturn has gone one step further: Recognizing that most consumers are uncomfortable with haggling over price, Saturn has adopted a no-haggling pricing system specifically designed to eliminate consumer discomfort and forestall buyer's remorse. Salespeople are being trained to reduce high-pressure selling and become consumer advocates. Such a nurturing relationship is important, because automobile consumers have lots of choices and can easily take their business elsewhere.

More and more businesses are also asking business/organization consumers to tell them what it will take to delight them. Fujitsu

Photo 3.1

Consumer satisfaction is growing in importance for all types of businesses. Saturn is known for its commitment to making customers feel like part of the family.

determined that their customers wanted powerful features, reliability, flexibility, and versatility, and then used this information to make a promise to consumers to deliver what they want (Photo 3.2). Consumer satisfaction can be both a selling advantage and a meaningful way to differentiate a product from the competition, in both personal use and business/organization consumer markets.

Deviant Consumer Behavior

It would be a mistake to assume that all consumers behave rationally, according to a single model of good consumer behavior. Just as there are unscrupulous businesspeople, there are personal use consumers who act in bad faith, destructively and sometimes illegally. **Deviant consumer behaviors** represent a variety of actions in the marketplace that deviate from norms expressed by other consumers, marketers, and society. Some personal use deviant behaviors, such as writing bad checks, not reporting billing and change errors, and switching price tags, are directed against the retailer. Other behaviors, such as alcohol and drug abuse, compulsive gambling, and compulsive shopping, are nonretailer directed.

deviant consumer behaviors   A variety of actions in the marketplace that are different from norms expressed by other consumers, marketers, and society.

Fraudulent consumer behaviors such as theft "rose 35% between the mid-1980s and 1990 and equals about 2% of all U.S. retail sales excluding gas and car purchases."[3] As many as 60 percent of all personal use consumers may shoplift at one time or another.[4] Some consumers cannot control their buying urges and pile up staggering

Photo 3.2

Businesses often ask customers what they want—then deliver. Here, Fujitsu shows its response to customer requests for telecommunications that are reliable, flexible, easy to use, and affordable.

debts. Compulsive buying may affect up to 6 percent of the U.S. population, or approximately 15 million Americans.[5] The more serious antiretailer deviant behaviors are estimated to cost each family in the United States an additional $300 annually.[6]

Deviant behaviors found among business/organization consumers include fraud, anticompetitive practices, deception, and theft. Marketers and marketing students must be aware that such behaviors exist and recognize that not all consumers behave as we want or expect them to behave.

Check Your Understanding
3.1

1. Why do some marketers prefer to mass market their products?
2. How are business/organization consumers classified?
3. Explain why consumer satisfaction is so important to marketers.

CONSUMER PURCHASE DECISIONS

Objective 2 Identify the characteristics of consumer purchase decisions.

Understanding consumers is one of the keys to marketing success.[7] Unfortunately, it is not always clear what consumers need and want, how they think and feel, or how they make purchase decisions. Personal use consumer preferences and behaviors can change rapidly and sometimes unexpectedly; conversely, when they are expected to change, they may not. Some personal use consumers want products that are not good for them, such as addictive substances like tobacco, alcohol, and narcotics, and foods high in calories, cholesterol, and fat. Other consumers purchase compulsively, spending far beyond what their budgets can handle. Consumer unpredictability and, sometimes, irrationality can complicate the marketer's job and increase the difficulty of making a successful consumer–product match.

Some business/organization consumers also make questionable purchase decisions, in which they obtain unsuitable or excessively costly products, or let personal friendships with salespeople dictate their purchase decisions. Many businesses fail to anticipate or respond to changes in market demand and may make inappropriate purchase decisions. Generally, most purchase decisions are made in a systematic manner, as shown in Figure 3.2.

Make, Lease, or Buy Decisions

Obvious differences between the two types of consumers exist, yet there also are many similarities that include buying many of the same products. Regardless of consumer type, *people* make purchase

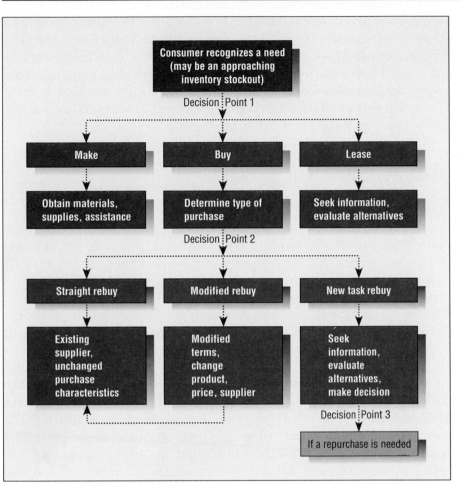

Figure 3.2

Consumer Purchase Decision
Points

decisions and their thoughts and responses are often the same, whether they are buying for themselves or for their business or organization.

Both types of consumers must decide whether to make, lease, or buy products. For example, many personal use consumers make their own clothing by purchasing raw materials (e.g., cloth, thread, buttons) and then using their talent and labor to construct finished products. Others prefer to purchase clothing from retail stores or directly through catalogs, or even lease special event clothing like tuxedos or ski outfits. Likewise, many businesses obtain raw materials and make products to use in their operations, in making other products, or for resale. Others buy or lease finished products. Leasing is becoming increasingly popular among both types of consumers. For example, automobile leasing at one time was almost exclusively a business/organization consumer decision; now it is an option used by many personal use consumers.[8]

Both personal use consumers and business/organization consumers engage in reciprocal transactions—barter or buy arrangements in which both parties benefit from product exchanges. For example, a computer store may swap a personal computer for advertising time at a local radio station, or a tire manufacturer may purchase company automobiles from an automobile manufacturer that buys its tires. These exchanges are acceptable as long as they do not unfairly restrict competition from other businesses.

Rebuy and New Task Decisions

In our chapter-opening story, Sara and Jay were purchasing products to use in operating their household. Many personal use consumer purchases are rebuys of routinely purchased products. For example, every week Sara and Jay typically buy two four-roll packages of the same brand of toilet paper. A really good special might convince them to stock up and buy more, perhaps even change brands.

Sara has a job as the purchasing agent for a local hospital. As a professional buyer, she purchases toilet paper in cases of 100 units, stocking the hospital's inventory for months at a time. Although the purchases differ in quantity and timing, they also are similar because both are **straight rebuys,** repeat purchases of products that are bought and consumed on a regular basis. (These are sometimes also called *standing orders.*) When inventory falls to a certain level, at home or in the hospital, a repeat purchase of the same product is made automatically from the same seller. Because it saves time and effort, businesses and organizations use straight rebuys when they are satisfied with the product, its price, and delivery conditions. Once the business is satisfied, there's no need to renegotiate price or product alternatives. Many routine purchase decisions are made by a purchasing agent, who doesn't consult anyone else. This may be secretaries ordering office supplies, which is only one part of their job, or professional buyers like Sara, whose full-time job is to make purchases for the hospital.

At the same time Sara is making straight rebuys for the hospital, she also is responsible for planning the purchase of a new magnetic resonance imaging (MRI) machine. Experts are called in to advise on the purchase because this sophisticated, highly complex machine represents a million-dollar investment. Representatives from the hospital's medical specialties who will use the machine participate in a collaborative decision, working together as a buying center for the hospital. This is a **new task buy,** a purchase made for the first time that requires gathering additional information and selecting among alternatives before making a purchase. The amount of information required in a new task buy depends on the product, cost, risk, and

straight rebuys   Repeat purchases of products that are bought and consumed on a regular basis; sometimes called *standing orders.*

new task buy   A purchase made for the first time that requires gathering additional information and selecting among alternatives.

Marketing Application 3.1

Personal use and business/organization consumers often use the same decision processes to make their purchases, and they frequently purchase the same categories of products. Someone at your school purchases paper, pens, and lightbulbs for the school. You may buy these same products for your personal use. To illustrate some differences between consumer types, contrast the purchase of any of these products by consumer types (personal use or business/organization). Consider quantity purchased, product features (number of items per package), storage, price, purchase frequency, and who makes the purchase decision. Ask a purchasing agent at a school, local government, or the business where you work about their purchasing procedures. How do they make routine purchases of such products as paper, pens, or lightbulbs? How do their purchases differ from those of a personal use consumer? Bring your findings to class for discussion. ■

situation. A high-risk, high-cost purchase of a unique or highly specialized product like an MRI machine requires greater effort than a new task buy of a low-risk, relatively low-cost product. For example, a self-serve photocopying business expanding into a self-serve fax business makes a new task buy of fax machines. The business's experience with similar products means that the buying task, although new, is relatively uncomplicated.

Personal use consumers also make new task buys, such as a first-time purchase of an automobile, home, or computer. The amount of time and effort spent in making the decision depends on the type of product, its complexity, its cost, and the risk associated with making a bad purchase decision.

Modified rebuys require greater effort than do straight rebuys, a need for more information, and consideration of alternatives, yet they typically involve less effort than do new task buys. A modified rebuy results from dissatisfaction with the existing product, price, terms of delivery, or suppliers, or a change in purchase specifications or operational needs. Frequently, all that is required is renegotiating the purchase from the existing supplier. Personal use consumers make modified rebuys when they change brands; for example, switching from one brand of jeans to another. Characteristics of the three types of purchase decisions made by business/organization consumers are shown in Figure 3.3.

modified rebuys Rebuys of alternative products resulting from dissatisfaction with some aspect of the existing product.

Participants in the Decision Process

A **buying center** is a more or less formal group of people who work together to make a purchase decision. In a business or organization, buying centers may be formed across departmental or functional

buying center A more-or-less formal group of people who work together to make a purchase decision.

Figure 3.3

Three Types of Purchase
Decisions

Variable	New Task Buy	Modified Rebuy	Straight Rebuy
Purchase frequency	Unique or very in-frequent	Fairly frequent to routine	Routine, automatic, recurring
Risk involved	Often high; may be low	Moderate to low	Low
Information needed	Often extensive	Moderate	Little to none
Alternatives considered	For high-risk buy, many	Few	No alternatives considered
Decision makers	Often a buying center	Depends on situation, one to many	One or only a few
Proportion of buys	Unique or infrequent	More frequent	Most purchases, very frequent for many consumers

lines for complex, high-cost, high-risk, and/or unique product decisions. Some buying centers operate on a regular basis. For example, the hospital's buying center made the MRI purchase decision; employees of a state's environmental protection department collaboratively make purchase decisions about products used in operating their offices.

A family acts as an informal buying center when family members participate in decision making. Family members influence decisions about such expensive purchases as a new car or vacation, as well as inexpensive purchases like which movie to rent or where to go for fast food. Buying center members in businesses, organizations, and families play certain roles, including:

The *initiator* who suggests the need to consider a purchase.

The *gatekeeper* who collects and distributes information.

The *influencer* who attempts to affect the decision (there can be more than one influencer).

The *buyer* who makes the purchase.

The *user* who uses the products (there can, of course, be more than one user).

Decision-Making Steps

Although straight rebuys are automatic, many businesses and organizations have formal, written, highly detailed directions for the steps to be taken when making new task or modified rebuys. Once a business, government, or other organization recognizes a need for a product, product requirements are identified and stated as product specifications that suppliers must meet. A search for suppliers is initiated. Interested suppliers submit proposals (bids) for the buyer to evaluate. (Governments often must advertise their product needs and formally invite suppliers to submit competitive bids for them. Many government contracts must be awarded to the lowest bidder in a sealed bidding process.) After a supplier is selected, final terms are set and, when all parties are satisfied, a written contract is signed. Periodic reviews are conducted to evaluate the adequacy of the product and supplier. Failure to satisfy a business/organization consumer can result in the supplier being denied a chance to bid on future contracts.

By contrast, most personal use consumer decisions are simple and routine, requiring minimal additional information or effort and few steps in the decision process. Relatively inexpensive and low-risk products such as groceries, leisure clothing, or cleaning services are simple decisions. Habit and brand loyalty (always buying the same brand) remove much of the effort from decision making, particularly for routinely purchased products, and reduce the number of steps between need recognition and purchase.

Other personal use consumer decisions are complex and not made easily or routinely, as illustrated in the model in Figure 3.4. These decisions involve extensive information search, the evaluation of alternatives, and more steps between the recognition of a need and the purchase that satisfies it. A new car purchase is a complex purchase decision in which the risks are much higher than they are from the purchase of breakfast cereal. In addition to the *financial* risk from a mistake, there is a *social* risk in purchasing a car that family and friends ridicule, a *physical* risk from an unsafe product, and a *time loss* risk if the automobile is unreliable and needs frequent repairs. Generally, the higher the risk is, the more steps are involved in the decision process and the more time is spent searching for information and identifying and evaluating alternatives. What risk is illustrated in Photo 3.3?

Check Your Understanding
3.2

1. Describe these alternatives: make, lease, or buy.
2. Contrast rebuy and new task buying decisions.
3. What is a buying center?

Figure 3.4

Consumer Purchase Decision
Model

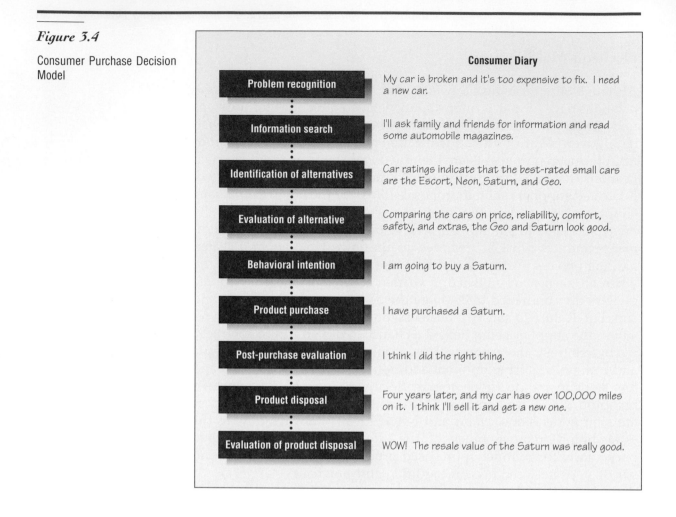

Consumer Diary

Problem recognition	My car is broken and it's too expensive to fix. I need a new car.
Information search	I'll ask family and friends for information and read some automobile magazines.
Identification of alternatives	Car ratings indicate that the best-rated small cars are the Escort, Neon, Saturn, and Geo.
Evaluation of alternative	Comparing the cars on price, reliability, comfort, safety, and extras, the Geo and Saturn look good.
Behavioral intention	I am going to buy a Saturn.
Product purchase	I have purchased a Saturn.
Post-purchase evaluation	I think I did the right thing.
Product disposal	Four years later, and my car has over 100,000 miles on it. I think I'll sell it and get a new one.
Evaluation of product disposal	WOW! The resale value of the Saturn was really good.

Photo 3.3

Hair colorings help consumers
avoid perceived social risks.

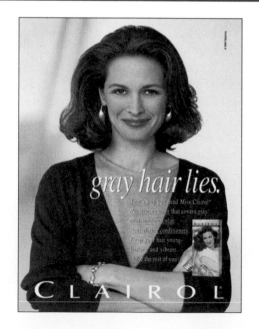

82

Marketing Application 3.2

Marketers sometimes use fear appeals to highlight risks to consumers, and then show how their products can counteract the risks and benefit consumers. Locate two fear appeal print advertisements in national publications, such as the one shown in Photo 3.4. To what types of risks do the fear appeals refer? Do the products represent complex or simple consumer decisions? How effective are the advertisements in influencing consumer purchase decisions? Bring the advertisements to class for discussion. ∎

Photo 3.4

Mild fear appeals put the advertiser in the role of helping the consumer solve problems, in this case, bad weather driving.

BETTER GRIP.

BUSINESS/ORGANIZATION CONSUMERS

Purchase decisions made by business/organization consumers are influenced by many factors. Some are long term, others are transitory; some are internally derived, others reflect external influences.

Objective 3   Describe influences on business/organization consumers.

Organizational Direction

When a business or organization states its mission, sets goals, and develops strategies, it also establishes a broad framework for its purchase decisions. For example, if a business sets out to be a low-cost, low-price leader in its industry and markets, its purchase decisions will reflect a low-cost priority. If the priority is to make high-quality offers, then the quality priority influences purchase decisions. These influences typically are long term and generated internally, as they reflect top-level strategic decisions.

Demand

Demand exerts a powerful force in purchase decisions made by businesses and organizations. **Derived demand** occurs when demand for

derived demand   Demand for one product increases the demand for other products.

one product increases demand for other products. When personal use consumer demand rises, so will demand for business products. In a growing economy in which home construction rises, increased home sales mean increased demand for furniture, washers, dryers, and other household goods. Personal use consumer demand fuels increased demand for industrial products as well as for products distributed by resellers. Derived demand is closely associated with business cycles. Consider what happens in a recession when the economy slows down—personal use consumer demand falls, which has repercussions all the way back to the businesses that supply raw materials for manufacturing. Derived demand in relation to a growth in home construction is outlined in Figure 3.5, showing the positive and negative effects.

Business/organization consumer purchases also are influenced by how sensitive demand is for their products when prices change. **Elastic demand** means that a change in price stretches demand: Demand rises when price falls, and demand falls when price rises, hence price and demand move in opposite directions. **Inelastic demand** means that demand remains the same regardless of price fluctuations over a broad range of price changes. This type of demand is seen for products that consumers consider essential, which means that they have a higher tolerance for price changes. **Fluctuating demand** reflects general economic conditions, in which demand usually rises when the economy is robust and falls when the economy is weak.

elastic demand   Demand changes when price does, and the two change in opposite directions.

inelastic demand   Demand remains the same, regardless of changes in price.

fluctuating demand   Demand rises and falls according to the state of the economy.

Figure 3.5

Effects of Derived Demand

EFFECTS OF DERIVED DEMAND		
Steps	Positive	Negative
1	Consumer housing purchases rise.	Consumer housing purchases fall.
2	New homes require new appliances like refrigerators.	Fewer new homes, fewer durable goods needed.
3	Demand for new refrigerators stimulates the manufacture of refrigerators.	Demand falls, manufacturing slows.
4	Manufacturer needs increase demand for parts and raw materials.	Manufacturers need fewer parts and raw materials.

Other Purchase Factors

Other influences on business/organization purchase decisions relate to the nature of the purchase situation. Although human emotions cannot be removed totally from business/organization buying, the assumption is that business/organization purchase decisions are far more rational than emotional, as reflected in advertising directed to business/organization consumers. (An example of a rational appeal for a printer purchase is shown in Photo 3.5.) Although a personal use consumer may make an **impulse purchase,** buying something on a whim, business/organization consumers are not expected to make such purchases. Nor are they expected to exhibit variety-seeking behavior, changing brands or purchasing habits out of boredom.

impulse purchase   Something bought on a whim.

Professional buyers, whose buying performance is evaluated by others, must be more knowledgeable about their purchases, weigh alternatives carefully in order to get the best deal, and frequently engage in negotiations with competing suppliers. Their buy decisions often are based on carefully designed specifications and technical requirements, particularly when the decision involves large sums of money and long-term commitments.

Many business/organization purchase decisions involve greater risk than do most personal use consumer purchase decisions. A wrong purchase decision may place the decision maker's career at risk as well as have financial repercussions for the business or

Photo 3.5

According to Texas Instruments, rational reasons for purchasing a new printer include compatability, performance, reliability, and value.

organization purchaser. This is particularly true with a purchase that represents a large sum of money, as with industrial or farm equipment.

A product's price affects both types of consumers; however, a product's price for the business/organization consumer often can be accounted for as a cost that can be passed along to the eventual consumer. However, costs that are too high cannot always be passed along, because they make a product's price uncompetitive. Just like personal use consumers, business/organization consumers have an incentive to negotiate the best possible price for the products they purchase in order to keep their operating costs down and, for business consumers, their profit margins up.

For the business/organization consumer, product quality often means how well a product conforms to technical specifications, sometimes with a zero tolerance for defects or errors. Quality and price are often considered jointly, and a trade-off may be made between the two by purchasing a product of somewhat lesser but still acceptable quality in order to save money.

Terms of delivery, training, warranties, guarantees, and set-ups are services that often accompany a product and provide a way to differentiate among comparable products. Service may be the deciding factor in making a business/organization purchase decision when other things are almost equal. For example, when a business is considering the purchase of new computers, if the prices, features, and quality of competing products are comparable, the supplier who offers services such as setting up the new computers, teaching employees how to use them, and offering a money-back satisfaction guarantee may get the purchase order.

Check Your Understanding 3.3	1. How can a mission statement direct purchase decisions?
	2. Explain the terms: *Derived, elastic,* and *inelastic demand.*
	3. Describe other purchase factors that influence business/organization consumers.

EXTERNAL INFLUENCES ON PERSONAL USE CONSUMERS

Objective 4 Recognize external influences on personal use consumers.

consumer behavior All the activities involved in selecting, purchasing, evaluating, and disposing of products.

Consumer behavior is all of the activities involved in selecting, purchasing, evaluating, and disposing of products. Some of these actions can be observed directly, whereas others cannot. Consumer behavior is influenced by both external and internal factors. External influences are more clearly recognizable than are internal influences, and may affect different consumers simultaneously, although not necessarily identically. External influences are grouped according to whether they are social (e.g., family, reference groups, class, culture), marketing (e.g., product, price, place, promotion), or situational (e.g., finances, time, weather) influences.

Social Influences

People exert social influences on other people's purchase decisions. Two of the most direct, small-scale, personal, and important social influences on consumers are families and reference groups. Family, friends, and co-workers often give purchasing advice, but it isn't always taken. Other social influences are large scale, less personal, and direct but still powerful. These include social class, microculture, and culture. For the most part, marketers have little if any control over large-scale social influences, yet it is important to understand how they affect consumer behavior.

Family   The family household is an intimate group, comprised of at least two or more people related by blood or marriage living together. Family purchasing decisions often are made collectively. In the 1950s, the American family was idyllically and often mistakenly described as an "Ozzie and Harriet" family of a dad who worked out of the home, a mom who was a homemaker, and two children. This nuclear family might have fit a television program, but even in the 1950s it didn't reflect single-parent families, childless families, multigenerational families, housemates, or families living in poverty.[9] Families are diverse and often fragile entities.

In the 1990s, the stereotypical nuclear family (working dad, homemaker mom, two kids) exists in less than 10 percent of American households.[10] Although the number of family households is declining, 97.3 percent of Americans live in households defined as one or more people who *may or may not be related* sharing a residence.[11] Households include unrelated housemates and communal living arrangements. Since the 1950s, the number of single-parent families has dramatically increased, particularly those headed by single women. (Note, however, that the number of single-parent households headed by males also is currently increasing.[12])

Marketers are interested in people's living arrangements and the stages through which they pass during a lifetime, because these stages represent different needs and purchase opportunities. Consider three different lifestages—young marrieds, full nest, and empty nest—that affect furniture purchases. When two people decide to marry, it often requires their moving into a larger space, which means they must buy new furniture. When they have a child it initiates a different set of purchase decisions, among them decisions to purchase children's furniture and perhaps move to a larger living space. An older couple whose grown children no longer live with them often move into a smaller living space, which necessitates selling their eight-person sofa and purchasing a two-person loveseat for their small condominium's living room.

demographics Statistics describing a particular population in terms of age, income, birth and death rates, and education level.

Marketers should pay close attention to consumer **demographics.** Demographics are statistics that describe a particular population by such numerical facts as age, income, birth and death rates, and education level. The U.S. government is the world's most prolific collector of demographic information, which marketers use extensively to develop greater knowledge about consumers. The importance of following demographic trends is illustrated by the impact of the **baby boomers,** a cohort of people born during the time following World War II (1946 to 1964) who have experienced the same historical events. Over the years, the force of this population bulge has influenced many marketing decisions. Baby boomers will become the wealthiest Americans ever, due to inherit over $6 trillion from their parents, who made good investments in the galloping economy of the 1950s and 1960s.[13] Aging baby boomers are fueling growth in many product categories, from golf-centered retirement communities to adult incontinence-care products.[14] From birth to death, the baby boomers represent a demographic phenomenon whose purchasing clout has challenged and enriched many marketers.

baby boomers People born from 1946 to 1964.

Marketers also are interested in how people make decisions together, in living groups as well as work groups. In some family households one or both parents dominate all family decisions, from large (e.g., what family car to purchase, where to take the family vacation) to small decisions (e.g., what foods and beverages to purchase). In an extended family of grandparents and other adults in the household, purchase decisions may also be influenced by these family members. Depending on the product being purchased, decision-making influence shifts among group members.

Family members often assume decision-making roles or patterns of behavior based on other people's expectations and tradition. Roles often are linked to one's gender, and typically convey information about status and power. A stereotypical mother's role in the nuclear family is that of food purchaser, whereas a stereotypical child's role is that of user of many products and influencer for others. Purchasing roles in family groups also have their counterparts in work and social groups.

A consumer may assume many different roles at the same time in the family, at work, and in social groups. Sara, from our chapter-opening story, is simultaneously a woman, wife, daughter, sister, aunt, hospital purchasing agent, jogging club member, choir member, and amateur artist. Her multiple roles sometimes conflict, but all

Marketing Application 3.3

Conduct an inventory of your roles. How many roles do you play? (For example, a male student also may be a son, husband, father, uncle, employee, religious group member, softball player, and band member all at the same time.) Do any of the expectations for your behavior in these roles sometimes conflict? How does your work role influence specific purchase decisions? Are there types of roles that you share with others? Could this commonality of role types be a useful basis for targeting consumers? Bring your role inventory to class for discussion. ■

of them exert both subtle and overt cues as to how she should behave and what she should buy in order to conform to her own and others' expectations.

Children are important targets for marketing actions because they are product users, initiate many decisions, influence even more, and often have a large amount of spending money at their disposal. Marketers often look at children as consumers in training, who can be influenced to develop a brand loyalty that may carry over into their later role as adult decision makers. It is estimated that children influence more than $132 billion in purchases annually in the United States.[15]

Traditional gender and family roles in the United States are constantly changing, as shown in Photo 3.7. In recent years fathers have been taking a more active role in raising their children; more parents are working at home, often running a small business; and more men are doing the household shopping, because 70 percent of American women hold jobs outside the home.[16]

Reference Groups Family and close friends make up a consumer's primary social groups, which often have an immediate, powerful impact on what the consumer purchases. Secondary social groups such as work groups, religious groups, sororities and fraternities, and clubs also influence consumer purchases. This is particularly true of aspirational groups—those to which the consumer already belongs or hopes to join. On the other hand, groups that the consumer wishes to avoid (avoidance groups) may have the opposite influence. For instance, if it is fashionable for a street gang to wear blue and gold jackets, a gang-avoider would never purchase clothing with these colors, so that he could avoid being identified as a gang member or sympathizer. The importance of reference groups can be seen in the power of opinion leaders, people who are highly regarded by group members and set the pace in consumer purchases

International Marketing Report

Children are heavily marketed to in the United States, as illustrated in Photo 3.6. Marketing to children is more stringently regulated and sometimes prohibited in Western Europe and other markets. The European Union has harmonized over 50 different country laws that restrict advertising to children. The European Association of Advertising Agencies has proposed a strict 12-point self-regulation code that does not allow children to verbally endorse, present, handle, consume, or compare products in advertisements. Under this code, many advertisements shown in the United States would be barred from countries in the European Union. ■

P. R. Cateora, *International Marketing,* 8th ed. (Homewood, IL: Irwin, 1993), p. 528.

Photo 3.6

Although some countries ban or restrict advertising to children, the United States allows it.

Photo 3.7

Changing family roles affect purchase decisions.

(as shown in Photo 3.8). If a group's opinion leader buys a leather coat, then others may follow his or her lead. Professional athletes, such as Michael Jordan, are opinion leaders for many teenagers, and their purchase decisions may be influenced by what the opinion leader says, does, and wears.

Class   Social classes in the United States are not as rigid as in other countries, yet even in America there are relatively homogeneous, stable groups of people with similar incomes, power, and prestige who hold related beliefs, attitudes, and social values. Consumers are characterized by their social class and often stereotyped, as in the assumption that upper-class consumers prefer fine wines and designer bottled waters whereas lower-class consumers prefer beer and sweetened cola drinks. Class influences store choice—for example, upper-middle-class consumers are associated with shopping at Saks Fifth Avenue and Tiffany's, whereas the lower-middle-class are more likely to shop Kmart and Wal-Mart. The United States is noted for its class mobility, in which an individual can move up by getting an education and a well-paying job, or move down by virtue of losing a job and income. Class cues are subtle signals alerting the consumer about what products a particular class is expected to purchase.

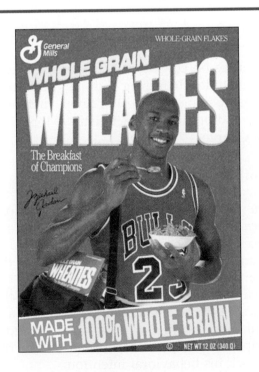

Photo 3.8

Popular figures who can influence consumer decisions are called opinion leaders.

Marketing Application 3.4

How multicultural is your city? For an illustration of multicultural influences on consumer behavior, look through your local telephone directory under the yellow pages heading for restaurants. Categorize the listings under cultural headings, for example: Chinese, Mexican, Thai, Greek, Japanese, and Italian. Count the number of entries that can be identified under each ethnic type. Are there any restaurants that advertise "American" food? What does your restaurant list suggest about the influence of culture on eating habits in your city? Find out the population characteristics of your city by using reference books or calling the chamber of commerce or local government. Compare the number of ethnic restaurants to the proportional representation of each culture in your city's population. How do they compare? What conclusions can you draw from your data about cultural influences on consumer behavior in your city? From your own experiences, do you believe these ethnic restaurants have altered their products in order to conform to American tastes? Is this a good marketing idea? ■

Microculture/Culture

The United States is a diverse union of people from many different cultural backgrounds. Large and small microcultures with distinctive characteristics, preferences, and sometimes languages thrive within the larger U.S. culture. Marketers often target their products specifically to consumers from a microculture. Culture and microcultural influences will be discussed at length in Chapter 5.

Marketing Influences

Marketing influences on consumer behavior are the marketing mix variables. These include advertising and sales promotions; store characteristics such as opening and closing times, merchandise mix, and location; pricing; and product characteristics. More will be said about these factors in Chapters 7 through 13.

Situational Influences

Consumers are influenced by nonmarketing factors, also called *situational influences,* that are beyond the marketer's control. These are circumstances that exist when the consumer is making a purchase decision and range from the weather, time of day, availability of transportation to reach a retailer, condition of the economy, or the consumer's finances. For example, Jay, from our chapter-opening story, is a stamp collector. He had planned to attend a stamp show in a nearby city but an ice storm closed the highway and he was unable to make the trip. The bad weather and resulting road conditions intervened to block his behavioral intention.

Marketing Application 3.5

Consumers, both personal use and business/organization, often must gather information to guide their purchase decisions. Product information can be obtained from knowledgeable salespeople, manufacturer-supplied information, U.S. government publications, and popular and trade publications. For some products, there is so much information that the typical consumer has difficulty evaluating it. As a test of this statement, go to your school library and find comparative information on the current model year of any two automobiles (foreign or domestic) in the $18,000 to $29,000 price range. Use publications such as *Consumer Reports, Consumer Digest, Road and Track,* and *Car and Driver.* Based solely on what you have read in these magazines, which car would you purchase, assuming money was not a limiting factor? What key information prompted your decision? What other sources of information, including people, would you seek out? Why? Bring your results to class for discussion. ■

Other situational influences are technological change, whether the purchase is a gift, or sudden changes in product supply. Technology changes rapidly, particularly in electronics, which may make a planned purchase obsolete. As for gifts, a consumer typically will spend more on a gift for a friend or loved one than on an obligatory gift for a person not well liked or known. Anticipated product shortages also influence purchases. News of the approaching winter storm that blocked Jay's trip to the stamp show also panicked consumers into stocking up on groceries, because they anticipated being stranded in their homes and unable to reach a grocery store for several days. Marketers often try to stimulate stock-up purchases by offering product price incentives.

Check Your Understanding 3.4

1. Describe the types of external influences on personal use consumer purchase decisions.
2. How can life stages influence a family's purchases?
3. Explain how roles, reference groups, and opinion leaders influence personal use consumers.

INTERNAL INFLUENCES ON PERSONAL USE CONSUMERS

Internal influences on consumer decision making, sometimes called *psychological factors,* are individual and unique. They cannot be seen but must be inferred by observing behaviors or using research techniques designed to uncover them.

Objective 5 Recognize internal influences on personal use consumers.

Needs and Motives

Needs are gaps between reality and a desired state that create a tension the individual seeks to release through goal-directed behavior. Needs can be primary (biogenic or physiological) survival needs for liquids, food, sleep, and shelter, or secondary needs that are social or psychological needs for financial security, social companionship, esteem, and accomplishment. An individual may experience multiple needs at any time, but some are more important than others. Obviously, a life-or-death need for water far exceeds a need for social acceptance, at least until the thirst is satisfied. Whatever the need, it can drive a consumer to make goal-directed, need-satisfying purchases. Motives are needs that have been energized and directed toward a goal.

Socially influenced needs are called *wants.* Needs can be socially modified by family, friends, and colleagues, as well as by marketing efforts. Advertisements often send signals to consumers about the needs that can be satisfied by purchasing and using certain products. Which need is being signaled for in Photo 3.9?

Involvement

Think back to our shoppers, Sara and Jay. Sara is an ardent 10K runner; she is passionately involved in her sport and regularly

---

Photo 3.9

Is this a primary or secondary need? Can it be socially influenced?

Reprinted by permission of Merrill Lynch, Pierce, Fenner & Smith Incorporated. Copyright 1992.

participates in out-of-state races. This activity is personally important to her and she seeks information relevant to her interests. Jay is a stamp collector. His involvement is quite different from Sara's, which means he is receptive to information relevant to his interests and unreceptive to information about activities that don't interest him. Involvement is an important concept in consumer behavior, because it explains many other factors and acts as a powerful information screen. By identifying people who are involved, marketers can direct their messages to those consumers who are receptive and avoid those consumers who are not.

Perception

Consumers select, organize, interpret information, and give meaning to it through the process called *perception.* Typically, consumers are very selective in their perceptions, which means that several consumers exposed to the same advertisement may have very different responses. This can be explained by determining whether or not these consumers are involved. Those who are involved will pay attention to the message they select to receive; uninvolved consumers may ignore the message.

Perception is a multistep process, as illustrated in Figure 3.6. A stimulus or cue (1) triggers the process. This may be an advertisement, a friend showing you a new purchase, the smell of popcorn popping in a shopping mall, or a taste picked up by a sensory receptor (2). Once the stimulus reaches the individual through one

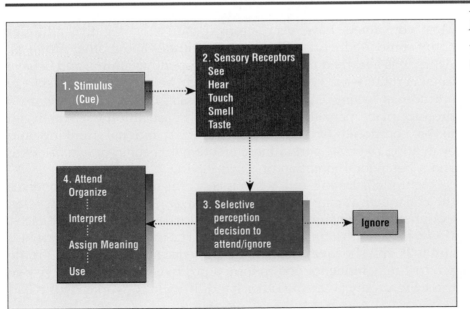

Figure 3.6

The Multistep Process of Consumer Perception

or more senses, the individual decides (consciously or unconsciously) to either receive or ignore it (3). This process occurs in a split second. If selected, the stimulus information is organized, interpreted, assigned meaning, and then used (4). Consumers selectively decide which information to process, whether or not to retain it, and how to interpret and use it. Often, the information is stored in memory until needed to assist in making a purchase decision.

Learning

Almost all consumer behavior is learned. You eat an ice cream cone for the first time, enjoy it, and store this learned positive information in your memory. The next time you are offered an ice cream cone, there's no delay in accepting it. On the other hand, if you have a negative experience, it is also learned, stored, and used at a later date in determining behavior. Any change in behavior that results from experience or the interpretation of experience is called *learning*. Learned information is stored in our memory to be retrieved for later use. You can't see learning take place, but you began learning at birth and won't stop until death. Knowing this, marketers try to educate consumers about their products. Advertisement repetitions rely on consumers' learning, storing information in memory, and then using it to make a purchase decision. Jingles, music, celebrities, and fragrances are used to aid consumers in learning about products, associating them in memory, and then recalling and using the information for a purchase.

Attitudes and Attitude Change

Most consumers have very strong positive or negative attitudes about some products and weak or no attitudes about other products. Attitude is a learned predisposition to respond to stimuli and behave in a certain way. Contemporary researchers commonly refer to attitude as feeling—an overall like, dislike, or neutrality toward a product, place, person, or situation. In the past, attitude was believed to be composed of three components: a rational thinking and evaluating *cognitive* part; a more emotional, feeling, or *affective* part; and a behavioral intention or *conative* part.

Attitude is lasting and, when it concerns a product that involves the consumer, it may be difficult to change. Attitudes may develop from both the consumer's own experiences and others' experiences. If your sister tries SnackWell's low-fat chocolate sandwich cookies and tells you she loves them, her experience and enthusiasm for the product may influence you to form a positive attitude before you've tried the product. On the other hand, if your co-worker had a bad

Career Watch

Manny Garcia has been a Burger King Corp. franchisee in Orlando, Florida, for over 23 years. He's seen marketing chiefs come and go and was understandably skeptical of the new marketing chief, Sid Feltenstein, when he came to visit Garcia. This was because Feltenstein was the firm's ninth marketing chief in the last decade. What sold Garcia was the way Feltenstein listened to customers and workers during his visits to Garcia's 41 area Burger King restaurants. Coming to the hamburger chain from marketing duties at Dunkin' Donuts and Procter & Gamble, Feltenstein had his work cut out for him. In the view of one marketing consultant, the chain has one longstanding problem: "It is perceived as a runner-up to McDonald's but has done little to capitalize on its second-place position, as Pepsi-Cola and Avis Inc. have done in their industries." Feltenstein is attacking the problem of consumer perceptions on many fronts, such as adding new products, dinner service, new distribution places (including selling burgers in kiosks in airports and truck stops), and cleaning up store landscapes and exteriors. ■

G. DeGeorge, "Sid Feltenstein Is Having It His Way," *Business Week*, November 23, 1992, pp. 64, 68; M. Prewitt, "Miami Subs Rekindles Growth with MG, III Buy," *Nation's Restaurant News* 28, no. 43 (October 31, 1994), pp. 3–5.

experience at a fast-lube shop, his negative experience may influence you to form a negative attitude about that particular shop, and so you avoid it.

Marketers often try to change consumer attitudes. Attitude change can be accomplished, but it is more difficult to do the closer the attitude is tied to the consumer's self-concept (i.e., the greater his/her involvement with the attitude object). Often it requires a combination of methods, including marketing communication in advertisements, salespeople, opinion leaders, and consumer word of mouth. Significant attitude changes have taken place in the United States over the last several decades, including our attitude toward smoking cigarettes. Despite the efforts of tobacco lobbyists, smoking among adults nationwide is on the decline. Attitude changes have also resulted in behavior changes about wearing seat belts and combining alcohol consumption and driving.

Personality

Each of us has a personality—the totality of all of the traits and experiences, preferences, and behaviors that make us unique and capable of self-reflection. Consumer behavior researchers have long sought connections between personality and consumer behavior, often fruitlessly. Personality traits such as self-confidence, creativity, stability, and sociability are often used to describe people. In essence, these traits describe what we are and only sometimes what we buy and why.

In Chapter 4, our focus shifts from understanding influences on consumer purchase decisions to a broader perspective of examining the interaction of marketing and society.

Check Your Understanding 3.3	1. What are needs? How are they related to motives? 2. How does involvement influence perception? 3. What is an attitude? Can consumer attitudes be changed?

Review of Chapter Objectives

1. *Describe the two segments of consumers.* There are far more personal use consumers than there are business/organization consumers. Personal use consumers make purchases for themselves, their families, and friends. Business/organization consumer purchases are for products used in production and operations, or for resale. Marketers apply knowledge of consumers when segmenting, targeting, and positioning their products. The goal is to identify those consumers who are most receptive and target the offer to them. Consumer satisfaction is very important, because dissatisfied consumers can easily find alternatives in the market. It is important to recognize that not all consumer behavior is "good," nor do all consumers behave as we wish them to in every situation.

2. *Identify the characteristics of consumer purchase decisions.* Consumers must decide whether to make, lease, or buy the products they need. If they buy, then it becomes a decision whether to make a straight rebuy, modified rebuy, or new task buy. Many purchase decisions are made in buying centers—groups of people who work together to make a purchase decision.

3. *Describe influences on business/organization consumers.* A business or organization's mission statement, goals, and strategies set a direction that carries through to influence purchase decisions. Derived demand that originates with personal use consumers has a ripple effect throughout the distribution and production systems and, thus, influences purchase decisions. Other considerations such as price, quality, and risk also influence business/organization purchase decisions.

4. *Recognize external influences on personal use consumers.* There are social, marketing, and situational influences on personal use consumers. Social influences include one's family, reference groups, social class, and cultural factors. Marketing influences are the ways product, price, place/distribution, and promotion are used. Situational influences vary widely and include such factors as the weather, time, and economic conditions.

5. *Recognize internal influences on personal use consumers.* Although internal influences cannot be seen, they are very powerful influences on purchase decisions. These factors include needs and motives, involvement, perception, learning, attitudes, and personality.

Key Terms

After studying Chapter 3, you should be able to define each of the following key terms and use them in describing marketing activities.

Target Marketing, page 71
Business, page 72
Organization, page 72

Positioning, page 73
Consumer Satisfaction, page 73
Cognitive Dissonance, page 73
Deviant Consumer Behaviors, page 75
Straight Rebuys, page 78
New Task Buy, page 78
Modified Rebuys, page 79

Discussion Questions

1. Explain why you think consumer behavior is such a puzzle to many marketers.

2. Can someone be both a business/organization and personal use consumer? Explain your answer.

3. What is deviant consumer behavior? Why is it important that marketers be aware of such behaviors?

4. Explain the difference between a make, lease, or buy decision by both consumer segments.

5. Pretend that your school is purchasing its first-ever schoolwide computer system. This system will be used for academic, administrative, research, and teaching purposes. Who should sit on the school's buying center committee?

6. Of the following product purchases, which has the highest financial risk, the highest physical risk, or the highest social risk?
   a. New clothes to wear on a first date.
   b. New 486SX personal computer.
   c. Fifteen-year-old used car.

7. Jim is walking through Cherry Blossom Mall. A pair of boots in a store window attracts his eye. He doesn't need boots, but decides to try them on. He likes them so much, he purchases them. Is this an impulse purchase? Explain your answer.

8. What is the baby boom generation? Why is it of such interest to marketers?

9. Who influenced your choice to attend school? What were your internal influences? Your external influences?

10. What is a multigenerational family? What different opinions might members of such a family give when faced with a decision about a family vacation?

What Do You Think?

David and Marylou Marsh Sanders own EcoSport, a New York–based organic clothing company. They connect to "green" consumers by offering clothing made only from certifiably organically grown cotton. They even have made a T-shirt for Greenpeace, the environmental activist organization. According to Marylou, marketing EcoSport's environmentally correct line is more than good business. "It's a product that only brings good karma." It's something you feel good about doing, so it's easy to do.

Although consumers express concern for the environment, a recent survey showed that only 11 percent were willing to pay 5 percent extra to purchase environmentally correct products. Why do you think consumers say one thing but won't follow through with their purchases? How would you identify a target market for

EcoSport's clothes? What characteristics do you think define their customers? What benefits are these consumers seeking? What related products might the Sanderses expand into while still serving the same customer base? Is this a good business to be in now? What do you think?

Sources: H. Schlossberg, "Makers of Organic Clothes Find Mainstream Outlets, *Marketing News* 27, no. 5, (March 1, 1993), pp. 1, 2; R. Mummert, "All-Natural Products," *Success* 40, no. 2 (March 1993), pp. 20–21.

Mini-Case 3.1

What Has Happened to the Fat-Conscious Consumer?

Are consumers giving up on low-fat and fat-free foods? Although this market is worth about $12 billion per year, there are indications that many consumers who once were anxious to reduce fat in their diet are now opting for taste, which means fats, salt, and sugar. Häagen-Dazs real cream ice creams outsell their healthier frozen yogurts by 13 to 1. Wendy's loaded cheeseburgers are outselling the "lite" version 3 to 1. Rice snack cakes, which are healthy but virtually tasteless, recently have lost three market share points. Healthy Choice, ConAgra's broad line of low-fat cookies, frozen desserts, frozen meals, and cheeses, is suffering slow and, in some categories, declining sales. Campbell Soup's best-selling new soup in 35 years is cream of broccoli. What's happening? Have consumers abandoned lite foods?

Indications are that consumers who have tried lite foods are now looking for something more. According to one food analyst, "There is definitely a trend toward the full-flavored foods." Another food marketer says, "People are not willing to compromise on flavor."

Case Questions

1. What do you think is happening to consumers' commitment to eating healthy?

2. If you were a marketer of a line of healthy foods, would you abandon the healthy food market?

3. Do you think this trend toward more flavorful foods will last? Why or why not? Can you explain your answer in terms of demographics?

Sources: S. W. Bhargava, "Gimme a Double Shake and a Lard on White," *Business Week*, March 1, 1993, p. 59; Y. Ono, "Think Thin? Not At Kraft, Home of Velveeta," *The Wall Street Journal*, January 25, 1995, pp. B1, 10; "U.S. Consumers Return to Indulgence," *Eurofood*, June 1994, pp. 7–8.

Mini-Case 3.2

Gender Differences Show Up in Consumer Behaviors

Research has shown that the supermarket is one place where gender differences between consumers are highly visible. Men generally can be separated into two kinds of grocery shoppers, those that are "lost in space" and efficiency experts who get in and out as fast as possible. Women, on the other hand, are generally more conscientious, seek sales and specials, make lists, and check the registers to ensure that prices are rung up correctly. Women also are more brand loyal. Younger men tend to use convenience stores more often, and men in general pay less attention to brands. They make last-minute emergency dashes to the supermarket without a list, which makes them particularly vulnerable to impulse purchases.

Gender differences also appear in how men and women use computers. Women tend to use computers as tools, sticking with older versions of software that get the job done. For men, computers are toys that need new software, games, and attention. Although women *use* computers, men *play* with them. According to W. M. Bulkeley, "Men seem to want computers to be their friends."

Gender differences also show up among business/organization consumers. For example, for female business travelers, security, service, and cost are more important factors in making a hotel selection than they are for male business travelers.

Case Questions

1. Do you think social pressures could have anything to do with these gender differences?

2. Are these gender differences important to marketers? Explain your answer.

3. Will some of these differences change as (1) more men have to do the grocery shopping and (2) more women have to use computers?

Sources: S. L. Hwang, "From Choices to Checkout, the Genders Behave Very Differently in Supermarkets," *The Wall Street Journal*, March 22, 1994, pp. B1, 10; W. M. Bulkeley, "A Tool for Women, a Toy for Men," *The Wall Street Journal*, March 16, 1994, pp. B1, 2; J. E. Rigdon, "Now Women in Cyberspace Can Be Themselves," *The Wall Street Journal*, March 18, 1994, pp. B1, 2; K. W. McCleary, P. A. Weaver, and L. Lan, "Gender-Based Differences in Business Travelers' Lodging Preferences," *Cornell Hotel & Restaurant Administration Quarterly* 35, no. 2 (April 1994), pp. 51–59.

Chapter 3 Notes

1. United States Department of Commerce, Bureau of the Census, *Statistical Abstract of the United States* (Washington, D.C.: U.S. Government Printing Office, January 1994), pp. 850–852.

2. E. E. Scheving, "Going Beyond Customer Satisfaction," in *Marketing 93/94*, ed. J. E. Richardson (Guilford, CT: The Dushkin Publishing Group, Inc., 1993) pp. 59–61.

3. D. Cox, A. D. Cox, and G. P. Moschis, "When Consumer Behavior Goes Bad: An Investigation of Adolescent Shoplifting," *Journal of Consumer Research* 17, no. 2 (September 1990), pp. 149–59.

4. D. L. Loudon and A. J. Della Bitta, *Consumer Behavior: Concepts and Applications*, 4th ed. (New York: McGraw-Hill, 1993), p. 648.

5. C. Arthur, "Fifteen Million Americans Are Shopping Addicts," *American Demographics* 14, no. 3 (March 1992), pp. 14–15.

6. M. R. Solomon, *Consumer Behavior* (Needham Heights, MA: Allyn and Bacon, 1992) p. 540.

7. L. Fortini-Campbell, *The Consumer Insight Workbook* (Chicago: The Lisa Fortini-Campbell Company, 1992).

8. A. Haas, "The New Era of Leasing," *Lexington Herald-Leader,* February 21, 1994, pp. 8–9.

9. J. Seligmann, "What Traditional Family? Debunking the Ozzie and Harriet Myth," *Newsweek,* December 7, 1992, p. 67; J. L. Zaichkowsky, "Consumer Behavior: Yesterday, Today, and Tomorrow," in *Marketing 93/94*, ed. J. E. Richardson (Guilford, CT.: The Dushkin Publishing Group, Inc., 1993), pp. 113–20; K. Ames, S. Lewis, P. Kandell, D. Rosenberg, and F. Chideya, "Cheaper by the Dozen: Hard Times Are Fueling Rising Numbers of Multigenerational Families," *Newsweek,* September 14, 1992, pp. 52–53.

10. Solomon, *Consumer Behavior,* p. 281.

11. "The Changing American Household," *American Households: American Demographics Desk Reference Series No. 3, American Demographics,* July 1992, p. 3.

12. J. Seligmann, D. Rosenberg, P. Wingert, D. Hannah, and P. Annin, "It's Not Like Mr. Mom," *Newsweek,* December 14, 1992, pp. 70–71, 73.

13. J. Warner, "The Family Fortune: 'Can We Talk?'" *Business Week,* March 1, 1993, pp. 106–7.

14. G. Stern, "Demographics Fuel Adult-Diaper Sales," *The Wall Street Journal,* March 20, 1992, pp. B1, 5.

15. J. U. McNeal, "The Littlest Consumers," *American Demographics* 14, no. 2 (February 1992), pp. 48–53.

16. L. Zinn, "Real Men Buy Paper Towels: More Ads Aim at the Guys Who Do the Household Shopping," *Business Week,* November 9, 1992, pp. 75, 76.

Market Analysis—A Broader Perspective

The Marketing Environment

After studying Chapter 4 you should be able to:

1. Define the dual roles of marketing in society: micromarketing and macromarketing.

2. Describe the rights, responsibilities, and ethical dilemmas of marketers.

3. Identify governmental controls on marketing.

4. Explain consumerism and the Consumer Bill of Rights.

5. Identify some important contemporary societal issues involving marketing.

A **society** is a political, geographical, and social entity that is defined by the rules, regulations, values, and behaviors its people accept and live by. The United States is a complex society made up of people from many different cultural and national backgrounds. This society of over 262 million people and thousands of businesses and organizations depends on marketing, yet at the same time it often directs serious criticisms at marketers and marketing activities.

Marketing activities are easily criticized because they are more visible to consumers than are most other business areas and because they deal with sensitive issues like pricing, advertising, and selling. Marketers often must make decisions in gray areas not clearly governed by laws or regulations or where regulations are not up to date or consistently enforced. This makes the marketer vulnerable to legal, regulatory, and ethical missteps. Marketers often face **ethical dilemmas,** difficult situations in which there are valid but conflicting alternatives and it may not be clear which action or decision is right. A small minority of marketers act illegally or unethically. However, problems can arise even for honest marketers because they are caught in a crossfire, balancing consumer demands for satisfaction against their company's demands for revenues. Honest marketers don't fail to do the right thing because they are evil; more likely it is because they have poor judgment, possess incomplete information, misunderstand, lack guidance, or fail to consider the decision's

society A political, geographic, and social entity defined by the rules, regulations, values, and behavior its people accept and by which they live.

ethical dilemmas Difficult situations in which there are valid but conflicting alternatives and it may not be clear which action or decision is right.

consequences. Whatever their cause, marketing mistakes hurt consumers, marketers, and, ultimately, society by undermining everyone's confidence in the marketing process. As you read this chapter and become familiar with the issues, ask yourself these questions: What is the role of marketing in society? Does marketing benefit or blemish society?

| *Making Ethical Marketing Decisions* | Ethan Nkwame turns from the chalkboard to face the participants in a conference on marketing ethics. "I've listed on the board some of the most critical ethical issues in marketing, from a study conducted in 1985. Look at the list (see Figure 4.1) and let's talk about the ones that are the most troublesome to you. Are these still the same issues you consider today? What has changed over the last few years? What hasn't changed?"

Jaye Baker reads the list and immediately raises her hand. "I was brought up to be a moral person. I try to do the right thing. Yet my manager is pressing me to increase sales and my competitors are out there trying to win over my customers with kickbacks and free tickets to basketball games. I feel I can't be a successful industrial salesperson if I'm honest. From my perspective, the biggest problems are *bribery* and *honesty*."

Next to raise a hand is Ted Chin. "I'm in advertising and my problem is clients who lie about their products. The Federal Trade Commission allows harmless exaggerated claims, but some of my clients want to go beyond exaggeration. It's sometimes hard to judge where exaggeration ends and misleading, deceptive *advertising* begins."

The last to raise a hand is Tina Stoltz. "You've all raised important issues from your perspective as marketers, but I think we need to look at these problems from the consumer's side. *Fairness* is a serious problem. Consumers need good information to make good decisions, yet they can't always get that information from salespeople or advertisements. There are too many *copycat products* on the market; often they're of *poor quality* and *overpriced*. Consumers are tired of *hard-sell* telephone calls at dinner time and junk mail. *Consumers no longer trust us.* That's the biggest ethical problem we face today." |

MARKETING'S SOCIETAL ROLES

Objective 1 Define the dual roles of marketing in society: micromarketing and macromarketing.

micromarketing The way marketing connects a business and its suppliers, distributors, and consumers in activities designed to deliver satisfaction.

macromarketing The way marketing contributes to our economic system and overall societal welfare by balancing supply and demand.

Marketing is important to society as it concurrently plays roles at the micro and macro levels. **Micromarketing** is the way marketing connects a business, its suppliers, its distributors, and consumers in activities designed to deliver satisfaction. This is the perspective that most consumers have of marketing on a personal, individual scale, and it is the focus of this book. There is also a much broader perspective, **macromarketing,** which is large scale and reflects how marketing contributes to our economic system and overall societal welfare by balancing supply and demand. The macromarketing system is composed of all the smaller micromarketing units that act to carry out society's orders. It is often difficult to determine with certainty where micro ends and macro begins. Many corporations have become so large that their marketing activities can have an impact on society. Likewise, similar actions of many marketers on the micro level can have larger, macro effects.

Question: Describe the job situation that poses the most difficult ethical or moral problem for you.	
Frequency	**Ethical Issue**
15%	Bribery
14	Fairness
12	Honesty
12	Pricing
11	Product
10	Personnel
5	Confidentiality
4	Advertising
4	Manipulation of data
3	Purchasing

Figure 4.1

Ethical Issues in Marketing (as cited in a survey of 281 members of the American Marketing Association)

Reprinted by permission of the publisher from "Ethics and Marketing Management: An Empirical Investigation," by Laurence B. Chonko and Shelby D. Hunt, *Journal of Business Research*, 13, pp. 339–59. Copyright ©1985 by Elsevier Science Research, Inc.

Micromarketing: The Individual Perspective

Micromarketing is seen from the perspective of the individual marketer, consumer groups, the business or organization, and the network of suppliers, distributors, and even the competitors that participate in or influence the business's marketing activities. The goal of the micromarketing system, particularly for those businesses and organizations that have adopted the marketing concept, is producing mutually beneficial exchanges with consumers. Determining whether marketing is a benefit or a blemish on the micro level means evaluating if marketing achieves the goals set for it by the individual business or organization; whether or not relevant consumers, suppliers, and distributors are satisfied; and the impact (if any) similar marketing activities have on society.

Although the marketing concept sounds like it should inspire businesses to always act in the consumer's best interest, not all companies have adopted the concept, nor do all companies that have adopted it know how to make it work. As a result, many consumers complain that, on a personal level, marketing is not working well for them. They complain about overpriced prescription drugs, poor-quality automobiles, annoying television advertisements, confusing food labels, and disposable diapers that clog landfills. These complaints show up in consumer protests and boycotts, consumer calls to businesses using 1-800 customer service lines, responses to consumer surveys and, ultimately, when dissatisfied consumers effectively lobby politicians, in new laws and regulations that control marketing activities.

In an ideal world, buyers and sellers at the micro level should be on a fair and equal footing, neither having an advantage over the other. In reality, the buyer (consumer) often is at a disadvantage. The seller may have information about product quality, obsolescence, or price that is not shared with the consumer and, therefore, undermines the consumer's ability to make an informed choice. Advertisers exaggerate the ability of their products to make you sexy, thin, or successful. High-pressure salespeople try to talk consumers into wanting products they don't need and can't afford. Instead of being mutually beneficial, some exchanges reflect a "let the buyer beware" attitude, in which the marketer puts profit ahead of customer satisfaction.

You might conclude from this analysis that there's lots of room for improvement on the micro level. Keep in mind, however, that not every consumer can be satisfied with each and every marketing encounter. Consumer satisfaction is a moving target. For example, although consumers might have been satisfied at one time with a record player, now they want a compact disc player; consumers want more than they sometimes need, generally prefer more over less, and expect an increasingly better standard of life. Although consumers may be satisfied generally, a few areas of dissatisfaction typically get the most attention. Only the most foolish marketer assumes that just because consumers are satisfied today they still will be satisfied by the same marketing mix tomorrow.

Marketing is boundary spanning, because it is the process that links the business directly in exchanges with its external environments, consumers, markets, and members of the marketing network (e.g., suppliers, distributors). As a result, marketers are often caught in a crossfire between consumers, who claim marketing should satisfy their needs, and the marketer's business, which claims marketing should generate revenue. Consumer satisfaction needs and business profit needs often seem to conflict, and the marketer is left trying to balance all claims and satisfy all parties. Criticisms of marketing can often be traced to a number of root conflicts involving the marketing mix variables shown in the following list. This list is not complete, but it does illustrate the types of complaints leveled at individual marketers, marketing managers, and the marketing activities of particular businesses or organizations.

- *Products* that are unsafe, identical to existing products, of poor quality, or environmentally unfriendly.
- *Prices* that are too high, covering inefficient business practices that raise costs of production, or prices that discriminate against the poor and disadvantaged.
- *Place* restrictions that limit where products are offered or when, or excessive use of intermediaries, which add to costs.
- *Promotion* that is overly aggressive and misleading, advertising, and telephones sales at meal time.

Consumer Insight

Marketers who adhere to the marketing concept put customer satisfaction first. They often publicize their commitment and encourage consumers to freely communicate with them about the products they purchase and whether or not they are satisfied. This has led some personal use consumers to become expert complainers who believe that their dissatisfaction deserves compensation by the offending business. Tips on profitable complaining techniques are even profiled in a monthly newsletter. One expert estimates her annual complaining income to be over $2,000. Even Ralph Nader, the embodiment of consumer advocacy, says that "he is often taken aback by how savvy, crafty and dauntless consumers have become." Mounting consumer awareness and occasional consumer militancy is also attributed to better consumer education as well as economic hard times. More often than not, a business will err on the side of the consumer and pay up even if the complaint is unjustified. This is judged to be a wiser alternative than to risk losing the lifetime value of the consumer's business. ■

E. Fenner, "Smart, Single and on Her Way to a Million," *Money* 23, no. 1 (January 1994), pp. 106–17; F. Bruni, "For Some Consumers, It Pays to Complain," *Lexington Herald-Leader*, February 27, 1994, p. J6.

- *Demand stimulation*, particularly of unwholesome demand, encouraging consumer materialism.
- *Privacy* issues involving marketing research and database marketing.

Marketing is not the only area of business criticized for its societal shortcomings. The overheated business environment of the 1980s also saw its share of abuses in finance, production, management, and human resources. Problems in the other business areas, however, do not excuse legal and ethical failings in marketing.

Another aspect of marketing's micro role is how businesses interact with other businesses, specifically their own suppliers and distributors, as well as competitors. Interactions within the marketing network can become disorderly, which has damaging results for consumers if they have to pay more because of marketing inefficiencies. Competition between sellers can lead to bitter rivalries that can upset consumers who won't tolerate what they perceive as unfair or excessively combative interchanges. Legal and regulatory oversight sometimes is needed to help keep competitive excesses under control.

Macromarketing: The System Perspective

There is an even broader role for marketing in a free market economy like that of the United States: Business is essential to the functioning of an entire economy, and marketing is the key business activity that evens out supply and demand imbalances by bringing sellers and buyers together. The vital role of marketing is being felt

Marketing Application 4.1

As a consumer, have you experienced problems in the marketplace? For example, have you bought a product that was unsafe? Do you know of two products that are identical except for their brand name and price? Are there advertisements (promotions) that you find objectionable? Have you been bothered by meal-time telephone sales calls? For each marketing mix category (product, price, place/distribution, promotion), describe a problem you've experienced and, if possible, identify the companies involved. Make a list and bring it to class to discuss and compare. From this class comparison, identify the most common types of marketing problems experienced. ■

even in the former Soviet Union. Great imbalances between supply (not enough, low quality, high priced, poorly distributed) and overwhelming demand in the former Soviet Union are very slowly being smoothed out. Marketing activities play a critical role in the process.

The U.S. government sets broad national goals; business provides what is needed to achieve the goals by creating jobs, raising capital, paying taxes, and producing products. Marketing is the mechanism by which business delivers a standard of living to society. Marketing exchanges encourage production, which provides consumers with choices, better products, and competitive prices. Marketing has tremendous power in a free market, but it also has a responsibility to operate within the law in a manner acceptable to the society that empowers it.

If marketing reflects society, then the societal values of honesty, trust, and fairness should also be key values in marketing. Critics of marketing at the macro level say it is not doing a good job of serving society honestly and fairly.[1] They complain that marketing costs too much and wastes resources through inefficiencies such as excessive numbers of brands and advertisements—that it stimulates unnecessary demand and undermines societal moral values by promoting materialism. **Materialism** is a preference for material possessions (goods and services) over spiritual and intellectual pursuits. Others believe that society is at fault. Society promoted materialism and prosperity after World War II as a solution for poverty, discrimination, and pollution without sacrificing an increasingly abundant range of product choices.[2]

Although marketing's success in its macro role is debated, it is clear that society has become so complex that it's difficult to imagine the economic system functioning without marketing. Marketing can deliver a good quality of life filled with many products that few of us would willingly give up; yet, at the same time, marketing is not serving other parts of society very well, particularly the poor, and those with physical disabilities and the disadvantaged. Criticisms

materialism   A preference for material possessions over spiritual and intellectual pleasures.

of marketing, both micro and macro, must be addressed, because if they are not resolved, they can undermine the credibility and effectiveness of all marketing activities.

1. Distinguish between the dual societal roles of marketing: micro and macro.
2. Should marketers be concerned when consumers believe that marketing is not working well for them? Explain your answer.
3. How does society benefit from marketing activities?

THE RIGHTS AND RESPONSIBILITIES OF MARKETERS

Because consumers and the economy benefit from marketing activities, our society encourages such activities by granting marketers broad rights.[3] Although there is no complete or generally accepted list of these rights, some timeless and generally accepted ones are presented in Figure 4.2. Generally, marketers may compete in any way as long as they do not break any laws, do adhere to existing rules and regulations, and don't harm consumers, society, or the competitive environment. When marketers overstep these rights, they may gain a short-term advantage, but in the long term they are usually punished.

Objective 2 Describe the rights, responsibilities, and ethical dilemmas of marketers.

Marketing's Societal Responsibilities

Along with rights, marketers also have responsibilities. At the same time that some business scholars criticize businesses for not being

Figure 4.2

The Rights of Marketers

THE RIGHTS OF MARKETERS				
Product	**Price**	**Promotion**	**Place**	**Services**
To introduce any product design, size, style, or color as long as it doesn't cause harm to consumers; to be able to withdraw or change products at any time.	To price the product as desired, as long as the price doesn't restrict competition or discriminate unfairly against consumers.	To promote products as much as desired in any medium for as long as needed, provided there is no deception or fraud.	To distribute products in any reasonable manner, offering products for sale wherever desired.	To offer product guarantees and services postsale, as desired or not.

Reprinted by permission of *Harvard Business Review.* An exhibit from "What Consumerism Means for Marketers," by Philip Kotler, May/June 1972. Copyright © by the President and Fellows of Harvard College; all rights reserved.

able to make the marketing concept work successfully, others believe that they should go even further and adopt the societal marketing concept. The societal marketing concept proposes that, in addition to operating by the marketing concept (see Chapter 1), a business should also operate in the public interest for the good of society. This requires making micro-level decisions that ultimately and collectively deliver benefits for society at the macro level. Individual marketers and businesses have conflicting views on what is best for society. Some short-term marketing activities can have long-term unintended consequences. Most macro-level societal problems are highly complex and long term, taking decades to resolve if they can be resolved at all. By adopting the societal marketing concept, marketers would have to ensure that their marketing activities serve society in such ways as protecting the environment, employing the hard-core unemployed, boycotting repressive political regimes in other countries, and producing only safe, healthful products.

Many businesses already demonstrate their concern for society. A recent survey showed that 76 percent of the business respondents believe that " 'good' companies have an obligation to 'give back to society,' " but they disagree on a definition of social responsibility.[4] Businesses are developing and offering consumer education programs, encouraging employees to become community volunteers on company time, operating consumer affairs information offices, promoting recycling programs, and removing roadside billboards. One Wall Street brokerage donates to charities half of the firm's commissions paid by buyers for new issue stocks and bonds—in 1991 this amounted to $300,000 for over 40 charities. Beneficiaries of this philanthropy include the Hearing Dog Program of Minnesota, the Downtown Women's Center of Los Angeles, and the Greater Boston Food Bank.[5]

Ben & Jerry's Homemade Inc., a Vermont producer of quality ice cream products, is known for its social conscience. The company pays more than market price for its milk because its owners, Ben Cohen and Jerry Greenfield (Photo 4.1), feel the Vermont dairy farmers need the money more than the company does, and the company gives away 7½ percent of pretax profits.[6] Celestial Seasonings's founder and CEO, Mo Siegel, has always embraced environmental activism for himself and the company.[7] You've probably enjoyed Newman's Own all-natural products (salad dressing, spaghetti sauces, popcorn, lemonade, and salsa). On every Newman's Own product, the label states, "Paul Newman donates all profits, after-taxes, from the sale of this product to educational and charitable purposes." Since Newman's Own was founded in 1982, Paul Newman has donated over $56 million to charity. For 1993, Paul Newman's charity donation amounted to over $7 million. Many smaller businesses contribute generously within their local commu-

Photo 4.1

Ben and Jerry's ranks high on a social audit of businesses whose actions benefit the community and society.

Photo 4.2

Newman's Own products also demonstrate a social consciousness.

nities, finding deserving outlets for their products, expertise, and, often, employees' time. For example, three Kinko Copy Center affiliates in California are active conservationists engaged in large-scale reforestation projects in their areas.[8]

Although social programs may be costly, they can also be beneficial marketing tools. By publicizing its social responsibility, the business may be carrying out the wishes of its owners and employees as well as attracting new investors and customers who share the company's social concern. The business may be able to head off

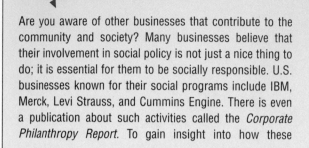

Marketing Application 4.2

Are you aware of other businesses that contribute to the community and society? Many businesses believe that their involvement in social policy is not just a nice thing to do; it is essential for them to be socially responsible. U.S. businesses known for their social programs include IBM, Merck, Levi Strauss, and Cummins Engine. There is even a publication about such activities called the *Corporate Philanthropy Report.* To gain insight into how these companies contribute to society, contact one of them through their public affairs office and ask for details on company philanthropy and volunteer programs. Alternatively, you might want to find out if any businesses in your community are involved in such efforts. Bring your results to class to help build a profile of how businesses can contribute successfully to the public good. ■

passage of new laws and regulations by acting rapidly and voluntarily to remedy what otherwise might be required by government. Finally, there is a strong incentive to make society better in the expectation that if life is better, demand will rise and greater profits will result. The Japanese use corporate philanthropy and social strategies to gain competitive advantage. Japanese businesses' contributions to charities are growing at about 20 percent annually. The Council for Better Corporate Citizenship, made up of 320 of the largest companies in Japan, finds ways for these companies to undertake social programs designed to make the world better.[9]

Marketing Ethics

Marketers must be knowledgeable of and adhere to the laws and regulations that govern marketing activities. Society also sets ethical standards for business conduct. Where marketing activities are not clearly governed by laws or regulations, the marketer sometimes faces tough ethical choices with no clear-cut correct alternative.

ethics The moral principles and values that both establish expectations for people's behavior and determine standards that set limits and define the boundaries of good and bad.

Ethics are the usually unwritten rules of conduct that a society enforces to maintain order, including such notions as fairness, honesty and trust, and adhering to proper conduct while avoiding the improper. Ethics are moral principles—values that establish expectations for people's behavior and determine standards that set limits and define boundaries where good becomes bad. The ethics of a society are taught to successive generations by parents, religious organizations, friends, and institutions including schools, businesses, and government. Just as people make laws that can eventually change, people formulate ethical standards that also can eventually change. Ethics often are situation specific, which sometimes makes it difficult to clearly determine the right and wrong of a situation.

International Marketing Report

Marketers also may face ethical dilemmas when they market internationally. Although kickbacks and bribes are illegal in the United States, they are common and expected in many other countries. Whether the practice is called Egyptian *baksheesh*, Kenyan *dash*, or Mexican *mordida*, American businesspeople are forbidden by the Foreign Corrupt Practices Act to use bribes to smooth the way for foreign business dealings. Laws against such payoffs are widespread; their enforcement often is noticeably lax. Corruption in China is common and predictable. Kickbacks are routinely demanded from foreign investors in Venezu-

ela. Bribery has become a serious problem in Russia, where many Russians seek payoffs for facilitating business ventures. The best advice for Western marketers doing business in any foreign country is if you are approached for a bribe, "Don't even think about it!"■

M. Elliott, D. Elliot, T. Padgett, J. Contreras, and R. Moreau, "Corruption: How Bribes, Payoffs and Crooked Officials Are Blocking Economic Growth," *Newsweek*, November 14, 1994, pp. 40, 42; V. Reitman, "To Succeed in Russia, U.S. Retailer Employs Patience and Local Ally," *The Wall Street Journal*, May 21, 1993, pp. A1, 8; A. A. Brott, "How to Avoid Bear Traps," *Nation's Business*, September 1993, pp. 49–50.

Ethical marketers have a social contract to adhere to the letter and spirit of the law, abide by rules and regulations, and, some believe, provide for the good of society. Ethical marketing behavior in the long run is also in the best interest of the business and marketer. However, the highly competitive, aggressive business environment of the 1980s appears to have undermined many marketers' decisions and called some of their behaviors into question. Sometimes personal standards of ethics were compromised in order to turn a profit. Bribes, deceptive promotions, copied products, and intellectual property infringements are examples of unethical and illegal misdeeds you may have read about in the popular business press. Other infringements may not have been illegal, but were still unethical.

In making difficult decisions in which the right answer may be unclear, the marketer might be wise to consider applying the Golden Rule ("Do unto others as you would have them do unto you"), the Mom Rule ("Do as you could explain to your mother in good conscience"), and the TV Rule ("Do as you could explain your actions on television without embarrassment to millions of people").

Professional Self-Regulation

Marketing is also regulated by codes of conduct and ethics that have been written and agreed to by trade associations, industries, store chains, and individual businesses. Many businesses and trade associations have responded to what appear to be increasing numbers of ethical and legal lapses by instituting codes of behavior that define more clearly what is and is not acceptable. The American Marketing Association has a code of ethics (see Figure 4.3) that marketers must

Figure 4.3 The American Marketing Association's Code of Ethics

Members of the American Marketing Association (AMA) are committed to ethical professional conduct. They have joined together in subscribing to this Code of Ethics embracing the following topics:

Responsibilities of the Marketer

Marketers must accept responsibility for the consequences of their activities and make every effort to ensure that their decisions, recommendations, and actions function to identify, serve, and satisfy all relevant publics: consumers, organizations and society. Marketers' professional conduct must be guided by:

1. The basic rule of professional ethics: not knowingly to do harm;
2. The adherence to all applicable laws and regulations;
3. The accurate representation of their education, training and experience; and
4. The active support, practice and promotion of this Code of Ethics.

Honesty and Fairness

Marketers shall uphold and advance the integrity, honor, and dignity of the marketing profession by:

1. Being honest in serving consumers, clients, employees, suppliers, distributors and the public;
2. Not knowingly participating in conflict of interest without prior notice to all parties involved; and
3. Establishing equitable fee schedules including the payment or receipt of usual, customary and/or legal compensation for marketing exchanges.

Rights and Duties of Parties

Participants in the marketing exchange process should be able to expect that:

1. Products and services offered are safe and fit for their intended uses;
2. Communications about offered products and services are not deceptive;
3. All parties intend to discharge their obligations, financial and otherwise, in good faith; and
4. Appropriate internal methods exist for equitable adjustment and/or redress of grievances concerning purchases.

It is understood that the above would include, *but is not limited to*, the following responsibilities of the marketer:

In the area of product development and management:

■ Disclosure of all substantial risks associated with product or service usage
■ Identification of any product component substitution that might materially change the product or impact on the buyer's purchase decision
■ Identification of extra-cost added features

In the area of promotions:

■ Avoidance of false and misleading advertising
■ Rejection of high pressure manipulations, or misleading sales tactics
■ Avoidance of sales promotions that use deception or manipulation

In the area of distribution:

■ Not manipulating the availability of a product for purpose of exploitation
■ Not using coercion in the marketing channel
■ Not exerting undue influence over the resellers' choice to handle a product

In the area of pricing:

■ Not engaging in price fixing
■ Not practicing predatory pricing
■ Disclosing the full price associated with any purchase

In the area of marketing research:

■ Prohibiting selling or fund raising under the guise of conducting research
■ Maintaining research integrity by avoiding misrepresentation and omission of pertinent research data
■ Treating outside clients and suppliers fairly

Organizational Relationships

Marketers should be aware of how their behavior may influence or impact on the behavior of others in organizational relationships. They should not encourage or apply coercion to obtain unethical behavior in their relationships with others, such as employees, suppliers or customers.

1. Apply confidentiality and anonymity in professional relationships with regard to privileged information.
2. Meet their obligations and responsibilities in contracts and mutual agreements in a timely manner.
3. Avoid taking the work of others, in whole, or in part, and represent this work as their own or directly benefit from it without compensation or consent of the originator or owner.
4. Avoid manipulation to take advantage of situations to maximize personal welfare in a way that unfairly deprives or damages the organization or others.

Any AMA members found to be in violation of any provision of this Code of Ethics may have his or her Association membership suspended or revoked.

Marketing Application 4.3

Do you belong to a professional organization that has a code of ethics? If so, bring a copy of the code to class. If not, locate a profession's code of ethics either from a professional in that field (e.g., a dentist, advertising account executive, physician), by contacting the head- quarters office of the profession, or through library research. Bring a copy of the code to class for discussion. Compare and contrast it with the American Marketing Association's Code of Ethics. ■

accept in order to become members of the association. A code of ethics for marketing represents a subset of all the codes that influence a marketer. In addition to the individual's ethical code, marketers also operate within the marketing codes of their employers, the ethical standards of their professional association, the industry ethical standards, the economic sector ethical standards, and the ethics of society. These standards can help guide the marketer through any difficult decisions that must be made.

Self-regulation is often undertaken to head off government intervention. For example, the four television networks (ABC, NBC, CBS, and FOX) and the movie industry were recently pressured by Washington to reduce gratuitous violence in their programs and films. To forestall government intervention, the networks took preemptive action to issue alerts prior to some programs. These printed messages that flashed on the screen stated "Due to some violent content, parental discretion advised." Rather than eliminate violence, they warned parents about it. Critics said this preemptive strike was not enough and government may still have to intervene.[10] Further complicating the issue, a federal appeals court has ruled that overly broad regulations restricting "indecent" television broadcasts during hours when children may be watching constitute an infringement of the First Amendment's guarantee of free speech. This may provide grounds for challenging restrictions on violent programming and advertisements.

Other forms of self-regulation include local Better Business Bureaus (BBB)—nongovernmental groups supported by local businesses that educate consumers, handle complaints against businesses, and arbitrate business disputes. Local BBBs are becoming more active in educating consumers against fraud through consumer councils, in which consumers pay a small membership fee to receive monthly bulletins about local scams, prepurchase product reports, assistance in resolving disputes, and direct help with purchasing questions.[11] Nationally, the Council of Better Business

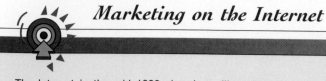

Marketing on the Internet

The Internet in the mid-1990s has been likened to the Wild West of early American history. It is an electronic frontier, a place in computer space where hard and fast rules are hard to find, behavior sometimes gets out of control, and things change by the hour. Remember, the Internet is a vast network of interlinked computer systems—ten thousand networks that link millions of computers worldwide. It is not owned or controlled by any single person, company, or organization, although it is subsidized by governments, universities, and businesses. Consumer behaviors are largely unregulated on the Internet, except for the minimal editorial control over their subscribers that can be exerted by commercial information services such as America Online (AOL). AOL and other companies provide a gateway to the Internet for a fee. Netiquette (etiquette on the Internet) and accepted rules of conduct are the only behavioral controls for most users.

Marketers, and others who are interested in developing the commercial potential of the Internet, are concerned about ensuring privacy in a place (the Internet) where there is **no** privacy, and security in a place that is hard to secure. For at least the near future, Net users must assume that any message they send can be intercepted and any visits to commercial locations (virtual stores) can be traced. Therefore, providing a credit card number when making a Net purchase raises the possibility that the number may be captured and then used fraudulently. Ensuring secure ways to make purchases on the Internet is a high priority. Currently, Internet purchases are usually paid for through such traditional channels as the telephone, fax, and even "snail mail" (letter). Concerned Internet user groups are studying the societal impacts of this technology and ways to civilize the Internet. Others fear that regulation will stifle the free exchange of information that has earned the Internet its reputation as the "Wild Wild Net." ∎

M. Meyer, A. Underwood, P. King, S. Rhodes, and D. Rosenberg, "Stop! Cyberthief!" *Newsweek* February 6, 1995, pp. 36–38; F. D. Zinn and R. C. Hinojosa, "A Planner's Guide to the Internet," *Journal of the American Planning Association* 60, no. 3 (Summer 1994), pp. 389–98; B. P. Kehoe, *Zen and the Art of the Internet: A Beginner's Guide to the Internet, First Edition,* INET_ZEN.TXT (electronic file transfer), January 1992; D. Pearl, "Government Tackles a Surge of Smut on the Internet," *The Wall Street Journal* February 8, 1995, pp. B1, 8; K. B. Sullivan, "Secure Internet Servers Just Around the Corner; By Early 1995," *PC Week* 11, no. 49 (December 12, 1994), pp. N1–2; J. Louderback, "The End of Internet's Age of Innocence," *PC Week* 11, no. 48 (December 5, 1994), pp. 158–59.

Bureaus, along with three advertising trade organizations, supports the National Advertising Review Board (NARB), which oversees complaints about advertising.

Check Your Understanding
4.2

1. What rights do marketers have in the United States?
2. Discuss marketing's societal responsibilities.
3. What kinds of ethical dilemmas do marketers sometimes face?

GOVERNMENT CONTROLS MARKETING THROUGH LAWS AND REGULATIONS

Objective 3 Identify governmental controls on marketing.

Even though it may appear that government is forever placing limits on business, in reality laws and regulations can't possibly cover everything that happens in the marketplace.

Marketing Application 4.4

Do you know how your local BBB works? Contact your local Better Business Bureau (BBB) and find out what services it offers both buyers and sellers. Does your local BBB have anything like a consumer council? Try to find out if consumer complaints are increasing in your community. If they are, what explanations are possible for the increase? ■

Laws

Laws are formal statements that guide actions and set limits and penalties for infractions. Common law built up through previous court rulings prevailed in the early years of American history; statutory or written law has governed U.S. businesses since the beginning of the 20th century. Other legal systems prevail in other parts of the world, primarily Napoleonic or code law, and Islamic law.

laws Formal statements that guide actions and set limits and penalties for infractions.

Society is made up of people; people make laws both to control and limit behaviors that they believe are harmful to society and to enforce society's standards. Laws also can be changed to reflect changes in the attitudes of a society. At one time, there was an amendment to the U.S. Constitution that forbade the sale of alcoholic beverages; this amendment was known as Prohibition. People found the law oppressive, there were widespread violations, and eventually Prohibition was repealed. Laws that restricted the voting rights of African-Americans and laws that segregated White and African-American students in different schools have been repealed. In other cases, laws have failed to keep up with public preferences. Some cities still have "blue laws" that prohibit Sunday retail sales. Most consumers today don't view Sunday sales as unethical, but some still do.

Marketers are bound by federal laws that have nationwide interstate jurisdiction, and state and local laws that have jurisdiction within states where the business operates. If you intend to begin a marketing career you must familiarize yourself with the federal, state, and local laws that will affect your marketing activities.

Illegal conduct occurs when a law is broken. Generally, what is illegal is also unethical.[12] However, unethical conduct is not automatically illegal—conduct may be unethical but legal if it violates a societal standard of acceptable behavior, yet breaks no written law. For example, the pharmaceutical industry is often criticized for price skimming—charging high prices for prescription drugs while claiming that the high prices are necessary to cover research and development

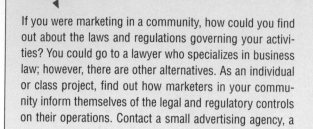

Marketing Application 4.5

costs.[13] Price skimming is not illegal, yet many people believe it is wrong if not unethical.

Federal Procompetitive and Consumer Protection Laws   Federal laws are designed to protect free market competition and consumers nationwide. Any business marketing its products in the United States is subject to these laws. As you look through the acts listed in Figure 4.4, notice how the names describe what the law regulates. Procompetitive laws begin with the Sherman Antitrust Act of 1890, which prohibits monopolies, trusts, and other conspiracies that restrain trade. Typically, legislation is passed to respond to a problem in the marketplace. The problems attacked by the Sherman Antitrust Act, Clayton Antitrust Act (1914), Robinson–Patman Act (1936), and Celler–Kefauver Act (1950) involve actions that make trade less competitive, such as discriminatory pricing, unequal treatment of customers, and corporate acquisitions designed to reduce the number of competitors. Other landmark acts directed against anticompetitive practices are the Lanham Act (1946), which gives trademark protection to businesses while protecting consumers from unknowingly purchasing fraudulently branded products; the Trademark Counterfeiting Act (1980), which prohibits marketing counterfeit products; and the Nutritional Labeling and Education Act (1990), which requires nutritional labels on foods and prohibits exaggerated health claims.

The Federal Trade Commission (FTC) Act (1914) created the FTC as a regulatory body to oversee marketplace activities and define uncompetitive actions. The Wheeler–Lea Amendment to it (1938) broadened FTC oversight to include activities that hurt consumers, even if they did not reduce competition. This extended FTC powers to outlaw false and deceptive advertising of foods, drugs, cosmetics, and health devices. More than any other federal agency, the FTC is most directly involved in marketing activities.

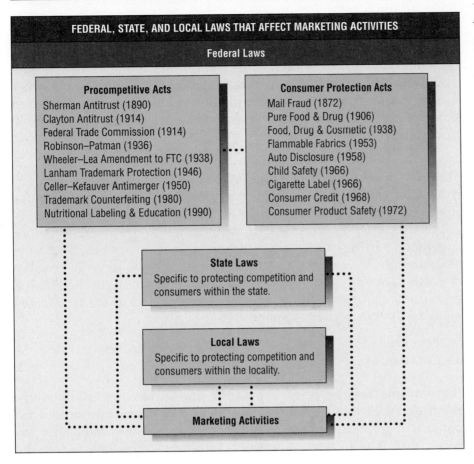

Figure 4.4

Federal, State, and Local Laws Govern Marketing Activities by Enforcing Procompetitive and Consumer Protection Acts

Another series of government actions in the late 1970s and early 1980s affected marketing activities enormously. These efforts were designed to deregulate American businesses and encourage competition. However, in some cases (notably airlines), deregulation has reduced the number of competitors, limited service to some areas, and raised prices. Deregulated industries include natural gas (1978), airlines (1978), motor carriers (1980), railroads (1980), and banks (1981).

Beginning with the Mail Fraud Act of 1872, written to protect unwary consumers from fraudulent product claims sent through the U.S. mail, many other laws have been passed to protect the public. The Pure Food and Drug Act (1906) and the federal Food, Drug and Cosmetic Act (1938) require foods, drinks, drugs, and cosmetics to be clean (unadulterated) and correctly labeled. Other consumer protection acts include those that protect the public from flammable fabrics (1953), require automobile manufacturers to disclose suggested retail prices on their cars (1958), prevent harmful toys and products from affecting child safety (1966), and force cigarette manufacturers to place health warning labels on every pack (1966). The Consumer Product Safety Commission was established in 1972 to regulate product safety.

Often, the courts must determine whether or not laws have been broken and, if so, the courts must set appropriate penalties. Courts also settle disputes between businesses over contracts and other business arrangements, hear complaints about copycat products and advertising,[14] and adjudicate consumer injury claims against businesses.

State and Local Laws State and local laws and regulations apply to intrastate and local marketing activities. These include controls for licensing, testing, and operating fees. State attorneys general actively oversee business performed in their states and sometimes work together to bring suit against illegal business activities that cross several state lines. Eleven state attorneys general recently collaborated in issuing a "Green Report," which defines how, in their states, environmental terms can be used in acceptable marketing practices so as not to mislead consumers.[15]

Regulations

regulations The rules, standards, and guidelines used by government agencies to implement laws.

Regulations are the rules, standards, and guidelines that government agencies issue to implement laws. Marketers are faced with copious regulations, some of which conflict, are outdated, not enforced, or administered unevenly. Like laws, regulations can be promulgated at the federal, state, and local levels. Federal regulations designed to limit marketing and protect consumers are only as strong as their enforcement by the executive and legislative branches. Regulatory agencies of the federal government issue and enforce guidelines for all interstate commerce and have jurisdiction over international businesses marketing products in the United States. Unfortunately, agency jurisdictions sometimes overlap and cause confusion and conflict for the marketer.

The federal agency exercising the greatest and broadest control over marketing is one already mentioned here—the Federal Trade Commission (FTC). Established in 1914 and strengthened by additional legislation in subsequent years, the FTC is charged with preventing unfair competition and protecting consumers and businesses against unfair and deceptive trade and advertising. Other federal agencies are more narrowly focused and lack the broad enforcement authority of the FTC. These include the Federal Food and Drug Administration (food, drugs, cosmetics, medical devices), the Environmental Protection Agency (automobile emission standards, waste disposal, environmental quality), the Consumer Product Safety Commission (health and safety of consumers in their homes), the National Highway Traffic Safety Administration (motor vehicle safety standards and recalls), the Interstate Commerce Commission (air, water, land, air transport), and the Federal Communications Commission (wire and television broadcast).

New product advances sometimes get ahead of regulations. For example, "cosmeceuticals" are a new group of products developed in the late 1980s.[16] The drug companies wanted to have these products labeled *cosmetics*, because they make the consumer more attractive. The Federal Food and Drug Administration (FDA) wanted them called *drugs*, because they are part drug as well as part cosmetic. The difference is that drugs must undergo far more rigorous safety and health testing than must cosmetics. The parties can't agree, so products like Johnson & Johnson's new anti-wrinkle drug Renova are called "cosmeceuticals." The rules covering this class of products still hadn't been drafted, even though the products were ready to be marketed.

A similar situation initially faced genetically engineered fruits and vegetables.[17] Based in part on consumers' unfamiliarity with genetic engineering and in part on a dose of skepticism, some consumers questioned the likelihood that products like Calgene's Fresh Flavr Savr tomatoes (Photo 4.3) could live up to the promise of fresher taste. However, reviews by the United States Department of Agriculture and the Food and Drug Administration, and regular monitoring through the regulatory process (as is done with most food products), support the continued development of genetically engineered food, and will go a long way to encourage consumers.

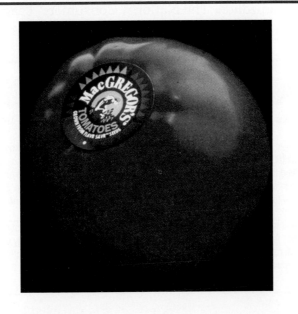

Photo 4.3

Products like MacGregor's tomatoes have led to a lively debate about genetically altered foods.

1. Compare and contrast laws and regulations.
2. Identify some federal laws that affect marketing.
3. What federal agency exerts the greatest control over marketing?

CONSUMERISM

Objective 4 Explain consumerism and the Consumer Bill of Rights.

It is easy to be lulled into thinking that all consumers have sufficient, accurate, and timely information, that products are equitably distributed and offered at fair prices in an adequate assortment for all consumers, and that all products perform as expected. Sadly, this is not always true. Through three periods in the recent history of the United States, as illustrated in Figure 4.5, public outcry over wrongful treatment of consumers has resulted in significant limits being placed on business and marketing.

consumerism The practice and policies of protecting the consumer.

Former U.S. Senator Charles H. Percy offered a widely used definition of **consumerism:** "a broad reaction against bureaucratic neglect and corporate disregard of the rights of the public."[18] Consumerism is not a single group; it is a constantly changing association of people, organizations, agencies, and even businesses that arises because people believe the imbalance in the market between buyers and sellers has gone too far. Typical outcomes include the passage of major new laws and the establishment of new regulatory controls.

The first consumerism period began at the turn of the century and lasted until America entered World War I. The first national consumer organization, The National Consumers' League (which is

Figure 4.5

Periods of Consumerism in the United States

Period	I	II	III
Length	1890s to World War I	Late 1920s to World War II	Late 1950s to late 1970s
Abuses	Mail-order fraud Tainted meat Child labor Unsafe products Unsafe medicines	High prices Poor quality products Unsafe cosmetics Unsafe drugs	Deceptive ads Unsafe products Environmental pollution Price gouging Harmful drugs
Major Outcomes	Meat inspection law Pure food bill Federal trade commission Procompetitive laws	Trademark protection Nutritional labeling laws Strengthened FTC Procompetitive laws Food and Drug Administration	Consumer Bill of Rights Many different consumer protection acts

still active), was founded in New York City in 1891.[19] Members protested mail-order fraud, tainted meat, spiraling prices, child labor exploitation, and outrageous claims for medical gadgets (Photo 4.4) and health cures by medical charlatans and patent medicine sellers. A catalyst spurring public outrage was the 1906 publication of Upton Sinclair's book *The Jungle.* This exposé of unsanitary conditions in the Chicago meat-packing industry shocked the country and prompted federal intervention to clean up businesses and protect consumers' health and safety. Outcomes of the first consumerism period include passage of meat inspection legislation and a pure food bill, as well as other laws designed to increase competition in the marketplace and protect consumers.

The second consumerism period rose along with prices during the Great Depression of the 1930s. Complex new products flooded the market and often didn't work as their manufacturers claimed. Consumer discontent over products and prices led to the formation of Consumer's Research, Inc., in 1929 as an independent product testing organization. Today it is Consumers Union, the publisher of *Consumer Reports.* Once again an exposé, this time of the cosmetic industry, led to public outcries and the passage of new laws and regulations designed to protect consumer health and safety. The second period ended abruptly when America went to war in 1941.

The third major consumerism period began in the late 1950s and lasted for over 20 years. A series of books, including Vance Packard's *Hidden Persuaders* (1957), attacking the advertising industry; Rachel Carson's *Silent Spring* (1962), describing businesses's degradation of

the environment through chemical dumping; Ralph Nader's *Unsafe at Any Speed* (1965), exposing unsafe practices in the automobile industry; and Jessica Mitford's *American Way of Death* (1967), describing profiteering in the funeral industry, enraged the public and prompted passage of a number of consumer protection laws. Also during this period, thalidomide, a drug prescribed in Europe for such early pregnancy symptoms as nausea, tragically resulted in thousands of infants born with deformed arms and legs, often no larger than stumps. This disaster led to stricter testing requirements for pharmaceuticals.

Responses during this period included new laws, rules and regulations, and the formation of consumer groups dedicated to protecting the wilderness, furthering consumer education, and protecting children's rights. Also, the first presidential message on consumer rights was delivered to Congress in 1962. It has come to be known as the Consumer Bill of Rights. Ralph Nader, a crusading consumer activist in the 1960s, still remains a champion of consumers. His nonprofit consumer organization recently published *The Frugal Shopper,* a book that advises consumers how to get the best buys and avoid wasteful spending. Some tips from his book appear in Figure 4.6.

The decades after the 1970s have been comparatively quiet consumerwise. During the 1980s, consumer protection by the federal government reached a low period as the Reagan administration's deregulation programs reduced the agencies' ability to enforce consumer protection laws. No major consumer legislation was

Figure 4.6

Tips from Ralph Nader's *The Frugal Shopper*

TIPS FROM "THE FRUGAL SHOPPER"

What to avoid:
- Credit cards with 18 percent interest rates when there are some with 12 percent available.
- Credit card insurance: price is high, benefits low.
- A lawyer who is not an expert in your specific area of need.
- A doctor who won't accept the assignment from Medicare.
- A loan with a prepayment penalty.
- Service contracts—if the warranty is not good enough to protect you, the product is probably shoddy.
- Banks that charge for automated teller services. These services lower labor costs for banks. Why should you pay more?
- Real estate agents who will not negotiate a commission.
- A house that you have not had inspected professionally.
- A car with a poor occupant injury history.
- Gas saving devices that do not work. Contact the National Technical Information Service in Springfield, Virginia, for details on these devices.
- Overpriced long distance phone service. Compare the programs of all the carriers before deciding.
- Energy-inefficient appliances. Bad for your pocketbook, bad for the environment.

Source: R. Nader and W. J. Smith, *The Frugal Shopper* (Washington, D.C. 1992).

passed during this time. In the late 1980s, the federal government returned to a more activist role, a trend that appears to be accelerating.

The Consumer Bill of Rights President John F. Kennedy sent a message to Congress in 1962 that has become known as the **Consumer Bill of Rights.** Kennedy was the first president to formally address the issue of consumer rights with Congress. The rights the president defined are shown in Figure 4.7. The president singled out food and drugs as needing new laws and regulations to protect public health and safety. The thalidomide tragedy became public knowledge while Congress was debating the president's message, and resulted in swift passage of expanded powers for the federal Food and Drug Administration.

Consumer Bill of Rights The right to have safe products, to be informed about products, to choose from among a variey of products, and to be heard and have complaints resolved.

In the last years of the 20th century, two additional consumer rights have been suggested as additions to President Kennedy's list. These are the right of consumers to enjoy a clean and healthful environment and the right of the poor and other minorities to have their interests protected.[20]

Although consumers' rights are more widely protected today than at any time in the past, abuses still occur with some regularity. Within the past several years, Volvo and its advertising agency were each fined $150,000 by the Federal Trade Commission for deceptively advertising that Volvos remained intact after "Bearfoot," a 13,000-pound monster truck, rolled on top of the cars. Only the Volvo car roofs survived, but they had been secretly reinforced to withstand the attack.[21] The three biggest baby food companies in the United States faced class action lawsuits claiming they had conspired to fix prices on their products since the 1970s.[22] The California Department of Consumer Affairs accused Sears, Roebuck & Co. of overcharging consumers 90 percent of the time at its auto-repair centers in what could be the "major auto-repair scam of the century."[23] Realizing the enormity of its mistakes, Sears apologized to the public.

CONSUMER RIGHTS ARTICULATED BY PRESIDENT JOHN F. KENNEDY
The right to have safe products;
The right to be informed about products;
The right to choose from among a variety of products;
The right to be heard and have complaints resolved.

Figure 4.7

The Consumer Bill of Rights

CONTEMPORARY ISSUES

Objective 5   Identify some important contemporary societal issues involving marketing.

Issues causing public concern sometimes involve marketers. Three controversial contemporary issues are green marketing, the marketing of harmful products, and marketing to children. Each reveals insights on how successfully marketing is interacting with society.

Green Marketing

green marketing   Marketing activities that are environmentally friendly rather than environmentally harmful.

Many marketers have jumped on the bandwagon of environmental concern. **Green marketing** is the term to describe the activities of marketers who offer products that are environmentally friendly rather than environmentally harmful. Such products are often labeled as being ozone-safe, recyclable, environmentally friendly, or biodegradable. In some cases, green marketing is insincere and represents only lip service and not substantive product advantages.[24] In other cases, marketers are caught in a crossfire when consumers claim they are environmentalists but still prefer products in single servings, plastic wrappings, and hard-to-recycle materials.[25] Being green isn't easy, even for large companies like McDonald's, which couldn't seem to satisfy anyone when it decided to change from polystyrene clamshell food containers to paper products.[26]

Green marketers develop products that are less toxic, can be recycled and reused, are of better quality and therefore often last longer, and are not overpackaged. Marketers are warned that they must offer products that live up to consumers' expectations, and be able to back up their claims to satisfy the FTC as well as environmental groups.

Consumer concern over the environment is rising, and marketers are paying attention. Melitta is offering a natural brown, unbleached coffee filter, Colgate has a tube of toothpaste that comes without an outer carton, and McDonald's carry-out bags have labels on the front reminding customers to recycle.[27] Marketers are advised to use less material to save space in landfills, use recycled materials in production processes, make products more durable and repairable, reuse, refill, and compost.[28] In the long run, businesses that are environmentally responsible and satisfy environmentally concerned consumers will be rewarded.[29] However, at this point the green market

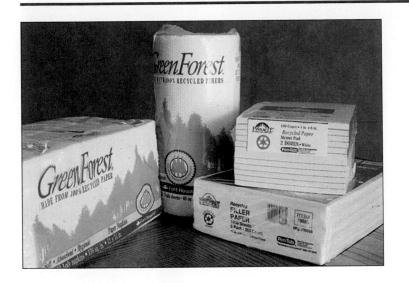

Photo 4.5

Recycled paper products appeal to consumers' desire to think "green."

is confusing, and some marketers are not doing a very good job justifying their green marketing claims.[30] For example, Mobil Oil Corporation has agreed to settle with the FTC over unproven claims that its plastic trash bags decompose quickly, and a consent decree has stopped Perrier from advertising that its water is natural.[31]

Marketing Harmful Products

Some products are marketed legally yet are harmful to consumers. Actions are being taken against many of the companies marketing harmful products. The U.S. Bureau of Alcohol, Tobacco and Firearms blocked the import of Black Death Vodka on the grounds that advertising about its name is misleading because the smiling skull logo "creates the impression of bubonic plague and poison, yet the bottle contains only vodka."[32] The vodka has a youthful target market and planned to use "hell-raising" musicians as product endorsers. The federal Food and Drug Administration is studying how industrial foam used in automobile filters and carpet-cleaning equipment came to be part of silicon breast implants.[33] Antismoking consumer groups are battling cigarette advertisements everywhere, even trying to ban cigarette ads from sports stadiums.[34]

Some marketers of harmful but legal products are trying to show greater social responsibility. For example, some alcohol marketers are encouraging their customers to drink responsibly. Yet this remains a very sensitive area, one about which marketing is often criticized. However, unless these products are made illegal, marketers will continue to have the legal right to offer them to consumers.

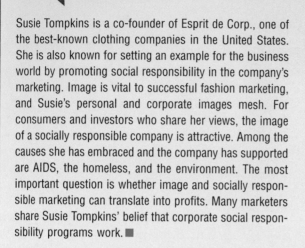

Career Watch

Susie Tompkins is a co-founder of Esprit de Corp., one of the best-known clothing companies in the United States. She is also known for setting an example for the business world by promoting social responsibility in the company's marketing. Image is vital to successful fashion marketing, and Susie's personal and corporate images mesh. For consumers and investors who share her views, the image of a socially responsible company is attractive. Among the causes she has embraced and the company has supported are AIDS, the homeless, and the environment. The most important question is whether image and socially responsible marketing can translate into profits. Many marketers share Susie Tompkins' belief that corporate social responsibility programs work. ■

L. Zinn, "Will Politically Correct Sell Sweaters?" *Business Week,* March 16, 1992, pp. 60–61; C. Miller, "Levi's, Esprit Spin New Cotton into Eco-Friendly Clothes," *Marketing News* 26, no. 9 (April 27, 1992), pp. 11–12;

A. B. Carroll and G. T. Horton, "Do Joint Corporate Social Responsibility Programs Work?" *Business and Society Review* 90 (Summer 1994), pp. 24–28; D. Bollier, "Do Business? Do Good? No. Do Both." *The New York Times* 143, Sec. 3 (September 18, 1994), pp. F11.

Photo 4.6

Some businesspeople, like Esprit's Susie Tompkins, teach corporate responsibility through their actions.

The dilemma involves the ethics of marketing unhealthy or threatening products.

Marketing to Children

Children can't evaluate advertisements with the same sophistication as can adults. They often can't distinguish where ads end and programs begin, which leaves them more vulnerable to influence. Television network commercials for upcoming telecasts that are highly violent and sexually explicit are aired even during children's programs.[35] Some marketing campaigns for harmful products like cigarettes are highly appealing to children, often using cartoon figures. Research has shown that children under the age of 13 are particularly susceptible to advertisements for Camel cigarette's mascot Old Joe Camel.[36] In some countries, marketing to children is restricted more severely than it is in the United States. Because marketers have failed to control and limit marketing to children, it is highly likely that greater restrictions will be considered in the future.

In Chapter 5 you'll learn how multicultural marketing is gaining in importance in the United States, and how international marketing presents great opportunities for both large and small marketers.

1. What is green marketing?
2. Should all products that *could* be harmful to *some* consumers be banned?
3. Should marketers be allowed to target children?

Review of Chapter Objectives

1. *Define the dual roles of marketing in society: micromarketing and macromarketing.* Marketing interacts with society at two levels. Micromarketing refers to the individual perspective of marketing at the business and consumer level. Macromarketing is a system perspective that relates to the broader economic system and how marketing contributes to delivering a standard of living for society by balancing supply and demand.

2. *Describe the rights, responsibilities, and ethical dilemmas of marketers.* Because marketing benefits individuals and society, marketers have certain rights to conduct marketing activities. Along with the rights go responsibilities. The societal marketing concept takes the marketing concept one step further by also requiring that marketing activities benefit society. There are strategic advantages for businesses that adopt societal strategies. Marketers who act ethically far outnumber those who do not. Marketers must make marketing mix decisions for which they are criticized, sometimes on ethical grounds. Marketers often face situations in which there is not an obvious right or wrong behavior, and they often face ethical dilemmas because laws and regulations governing business activities are not always clear. Marketers must balance both the needs of consumers and the revenue needs of their business, which, if they conflict, can cause ethical dilemmas.

3. *Identify governmental controls on marketing.* There were few restrictions on marketing prior to the end of the 19th century. This changed over the next century, as consumerism prompted government responses, including the passage of laws to protect competition and consumer health and safety. Regulatory agencies, including the Federal Trade Commission, were created to enforce laws and issue standards for marketing conduct. Laws and regulations are designed to protect competition and consumers, but they sometimes fail to keep up with changes in society and technology.

4. *Explain consumerism and the Consumer Bill of Rights.* Consumerism is a broad reaction against bureaucratic neglect and corporate disregard of the rights of the public. Consumerism is not a single group; it is a constantly changing association of people, organizations, agencies, and even businesses that arises because people believe the imbalance in the market between buyers and sellers has gone too far. The Consumer Bill of Rights was articulated by President John F. Kennedy in a message to the Congress in 1962.

5. *Identify some important contemporary societal issues involving marketing.* Important contemporary issues involving marketing are green marketing, marketing harmful products, and marketing to children. Although marketing has made many positive and constructive contributions in all three areas, there is considerable room for improvement.

Key Terms

After studying Chapter 4, you should be able to define each of the following key terms and use them in describing marketing activities.

Society, page 105
Ethical Dilemmas, page 105

Micromarketing, page 106
Macromarketing, page 106
Materialism, page 110
Ethics, page 114
Laws, page 119

Regulations, page 122
Consumerism, page 124

Consumer Bill of Rights, page 127
Green Marketing, page 128

Discussion Questions

1. Why is the buyer (consumer) often at a disadvantage in an exchange with a seller?

2. Identify some of the criticisms leveled at marketing, and discuss how they might be corrected.

3. Should consumers be satisfied all the time? Should the marketer work to accomplish this goal? Explain your answers.

4. What is materialism? Is it good or bad?

5. What are some types of controls on marketing?

6. Explain how some things that are unethical might still be legal.

7. Are all marketers evil? If not, what explanations could be offered for the mistakes they make?

8. Is price skimming illegal? Is it ethical? Is it good marketing?

9. Discuss how marketers are often caught in crossfires. Explain how this can affect their ability to make the right decisions.

10. Compare and contrast the societal marketing concept and the marketing concept. Do you think that the societal marketing concept will be readily accepted by all businesses? Why or why not?

What Do You Think?

Consumers Digest and *Consumer Reports* are two different consumer publications. *Consumer Reports,* the more famous of the two consumer magazines, will not accept any advertising or free products and will not allow a business to use its ratings in their advertising. It works hard to maintain its objectivity and accepts no ads from advertisers. It buys all products tested on the open market and does not accept special treatment or discounts. *Consumers Digest* accepts advertisements and even products,

and solicits ads from marketers whose products have been rated "Best Buys." Some marketers claim that being awarded a "Best Buy" rating made them prime targets for ad space sales calls. The magazine denies that its objectivity is being compromised by these actions. Should consumer product testing magazines accept products and advertisements? What do you think?

Sources: S. L. Hwang, "Consumers Digest Mines Its Best-Buy List," *The Wall Street Journal,* September 1, 1992, pp. B1, 6; *Consumer Reports 1995 Buying Guide.* (Yonkers, NY: Consumers Union, 1995), p. 8.

Mini-Case 4.1

Diet Disasters: The FTC, FDA, and Others Take Action

Americans have an obsession about being thin, which often seems to destroy their judgment and make them particularly susceptible to aggressive diet marketing. From diet skin patches to liquid diets, over-the-counter diet pills, and spas, evidence indicates that despite all the marketing claims to the contrary, 95 percent of the estimated 50 million Americans who are dieting this year won't be able to keep the lost weight off.

In light of recent reports that hit the diet industry hard, the FTC is joining forces with the Food and Drug Administration and the National Association of Attorneys General to evaluate the marketing of diet aids and determine what actions should be taken to clean up the market and protect consumers. Consumers spend a huge amount of money on these products, and not only do most of them not work, some are potentially harmful.

A crosscurrent to this situation is that Americans are getting fatter and not thinner. As baby boomers age, more will be looking for quick fixes to middle-age spread. The thin obsession will probably continue, despite the mounting evidence that most dieting just doesn't work and it is genes and body type, not dieting, that determine thinness. The latest trend appears to be to abandon diet classes for health clubs and self-help fitness books and videotapes.

Case Questions

1. Why is there such an obsession with thinness in the United States?

2. Is diet marketing legal? Is it ethical?

3. Do you thing the antidiet movement in the United States will grow? Explain your answer.

Sources: C. Miller, "Anti-Diet Forces, Health Report Assail Weight-Loss Programs," *Marketing News* 26, no. 11 (May 25, 1992), pp. 1, 14; D. Machan, "Where Have All the Dieters Gone?" *Forbes* 153, no. 4 (February 14, 1994), pp. 46–47; K. L. Alexander, "A Healthy Kick at Weight Watchers," *Business Week,* January 16, 1995, p. 36.

Mini-Case 4.2

Fear Appeals Sell Products

Real people who have died of carbon monoxide poisoning are pictured in television commercials for carbon monoxide detectors. People who survived terrible automobile crashes because they were driving a certain brand of car silently look out at you from television or magazines or newspapers in ads for some of those cars. A husband and wife survey the smoldering wreckage of their home in one ad; in another, a mother and daughter sit at their kitchen table and mournfully talk about a friend who died without enough life insurance. Marketers increasingly are using real people in real-life situations to sell products—among them poisonous gas detectors, automobiles, and fire and life insurance. These fear appeals are particularly effective because they are using people just like the audience members. They provide a not very subtle reminder of how vulnerable we are to life's unexpected tragedies. Some people call these ads "slice-of-death" or "living dead" appeals; others call them just plain scary.

Marketers use emotions to communicate with consumers. For example, flowers are marketed for happy occasions as well as to convey regret; telephone companies position their service as a way to share experiences with loved ones. However, many current fear appeals go beyond the boundaries of previously gentle tugs on the emotions. Guns marketed to women are hard sell rather than soft sell, playing on fears of violence and danger. Even cellular phone companies have changed the initial positioning of their products from business purposes to safety concerns, particularly for women drivers who often are in their cars alone at night. These appeals sell products, but do they also take advantage of consumers' vulnerability and anxiety?

Case Questions

1. Do all consumers react to fear appeals in the same way?
2. Are fear appeals legal? Are they ethical?

3. Do fear appeals exploit consumers' weaknesses, or do they instead use powerful images to market important products?

Sources: P. Thomas, "Taking Up Arms Against a Sea of Troubles," *The Washington Post National Weekly Edition* 11, no. 15 (February 7–13, 1994), p. 31; B. Meier, "Marketers Prey on Feelings," *Lexington Herald-Leader*, January 4, 1994, p. 4 Today; K. Deveny, "Marketers Exploit People's Fears of Everything," *The Wall Street Journal*, November 15, 1993, p. B1; C. Goerne, "Gun Companies Target Women; Foes Call It 'Marketing to Fear,' " *Marketing News* 26, no. 18 (August 31, 1992), pp. 1, 2, 8.

Chapter 4 Notes

1. E. R. Corey, "Marketing Managers: Caught in the Middle," in *Ethics in Marketing*, ed. N. C. Smith and J. A. Quelch, (Homewood, IL: Richard D. Irwin, 1993), pp. 37–45.
2. R. J. Samuelson, "How Our American Dream Unraveled," *Newsweek*, March 2, 1992, pp. 32–39.
3. P. Kotler, "What Consumerism Means for Marketers," *Harvard Business Review*, May–June 1972, pp. 48–57.
4. C. Caggiano, "Is Social Responsibility a Crock?" *INC.* 15, no. 5. (May 1993), p. 15.
5. F. R. Bleakley, "Firm's Generosity Generates Business, Worries Wall Street," *The Wall Street Journal*, July 7, 1992, pp. C1, 25.
6. S. Alexander, "Life's Just a Bowl of Cherry Garcia for Ben & Jerry's," *The Wall Street Journal*, July 15, 1992, p. B3; E. Hitchner, "We All Scream for Ice Cream," *National Productivity Review* 14, no. 1 (Winter 1994), p. 114; G. Smith and R. Stodghill II, "Are Good Causes Good Marketing," *Business Week*, March 21, 1994, pp. 64–65.
7. S. D. Atchinson, "Putting the Red Zinger Back into Celestial," *Business Week*, November 4, 1991, pp. 74–78; D. Stipp, "Small Companies See Growth Potential in Preventing Environmental Problems," *The Wall Street Journal*, June 1, 1992, pp. B1, 2.
8. E. E. Spragins, "Making Good," *INC.* 15, no. 5 (May 1993), pp. 114–22; P. Hise, "Charity Begins at Home," *INC.* 15, no. 4 (April 1993), p. 50; P. Hise, "They Recycle Whole Trees," *INC.* 15, no. 6 (June 1993), p. 49.
9. B. Hutton and A. R. Wildt, "Conference to Examine Corporate Social Policy," *Marketing News* 26, no. 1 (January 6, 1992), p. 32.
10. H. F. Waters, D. Glick, C. Friday, and J. Gordon, "Networks under the Gun: Broadcasters Have Promised to Clean Up Their Act. Critics Say Don't Believe the Hype," *Newsweek*, July 12, 1993, pp. 64–66; K. Goldman, "Networks' Plan for TV Program Warnings May Backfire," *The Wall Street Journal*, July 1, 1993, pp. B1, 9; "Rules Restricting Indecency on TV Are Struck Down," *The Wall Street Journal*, November 24, 1993, p. B7; E. Jensen, "Violence Advisory Set for Unveiling by Four Networks," *The Wall Street Journal*, July 1, 1993, p. B8.
11. T. R. Hill, "Program Seeks to Educate Consumers Against Fraud: Project of Better Business Bureau Offers Monthly Publications, Alerts," *Lexington Herald-Leader*, July 7, 1993, p. B5.
12. N. C. Smith, "Ethics and the Marketing Manager," in *Ethics in Marketing*, ed. N. C. Smith and J. A. Quelch, (Homewood, IL: Richard D. Irwin, 1993), pp. 10.
13. C. Miller, "Drug Marketers 'on the Alert': Tighter Restrictions Possible under Clinton Presidency," *Marketing News* 27, no. 1 (January 4, 1993), pp. 1, 10.
14. L. Bird, "Thompson Is Named in Copycat Lawsuit," *The Wall Street Journal*, July 13, 1992, p. B3.
15. M. P. Cronin, "Green Marketing Heats Up," *INC.* 15, no. 11 (January 1993), p. 27; J. Saddler, "FTC Issues a 'Green-Marketing' Guide to Help Prevent Deceptive-Ad Charges," *The Wall Street Journal*, July 29, 1992, p. B5.
16. "Mirror, Mirror," *The Economist* 327, no. 7807 (April 17, 1993), p. 62.
17. C. Miller, "Food Fight Rages over Bioproducts," *Marketing News* 28, no. 6 (March 14, 1994), pp. 1, 19; C. Miller, "Midwest Will Be Test Market in '93 for Genetically Engineered Tomatoes," *Marketing News* 26, no. 19 (September 14, 1992), pp. 1, 20–21.
18. J. F. Engle, R. D. Blackwell, and P. W. Miniard, *Consumer Behavior*, 6th ed. (Hinsdale, IL: Dryden, 1990), p. 759.
19. R. O. Herrmann, "The Consumer Movement in Historical Perspective," in *Consumerism: Search for the Consumer Interest*, 3rd, ed. D. A. Aaker and G. S. Day, (New York: Free Press/Macmillan, 1978), pp. 27–36.
20. Engle, Blackwell, and Miniard, *Consumer Behavior*, p. 759.
21. R. Serafin, "No More 'Monsters': Volvo Carefully Documents New Advertising," *Advertising Age*, September 23, 1991, pp. 1, 42; " 'Monster' Truck Puts Pedal to Volvo Metal," *The Orlando Sentinel*, November 10, 1990, p. A20.

22. R. Gibson, "Firms Are Alleged to Have Fixed Baby Food Prices," *The Wall Street Journal,* January 18, 1993, p. C15.

23. T. Yin, "Sears Is Accused of Billing Fraud at Auto Centers," *The Wall Street Journal,* June 12, 1992, pp. B1, 6.

24. T. B. Wheeler, "Green Products Offer Just Pitch for Green Cash," *Lexington Herald-Leader,* October 6, 1991, p. E1.

25. H. Schlossberg, "Products Must Live Up to Expectations," *Marketing News* 26, no. 23 (November 9, 1992), pp. 9, 13.

26. "Food for Thought," *The Economist* 324, no. 7774 (August 29, 1992), pp. 64, 66.

27. J. Ottman, "Consumer Attitude Shifts Provide Grist for New Products," *Marketing News* 27, no. 1 (January 4, 1993), p. 16.

28. J. Ottman, "Use Less, Make It More Durable, and Then Take It Back," *Marketing News* 26, no. 18 (August 11, 1992), p. 13.

29. C. Frankel, "Blueprint for Green Marketing," *American Demographics* 14, no. 4 (April 1992), pp. 34–38.

30. J. Wasik, "Market Is Confusing, but Patience Will Pay Off," *Marketing News* 26, no. 21 (October 12, 1992), pp. 16–17.

31. "Mobil Oil Corp. Agrees to Settle with FTC over Trash Bag Claim," *The Wall Street Journal,* July 28, 1992, p. B4.

32. L. Bird, "New Vodka Sold as Black Death Riles Regulators," *The Wall Street Journal,* April 3, 1992, pp. B1, 8.

33. T. M. Burton, "How Industrial Foam Came to Be Employed in Breast Implants," *The Wall Street Journal,* March 25, 1992, pp. A1, 4.

34. S. L. Hwang, "Some Stadiums Snuff Out Cigarette Ads," *The Wall Street Journal,* July 17, 1992, p. B3.

35. M. Silver, S. Burke, J. Sieder, and K. Glastris, "Troubling TV Ads," *U.S. News & World Report,* February 1, 1993, pp. 65–67.

36. G. Levin, "Poll Shows Camel Ads Are Effective with Kids," *Advertising Age,* April 27, 1992, p. 12.

Multicultural and International Marketing

Chapter Objectives

After studying Chapter 5 you should be able to:

1. Explain why marketers should develop cultural understanding.

2. Identify the three largest ethnic microcultures in the United States.

3. Discuss why and how businesses go international.

4. Describe the environment of international marketing.

5. Analyze the contemporary issues facing international marketers.

*I*n the past 10 years, nearly 10 million immigrants have arrived in the United States. Current trends indicate that by the year 2050, Asians, Hispanics, African-Americans, and other non-Caucasian groups could represent 47 percent of the total U.S. population, which will increase to 383 million people from the current 262 million people.[1] This multicultural diversity presents challenges and opportunities for marketers. In light of the importance of multiculturalism as a social force worldwide, this chapter first examines culture and the dominant ethnic microcultures of the United States, and then it addresses international marketing, in which culture is one of several key factors affecting marketing decisions. As you read the chapter and learn about multicultural and international marketing, consider the question, will growing multicultural diversity in the United States affect the international marketing efforts of U.S. businesses?

<table>
<tr><td>

Cultures Collide at a
Backyard Barbecue

</td><td>

On a summer afternoon, a group of Japanese and American men sitting in lawn chairs in a circle are discussing how they can make quality controls more rigorous for the parts they supply to the multibillion-dollar Japanese automobile plant 30 miles away. In another tight circle, Japanese and American women are talking about children and where to buy the best farm-fresh vegetables. The American host is busy cooking hot dogs and hamburgers on the grill, while his wife lays out delicious homemade American picnic favorites on the long table set up in the yard. When the food is ready, she calls out for everyone to come help themselves. The American men and women and the Japanese women get up and move toward the table. The Japanese men remain in their comfortable chairs, waiting for their wives to bring them food. The American hostess is not at all surprised by the response of the Japanese men. She laughingly calls out to them, "Come on, you're in America now, you have to serve yourself! If you don't come up here and get your own food, you'll starve." What do you think happens next?

</td></tr>
</table>

DEVELOPING CULTURAL UNDERSTANDING

Objective 1   Explain why marketers should develop cultural understanding.

cultural blinders   A preferential view of one's culture that blinds the observer to the value of the ways of another, different culture.

culture   The social insitutions, values, beliefs, attitudes, customs, languages, and preferences that a group uses to solve problems and keep order.

socialization   A learning process through which people learn acceptable ways to think and behave.

self-reference criterion   A reaction to one's personal and cultural background.

If you've visited a racetrack you may have seen a horse wearing blinders—headgear placed along the horse's head to keep its eyes focused on the track ahead and virtually blind to everything else. Some people wear **cultural blinders,** meaning that their view is restricted to accepting only what their culture considers acceptable, so that they cannot see or readily accept other cultures' ways. Often, this results in a prejudiced view of others' ways of thinking and behaving. Americans would consider the Japanese men's behavior at the picnic in the chapter-opening story as strange by *American* standards. The Japanese women at the picnic thought their husbands' behavior was perfectly normal, by *Japanese* standards.

Culture is how a society lives through its social institutions, values, beliefs, attitudes, customs, languages, and preferences—how its people solve problems, regulate interactions, establish order, and avoid chaos. Culture is dynamic and evolves to meet people's needs. It teaches people acceptable ways to think and behave through a learning process called **socialization.** Unfortunately, becoming socialized to one's own culture sometimes results in learning to be less sensitive to others' cultures, which can lead to serious misunderstandings. An unconscious reference to one's own cultural background and values, called the **self-reference criterion,** is a cultural bias reaction that may undermine one's ability to make an objective decision.[2]

Let's return to our picnic. The outcome of the hostess's statement was a moment of silence, followed by everyone sharing a good laugh. The Japanese were amused by the example of American extroversion, and everyone applauded when the Japanese men left their lawn chairs and got their own food. It helped that these people already were well acquainted, and liked and respected one another. Otherwise, the outcome might not have been as pleasant. **Culture clash,** in which people from different cultures fail to understand and accommodate patterns of behavior and attitudes unlike their own, can create hurt feelings in social situations and disaster in business deals.

culture clash Failure of people to understand and accommodate patterns of behavior and attitudes of people from a different culture.

Macroculture and Microculture

The **macroculture** of the United States represents our entire society of over 260 million people with its predominately Caucasian, Anglo-Saxon majority. In the 1990 census, about 13 million Americans described their family's origins as from the United States. Others claimed ancestry from Italy (almost 15 million), England (32.7 million), Ireland (38.8 million), and Germany (close to 60 million).[3]

macroculture An entire society.

To outsiders, the United States may appear to be a fairly uniform place, where people share the American culture, have similar likes and dislikes, and lead similar lives. However, the United States is a **multicultural society** made up of groups of people from many cultures representing different backgrounds, preferences, and lifestyles.

multicultural society A society made up of cultures representing different backgrounds, preferences, and lifestyles.

Smaller but distinguishable groups within a macroculture are called **microcultures.** All Americans are members of many microcultures, whether they are defined by ethnic origin, gender, race, religion, age, geography, economic status, or some other defining characteristic that they share. These groupings correspond to the segmentation bases covered in Chapter 3.

microculture A small, distinguishable group within a macroculture.

Photo 5.1

Consumer diversity reflects the richness of American society.

Ethnic Microcultures   Marketers are growing more interested in ethnic microcultures because they can exert powerful influences on their members, particularly on their purchasing preferences and habits. In the United States, some ethnic microcultures and their purchasing power are growing more rapidly than is the Caucasian majority.

Through family and business connections, members of ethnic microcultures often facilitate access to the cultures and countries from which they've come. In the next century, this may give an international marketing advantage to some American businesses that employ Asian-Americans or Hispanic-Americans. This is because the Asian–Pacific and Mexico–Latin American regions are prime targets for American exports. Finally, the U.S. workforce also is becoming more diverse, which means people from different ethnic backgrounds are often the targets of business/organizational marketing efforts, as well as being employees and employers.

Core Values

If you were asked to describe a typical American, what would you say? This is difficult, because Americans come from so many different ethnic backgrounds. In fact, the United States has absorbed more immigrants than has any other country in the world, and assimilated them (more or less) into the majority American culture.[4]

values What a society holds in high esteem.

Values are the things a society holds in high esteem. Enduring, widely shared core or universal values form the building blocks of a nation's character and define that nation to the rest of the world. Some say that the most deeply held American values are family, religion, and love of country.[5] Other core American values are shown in Figure 5.1. These core values are not held by everyone, but represent values *generally* associated with Americans. These values also are evolving. For example, one in three Americans is a baby boomer. As baby boomers enter their more sedentary middle age, youthfulness and fitness core values may change. As the United States becomes more diverse, core values of immigrants influence the macroculture even as the immigrants are being socialized and assimilated into the American culture.

homogeneous Culturally alike.
heterogeneous Ethnically diverse.

Japan's population is **homogeneous,** or more culturally alike than the ethnically diverse (**heterogeneous**) population of the United States.[6] Important Japanese core values are teamwork and cooperation for the collective good. Loyalty to one's group and discipline are demanded. The Japanese often say, "The nail which stands up gets beaten down." Compare this to the American core value of individualism, and you begin to see why American and Japanese people often find it difficult to understand one another.

Marketing Application 5.1

Do you agree with the list of American core values shown in Figure 5.1? Are these values characteristic of *most* Americans? Because advertising is often considered to be a mirror of society, take the list of core values from Figure 5.1 and evaluate several full-page print advertisements in some current popular magazines such as *Cosmopolitan*, *Business Week*, and *Newsweek*. Can you find advertisements in which the message (copy) and/or visual images (art) appeal to one or more of the core values? Are there other core values that the advertisements appear to reflect? Bring your analysis to class for discussion. ▪

Value	Characteristic
Achievement and success	Protestant work ethic, hard work brings success
Activity	Keep busy, be involved
Efficiency and practicality	Down-to-earth, get it done, can do
Progress	New and improved
Material comfort	The good life, convenience products, feel-good products
Individualism	I've got to be me, self-sufficiency
Freedom	Democracy, broad latitude in choice, speech
External conformity	Being one of the group
Humanitarianism	Generosity, helping your neighbors, being there in an emergency
Youthfulness	Stay young
Fitness and health	Stay fit

Figure 5.1

Core American Values

Source: L. G. Schiffman and L. Kanuk, *Consumer Behavior,* 5th ed. © 1994, pp. 424–37. Adapted by permission of Prentice Hall, Englewood Cliffs, New Jersey.

Marketers must understand the culture and core values of the ethnic groups they are targeting, regardless of whether the cultures are macro or micro, or domestic or international. Because culture provides a strong influence on consumer decisions, marketers who fail to study and understand a culture and its core values are ill equipped to identify and satisfy that culture's consumer needs or conduct business dealings with members of that culture. This also includes knowing when it is appropriate and more effective to target your offer to the mass market. Sometimes cultural differences are ignored, either because they are not highly significant for a particular product or it is not cost effective to use target marketing.

The Importance of Language

"Language is one of the strongest forces unifying or separating communities."[7] In some parts of the United States, particularly large urban areas (e.g., New York, Los Angeles, Miami) and the states of California, Texas, and Florida, marketers often must be fluent in Spanish in order to accommodate consumers who cannot or prefer not to communicate in English. Some consumers are linguistically isolated, without a single member of their household over the age of five able to speak English. As a result, some businesses run preemployment language checks for jobs requiring bilingual fluency, to ensure that their employees can communicate with their Spanish-speaking customers.[8] Linguistic isolation also presents marketing opportunities. In New York City, Time Warner Cable offers separate pay cable channels with programming in Japanese, Korean, Hindi, Arabic, and Chinese. Bi- and trilingual employees serve their customers.[9] Large ethnic enclaves are often served by ethnic directories, including telephone Yellow Pages published in Spanish, Chinese, Vietnamese, Farsi, Korean, and other languages.[10]

In Japan, English is often used on products to convey an image of Western stylishness. Unfortunately, some translations are quite bad, resulting in a fractured English often called *Japlish*.[11]

Marketers must also be careful about their unspoken, silent body language. It is estimated that 60 percent of all communication is nonverbal.[12] This includes how close you stand to your customer, whether or not you touch a colleague's shoulder, your sense of time, and your face movements and hand gestures in a meeting. For example, "OK" (making a circle of one's thumb and first index finger) is a common gesture in the United States, yet it does not mean OK in Australia, Germany, Brazil, or Russia, where the gesture is considered obscene. Among Latinos, the personal embrace (or *abrazo*) among men is a standard greeting; among Anglo men in the United States, usually it is not.

Check Your Understanding
5.1

1. Compare and contrast the U.S. macro- with the principal U.S. microcultures.
2. What is the self-reference criterion and why is it important?
3. Why is language an important element in culture?

Cultural Sensitivity

Cultural sensitivity means viewing people from other cultures objectively, respectfully, and nonjudgmentally. Growing diversity in the United States is straining some Americans' tolerance of differences as the perception of the United States as a Caucasian, Anglo nation fades. Immigration is at its highest levels since the 1890s, and, whereas earlier immigrants were rapidly assimilated into the American melting pot, current immigrants generally are not assimilating as rapidly or willingly.[13] Instead of a melting pot, some people now characterize the United States as a mosaic of many different tiles, a rainbow, or a salad bowl.

Each great immigrant wave has changed American culture. Colonists (largely English and Dutch) made up the first wave, and their arrival had grievous consequences for Native Americans as the new nation was built. The Colonists were followed by Africans brought to the New World as slaves. A third wave, in the mid-1800s, was mainly Northern European (German and Irish), followed in the late 1800s by immigrants of Italian and Eastern European ancestry. The fifth wave, which began in the mid-1960s as a result of changes in U.S. immigration law, was and continues to be overwhelmingly Asian and Hispanic.[14] Whereas other major industrialized nations' populations are aging, the recent influx of young Asians and Hispanics, who tend to have larger families, will fuel a U.S. population surge in the 21st century.[15] Like previous immigrants, these new citizens will reinvigorate American society.

Because of growing workforce diversity in the United States, greater cultural sensitivity is also required when marketing to business/organizational consumers.[16] Miami has more foreign-born residents than does any other major American city. Hispanics make up 49 percent of Dade County, Florida, and exert significant business clout.[17] American companies are becoming more culturally diverse in their executive ranks, and recruit domestically and internationally to find people who are internationally minded.[18]

As more businesses go international, opportunities for marketers will increase; hence, developing cultural sensitivity also makes good sense professionally.[19] Many of you will work for a foreign-owned business in the United States sometime in your career. You already have if you've worked for Burger King, Macmillan Publishing Company, Firestone Rubber, CBS Records, Ann Taylor, 7-Eleven Stores, Bantam Books, Baskin-Robbins, Carnation Company, or Pillsbury.[20]

Stages of Cultural Perception   Cultural differences between buyer and seller may result in culture clashes if there is a lack of cultural understanding. Astute businesses realize that it is wise to train

cultural sensitivity Viewing people from other cultures objectively, respectfully, and nonjudgmentally.

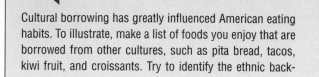

Marketing Application 5.2

marketers to understand other cultures. There are four stages of cultural perception:[21]

1. Ignorance.
2. Awareness.
3. Knowledge.
4. Understanding.

The challenge is to train marketers to move from stage 1 (ignorance), where they are liabilities, to stage 4 (understanding), where they are effective in connecting with consumers and facilitating exchanges.

cultural borrowing Adopting elements from another culture.

cultural change Changes resulting from cultural borrowing.

Marketers as Culture Change Agents   Cultures borrow from one another, some more than others and not always willingly. **Cultural borrowing** occurs when elements from one culture are adopted and (usually) adapted by another. The United States is particularly rich in cultural borrowings because of its immigrant history. This is reflected in language, food, clothing, and other aspects of daily life. **Cultural change** refers to how these borrowed elements can change the culture that borrows them. For example, contemporary Russian culture is being changed by Western brands like Gillette, Reeboks, McDonald's, and Colgate, as well as by the television advertisements and billboards promoting them.[22] "Modre Svetlo!" Kmart Corp.'s blue light specials, are changing local culture through Kmart's 13 new stores in formerly Communist Czechoslovakia.[23] Chinese consumers are exposed to Western brands advertised on outdoor billboards as well as on television, which can reach 600 million viewers at once.[24] South Korea, with its highly conservative Confucian culture, is experiencing its first advertisements featuring nude bodies selling body shampoo, clothing, and even environmentally friendly computers.[25]

American pop culture is in great demand worldwide, and changes cultures wherever it appears. The Japanese embrace Americana through their patronage of Tokyo Disneyland, Coca-Cola, McDonald's, KFC (formerly Kentucky Fried Chicken), and Toys "Я" Us. On the other hand, the French are far less enthusiastic about

Photo 5.2

Two well-known Western products advertised together—cultural borrowing at work.

American culture, often because their government periodically challenges what they perceive as American cultural imperialism.

Cultural changes are accelerated through licensed consumer products (Mickey Mouse watches), culture-driven products (Levi's jeans, McDonald's hamburgers), and movies, music, television programs, and other forms of entertainment. MTV Europe, which reaches over 120 million homes, is the first pan-European television station and a vehicle that is spreading American culture among young people. When the border between West and East Germany was first opened, the two things most East Germans asked for when they reached West Germany were oranges and records.[26]

LARGE ETHNIC MICROCULTURES IN THE UNITED STATES

Marketers are recognizing the value of targeting ethnic microcultures, particularly the largest ones in the United States: African-Americans, Hispanic-Americans, and Asian-Americans. These ethnic groups are

Objective 2 Identify the three largest ethnic microcultures in the United States.

unevenly spread across the country, tending to concentrate in urban rather than rural areas. Generally, consumers within an ethnic microculture may share some preferences for products, stores, and services; however, individual differences still occur. Figure 5.2 compares some characteristics of these three important groups.

African-Americans   African-Americans, currently the largest ethnic microculture, constitute 12 percent of the U.S. population, but their numbers are not increasing as fast as those of Asian and Hispanic groups because of the latter two's high immigration rates. The 30 million African-American consumers represent over $260 billion annually in purchasing power. On the average, the African-American population is younger and poorer than are Whites. However, there is a growing African-American middle class, and the number of African-American families with annual incomes of $50,000 or more increased by 50 percent during the 1980s, rising to

Figure 5.2

Microculture Characteristics of Interest to Marketers (from a survey of 3,500 people and data from the U.S. Bureau of the Census and the Urban Institute)

Characteristics	African-Americans	Hispanic Americans	Asian Americans
Prefer to purchase products made in the United States	58%	N/A	25%
Have bank account	60	< 50%	87
Own home	40	42	44
Select a store based on quality of its products	76	72	66
Select a store based on price of products	24	28	34
Top leisure activities mentioned:			
Watching TV	66	63	58
Going shopping	50	51	38
Reading	48	N/A	39
Partying with friends	39	N/A	N/A
Cooking	N/A	46	N/A
Radio listening	N/A	13 higher than general population	N/A

Sources: C. Miller, "Researcher Says U.S. Is More of Bowl Than a Pot," *Marketing News* 27, no. 10 (May 10, 1992), p. 6. Used with permission. A. Gerlin, "Radio Stations Gain by Going after Hispanics," *The Wall Street Journal*, July 14, 1993, p. B1. Reprinted by permission of *The Wall Street Journal*, ©1993, Dow Jones & Company, Inc. All Rights Reserved Worldwide.

Consumer Insight

Targeting ethnic consumers in the United States can pay large dividends. Although Mattel had had Afrtican-American Barbie dolls in the 1980s, it wasn't until 1990 that Mattel launched advertising campaigns for its other multicultural dolls, hoping to capitalize on growing ethnic spending power in the United States. The Barbie doll, a best-seller for Mattel for over 30 years, is now sold in over 100 countries and comes in Hispanic, African-American, and Asian versions, as well as the original blue-eyed Anglo version. Procter & Gamble sponsors such Hispanic events as the Miami Carnaval Festival and is the top advertiser on

Hispanic radio. During the 1993 baseball All-Star game, Nike broadcast a 30-second commercial nationwide on CBS in Spanish with *English* subtitles. The advertisement was shown at the same time on Hispanic networks Univision and Telemundo in the United States without subtitles. The same ad was shown on television networks in Central and South America with the company slogan, "Nike. Just Do It!" in English. ■

D. N. Berkwitz, "Finally, Barbie Doll Ads Go Ethnic," *Newsweek,* August 13, 1990, p. 48; K. Goldman, "Nike Will Premier Commercial in Spanish with English Subtitles," *The Wall Street Journal,* July 12, 1993, p. B3.

1.6 million families.[27] Because African-Americans speak English, it is too easy to assume that they can be reached by mass marketing targeted to Anglo-Americans. Mass marketing works for some products; for others, targeting is required. Although African-Americans aren't identical in their purchasing preferences, they generally are brand loyal, prefer products made in the United States, and seek quality products.

Hispanic-Americans There are about 25 million Hispanics in the United States, a number slightly less than the population of Canada. It is the fastest-growing segment of the U.S. population, increasing 53 percent between 1980 and 1990, and expected to double by 2006. Hispanics have about $200 billion in annual purchasing power.[28] Their incomes and purchasing power vary, and include successful Cuban-Americans in Miami and Mexican-Americans in Texas and California. Many Hispanics are linguistically isolated, which explains the growing popularity of Hispanic radio stations. Generally, they are very family oriented and brand loyal, and seek quality products.[29]

Asian-Americans Asian-Americans also are a heterogeneous microculture, representing many different backgrounds and languages. Most Asian-Americans settle along the coasts, particularly the West Coast. The Asian population in metropolitan Washington, D.C., doubled in the 1980s. Asians and Pacific Islanders are the most rapidly growing population segments. Like Hispanics, generally

Photo 5.3

This billboard targets the large Vietnamese-American market.

Photo 5.4

Mattel's Shani doll was developed to tap the African-American consumer market.

they are family oriented. Asian-Americans tend to retain their native language longer and are the most highly educated of the dominant ethnic microcultures in the United States.

Check Your Understanding 5.2

1. Define the term *cultural sensitivity* and explain its importance to marketers in a multicultural society.

2. Are marketers culture change agents? Explain your answer.

3. Identify the largest ethnic microcultures in the United States and describe some of their characteristics.

Marketing Application 5.3

Some of America's most valuable companies reap significant profits from international marketing. This includes such giants as General Electric, American Telephone and Telegraph (AT&T), Wal-Mart Stores, Coca-Cola, Philip Morris, General Motors, Procter & Gamble, DuPont, Pepsi-Co, IBM, and Motorola. Select one of these companies (or a different one, if you prefer) and use the *Business Periodicals Index* or an electronic periodicals index in your school or public library to find recent magazine or journal articles that tell more about that company's recent international marketing activities. Bring the information to class for discussion. For students interested in working abroad, this is a good opportunity to investigate potential employers. ■

"America's Most Valuable Companies," *Business Week,* March 28, 1994, pp. 73–142.

MARKETING ABROAD

Domestic marketing is marketing within a business's *home country.* When a business offers its products across national borders, usually to two or more other *host countries,* it is engaged in **international marketing.** To **export** means offering finished products, supplies, and raw materials to markets in other nations; to **import** means bringing finished products, supplies, and raw materials into your home country domestic market. The United States is a dominant force in world trade as the world's largest exporter and importer. Although exports leaving the United States are worth over $400 billion annually, the value of imports is even greater; therefore, the United States is running a **trade deficit** (imports greater than exports) and, consequently, is the world's largest debtor nation.

Major U.S. trading partners are Canada, Japan, Mexico, the United Kingdom, and Germany. Top U.S. exporters by volume of sales are Boeing, General Motors, General Electric, IBM, Ford, Chrysler, and McDonnell Douglas.[30] Many small and mid-size businesses are also profitably marketing internationally. For example, Vita-Mix Corp., a small Ohio-based blender manufacturer, began marketing abroad in 1991; by 1992, international sales from 20 countries accounted for 20 percent of the firm's total sales.[31] Export growth is high in medical products, environmental systems, consumer goods, and scientific instruments, as well as raw materials.

Going International

Not all businesses belong in international markets. However, there are good reasons why many businesses should consider international

Objective 3 Discuss why and how businesses go international.

domestic marketing Marketing within a business's home country.

international marketing Marketing across national borders.

export To offer finished products, supplies, and materials to markets in other nations.

import To bring finished products, supplies, and raw materials into the domestic market.

trade deficit The imbalance occurring when the value of imports is greater than the value of exports.

Consumer Insight

The majority of exporters are small with sales of $5 million to $300 million annually. Small businesses can market faster internationally, with fewer resources and costs than at any time in the past, mainly because they can use international toll-free 800 numbers, fax machines, and air express; speak English, the language of international business; and enjoy lower labor costs along with increasing productivity and quality in the United States. Because of their smaller size and flexibility, they can adapt to the needs of their international markets, arrange schedules, change products, and maintain close personal rela-

tionships with international buyers. Small Asian-American entrepreneurs on the Pacific Coast and Hispanic-Americans in California, Texas, and Florida are spurring exports to Asia and Latin America, while the Polish, Lithuanian, and Ukrainian communities in Chicago, Milwaukee, and Cleveland are encouraging exports and investments in Eastern European countries. ■

W. J. Holstein and K. Kelly, "Little Companies, Big Exports," *Business Week*, April 13, 1992, pp. 70–72.

marketing. Some of the best reasons are to generate revenue, escape domestic competition, prolong product life, receive tax incentives, and dispose of discontinued surplus goods. The U.S. domestic market is the world's most desirable market but, as a result, it is extremely competitive and, in many product classes, saturated. International markets offer opportunities to increase sales, which may allow for production economies at home as well as extend product life and bring new product ideas back to the domestic market. By being in more than one market, a business spreads its risks. It can also better serve its domestic business customers who have gone abroad. Some countries offer tax incentives to companies willing to enter their markets. Finally, products that are not salable in the domestic market may be sold abroad. However, marketers should not go international with unsafe products, products that are being dumped (sold below fair market price or production cost), or inferior-quality products that could ruin a business's reputation.

Any business considering international marketing must carefully consider the risks and possible benefits. Some international marketers say that the best reason to compete abroad is because it makes your business better at home. Your business becomes more sophisticated because of sharpened competitive skills, better planning, and exposure to new products and ideas.[32]

A small to mid-size business going international can get help from a variety of sources, as illustrated in Figure 5.3. The U.S. Department of Commerce has offices in most large American cities and over 130 cities abroad and provides information on exporting, market research, sales leads, trade shows, and matchmaker trade

Marketing on the Internet

The Internet has no global boundaries. It already connects over 30 million users in 75 countries with full Internet services and users in 77 more countries with E-mail service. The world is becoming a much smaller place as people and organizations gather information, transmit messages, and make transactions in cyberspace without regard to physical and cultural boundaries.

As the Internet gets even easier to use, more consumers worldwide will jump on board. Commercial sites on the World Wide Web have grown from 9,000 in 1991 to over 22,000 in 1995 with even faster growth predicted for the last years of the 20th century. According to Bill Washburn, former executive director of Commercial Internet Exchange, a major Internet trunk service, "With the Internet, the whole globe is one marketplace." Comprehensive lists of current commercial sites can be found at various places on the Internet, including the address http://www.directory.net./dir/directory.html. Soon, Inter-

net users will be able to enjoy two-way audible conversations in real time using software developed by companies such as VocalTec. Inc., a small Israeli firm.

The implications for international marketing are clear: the Internet has the potential to reduce or eliminate many differences between marketing domestically and internationally. The implications for cultural diversity, however, are less clear. Some social scientists claim that many of the earth's languages are being lost because children learn English as their primary language rather than their native tongue. Since English has become the worldwide language of business, the Internet will probably accelerate this trend toward linguistic homogeniety. ■

J. H. Verity and R. D. Hof, "The Internet: How It Will Change the Way You Do Business," *Business Week,* November 14, 1994, pp. 80–88; W. M. Bulkeley, "Hello, World! Audible Chats On the Internet," *The Wall Street Journal,* February 10, 1995, pp. B1, 4.

mission programs. Additional information is available from the Commerce Department's local trade specialists and small business administration offices. The U.S. Department of Agriculture offers programs to help businesses market agricultural products abroad. Most states offer some international marketing assistance, as do many large accounting and consulting firms and some banks. There are books on the subject, as well as periodicals and computer software. Business associates who are already marketing internationally can be good sources of information, as are trade associations and networks formed with others in the same industry who are also preparing to go international. Finally, foreign-born employees of American businesses often are a good source of information about their homelands, and sometimes have valuable contacts there.

The International Marketplace

Many small to mid-size businesses become international marketers almost by accident when they receive an unsolicited order from an international buyer or inquiries from an agent interested in representing the company overseas.[33] Although it is getting easier for U.S.

Marketing Application 5.4

What assistance is available for businesses that are considering going international? Make a list of possible sources of international marketing information at the local, state, and national levels that are listed in your local telephone directory. For example, is there a listing for a small business development center, city or state trade office, a world trade center branch, or a U.S. Department of Commerce office? Bring your list to class and compile a complete inventory of sources. Which source would you contact first? Why? ■

Figure 5.3

Sources of Assistance for Learning More about Marketing Abroad

Source	Type of Assistance
U.S. Department of Commerce: U.S. and Foreign Commercial Service; Small Business Administration	Consulting, publications, seminars, trade missions, assistance in networking, trade shows, distributor lists, 1-800-USA-XPOR for export guide
U.S. Department of Agriculture	Assistance with marketing agricultural products
State trade offices	Depends on each state
World trade centers	Cities in United States and abroad; seminars, trade missions, database assistance
Export management companies	U.S. companies specialized by product classes and country groups will market products abroad on commission or buy/sell agreement
Export trading companies	Take titles and sell abroad
Major accounting firms	International trade department; consulting services, seminars, publications
Popular press publications	Guides to markets and how to go international, trade journals
Business peers	Industry trade associations, networks, consulting services
Computer software	Export-automation software from various firms, information from International Trade Facilitation Council

businesses to market internationally, relatively few choose to do so. A recent survey of small business executives in the United States revealed that only 18 percent say they are doing any exporting.[34] One reason for this lack of interest is the size and attractiveness of their own domestic market.

International Marketing Report

For many businesses, their first international marketing experience is exporting to Canada, the second largest country (by land area) in the world. Canada and the United States have a very close trading relationship; each is the other's best market and trading partner. Seventy percent of Canada's imports are from the United States; the United States is the destination for more than 75 percent of Canada's exports. Some of the hottest markets for exports to Canada are electronic components, computers, building products, and auto parts. There has been a 35 percent increase in the volume of U.S. exports to Canada

since the enactment of the United States–Canada Free Trade Agreement (FTA) on January 1, 1989, and an even greater increase is expected with the implementation of the North American Free Trade Agreement (NAFTA). ■

"INC.'s Going Global: Canada," *INC.* 15, no. 6 (June 1993), insert No. 1; H. Schlossberg, "North American Marketers Await Trade Pact: Canadians Are Cautious, but Hopeful," *Marketing News* 27, no. 10 (May 10, 1993), pp. 1, 17; A. C. Samli, R. Still, and J. S. Hill, *International Marketing: Planning and Practice* (New York: Macmillan, 1993), p. 165; A. Warson, "Tapping Canadian Markets," *INC.* 15, no. 3 (March 1993), pp. 90–91.

The Triad: North America, Europe, Japan The world's population of about 5.5 billion people live in over 200 countries. Although wealth obviously is not evenly distributed worldwide, the potential size of international markets is a strong incentive for many U.S. businesses to go abroad. Three industrialized trading blocs—the Triad—dominate the volume of world trade, although they represent only a small part of the world's land mass and population. The Triad are the United States, Canada, and Mexico (NAFTA); the European Union; and Japan. As you might imagine, competition within their domestic markets and between the members of the Triad is fierce. For this reason, many marketers are turning their attention to emerging markets.

Emerging Markets Markets that are growing and represent great potential are called *emerging markets.* China is perhaps the last major marketing frontier, and it is booming.[35] About 1.2 billion people live there, one-fourth of all consumers in the world, yet only around 100 million are currently affluent enough to purchase Western products; most Chinese, particularly those living in the rural areas, are poor.[36] The country is ruled by the Chinese Communists, who are often condemned for human rights violations, such as the 1989 massacre in Tiananmen Square. With its rapidly growing economy, China is emerging as a world-class economic and, perhaps, military power.[37]

Western and Japanese businesses are aggressively marketing in China because of its current size and potential. For example, China is Motorola's largest market for cellular telephones outside the United States; Xerox Corporation's sales of personal computers in China rose 20 percent between 1991 and 1992; China is Boeing's second largest market; AT&T recently signed a contract with China for over $1 billion for communications equipment, research, and development; and Coca-Cola is building at least 10 bottling plants in China's interior cities (see Photo 5.5).[38]

China is not the only Asian nation attracting marketers. Members of Asean, the Association of Southeast Asian Nations (Indonesia, Singapore, Thailand, the Philippines, Malaysia, and Brunei), are becoming top trading partners for American businesses.[39] Although it's roughly the same size as the European Union (about 330 million people), Asean consumers do not have the same spending power as Europeans, and the distribution of affluent consumers able to afford Western products is uneven. Many problems confront U.S. marketers in Asean countries, including religious and racial strife, poor roads, jammed ports, and clogged airports. However, opportunities exist for businesses willing to undertake the challenges in this growing region.

The Indian subcontinent, home to over 900 million people, is also an emerging market. India became independent from Britain over 50 years ago and is just now beginning to break free of the highly restrictive British-style bureaucracy that controlled and dampened Indian business activities. India is a land of contrasts: Although roughly 25 percent of the population live in poverty, at least 40 million Indians are "super-haves," high-end consumers with annual incomes equivalent to the purchasing power of Americans in the $600,000 income bracket. About 150 million Indian consumers have the equivalent of $20,000 in annual United States income purchasing power. The Indian middle class is larger than the entire population of the United States. Major international companies already invested in India include General Electric, General Motors, Motorola, Coca-Cola, PepsiCo, and Philip Morris.[40]

Eastern Europe (former East Germany, Czechoslovakia, Poland, Hungary, Yugoslavia, Romania, Bulgaria, and Albania) and the

Photo 5.5

China's economic growth and huge market potential will continue to attract international businesses.

republics of the former Soviet Union combined have an estimated 350 million consumers. In some of their languages, there isn't even a word for marketing. The free market is a totally new concept for these countries, yet PepsiCo and Coca-Cola already are there, battling for market share. For years, Pepsi was the dominant Western soft drink in Eastern Europe and the Soviet Union. Germany is Coke's largest European market, and the company expects that Coke will easily dominate the former East German market.[41] Eastern Europe and the former Soviet Union are volatile and very bureaucratic: some governments are unstable; there are noncompetitive industries, environmental degradation, people unused to capitalism and a free market, high inflation, high unemployment, lack of hard currency, and distribution difficulties.

As Mexico opens to U.S. and Canadian marketers under the NAFTA agreement, it will be a gateway to Latin and South America. The 1990 Latin American population was about 448 million. There are four major marketing arrangements in the area that show a high degree of cooperation among nations, a growing population, and democratically elected governments in almost all countries.[42] Many countries are privatizing their previously government-controlled industries, and Western investors are responding.

Check Your Understanding 5.3

1. Why should businesses consider going international?
2. What kind of help can businesses get in going abroad?
3. What is the Triad? What are the emerging nations?

BECOMING AN INTERNATIONAL MARKETER

International marketing is not just domestic marketing extended unchanged to other countries. An additional layer of complexity is added with each country targeted.

Objective 4 Describe the environment of international marketing.

The International Marketing Environment

The marketer must evaluate many factors before going international. Consumer demand and consumer characteristics affect the product offer. The marketer must analyze the level of direct and indirect competition, the availability of suppliers and distributors, and the market's technology level, infrastructure, geography, and climate.

Culture Factors Just as it is important to understand the different cultures *within* a domestic market, it is equally important to understand the macroculture and dominant microcultures of international markets. For example, consider what might happen if an advertisement targeted to a very conservative society didn't take into account the cultural norms of that society. If, for instance, an advertisement showing men and women touching in public was used in predominantly Muslim countries, the advertiser would run the risk of insulting and offending a large portion of the population. This, in turn, could be very damaging to sales in that country. It is up to marketers to research and understand the norms of other cultures to avoid this type of mistake. Many marketing mistakes have been made because of a lack of cultural understanding; most of these mistakes could have been avoided. Some past international marketing mistakes are shown in Figure 5.4.

Political/Legal Factors   Each country has laws, rules, and regulations that govern, encourage, and restrict business within its borders. This is true also in free trade areas in the European Union and North America (United States, Canada, and Mexico). In addition, each country has a political system that the marketer must examine in order to determine its stability and attitude toward the United States. Countries with governments hostile to the United States or where there is political strife are not always inviting places for international marketers.

Figure 5.4

Language-to-Language Mistakes

In Spanish, Chevy's Nova automobile translates to "doesn't go."

In Spanish, Ford's Fiera truck translates to "ugly old woman."

In Mexico, Ford's Caliente automobile is slang for "street walker."

In German, Sunbeam's Mist-Stick hair curling iron translates to "manure wand."

In Taiwan, Pepsi's "Come alive with Pepsi" translates to "Brings your ancestors back from the grave."

In China, the calligraphy for Coca-Cola translates to "Bite the wax tadpole."

In Arabic-speaking countries, the Jolly Green Giant translates to "Intimidating green ogre."

In Spanish-speaking Latin American countries, Braniff Air Line's "Fly on leather" advertisement for its comfortable leather seats translates to "Fly naked."

In Spanish, Coor's beer slogan "Get loose with Coors" translates to "Get the runs with Coors."

In Swedish, Kellogg Bran Buds translates to "Burned Farmer."

Marketing Application 5.5

A good way to learn about people from other countries is to conduct cross-cultural interviews. Imagine that you are a marketer of jarred, boxed, and fresh (requires refrigeration) baby food, who is thinking about going international. You have scheduled meetings with businesspeople (male and female) from each of the countries you are considering. What questions should you ask these business-people? Decide what information you need, then develop a short list of questions that will help you make a market selection. For example, if products require both store and home refrigeration, what questions must you ask related to refrigeration? What questions must you ask about consumers? Bring your question list to class for discussion. ■

Economic Factors Marketing must generate revenues. Therefore, marketers must target international markets that are sufficiently affluent to allow consumers to purchase American products. When marketers consider entering a country, several measures of the country's economic health are usually evaluated, including the **standard of living,** which reflects what kinds of products are consumed, their quality, and quantities; and **gross domestic product (GDP),** which is a composite figure indicating the total value of the products produced annually by the country. Both standard of living and GDP figures can be obtained from the United Nations. These figures must be evaluated carefully, because they can be misleading, particularly if a country has a small elite class that holds most of the country's wealth. A very uneven distribution of wealth distorts averages and indicates a much larger consumer class than is actually there.

Another indicator of a country's economy is its level of economic development. Factors frequently used to determine economic development level are per-capita income, educational levels, technology, and purchasing power. The world's countries are often grouped according to their level of economic development. One classification method groups countries as *industrialized* (e.g., United States, Canada, Japan, the European countries), *developing* (e.g., India, South Korea, and many South American countries), and *less developed* (e.g., many Asian and African countries). Nine out of ten countries are classified as developing. Another measure of a country's economy is its financial situation, in particular whether the currency can be exchanged for products and whether financial institutions have the ability to support international marketing efforts.

standard of living A measure of a country's economic health reflecting the kinds of products consumed, their quality, and quantities.

gross domestic product (GDP) A composite figure indicating the total value of the products produced annually by a country.

Entry Strategies

Once a company makes the decision to market abroad, the next step is deciding how to do it. Entry strategies differ in the level of commitment required, risk, and the degree of control the business retains over its marketing mix. Opportunities must be carefully evaluated. This requires collecting information about each potential market's environments and forecasting current market demand, market potential for your products, the kinds of profits that can be made, and the level of risk. Accurate information can be obtained from the U.S. government, the United Nations, most Western European countries, and Japan. Information from most other countries is dated and often incomplete. Some businesses sell research information to be used for these purposes.

Barriers to Entry   Trade is not free throughout the world. Many countries erect barriers to stop foreign products from being imported and undermining protected domestic industries. Protecting domestic business at the expense of foreign business is called **protectionism.** A common complaint against the Japanese is that their markets are closed, particularly to many U.S. products, which accounts for a large United States–Japan trade imbalance. Some frequently used reasons for protectionism are:

protectionism   Protecting domestic business at the expense of foreign business.

- To protect an infant industry.
- To protect the home (domestic) market.
- To keep needed money at home.
- To encourage the accumulation of capital.
- To maintain the citizens' standard of living.
- To conserve the country natural resources.
- To maintain employment.
- To ensure the national defense.
- To increase the size of the home country business.

The only valid arguments are the protection of infant industries, national defense, the need to industrialize underdeveloped countries, and, possibly, the conservation of natural resources.[43] Protectionism can result in higher prices for home country consumers because it stifles competition. It may also blind protected businesses to the need to become more competitive.

tariff   A tax on selected imports, designed to protect native industries.

A common form of barrier is a **tariff,** a tax on selected imports designed to protect native industries. There also are many types of nontariff barriers including import quotas, embargoes, exchange controls, and local content laws. These are identified in Figure 5.5.

GATT   The General Agreement on Tariffs and Trade, an asociation of 103 nations representing 80 percent of the world's trade, which is attempting to eliminate trade restrictions and encourage open markets.

The General Agreement on Tariffs and Trade (**GATT**) is an association of 103 nations, representing approximately 80 percent of the world's trade, that is attempting to eliminate trade restrictions and encourage open markets. The Uruguay round of world trade

Tariffs
Taxes applied on imported goods to restrict their being brought into a country.

Nontariff Barriers	
Quota	Physical limits on the amount of specific goods that can be brought into a country.
Embargo	Ban on importing some products or a ban on letting some products leave a country.
Exchange controls	A limit on the amount of currency that can be exchanged.
Product standards	Set of requirements for products in such areas as electrical plugs, machine tools, and weights and measures.
Licensing	Licensing of primarily imports in order to control inflow of products.

Figure 5.5

Barriers to Entry

talks began in 1987 and finally resulted in a signed agreement seven years later. Because the talks proceeded at a snail's pace, GATT is often called the General Agreement to Talk and Talk. GATT will be replaced by the World Trade Organization, which will continue to work toward liberalizing world trade and lowering trade restrictions.[44]

Entry Alternatives Exporting is the least risky entry alternative. **Indirect exporting** means that the company assigns its products to an agent, who takes on the responsibility of marketing the products abroad, and is paid either by commission or through a buy-sell agreement in which the agent purchases the products and resells them. This alternative carries the least risk, but also offers the least control for the business over product marketing. **Direct exporting** requires the business to take greater control of its marketing mix, which also increases the risk.

Alternatively, the business may enter into a **joint venture** arrangement by which it works with another company (or even several others) to market products abroad. This way the risk is shared; however, so is control. Many businesses seek international joint venture partners for their expertise and established distribution systems. The NBC television network is expanding internationally through many joint ventures. The company recently entered into an alliance with TV Azteca in Mexico in anticipation of rapid growth in television advertising with the implementation of NAFTA.[45] Through **direct ownership,** the company owns the production facilities and manufactures and markets products abroad without partners. This means that the company has full control, but also takes all the risk.

indirect exporting Assigning products to an agent who markets the products abroad.

direct exporting Keeping international marketing tasks within a parent company.

joint venture Companies working together to market products abroad.

direct ownership A company owns production facilities and manufactures and markets products abroad without partners.

Going Global There are different levels of involvement in international marketing. Limited international marketing means that the business offers its products in only a few foreign markets. A multinational business markets to many different countries around the world. **Global marketing,** a term first described by Ted Levitt, is conducted by a business that uses a standardized marketing approach in all the countries in which it markets on the principle that the world is really just one market. This assumes that "Consumers everywhere want high quality goods at a fair price ... [therefore] companies need global strategies to exploit this homogeneity."[46]

global marketing The use of a standardized marketing approach in all countries, based on the principle that the world is really just one market.

Few companies are truly global by Levitt's definition. Even Coca-Cola, McDonald's, Nike, and Disney make adaptations to local markets.[47] McDonald's offers spaghetti in the Philippines because it is cheaper than meat sandwiches. In Japan, there is a McDonald's breakfast entrée of two rice balls and a cup of miso soup, as well as a cheese Katsu burger (actually roast pork), fried rice, and a teriyaki McBurger.[48]

Marketing Mix Strategies

The marketing mix variables are discussed in depth in Chapters 7 to 13. International marketing mix decisions (product, price, place/distribution, promotion) center on whether to *standardize* (global strategy), *customize* (local strategy), or *mix* (combine the two). Most large companies use a mixed approach of "think global, act local," which means that although they may aspire to the global goal of standardization and centralization to become more efficient, they realize that local differences must be accommodated in order to sell their products.

A product that is not changed and is marketed the same in both domestic and international markets is a *straight product extension*. A product that is changed to accommodate a culture, language, standards, or some other specific country requirement is a *product adaptation*. In some cases, a product must be simplified because it is too complex for the technology in a particular market. This is a *backward invention*. If the product must be made more technically sophisticated for an international market, it is a *forward invention*.

It is almost impossible to standardize prices unless the products are sold in a free trade area. Therefore, price setting is a particularly difficult task because so many elements must be considered, including tariffs, transportation, distribution, currency exchange rates and stability, risk, competition, and so on. Sometimes a product's price is undercut if **dumping** occurs, when a company sells a product abroad at a lower price than the product is sold for in the company's home market (plus costs for sales abroad) or lower than the cost of production. Because of the lack of a single definition for dumping, it is a difficult charge to prove. In legal terms, it must be shown that a dumped product has caused harm to host country businesses.

dumping The selling of a product abroad at a price lower than it is sold for in the company's home market or lower than the cost of production.

Distribution is more complex internationally than domestically. This includes not only the transportation and handling of goods, but also decisions about whether or not to use intermediaries (wholesalers and retailers) brought from the home country or host country distribution networks.

Many marketers run into trouble when they promote their products internationally. Standardized advertising is difficult unless the product is culturally insensitive, such as industrial and agricultural products. For products that are highly culturally sensitive, such as personal use consumer products, it is far more difficult to standardize. Other decisions involve whether to hire and train host country salespeople or use salespeople brought from home or another international office. Sales promotions are popular in the United States but may be illegal in other countries. Direct marketing can be far more complicated abroad, particularly in countries without dependable telephone or mail service.

Check Your Understanding
5.4

1. Is international marketing more complex than domestic marketing?
2. What are some common barriers to entry?
3. What is global marketing?

CONTEMPORARY ISSUES IN INTERNATIONAL MARKETING

It is impossible to foresee what international marketing will be like in the next century, but it appears that the world is moving toward establishing three large free trade areas (FTA). Unless efforts to encourage worldwide free trade are strengthened, the next century may be dominated by the North and South American FTA, the European FTA (Western Europe and parts of Eastern Europe), and a Pacific Rim FTA bloc dominated by Japan and possibly China.

Objective 5 Analyze the contemporary issues facing international marketers.

NAFTA

Many U.S. and Canadian marketers didn't wait for the official 1993 ratification of NAFTA between the United States, Canada, and Mexico, which created the largest free trade area in the world. Coca-Cola, Kmart, Sears, Arby's, and PepsiCo were in place well before ratification, betting that free trade with Mexico would create a new market of consumers affluent enough to be able to afford their products.[49] A Mexican Spanish-language media group had already put together a media network called Televisa, which operates from

Connecticut to Chile with an audience of over 340 million Spanish-speaking consumers. Televisa illustrates the belief of many that NAFTA will open the door to the whole of Latin America.[50] Some Americans fear that U.S. manufacturing jobs will be lost to Mexico under NAFTA; many marketers believe that any losses will be offset by gains through growth of a middle class eager to buy U.S. products. Environmental concerns slowed ratification of the treaty but did not slow businesses seeking opportunities in Mexico.

European Integration

On December 31, 1992, the 12 nations of the European Union formally established a free trade zone among their countries. This economic integration abolished border stoppings, established communitywide product standards, and generally encouraged the free passage of people, capital, and products within its borders. Members of this 320-million-person free trade area are Belgium, Denmark, France, Germany, Great Britain, Greece, Ireland, Italy, Luxembourg, the Netherlands, Portugal, and Spain. Although it is often called the "United States of Europe," there is no common language uniting these countries, nor is there one federal government. The road to economic integration has been bumpy, particularly in the area of social policies and currency. West Germany was distracted by its reunification with East Germany, which turned out to be far more costly than expected. Many people expect that the Chunnel (the tunnel under the North Sea linking France and England) will symbolically boost the further integration of European economies.

Photo 5.6

The port of Miami is a bustling center of export and import to markets in Latin and South America.

Photo 5.7

With the new Chunnel, or Euro Tunnel, providing a link between Great Britain and continental Europe, prospects look good for continued growth of the European single market.

The Pacific Rim

Many international trade experts believe that the 21st century will be dominated by nations that rim the Pacific Ocean. In addition to the heavily industrialized countries of Japan, New Zealand, and Australia, the area is home to such rapidly industrializing countries as South Korea and Taiwan, as well as the city-states of Hong Kong and Singapore. Commercially profitable markets are also developing in the Philippines and Malaysia. Much is expected of the Vietnamese market. However, overshadowing all these markets is Japan.

By the end of World War II, Japan's industrial base was shattered. Its remarkable industrial rebirth, aided by the United States, has brought it to the point where it is a major international marketer. Its strong home market is protected from imports. *Keiretsu*—vast alliances of interconnected networks of businesses with overlapping directors tied to a bank and numerous core companies—share information, financing, and research and development while restricting imports. *Keiretsu* such as Sumitomo, Mitsui, and Mitsubishi provide mutual support and safety nets for affiliated businesses in hard times.[51] Because their actions often block imports, *Keiretsu* are criticized for increasing costs for Japanese consumers. Japan's trade imbalance with most industrialized nations is a matter of concern, and considerable pressure is being applied on Japan to open its market and accommodate freer trade.[52]

Chapter 6 examines some of the skills and technologies that modern marketers must apply in order to be competitive domestically and internationally.

Career Watch

Scott Montgomery, of Cannondale Japan, has been successful in marketing his company's high-performance mountain and racing bikes in Japan. Scott maintains that the key to successful marketing in Japan means getting closer to the customer. Instead of forming a joint venture with a Japanese company, he set up a wholly owned subsidiary of Cannondale Corporation, based in Georgetown, Connecticut. Rather than pay high rents in Tokyo, he set up shop 20 miles outside Osaka, close to local suppliers. To get the bikes into stores, he hired two Japanese-speaking American professional bicyclists to spearhead sales and promotions. By working directly with bicycle dealers, the company gets feedback about Japanese consumer preferences, which it incorporates into product modifications. Bike sales (average price per bike: $1,500) have quadrupled in one year. Montgomery's advice to marketers entering the Japanese market is "Just get out there and sell. Japanese genuinely appreciate it if you make the effort here." ■

D. L. Boroughs, "Cannondale Pedals Its Way to the Top; The Bike Maker Has Made Big Inroads in Japan," *U.S. News & World Report* 116, no. 1 (January 1, 1994), p. 53; R. Stodghill II, "Joe Montgomery's Wild Ride: As Sales Climb, Will Cannondale's Do-It-All Founder Switch Gears?" *Business Week,* April 19, 1993, p. 50; A. Tanzer, " 'Just Get Out and Sell,' " *Forbes* 150, no. 7 (September 28, 1992), pp. 68, 72.

Photo 5.8

Scott and Joe Montgomery of Cannondale believe in direct communication with the customer—on the customer's terms and turf.

Check Your Understanding 5.5

1. Discuss different product alternatives that can be offered to international markets.
2. Why is pricing more complex in international markets?
3. Describe the contemporary issues involved in international marketing.

Review of Chapter Objectives

1. *Explain why marketers must develop cultural understanding.* Marketers must develop cultural understanding because the United States is becoming more culturally diverse and more internationally minded. Cultural insensitivity can lead to misunderstandings and marketing disaster. A marketer can't get close to consumers if their cultures clash.

2. *Identify the three largest ethnic microcultures in the United States.* The three largest ethnic microcultures in the United States are African-Americans, Hispanic-Americans, and Asian-Americans. Asians and Hispanics continue to immigrate in large numbers. Although these groups are not homogeneous, ethnic background often influences consumer purchase decisions. Hispanics and Asians are important in international marketing, both as entrepreneurs exporting back to their home countries and as business contacts.

3. *Discuss why and how businesses go international.* Businesses go international for a variety of reasons, but the simplest explanation is for profits. The U.S. domestic market is highly competitive and saturated. Going international is getting easier even for small to mid-size companies. Therefore, it is expected that more busi-

nesses will look abroad for their growth in the next century.

4. *Describe the environment of international marketing.* International marketing is not identical to domestic marketing. Complexities are added with each country market. In addition to evaluating cultural differences, the marketer must also analyze demand potential, competition, costs, and risks among other factors.

5. *Analyze the contemporary issues facing international marketers.* The most timely contemporary issues relate to the growing pattern of cooperative trade agreements among nations, particularly the North American Free Trade Agreement and the European Union. Another issue is the emergence of the Pacific Rim nations. International marketers also must be aware of opportunities in Latin America.

Key Terms

After studying Chapter 5, you should be able to define each of the following key terms and use them in describing marketing activities.

Cultural Blinders, page 138
Culture, page 138
Socialization, page 138
Self-Reference Criterion, page 138
Culture Clash, page 139
Macroculture, page 139
Multicultural Society, page 139
Microculture, page 139
Values, page 140
Homogeneous, page 140
Heterogeneous, page 140
Cultural Sensitivity, page 142
Cultural Borrowing, page 144
Cultural Change, page 144

Domestic Marketing, page 149
International Marketing, page 149
Export, page 149
Import, page 149
Trade Deficit, page 149
Standard of Living, page 157
Gross Domestic Product (GDP), page 157
Protectionism, page 158
Tariff, page 158
GATT, page 158
Indirect Exporting, page 159
Direct Exporting, page 159
Joint Venture, page 159
Direct Ownership, page 159
Global Marketing, page 160
Dumping, page 160

Discussion Questions

1. What are the three largest ethnic microcultures in the United States?

2. What is the difference between a macroculture and a microculture?

3. Explain what is meant by the term *multicultural society.*

4. What are American core values? Explain how they are used in describing a nation.

5. Compare and contrast the terms *homogeneous* and *heterogeneous.*

6. Do you think body language is important in marketing? Explain.

7. Can cultural sensitivity be overdone? Might it threaten the unity of the United States if immigrants don't assimilate?

8. Are marketers culture change agents? Could this be the case even in the United States? Explain.

9. How are recent immigrants to the United States contributing to international marketing?

10. Why do businesses go international? Describe the important factors a marketer must consider when going international and selecting target markets.

What Do You Think?

Many human rights activists believe that trade with China should be restricted until the Chinese Communist government makes substantive improvements in its human rights record. They even suggest that trade sanctions should be imposed if China doesn't release its imprisoned political dissidents. Others believe it would be a mistake to cut off or severely restrict trade with China, because the ones who would be hurt most would be Chinese entrepreneurs and those leading the way to a free market economy in China. They argue that the road to democracy in China is through economic reform and trade. What do you think?

Sources: J. Klein, "The Rites (and Wrongs) of Spring," *Newsweek,* (March 28, 1994), p. 30; L. Kaye, "Commerce Kowtow: Human Rights Concerns Lost in Rush of U.S. Deals," *Far Eastern Economic Review* 157, no. 36 (September 8, 1994), p. 16.

Mini-Case 5.1

Pier 1: Retailer of Global Goods Goes International

Pier 1 is the largest marketer of home furnishings in the United States. For over 30 years, the company has offered goods from 44 countries to Americans eager to outfit their homes with such exotic items as Italian dinnerware, Chinese baskets, Indonesian rattan chairs, and Japanese sake cups. Despite the high failure rate of retailers trying to take their retailing concepts abroad, Pier 1 will try to export its unique shopping experience, but adapt it to local tastes. For example, instead of marketing Asian goods in Asia, Pier 1 will stock its Asian stores with American goods and Native American artifacts. The goal is the same as in the United States: to give shoppers a chance to purchase unusual, moderately priced products designed to satisfy their wanderlust.

Based in Fort Worth, Texas, the company plans to have about 100 stores open outside North America by the year 2000. Stores were opened in Great Britain in 1992, and two were planned for Puerto Rico by the end of 1993 with 13 to 15 more expected by 1996. Others are planned for Mexico. Because the Puerto Rican market resembles

Photo 5.9

Pier 1's ongoing mission is to bring international products to international markets.

Florida's, Pier 1's CEO believes that the inventory used in the United States for Cubans and other Hispanic-Americans can be brought to the islands unchanged. Puerto Rico is seen as the stepping stone leading to other Latin American markets, and the United Kingdom is the gateway to expansion onto the rest of the European continent.

Case Questions

1. What do you think of Pier 1's plans? Is their strategy an example of "Go global, think local?"

2. Would you recommend that Pier 1 find a local partner in the countries where it plans to open stores? Explain your answer.

3. Is the plan to market to Puerto Rico the same way Pier 1 markets to Florida a good one? Explain.

Sources: S. A. Forest and R. Golby, "A Pier 1 in Every Port? The Retailer Will Push Its Global Wares in 250 Stores Overseas," *Business Week,* May 31, 1993, p. 88; A. L. Stewart, "U.S. Puts Pier Pressure on Europe's Retailers," *Marketing News* 27, no. 16 (August 2, 1993), pp. 6–7; A. Feldman, "But Who Is Minding the Store?" *Forbes* 152, no. 12 (November 22, 1993), pp. 47–48; A. L. Choo, "Asian Crafts Lend Flavor to Pier 1's Home Bazaar," *The Asian Wall Street Journal* 16, no. 37 (September 12, 1994), p. 4.

Mini-Case 5.2

Joint Ventures at Home and Abroad

Today's business climate is a risky one. Therefore, businesses both at home and abroad are increasingly seeking joint venture partners to develop projects. Domestically, a joint venture between Spiegel and *Ebony* magazine teams a huge cataloger and a magazine to direct market clothing to African-American women. Hanover Direct and Essence Communications (the parent companies of Spiegel and *Ebony*) also have joint ventured to mail an apparel catalog to *Essence* magazine's subscriber list. Both catalogs offer clothing styled and sized for African-American women.

Internationally, even a giant corporation like AT&T is teaming up with joint venture partners to modernize China's telephone system. It already has joint venture partnerships with companies in Canada, Poland, India, Russia, and the Ukraine. PacTel Corporation, a California company, also has gone international through joint venturing.

It has established cellular licenses in Japan, pager systems in Thailand, and a credit card confirmation program in South Korea.

Case Questions

1. What do you think of joint ventures? What are the benefits and shortcomings?

2. What can a catalog company gain from forming a joint venture partnership with a magazine targeted to African-American women?

3. What can AT&T gain from having joint venture partners in China?

Sources: J. Schmeltzer, "Spiegel, Ebony Team Up to Target Key Market," *Lexington Herald-Leader*, August 8, 1993, p. 8; B. Ziegler, "AT&T Reaches Way Out for This One," *Business Week*, March 8, 1993, p. 83; D. Kaufman, "Playing by the Rules," *Link* 5, no. 6 (June 1993), pp. 17–19, 26.

Chapter 5 Notes

1. C. Farrell, "Shut Out Immigrants and Trade May Suffer," *Business Week*, July 5, 1993, pp. 82, 84; B. Bremner and J. Weber, "A Spicier Stew in the Melting Pot," *Business Week*, December 21, 1992, pp. 29–30.

2. P. R. Cateora, *International Marketing*, 8th ed. (Homewood, IL: Richard D. Irwin, 1993), p. 15.

3. S. J. Ungar, "Painting the U.S. by Number," *The Washington Post National Weekly Edition* 11, no. 25 (April 18–24, 1994), p. 36.

4. K. W. Reyes, "The Fabric of a Nation," *Modern Maturity* 35, no. 3 (June–July 1992), p. 24.

5. J. Schwartz and S. Krafft, "Managing Consumer Diversity: The 1991 American Demographics Conference," *American Demographics* 13, no. 8 (August 1991), pp. 22–29.

6. "Japan: Outsiders All," *The Economist* 326, no. 7794 (January 16, 1993), p. 36.

7. V. Terpstra and K. David, *The Cultural Environment of International Business*, 3rd ed. (Cincinnati: South-Western, 1991), p. 28.

8. C. Miller, "Employees Tested for Language Skills as Marketplace Goes Global," *Marketing News* 27, no. 10 (May 10, 1993), p. 7.

9. "Ethnic Channels Fill a Gap as Cable Television Capacity Mushrooms," *The Wall Street Journal*, April 15, 1993, p. A1.

10. C. Laughlin, "Speaking in Tongues," *Link* 5, no. 9 (October 1993), pp. 13–17.

11. Y. Ono, "A Little Bad English Goes a Long Way in Japan's Boutiques," *The Wall Street Journal*, May 20, 1992, pp. A1, 6.

12. J. Clark, "Watch Your Body Language if You Go Abroad," *Lexington Herald-Leader*, November 10, 1991, p. H6.

13. "Life, Liberty and Try Pursuing a Bit of Tolerance Too," *The Economist* 324, no. 7775 (September 5, 1992), pp. 19–21.

14. "The New Americans: Yes, They'll Fit in Too," *The Economist* 319, no. 7706 (May 11, 1991), pp. 17–20.

15. "People-Power," *The Economist* 325, no. 7788 (December 5, 1992), p. 29.

16. E. E. Spragins, "The Diverse Workforce," *INC.* 15, no. 1 (January 1993), p. 33.

17. G. DeGeorge, "Armageddon—or Shining City of the Future," *Business Week*, July 13, 1992, p. 122.

18. J. S. Lublin, "Foreign Accents Proliferate in Top Ranks as U.S. Companies Find Talent Abroad," *The Wall Street Journal*, May 21, 1992, pp. B1, 7.

19. P. Oster, D. Woodrull, N. Gross, S. Bhargawa, and E. Lesly, "The Fast Track Leads Overseas," *Business Week*, November 1, 1993, pp. 64–68.

20. Cateora, *International Marketing*, p. 7; P. Kotler and G. Armstrong, *Principles of Marketing*, 6th ed. (Englewood Cliffs, NJ: Prentice Hall, 1994), p. 612.

21. A. C. Samli, R. Still, and J. S. Hill, *International Marketing: Planning and Practice* (New York: Macmillan, 1993), p. 40.

22. "From Billboards to TV, Western Culture Leaving Its Mark on Moscow," *Lexington Herald-Leader*, May 10, 1993, p. A3.

23. "Blue Light Flashing in Czechoslovakia," *Lexington Herald-Leader*, December 26, 1992, p. A4.

24. S. Strasser, "Where the Admen Are," *Newsweek*, March 14, 1994, p. 39.

25. N. J. Cho, "South Koreans Are Offered Naked Truth in Advertising but Some Find It Hurts," *The Wall Street Journal*, May 10, 1994, p. A8.

26. J. Huey, "America's Hottest Export: Pop Culture," *Fortune*, December 31, 1990, pp. 50–60; J. B. Levine, "Cable Has a New Frontier: The Old World," *Business Week*, June 28, 1993, p. 74; B. Powell and F. Shaw Myers, "Death by Fried Chicken: Western Foods Are a Hazard to Japanese Health," *Newsweek*, September 24, 1990, p. 34.

27. "Black Is Bourgeois," *The Economist* 324, no. 7766 (July 4, 1992), p. 28; C. Miller, "Researcher Says U.S. Is More of a Bowl Than a Pot," *Marketing News* 27, no. 10 (May 10,

1993), p. 6; M. F. Riche, "We're All Minorities Now," *American Demographics* 13, no. 10 (October 1991), pp. 26–34; M. Mallory and S. A. Forest, "Waking Up to a Major Market," *Business Week,* March 23, 1992, pp. 70, 73.

28. A. Gerlin, "Radio Stations Gain by Going After Hispanics," *The Wall Street Journal,* July 14, 1993, pp. B1, 8; L. E. Wynter, "Business and Race," *The Wall Street Journal,* July 30, 1993, p. B1; H. F. Waters, "Listening to Their Latin Beat," *Newsweek,* March 28, 1994, pp. 42–43.

29. B. Bremner and J. Weber, "A Spicier Stew in the Melting Pot," *Business Week,* December 21, 1992, pp. 29–30; C. Miller, "Advertising in Hispanic Media Rises Sharply," *Marketing News* 27, no. 2 (January 18, 1993), p. 9; Gerlin, "Radio Stations Gain," pp. B1, 8; C. Miller, "Study: Shopping Patterns Vary Widely among Minorities," *Marketing News* 27, no. 2 (January 18, 1993), p. 11; Miller, "Researcher Says U.S. Is More of a Bowl Than a Pot," p. 6.

30. T. Eiben, "U.S. Exporters on a Global Roll," *Fortune* 125, no. 13 (June 29, 1992), pp. 94–95.

31. W. J. Holstein and K. Kelly, "Little Companies, Big Exports," *Business Week,* April 13, 1992, pp. 70–72.

32. J. Hyatt, "The G Factor," *INC.* 14, no. 1 (January 1992), pp. 68–73.

33. Samli, Still, and Hill, *International Marketing,* p. 165.

34. S. Woolley, "Shaping Up by Shipping Out," *Business Week,* April 19, 1993, p. 119.

35. V. Reitman, "Enticed by Visions of Enormous Numbers, More Western Marketers Move into China," *The Wall Street Journal,* July 12, 1993, pp. B1, 6.

36. S. Strasser and B. Powell, "What Asia Wants from America," *Newsweek,* July 12, 1993, pp. 40–45.

37. Ibid.

38. P. Engardio, L. Curry, and J. Barnathan, "China Fever Strikes Again," *Business Week,* March 29, 1993, pp. 46–47.

39. J. P. Quinlan, "Going to Market in the East," *The Wall Street Journal,* January 4, 1993, p. A8; H. Rowen, "Asia Major," *The Washington Post National Weekly Edition* 10, no. 38 (July 19–25, 1993), p. 5.

40. P. Fuhrman and M. Schuman, "Now We Are Our Own Masters," *Forbes* 153, no. 11 (May 23, 1994), pp. 128–38.

41. W. Konrad and I. Reichlin, "The Real Thing Is Thundering Eastward," *Business Week,* April 13, 1992, pp. 96–98.

42. Cateora, *International Marketing,* Chapter 9.

43. Ibid., p. 41.

44. _____ "Free Trade or Foul?" *The Economist* 331, no. 7858 (April 9, 1994), p. 13.

45. E. Jensen, "NBC Creates Broad Alliance with TV Azteca," *The Wall Street Journal,* May 16, 1994, pp. A3, 6.

46. T. Levitt, "The Globalization of Markets," *Harvard Business Review,* May–June 1983, pp. 92–102; K. H. Hammonds, "Ted Levitt Is Back in the Trenches," *Business Week,* April 9, 1990, pp. 82–84.

47. T. W. Ferguson, "Nike Seems to Be Doing It Right (and Left)," *The Wall Street Journal,* July 14, 1992, p. A15.

48. K. Morgan, "Fast Food Goes Global: Make Mine a Whopper with Beets, Hold the Egg," *Lexington Herald-Leader,* May 2, 1992, p. D5; Y. Ono, "Japan's Fast Food Companies Cook Up Local Platters to Tempt Local Palates," *The Wall Street Journal,* May 29, 1992), pp. B1, 5.

49. C. Miller, "North American Marketers Await Trade Pact," *Marketing News* 27, no. 10 (May 10, 1993), pp. 1, 10.

50. "Television in Mexico: Changing Channels," *The Economist* 327, no. 7809 (May 1, 1993), pp. 76, 77.

51. W. J. Holstein, "Japan's Ties That Bind," *Business Week,* May 10, 1993), p. 10.

52. R. Neff, "For Bankrupt Companies, Happiness Is a Warm Keiretsu," *Business Week,* October 26, 1992, pp. 48, 49.

Marketing Research and Information Technology

Chapter Objectives

After studying Chapter 6 you should be able to

1. Explain why information is so important to marketers.

2. Understand that all marketers need information.

3. Describe a marketing information system (MIS) and explain how it works.

4. Identify the steps in marketing research.

5. Discuss how recent advances in information technology are pushing marketing in new directions.

*M*arketers are told repeatedly that they must focus on the customer, get close, identify his or her needs, and then find out a way to satisfy them. This sounds great in an abstract sense, but how do you do it? With all the different consumers in the marketplace, how do you get the right information to make the right marketing decisions? As you read this chapter and become familiar with the skills and technologies marketers employ to collect, evaluate, and use information, consider the question "How can information be used by marketers to gain competitive advantage?"

Isabelle Ono, a second generation Japanese-American, is the marketing manager of a small health foods business headquartered in Harlan, Tennessee. She has heard from relatives in Japan that consumers there are losing confidence because the economy is not doing well. Many people are avoiding stores, preferring to spend their money on less expensive products sold door to door. From her readings about Japan, Isabelle has discovered that Japanese health researchers and government officials are voicing concern about the people's intake of additive-rich, high-fat foods like *tiramisu,* a very popular dish made primarily from chocolate, cream cheese, and sugar.[1] Linking these two streams of information—successful door-to-door selling of products and concern about nutrition—she begins to see an opportunity for her company. They could form a joint venture partnership with a company such as Amway to distribute their health foods in Japan. Amway, an Ada, Michigan, company, sells its products in Japan through independent Japanese marketers going door to door. This is the way products were sold for years in the United States before large numbers of women joined the out-of-home workforce. Because Amway is Western, it has a desirable image and is a great success among Japanese consumers.[2] In talking it over with her boss, both agree they need more information before deciding if Japanese consumers are a good export target market for their firm's products and if Amway is a potential partner.

THE INFORMATION EXPLOSION

Objective 1 Explain why information is so important to marketers.

information Knowledge that can be used to solve a problem.

data The raw materials that make up usable information, such as facts, figures, observations, and reports.

Isabelle, like most marketers, needs more information before she can make a marketing decision. **Information** is knowledge that can be used to solve a problem, such as helping marketers make a decision about whether or not to market their company's products in a market and how to market them. **Data** are the raw materials that make up usable information including facts, figures, observations, reports, research results, documents, and other items converted to a form that can be used to reduce the risk of making a bad marketing decision. Often the terms *information* and *data* are used interchangeably. However, most marketing professionals make a distinction between the two.

In order to be useful, information must be current, reliable, suitable, sufficient, affordable, and available. The marketplace is changing so rapidly that any business failing to continuously collect and use information courts disaster. Good information wisely used can help the marketer identify profitable windows of opportunity and avoid threats to the business's survival. However, the information explosion has also resulted in a tidal wave of information that threatens to overwhelm decision makers. Instead of eliminating hard copy documents, the computer, copier, and fax machine seem to encourage the production of even more documents, most of them on paper.

The world is in the midst of an information explosion, fueled by continuous advances in computer technology. The computer has revolutionized business and society over the past 30 years. Today, for

Marketing Application 6.1

Isabelle must collect information that will help her decide whether Japan is a good opportunity or the opening of a trap door to disaster. Put yourself in the place of an information collector, a disposable diaper marketer who wants to expand into new markets in selected cities in the states of Kentucky, Indiana, and Louisiana. Before you can identify which markets to enter, you must first decide what *kind* of information you must collect to make the location decision. Brainstorm either independently or with several classmates; make a list of the categories of information you'll need. For example, one broad category is population demographics. You'll need information about specific parts of the population that will help you forecast demand for your product now and in the future. Identify as many different kinds of information categories as possible. In a later Marketing Application you'll be asked to brainstorm sources for this information. ■

around $2,000 a business can purchase a desktop personal computer (see Photo 6.1) with the same power as the enormous room-sized mainframe computers of the 1960s. Some of the tasks these machines can perform for marketers are identified in Figure 6.1. The downside of the computer revolution is that so much information is being generated that it overwhelms the capacity of many marketers to manage it.

Photo 6.1

Reasonably priced personal computers are revolutionizing the workplace.

Figure 6.1

Some Marketing Tasks
Performed Using Computers

Task	Description
Word processing	Manipulation of written word allows for great flexibility in document preparation and revision, storage, and retrieval.
Spreadsheet calculations	Electronic ledgers allow fast calculations, graphic presentations, statistical analysis, "what if . . ." scenarios based on changing factors.
Database management	Compilation, revision, and manipulation of information in electronic Rolodex form.
Advertising design/layout	ClipArt, original designs, paint and draw programs for visual images, type and spatial relationships, all with a laser printer can create camera-ready print advertisements.
Desktop publishing	Printshop capacities allow for page setups in various column formats, includes art.
Inventory control	Tracking systems for inventory and automatic reordering.
Statistical analysis/ forecasting	Data sorting, testing for significance, trends, market calculations, forecasting demand, sales.
Sales force management	Efficient development of sales routes, sales force tracking, sales records management.
Financial control/ budgeting	Accounting and tax records, sales forecasts, budget tracking.
Intra-/interoffice communication	Regulates document flow, electronic mail, paperless communication.

hardware   Equipment, such as computers, printers, and scanners.

software   Computer programs that perform such functions as spreadsheets, word processing, and database management.

Another difficulty is technology overkill. In the rush to jump aboard the computer bandwagon, some marketers purchase **hardware** (computers, printers, scanners, and associated devices) and **software** (programs such as spreadsheets, word processing, database management, and statistical analysis) too sophisticated for their needs. Keep in mind that not all marketing tasks and decisions require super-sophisticated computer technology.

MARKETING IS INFORMATION INTENSIVE

Objective 2   Understand that all marketers need information.

Marketing is an information-intensive process. It takes considerable skill, based on experience and judgment, for marketers to use information wisely in planning, program implementation, management, and control. The top 10 information needs for marketers, shown in the survey results in Figure 6.2, have remained constant

Consumer Insight

Consumers, both business and personal use, are becoming more knowledgeable about computer hardware and software. A recent study of over 4,500 people shopping for computer products at various retail outlets showed that 85 percent consider themselves computer literate. These are not impulse shoppers; they are deliberate and well informed. Over 60 percent are college educated, with average household incomes of over $50,000. Most use their computer daily, often in home offices. This new breed of computer-literate consumer (the Techno-Savvies) represents a hot target market for many computer-related products.■

C. Miller, "Study Says PC Shoppers Are Knowledgeable and Experienced," *Marketing News* 27, no. 20 (September 27, 1993), p. 5; L. Bird, "Techno-Savvies Are New Target of Advertisers," *The Wall Street Journal,* January 11, 1994, pp. B1, 3.

Figure 6.2

Information Needs of Marketing Managers

Rank	Main Information Needs
1	Improving new product development
2	Improving the use of market information
3	Measuring and managing brand equity
4	Market orientation and bottom line
5	Market segmentation and implementation
6	Identifying, anticipating, and responding to competitors
7	Understanding buyer behavior
8	Strategic new product issues
9	Integrating marketing mix
10	Service quality/performance links

Source: J. Honomichl, "Time Is Ripe to Overhaul Traditional Marketing Research Departments," *Marketing News* 27, no. 12 (June 7, 1993), pp. H34–39. Used with permission.

and consistent. These are the information needs of managers responsible for marketing entire lines of their corporation's products. The information needs of small business marketers or the marketing manager of one store in a chain may be quite different. However, they all use information to aid in making decisions about the marketing mix variables (Four Ps), markets, consumers, and the way their businesses are run. **Descriptive information** describes what consumers do, buy, and say; **prescriptive information** helps marketers make decisions and solve marketing problems.

descriptive information What consumers do, buy, and say.

prescriptive information Information that marketers use to make decisions and solve marketing problems.

Marketing on the Internet

An enormous amount of information is available for retrieval and transmission on the Internet, and the amount is growing daily. Personal use consumers and business/ organization consumers can readily access enormous libraries, such as the Library of Congress, as well as financial information services such as Dow Jones, news services such as Reuters, and specialized databases such as Nexis and Lexis. Many Americans are overwhelmed by the amount of information that is suddenly within reach of their computer keyboard, modem, and telephone line. Coupled with information arriving via fax machines, voice mail, and routine E-mail, many consumers find that they need help.

Electronic assistants, also called help desk software, are among the latest technological developments to lend a helping hand in information management. One program, called Wildfire, recognizes the spoken word and acts as an information filter. It can, upon command, route incoming calls to a car phone, reroute E-mail, fax messages, and place priorities on incoming messages following preprogrammed instructions. BeyondMail, another information manager, or cyber servant, can filter out and automatically delete electronic junk mail.

Advanced systems currently under development will be able to search the Internet for information about products, initiate comparative shopping, and report the results. Other systems can be programmed to monitor news retrieval databases on the Internet and pick out information of interest to retain and deliver as text. These systems hold out the hope of establishing order over the growing information chaos on the Internet. ■

K. Hafner, "Have Your Agent Call My Agent: Info Glut," *Newsweek,* February 27, 1995, pp. 76–77; "Is There Gold in the Internet?" *The Economist* 332, no. 7880 (September 10, 1994), pp. 73–74; T. S. Bowen, "Help Desks Reach Out to Users; Lower Pricing and E-Mail Systems Aid IS Expansion," *PC Week* 11, no. 41 (October 17, 1994), pp. 43–45; R. Tetzeli, "Surviving Information Overload," *Fortune* 130, no. 1 (July 11, 1994), pp. 60–65.

Some information, such as check-out scanner reports on retail sales, is collected routinely, even on a daily basis. Other information, such as tests to determine viewer recall of last night's televised advertising messages, is gained from research conducted only when there is a "need to know." In a recent survey of 173 chief executive officers (CEOs) of companies with $10 million or less in annual sales, the CEOs reported spending on average one to six months and less than $5,000 on market research before launching a new product.[3]

Figure 6.3 shows a continuum of the timing of information collection. Routine information is collected regularly; there is more certainty about what to collect, when and how, and the costs involved. The collection costs are known, because the task is standardized. Information collected less regularly increases collection costs and the length of time needed for collection. Some information is simply not accessible. Other information may be so expensive that collection costs outweigh the benefits of collecting it.

Managing Information

Marketers must manage information in order to ensure that the correct information is collected and made available when and where

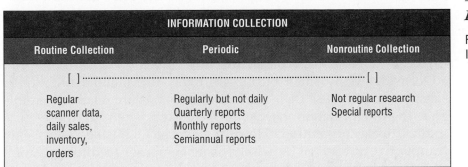

Figure 6.3

Frequency of Marketing
Information Collection

Figure 6.4 A Marketing Information System (MIS)

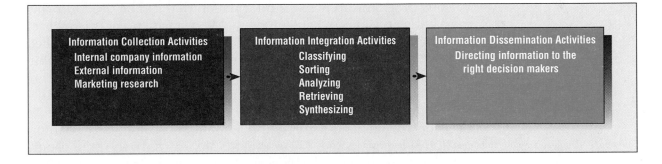

it is needed. **Information overload** occurs when the mass and disorganization of information overwhelms and jeopardizes good decision making instead of aiding it. A popular response to the problem of information management is to create a marketing information system (MIS), as outlined in Figure 6.4 and discussed in the next section.

information overload A situation that exists when the quantity and/or disorganization of information overwhelms and jeopardizes good decision making.

Check Your Understanding
6.1

1. What is information, and how is it used in marketing?
2. Explain this statement: "Marketing is information intensive."
3. Why must marketers be concerned about managing information?

MARKETING INFORMATION SYSTEMS (MIS)

Most but not all modern marketing information systems are computerized. Before the widespread adoption of computers in business, marketers manually performed the same kinds of tasks that are

Objective 3 Describe a marketing information system (MIS) and explain how it works.

accomplished today by a computer-based MIS. They gathered information, integrated it in that most incredible computer, the human mind, and used the results to make marketing decisions such as when to launch a new product and how much to charge for it, where to locate a new retail outlet, or how much to spend on print advertising. Many small businesses today use manual MISs quite satisfactorily, because their marketing decisions are relatively simple and their information needs are few (compared to those of a multinational corporation). However, even small businesses can gain competitive advantage by wisely using computer technology. Computers can add breadth, speed, and organization to the marketer's skills, intuition, and judgment. A computerized MIS cannot replace a marketer's skills, but computer technology can enhance them, if used correctly.

marketing information system (MIS) A process for making marketing decisions using computers, in which information is collected, analyzed, and disseminated or distributed.

A **marketing information system (MIS)** is a process by which one or more people work, usually with computer hardware and various programs, to manage information that can be used to make marketing decisions. A contemporary MIS is made up of three sets of activities: *information collection, information analysis* (sometimes called *information integration*), and *information dissemination.* A smoothly operating MIS should reduce the time needed for information collection, speed the decision-making process, save money by reducing labor costs, improve the quality of the information available to decision makers, and increase the amount and complexity of information being evaluated. These benefits are realized *only* if the people running a computerized MIS correctly instruct the machines, collect the right information, and use the analyzed information output wisely.

Information Collection Activities

Information collection is like vacuum cleaning—you steadily scoop in information and, in a MIS, route it to the next MIS function. Before you can begin collecting, you must decide what information is needed and whether or not it is readily available.

quantitative Objective facts and figures.

There are three commonly used sources of information: internal company records, external information, and results of marketing research. Both quantitative and qualitative information are usually collected from primary and secondary sources. **Quantitative** information includes objective facts and figures, statistical reports, sales data, scanner records, and other numerical items that answer how much, how many, and when questions. **Qualitative** information is more subjective and includes information collected by salespeople, summaries of conversations with customer service representatives, analyses of competitors' actions, observations made by suppliers

qualitative Subjective information, such as observations and anecdotal reports.

and members of the distribution chain, anecdotal reports, and casual accounts of events occurring in the environment. Qualitative information seeks to answer why questions. **Primary data** are collected specifically for the task or problem at hand. Reports and other materials collected for other purposes than the one specifically at hand are called **secondary data.**

primary data Data collected specifically for the immediate task or problem.

secondary data Data collected for purposes other than the immediate task or problem.

Internal Company Information Internal company information includes routinely collected accounting records, such as daily sales receipts, weekly expense records and profit statements, production and shipment schedules, inventory records, orders, monthly credit statements, and quarterly and biennial reports. Field salespeople are increasingly likely to have portable personal computers, pagers, and personal digital assistants (PDAs) to log in data for immediate transmission back to the company or customers, and to receive information from the company and customers.[4] Technology is revolutionizing the selling process. Most companies collect an abundance of information on a regular basis that can also be used in making marketing decisions.

External Information In most marketing decisions it is important to determine what is happening in the business's external environment, particularly anything that involves the competition, the economy, and consumers. External information can be obtained from many sources. Some of the most commonly used sources are commercial intelligence, trade shows, trade journals, the government, private publications, commercial data suppliers, and the popular press. Many companies purchase their competition's products and then perform "autopsies" to find out what makes them tick so they can improve on them. Marketers attend trade shows and read trade journals to keep an eye on the competition. Information can be purchased from information brokers—individuals and companies who help businesses by electronically searching information bases for useful data (see Photo 6.2).[5] Valuable information can be obtained by training salespeople to listen to and observe customers, suppliers, members of the distribution system, and the competition, and then contributing this intelligence to the MIS. The intent should be to obtain usable commercial intelligence (information that is available to the public) and *not* to conduct commercial espionage (stealing information not available to the public). The latter is unethical and illegal.[6] Marketers should be savvy enough to realize that as they are collecting information about their competition, the competition is probably collecting information about them.

The Internet may become the ultimate information source. It already provides access to information provided by government

Photo 6.2

Information services like Dow Jones provide up-to-the-minute information on any topic or trend. Now, marketers can get this information on-line.

(.gov), commerce (.com), universities (.edu), and individuals. Marketers can use this information to perform environmental analysis and market research.

Information Analysis (Integration) Activities

In many situations, a marketer can take the information that has been collected, study it carefully, analyze it in light of a career's worth of experience and judgment, and then apply the results directly to a marketing problem. However, in large businesses it is more likely that the complexity and vast amount of information to be analyzed necessitates using computer technology to integrate various streams of information, establish relationships, and provide analysis and directions on where to proceed with the decision making.

A complex analysis may require the use of intricate mathematical models to draw trends out of the data, such as tracking sales over a period of years or searching out relationships between a product's price and the quantity sold or the amount spent on advertising compared to sales. In these cases, the computer organizes data and sorts and retrieves it much faster than does the human mind.

Marketing Application 6.2

In Marketing Application 6.1, you were asked to identify the kinds of information that a disposable diaper marketer would need in order to decide what new markets to enter with this product. Now you need to determine *where* the information can be found. We'll assume that you've already collected internal company information. What about external sources? The first place to look is at secondary sources—information originally collected for a purpose other than your diaper problem. Census information about possible targets is extremely important and will probably be your first data source. You can go to the *Statistical Abstract of the United States,* a sourcebook for government reports, to a computer database, such as *PC USA,* or to the Internet. Because it is important for marketers to understand *how* and *where* to collect information, locate a copy of the *Statistical Abstract* in your school or local public library. How much of your information needs can be met through leads provided in this sourcebook?

The Statistical Abstract is on the Internet at the address gopher://gopher.census.gov. Enter the Main Data Bank, a menu leading to other directories, then enter the Statistical Abstract of the United States and locate the directory of State Profiles. Access the files for the states of Kentucky, Indiana, and Louisiana. Remember, you have taken the role of a marketer of disposable diapers looking to identify the best city markets in these states. What relevant information is available in the State Profile files? Which two states look to have the best markets? Why? Bring your analysis to class for discussion. ■

Inexpensive computer software for spreadsheets and statistical packages can develop "what if" scenarios in which marketers can alter factors to see effects on future demand. For example, you can project the effect on sales over the next three months if a product's price is raised 5, 7, 8, or 10 percent.

Some software allows marketers to estimate the effect of various promotional efforts on sales.[7] Digital maps combined with customer database information in computer mapping software can be used to pinpoint locations for new retail outlets.[8] Applied intelligence software, known as *neural nets,* are used by mail-order retailer Spiegel, Inc., to identify potential buyers for direct mail efforts. The software analyzes a large number of factors in a vast customer database to separate hot repeat purchasing prospects from one-time buyers.[9]

Advanced computer programs can take the data analysis results and use this information to suggest answers to marketing problems. These sophisticated prescriptive systems, known as *marketing decision support systems (MDSS),* are typically found in extremely large, complex marketing-driven corporations. An MDSS uses mathematical models and simulations to develop decision alternatives and select the best choice of action for the marketer to take. However, the state of current MDSS technology means that these systems are often very complex, difficult to use, and expensive, which limits their widespread adoption.

Instead of a quantitative data analysis, the marketing decision may call for a qualitative approach, using subjective judgments of experts such as salespeople, making observations of consumers, or conducting interviews with suppliers. Information analysis usually includes both quantitative and qualitative approaches.

Information Dissemination Activities

After the information has been analyzed and converted to a usable form, the next step is to make sure that it gets to the right decision maker(s). This isn't always as easy as it appears. If the same marketer is performing all three MIS activities in a small business, then dissemination is no problem. However, in larger businesses where there are many people involved in various phases of MIS activities, dissemination becomes far more complicated, involving hard-copy written reports, E-mail, faxes, or oral presentations.

workflow automation   A system using computer software to distribute information.

Because information spends most of its time moving from desk to desk, office to office, and person to person, it is often delayed in reaching the right person and may lose some or even all of its value. **Workflow automation** offers an approach and computer software that gets information to the right person. The approach requires an in-depth study of the business's information flows and procedures and the design of new information routes. Workflow software converts paper documents to electronic files, automatically routes files to the right decision maker(s), tracks the flow, and facilitates multiple-person access to the information. Lotus Development, Microsoft, and WordPerfect as well as IBM, Xerox, and Unisys offer workflow systems. In smaller businesses, a manual analysis of workflows may lead to more efficient information dissemination.[10]

Check Your Understanding
6.2

1. Describe what takes place in a marketing information system.
2. Identify sources for information collected internally in an MIS.
3. Distinguish between commercial intelligence and espionage.

MARKETING RESEARCH

Objective 4   Identify the steps in marketing research.

Marketing has made a significant contribution to business and society through the advancement of marketing research techniques. According to the American Marketing Association:

> Marketing research links the consumer, customer and public to the marketer through information—information used to identify and

define marketing opportunities and problems; generate, refine and evaluate marketing actions; monitor marketing performance; and improve understanding of marketing as a process. Marketing research specifies the information required to address these issues; designs the methods for collecting information; manages and implements the data collection process; analyzes the results; and communicates the findings and their implications.[11]

Marketing research should be conducted whenever information is needed. The goal is to conduct a systematic, objective, bias-free inquiry that can withstand careful scrutiny. Although in many large businesses research is an ongoing process, each research project typically is directed toward seeking new information to solve a unique problem or make a specific decision.

Marketing research is not always correct or interpreted properly, as demonstrated by the marketing research results that encouraged Coca-Cola marketing managers to launch New Coke.[12] Project Kansas, a two-year Coca-Cola marketing research program, was designed to determine consumer willingness to accept a "New Coke" taste. It involved surveys, focus groups, and blind taste tests with over 200,000 consumers in 10 major U.S. test market cities over a two-year period. The research question of "Do consumers prefer the new, sweeter taste?" did not address the even more important question of "Will consumers like New Coke enough that they will *prefer* it to the familiar 'Old Coke?'" The researchers failed to tell consumers that by selecting one cola they would lose the other. They didn't recognize that taste was only one element affecting consumers' cola choice.[13] Consumers began expressing their displeasure within 24 hours of the announcement that New Coke would *replace* Old Coke. The Coca-Cola researchers failed to understand the symbolism attached to the brand name: Coca-Cola is a part of American history and symbolizes the American way of life. Over 40,000 consumers sent negative letters to the company protesting the removal of traditional Coca-Cola from the market; the phones at Coca-Cola headquarters in Atlanta buzzed for days. The rest is history. The protests led to the return of "Old" Coke as Coke Classic and the eventual decline of the New Coke name and product.

Uses of Marketing Research

The AMA definition clearly specifies how marketing research is to be used. First and foremost, it is an information link connecting consumer needs and what the marketer has to offer. Research results are used to make marketing mix decisions, oversee the implementation of marketing programs, evaluate outcomes, monitor performance, and control expenditures. Marketing research broadly includes re-

market research   Research performed to answer questions about market potential, share, targets, sales, and other issues related to specific markets.

advertising research   Research on ad and copy effectiveness, recall, and media choice.

consumer behavior research   Research about consumers and their behavior and preferences in the marketplace.

search in all marketing activities. **Market research** is more narrowly defined as research performed to answer questions about market potential, share, targets, sales, and other issues related to specific markets. **Advertising research** is research on such advertising issues as ad and copy effectiveness, recall, and media choice. **Consumer behavior research** answers questions about consumers and their behaviors and preferences in the marketplace. Research is also performed on each marketing mix variable, for example, product research on packaging, testing, and new product development; price research on pricing issues; and place research on retail store location choice, stocking, and distribution issues.

Who Performs Marketing Research?

In a large business, there may be a separate department whose sole job is to perform marketing research. This may be several or several hundred people. Marketing managers may conduct marketing research as part of a unique, special project. This was the case with Diners Club of Argentina. When their credit card business suddenly became threatened with the entrance of 11 new, rival cards into the market over a two-year period, the company went to its customers to find out what was necessary to keep their loyalty. This customer service research was performed by 130 company executives in the top four levels of management, including the Diners Club CEO. Each executive took a list of 80 randomly selected customers to contact, using a standard series of survey questions. The information collected was current and personal, and provided the executives a unique closeness to their customers that couldn't be matched by an objective research report.[14]

In mid-size businesses, people within the marketing department may specialize in marketing research or they may be responsible for contracting outside the company for the services of a commercial marketing research company (see Photo 6.3). There are over 1,000 independent marketing research companies in the United States. The 1993 revenues of the top 50 firms exceeded $3.7 billion.[15]

In a small business, marketing research may be conducted in a much less formal way, sometimes by the owner, who performs research for the same reasons as larger businesses but not as extensively and usually not as regularly. Many small-scale studies are very useful to the marketer. These smaller-scale research efforts are usually performed in-house by the marketer, cost much less than hiring a commercial marketing research firm, and allow for closer control over the research process.[16] Getting information directly from customers can provide fruitful feedback for a small business, letting marketers know what they are doing right or wrong. As Deck

International Marketing Report

Some of the giants of marketing research in the United States are expanding rapidly into international markets. Gallup claims it is the first and only licensed marketing research company in China. Along with its joint venture partner, Gallup has offices in Beijing and 18 branches throughout the country. A recent study completed by Gallup for the Chinese confectionery industry indicated considerable differences between consumers in different parts of the country. Chinese in the south like a sweet taste; northern Chinese like sour. Therefore, the same candy bar recipe can't be used in both north and south.

Nielsen makes 60 percent of its revenues abroad and is extending its grocery scanner service to Europe. Information Resources Inc. is in joint ventures with other research companies in Europe, the Pacific Rim, and Latin America. Its customers in the United Kingdom include Gillette, Helene Curtis, and Phillips Lighting. ■

C. Miller, "China Emerges as Latest Battleground for Marketing Researchers," *Marketing News* 28, no. 4 (February 14, 1994), pp. 1–2; C. Miller, "New Battleground Looms for IRI and Nielsen," *Marketing News* 28, no. 9 (April 25, 1994), pp. 1, 3; M. Landler, "The 'Bloodbath' in Market Research," *Business Week*, February 11, 1991, pp. 72, 74.

Photo 6.3

Market research companies and services take care of the time-consuming tasks involved in gathering large amounts of information.

House, Inc., discovered through customer surveys, customers could provide information for all facets of their home design and building business. Surprisingly, instead of liking the freedom of choice that the company provided, Deck House's customers were overwhelmed by the number of decisions they had to make when building a new home. As a result, the company has designed a new line of homes that are more standardized, less costly, and require fewer consumer choices.[17] Electronic Controls Co. (ECCO) uses customer complaint surveys to tabulate complaints and identify problems. ECCO identifies the most common complaints from their business customers and then assigns teams to solve the problems. As a result of these efforts, complaints have gone down.[18]

Steps in Marketing Research

Marketing research is systematic, the process is careful and orderly, and it proceeds methodically through a well-defined series of steps:

1. Identify the problem—state the research question.
2. Develop a plan—state how the answer is to be found.
3. Execute the plan—collect the information.
4. Analyze and interpret results—conduct statistical analysis and draw conclusions.
5. Report findings and recommendations—what should be done in order to solve the problem.

The first step, defining the problem, also shows the complexity of the project. If the problem is too complex and beyond the marketer's research capacities, it must be redefined, broken into smaller parts, or the marketer should seek outside help. In addition to commercial marketing research companies, research help often can be arranged through university marketing professors or independent marketing consultants. **Exploratory research** may be conducted in order to search for information that will help redefine or clarify the problem. This is often a preliminary step done before conducting more sophisticated descriptive or causal research after the problem has been clearly stated. Descriptive research is designed to describe a situation; causal research attempts to find a cause–effect relationship between factors.

exploratory research Research conducted to collect information to help redefine or clarify a problem.

Once the problem has been identified, a plan is developed for conducting the research. This includes identifying information needs (Marketing Application 6.1) and information sources (Marketing Application 6.2) and writing a plan to guide how the work is to be accomplished. For example, answering the question "Why are we losing market share?" may require pursuing several avenues of research concurrently. This can involve a customer survey, an experiment to determine if the product's price is reasonable, observations of in-store consumer behaviors, and interviews with members of the distribution channel that moves the product from producer to consumer.

After the research plan is approved, it is executed. Usually the first activity is to collect and analyze secondary data. A number of very good guides to secondary sources are available in most school and city libraries.[19] Other sources can be identified with the assistance of a business librarian or through a local small business development center. Many companies provide secondary data on computer disks or tapes. The Internet has many avenues for exploring secondary sources.

When a research question cannot be answered using only secondary sources, the research continues with the next step, collecting primary data. At the conclusion of the data collection, all of the data are analyzed. This requires a systematic analysis and often statistical analysis of the quantitative and qualitative data. Computer software can quickly process large numerical data sets and produce results. However, it is still up to the marketer to interpret the results and make sense of them. The final step in marketing research is to communicate the research findings and recommendations on future actions to the people responsible for making marketing decisions. As shown in Photo 6.4, sometimes research results are communicated directly to consumers.

Special Considerations

Although this chapter only presents a brief overview of marketing research, it is important to note several important considerations.

Photo 6.4

The results of customer satisfaction surveys can be used as powerful product promotions. Here, Infiniti shares the results of some impressive market research data.

Researchers must be concerned that their efforts have validity, reliability, and generalizability. Research that falls short on any of the three must be used *only* with the utmost caution, if at all.

validity   Measuring what you are trying to measure by asking the right questions and collecting the right information for the problem.

Validity means truly measuring what you are trying to measure; asking the right questions and collecting the right information for the problem. Irrelevant or incorrect information can obstruct problem solving rather than enhance it. For example, when the goal is to determine whether or not a product advertisement moves consumers to purchase the product, a valid measure determines whether or not there is a link between the advertisement and product sales. A measure that asks only whether or not consumers *like* the advertisement is not valid if it fails to establish the link between the advertisement and sales.

reliability   Accuracy and consistency, characterized by lack of bias and freedom from random error.

Reliability indicates that the data are accurate, without bias, and free from random error. If you perform the same research again under identical circumstances and make the same measurements, the results will be the same because the data are consistent. For example, a survey of women 25 to 40 years old indicates that 53 percent work full time out of the home. A reliable survey will show the same results if the same population is surveyed again several weeks or months later.

generalizability   Occurs when data come from a representative, randomly selected sample population and the results can be projected from the sample to the greater population that the research was designed to test.

Generalizability means that the data come from a representative sample population, so that the results can be projected from the small research population to the greater population or universe that the research was designed to test. For example, only 2,000 people may participate in a national survey, but if these people are randomly selected yet representative of the population as a whole, the survey results should represent the entire population, with a small margin of error. If too few subjects are used in the research or the sample is not representative of the universe from which it is drawn, then the research results will be biased or skewed. Results that are not representative cannot be applied to the population.

Primary Research Designs

Primary research is original research designed to collect data unique to the project. There are a number of different approaches to the collection of primary data.

- *Qualitative research* uses such methods as individual interviews with consumers, focus group interviews, projective techniques, and consumer ethnography (in which a trained observer views the consumer in a situation, such as cooking or shopping, to determine how products are used). Although these methods get close to the consumer, it is more difficult to interpret the results because they are subjective and typically involve fewer subjects than does quantitative research. A focus group is a group interview, with 8 to 12 participants, led by a moderator who guides the discussion. Focus groups are popular despite their expense and the difficulty of generalizing results from a small focus group discussion to a population. Another popular qualitative method is the direct observation of shoppers' store traffic patterns, using electronic surveillance equipment or direct observers stationed at vantage points in various locations throughout a store. Mystery shopping, where store employees visit retail stores posing as customers in order to critique store operations, is experiencing a resurgence of interest. Banks, hospitals, and even U.S. military base stores are using this technique.[20]

- *Quantitative research* is objective, numerically based, and lends itself to statistical analysis. Quantitative techniques include various types of surveys (e.g., in person, mail, telephone, fax, or computer), experimentation, and case studies. Surveys tend to be on a large scale; some involve thousands of people. A growing problem with the use of survey research involves people who refuse to cooperate. If there are too many noncooperators, survey results may be biased and, therefore, unusable. An example of a survey used by a national magazine to poll its readers is shown in Figure 6.5.

Check Your Understanding 6.3

1. What is marketing research? What are market and advertising research?
2. Identify the steps in marketing research.
3. Compare and contrast primary and secondary data/research.

ADVANCES IN INFORMATION TECHNOLOGY

The end of the 20th century and the beginning of the 21st century are often characterized as the dawn of the information age. Information technologies are changing the way marketing is practiced. Given the rapidity with which the information age is proceeding, even greater technological advances are doubtlessly just on the horizon. Marketing is benefiting from vast amounts of descriptive information being generated about consumers, as well as from prescriptive computer systems that take the descriptive information and recommend the best decision to solve a marketing problem.

Objective 5 Discuss how recent advances in information technology are pushing marketing in new directions.

Figure 6.5   What Are Your Family Values

Teachings kids right from wrong, respect for others, and the value of work is a tough job for today's parents.

True family values are not found in a TV show or a political slogan. Values are the deeply held attitudes and beliefs that matter most to parents and that they hope to pass on to their own children. *Parents* wants to know what your values are and how you're transmitting them to your kids. Please fill out this survey and return it to "Values Poll," c/o *Parents*, 685 Third Avenue, New York, NY 10017. The deadline for all surveys is December 31, 1994. Please do *not* include any materials unrelated to the survey. Your name and address are not required, but if you're willing to be interviewed, please include that information and a daytime telephone number. We will report the survey results in a future issue.

(Answer questions by circling the number that best reflects your view.)

1. Which of the following positions is closest to your own in terms of parents' teaching their children values? (Choose one number only.)

- I want my children to have values identical with or very similar to my own 1
- I want my children to have a firm set of values, but I don't mind if their values differ significantly from my own 2
- I am not so concerned about my children's values; it's more important that they get a good job, find a good mate, and so on 3
- Not sure 4

2. Do parents need to make a special effort to ensure that their children acquire values, or do children automatically acquire the dominant values of the household in which they grow up?

- Parents need to make a special effort 1
- Children automatically acquire values 2
- Not sure 3

3. Do you think it's harder now for parents to instill values in their children than it was when you were growing up?

- Yes 1
- No 2
- Not sure 3

4. How important is it for parents to teach their children each of the following values? (Circle one number in each row.)

	One of the most important	Important but not essential	Not very important	Not sure
Religious beliefs	1	2	3	4
The importance and necessity of hard work and delaying gratification	1	2	3	4
The importance of education	1	2	3	4
Basic ideas of right and wrong	1	2	3	4
The importance of each individual's achieving his or her full potential	1	2	3	4
Appreciation of art and culture	1	2	3	4
Tolerance for people of different races, ages, values, and so on	1	2	3	4
Standards concerning sexual behavior	1	2	3	4
Patriotism	1	2	3	4
The importance of marriage and family	1	2	3	4
The value of friendship	1	2	3	4
Good manners and appropriate social behavior	1	2	3	4
The importance of being financially independent and secure	1	2	3	4
The importance of ecology and of preserving our planet	1	2	3	4

Source: "What Are Your Family Values?" *Parents,* December 1994, p. 57. Used with permission.

Electronic Measuring Devices

One of the challenges facing marketers is trying to describe and measure consumer attitudes and behaviors so they can use the information to stock shelves, design new products, redesign old products, and market them. To keep track of what people watch on television, Nielsen Media Research uses special people meters, electronic readers that attach to a home television set and automatically

Marketing Application 6.3

This exercise is a mini-research project designed to give you a feel for marketing research. A recent survey of Americans provides mixed news about consumer lifestyles. Some encouraging signs that consumers are living healthier lives include increased use of seat belts and smoke detectors, and decreased tobacco and alcohol use. The discouraging news is that Americans weigh more, exercise less, experience more stress, and get less sleep.

Study the survey information provided in Figure 6.6; note how the numbers change over the two data collection periods, 1983 and 1992. Determine whether this information fits your class. As a class project, write a question

for each item (numbers one through seven). For example, for the first item (seat belt use) your question might be "Do you use automobile seat belts?" with response categories "yes" and "no." Working together as a class, construct a seven-question survey, one question for each item; duplicate enough typed copies for everyone in your class, administer it *anonymously,* tally the results, and, for each question, determine whether the class average is close to the national average for 1992. What can you conclude from the information you've collected? Is your class a bunch of couch potatoes or a good target market for exercise and fitness products? ■

Figure 6.6

Annual
National Healthy
Lifestyles Survey
Comparison between
1983 and 1992

Item	Consumer Lifestyle Behavior	1983	1992
1.	Use seat belts	19%	70%
2.	Weigh more than recommended weight	58	66
3.	Use smoke detectors	67	90
4.	Get six hours or less of sleep/night	25	33
5.	Don't drink alcohol (wine, beer, etc.)	34	40
6.	Feel stress almost every day or several days/week	28	33
7.	Exercise strenuously at least three times/week	37	33

Source: S. Rich, "Are Healthy Lifestyles Just Another Hula Hoop? A Survey Finds That Fewer Americans Are Holding the (Waist) Line on Good Habits," *Washington Post National Weekly Edition* 10, no. 21 (March 22–28, 1993), p. 37.

note what is being viewed. Nielsen has plans to advance this measuring capacity by installing special television meters in homes of Nielsen families who agree to participate in the studies. These meters will recognize each family member by his or her facial characteristics, and record not only what program is being watched, but *who* is watching it.[21]

Another electronic measuring device is the smart card, a computer the size of a standard plastic credit card. However, in this case, it is a smart microchip that allows the user to charge purchases, dial a telephone, pay for products at vending machines, make reservations, and store and manipulate up to 1,000 pages of text information. Already used by millions of consumers in Japan and Europe, these cards help retailers collect information on the card's user, providing purchase information for the marketer's customer *database,* a computerized storehouse of information that can be entered, changed, and used for marketing purposes. In some parts of the United States, medical data are being entered on smart cards that the patient carries in a wallet or purse. One smart card can hold a patient's entire medical history.[22]

Scanners

You are probably familiar with the check-out scanners used in 80 percent of U.S. supermarkets and 50 percent of retail stores.[23] Scanners are laser readers embedded in the counter to read bar codes (see Photo 6.5)—universal product codes (UPC) of narrow and broad lines—on products as they pass over the reader. Types of information captured include brand names, manufacturer, size, price, and, in the case of smart card users, purchaser identification. Information Resources, Inc., makers of InfoScan, buys raw scanner data from 2,700 supermarkets in 66 different markets. Nielsen Marketing Research USA tracks 3,000 supermarkets in 50 markets. Other, smaller research firms also collect these data for marketing reports they sell to others. When grocery store data are coupled with research on neighborhoods (including what television programs these consumers watch), then "store specific marketing" can be initiated. Scanners are also becoming widely used in Europe, particularly in countries with the largest expenditures for marketing research, such as France, Germany, and the United Kingdom.[24]

Scanners are even used to track tourist movements in Florida. When tourists redeem coupons dispensed through discount travel

---

Photo 6.5

Bar codes, used on products from college textbooks to strawberries, provide valuable sales and market trend information.

clubs, their movements and travel preferences are recorded electronically. Each coupon they redeem is marked with a code number for the merchant and tourist.[25] Scanners are used for inventory and distribution control. Federal Express is probably the largest user of bar codes and scanners in the world. Federal Express uses them to track and direct the flow of packages and shipments.

Smart cards are designed to work with scanners. These electronic purses are plastic electronic payment cards with a running cash balance embedded in their memory. As a purchase is made, the smart card is scanned in a reader. Each purchase draws down the balance until the card zeros out. The consumer can replenish the card at a bank or vending machine.[26]

Fax

Facsimile, or fax, machines seem to be everywhere. Connected by personal computers to telephone answering machines, faxes allow a marketer to tap into national and international electronic information databases. Faxes are used to administer surveys, send promotions directly to a consumer's office or home, confirm and make orders, and permit shopping and publishing on demand at the consumer's convenience.[27] New uses for fax technology are being identified on a regular basis. Its uses in marketing are just beginning to have an impact.

Photo 6.6

The fax machine is an indispensable tool to marketers for getting information into the right hands instantly.

Career Watch

Barbara Bryant, former director of the United States Bureau of the Census during the 1990 census, came to the job through her experience as a marketing researcher with Market Opinion Research in Detroit. The director is in charge of "150 surveys annually, constantly monitoring: The United States economy and its retail, wholesale and manufacturing sectors; demographic updates on 70,000 households; the United States minority population; housing, crime, unemployment and agriculture in America." The bureau has maps that define every city block in the United States, and computer-based census data that can be searched to provide extensive information of value to direct marketers and marketing researchers. A staff of almost 10,000 makes the Bureau of the Census the U.S. government's biggest statistical agency. ■

B. E. Bryant, "Reflections of the Census Director," *American Demographics* 15, no. 3 (March 1993), p. 13; H. Schlossberg, "Even Amid Controversy, Bryant Finds Census Work Enjoyable," *Marketing News* 25, no. 7 (April 1, 1991), p. 2.

Virtual Reality

Computer-generated images made their first appearance in arcade games. Much more complex virtual reality (VR) systems now are being used in a variety of business applications. There are different approaches to VR, but generally it refers to a sophisticated 3-dimensional graphics system created through computer images and extensive information databases. VR systems relay multisensory information to the viewer to provide a simulation of a real visual and aural image. Sometimes called *applied reality,* various VR systems are showing up in product development (showing engineers and designers exactly how a new product may look and work) and for studying the behavior of consumers in shopping situations. The Visionary Shopper software feels like a shopping experience for the consumer and allows marketers to test the appeal of packaging, shelf layout, and in-store promotions.[28]

The Internet and the Information Highway

Most people are fascinated by the idea of an information superhighway but aren't sure what it means. The information superhighway will be an interactive electronic communication network that delivers various kinds of services to subscribers. It is unclear whether the Internet is an entry ramp to the highway or the foundation on which the highway is being built. Many businesses expect to realize cost savings and expansion opportunities by using the highway. On-line services such as Prodigy, CompuServe, and America Online already function as entry ramps to some of the services. Many business applications are already functioning. For example, in some areas of the country, Realtors already are using an electronic system that matches prospective home buyers with homes on the multiple listing service and renters with available apartments. Consumers and Realtors view digitized pictures of prospective choices before narrowing the list to those homes or apartments that will actually be visited.[29]

Review of Chapter Objectives

1. *Explain why information is so important to marketers.* The computer has revolutionized the way information can be collected, sorted, analyzed, and stored. Computers have an immense capacity to collect, store, analyze, and report information. This presents marketers with both a tremendous opportunity and a considerable problem. The opportunity is to use information wisely to get closer to the customer and do a better job of developing satisfactory products. The problem is that this same abundance of information creates an overload situation—instead of enhancing marketing decisions, this abundance can overwhelm the marketer, which can jeopardize good decision making.

2. *Understand that all marketers need information.* To create targeted marketing plans, marketers take in a variety of information about the marketing mix variables (the Four Ps), consumer needs, wants, and behaviors and the businesses' environment. Information is broken down into two categories: descriptive and prescriptive. Information must be managed and organized to make it most useful and accessible.

3. *Describe a marketing information system (MIS) and explain how it works.* Some marketers use marketing information systems, most frequently computer-based systems designed to systematically collect, analyze, and disseminate information to the right person to enhance his or her decision-making and problem-solving abilities. Valuable information can be collected from within the company through the development of marketing intelligence systems. Often, this means training salespeople, customer service representatives, and others to listen closely, observe, and report what they see and hear. Additional information is obtained from external sources and by conducting marketing research.

4. *Identify the steps in marketing research.* Marketing research is a systematic, methodical, objective method for collecting information to be used in marketing decision making and problem solving. Most companies perform marketing research as the best way to collect objective information about consumers, markets, the marketing mix variables, the competition, and the environment.

5. *Discuss how recent advances in information technology are pushing marketing in new directions.* Advances in information technologies are revolutionizing business and society. Two advances of particular importance to marketers are electronic measuring devices and scanners. Both are designed to collect descriptive information about consumer behaviors. Other advances include virtual reality and, of course, computers and the Internet.

Key Terms

After studying Chapter 6, you should be able to define each of the following key terms and use them in describing marketing activities.

Discussion Questions

1. Explain this statement: "We are in the midst of an information explosion."

2. What do computers have to do with the information explosion?

3. Distinguish between computer hardware and software.

4. Explain what is meant by the term *marketing information system.* How could a small business marketer put such a system to good use?

5. Describe the three common sources of information collected by marketers.

6. Contrast primary and secondary data, and primary and secondary research.

7. Describe the steps in marketing research.

8. What three research considerations are very important to the marketer and underlie his or her confidence in research results?

9. Why are customer surveys such a popular form of marketing research?

10. What are some of the new technologies affecting marketing?

What Do You Think?

Marketing research in the United States tends toward large-scale studies, often consumer surveys of people who may not even be using the researcher's product. The Japanese approach the task from a different perspective: They prefer to go directly to the members of the business's distribution channel, visiting the people who move their products from production to consumer. It is not at all uncommon for mid-level marketing managers and even top management to systematically visit the people most intimately involved with their products. If consumer surveys are performed, it is of consumers who have already purchased the products. Japanese researchers get close to actual customers, not masses of potential buyers. What do you think of this type of research? Are the Japanese the only marketing researchers to use it?

Source: M. Czinkota and M. Kotabe, "Product Development the Japanese Way," *Journal of Business Strategy* 11, no. 6 (November–December 1990), pp. 31–37; J. K. Johannsson and I. Nonaka, "Marketing Research the Japanese Way," *Harvard Business Review,* May–June 1987, pp. 16–18, 22.

Mini-Case 6.1

Vons Does It the Customers' Way

Every week 5 million Southern Californians go shopping for their groceries at a Vons. Vons's management has found a competitive advantage for their grocery stores that is very different from their competitors. Instead of offering "cookie cutter" stores with a single format in which all stores are stocked alike, each Vons store is tailored to the ethnic backgrounds and lifestyles of its neighborhood. Vons relies on customer and demographic surveys as well as data from inventory movements to determine store formats. Hispanic neighborhood stores are heavy on chilies and fresh tortillas; affluent neighborhoods have sushi and smoked stuffed sausages.

Vons has also invested heavily in computer technology. Prices on the shelf and at check-out can be changed electronically by hitting a few keys on a computer keyboard. Customer checks are automatically authorized by electronic readers at the check-outs that also keep track of individual purchases. This information is used to tailor direct-mail promotions to shoppers, informing them of specials that should be of particular interest to them. Although information technology plays a big part in marketing decisions at Vons, the bottom line is their operating philosophy: "Keep the focus on the customer and you can never go wrong." That and the wise use of information technology are a winning combination.

Case Questions

1. Could the Vons approach be used in *all* supermarkets?

2. Could Vons carry this customization process too far? Explain your answer.

3. Are there any consumer privacy issues involved in this case? Explain your answer.

Sources: "How Vons Makes It Work," *Progressive Grocer* 73, no. 10 (October 1994), p. S8; L. Freeman, "Supermarkets Sift Through Data: Work Needed to 'Take these Card Programs to the Next Level,'" *Advertising Age,* October 10, 1994, p. 16; M. J. McDermott, "Marketers Pay Attention! Ethnics Comprise 25% of the U.S.," *Brandweek* 35, no. 29 (July 18, 1994), p. 26; T. Gutner, "'Focus on the Customer,'" *Forbes* 152, no. 3 (August 2, 1993), pp. 45–46.

Mini-Case 6.2

Marketing Research Serves Different Needs

Mecklenburg Community Church and Willow Creek Church are two of the growing number of religious institutions in the United States using marketing research. Mecklenburg hired a marketing research firm to find out what consumers wanted in a church, and then tailored its approach to the research results. The target market of people who were not already members of a church wanted contemporary music, a relaxed dress code, and relevant sermons. Sixteen months after opening its doors, Mecklenburg had almost 400 members, only 20 percent of whom had previously belonged to a church. Willow Creek Community Church's marketing research found that people didn't like frequent requests for money, dull music, and boring sermons. As a result, the church adopted a multimedia approach using videos, contemporary music, and drama. The new Willow Creek Church draws about 15,000 people to weekend worship services and 5,000 to 7,000 to weekday services.

Case Questions

1. Many churches are using marketing research, advertisements, and direct marketing to reach their markets. Do you think there is any opposition to churches using marketing? What might be the basis for this opposition?

2. If a church decides to use a marketing research survey to determine its market's preferences, who should be surveyed? Should only current members be questioned? Explain your answer.

Sources: C. Miller, "Churches Turn to Research for Help in Saving New Souls, *Marketing News* 28, no. 8 (April 11, 1994), pp. 1, 2, 5; C. Miller, "Church Keeps Message but Changes Medium," *Marketing News* 28, no. 8 (April 11, 1994), pp. 5, 7; D. Sullivan, "Targeting Souls," *American Demographics* 13, no. 10 (October 1991), pp. 42–48.

Chapter 6 Notes

1. B. Powell and F. Shaw Myers, "Death by Fried Chicken: Western Foods Are a Hazard to Japanese Health," *Newsweek,* September 24, 1990, p. 34; "Japan's Wary Shoppers Worry Two Capitals," *The Wall Street Journal,* April 26, 1993, p. A1.

2. Y. Ono, "U.S. Cosmetics Firms Take Cases to the People," *The Wall Street Journal,* July 21, 1993, p. B1.

3. S. Greco, "What Do You Spend on Market Research," *INC.* 24, no. 7 (July 1992), p. 117.

4. J. W. Verity, "Taking a Laptop on a Call," *Business Week,* October 25, 1993, pp. 124–25; A. LaPlante, "It's Wired Willy Loman!" *Forbes ASAP,* April 11, 1994, pp. 46–55; P. Eng, "Smart, Useful—And They Won't Put a Sag in Your Suit," *Business Week,* May 30, 1994, pp. 141–42; K. Siegal, "Notebooks Find a New Home with Realtor," *PC Week* 11, no. 27 (July 11, 1994), pp. 43–44.

5. J. R. Emshwiller, "Firms Find Profits Searching Data Bases," *The Wall Street Journal,* January 25, 1993, pp. B1, 2.

6. S. M. Eby, "Pssssst! (Do You Want to Know a Secret?)," *Small Business Success,* supplement to *INC.,* 1987, pp. 6–7.

7. B. Spethmann, "Category Management Multiplies: Marketers Invest in Technology to Woo Retailers," *Advertising Age,* May 11, 1992, p. 42.

8. E. Schine, "Computer Maps Pop Up All over the Map," *Business Week,* July 26, 1993, pp. 75–76; A. Classe, "Mapping out the Future," *Computing,* May 12, 1994, pp. 37–38.

9. E. I. Schwartz and J. B. Treece, "Smart Programs Go to Work: How Applied-Intelligence Software Makes Decisions for the Real World," *Business Week,* March 2, 1992, pp. 97–105.

10. J. W. Verity, "Getting Work to Go with the Flow," *Business Week,* June 21, 1993, pp. 156, 161; L. O. Levine and S. S. Aurand, "Evaluating Automated Work-Flow Systems for Administrative Practices," *Interfaces* 24, no. 5 (September–October 1994), pp. 141–52.

11. "New Marketing Research Definition Approved," *Marketing News,* January 2, 1987, p. 1.

12. R. F. Hartley, "Coca-Cola's Classic Blunder," in *Marketing Mistakes,* 4th ed. (New York: Wiley, 1989), pp. 221–36.

13. C. Anderson, "Processing the New Coke Fiasco," *Science* 261 (September 3, 1993), p. 1271.

14. M. E. Raynor, "Fantastic Things Happen When You Talk to Customers," *Marketing News* 27, no. 4 (February 15, 1993), p. 13.

15. J. Honomichl, "Combined Revenues for '93 Hit $3.7 Billion," *Marketing News* 28, no. 12 (June 6, 1994), pp. H2–4.

16. F. Karakaya, "Marketing Research: A Pocket Guide for Managers," *SAM Advanced Management Journal* 56, no. 3 (Summer 1991), pp. 34–40.

17. T. Lammers, "The Smart Customer Survey," *INC.* 14, no. 11 (November 1992), pp. 133–35.

18. J. Finegan, "The Rigorous Customer-Complaint Form," *INC.* 16, no. 3 (March 1994), pp. 101–3.

19. D. Crispell, "How to Hunt for the Best Source," *American Demographics,* September 1989, pp. 46, 48.

20. E. Larson, "Attention Shoppers: Don't Look Now but You Are Being Tailed," *Smithsonian* 23, no. 10 (January 1993), pp. 70–79; M. J. McCarthy, "James Bond Hits the Supermarket: Stores Snoop in Shoppers' Habits to Boost Sales," *The Wall Street Journal,* August 25, 1993, pp. B1, 8; K. Helliker, "Smile: That Cranky Shopper May Be a Store Spy," *The Wall Street Journal,* November 30, 1994, pp. B1, 6.

21. M. Burgi, "A Battle of Meter Readers: New Company Says Passive Audience Measurement Is Ready," *Media Week* 4, no. 45 (November 21, 1994), pp. 3–4; T. R. King, "Keeping Track (of what viewers watch)," *The Wall Street Journal*, September 9, 1994, p. B12.

22. M. Rogers, "Smart Cards: Pocket Power," *Newsweek*, July 31, 1989, pp. 54–55; W. M. Bulkeley, "Get Ready for 'Smart Cards' in Health Care," *The Wall Street Journal*, May 3, 1989, p. B5.

23. G. G. Marcial, "Scanning the World," *Business Week*, March 8, 1993, p. 81.

24. T. Seideman, "Bar Codes Sweep the World," *Invention and Technology*, Spring 1993, pp. 56–63; S. Caminiti, "What the Scanner Knows About You," *Fortune* 122, no. 14 (December 3, 1990), pp. 51–52; M. J. Fahey, "Timekeeping Software Solves Agency's Tracking Problems," *Marketing News* 25, no. 22 (October 28, 1991), p. 12; T. Moore, "Different Folks, Different Strokes," *Fortune*, 1985, pp. 65, 68; G. J. Eskin, "POS Scanner Data: The State of the Art in Europe and the World," *Marketing and Research Today* 22, no. 2 (May 1994), p. 107.

25. W. L. Seldon, Jr.,"Bar Code Technology Helps Track Florida Tourists," *Marketing News* 24, no. 23 (November 12, 1990), pp. 8–9; P. Beall, "Where Technology Meets the Tourist," *Orlando Business Journal* 11, no. 15 (September 16, 1994), pp. 23–25.

26. R. L. Hudson, "Europe Adds Brains to Its Smart Cards in 'Electronic Purses,' " *The Wall Street Journal*, April 11, 1994, p. B10.

27. W. M. Bulkeley, "Faxes Prove to Be a Powerful Tool for Setting Up Electronic Markets," *The Wall Street Journal*, July 28, 1992, p. B6; L. G. Coleman, "Report: It's a 'Wild' Fax Future for Marketers," *Marketing News* 25, no. 22 (October 28, 1991), pp. 5, 11.

28. H. Schlossberg, "Shoppers Virtually Stroll through Store Aisles to Examine Packages," *Marketing News* 27, no. 12 (June 7, 1993), p. 2; J. J. Keller, "In 'Virtual Office,' High-Speed Lines Rule," *The Wall Street Journal*, May 17, 1993, pp. B1, 5; D. C. Churbuck, "Applied Reality," *Forbes* 150, no. 6 (September 14, 1992), pp. 486–90; J. O'C. Hamilton, E. T. Smith, G. McWilliams, E. I. Schwartz, and J. Carey, "Virtual Reality: How a Computer-Generated World Could Change the Real World," *Business Week*, October 5, 1992, pp. 97–105.

29. P. Eng, "On-Ramps to the Info Superhighway," *Business Week*, February 7, 1994, pp. 108–9; T. L. O'Brien, "Small Businesses View Information Highway as an Aid," *The Wall Street Journal*, February 9, 1994, p. B2; S. Woolley, "The *Real* Home-Shopping Network," *Business Week*, February 21, 1994, p. 85.

P A R T

3

The Marketing Mix

Understanding Product

Chapter Objectives

After studying Chapter 7 you should be able to:

1. Recognize the nature of product.
2. Describe the total product concept.
3. Identify different perspectives on product.
4. Explain the issues involved in making product decisions.
5. Describe how product assets are protected.

*P*roduct is the first of the marketing mix variables you'll learn about, because it is the focal point for decisions involving the other marketing mix variables. Price, place, and promotion are product-specific in that each is tailored to a particular product category, item, line, or market. A product is the offer sellers make to potential buyers. Products are more than just tangible goods, such as a T-shirt you can feel, wear, and store; products also are services, ideas, places, people, entertainment, and anything that can be offered in exchange for something of value.

The continual search for products that satisfy consumers and profit the business is an expensive and time-consuming challenge for most companies. Few businesses can survive for long without new products to entice consumers who are increasingly more demanding. Some marketers even believe that satisfying consumers is no longer enough—products now must *delight* them.[1] Marketers strive to differentiate their products from the competition, to make them stand out on the shelf and in the consumer's mind, so that their product is chosen when a purchase is being made.

This chapter presents the different aspects of the product variable and sets the stage for the examination (in later chapters) of price, place, and promotion. In most industrialized countries (including the United States), the national economy has evolved, from being dominated first by agricultural products, then by manufactured goods, and now by services, and in the future, by information. As you learn about products, consider the question "What product opportunities will emerge in the next century?"

Marge and Karen are visiting New Orleans for the first time. In the French Quarter, they drop into one of the many T-shirt shops dotting Bourbon Street and each purchases a preprinted souvenir T-shirt reading "Let the Good Times Roll." At the same time in Maryland, Sam and Tai Chu are having Baltimore souvenir T-shirts custom printed with their names, the date, and a picture of a Maryland crab. Men and women, young and old alike, are purchasing and wearing T-shirts from Somalia to Singapore, Paris to Pakistan.

The T-shirt is the "Big Mac of the international clothing industry." In 1990, over one billion T-shirts were sold in the United States alone. T-shirts are mass produced, but are also customized with pictures and sayings from the cute to the obscene. They reflect an individual's and society's attitudes, beliefs, and behaviors. The oldest T-shirt in the Smithsonian Institution's collection is a child's T-shirt from the 1948 presidential campaign that reads "Dew-It With Dewey."[2] Writings on contemporary T-shirts (Photo 7.1) present a social commentary of the times. Whatever you think of T-shirts, for many marketers they are T-errific!

THE NATURE OF PRODUCTS

Objective 1 Recognize the nature of product.

A *product* is anything offered to buyers to satisfy their wants and needs in exchange for something of value. Product buyers are personal use consumers and business/organization consumers. Products come in many forms, from tangible goods that can be physically felt to intangible services and ideas. Products provide values that are functional—related to product form and use—as well as benefits that are social, symbolic, and psychological.

For personal use consumers in particular, product is a complex bundle of benefits. Take the case of the automobile. The functional

Photo 7.1

T-shirt slogans reflect what is on consumers' minds in the United States and abroad.

unit transports a person to work; it also communicates information about social status, symbolizes an achieved or sought lifestyle, and facilitates interactions and belonging. When consumers purchase automobiles, they are buying far more than just metal, glass, plastic, and rubber. Charles Revson, founder of Revlon cosmetics, recognized the complexity of his products when he said, "In the factory we make cosmetics. In the stores we sell hope."[3]

Some products have a deep association with a country's culture. For example, the Japanese take rice, an agricultural product, very seriously because of its association with Japan's religious and cultural heritage. The Japanese government historically has banned foreign rice imports and protected domestic production. A recent failed rice harvest, however, forced the government to allow imports in order to avoid shortages. This action prompted hoarding and price gouging by Japanese who are leery of buying foreign rice even in an emergency.[4]

Many products are mass produced with few, if any, variations. Other products are customized to satisfy niches of consumers or even individuals. Although Citicorp mass markets only two variations of its credit cards, the Classic to the general public and the Preferred to affluent consumers, Advanta Corp.'s MasterCards and Visas are micromarketed to highly select consumer targets. High technology and extensive consumer credit databases allow Advanta to tailor individual product offers. It may have 30 different interest rate and term offers distributed in any direct mailing. Advanta has found product customization to be more profitable than product standardization.[5]

Product Differentiation

Product differentiation means using the marketing mix variables to make a unique product offer that stands out from the competition. This strategy is aggressive in that it focuses on besting the competition while still satisfying consumers and gaining higher profits.[6] The tools used to differentiate products include branding, quality, image, product features, packaging, location, promotion, innovation, and different service levels. Consumers who perceive that a product is unique in serving their needs often become brand loyal and are more willing to pay a premium price in order to gain the product's benefits. Examples of successfully differentiated products include Perdue chickens, Hershey's chocolates, Lands' End clothing, and Lexus automobiles.

product differentiation Using the marketing mix variables to make a unique product offer.

Products Classified

Most professions and academic disciplines classify the items of greatest interest to them in an effort to facilitate understanding, establish relationships, and advance the field. Marketing is no exception. Products are classified in a number of different ways for these reasons and also because similar products often benefit from the same general type of price, place, and promotion decisions. Therefore, identifying a product's characteristics aids in making decisions about how best to use the other marketing mix variables.

Goods and Services   Goods and services comprise the bulk of the product offers in the contemporary marketplace. In the early days of the marketing discipline, the definition of product only included goods. Within the past 20 years, however, the definition gradually has been expanded to include services as well as other product types. It makes a considerable difference to the marketer whether a product is a good, service, or mixture of the two, because many marketing mix decisions are contingent on a product's classification.

Products are classified along a continuum (shown in Figure 7.1) anchored at one end by "pure" goods and at the other by "pure" services. The characteristics associated with goods or services become more pronounced as the product approaches either "pure" extreme.

Although services will be discussed at greater length in Chapter 14, they are included here to both emphasize their importance and serve as a contrast to goods marketing. The U.S. economy is dominated by services, as are the economies of most fully industrialized nations. Consumers in these countries demand products that make their daily home and work lives easier and more productive. As a result of the proliferation of services, many college marketing majors find rewarding careers in services marketing.

goods   Physical products that can be felt, stored, inventoried, mass produced, transported, tested in advance, or purchase and quality controlled.

durable goods   Long-lasting goods that are replaced infrequently, such as washing machines, lawn mowers, and home freezers.

nondurable goods   Goods that are replaced frequently, such as laundry detergent, clothes, and perishable food.

services   Activities that are performed for a customer, such as cutting hair, counseling, or entertaining.

Goods, like this textbook or the chair you are sitting on, are physical products that can be felt, stored, inventoried, mass produced, transported, tested in advance of purchase, and controlled for quality. Goods are further distinguished by whether they are **durable goods,** which are long lasting and replaced only infrequently, such as washing machines, lawn mowers, and home freezers; or **nondurable goods,** that are replaced frequently, such as laundry detergent, rapidly outdated faddish clothing, or food perishables with a short shelf life, like milk and eggs. On the other hand, pure **services** are performances, such as cutting a customer's hair, counseling people through a troubled marriage, or attending a symphony or play. The customer is a participant in the service performance. Pure services cannot be stored, inventoried, mass produced, transported, tested in advance, or controlled through standardized quality checks.

Many products are a mixture of goods and services. Your automobile is a tangible good, yet it comes with a service warranty.

PRODUCTS ARE EVALUATED BY WHERE THEY FIT ALONG THIS CONTINUUM		
Pure Goods	**Mixed Goods/Services**	**Pure Services**
[ ]···[ ]		
Tangible physical features		Intangible products are experienced
Can be felt		
Can be stored		Cannot be stored
Can be inventoried		Cannot be inventoried
Supply/Demand balanced		Supply/Demand often becomes unbalanced
Manufacture and consumption separate		Production/Consumption inseparable
Can be mass produced		Cannot be mass produced
Quality can be controlled		Quality is less controllable
Consumer can try or test in advance of purchase		Performance cannot be tried out before delivery
EXAMPLES		
Notebook paper	Truck with service warranty	Haircut
Textbooks		Marriage counseling
Hammer	Automobile rental	Tax audit
Chair	Motel room	Live classroom teaching
Lightbulb	Cellular phone	Opera performance

Figure 7.1

The Goods/Services Product Continuum

Service performed on an owned car is an owned-goods service; a rented-goods service is performed on a rented car. In either case, when an automobile is repaired, the service performed on it often includes using tangible goods, such as adding oil, installing a replacement part, and so on.

Personal Use Consumer Products An article published in the *Harvard Business Review* in 1923 by Melvin Copeland was the first to present a classification system for merchandise sold in retail stores.[7] Copeland's product classification by buyer habits (Figure 7.2) is still used with only minor modifications, the most notable being an expansion of the system to include both goods *and* services.

It is important to emphasize that this classification is based on buyer habits—the consumer's view of the purchase. This suggests a

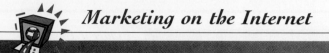

Marketing on the Internet

What kinds of products are being sold on the Internet? It's almost easier to ask for a list of what *isn't* being sold! Although Internet commerce is still in its infancy, success stories about businesses using the Net to sell their products to purchasers around the world are increasing. For example, businesses on CompuServe's Electronic Mall are selling products to CompuServe subscribers in over 100 countries. Florida Fruit Shippers has been selling fruit on the Electronic Mall since 1985. About 60 percent of their annual sales are on-line. Computer Express does about 50 percent of its business through CompuServe. As might be expected, lots of computer software is being sold on the Internet along with communications services, computer hardware, and business services.

Spiegel Inc. and Time Warner Inc. are developing a site on the World Wide Web where they will offer products from 10 upscale catalog retailers including Spiegel, Sharper Image, Crate & Barrel, Williams-Sonoma, Nature Co., Bombay Co., Neiman Marcus Group Inc., and Eddie Bauer. Many banks and other financial institutions are on the Internet, offering their financial products for sale along with product information. Products for business/organization consumers can be located at such sites as http://www.globalx.net for the GLOBAL-X-CHANGE. A buyer's guide for industrial products is located at Industry Net address http://www.industry.net. ■

G. A. Patterson, "Spiegel and Time Warner to Scale Back Cable Shopping Venture, Use Internet," *The Wall Street Journal,* January 30, 1995, p. B5; S. Greco and K. Carney, "Overseas Sales On-Line," *INC.* 16, no. 14 (December 1994), p. 124.

source of considerable classification variation, at the least by the same consumer at different times and among many different consumers. Take the case of nylon stockings (panty hose). For everyday wear, the consumer is satisfied to purchase nylons as inexpensively as possible in the grocery store. For more important occasions, such as a date or having dinner in a nice restaurant with friends, the consumer may purchase more expensive nylons at a local department store. For her wedding day, the consumer makes a special trip to a specialty bridal store to purchase real silk stockings. Knowledge of how consumers view these purchases is used by the marketer in making decisions about how to package and price the product, where to offer it, and how to promote it. Each decision is designed to enhance the product offer as well as alter the product if needed to better accommodate consumers.

Services also may be classified according to how consumers buy them. An everyday haircut may be offered by a national chain for $7 a cut, no appointment, no waiting. For a haircut before a job interview, the consumer shops around and goes to a department store styling salon for a more expensive and stylish cut. Finally, for a really special event, like a wedding day, nothing will do except getting a specialty fashion cut at a private salon.

Business/Organization Products Goods and services are purchased by business and organization consumers for use in manufacturing

Product Class	Description
Convenience goods	Easily accessible, familiar, and frequently purchased products such as canned soup, lightbulbs, razor blades, and toothpaste
	Low price, minimal effort to seek new information, frequent substitutions
	Outlets: grocery and drug stores, convenience stores, widespread distribution
	Staples: bread, milk, toilet paper Impulse: candy bars, chewing gum, tabloid newspapers Emergency: candles in stormy weather, umbrellas
Shopping goods	Less frequently purchased, consumer seeks to compare prices and styles. Comparison shopping for such goods as name brand clothing (Donna Karan, Calvin Klein), cookware (Corning Ware), household items
	Outlets: department stores, mall shops, smaller number of outlets than convenience goods
Specialty goods	Requires special effort to shop in a particular store: decorator furniture, expensive electronic goods, designer clothing and jewelry, gourmet foods; brand names like Tiffany, Saks Fifth Avenue are important; shopping is far less frequent, prices are often very high, substitutes are usually not accepted
	Outlets: selected distribution, often exclusive to only a few stores
Unsought goods	Either consumer doesn't know about these products and, therefore, doesn't seek them out, or the consumer does know about them and ignores them
	Examples include burial plot, casket, cancer insurance policy

Figure 7.2

Product Classification by Consumer Buying Habits: Personal Use Consumers

and production processes, as well as to operate the business and for resale. The same product purchased by personal use consumers may also by purchased by businesses and organizations. For instance, consider the rise in popularity of label markers. As their advertisements state, the Electronic Labeling System is recommended for "virtually any home, office or commercial application!"

Goods and services used by businesses and organizations are also called **industrial products.** The classification system for industrial products shown in Figure 7.3 is based on such factors as product costs, complexity of the purchase decision, and how the products are used in the business. Industrial products exhibit a considerable range from relatively low-priced, low-complexity raw materials

industrial products Goods and services used by businesses and organizations.

Figure 7.3 Industrial Products Classification

PRODUCTS CLASSIFIED BY THEIR USE IN BUSINESS/ORGANIZATION PROCESSES					
Materials/Parts		Capital Items		Supplies/Services	
Raw materials; farm products like barley, wheat, meat; natural materials like wood, oil, coal, other minerals	Manufactured parts and components like aluminum and steel for automobile frames	Installations, plants, assembly lines	Accessory equipment like trucks, tractors	Maintenance equipment supplies, repairs, office supplies	Business services like program auditing, tax accounting, temporary help placement services

taken into production in order to create manufactured products, to high-priced, complex installations, supplies, and business services.

Check Your Understanding 7.1	1. Explain this statement: "The T-shirt is the Big Mac of the international clothing industry." Do you agree or disagree?
	2. Provide your own definition of *product*.
	3. Distinguish between the nature of goods and services, and personal use and business/organization products.

THE TOTAL PRODUCT CONCEPT

Objective 2 Describe the total product concept.

augmented product What the consumer expects beyond the core product and the seller adds to make the offer more attractive.

The total product or whole product offer is often represented as the sum of three parts (see Figure 7.4). At the *core* is the basic product, for example, a perfume is a mixture of chemicals, and an air conditioner is mechanical components and materials built to exact production specifications. The **augmented product** is what the consumer expects beyond the core and the seller adds to make the offer more attractive and differentiate it from the competition. Obviously, the augmented product varies with the type of product offered. In the case of White Diamonds perfume (Photo 7.2), the augmented or extended product includes the brand name, a very stylish glass container designed with diamondlike objects embedded in a metallic bow, elaborate packaging, a glamorous image, and the intimation of status and quality associated with a premium-priced product. The augmented air conditioner also offers delivery terms, installation, a warranty or service contract, payment arrangements, and written instructions on product use. The features emphasize what consumers value in such products: reliability, efficiency, and

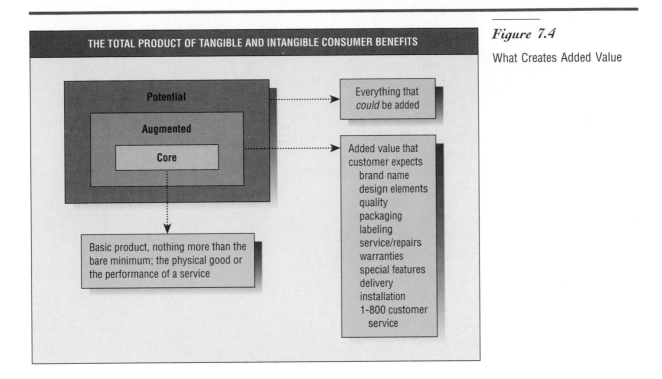

Figure 7.4

What Creates Added Value

Photo 7.2

The total product concept of White Diamonds includes the core product, the augmented product, and the potential product.

service. Finally, there is the **potential product,** what *might* be added to increase the value of the offer for the consumer. This potential often is commercialized as a "new and improved" version.

Some marketers find profits in product repairs. Once an electronic product goes off warranty, it often is difficult to find a retailer

potential product   What might be added to increase the value of the offer for the consumer; often what is called the "new and improved" version.

willing and able to perform repairs. Radio Shack recognizes this as an opportunity and is committed to making the 6,700-store chain the number one consumer electronics repair center, with projected annual volume of $500 million within five years.[8]

Marketing opportunities also exist for product disposal and recycling. Because of environmental concerns, particularly declining landfill capacity, many cities and states are enacting more stringent product disposal requirements. As a result, more products and packages are being produced partly or solely from recycled materials, and disposal instructions are often incorporated into product usage information.

Check Your Understanding 7.2

1. What is the core product?
2. What is the augmented product?
3. What is the potential product?

PERSPECTIVES ON PRODUCT

Objective 3   Identify different perspectives on product.

What a product appears to be depends to a great extent on whose product perspective is taken, as shown in Figure 7.5. All the perspectives are important and, depending on the situation, at any time may dominate product decisions. For marketing-driven businesses that operate by the marketing concept philosophy, all things being equal, the customer's perspective should be paramount (although it often isn't).

Government views product as something to be monitored to ensure consumer safety and the perpetuation of the free market. Federal agencies regulate product contents, labeling, packaging, transport, claims, and sale. They can mandate product recalls as well as termination. State and local governments oversee products offered within their jurisdictions. Complaints about products are made to local Better Business Bureaus, state departments of commerce, and state attorneys general, as well as directly to federal agencies.

From the competition's perspective, product is something to be closely observed, sometimes dissected, copied, and, if possible, driven from the marketplace. The competition views some products as more of a threat than others. This reflects whether or not the products are in direct competition with one another, as is the case of Coca-Cola and Pepsi. Indirectly competing products may also be viewed as threats, as is the case of carbonated colas and bottled waters or fruit drinks. Many competing products are considered parity products, which means there are few features to distinguish them from one another. This often results in ferocious price compe-

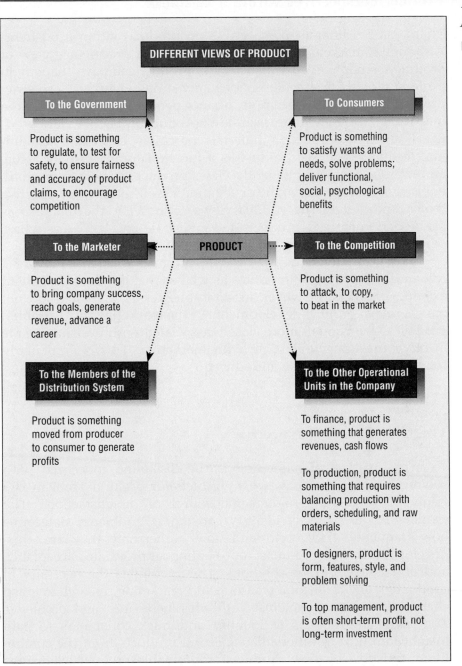

Figure 7.5

Perspectives on Product

tition as competitors seek to differentiate their products using a tool (price) that attracts consumers.

To members of a product's distribution system, products are their reason for being. Product sales provide revenue and profit. Products are what they move through the channel of distribution and, ultimately, offer to the consumer.

Product Perspectives within a Business

There can be different perspectives on product within a business. Although a marketer may take a personal and proprietary view of product, perhaps because a successful product can pave the way to professional advancement, other equally strong views also can sway product decisions. For example, finance people view product as the mechanism for generating cash flow; production people view product in terms of production materials, processes, costs, and scheduling; design people see product as a functional and aesthetic issue; and top management frequently views product as short-term profit, not long-term investment. By developing a well-rounded perspective that acknowledges the various views collectively, the marketer is positioned to manage products and anticipate problem areas where perspectives may conflict.

Marketers should be involved in product decisions, playing a role in developing new products as well as making decisions about existing products. However, in some businesses marketers do not have a role in product development. Of the marketing mix variables, product alone is often more closely associated with decisions made in other operating units than with marketing. This is particularly true before the product is introduced.

The Consumer's Perspective

To many marketers, marketing is the discipline concerned with solving people's problems with products for profit; a problem is a frequently occurring, bothersome source of dissatisfaction.[9] The challenge is to correctly identify consumers' problems, determine how frequently they occur and how bothersome they are, then develop and offer products representing appropriate, acceptable, and, if possible, unique solutions. This highlights the necessity of conducting environmental scanning and marketing research to grasp changes in consumer interests, attitudes, behaviors, and problems. The marketer's goal is to identify and track consumers to gain insight into how to differentiate existing products from the competition and develop new products or profitable product extensions that establish a competitive advantage.

Sometimes, however, consumers don't realize that they have a problem or a need. If businesses relied solely on consumers for product development ideas, the microwave oven, videocassette, facsimile (fax) machine, personal computer, and other products might never have been invented, because most people couldn't conceive of the product concept.

Marketing Application 7.1

"It isn't always clear what consumer problem a product is designed to solve." Test this statement yourself or as a group. Consider the following list of personal use consumer products. What problem is each trying to solve? Try to identify a primary problem-solving feature in each product, and then evaluate how successfully the problem is solved by the product, using a scale of 1 (very unsuccessful) to 10 (extraordinarily successful):

- Automobile.
- Microwave oven.
- Telephone answering machine.
- Automobile insurance policy.
- Videocassette recorder (VCR).
- Automobile air bags. ∎

Business/organization consumers also have needs and problems that products are designed to solve. These product opportunities often are quickly recognized and acted on, because of the close association between consumer and supplier. They also may require product customization to accommodate consumer specifications.

Check Your Understanding 7.3

1. What product perspective should a business take? Explain your answer.
2. What is the government's perspective on product?
3. Explain why there may be different perspectives on product within a business. Why might this result in conflict?

PRODUCT DECISIONS

Marketers must make a number of important product decisions, whether they are responsible for marketing one product or several hundred. Understandably, the complexity of the decisions, the number of people involved in the decision process, and the length of time needed to make the decision are different in a small business marketing only one or relatively few products than they are in large, marketing-driven companies like Procter & Gamble or Kraft General Foods. Yet, the types of decisions made are remarkably similar and involve the areas identified in Figure 7.6. These decisions contribute to the development of a **product strategy,** the planning efforts designed to bring products from the idea stage to commercialization, with the goal of differentiating or setting them apart from the competition and gaining sustainable competitive advantage and higher profitability.

Objective 4 Explain the issues involved in making product decisions.

product strategy The planning efforts designed to bring products from the idea stage to commercialization.

Figure 7.6   Product Decisions

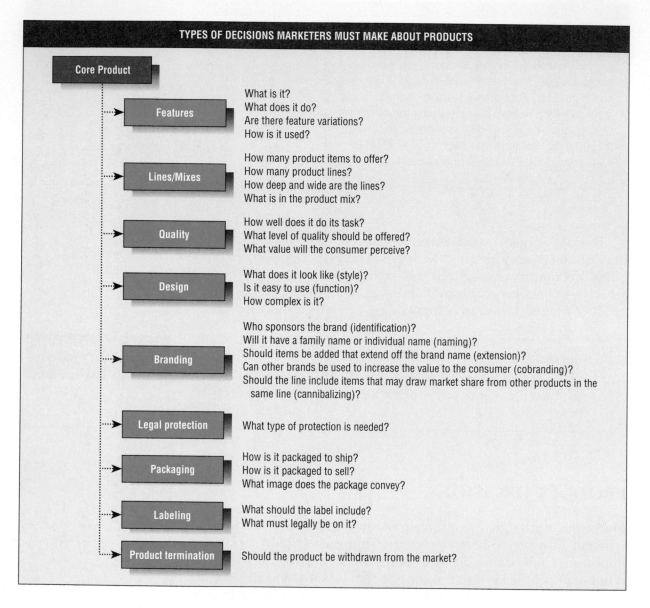

TYPES OF DECISIONS MARKETERS MUST MAKE ABOUT PRODUCTS

Core Product

Features
What is it?
What does it do?
Are there feature variations?
How is it used?

Lines/Mixes
How many product items to offer?
How many product lines?
How deep and wide are the lines?
What is in the product mix?

Quality
How well does it do its task?
What level of quality should be offered?
What value will the consumer perceive?

Design
What does it look like (style)?
Is it easy to use (function)?
How complex is it?

Branding
Who sponsors the brand (identification)?
Will it have a family name or individual name (naming)?
Should items be added that extend off the brand name (extension)?
Can other brands be used to increase the value to the consumer (cobranding)?
Should the line include items that may draw market share from other products in the
    same line (cannibalizing)?

Legal protection
What type of protection is needed?

Packaging
How is it packaged to ship?
How is it packaged to sell?
What image does the package convey?

Labeling
What should the label include?
What must legally be on it?

Product termination
Should the product be withdrawn from the market?

Product Features

The first decision is to select product features that solve consumers'
problems and serve their needs. This requires establishing what the
product is, what the consumer wants it to do, and how it is to be
used. The electronics industry is particularly guilty of ignoring
consumers and offering user-unfriendly products that are overly
complex and overdesigned, with features consumers neither want

Marketing Application 7.2

How easy are products to use? Working with the other students in your class, have each person answer the following questions:

1. What one product (such as a television or a computer) do you personally find the most difficult to use?

2. What is there about this product that makes it so hard to use?

Analyze the responses and identify the most common complaints. You can extend this research outside of class by asking the same two questions of 10 other people. Summarize your results and bring them to class for discussion. How might the marketers of these products make their products more user-friendly? ■

nor understand. As a result, many consumers can't program their VCRs or operate their camcorders or computers. Stephen Wozniak and Steve Jobs, founders of Apple Computer, recognized the need for a user-friendly operating system when they designed the Apple computer, which uses pictures (icons) and a mouse rather than complicated typed commands.

Too few American companies watch people using their products and then make products with features that fit the actual use. General Electric is one of the few that does, and the result is a marketing success: the toaster oven that allows consumers to both toast and heat foods.[10] Similarly, Sharp Corporation and Matsushita Electric Industrial Company redesigned their camcorders to make them simpler to use, ending up with imaginative and attractive products that eliminated features customers didn't want.[11]

Ideas for products often come from the inventor's own needs. Lounge Lokrs is a safe place to store a swimmer's stuff while he enjoys a dip in the pool.[12] It is a safe, featuring a tough plastic drawer that is installed under outdoor pool chairs. The key to the drawer's lock is attached to a waterproof nylon wristband the swimmer can wear in or out of the water. This solves the problem of not having a safe place to temporarily store suntan lotion, books, a handkerchief, or keys while swimming.

Other product feature decisions concern whether or not variations will be offered. For example, automobiles are offered in stripped-down versions with few added options, whereas loaded editions have many options, from power-driven sun roofs to seats that heat and massage the driver's back.

One product feature that eventually will be standard on all products is bound to shock most Americans. Worldwide, the United

Consumer Insight

Chrysler Corporation's Dodge Ram truck illustrates how getting close to consumers can pay off. The Dodge Ram is a full-size pickup truck, with an optional V-10 engine, introduced into a market dominated by Ford and Chevy. In order to develop product features to differentiate the Ram truck from Ford and GM models, Chrysler designers traveled around the United States, photographing hundreds of pickup trucks in use by consumers performing their daily tasks. They found that many large trucks are used by contractors as "rolling offices," so they added such features as space for a computer and an extra cigarette lighter socket specifically for cellular phones. The sleek interior contains a driver-side air bag, large storage areas, and an optional four-wheel antilock brake system. One automobile analyst calls the truck "stunning" and forecasts sales of more than 200,000 units a year. ■

D. Lavin, "Dodge Hopes New Ram Picks Up Sales" *The Wall Street Journal,* May 6, 1993, p. B1; K. Kinter, "Mobile Office in Transit as Carmakers Join Race," *Advertising Age* 65, no. 11 (March 14, 1994), p. 56.

States and Liberia are the only countries that do not use the metric system of meters, grams, and liters.[13] American products designed for export already must be made and sold in metric units. In order to speed the metric conversion, the U.S. government is taking two dramatic steps. By 1996, all road signs on federally funded highways will be metric, and going from miles to kilometers is just the beginning. Soon, all products sold to the U.S. government must be measured in metric units.[14] Businesses will have to adjust and the public will eventually follow, since the government is the largest employer in the United States and the biggest customer in many product categories.

Product Lines and Mixes

product line A group of several related products that accommodate different levels of consumer need.

When a business offers several related products, the products are considered part of a **product line** designed to accommodate different levels of consumer need. The Bayer Select product line has individual product items that specifically treat headache, arthritis, menstrual, sinus, or nighttime pain. "Because all pain is not the same," as Bayer's ads state, each item in the line possesses unique features designed to attack a specific type of consumer pain problem (and Bayer competitor). Introducing the line cost $116 million in advertising and promotion, which makes the Bayer Select line the most expensive product launch to date in Bayer's history.[15]

Many small businesses start out marketing only one product, such as custom-printed T-shirts. As the business grows, new products are added: usually items with different features in the same line, or sometimes a new, related line, for example, a line of sweatshirts and a line of lounge pajamas that are all in the same **product category** of related offers (in this case, casual clothing). The **product mix** is all of the business's offerings, product lines, and product items. At least at its beginning, a small business rarely has more than a few product items and lines. However, Procter & Gamble or another large marketing-driven business has many product items within a large number of different product lines in separate categories (laundry detergents, disposable diapers, shampoos, prepared foods, etc.). P&G has great product **width** and **depth:** *Width* refers to the number of different lines in the mix; *depth* refers to the number of items within a line.

product category Items in a different but related product line, or in the same product line but having different features.

product mix All of the business's offerings, product lines, and product items.

width The number of different lines in the mix.

depth The number of items within a line.

Quality

Quality has many meanings. In production, *quality* refers to zero defects or conformity to exact manufacturing and production specifications. Many U.S. firms are becoming more quality conscious, and an increasing number are voluntarily seeking ISO 9000 registration. In the late 1980s, the International Organization for Standardization (ISO) issued a series of guidelines for evaluating whether goods producers and service organizations satisfy quality management and assurance standards. ISO 9000 registration procedures require that an independent registrar audit and inspect a business's production processes, customer service, and marketing activities. The ISO quality standards have been endorsed by over 50 countries, including the United States and the European Union. Europe is rapidly moving toward requiring ISO 9000 registration for companies doing business in many of its major industries. The U.S. government is also integrating these standards into its requirements for businesses selling products to government agencies.[16]

To the personal use consumer, quality is less tangible and more difficult to define, yet most people are confident they know a quality product when they see it. Marketers realize that quality is a good way to promote their products, as shown in Photo 7.3. A commonly held misperception is that consumers always desire the best-quality product. The success of generic (unbranded) food products demonstrates that many consumers are willing to make a trade-off between price and quality by purchasing a product of acceptable, but not superior, quality at the right price.

Consumers want *value* in a product—their evaluation of the relationship between the product's *relative* price, quality, and image. **Image** is how the brand appears to the customer through such details as colors, use of symbols, packaging, displays, price, and how and where it is sold and advertised. The goal of the marketer is to

image How the brand appears to the customer through such details as colors, use of symbols, packaging, displays, price, and how and where it is sold and advertised.

Consumer Insight

Small and mid-size businesses are also being pressed to improve product quality. All businesses that market products in the European Union are strongly advised to seek ISO 9000 registration or risk becoming noncompetitive. Smaller firms that supply large corporations must establish quality standards for their products to avoid losing contracts. For example, Toyota Motor Manufacturing, U.S.A. (TMM) has won the J.D. Power and Associates gold plant award twice in recognition of the high-quality product manufactured in the company's Kentucky plant. The Power survey of customer satisfaction with initial car quality consistently rates Toyota products at the top among major car brands. Cornerstones of the Toyota

quality program are continuous improvement in the product and its production and high-quality standards for the products that its 174 American suppliers provide TMM. Many of these suppliers are small to mid-size businesses that specialize in one or a related group of product lines, such as windshields, rear-view mirrors, and reflectors. ■

C. Miller, "ISO Status Not Only for Big Firms," *Marketing News* 27, no. 4 (February 15, 1993), p. 6; C. P. Prather, "Remaining Positive and Leading Kentucky into the Future," *The Lane Report* 10, no. 1 (January 1994), pp. 49–51; D. Lavin, "J. D. Power Study on Initial Car Quality Reports Slight Decline in Model Year," *The Wall Street Journal*, May 27, 1994, p. B4.

Photo 7.3

Product quality is a powerful promotion tool. Ford's slogan underlines the company's sense that consumers value quality above all else.

convince consumers that a particular product offer is an exceptional value. Value differentiates the product from the competition. Take the case of General Motors, whose product strategy for the Chevrolet Cavalier is to present the car as "value priced." Consumers evaluate both the value proposal *and* the car when they make their purchase

What does quality mean to you? Consider all the products that you're familiar with and select five that you believe are of very high quality. (You don't have to personally own or have used these products.) For each product, identify the reasons why you believe it is a quality product. Bring your list to class to compare with others'. What features set these high-quality products apart from lesser-quality products? Are the quality features convincing enough that you and other consumers would be willing to pay a higher price for the products? ■

decision. Advertised as "the lowest-priced car in America with antilock brakes," not only are the antilock brakes standard, but so are air-conditioning and automatic transmission, which, to many consumers, makes the Cavalier a very good value.[17]

Design

Is Levi's 501 jeans the best-designed product in the history of American commerce? Some people believe that Levi's is the pinnacle of good product design.[18] Design affects product from the core to the augmented and potential product. It is an essential tool of the big business as well as the small—a competitive tool for communicating how the business and its products intend to satisfy consumers, differentiate themselves from the competition, and gain competitive advantage. Industrial design successes like Chrysler's LH cars, Apple's PowerBook, the Reebok Pump sneaker, and the Gillette Sensor razor (shown in Photo 7.4) are also billion-dollar marketing successes.[19]

Design is how a product functions to solve a consumer problem. It is more than style or outward appearance; it is *usability* that should discourage overdesign. Good design requires getting very close to consumers and observing their behaviors in order to weave this knowledge into products that are easier to use, perform better, and are aesthetically pleasing. Design decisions also extend to packaging and graphics (discussed in a later section).

design   How a product functions to solve a consumer problem.

Branding

A brand has been called "a company's most important asset."[20] Just as cattle are branded to identify ownership, so are products. A **brand** is something (name, symbol, design, or other element) that identifies one seller's product and differentiates it from all others. A **brand name** is the spoken version of the brand identification (e.g., Coke,

brand   A name, symbol, design, or other element that identifies one seller's product and differentiates it from all others.

brand name   The spoken version of the brand identification (e.g., Coke, Tide, MasterCard).

Photo 7.4

This product was designed specifically for women, reflecting the marketers' awareness of segment-specific needs.

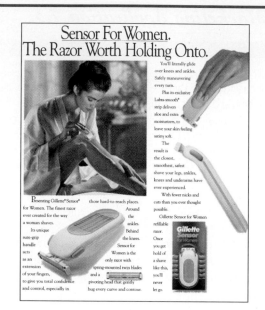

brand mark   A visual brand identification, like the NBC peacock, Apple Computer's apple, or Quaker Oats's Quaker.

service mark   Brand identification for services.

brand equity   The added financial value of owning a popular brand with a valuable image.

Tide, MasterCard); a **brand mark** is the unspoken brand identification, like the NBC peacock, Apple Computer's apple, or Quaker Oats' Quaker man (see Photo 7.5); and a **service mark** is the brand identification for services. **Brand equity** is the added financial value that a company accrues by virtue of owning a popular brand with a valuable image. To illustrate, one business publication in 1992 placed a value of $31.2 billion on Marlboro, which it called at that time the "world's most valuable brand name."[21] Second on the list was the Coca-Cola brand name, valued at $24.2 billion. As Dole and Del Monte have discovered, brand names can even be successfully attached to fresh produce.

Brand Decisions   For the small business marketer offering products in a local market with a limited distribution system, brand decisions are far less complicated than they are for a regional, national, or international marketer. However, most of the kinds of decisions to be made are quite similar: selecting a name, seeking legal protection for it, deciding whether or not to develop brand extensions or undertake cobranding, and determining if a premium price can be charged for the brand. Other decisions are different because of the additional layers of decision-making complexity frequently found in large businesses.

Less than two decades ago, manufacturer's national brands were virtually uncontested in the marketplace and earned good profits even though they were premium priced. Consumers with **brand loyalty** preferred and bought national brands because the brands

brand loyalty   Repeated purchases made by consumers on the basis of brand name.

Photo 7.5

Products are often identified by their specific brand marks, like this famous one.

gave good value and saved shoppers time and energy by eliminating the need to search for alternatives. Today, however, the situation has changed for many national brands. Private-label store brands are challenging them in many product categories, particularly in grocery products. Identifying the product's backer, the national manufacturer itself, or a member of the distribution system is a key decision for marketers.

Most national manufacturers still use a **national** (manufacturer's) **brand** strategy, like Kellogg's Corn Flakes, Diet Coke, Quaker State Motor Oil, or Procter & Gamble's Tide. Others sell their products to distributors, such as Kroger, Sears, and Kmart, who place their name on the product as a **store brand** (private label). For example, Kmart puts its name on products from curtains to potting soil; Kroger has several different levels of branding at different prices, using Cost Cutter and its own name on grocery products. Finally, because of growing consumer preferences for less expensive store brands, many

national brand   Products distributed and known nationally.

store brand   Products sold by national manufacturers to distributors who put their own name on the product.

Store brands are eroding national manufacturer brands in international markets. Private store brands account for as much as 32 percent of supermarket sales in Britain and 24 percent in France. Japanese consumers, known for being quality-conscious shoppers, are discovering cost savings in private labels. Japanese supermarket chains are launching private labels at bargain prices without compromising on quality, which is hurting Japanese national brands as well as U.S. national brands sold in Japan. In the United Kingdom, private labels dominate grocery store shelves and are credited with increasing profit margins to as high as eight times the typical U.S. margin of 1 percent.

National brands in the British market are weaker than in the United States, mainly because British television is almost commercial-free. In Canada, private-label sodas are aggressively cutting into the market share of Coca-Cola and Pepsi, and now represent about 25 percent of the soft drink market. ∎

P. Oster, G. Saveri, and J. Templeman, "The Eurosion of Brand Loyalty," *Business Week,* July 19, 1993, p. 22; E. de Lisser and K. Helliker, "Private Labels Reign in British Groceries," *The Wall Street Journal,* March 3, 1994, pp. B1, 8; Y. Ono, "The Rising Sun Shines on Private Labels," *The Wall Street Journal,* April 26, 1993, pp. B1, 6; L. M. Grossman, "Upstart Brands Challenge Coke, Pepsi in Canada," *The Wall Street Journal,* March 3, 1994, pp. B1, 8.

mixed branding Manufacturers offer their products under their own national brand name and through store brands.

national manufacturers follow a strategy of **mixed branding** by which their products are offered under their own national brand name and through store brands. Kraft, Borden, Playtex, and Nestlé all have divisions for private-label brands in addition to their regular national brands.[22] Often, they end up competing with their own national premium brands.

Store brands account for slightly over 18 percent of all products sold in grocery stores. Their sales in 1993 were up 3.2 percent over 1992, totaling $6.78 billion.[23] In response, some large national brands are cutting prices to compete with their private brand rivals.

Now let's examine branding issues more closely.

• *Naming:* The most effective brand names are short, easy to pronounce and remember, appropriate to the product, and distinctive, and travel well so they can also be used internationally. Good examples include Bounce dryer sheets, Energizer batteries, Healthy Choice reduced-fat and reduced-sodium foods, Defend flea and tick protection for dogs, KinderCare child learning centers, and Ziploc resealable bags (see Photo 7.6). Companies often seek assistance from a professional naming company in naming a product and, sometimes, a business.

Sometimes naming a product can have disastrous results. After spending thousands of dollars generating names and testing them on consumers, Bic Corporation named one of its new line of Wavelength Soft Feel pens "Spaz." Analysts estimate that millions of dollars probably were earmarked to launch the product; at least $2 million was designated for advertising. The name may have been

Photo 7.6

Effective brand names are short, memorable, and descriptive—Ziploc says it all.

appealing because it is short, memorable, and appears to be popular among young consumers; however, it is also a word that can be used to make fun of people with disabilities. After reading about the product, the mother of a young man with cerebral palsy wrote the company to complain that the name is highly offensive. The same day the letter was received, the name was changed to "Boppers."[24]

• *Extending:* A **brand extension** offers additional products in the same product category under the original brand's name. Dial bath soap has been extended to include Dial soft hand soap and Dial deodorant; Coca-Cola extended original Coke to Diet Coke, Cherry Coke, and Diet Cherry Coke; and Cheerios grew to include Multi Grain, Apple Cinnamon, and Honey Nut. Marketers use brand extensions mainly because the estimated cost of establishing a totally new brand name is so high (from $50 to $150 million). The original may suffer if the extension fails, or a brand name may be extended so far that it is overused and becomes trivialized.

brand extension Inclusion of additional products in the same product category under the original brand's name (e.g., Dial bath soap extended to Dial deodorant).

• *Cobranding:* **Cobranding** means double branding products, piggybacking one distinctive brand onto another. General Mills's Betty Crocker Supreme M&Ms Cookie Bar is cobranded with M&Ms candies, Pop-Tarts are filled with Smucker's fruit, and Ben & Jerry's and other ice cream companies have Heath Bar–flavored ice cream. If the cobrand is not owned by the original brand, a royalty is paid to the trademark owner. Cobranding spread from grocery products to credit cards and other products. Citibank cobrands its Visa and MasterCards with Ford Motor Company, American Airlines, MCI,

cobranding Double branding or piggybacking of one distinctive brand onto another.

Marketing Application 7.4

Naming a product (or company) doesn't appear to be a difficult task, but it is! Try your hand at it individually or with a class team. The product is completely new to the U.S. market. It is a microwave that heats *or* cools at the flip of a switch. Place a cup of water inside and it will either heat to boiling or cool to ice in a matter of seconds. What are you going to name this revolutionary new product? Brainstorm with several others in your class and bring the best product names to class. ∎

Photo 7.7

Cobranding links national manufacturers' brands in a joint effort to make the product more attractive to consumers.

and Apple Computer. American Express is planning to issue 10 to 15 new cobranded credit and charge cards within the next several years.[25]

• *Cannibalizing:* When PepsiCo launched Pepsi Clear, a clear and caffeine-free carbonated beverage, it ran the risk of **cannibalizing** sales of Pepsi and Diet Pepsi, stealing market share from one or more of its own brands by another of its brands in the same category.[26] Companies offer several product items in the same category that are substitutes for one another in the belief that, by doing so, a bored consumer shopping around may select the marketer's other product in the line, and hence the sale stays in the "family."

cannibalizing   Stealing market share from one or more of a company's own brands by another in the same category.

Product Termination

Product termination is among the most difficult product decisions. Withdrawing a fad product from the market after it has run its course is far easier than deciding when to terminate a product whose profitability is fading but still has name recognition. Heroic efforts are often undertaken to attempt to revive a failing brand. Brand revitalization efforts often include reformulation, increased advertising and sales promotions, and price reductions. The challenge is to recognize when to *terminate*—in other words, to withdraw the product from the market when the costs of maintaining it exceed the potential profits.

Check Your Understanding 7.4

1. Discuss the types of product decisions that must be made.
2. Explain the difference between national manufacturer's branding and store branding.
3. Discuss the difficulty of defining quality.

PROTECTING PRODUCT ASSETS

If everyone knew the formula for Coca-Cola, it would no longer be a secret. Without legal protection, Coca-Cola could not defend its distinctive recipe, a valuable asset that differentiates it from other colas and gives it a competitive advantage. Ingredients, computer programs, publication subscriber lists, trade characters, processes, procedures, and other assets are secrets that companies zealously guard.[27] There are four approaches to protecting product assets: patents, copyrights, trademarks, and trade secret protection.

Objective 5 Describe how product assets are protected.

Even when products are legally protected, product espionage still occurs. Technology has advanced to the point where products can be copied in several hours and reach the market within a month. High-tech piracy is estimated to cost U.S. businesses up to $40 billion in lost sales, royalties, and licensing fees annually.[28]

Packaging

Packaging is often called "the last five seconds of marketing," to indicate how little attention is paid to it; however, this is changing. Marketers are finding that package redesign is a cheaper alternative to increasing expenditures for coupons, advertising, and other promotions. The cost of repackaging a small regional brand may be several hundred thousand dollars, and a large national brand may cost $500,000 or more, whereas developing and launching a new product could cost many times that.

Packaging is a product's individual delivery system that gives it shelf appeal and, in some cases, a differential advantage over the competition (Photo 7.8). It conveys an image, like the sense of

Photo 7.8

Energizer makes a point of focusing on its environmentally responsible packaging—a bonus for green-minded consumers.

(Excess Packaging Not Included)

When Energizer traded cardboard for a simple shrink wrap, 70% of the overall packaging waste was immediately eliminated. What's left is an innovative, environmentally responsible package that is now being added to our product line. It may not save the Earth, but Energizer believes that even small changes can make a powerful difference.   *Energizer*

elegance that many perfumes and cosmetics strive to achieve. It can capitalize on nostalgia, as in the case of Coca-Cola bringing back its famous patented contoured bottle in a 20-ounce recyclable plastic version.[29] Crystal Pepsi is packaged in a transparent bottle, a container designed to emphasize its pure and clear features. The Itty Bitty Book Lamp is packaged, appropriately enough, in a hollow book-shaped package box that provides a bit of whimsy along with an innovative and useful product.[30]

Packaging decisions are about shapes, colors, enclosures, instructions, closures, labels, graphics, and shipping cartons. A package functions in many different ways. It:

- Visually represents that product through design and graphics.
- Contains the product.
- Protects the product on the shelf, in transit, in storage, and during use.
- Distinguishes the product from its competition.

In Japan, the package is an art form that must be understated to be effective.[31] Packaging must ensure that the product can be seen. There are about 25,000 items in a typical grocery store; shoppers spend an average of 20 minutes in a store; and 80 percent of shoppers make a final decision on what they're buying while in the store.

Packaging informs, persuades, and reminds consumers when they see it in a retail store, a catalog, or even their home. Packaging

Marketing Application 7.5

The U.S. Food and Drug Administration (FDA) issued sweeping new rules for food labels required for all foods sold in the United States after August 18, 1994. These labels have to list the food's contents and tell exactly the amount of fat, cholesterol, calories, and nutrients found in each serving. Low-fat foods must contain less than three grams of fat per serving. Healthy foods must have only small amounts of fats, cholesterol, and sodium, and contain some helpful ingredients. This kind of information should benefit consumers, but the question is will it? Will consumers be able to read and understand the new labels? To see for yourself, on your next trip to the supermarket compare the labels on several different brands of potato chips. Are the labels easy to read? Can you easily make a comparison between the contents of the different brands? If there is a brand labeled low-fat or lite, compare its label to that of the regular chips. How do they differ? Bring your results to class for discussion.■

works to promote a product 24 hours a day. It should be integrated with the other elements used to promote a product in order to present consumers with a coordinated, consistent image.

Overpackaging is a growing concern for many consumers and marketers. Environmental considerations are prompting marketers to abandon excess packing materials (Photo 7.8), use paper instead of plastic, and recycle when possible. Some packages are recycled through multiple product uses.

Labeling

The label is often integrated into the package, although many products still have traditional paper or plastic labels stuck to the container. Food product labels must give consumers information they need to make decisions. The U.S. Food and Drug Administration (FDA) determines exactly what food labels should say, particularly regarding health claims. A uniform system of food labeling has been cleared to carry out the 1990 Nutrition Labeling and Education Act,[32] and, for the first time, the FDA has issued proposals to require the source of bottled water to be identified on the bottle.[33]

Check Your Understanding 7.5

1. Why is it important to protect product assets?
2. Why is packaging often called the "last five seconds of marketing"?
3. What does a label do for consumers?

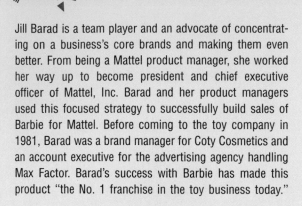

Career Watch

Jill Barad is a team player and an advocate of concentrating on a business's core brands and making them even better. From being a Mattel product manager, she worked her way up to become president and chief executive officer of Mattel, Inc. Barad and her product managers used this focused strategy to successfully build sales of Barbie for Mattel. Before coming to the toy company in 1981, Barad was a brand manager for Coty Cosmetics and an account executive for the advertising agency handling Max Factor. Barad's success with Barbie has made this product "the No. 1 franchise in the toy business today."

Considering that the average American girl now owns about seven Barbies and that Barbie sales boosted Mattel revenues for 1992 to $1.8 billion, Barad's product philosophy appears to be a perfect match with her core product and company. In 1993, she was recognized as one of the 10 most admired women managers in America. ■

J. A. Oliver, "Mattel Chief Followed Her Instincts and Found Success," *Marketing News* 26, no. 6 (March 16, 1992), p. 15; "The 50 Most Beautiful People in the World," *People* 41, no. 17 (May 9, 1994), p. 54; C. Willis, "The 10 Most Admired Women Managers in America," *Working Woman* 18, no. 12 (December 1993), p. 44.

Review of Chapter Objectives

1. *Recognize the nature of product.* Product is a very complex concept, particularly for personal use consumers who look at products as bundles of benefits. Products include goods and services as well as many other offers. Products are designed to satisfy the needs and solve the problems of consumers, personal use or business/organization. Marketers differentiate products in order to best the competition, satisfy consumers, and earn higher profits.

2. *Describe the total product concept.* Product is more complex than the consumer's initial perception. It is often represented as being composed of a core, augmented, and potential parts. The core is the basic good or service. The augmented product is what the consumer expects beyond the core and the seller adds to make the offer more attractive; this includes warranties, parts, instructions, packaging, delivery, and special services. The potential product is what *might* be added to increase the value of the offer for the consumer.

3. *Identify different perspectives on product.* There are many different perspectives on product, but for marketing-driven businesses, the consumer's perspective should come first. However, the perspectives of the government, the competition, and the members of the distribution channel must also be considered. Different perspectives on product *within* the business sometimes can be a point of conflict.

4. *Explain the issues involved in making product decisions.* Product strategy encompasses all of the planning and development efforts required to bring a product from the idea stage to the commercialization stage. Among the decisions that must be made, those concerning product features, quality, design, and brand are among the most important. Product decisions also must be made for existing brands. One of the most difficult decisions to make is when to terminate a product.

5. *Describe how product assets are protected.* Products, particularly, nationally branded products, are protected legally to discourage copying. Packaging also protects products, as well as promotes them. Labeling provides information to consumers and helps avoid product misuse or misunderstanding.

Key Terms

After studying Chapter 7, you should be able to define each of the following key terms and use them in describing marketing activities.

Discussion Questions

1. Explain the concept of product as core, extended, and augmented parts.

2. Identify some tools used to differentiate products.

3. Why is it important to distinguish among various types of products?

4. Describe Copeland's classification system and explain its importance to a marketer.

5. Discuss the types of product decisions that a marketer must make. Are all of the decisions made solely by marketers? Explain.

6. What is a product line? Give an example of one.

7. Compare and contrast: product line, product category, product mix.

8. What is value? Why is it important to the consumer? To the marketer?

9. If you were marketing national manufacturer's brands, how might you feel about private-label brands?

10. What is cobranding?

What Do You Think?

Is more of a product always better? A highly publicized path on the information highway is forecast to contain 500 television channels. However, a recent nationwide survey of more than 4,000 adults and children indicates that more is not always better when it comes to television viewing alternatives. Subscribers to premium cable channels have more viewing choices but are less satisfied than are viewers with basic cable who have far fewer choices. Some pilot studies indicate that when consumers can order movies on demand, they often respond by dropping their premium cable subscriptions. More channels may frustrate viewers more than benefit them. What do you think?

Sources: F. Rose, "Big Survey Casts Doubt on Future of 500 Channels," *The Wall Street Journal,* May 24, 1994, p. B6; W. M. Bulkeley, "Can the Exalted Vision Become Reality?" *The Wall Street Journal,* October 14, 1993, p. B1.

Mini-Case 7.1

The Best Brand in the World?

According to Total Research Corporation's annual EquiTrend survey of 2,000 consumers, the top 10 quality brands are Walt Disney World amusement parks, Disneyland amusement park, Kodak film, Hallmark cards, Mercedes-Benz automobiles, Fisher-Price toys, Reynolds Wrap aluminum foil, AT&T long distance, Levi's jeans, and Ziploc resealable bags. Consumers were asked to rate nearly 200 national and international brands for product quality on a 10-point scale, from poor to extraordinary. Although Coca-Cola didn't make the top 10, it has been called "the world's best brand." Coca-Cola, one of the largest companies in the United States, has a market value close to $60 billion. More than 80 percent of its profits come from international operations where, in many countries, Coca-Cola represents American culture and is a symbol of upward mobility.

Case Questions

1. What value is there to a brand in being named to a top 10 list like EquiTrend's?

2. Explain Coca-Cola's popularity worldwide.

3. Discuss possible meanings for the statement, "Coca-Cola is the *best brand* in the world."

Sources: C. Miller, "Upscale Brands Regaining Popularity," *Marketing News* 28, no. 11 (May 23, 1994), p. 3; J. Huey, "The World's Best Brand," *Fortune*, May 31, 1993, pp. 44–54.

Mini-Case 7.2

Buyers and Marketers Beware: Fakes Flood Markets

It is estimated that the traffic in counterfeit products worldwide tops $200 billion annually. Although product counterfeiting is considered a victimless crime because businesses and not individuals suffer, it is costly to both buyers and marketers. Buyers are duped into buying cheap products with designer labels or name brands only to find that the fakes are often grossly inferior to the real thing. Marketers lose profits, and they risk losing brand equity through negative word of mouth about poor-quality products wearing their brand name. Fake products are found in almost every product category, from automotive parts to designer handbags to nuclear power plant reactor fasteners to fashion clothing to computer software to ulcer drugs to airplane engine bolts.

Experts say that the volume of counterfeit products is growing; doubling in the past five years and forecast to double again in the next five. Counterfeiting production facilities are about evenly split between the United States and abroad. Some governments condone product counterfeiting for export, because it employs local labor and is a profit center for struggling industries. In China, an estimated 30 factories produce about 80 million compact discs annually, although China's domestic market for CDs is only three million. Some factories make both legal and illegal CDs. Pursuit and prosecution of counterfeiters in China has been half-hearted at best. In the United States, some states are cracking down on counterfeiters, stiffening penalities of fines and prison time.

Case Questions

1. Who should bear the responsibility for defective fake products—the owner of the brand name or the counterfeiter?

2. Why might some consumers want product counterfeiting to continue?

3. What, if anything, can governments do to stop the flow of counterfeit products?

Sources: J. Levine and N. Rotenier, "Seller Beware," *Forbes* 152, no. 10 (October 25, 1993), pp. 170, 174; M. W. Braichli, "Fake CDs Are a Growth Industry in China," *The Wall Street Journal,* February 11, 1994, pp. B1, 10; A. Meadus, "Counterfeit Crackdown Gets Tougher," *WWD* 168, no. 75 (October 17, 1994), p. 12.

Chapter 7 Notes

1. H. Schlossberg, "Dawning of the Era of Emotion," *Marketing News* 27, no. 4 (February 15, 1993), pp. 1, 2.

2. J. D. Reed, "Hail to the T, the Shirt that Speaks Volumes," *Smithsonian* 23, no. 1 (April 1992), pp. 97–101.

3. J. A. Czepiel, *Competitive Marketing Strategy* (Englewood Cliffs, NJ: Prentice Hall, 1992), p. 67.

4. P. Blustein, "Going Against the Grain," *The Washington Post National Weekly Edition* 11, no. 21 (March 21–27, 1994), p. 17.

5. P. Pae, "Advanta Finds Edge with Careful Customer Screening," *The Wall Street Journal,* April 8, 1993, p. B4.

6. S. P. Schnaars, *Marketing Strategy: A Customer-Driven Approach* (New York: Free Press, 1991), pp. 117–18, 132.

7. M. T. Copeland, "Relation of Consumers' Buying Habits to Marketing Methods," *Harvard Business Review* 1, no. 3 (April 1923), pp. 282–89.

8. S. A. Forest, "Radio Shack Goes Back to the Gizmos," *Business Week,* February 28, 1994, pp. 102–3.

9. K. J. Clancy and R. S. Shulman, *The Marketing Revolution: A Radical Manifesto for Dominating the Marketplace* (New York: HarperCollins, 1991), p. 17.

10. H. Schlossberg, "On a Crusade for Better Design: Consumers Fed Up with Complexities of Products," *Marketing News* 26, no. 7 (March 30, 1992), pp. 1, 15.

11. D. P. Hamilton, "Japanese Focus on Simpler Camcorders," *The Wall Street Journal,* May 3, 1993, p. B1.

12. J. Applegate, "Poolside Problem Leads to Lockers on Lounge Chairs," *The Washington Post* 116 (June 7, 1993), p. WB8.

13. S. C. Fehr, "We're Miles Away from Knowing Metric," *Lexington Herald-Leader,* August 26, 1992, pp. A3, 6, L. M. Litvan, "Sizing Up Metric Labeling Rules," *Nation's Business* 82, no. 11 (November 1994) p. 62.

14. O. Port, "In a New Metric Push, Uncle Sam Goes the Whole Nine Yards," *Business Week,* May 16, 1994, p. 91; M. Haggerty, "A Federal Agency Turns Its Builders into Meter Readers," *The Washington Post* 117, (February 2, 1994), p. F1.

15. K. Deveny, "Ibuprofen's Success Pains Aspirin Makers," *The Wall Street Journal,* January 12, 1993, pp. B1, 3.

16. T. R. Hill, "New Mark of Quality: ISO 9000 Offers Internationally Recognized Bench Mark Sought by Businesses," *Lexington Herald-Leader,* July 28, 1993, p. C7; C. Miller, "U.S. Firms Lag in Meeting Global Quality Standards," *Marketing News* 27, no. 4 (February 15, 1993), pp. 1, 6.

17. J. B. White and O. Suris, "GM, Pitching Value, Scores Cavalier Upset," *The Wall Street Journal,* May 11, 1993, pp. B1, 2; R. Serafin, "U.S. Cars Build Share with Value Pricing," *Advertising Age* 64, no. 29 (July 12, 1993), p. 4.

18. G. Gendron, "Confessions of a Passionate Shopper," *INC.* 15, no. 1 (January 1993), pp. 89–99.

19. B. Nussbaum, "Hot Products: Smart Design Is the Common Thread," *Business Week,* June 7, 1993, pp. 54–57.

20. E. Selame and G. Kolligian, "Brands Are a Company's Most Important Asset," *Marketing News* 25, no. 19 (September 16, 1991), pp. 14, 19.

21. S. Elliott, "What's in a Name? Perhaps Billions," *New York Times* 141 (August 12, 1992), p. C4.

22. G. Stern, "Big Companies Add Private-Label Lines That View with Their Premium Brands," *The Wall Street Journal,* May 21, 1993, pp. B1, 10.

23. K. Deveny, "Bargain Hunters Bag More Store Brands," *The Wall Street Journal,* April 15, 1993, pp. B1, 10.

24. "Bic Drops 'Spaz' After Mother of Disabled Boy Is Offended," *Marketing News* 28, no. 11 (May 23, 1994), p. 7; "Commentary: Penning the Wrong Word," *Marketing News* 28, no. 11 (May 23, 1994), p. 4.

25. G. B. Knecht, "American Express Embraces Co-Brands," *The Wall Street Journal,* February 17, 1994, pp. B1, 6; R. Gibson, "Co-Branding Aims to Double the Appeal," *The Wall Street Journal,* August 3, 1993, pp. B1, 8.

26. L. Zinn, "Pepsi's Future Becomes Clearer," *Business Week,* February 1, 1993, pp. 74–75.

27. M. S. Lans, "Protecting Trade Secrets Helps Maintain Marketing Edge," *Marketing News* 27, no. 11 (May 24, 1993), p. 13.

28. B. Nussbaum, "Design Patents: How the Courts Help the Copycats," *Business Week,* November 5, 1990, p. 105.

29. M. J. McCarthy, "Coca-Cola Introduces Marketing Gimmick: Its Famous Old Bottle," *The Wall Street Journal,*

January 12, 1993, p. B3; C. Miller, "The Shape of Things: Beverages Sport New Packaging to Stand Out from the Crowd," *Marketing News* 28, no. 17 (August 15, 1994), pp. 1–2.

30. B. Nussbaum, "For Noel Zeller, Good Design Is Just the Beginning," *Business Week*, November 5, 1990, pp. 104–8; G. Morgenson, "Is Your Product Your Advocate?" *Forbes* 150, no. 6 (September 14, 1992), pp. 468–52.

31. H. Schlossberg, "Effective Packaging 'Talks' to Consumers," *Marketing News* 24, no. 16 (August 6, 1990), pp. 6–7.

32. R. Gutfeld, "Food-Label 'Babel' to Fall as Uniform System Is Cleared," *The Wall Street Journal*, December 3, 1992, pp. B1, 7; J. Carey, "Food Labeling: The FDA Has the Right Ingredients," *Business Week*, November 23, 1992, p. 42; C. Miller, "Food Industry Faces Sweeping Label Requirements," *Marketing News* 28, no. 12 (June 6, 1994), pp. 5, 12; "New Food Labels: At Last, You Can Trust Them—Most of The Time," *Consumer Reports* 59, no. 7 (July 1994), pp. 437–38.

33. "FDA Proposes Rules Governing Labeling of Bottled Water," *The Wall Street Journal*, December 31, 1992, p. B8.

Product Processes

Chapter Objectives

After studying Chapter 8 you should be able to

1. Explain how businesses obtain products.
2. Characterize the new product development process and explain the importance of new products.
3. Recognize the methods used to describe consumer responses to products.
4. Compare different product management strategies.
5. Identify contemporary product issues.

*N*ew products are frequently called the lifeblood of a company. They promise profits, growth, and survival; all too often they deliver costly failure. You've probably read about spectacular product failures and their estimated costs: the Ford Edsel ($250 million), RCA Videodisc ($200 million), or Time's *TV-Cable Week* magazine ($47 million), among others. Most new product ideas never survive the development process. Of the new products that do make it to market, only a little more than half survive five years. Some people believe the current new product failure rate approaches 80 percent compared to 70 percent from 1960 to 1990.[1] This chapter presents the processes involved in obtaining and managing products. As you learn about product processes, consider this question: "If new products are so crucial to business success (if not survival), why do so many of them fail despite efforts to ensure their success?"

Donna Martin owns and operates a successful women's specialty clothing store in an upscale community near a large metropolitan area. At the end of each workday, she and her assistants inspect and clean the garments that had been tried on that day. Her biggest cleaning problem is the white deodorant residue left on dresses, blouses, and sweaters by many of her customers as they try on the garments. Donna and countless others who sell clothing retail wish deodorant makers would get the message and develop a deodorant that wouldn't leave white smudges.

OBTAINING PRODUCTS

Objective 1 Explain how businesses obtain products.

When marketers perceive an opportunity, new products quickly emerge. Ban Clear is an example of a new product designed to solve a specific consumer problem. Ban marketers listened to consumers like Donna in the chapter-opening story and discovered the most bothersome problem with deodorants is the white chalky residue left on skin that often transfers to clothing. The resulting problem solver is a clear product with no residue. Ban's advertising campaign slogan "Don't Mess That Dress" neatly sums up the advantages of Ban Clear.[2]

Degrees of Product Newness

Newness is a matter of perspective: new to whom? A product may be new to the business offering it, to consumers, to an industry, even to a country. A brand may be new, although the product itself is not. A product modification may be new to a brand, yet old to the market (see Photo 8.2). An old product may be reintroduced and extolled as new and improved, although the change is often hardly noticeable to consumers. Secondhand markets for products, from automobiles to clothing and furniture, represent used products that are new only to the latest purchaser.

The Federal Trade Commission (FTC) defines *new* as lasting six months after a product's regular commercial interstate distribution; however, the meaning of "regular" is vague and confusing. Fewer than 10 percent of new products are true innovations.

continuous product innovations Products that differ only slightly from existing ones and require little if any effort by the consumer to learn their use.

discontinuous product innovations Revolutionary new products that are unique or extremely different from existing products and require a considerable effort to learn their use.

Product newness is often classified according to how revolutionary or evolutionary the product is compared to other similar products already being offered. Most new products are **continuous product innovations,** products that differ only slightly from existing products, require little if any effort by the consumer to learn their use, and are minimally evolutionary in design (e.g., Multi Grain Cheerios, 486K microchip). At the opposite extreme, **discontinuous product innovations** are revolutionary new products that are unique or extremely different from existing products and require consider-

Consumer Insight

Ban Clear is only one of many new health and beauty products with a pure and natural selling point. The number of these products being marketed increased by 44 percent in one year, with 575 launched in 1992. This illustrates the growing profitability of new "detox" products aimed at reducing the number of chemicals in everything from cleaning materials to cosmetics and clothing. Like the marketers at Del Laboratories Inc.'s Naturistics brand, other pure-product marketers also are counting on the detox movement being a trend and not a short-term fad. Naturistics brand women's toiletries, launched in 1991, has already expanded its line of products from 37 items to over 200. (See Photo 8.1.) Clear products won't survive if they are just a fad and capitalize on their association with purity without solving consumer problems.

Product proliferation is a constant in the marketplace; one successful product typically inspires a host of imitations. Some observers believe that clear products *are* a fad, undermined by the number of me-too products and a concept that is just stretched too far. Although clear may be appropriate for deodorants, the value of clear gasolines, clear beers, or clear colas to consumers is more murky. Fad marketing may have an initial appeal to consumers but no lasting power. Marketers ignore a fad at their own risk, however, because even a short-term popular fad can result in considerable profit to early market entrants.■

K. Deveny, "Putting It Mildly, More Consumers Prefer Only Products That Are 'Pure', 'Natural,'" *The Wall Street Journal,* May 11, 1993, pp. B1, 8; K. Deveny, "For Growing Band of Shoppers, Clean Means Green," *The Wall Street Journal,* April 6, 1993, pp. B1, 7; K. Deveny, "Anatomy of a Fad: How Clear Products Were Hot and Then Suddenly Were Not," *The Wall Street Journal,* March 15, 1994, pp. B1, 5; T. Triplett, "Consumers Show Little Taste for Clear Beverages," *Marketing News* 28, no. 11 (May 23, 1994), pp. 1, 11.

Photo 8.1

Be clean *and* concerned about the environment.

Photo 8.2

Ben and Jerry's took a calculated risk when introducing their new smooth flavors.

International Marketing Report

Mars Inc.'s Snickers is an old favorite in the United States; in Russia, it is a new brand. A 1992 Gallup survey found that when Russian consumers were asked to identify their favorite candy bar, only 5 percent named Snickers. Mars used extensive brand advertising to introduce Snickers to the Russians and, a year later, brand name recognition had risen to 82 percent! Russia's 218 million consumers are a highly desirable if risky market for Western brands, most of which are new to Russia. Many Western businesses are willing to take the risk. Procter & Gamble has introduced Oil of Olay cream (Oil of Ulay in Russia) and Head & Shoulders; Unilever has introduced Lux soap and Signal toothpaste; Cadbury Schweppes has introduced its Time Out candy bar.■

P. Kranz, "In Moscow, the Attack of the Killer Brands," *Business Week*, January 10, 1994, p. 40; V. Reitman, "P&G Uses Skills It Has Honed at Home to Introduce Its Brands to the Russians," *The Wall Street Journal*, April 14, 1993, pp. B1, 3; "Cadbury Schweppes," *Investors Chronicle* 109, no. 1391 (September 16, 1994), p. 53.

dynamically continuous product innovations Products that are different from existing products but not unique.

able effort to learn their use (e.g., CD player, microwave oven) when they are first introduced. In between the evolutionary and revolutionary innovations are **dynamically continuous product innovations** that are different from existing products but not dramatically so (e.g., portable personal computers, telephone answering machine). Many products evolve over time, so that if you compared today's version to the original the change would be quite striking. Personal computers illustrate this point. The first PCs were primitive compared to current versions, which are more versatile and powerful, smaller, and cheaper.

Product Strategies

Some common business goals are for growth, profitability, or market share protection. A number of paths may be taken to achieve such goals; one path is to adjust the marketing mix for existing products. The product remains unchanged while the other marketing mix variables vary. For example, the *price* of a product can be raised even though the product is unchanged. (However, this can result in increased profits only if consumers accept the price change.) Alternately, the price can be lowered with the expectation that a greater volume will be sold, thereby increasing profits and protecting market share. The product distribution strategy can be changed, increasing the number of *places* where the existing product is offered or pursuing new markets entirely. Product *promotion* can be increased through more advertising, different sales promotions, or direct mailings.

Marketing Application 8.1

On your next regular trip to a supermarket, select five product categories (e.g., canned vegetables, dry cereals, jams and jellies, laundry detergents, etc.) and, in each category, look for brands that claim they are new and improved, or use words to that effect. Are the new and improved claims spread evenly over all categories, or do they appear to cluster within certain product categories, such as laundry detergents? What might explain your findings? Bring the results of your research to class for discussion. ∎

At the same time businesses are altering marketing mixes for existing products, most also seek to obtain new products. These *product* strategies include the following.

Revitalize Reformulate, repackage, and relaunch an old product, then introduce it as "new and improved." This is the strategy used by Dial Corporation to revitalize Breck shampoo. Bought by Dial in 1990, the Breck line was relaunched in 1992 as a premium brand. A year later Breck had captured only 1.1 percent of the $1.53 billion shampoo category, despite a $50 million advertising campaign and a lingering favorable consumer image.[3] Blaming brutal competition for the failure of the brand to ignite nationwide, Dial relaunched Breck for the second time as a regional brand, value priced at less than the first relaunch.[4] Of the 15,866 health, beauty, household, food, and pet products introduced in 1992, nearly 70 percent were revitalizations with new packages, sizes, formulas, or varieties.[5]

Revitalization sometimes means a decrease in product size while the price stays the same or increases. Either way, the consumer gets less product for the same or a greater price. For example, Brut deodorant spray shrank from a five- to a four-ounce can and Velamints shrank from 0.85 ounces to 0.71 per package, yet their prices did not change.[6]

Extend Stretch a popular brand name to other products, often while also identifying new uses for the same product completely. This is typically less costly and less risky than launching a new product. For example, although Dial Corporation has not had great success with its relaunch of Breck shampoo, it is successful with line extensions, extending Dial bar soap to Dial Plus moisturizing soap as well as liquid soaps and antibacterial soaps, including Dial for Kids.[7] There are 20 varieties of Kleenex facial tissues, from lotion-rich tissues to

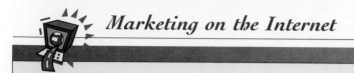

Marketing on the Internet

More new products (goods and services) are being offered on the Internet each day. A group of around 30 large banks, and research and other financial organizations has formed The Financial Services Technology Consortium to study how they can develop the commercial potential of the Internet. Banc One Corp. is one of the members. Its management believes that the way banks interact with their customers will change because of the Internet. The Internet will become an important tool that financial institutions can use to stay in touch with customers and service accounts.

Financial services are already available on the Internet's World Wide Web. Financial products being offered include information sources for market traders, economics working papers, economic bulletin boards and time series data, stock market quotes and reports, mutual fund information, the Securities and Exchange Commission's EDGAR database, and the GNN Personal Finance Center—a financial product cyberstore.

Most banks, however, have hesitated about offering their services on the Internet, because of concern over the security of funds handling. A Kentucky-based bank planned to lead the way by joining the Internet in the spring of 1995. The new cyberbank's services were to be accessible to anyone with access to the World Wide Web. A North Carolina bank also has plans to open an Internet bank in 1996.

The Kentucky-based cyberbank plans to begin by offering checking and money market account services. It will be managed through SecureWare, Inc., in Atlanta. Security will be established through the use of passwords and encryption—scrambling data in order to prevent unauthorized users from intruding into secured accounts. This is the same encryption technology used by the U.S. Department of Defense to safeguard information transmission. All bank records will be kept by a bank data processing company in Wisconsin. Bank customers will have 24-hour access to their accounts, along with automated teller machine cards and direct deposit capabilities, and eventually, will be able to have account information downloaded from the cyberbank directly into a personal computer for use in personal finance software.

Michael Neubarth, editor of Internet World magazine, says that more banks can easily be supported on the Internet. "There will soon be 50 million people on the Internet, most of them in the United States. It's a very large market, and they won't all want to use one bank." ∎

J. Jordan, "Pineville Bank to Join the Internet," *Lexington Herald-Leader*, March 2, 1995, p. A13; T. Pack, "How It Works," *Lexington Herald-Leader*, March 2, 1995, p. A13; F. Brown, "Surfing the Internet for Trading Jewels," *Internet Interactive Marketing*, 1994; B. Orr, "Banking on the Internet," *ABA Banking* 86, no. 11 (November 1994), p. 67; J. Kutler, "Banc One Joins Group Exploring Internet Use," *American Banker* 159, no. 204 (October 21, 1994), p. 14.

"man"-size boxes and Kleenex for the nursery.[8] Arm & Hammer has extended its baking soda for use as a freshener in the refrigerator, a carpet deodorizer, and, now, as an antiperspirant deodorant.[9] RJR Nabisco is extending several of its popular cookie brands to breakfast. Oreo, Chips Ahoy!, and Nutter Butter granola bars and Snack-Well's Cereal Bars seek to capture part of the growing market of adult morning snackers who are also health conscious. Nabisco is leveraging its popular cookie brands to gain quick market acceptance.[10]

It is estimated that from 75 to 86 percent of all new products launched in 1993 were extensions. However, line extensions don't always work, often because consumers won't accept the leap from the original product to the extended one. For example, RJR Nabisco

Marketing Application 8.2

On your next shopping trip to a grocery or drug store, check the analgesic (aspirin, acetaminophen, ibuprofen) shelves for private labels that mirror national manufacturer's brands. Find one that looks much like one of the well-advertised, popular national brands. How much alike are the two in their name, ingredients, packaging, and price? If you weren't looking closely when you reached for a national brand, might you pick up a private label by mistake? Who benefits if you make this mistake? Bring the results of your analysis to class for discussion. ■

tried and failed to extend A.1 steak sauce to A.1 poultry sauce. Sterling Winthrop, a Kodak unit, spent over $116 million launching its Bayer Select line of 11 products, but captured only a 1 percent market share. Analysts believe that this extension compromised the brand equity of the mother brand, Bayer aspirin, which experienced a 7 percent market share slip.[11]

Acquire Buy another business for its brands; therefore, the brand is new to the company but not the market. For example, PepsiCo's Frito-Lay has acquired a product new to its business through the purchase of Smart Food popcorn.[12] Popcorn complements the company's potato chips, corn chips, and other snack food lines. By using this strategy, a business obtains a new product while also eliminating a competitor.

Duplicate Copy a product with or without modification. Perrigo Company, a nonprescription drug maker, sells its products to retail chains like Wal-Mart, Rite Aid, and Kmart Corp., who market the drugs in their stores under private store labels.[13] The company's chemists take existing over-the-counter drugs apart and reformulate them with slight modifications. Major lawsuits from national brand drug companies like American Home Products and Warner-Lambert indicate that some companies believe Perrigo is knocking off their brands, right down to similar names and packaging. Perrigo persists in pushing the limit, getting as close to national brands as possible, because consumers like the lower prices and believe the quality is as good as the national brands. Retailers like Perrigo because the company is fast and flexible, and able to respond quickly when retailers request special orders of its brand equivalents.

Cooperate Enter into a joint venture with one or several other companies to develop a new product and share the development costs and risks. IBM, Apple Computer, and Hewlett-Packard are working together to develop a new computer operating system that will both make moving from one software program to another faster and easier, and lower barriers to sharing information between application systems.[14]

A growing number of companies enter into agreements with foreign businesses to obtain products by importing them. For example, Multivision S.A., a Mexican business, has entered into an agreement with Blockbuster Entertainment Inc. to obtain entertainment products. Multivision S.A. provides electronic access to a cable and satellite television system seen in over 2 million Latin American homes. Blockbuster provides programs from its more than 12,000-hour library, including such popular television series as "The Streets of San Francisco" and "Little House on the Prairie."[15]

Generate   Produce a new product. This is the product strategy with the highest risk and cost. For example, Quaker Oats Company has developed an adult energy drink as an alternative morning beverage. SunBolt contains carbohydrates, caffeine, and vitamin C for a morning picker-upper.[16] The company is counting on consumer acceptance of the product despite a multitude of direct and indirect competitors. Unilever has introduced Mentadent, a combination of fluoride, baking soda, and peroxide, for a new fizzy toothbrushing experience.[17] Mattel's new toy cars, called Top Speed, have a unique suspension system and are powered by a rubberband that allows them to streak on a track, leap, loop, and race through plastic tubing.[18]

Photo 8.3

Campbell's product line extension strategy—to go beyond chicken noodle soup—offers something for every consumer.

1. Why are new products called the "lifeblood of a company"?
2. Explain this statement: "Newness is a matter of perspective."
3. Discuss the different ways a business may obtain products.

NEW PRODUCT DEVELOPMENT

A new, unique product that consumers love can mean big profits and a sustainable competitive advantage, at least until the product is copied and lower-priced versions hit the market. Some companies are product innovators, developing and introducing new products on a regular basis, enjoying the profits that come with market leadership, but also paying a steep price for aggressive research and development activities. Other businesses are me-too specialists, content to make their profits by copying market innovators. These businesses often concentrate on regional markets. Although their research and development costs are less than the market innovators', so are their profits.

Objective 2 Characterize the new product development process and explain the importance of new products.

It is not unusual for a new product to cost a business from $20 million to over $100 million for product development and a national launch. Despite the costs and risks, many businesses at the forefront of their industries must innovate to survive. American businesses lost the competitive edge in inventiveness to the Japanese during the 1980s. However, in 1993 IBM was granted more patents (1,088) from the U.S. government than any other company. IBM's annual product research and development budget exceeds $6 billion. This feat represents the first time since 1985 that an American company topped the patent-granting list. However, 7 of the 10 top companies on the 1993 list are Japanese.[19]

SunBolt, Mentadent, and Top Speed are all new products for personal use consumers from major national companies. They are continuous product innovations that don't require much effort by consumers to figure out how to use them. What are their chances for success? That depends on consumers and whether or not the products satisfy their needs and preferences, including a desire for variety. It depends on product prices, the places where the products are offered, and how successfully promotions communicate product value to consumers. It depends on the competition and factors in the environment.

A great amount of time, money, and effort goes into new product development. For example, it took many years to produce and market Hershey's Hugs, a Hershey's Kiss made with white chocolate

Photo 8.4

Hershey's took a tried and true familiar product, the Hershey's Kiss, and gave it a new twist to create Hershey's Hugs.

swirled with milk chocolate. This process required the development of a new manufacturing technology and tens of millions of dollars. The candy, introduced in August 1993, was a success.[20]

Steps in Product Development

Product development typically proceeds through a series of interrelated steps, as outlined in Figure 8.1. These activities are not isolated and often overlap, occurring simultaneously rather than in a rigid sequence. The steps are discussed in the following section from the perspective of the development of a national brand; however, the discussion is equally applicable, on a smaller scale, to local and regional new product development processes. When it comes to new products for business/organization consumers, the consumer often becomes more intimately involved in the process, sometimes specifying from the start exactly what is sought from a new product.

Opportunity Scanning Businesses constantly monitor consumer behaviors and the environment in order to identify gaps in the market that represent product opportunities. Opportunity scanning is the first step in product development. Many opportunities are identified through personal experience and observation, reading business papers and trade journals, studying industry reports and U.S. census data, and attending trade shows and professional meetings. Opportunities often result from scanning the competition and analyzing their product offers. Salespeople are a good source of information, as are customer service representatives who take calls on a business's 1-800 number and the customers who make these calls, often to complain about a product. Suppliers, as well as wholesalers and retailers, are also sources of new product ideas.

Figure 8.1 The New Product Development Process

STEPS IN THE NEW PRODUCT DEVELOPMENT PROCESS	
1. Opportunity Scanning Determine what gaps exist in the market—unmet consumer needs that might be met by product offers that the business has the competency to produce	**5. Market Analysis and Marketing Plan Development** Conduct thorough evaluation of marketability of the product, develop marketing plan
2. Idea Generation Brainstorm ideas for new products, don't throw out any yet, seek quantity not quality	**6. Product Production** Produce product in sufficient amounts to test
3. Idea Screening Take ideas and screen them for feasibility and profitability, rank order best ideas, and select one or a few for testing and development	**7. Test Marketing** Test on consumers (potential customers) either through a traditional test market in the field, simulated test market, or mini-test market
4. Concept Testing Try out the concept on consumers, make a prototype, develop the concept further	**8. Commercialization** If test market results warrant, launch product and evaluate results so that any necessary changes may be made

A recent change in consumer behavior presents an opportunity and challenge for some businesses. This change relates to what women are *not* wearing on their legs. For example, sales of women's hosiery dropped from 936 million pairs sold in 1987 to 672 million pairs sold in 1993.[21] This information suggests a product opportunity for hair removal systems for women who prefer bare legs. Let's follow through the steps in new product development to see what happens as this information is used to bring a hypothetical new product to market.

Idea Generation   The idea generation step uses information obtained in opportunity scanning and relates these opportunities to the business's core competencies—what it does best. People from many functional areas are often brought in to contribute their expertise and brainstorm ideas for new products. This includes marketers (particularly from sales and promotions) as well as designers, engineers, production people, quality-control specialists, and others. Sometimes a business will hire a new product development specialist to act as a facilitator, drawing ideas out of the various participants. The goal is to produce as many ideas as possible and not judge them at this time; quantity is preferred over quality. Being nonjudgmental rouses people to generate ideas, piggyback new ideas onto others, and make creative leaps in entirely new directions.

Let's say that the drop in panty hose sales presents an opportunity for a hair removal products business. Brainstorming by one of their product development teams generates ideas about new shaving systems for women. The team comes up with such ideas as a shaver with a built-in shaving cream dispenser that releases creme as the shaver is in use, a built-in light that makes it easier for the user to see what she is doing, a handle contoured to fit a woman's hand, a broad head to lessen shaving time, a nonslip rubber handle for safer use, a dispenser for shaving cream mixed with skin softener, and an elasticized wrist strap so that if the shaver is dropped it bounces back to the user's hand. No idea, no matter how outrageous, should be dismissed at this stage.

Idea Screening The ideas that were generated must be evaluated. This is idea screening, and the goal is to refine the ideas, eliminate the bad ones, identify the good ones, and then rate them according to their marketability, produceability, and potential profitability. Ideas usually are dropped when they don't fit what the business does best. Ideas are eliminated when they aren't technically feasible or are too costly, might harm existing brands, or can't satisfy government regulations. Product potential is projected to evaluate profitability and market size. The competition, both direct and indirect, is identified, and the costs of being competitive are estimated. Safety and liability issues are explored, along with whether or not the product can be patent protected. At the conclusion of this step, the most promising idea should be ready for testing and development.

Let's say that the top-rated idea is a combination of several of the best concepts: a shaver with a nonslip contoured handle, broad head, and light. This product will fill a gap in the market. It is compatible with the products already being produced by the business. It will be simple to produce and use. Because there is nothing identical to it on the market, it can be patented. It can be promoted as a safer alternative to existing shaving systems because it includes a light to help the user see what she is doing. Although there is considerable direct competition from existing shavers and indirect competition from chemical depilatories, this product is unique and will deliver a competitive advantage. Although the product development team is enthusiastic about the product concept, the next step is to test the product concept on consumers to see if they think the concept is on track.

Concept Testing Will consumers like the idea? That is the question that must be answered through concept testing. Typically, a model of the product or a detailed description and visual representation of the product concept is presented to members of the potential target market. Sometimes target consumers are interviewed during mall intercepts. Shoppers are stopped, asked to participate in a consumer survey, familiarized with the product concept, then asked such questions as: Does the product concept make sense? Is it unique? Do you see a benefit from using this product? What can be done to improve this idea? What kind of consumer will use this product? How likely are you to want to purchase and use this product? How much are you willing to pay for it? What do you use now? Again, caution must be maintained in analyzing concept test results. Consumers often are highly enthusiastic about inventive new products but, when it comes to making the change from an old familiar product, their purchase reflects the pull of the familiar.

Let's say that women shoppers between the ages of 20 and 45 are sought to participate in a concept test of the shaver. They are shown pictures of the proposed product or a full-scale model and asked questions like the ones stated earlier to determine whether or not this is a good product concept. Focus groups (directed group interviews) are held with small groups of women to collect their responses to the concept. Concept test results are analyzed to discover whether or not this concept is viable. If the results are negative, the concept will either be reworked and tested again, or dropped.

Market Analysis and Marketing Plan Development   If the concept test is a success, consumers are enthusiastic about the product, and they say they'd buy it, the next step is to conduct a comprehensive market analysis and develop a marketing plan. This includes projecting costs of production and introduction, timetables for bringing

Photo 8.5

The development team for Mattel's Top Speed cars went through all the stages of new product development to create a toy to rival Barbie.

the product to market, a promotions budget, delivery systems for getting the product to retailers, analysis of the competition and their response to the product introduction, and estimates of market size and profit potential. The outcome of the market analysis is the development of a comprehensive marketing plan that must be compatible with the overall business plan. The marketing plan provides details about product features, brand name, packaging, prices, distribution, and promotion. Even with good results from the concept test, if the market analysis shows that the costs and risks outweigh potential benefits, the process should be stopped before it proceeds further. Often this is the point at which higher management gets involved and gives a go/no-go decision to the product development team.

Let's say that the market analysis for the shaver is very encouraging. Suggested prices are set at $15.95 per unit for an introductory package of the shaver base, three refill blades, and light. Additional refills are priced at $3.95 per package of five blades. The shaver is given the company brand name and called Smooth 'n Easy. It will be promoted as a revolutionary new shaving system for women with a built-in light to guide their way to smooth-as-silk legs. The product will be distributed through existing dealer networks and featured in department stores, beauty salons, and chain drug stores. The product introduction (rollout) will be launched by a national advertising campaign using television and magazine advertising along with a direct mailing of coupons to a select mailing list of 3 million women between 21 and 45 years old with family incomes above $25,000. A patent application for the unique lighting system has been registered.

Product Production   Enough of the product must be produced so that it can be tested by consumers. The details of the marketing plan are developed so that when the product is tested, consumers will be evaluating a finished product with the brand name, package, promotion campaign, price, and place that will be used for the product launch.

Let's say that an initial production run of Smooth 'n Easy Shavers is set at 125,000 units of the special introductory package. Although the cost of such a small run is high, there must be sufficient numbers of shavers to test market them on consumers.

test market A group of consumers in one or several cities who determine purchase responses by trying a product or the idea of a product.

Test Marketing   A **test market** requires offering a complete, finished product to a group of consumers in one or several test market locations to determine purchase responses. Many businesses have gotten away from traditional test markets—they are expensive to run and require a series of complicated decisions regarding where to test, how to test, and for how long. In addition, a test market alerts the competition to the new product. Frequently, the competition may respond by trying to muddy the test market results through price cuts, special offers, increased advertising, and other incentives designed to move their products and undercut sales of the test market product.

A less costly and less risky alternative is to test the product in selected stores in selected test market cities. Cooperating retailers display the product and scanner tape printouts track sales. Some tests are conducted in laboratory simulations, where consumers are given a small amount of money and asked to either spend it on any of the products offered or pocket it. In this highly controlled model shopping trip, consumer purchases simulate their real-world decisions.

Let's say that Smooth 'n Easy is test marketed in two mid-size U.S. cities, one in the Midwest and the other in the Southeast. Each has a population of about 250,000. The product is distributed as proposed, and supported by commercials in the local media and with a direct mailing of $1.00-off coupons. The test runs eight weeks and is closely monitored to track sales of Smooth 'n Easy and competing products. At the end of the test, a comprehensive analysis is conducted and the results used to make necessary changes in the marketing mix before commercialization.

Commercialization The culmination of the new product development process is the product launch—its introduction to the market. This assumes that the test market results have been satisfactory and production is ready to begin. An important part of this stage is monitoring the product after it has been launched. Corrections in the marketing plan, through product changes or alterations in price, place, and promotion, may be made if initial results indicate problems in consumer acceptance.

Let's say that the time has come to roll out Smooth 'n Easy nationally. A media blitz announces the product on national television and in various women's magazines prior to the launch. As product awareness builds in the target market, the product is distributed throughout the country and sales begin to climb.

Identify the steps in the new product development process and explain what happens in each step.	**Check Your Understanding** *8.2*

Teamwork in Product Development

In most companies it certainly takes more than one person to develop a new product; in large businesses, it could take hundreds or more. In the past, new product development was a compartmentalized process with little interaction or cooperation among design, engineering, marketing, and others. In part because of the success of Japanese new

Consumer Insight

Innovative new products also come from small and mid-size businesses. William and Jim Staber have developed a European-style washing machine that rotates clothing on a horizontal axis. Their design saves water and is more energy efficient. The designers claim it uses as much as 75 percent less detergent to get clothes clean. In order to make it more appealing to American consumers, the machine's size was increased to be comparable to existing vertical axis washing machines, and it is top loaded. The clothes basket is six-sided instead of round. The product was developed by a small team working with a small product development budget. They had to research the market and determine consumer reactions to the innovative product. Because many small businesses are unable to finance national or even regional product launches, they often must raise cash through public offerings of stock, seek a joint venture partner willing to invest in the business, or agree to being bought out by a large company who will commercialize the product. ■

R. L. Rose, "A Small Company Puts a New Spin on Washers," *The Wall Street Journal*, March 21, 1994, pp. B1, 10.

product development teams, the team concept is growing in popularity in the United States. Examples include simultaneous engineering and cross-functional teams, in which engineers, marketers, purchasers, and professionals from other operational areas work together at the same time on new product development.[22]

Top Speed, a new toy car from Mattel, was developed by a team in an astonishingly short five months. This feat required the close cooperation of a product development team that included toy designers, former automobile designers, engineers, artists, computer modelers, and marketing experts.

New food products increasingly result from tech team development efforts. It is claimed that using a tech team can cut the normal new product development time in half.[23] Tech teams may include a brand manager, research and development formulator, production manager, and marketing research manager. Such teams function as product entrepreneurs, completely responsible for the product's development and success, working within their own budget. Their meetings are informal, with the brand manager taking a lead role. Sometimes consumers are brought in to participate in product development, providing their perspective in each stage of the process.

Product Failures

New products fail for many reasons, such as:

- Poor quality.
- High price.
- Redundancy (me-too).
- Bad timing.

- Too small a target market.
- Wrong target market.
- Product far away from business's strengths.
- Organizational inflexibility.
- No consumer input.
- Lack of leadership and product champion.
- Problems with other elements of marketing mix.

Perhaps most troubling is the view expressed by 166 managers, from 112 leading manufacturers and retailers, who participated in surveys and in-depth interviews on the topic of new product failures. The lack of strategic direction and commitment from top management, who seem not to view new products as a priority, is cited as a significant factor contributing to high new product failure rates.[24] These top managers press for short-term earnings when new products are really long-term investments.

On the other hand, products that are successful seem to be so because they offer clear advantages over the competition's products. They give good value for the price, fit well with existing ways that consumers use products, are not too complex to use, and can be tried out before being purchased through sampling or prepurchase testing. These products are truly new—the newness is obvious and not a sham. They are fully supported by the company and timed right for the market.

Sometimes there is no hope for a product; it cannot be made profitable. In this case, the marketer has to decide whether or not to drop the product entirely or try to revitalize and relaunch it. Procter & Gamble, faced with having to cut costs in order to strengthen its retail position, plans to drop as many as 25 percent of its unproductive items, different sizes, and varieties of brands.[25]

Less often, a company will be accused of having too many products. In the very slow-growing soft drink business, PepsiCo has taken the lead in introducing new products in an ambitious program that includes fruit juices, iced tea, sports drinks, and clear colas. Although short-term profits are good, analysts fear that the glut of new products will divert consumer attention away from the mother brands, Pepsi and Diet Pepsi, which generate 60 percent of the company's earnings. Any erosion of brand loyalty to the mother brands could have dire results in the future.[26]

Ensuring Product Success

Because the cost of product failure is so high, many businesses are making an aggressive attempt to reduce the rate of new product failure. The new product success rate can be improved by:

- Consulting customers at every stage of the development process.

- Setting realistic goals for profit and market share.

- Having research, marketing, and manufacturing cooperate on the project from the start.

- Not letting the project snowball—have checks at several points where the project is evaluated and go/no-go decisions are made.

- Test marketing the product long enough to get an accurate reading of consumer acceptance.

- Autopsying the flops: find out what went wrong and don't make the same mistakes twice.[27]

Check Your Understanding 8.3

1. What advantages do multifunctional development teams have in the development of new products?
2. Provide several explanations for why products fail.
3. What steps can be taken to ensure product success?

UNDERSTANDING CONSUMER RESPONSES TO PRODUCTS

Objective 3   Recognize the methods used to describe consumer responses to products.

Marketers gather specific information about how a certain product is being accepted by consumers by using some of the techniques discussed in Chapter 6. However, it is also important to develop a broader knowledge about how consumers respond to products generally.

Adoption and Diffusion

On the individual level, consumers exposed to new products typically progress through a series of psychological and behavioral stages (Figure 8.2) called the **product adoption process.** The individual must first become aware of the new product, probably from advertisements or other promotions, then move through the interest and evaluation stages to trial, which can be encouraged by providing free samples and coupons, and then adoption. How rapidly a consumer travels through the stages and whether or not the adoption stage is ever reached depends on the individual, the product, marketing activities, and the situation. However, the adoption process is generally a good representation of how most consumers respond when faced with new products.

product adoption process
Stages from becoming aware of a product to adopting it.

Figure 8.2   The Product Adoption Processes

STEPS AN INDIVIDUAL CONSUMER IS EXPECTED TO GO THROUGH WHEN FACED WITH A NEW PRODUCT	
1. Awareness Consumer first notices the new product; it is new to the consumer	**5. Decision** The consumer likes the new product
2. Interest The product is interesting to the consumer	**6. Adoption** The consumer accepts the product and becomes a regular user
3. Evaluation The consumer evaluates the product and decides whether or not to try it	**7. Post-Adoption Confirmation** Regular use convinces the consumer the new product is a good choice
4. Trial The consumer tries the product perhaps through a store sample, at a friend's home, or at work	

It is also generally known how innovations diffuse through society—a process of consumer acceptance called the **diffusion of innovations.** There are groups of consumers who are always the first to try new products. These are innovators: risk takers whose characteristics often can be predicted by their lifestyles, income, and status. As shown in Figure 8.3, innovators make up less than 3 percent of the population. By far the largest groups are the early and late majority, consumers who comprise almost 70 percent of the population and are the mass market. The laggards are the very last to adopt a new product, if they ever do. These categories of adopters are not static. Whereas music enthusiasts may be early adopters of new sound technology, the same consumers may be laggards or even nonadopters of new ski equipment. What the general diffusion response indicates is that for any product category, there is a potential mass market of about 70 percent of all consumers in the market who are the target for businesses seeking widespread product acceptance.

diffusion of innovations The process of product acceptance within society.

The Product Life Cycle

As any new product is adopted by consumers it diffuses through the market and a life cycle can be described for it. The **product life cycle (PLC)** is derived from the diffusion curve and is a descriptive, not prescriptive, device. It says that all products go through some variation of a cycle patterned after a traditional biological life cycle

product life cycle (PLC) Cycle in which products are introduced, grow and accrue profits, reach maturity, and decline.

Figure 8.3

The Diffusion of Innovations through Society

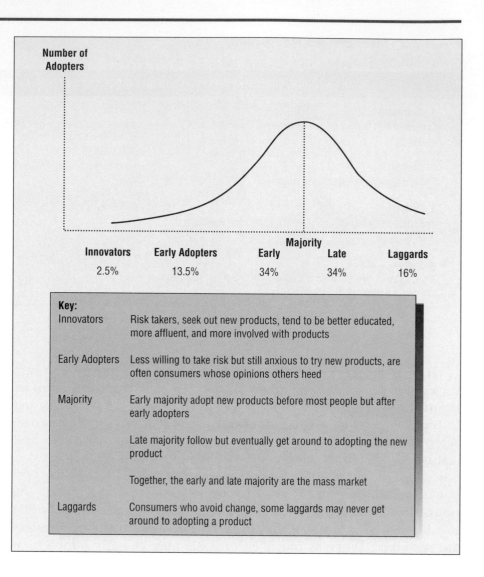

(see Figure 8.4). Products are introduced, begin to grow and accrue profits, reach maturity (which may last for varying lengths of time), and, at some point in time, decline. Unless revitalized, they will finally be removed from the market.

A fad product has a very abrupt PLC, rising and falling sharply. A durable product like a washing machine or refrigerator has an extremely long maturity stage. A failure like the Edsel may never leave the introduction phase and has only a short rise and fall; it never experiences growth or maturity before being dropped.

Considerable debate rages in marketing about the value of the PLC. Other than as a descriptive tool, how can it be used and at what level does the PLC apply? Is it a useful tool for individual brands,

Marketing Application 8.3

Are you an early adopter of any products? Are there products that you have not yet adopted? As a class project, construct a short survey to determine adoption patterns. For example, ask whether or not a particular product has been purchased. If not, the consumer is a nonadopter or a laggard. If the product was purchased, was it as soon as the product was introduced, after several months, or years? Ask the same questions for each of the following products: Microwave oven, VCR, cellular telephone, personal computer, hand-held calculator, and fat-free cookies. Make sufficient copies of the survey to administer it in class. Analyze the results. What can you conclude about product adoption patterns among your classmates for these products? ■

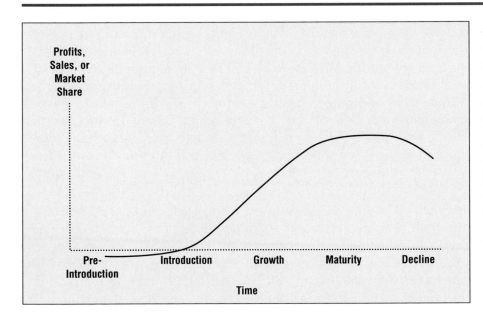

Figure 8.4

The Product Life Cycle Concept

The product life cycle (PLC) is a descriptive presentation of the stages a product passes through over the span of its presence in a market. There is considerable disagreement over the level of product for which the PLC is designed: brand (e.g., Toyota Camry is the brand within the line); product form (e.g., sedan is a variation of automobile); or product class (e.g., automobile is a product category).

products, or a product category? This is an important question, because marketing mix decisions are different in each stage of the life cycle:

Pre-introduction This is the product development stage discussed earlier in the chapter. Because the product is not yet offered for sale, there are no revenues, profits, or market share. Consumers cannot adopt the product yet and there is no diffusion through the market. However, costs are incurred as the product concept is developed, tested, and, finally, commercialized. Promotion costs rise as awareness-building promotions are developed and produced; media are selected and bought.

Introduction   Commercialization has taken the product to market. It is offered for sale locally, regionally, nationwide, or internationally. Innovators may rush to purchase the product, but initial sales usually are slow; therefore, costs are still high and not yet recovered through revenues and profits. Market share is extremely low.

If the product is really popular, the introduction stage may be quite short. For less popular products, introduction may drag on, with low sales and profits. Many products never make it out of introduction and are withdrawn. Expenditures are typically high for promotions, including advertising, point-of-purchase displays, coupons, samples, and direct marketing. A special introductory price may be offered to speed market penetration. Alternately, if the product is desirable and unique, price skimming may be used to extract a high profit before knockoffs enter the market and the price drops.

Growth   The early majority are now purchasing the product, and the product's market share is rising along with sales, revenues, and profits. Costs of production should come down as economies of scale kick in. Because costs are coming down, the price may be reduced to speed diffusion. In addition to growing numbers of first-time purchasers, many consumers are making repeat purchases. New product features may be added in order to stimulate innovator repurchases. Promotions continue, often shifting toward price promotions and away from awareness-building advertising.

Maturity   The late majority are making their purchases, and sales are flattening out. Product imitators enter the market, lowering profits and forcing further price reductions. More sales are to repeat purchasers. The laggards are finally making their purchases and the product is diffused throughout the market. Because so many imitators have entered the market, there is usually a shakeout and the weaker competitors are forced to exit. Reminder advertising along with price promotions often are used to stimulate repurchases.

Decline   If there is no effort to rebuild sales, the product will eventually enter a period of decline. This is characterized by decreasing sales, revenues, and profits. If the life cycle is not extended through product revitalization, the business must decide how long it will leave the product unsupported before finally withdrawing it from the market.

The International Product Life Cycle

Think back on the discussion of product newness as a function of perspective, and it is easy to understand why products are exported to other countries in order to extend their life cycle. Many products (and brands) are new in other countries even as they are maturing or declining domestically. When they are exported, it often represents a new product introduction and the beginning of a new life cycle. This was the case for Snickers and many other Western brands when they were first introduced to the Russian market. There are still many markets abroad where American brands are new, and their newness represents an excellent opportunity to extend their profitability.

Product Positioning

Another important consumer response to products involves brand comparisons. *Positioning* refers to the image or mental view that consumers form about products. This perception is strongly influenced by marketers and their use of the marketing mix. **Perceptual maps** (Figure 8.5) are plots of how consumers perceive different products or brands in relation to one another on several key measures that are important to the consumer. For example, consumers are asked to compare various restaurants along such dimensions as price (low/high) and speed of dining (fast/slow). The responses are combined and computer analyzed to form a product positioning or perceptual map. This map is an aggregate plot of consumers' comparison judgments that also indicates the size of each group of consumers who share the perceptions. Such a map helps marketers understand how consumers view products or brands comparatively. This knowledge can be used to help manage a brand by developing insights on where to position new products at introduction and how to develop advertising appeals targeted to various consumer segments.

perceptual maps Plots of how consumers perceive different products or brands in relation to one another along several key measures.

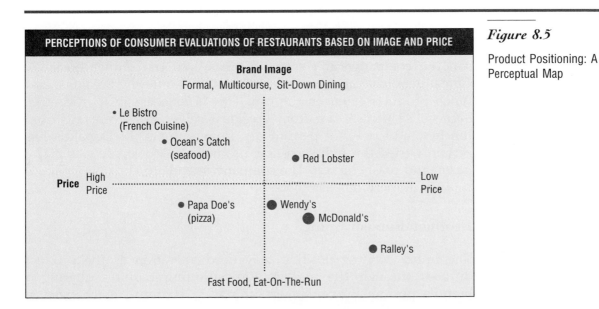

PERCEPTIONS OF CONSUMER EVALUATIONS OF RESTAURANTS BASED ON IMAGE AND PRICE

Brand Image
Formal, Multicourse, Sit-Down Dining

• Le Bistro
(French Cuisine)

● Ocean's Catch
(seafood)

● Red Lobster

Price High Price .... Low Price

● Papa Doe's
(pizza)

● Wendy's
● McDonald's

● Ralley's

Fast Food, Eat-On-The-Run

Figure 8.5

Product Positioning: A Perceptual Map

Marketing Application 8.4

To see the principle behind a positioning or perceptual map, develop one yourself. Figure 8.6 provides the outline of a perceptual map with two key dimensions that are usually of importance to car buyers: price (expensive to affordable) and image (sporty to family sedan). Your task is to locate each of the following automobiles in the spot on the map where you believe it belongs: Toyota Camry, Ford Taurus, Dodge Shadow, Nissan Sentra, Jaguar, and Mazda Miata. Bring your work to class to compare. What insights might a Mazda Miata marketer make from this type of comparison? ■

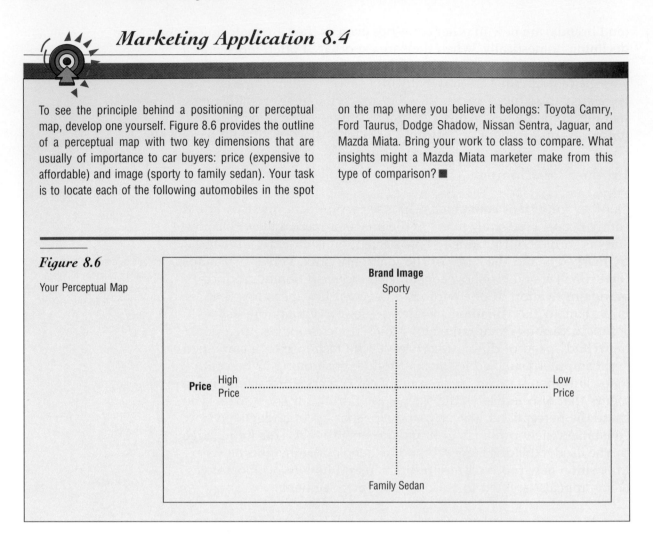

Figure 8.6

Your Perceptual Map

Consumer perceptions about McDonald's appear to be the reason the company can't seem to break into the dinner business. Consumers have an image of McDonald's as offering breakfast and lunch products eaten on the run. This is reflected in its revenues, because 25 percent are from breakfast sales, 55 percent are from lunches, and only 20 percent are from dinners. McDonald's has certainly tried through such new products to McDonald's as pizza, pasta, and roast chicken. The company intends to keep on trying to capture dinnertime customers.[28]

Product Repositioning

repositioning Altering a brand's position in consumers' minds in response to changes in consumer demands and events in the environment.

The initial product position may need alteration as the product diffuses through the market. **Repositioning** requires altering a brand's position in consumers' minds in response to changes in consumer demands and events in the environment. For example, JCPenney changed its image by repositioning itself as a medium-price fashion store for women's clothing. Over the years, Toyota has repositioned the Camry from its initial introduction as an economy car to its current position as a higher-priced family sedan.

1. Describe the product adoption process.
2. What is the product life cycle?
3. Explain the concepts of product positioning and repositioning.

PRODUCT MANAGEMENT

Once a product is launched, it must be managed. Sometimes this is done by the same person or team who developed the product; other times the job passes to managers whose task is to guide the product after introduction to profitability.

Objective 4 Compare different product management strategies.

There is no single form of product management that fits all products and businesses. Procter & Gamble pioneered the use of a **brand manager,** a mid-level professional assigned to a brand as its champion, monitoring sales, planning changes in the brand's marketing mix, developing responses to the competition, allocating resources, and deploying people to ensure the brand's profitability. The brand management system is narrow and can pit brand managers against one another within the same company as they compete for resources and support.

brand manager A mid-level professional having overall responsibility for a brand, including monitoring sales, planning changes in the brand's marketing mix, developing responses to competition, allocating resources, and deploying people to ensure the brand's profitability.

According to a survey by the Boston Consulting Group, in the 1980s, 90 percent of the consumer goods companies surveyed revealed they had restructured their marketing departments, often eliminating the brand manager system and replacing it with a category manager or a business group.[29] A **category manager** manages a unit of products in a category, such as laundry detergents, processed food, or diapers. It requires managing many brands in a category instead of one. Another product management alternative is the **business group,** a multifunctional team of professionals from marketing, production, and other areas who manage a group of products and concentrate on consumer research and product development.

category manager One person responsible for all the products in a category, usually with many brands.

business group A multifunctional team of professionals from marketing, production, and other areas who manage a group of products and concentrate on consumer research and product development.

Many of the changes in product management result from the decline of national brands and the shift of power to retailers from manufacturers. This does not mean that marketing is being deemphasized; to the contrary, a recent study by a major accounting firm found that "marketing as a discipline is more vital than ever," but the marketing department as a self-contained unit is threatened.[30]

CONTEMPORARY PRODUCT ISSUES

As you have learned, product *is* a highly complex subject. This and the previous chapter have identified many important product issues. Other issues also are of concern and deserve mention. These include the following.

Planned Product Obsolescence   Consumers continue to complain about products that seem to self-destruct prematurely. With the growing emphasis on quality, marketers must heed the warnings and incorporate durability and reliability into product features in many product categories.

Consumer Rights   According to the Consumer Bill of Rights, consumers have the right to choose, to be safe, and to be fully informed. These issues directly relate to product decisions involving the product mix, features, packaging, and labeling. The Consumer Product Safety Commission (CPSC) was established in 1972 to oversee product safety. CPSC has the authority to issue recalls, ban product sales outright, and maintain a consumer hot line for product safety complaints. The National Highway Traffic Safety Administration (NHTSA) and the Food and Drug Administration (FDA) also regulate product safety. NHTSA regulates transportation vehicles and systems; the FDA regulates foods and pharmaceutical products.

Product Recalls   Manufacturers often voluntarily recall their products when a problem is found; for example, Frito-Lay quickly recalled bags of Cheetos after pieces of glass were found in a mixing vat, Nestlé recalled Perrier after finding traces of benzene in some of its bottles, and Toyota recalled its Camry sedan because of faulty door locks.[31] Marketers may also be forced to recall their products because of government intervention. Of the two routes, a voluntary recall impresses consumers more than a government-mandated one. A voluntary recall suggests to consumers that the business is genuinely concerned about their health and safety. In any case, swiftly removing defective products from the market should be a priority for all marketers.

Recalls are becoming a marketing opportunity for some companies as they seek to satisfy consumers. Chrysler has conducted marketing tests to determine which vehicle recall system consumers like best from among the alternatives: when consumers drop off their vehicle for correction of the recall problem they get freebies such as a car wash and a loaner, or someone from the dealership picks up and returns the recalled vehicle.[32]

Career Watch

When she was four years old, Mary Rodas first went to work for Catco, Inc., a $70 million New York–based toy company. She began as an official toy tester and, by the age of 14, was appointed vice president of marketing, the youngest corporate vice president in the United States. Barbara Carver, Catco's president, says that "Mary has caused the company to change direction more than once with her comments and insight. Though she may not really know it, Mary has an instinct and natural interest in her products that most people just don't have." Mary decries the loss of the word *fun* from toys, and wants to make sure that high-tech doesn't mean leaving the kids behind. She has been instrumental in new product development, including the company's highly successful launch of the Balzac Balloon Ball. She even appears in commercials for the product and has traveled abroad to promote it. Her memories of childhood, along with extensive research on how kids play, has helped make Mary a key to Catco's success in developing toys that kids enjoy and parents will buy. ■

A. Cohen, "Whiz Kid," *Sales and Marketing Management,* June 1994, p. 92; B. Kanner, "Little Miss Marketer," *New York* 26, no. 48 (December 6, 1993), p. 90.

Photo 8.6

Mary Rodas, head of Catco.

Product Liability Who is liable when a product fails to deliver as promised or causes injury? Businesses are liable if their products cause injury. However, state liability tests vary with some requiring proof that products are poorly designed or manufactured; others assess liability even if there is no negligence.

Check Your Understanding
8.5

1. Why do products need to be managed?
2. Discuss the difference between a brand manager and a category manager.
3. Identify several contemporary product issues.

Review of Chapter Objectives

1. *Explain how businesses obtain products.* Businesses obtain new products in many different ways; sometimes many ways are used concurrently. These include revitalization, product extensions, acquisition, copying, cooperation through joint ventures, and generation of new products.

2. *Characterize the new product development process and explain the importance of new products.* Developing new products requires proceeding through a process that begins with idea generation. The ideas are screened, and then the best concept is tested on a sample of consumers. If the results are promising, a complete market

analysis is performed and a marketing plan developed. Some of the product is produced and tested again on a larger number of consumers. If everything is positive, commercialization occurs and the product is introduced to the market. New products are vital to the continued competitiveness of a business. Consumers expect new and improved products.

3. *Recognize the methods used to describe consumer responses to products.* Marketers must understand and record consumer responses to products. Some responses include how products are adopted by consumers and diffuse through society; stages in a product life cycle, which reflect rates of adoption and diffusion; and how consumers perceive products in their minds through product positioning and repositioning processes.

4. *Compare different product management strategies.* There is no single best way to manage a product. Some businesses use a brand manager, whereas others use a category manager or a business group.

5. *Identify contemporary product issues.* Several important issues involving products are product obsolescence—products that don't last and seem to self-destruct—consumer rights to safe products and product information, product recalls, and product liability.

Key Terms

After studying Chapter 8, you should be able to define each of the following key terms and use them in describing marketing activities.

Continuous Product Innovations, page 236

Discontinuous Product Innovations, page 236

Dynamically Continuous Product Innovations, page 238

Test Market, page 248
Product Adoption Process, page 252
Diffusion of Innovations, page 253
Product Life Cycle (PLC), page 253
Perceptual Maps, page 257
Repositioning, page 258
Brand Manager, page 259
Category Manager, page 259
Business Group, page 259

Discussion Questions

1. Why is product newness a matter of perspective?
2. Compare and contrast the three levels of product newness.
3. What are the ways businesses obtain products?
4. Why would a business copy other businesses' products?
5. Describe the product strategy with the greatest inherent risk.
6. Compare and contrast idea generation and idea screening.
7. How are product concepts tested?
8. What is a test market?
9. Why do so many new products fail? What can be done to reverse this trend?
10. Compare and contrast such consumer responses to products as adoption, diffusion, and positioning.

What Do You Think?

Procter & Gamble is best known for marketing such workhorse brands at Tide, Crest, and Pampers. The company also has considerable marketing expertise with low-priced perfumes, such as Navy, California, and Old Spice.

Now, Procter & Gamble is trying to market luxury perfumes. Laura Biagiotti's Venezia was the first. Offered in such fine stores as Sak's Fifth Avenue, Lord and Taylor, and I. Magnin, the product rollout was expected to reach over 1,200 stores in the United States after one year. It is said that the company earmarked about $15 million for advertising in the first year of the product launch. P&G also entered into an agreement to sell another luxury perfume under the Ferragamo name. What do you think are its chances for success with luxury products?

G. Stern, "Proctor Senses Opportunity in Posh Perfume," *The Wall Street Journal*, July 9, 1993, pp. B1, 5; "P&G to Develop Luxury Perfume with Ferragamo," *The New York Times*, July 12, 1994, p. C4.

Mini-Case 8.1

Gillette's "Sensor for Women" Takes a Big Slice of the Market

In 1989, Jill Shurtleff, the only woman designer in Gillette's shaving division, was assigned the task of evaluating the women's shaving market. Her conclusion that women's shavers were "ergonomically terrible for women" resulted in the subsequent design and commercialization of Sensor for Women. In the first six months after its launch, the razor sold 7.6 million units, reached sales of $40 million, and achieved a 60 percent market share! Despite the fact that women shave far more skin surface than do men (412 square inches compared to 48), women shave less frequently and replace their blades only 10 times each year, compared to an average of 30 times for men. Men, who often learn to shave from their dads, have a different attitude about shaving than women, and usually think of having to shave one's legs as "gross." Many women find shaving somewhat embarrassing, a very personal chore for themselves, but enjoy watching men shave because it's sexy.

Case Questions

1. Most new products "wear out" after a relatively short time, particularly when their reign as market leader is threatened by knockoff me-too products. What can Gillette do to extend the success of the Sensor for Women and repel knockoffs?

2. If a *brand* life cycle were drawn for Sensor for Women, what stage would it be in? Explain your answer.

3. Considering the brand's market share, where is it in both the adoption and diffusion of innovations processes?

Sources: K. Deveny, "Sensor Gets Big Edge in Women's Razors," *The Wall Street Journal*, December 17, 1993, pp. B1, 12; M. Maremont, "A New Equal Right: The Close Shave," *Business Week*, March 29, 1993, pp. 58–59; L. Freeman, "Sensor Still Helping Gillette Fend Off Razor Challenges," *Advertising Age* 65, no. 41 (September 28, 1994), p. 21.

Photo 8.7

A closer look at the Sensor razor for women and its proud designer Jill Shurtleff.

Mini-Case 8.2

Brands Have Personalities, Too

People's personalities reflect characteristics that determine how they will respond to events in their environments. Personality reflects individual differences. Although personality is consistent and enduring, it can also change. Brands take on human personalities in consumers' minds. Brand personality is part of a brand's image, and marketers believe it must be carefully managed in order to build brand equity. Consumer research is often used to help brand managers understand how consumers view their brands and competing brands. For example, focus group participants are asked to cut out pictures that represent how a particular brand would look and behave if it were a person. Using this process, Whirlpool found that their two appliance brands have different personalities. Whirlpool's KitchenAid brand is perceived as being a modern professional woman, competent, aggressive, smart, sophisticated, glamorous, wealthy, innovative, and elegant. On the other hand, the Whirlpool brand is gentle, motherly, sensitive, quiet, good natured, flexible, cheerful, and creative. By identifying a brand's personality, marketing promotions and brand communications can focus precisely on those personality characteristics that appeal to buyers. This extends to the selection of a spokesperson, copy, and selling approach.

Case Questions

1. Why should a brand's personality be managed? What might happen if it were not managed correctly?

2. Brands are also associated with colors. Can you think of some brands that are associated with certain colors?

3. For each of the following brands, think of one adjective that describes the brand's personality (use stream-of-consciousness thoughts to select the first adjective that pops into your mind): Coca-Cola, Jell-O, Mr. Coffee, Betty Crocker, IBM, Apple Computer, and Disney.

Sources: L. G. Schiffman and L. L. Kanuk, *Consumer Behavior*, 5th ed. (Englewood Cliffs, NJ: Prentice Hall, 1994), Chapter 5; T. Triplett, "Brand Personality Must Be Managed or It Will Assume a Life of Its Own," *Marketing News* 28, no. 10 (May 9, 1994), p. 9.

Chapter 8 Notes

1. D. B. Wolfe, "Why Marketing Executives Aren't Thinking Straight," *Advertising Age* 65, no. 47 (November 7, 1994), p. 34; M. Millstein, "Better System Is Urged for Product Launches," *Supermarket News* 44, no. 10 (March 7, 1994), p. 25.

2. V. Reitman, "Transparent Brands Are Clearly Trendy," *The Wall Street Journal*, May 21, 1992, p. B1; "Bristol Myers to Roll Out New Clear Ban," *ADWEEK* Eastern Edition 34, no. 10 (March 8, 1993), pp. 36–37.

3. P. Yoshihashi, "Reviving Breck: New Bottles, No 'Girls,'" *The Wall Street Journal*, June 1, 1993, pp. B1, 5; C. Goerne, "Dial Repositions Breck as a Premium Brand," *Marketing News* 26, no. 10 (May 11, 1992), p. 6.

4. A. Barrett, "Dial Succeeds by Stepping in Bigger Footsteps," *Business Week*, June 13, 1994, pp. 82, 84.

5. C. Miller, "Little Relief Seen for New Product Failure Rate," *Marketing News* 27, no. 13 (June 21, 1993), pp. 1, 10–11.

6. "New and Improved Twaddle," *Business Week*, November 1, 1993, p. 8.

7. Barrett, "Dial Succeeds," pp. 82–84; "Baby Boom Sees U.S. Marketers Exploiting Children's Potential," *Cosmetics International* 18, no. 421 (October 25, 1994), p. 8.

8. E. Shapiro, "Consumers Leaving New Twists on Old Products on the Shelves," *The Wall Street Journal*, February 1, 1994, pp. B1, 2.

9. "A Second Career for Some Old Warhorses," *Business Week*, May 30, 1994, p. 8.

10. S. L. Hwang, "Nabisco to Bring Top Cookie Brands to Breakfast Line," *The Wall Street Journal*, February 23, 1994, p. B5.

11. J. Weber and Z. Schiller, "Painkillers Are About to O.D.," *Business Week*, April 11, 1994, pp. 54–55.

12. Miller, "Little Relief Seen," pp. 1, 10–11.

13. G. Stern, "Perrigo's Knockoffs of Name-Brand Drugs Turn into Big Sellers," *The Wall Street Journal*, July 15, 1993, pp. A1, 5.

14. F. Guterl, "The Keys to the Future: Object Programming," *Business Week/The Information Revolution 1994*, pp. 60–64; L. Aragon, "A United Front," *PC Week* 11, no. 24 (June 20, 1994), p. A5.

15. E. Jensen, "Cable Concerns Explore Export of Programs," *The Wall Street Journal*, April 18, 1994, pp. B1, 6.

16. "Quaker Oats to Unveil Adult 'Energy Drink' for Breakfast Buzz," *The Wall Street Journal*, June 2, 1994, p. B5; "Sun Bolt May Open Distribution for Gatorade," *ADWEEK* Eastern Edition 35, no. 23 (June 6, 1994), p. 3.

17. L. Bird, "Consumers Smile on Unilever's Mentadent," *The Wall Street Journal*, May 31, 1994, p. B9; P. Sloan, "New Toothpastes Ready: Colgate, Unilever Have Big Plans for Products," *Advertising Age* 65 no. 4 (January 25, 1993), p. 2.

18. E. Schine, "Mattel's Wild Race to Market," *Business Week*, February 21, 1994, pp. 62–63.

19. D. E. Kalish, "IBM Unseats Japanese as Most Inventive Company," *Marketing News* 28, no. 4 (February 14, 1994), p. 9.

20. J. G. Brenner, "Candy Is Dandy, but Slow," *Washington Post National Weekly Edition* 10, no. 46 (September 13–19, 1993), p. 21; C. Fisher, "Line Extensions No Recipe for Success in Candy," *Advertising Age* 65, no. 5 (January 31, 1994), p. 3.

21. G. Slutsker, "The Naked Truth," *Forbes* 152, no. 4 (August 14, 1993), p. 94.

22. J. S. Lublin, "Best Manufacturers Found to Triumph by Fostering Cooperation of Employees," *The Wall Street Journal*, July 20, 1993, p. A2; "The Team Dream: Management Specialists Agree that 'Teamworking' Helps Japanese Firms to Develop Better Products and Get Them to Market Faster. But Many Western Companies Are Finding It Hard to Follow Their Example," *The Economist* 324, no. 7775 (September 5, 1992), p. 69.

23. R. J. Tucker, "'Tech Team' Speeds Product Development," *Marketing News* 28, no. 11 (May 23, 1994), p. 9.

24. Miller, "Little Relief Seen," pp. 1, 10–11; C. Miller, "Survey: New Product Failure Is Top Management's Fault," *Marketing News* 27, no. 3 (February 1, 1993), p. 2.

25. "Procter & Gamble Dropping Products," *Lexington Herald-Leader*, August 3, 1992, p. A5; N. O'Leary, "Cut and Run: As Major Marketers Eliminate Second-Tier Brands, Their Agencies Are Forced to Scramble and Adjust," *ADWEEK* Eastern Edition 35, no. 16 (April 18, 1994), p. 26.

26. L. Zinn, "Does Pepsi Have Too Many Products?" *Business Week*, February 14, 1994, pp. 64–66.

27. C. Power, K. Kerwin, R. Grover, K. Alexander, and R. D. Hof, "FLOPS: Too Many New Products Fail. Here's Why—And How to Do Better," *Business Week*, August 16, 1993, pp. 76–82.

28. M. Berss, "Empty Tables," *Forbes* 152, no. 13 (December 6, 1993), pp. 232, 235.

29. "Death of the Brand Manager," *The Economist* 331, no. 7858 (April 9, 1994), pp. 67–68.

30. Ibid.

31. "Frito-Lay Unit Recalls Bags of Cheetos in Seven States," *The Wall Street Journal*, December 31, 1992, p. B3; J. Mitchell, "Door Locks on Toyota Cars Studied by U.S.," *The Wall Street Journal*, August 18, 1992, pp. B1, 6; A. Miller, F. Gleizes, and E. Bradburn, "Perrier Loses Its Fizz," *Newsweek*, February 26, 1990, p. 53.

32. R. L. Simison, "How a Recall Becomes a Marketing Opportunity," *The Wall Street Journal*, February 18, 1994, p. B1.

CHAPTER

9

Understanding Price

*M*ost consumers, both personal use and business/organization, complain about price at one time or another—usually that prices are too high, rarely that they are too low. Most marketers complain about the difficulty of pricing products *right* and the challenge of getting a high enough price for their products. Price is more than the dollars, pesos, or yen that must be given up in exchange for a product: Consumers evaluate a product's value and quality by its price, particularly when other information is absent. Price is a powerful marketing tool. It generates revenue, communicates information about the product and company, and can be used to build both. It can be changed quickly, often with relatively little effort, which is an advantage for both the marketer and his or her competition. Yet, it is difficult to set the right price for a product. A good product that is priced wrong can be a marketing disaster; priced right, it can be a huge success. As you learn about price in this chapter, consider this question: Why is it so difficult for marketers to arrive at the *right* price for a product?

Price Is More Than a Number	Corrine Blair is shopping for a new winter skirt, even though it's the end of July and 90 degrees outside. As she browses in air-conditioned comfort in a local enclosed mall, she finds the perfect skirt, a red wool plaid. The only problem is the price. But Corrine is a savvy shopper and knows that $62 is the skirt's price *today*. If she comes back in three or four weeks, the price will be much lower. However, she also realizes that she risks not being able to find the skirt in her size later in the season. The longer she waits, the lower the price and the greater the chance that her size will be sold out. She decides to have a soft drink and consider the purchase. She finds a vending machine in the mall's food court and pays for her drink with a dollar bill, getting back some change. She doesn't hesitate about paying for the drink because she wants it now and knows the price is standard for similar products. As she drinks the soda, her eyes wander to a nearby store whose entrance is covered with a banner announcing, "All Summer Clothes 50%–75% Off!" Corrine quickly finishes her soda and heads for the sale, thoughts of the $62 skirt temporarily out of mind as she begins to hunt for bargains, clothes she can wear right now or store to wear next spring.

WHATEVER IT'S CALLED, IT'S PRICE

Objective 1 Explain how different perspectives on price influence the pricing process.

Corrine is about to decide whether or not she'll give up $62 in order to take immediate possession of the red wool skirt. By allocating the money for the skirt, she'll forgo the opportunity to use it for other purposes. On the other hand, if she indulges in too much bargain shopping at the summer clearance sale, she may avoid having to make the red skirt decision because she will have financially overextended herself on end-of-season bargains. Consumers constantly face decisions like this in the marketplace, choices involving price.

Most commonly, price is thought of in terms of currency, U.S. dollars and cents. In addition to our common definition of the term, *price* indicates the value of the things traded in a marketing exchange, a measure of what must be given up in order to take possession or use of something else. The price of a bushel of apples might be $6 or alternately, in nonmonetary terms, it may require exchanging a bale of hay, helping mow a lawn, or baking an apple pie in exchange for the bushel. Nonmonetary exchanges are called **barter,** the trading of products, labor, or other items or services of value for possession or use of something else. Barter is an ancient form of exchange that still thrives today, even in fully industrialized countries like the United States. Often a business will barter for advertising time on radio or television stations, not paying in currency but trading some of its products as the price for the advertising exposure. PepsiCo, a U.S. multinational corporation, bartered with the former Soviet Union to exchange Pepsi syrup for vodka because, at the time, the Soviet currency could not be used in trade.

barter A nonmonetary exchange, involving the trading of products, labor, or other things of value for possession or use of something else.

Where can U.S. dollars, known popularly as "greenbacks," be used to make purchases? It appears everywhere in the world! About $300 billion in U.S. currency is in circulation and the Federal Reserve estimates that nearly two-thirds of it has gone overseas. The dollar is the currency standard in many emerging markets. Many businesses abroad demand payment in American dollars. To get into a nightclub in Ho Chi Minh City, Vietnam, you have to pay a $4 cover charge in greenbacks; a Zhiguli automobile in Russia is priced at $5,000 American dollars; and just about everything in the classified ads in the Sao Paulo, Brazil, Sunday paper is priced in U.S. currency. Why is the U.S. dollar so highly valued? Several reasons are offered. The dollar is stable now that inflation appears to be under control, while many other currencies are unstable, particularly in developing nations. It is the single most recognizable currency worldwide, and there is a lack of competition; the Japanese are closely controlling the international circulation of the yen and, at least in Russia, there is a historical reluctance to use the German mark. Even Cuba's Fidel Castro has legalized the use of the dollar in an attempt to prop up the island nation's economy. Confidence in the dollar is making it the first worldwide currency.■

M. McNamee, "Emerging Nations Can't Get Enough Greenbacks," *Business Week*, April 4, 1994, p. 28; O. Ullman, P. Engardio, P. Galuszka, and B. Hinchberger, "The Global Greenback," *Business Week*, August 9, 1993, pp. 40, 44.

Price is known by many different names. The price to attend school is tuition. When your dentist cleans your teeth, the price is a fee for service. If you run a red light and are caught, a ticket is the price you pay. The price of your apartment is the rent. The price of an airline ticket is a fare. The price to drive the New Jersey Turnpike is a toll. All of these designations are synonyms for the same thing: price. Can you think of others?

Events of the past two decades help explain why price has grown in importance to marketing. The 1970s and 1980s were decades of brisk growth in businesses, costs, and prices. Two oil supply disruptions stimulated a period of hyperinflation that propelled higher prices, and consumers became more price sensitive. In the 1980s, a flood of new products entered the market and the increased competition tended to lower prices and encourage consumers to shop around, looking for the best deal. The recession at the end of the 1980s into the early 1990s seriously undermined **consumer confidence** (the positive or negative feelings consumers have about the present, the future, their job security, and their spending ability) and increased pressure on marketers to avoid raising prices. With falling consumer confidence, more consumers switched from national brand products to store brands in an effort to achieve price savings. At the same time, deregulation of many domestic industries (e.g., airlines, trucking, banking) increased price competition, sometimes with near-disastrous results.[1] Finally, foreign competitors enjoyed price advantages by selling their products in the U.S. domestic market when, for at least a short period, the dollar strengthened and the relative price of imported products fell.

consumer confidence The positive or negative feelings consumers have about the present, the future, their job security, and their spending ability.

PERSPECTIVES ON PRICE

Objective 2 Describe how pricing decisions are made.

Just as price has many names, it also has different meanings, depending to a great extent on whose perspective is taken (as shown in Figure 9.1). These perspectives also influence the marketer's price decisions.

The principal meaning of price to the marketer is reflected in the relationship of profit to revenue and costs. As shown in the following equation, profit is total revenue minus total cost:

$$\text{Profit} = \text{Total Revenue} - \text{Total Cost}$$

Total revenue is the price per unit times the number of units sold.

$$\text{Total Revenue} = \text{Price per Unit} \times \text{Units Sold}$$

Total cost is all costs that remain constant regardless of how many units are produced plus variable costs that change with the number of units produced. When fixed costs are high, the business is pressed to increase production in order to achieve economies of scale, eliminate slack resources, and spread fixed costs over a greater number of units produced.

$$\text{Total Cost} = \text{Fixed Costs} + \text{Variable Costs}$$

Because price is a complex concept, with many different perspectives on it, the marketer must weigh each when considering initial price decisions and, later, when making price changes.

Consumers

Price is a signal about a product that consumers interpret to indicate the product's value and quality, particularly in the absence of other information. Most consumers develop their own unique perspective on price, a subjective, psychological view that helps them simplify their purchase decisions. Whether price is even evaluated depends also on the consumer's needs or wants for the product. For couples anxious to cure their infertility, the $1,400 per month price of Pergonal, an ovulating-enhancing hormone, is a good value if it results in a successful pregnancy. For the consumer who needs a contraceptive and not a fertility drug, the product won't even be considered, which means that price is not an issue in the purchase decision.[2]

Some consumers are price conscious, sensitive enough to price that they shop around for deals or price savings and often willingly give up some quality in order to get what they believe is a good

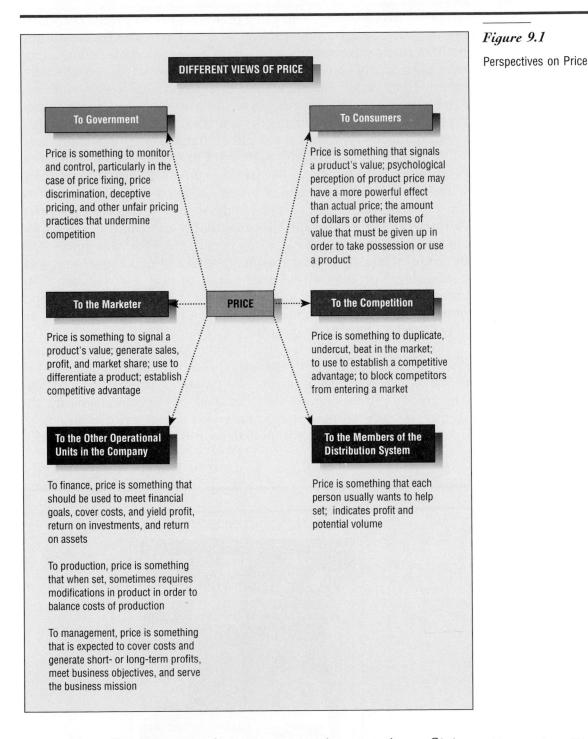

Figure 9.1

Perspectives on Price

DIFFERENT VIEWS OF PRICE

To Government

Price is something to monitor and control, particularly in the case of price fixing, price discrimination, deceptive pricing, and other unfair pricing practices that undermine competition

To Consumers

Price is something that signals a product's value; psychological perception of product price may have a more powerful effect than actual price; the amount of dollars or other items of value that must be given up in order to take possession or use a product

To the Marketer

Price is something to signal a product's value; generate sales, profit, and market share; use to differentiate a product; establish competitive advantage

PRICE

To the Competition

Price is something to duplicate, undercut, beat in the market; to use to establish a competitive advantage; to block competitors from entering a market

To the Other Operational Units in the Company

To finance, price is something that should be used to meet financial goals, cover costs, and yield profit, return on investments, and return on assets

To production, price is something that when set, sometimes requires modifications in product in order to balance costs of production

To management, price is something that is expected to cover costs and generate short- or long-term profits, meet business objectives, and serve the business mission

To the Members of the Distribution System

Price is something that each person usually wants to help set; indicates profit and potential volume

price. Not all consumers, however, are price conscious. **Status conscious** consumers use price as a surrogate for prestige or social prominence, flaunting the high price they are able to pay for a house, automobile, article of clothing, restaurant meal, or vacation as a measure of their social status. Status products are priced accordingly,

status conscious This describes consumers who use price a a surrogate for prestige or social prominence, flaunting the price they have paid as a measure of their social status.

to appeal to consumers who value premium-priced products and the high-quality image they project (see Photo 9.1). To complicate matters further, consumers who are price conscious for some products, particularly convenience products, may be status conscious for others (e.g., automobiles) and fashion conscious about clothing. Price perception and purchase behavior vary not only by consumer type but also by product category, purchase situation, and timing.

price comparison Evaluation of the value of a product according to its price in comparison to similar or even alternative products.

price range The span of prices that a consumer is willing or able to pay.

price floor The lowest price acceptable to a consumer.

price ceiling The highest price that a consumer is willing or able to pay.

Consumers typically make **price comparisons,** evaluating the value of a product according to its price in comparison to similar or even alternate products. Likewise, consumers typically view price within a **price range,** a span of prices anchored at the lower end by a **price floor,** the lowest acceptable price, and at the top by a **price ceiling,** the highest acceptable price that a consumer is willing or able to pay. Consumers have price floors because they use price as an indicator of quality. Most consumers are unwilling to take the risk of purchasing a product whose price is ridiculously low, because their perception is that such a cheap product gives poor value and probably is a waste of money; therefore, a price floor might also be judged to be a quality floor.

Price is an allocation device—it rations products among consumers in the marketplace and, when the price is right, clears the market to make way for new products. By paying a product's price, the consumer's purchasing power is reduced by that same amount. To all but the very wealthiest consumers for whom price is no object, limited resources force consumers to set purchase priorities. Usually

Photo 9.1

Some consumers have the income to purchase products at prestige prices.

Marketing on the Internet

How much are you willing to pay to get connected to the Internet? Faculty, students, staff, and others associated with a college or university can usually connect to the Internet free, as do government users. Internet connections for businesses and organizations and most personal use consumers are made through a commercial on-line service, such as America Online (AOL), CompuServe, or Prodigy.

Trying to figure out which on-line service to subscribe to can be hard for consumers because of the different pricing schedules. There is usually an initial fee to open an account, then various service plans are offered at different prices per service along with an assortment of prices per hour of connection time. Sometimes there is a flat fee for a set number of connection hours, then an additional price per hour is added on when the base hours are exceeded. Complicated pricing schedules make comparing the different services almost impossible. One thing seems certain though: when Microsoft enters the market with its planned Marvel on-line subscription service,

prices at the other on-line services will probably fall as they try to compete with Microsoft's pricing clout.

From a commercial perspective, there is also a price to be paid to operate a business site on the Internet's World Wide Web. A business can set up a home page on the World Wide Web for as little as several hundred dollars a month. To operate a site at the Electronic Newsstand costs about $17,500 annually. On CompuServe, rent in the Electronic Mall starts at about $20,000 per year. Many businesses will set up Web sites for others for a price. As more businesses and organizations hop on board the Internet, the prices currently charged for sites will probably come down. ■

J. Sandberg, "Microsoft to Unveil Its On-Line Service, Marvel, at Comdex; Rivals Update Their Offerings, Cut Prices in Preparation," *The Wall Street Journal,* November 8, 1994, p. A3; P. H. Lewis, "A Cyberspace Atlas: America Online," *The New York Times,* November 15, 1994, p. B10; P. Huber, "Madison Avenue Meets the Net," *Forbes* 154, no. 14 (December 19, 1994), p. 306; "Electronic Media: What You See Is What You Get," *INC.* 16, no. 12 (November 1994), p. 130.

this means that the **law of demand** holds in predicting that when prices rise, consumer demand usually falls; conversely, when prices fall, consumer demand usually rises (as shown in Figure 9.2).

law of demand The hypothesis that when prices rise, consumer demand falls, and vice versa.

Looking at Figure 9.2 more closely, we can see the law of demand in action, based on these calculations:

At P_1 of $300/unit, a total of 6,000 units are sold (Q_1). Demand is for 6,000 units.

At P_2 of $200/unit, a total of 19,000 units are sold (Q_2). Demand rises to 19,000 units.

Using the relationship Revenue = Price per unit × Units sold (Q),

$$R = P \times Q$$
$$R_1 = \$300 \times 6{,}000 = \$18{,}000$$
$$R_2 = \$200 \times 19{,}000 = \$38{,}000$$

Usually, but not always, price and demand move in opposite directions, with consumers purchasing greater quantities at a lower

Figure 9.2

A Typical Price–Quantity Relationship, as Shown in a Downward-Sloping Demand Curve

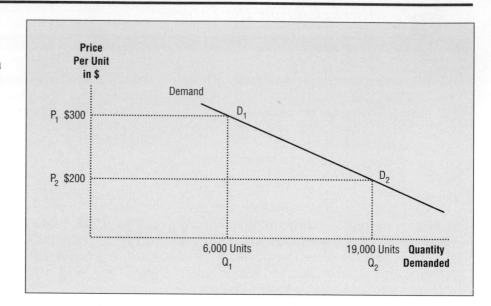

necessities Products that consumers consider indispensible, such as milk or gasoline.

inelastic demand Situation existing when a change in price does not affect demand, as for essential products.

price than at a higher price. In the case of **necessities,** products that consumers consider indispensable (e.g., milk, gasoline, and urgent medical treatment), a price rise doesn't dampen demand, at least not until a critical point is reached. These are **inelastic demand** products, meaning that a change in price *does not* result in a comparable percent change in demand; consumers are relatively insensitive to price changes for products they consider essential and must purchase. Consumers are more price sensitive to *elastic demand* products that are not essential and for which many substitutes or alternatives exist (see Photo 9.2). Demand is elastic for such products as high-fashion clothing, music cassette tapes, luxuries, and consumer electronics; hence, when a price changes consumer demand changes by a greater amount. For example, if price is dropped 5 percent, demand is expected to increase by more than that, and vice versa.

Price elasticity depends on how badly the consumer needs and wants the product, whether or not acceptable substitutes are readily available at acceptable prices, product supply, and the number of consumers in the market who are seeking the same product. If a consumer wants or needs the product badly enough, often he reluctantly pays the asked price. The concept of elasticity is often used to predict how consumers *might* react to a price change. Typically, elasticity changes as a product matures through its life cycle. In the later stages, when competition increases and substitute products enter the market, demand becomes more elastic as consumers can shop, seeking the best deal.

Photo 9.2

The Waldorf Astoria in New York City is a prime example of a luxury product with elastic demand.

Brand-loyal consumers are willing to pay more for national brands at what they consider a fair price because they are confident that national brands are better-quality products, more reliable and consistent. These consumers trade a higher price to eliminate the uncertainty and risk of trying products that are unknown to them. Alternatively, other consumers may value such nonprice factors as service, convenience, and location. Generally, consumers exhibit considerable variety in their perspectives on price and flexibility according to the purchase situation.

In the absence of direct indications of a product's quality, consumers often use price as a quality indicator. This means that when information about such things as reliability, durability, and safety are absent, price becomes a proxy for them. For the most part, consumers perceive that a higher price signals a product of higher quality; a lower price indicates lower quality. This is still an area of controversy, because the true nature of the price–quality relationship is not well defined.

Government

Government pays very close attention to product pricing, often aggressively regulating it, because price is an important factor in the efficient functioning of the marketplace. Price brings supply and demand into balance and clears the market of excess products (see Figure 9.3). Knowledge of how consumers respond to price generally provides some guidelines about how much of a product will sell at various prices. Generally, consumers purchase more at lower prices; thus, a lower price clears supply from a market. Consumers purchase

Figure 9.3

Price Can Act to Clear a
Market: Interaction of Supply
and Demand

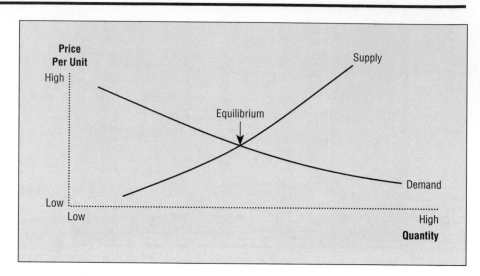

less at higher prices. However, producers generally prefer to make
fewer units to sell at a higher price. Equilibrium occurs where supply
equals demand—where the market's preferences and the producer's
preferences coincide. Price even has a public policy role through
government's regulation of price in monopolies, such as power utilities and mass transit systems, and through price guarantees to support agricultural commodities. Governments set tuitions for state-
supported public colleges and universities, and establish tax rates and
licensing fees.

The marketer's pricing authority is limited by government
through such legal controls as the Sherman Antitrust Act, the
Robinson–Patman Act, and the regulations set by the Federal Trade
Commission (FTC). Government's perspective is that business must
be scrutinized regularly to guard against anticompetitive and harmful pricing practices. Some pricing practices that concern government are identified in Figure 9.4.

Government sets guidelines for how price is advertised, which is
particularly relevant to advertising used in the illegal practice of bait
and switch. The FTC, state attorneys general, and Better Business
Bureaus handle advertised price complaints.

Governments play a role in maintaining the stability of their
national currencies internationally. A strong U.S. dollar relative to
other currencies means that prices for American products sold
abroad rise relative to local products, making them less competitive,
while products imported to the United States become cheaper. The
opposite occurs when the value of the American dollar falls and
American products sold abroad become a bargain. At the same time,
the prices of international products sold in the United States in-

Figure 9.4 Problem Areas in Pricing

ILLEGAL PRICING PRACTICES

Price Fixing

Illegal collective price setting or the use of price setting agreements by members of a channel of distribution or among retailers, wholesalers, and manufacturers. Forbidden under the Sherman Antitrust Act and the Federal Trade Commission Act.

Deceptive Pricing

Practices designed to deceive consumers, like bait-and-switch where the consumer is baited into a store with a low price and then pressured to buy at a higher price. Or the use of phony base list prices to fool a consumer into believing that a markdown price is a bargain. Illegal as governed by the Federal Trade Commission Act.

Predatory Pricing

Selling products below cost to drive competitors out of business. Illegal in 23 states that have unfair pricing practices laws. Complaints may be filed with the Federal Trade Commission (FTC) or the state attorney general. Most states require a minimum amount of markup over costs in order to maintain a floor on prices. These practices are denied under the Sherman and FTC Acts.

Discriminatory Pricing

The Robinson–Patman Act (1936) forbids manufacturers and wholesalers from selling products of like quality at different prices within a relatively short timespan to different members of a channel of distribution if such actions are unrelated to costs and negatively affect competition. This legislation was originally designed to protect small retailers from larger grocery stores that could force price deals because of their size.

crease, making them more expensive. For example, because the U.S. dollar weakened against the Japanese yen in a six-month period in 1993, prices for American products sold in Japan fell sharply (see Figure 9.5).[3] At any time, product prices vary significantly across the globe, reflecting exchange variations as well as the cost of doing business internationally.

The Marketer and the Business

The business perspective on price should be, but often isn't, that price is the key element of the marketing mix that influences revenue and profit directly and quickly. For most marketers, price is a dynamic element in the strategy to achieve the marketing objectives set for a product; for some, price is a passive response designed to maintain the status quo. Most businesses cannot survive for long if their products are priced below the cost of production, nor can they generate acceptable revenues if their products are priced too high for the market.

Businesses set different objectives for price. Lower prices may be used to establish volume leadership and increase sales and market share by getting more consumers to make purchases. Higher prices are used to establish quality leadership. Aggressive pricing is used as a competitive tool, to meet or beat the competition. Price objectives also include generating enough revenue to achieve stability and survival or to accomplish societal goals.

DROPS IN PRICES FOR U.S. PRODUCTS MARCH THROUGH SEPTEMBER 1993			
	PRICE		
	March	September	Price Change
Wine	$ 17.14	$ 14.28	− 16.7%
Sport shirt	92.48	84.76	− 8.3
100 grams of beef (3.5 ounces)	3.86	3.33	− 13.7
Apple PC	2,266.00	1,600.00	− 29.4*
* Prices fell in the product category, adding to the decline due to the weakened dollar.			

Source: W. Spindle, "Can't Get Enough of That Super-Yen," Reprinted from October 4, 1993, (p. 50) issue of *Business Week*, by special permission, copyright ©1993 by McGraw-Hill, Inc.

Marketers use price to differentiate their products from others. For example, Joy, often advertised as the most expensive perfume in the world, is sold in exclusive department stores like Saks Fifth Avenue. This sets Joy apart from perfumes discount priced in the neighborhood grocery store. Price signals consumers about a business's mission; for example, there's a difference between warehouse clubs that offer products in large quantities at discount prices and gourmet shops that sell select products at premium prices in small quantities.

Businesses use price to reward members of their channel of distribution (wholesalers, retailers, suppliers) or punish them. By offering price incentives, particularly in the form of discounts, producers can encourage the cooperation of the channel members who distribute their products. Often this means getting retailers to give the product better or more shelf space, stock up on the product, or move more product through the channel of distribution.

Price can be used as a weapon against the competition. Wal-Mart uses an aggressive price competition strategy and states that "the company bases its prices on how much competition it faces: More competition, lower prices; less competition, higher prices."[4] Wal-Mart has been accused of predatory pricing by pharmacies for selling products below cost.[5] American Airlines discovered that price cuts may prompt competitors to begin crying "foul" and pursue predatory pricing claims in the courts.[6]

Different operational areas of a business typically have different perspectives on price. Although not necessarily conflicting, different perspectives should be considered in the price setting process. For example, production people may provide insights on ways that production costs can be trimmed in order to avoid raising a product's price, yet maintain revenue expectations.

Ethical Concerns over Price   Marketers are faced with ethical dilemmas in many pricing situations. For example, because policymakers have not intervened aggressively in placing limits on pharmaceutical prices in the United States, drug prices have become an area of considerable anguish to many people. Between 1987 and 1992, prices for one heart drug increased 159.4 percent, an anxiety drug rose 139.2 percent, and an arthritis medicine jumped 126.4 percent.[7] Although the drug companies claim they need high prices to support costly research, others claim their prices are excessive.

Some consumer advocates claim that consumers are being deceived by marketers who use packaging to conceal price hikes; the volume is reduced but not the price or packaging. Marketers are also criticized for using prestige pricing (above the market average) for products whose value is not commensurate with its price.

Tweeter etc., a stereo and television retailer in New England, takes positive steps to act in the best interests of the consumer. In order to deliver on their low-price guarantee, their marketing staff tracks the competition in a 25-mile radius. If they find that the price of one of their products has been beaten, they enter the information in a computer that tracks the names of customers due a refund, and checks are automatically mailed out. Tweeter etc.'s staff monitors newspaper ads only and the item must be for $50 or more, yet they still make an admirable effort to deliver the promised low price.[8]

The Competition

To the competition, price is a weapon that can legally be used against others to gain market share, sales, and revenue; establish a competitive advantage; and ensure survival. Price is used as a tool to stimulate consumer demand for one's own products at the expense of the competition. Because price can be changed rapidly, it is a logical and effective tool to match or beat the competition. On the other hand, it is often difficult to gain information about the competition's pricing strategy, because so much of what passes as competitive pricing often is more like guesswork.

What the competition does with its prices can have an immediate and dramatic impact on your product's sales and revenue production. Therefore, it is vital that competitive pricing information be collected on a routine basis. One popular method for doing this at the retail level is to send comparison shoppers to stores to personally observe what prices are being charged. You can also scan the competition's advertising. Information about pricing can be found in trade journals, business publications, and U.S. government publications.

Marketing Application 9.1

Take the role of a comparison shopper. On your next trip to the grocery store, check out the prices on two-liter bottles of sodas. Compare the prices of national brands like Coca-Cola and Pepsi with store brands or a private label brand. When you have made your comparisons, write out a brief evaluation of the prices. Who is the price leader? How much of a difference in price is there between the competitors? How do the prices of the national brands and the store brands compare? Are any of the sodas priced much lower than the others? Bring your observations to class to compare. To help make this task easier, prepare a data matrix in advance with spaces to fill in the information you will be collecting. Pattern your data matrix after the example provided. ■

PRICE COMPARISON

Date conducted: _____   Store: _____
Product category: Two-liter carbonated sodas

SODA TYPE	PRICE	BRAND NAME
(cola, other)	(2-liter)	(National, store, other)

price war   Aggressive price cutting among competitors.

When aggressive price competition gets out of hand, it can escalate into a **price war,** in which competitive rivals intensify their price cutting to match and exceed one another, often benefiting the consumer (at least in the short term) while inflicting damage on one another and themselves through drastically reduced revenues. It is estimated that a Standard & Poor's 1000 company must increase its sales volume 12 percent in order to offset revenue losses from a 3 percent price cut.[9] Because consumers don't automatically increase their spending just because a product's price is cut, extreme and prolonged price competition can be harmful. For example, one tuna price war ran for over five years and finally forced a rollback to price levels from the previous decade, resulting in vastly reduced revenues for the warring companies.[10]

Few if any products are unique. Therefore, most products face many competitors at any one time. It is critical to identify this competition and assess their products and prices on a routine basis. A thorough evaluation of the competitive pricing situation may determine that price competition is a less desirable alternative than some form of nonprice competition.

nonprice competition   A rivalry that deemphasizes or ignores price differences and emphasizes nonprice factors.

Nonprice Competition   If price competition is not desirable or feasible, perhaps because the marketer fears getting involved in a price war, then the alternative is to engage in **nonprice competition.** Although it may be more difficult and take longer to differentiate products by something other than price, nonprice competition has the advantage of being harder for a competitor to match. Payless Cashways, Inc., found it couldn't compete against Home Depot, a "category killer" in tools with warehouse stores averaging 100,000 square feet of merchandise. Instead, Payless Cashways changed their focus to concentrate on professional builders who want high-quality tools for their work. Where price competition would have been a disaster, nonprice competition meant the development of a profitable market niche.[11]

Nonprice competition typically deemphasizes or ignores price differences between products and emphasizes such things as special or unique product features, extra-fast delivery, free delivery, an extended warranty, and no interest payments or even no payments for a predetermined time period. These nonprice factors differentiate a product from its competition and serve as the basis for promotions to inform consumers of nonprice merits (see Photo 9.3). An alternative to nonprice competition is to use a combination of price and nonprice competition that capitalizes on the advantages of both alternatives, to the detriment of the competition.

Channel of Distribution Members

A channel of distribution is made up of a producer at one end, a consumer at the other, and members in between who are responsible for getting a product from one end of the channel to the other. Each intermediary typically wants a say in the pricing of the products they handle, often adding a **markup** or price increase to a product's base price as it passes through their hands. Channel of distribution members rely on price to generate revenues and profit. Therefore,

markup Price increase.

Photo 9.3

In both of these examples, safety, rather than price, is the competitive focus.

their perspective on price is like that of the business and marketer, except that conflicts may arise as to the best way to price in order to ensure that everyone profits.

Some retailers are pushing price to the limit through single-price stores that offer everything at one price, often only one dollar.[12] These retailers purchase products opportunistically from manufacturers and other retailers at the end of the season, as close-out items, or as discontinued products. As a result, their product assortment often is highly varied, from silk ties to potato chips, and constantly changing. Both the price and the variety of the changing product assortment add to consumer excitement about this tribute to frugal shopping.

Check Your Understanding *9.1*	1. Describe some of the meanings commonly applied to *price*.
	2. Explain this statement: "Price is a matter of perspective."
	3. Discuss the various perspectives on price.

OTHER INFLUENCES ON PRICE

Objective 3   Discuss further influences on price.

A product's price cannot be set in a vacuum, free from influence. All of the different perspectives on price (consumers, the government, other operating units in the business, the competition, members of the channel of distribution) influence price. Indeed, price is a function of many factors, as illustrated in Figure 9.6.

cost plus pricing   Price setting that covers costs plus an extra increment to deliver profit.

Cost is a powerful influence on price. Price and costs are inextricably linked. In fact, most pricing is done on a cost coverage basis, often called **cost plus pricing**, where price is set to cover costs plus an extra increment to deliver profit. Typically, price changes as costs change. For example, if production costs rise, the additional costs of production are passed along to consumers as price increases, unless there are compelling reasons not to raise price (perhaps cutthroat competition). This holds whether the increased costs are externally related (perhaps through a government-mandated rise in the gasoline tax) or internally related (as in the case of salesperson wage hikes). Many of these costs are part of the uncontrollable environment businesses face.

There are alternatives to price increases to offset higher costs. One is to attempt to reduce other associated costs, perhaps in the area of promotions, by reducing or shifting advertising expenditures. Another response is to change the product itself, offering fewer options or services to offset cost increases. Honda wants to keep the price of its newly redesigned Accord down, so it has drastically reduced the cost of producing the car, even though many costs had risen since the last remodeling.[13]

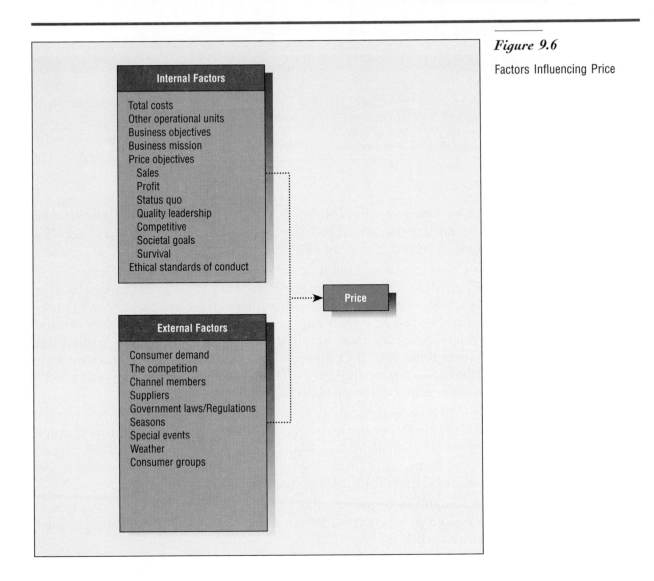

Figure 9.6

Factors Influencing Price

Other influences on price also occur on a regular basis. Some of the most important are:

• *The economy:* The health of the economy affects price decisions as well as demand and supply. Price influences the economy as acceptable prices clear the market. Products acceptably priced are more likely to be purchased, which requires more products to be made to replace them. Price moderates supply and demand, but is also influenced by such economic factors as inflation (rising prices), recession (stagnant economic growth), and shortages caused by nature or politics, as in the oil shortages instigated by the Organization of Petroleum Exporting Countries (OPEC).

• *Seasons:* In many product categories, particularly clothing, the change of seasons influences product price. In the chapter-opening

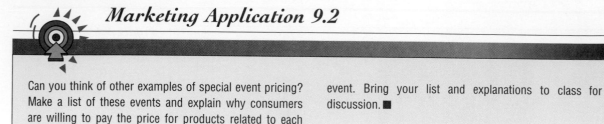

Marketing Application 9.2

Can you think of other examples of special event pricing? Make a list of these events and explain why consumers are willing to pay the price for products related to each event. Bring your list and explanations to class for discussion. ■

story, the consumer is faced with a decision to buy clothing in advance of the season at full price or, instead, pay a reduced price for end-of-season clearance clothing.

• *Special events:* Holidays and special events can influence price. The price of Halloween candy before the holiday is higher than the discounted price after the holiday when the same candy can often be purchased at less than half price. Roses are priced higher around Valentine's Day than at other times. Hotels in cities hosting the Super Bowl, World Cup soccer matches, or Olympic Games increase their rates during the events. This illustrates the greater value placed on a product when demand is high and supply is low.

• *Nature:* Nature can influence price. Hurricane Andrew in the fall of 1992 influenced prices for building supplies in the devastated areas. The great Midwestern flood in the summer of 1993 caused some commodity prices to rise. The Los Angeles earthquake of 1994 affected prices for building materials, housing, and insurance.

• *Suppliers:* Suppliers affect production costs and the list price of finished products through the pricing of raw materials and supplies provided to producers.

Check Your Understanding 9.2

Describe the many factors that influence price.

MAKING PRICING DECISIONS

Objective 4   Describe the four decisions made during pricing.

How are prices set? Some marketers will tell you that they set the prices for their products according to what the market leader does, to cover costs, and to provide a desired profit. Others state that they price "by the seat of their pants," perhaps using this year's prices with a markup for next year, without giving much thought to what they want price to accomplish for their business.

Given the significance of price in generating revenues and profit, more marketers are recognizing that pricing must be a systematic, organized process with price objectives that complement the business's objectives. A recent survey of 172 chief executive officers (CEOs), 75 percent of whom represented businesses with sales less than $20 million annually, found that 52 percent of the respondents priced their most recent new product to cover costs and make a fair profit, 50 percent charged what the market would bear, 37 percent matched their competitors' prices, 22 percent priced equal to related product prices, and 9 percent used best guesstimate pricing.[14] Multiple responses account for a total greater than 100 percent.

The pricing process often includes marketers and others from operational areas directly involved with the product, as well as representatives from the distribution system. The entire array of factors that influence price must be considered, including consumer demand, product life cycle stage, production costs, government regulations, state of the economy, and the competition's pricing of identical, similar, or alternative products. Whether pricing is undertaken by top management or a pricing team of middle-level managers, industrial salespeople in the field, or the owner-operator of a small business, the process typically proceeds more or less formally through a series of decisions. The steps in the pricing decision process are: set objectives, establish a pricing strategy, select pricing tactics, and make adjustments. These are discussed in the following sections.

Information Used in the Pricing Process

Information from internal and external sources must be gathered and evaluated throughout the pricing process and the product's life. Although large businesses routinely scan their environments for the kind of information needed in making sound pricing decisions, smaller businesses are at a disadvantage when doing so because they often lack needed resources to mount a regular, comprehensive information collection effort. However, even the smallest business can obtain valuable information from its salespeople, suppliers, and customers about demand for its products, as well as information about the competition. (See Figure 9.7.) Industry data are available in trade journals, government publications, and the general business press. Commonly used information sources are *internal business documents* (e.g., salespeople reports, previous pricing policies) and *external reports* on the economy, competition, consumers, and industry (e.g., from the U.S. Department of Commerce, trade journals, business publications, industry associations, and distributor's reports).

Figure 9.7

Prices are determined after making decisions in four areas.

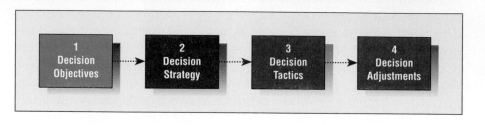

Regular monitoring is needed after a price has been set and the product offered, particularly to determine whether or not price objectives are being met and if price adjustments should be made. Some types of information used in price evaluation include *sales data* to indicate consumer acceptance/rejection of the product at various times; *consumer reactions* to the price, often obtained through survey research, focus groups, and other types of customer contacts related to measures of consumer demand; *cost data* to monitor the costs of production and marketing over the long run; *economic data* to evaluate changes in the economy, particularly recession, inflation, or shortages that may require price responses; *data on the competition,* tracking price adjustments on their products that may need a price response from you; and *legal/regulatory changes* on the local, state, and/or national levels that affect price.

Decision 1: Objectives

It is essential to consider what is expected of price before one can be set for a product or product line. In order to be most effective, pricing decisions must be goal directed, designed to achieve a particular end, and not be arbitrary or undefined. A business may adopt multiple objectives for price; the key is to take the time to evaluate what it is that you want price to do for your business. Because of the broad nature of the price decision and its relationship to the business mission, the price decision is often made by top management in large businesses and by the owner-operator in smaller businesses. Although there are a number of pricing objectives on which a business may decide, the principal ones are related to *covering costs, maximizing profit,* and *meeting or beating the competition.*

Decision 2: Strategy

Based on the objective(s) set for price, as well as an evaluation of available information, the next step is to decide on a price strategy. Strategy is a broad decision about the type of pricing to use to achieve the objectives set for price, and it reflects whether you are pricing a new product, a single product, or an entire line of products.

For a *new product* entering the market for the first time, two broad strategies with opposing philosophies are frequently used. One is **skimming pricing,** which follows the pricing philosophy of attempting to skim the cream off the market. A high price is charged for a unique or very desirable product with the knowledge that it will attract a profitably sized group of innovators, fashion leaders, or image-conscious consumers who are highly motivated to purchase it. The price often is reduced as soon as competition heats up. When pricing unique products, the challenge is to set a price high enough to skim, yet not so high that it stifles demand.

The second broad strategy—**penetration pricing**—is the philosophical opposite of skimming. This strategy sets price low in order to quickly penetrate the market and attract as many consumers as possible to build volume. A low price may also serve as a barrier to competition, because later entrants to the market may not have the ability to steal market share unless they lowball (seriously undercut) price or offer extremely desirable product advantages. AT&T used a penetration pricing strategy with its Universal card by initially offering the card at no annual fee for life. In under two years, over 11 million consumers signed up for the card, 5.8 million in the first year alone. With a higher quality customer base than the other credit cards, its profitability seems assured.[15]

Strategies for *existing products* focus on price level and form. A very broad decision concerns **price level** strategy, deciding where price will be set in relation to similar products on the market. Products can be priced *at* market level (comparable to the average competitive price); *above* the market (at the high end, with prestige or premium pricing); and *below* market (discount). Above-market pricing is used for products like designer clothing. Clothes priced at the market level are found on the racks in full-service department stores. Clothing priced below market level is found at discounters like Kmart and stores that sell seconds, overruns, or season remainders. Likewise, it must be determined if the price strategy form will be flexible or stable. A **flexible pricing** strategy changes price as factors in the environment (both internal and external) change. A **stable pricing** strategy resists changes, maintains a price status quo, and tries to avoid costly price wars.

Often, a product will be offered in a number of different versions designed to appeal to different market segments. This is called *product line pricing.* For example, Toyota has a car line that includes Paseo, Tercel, Corolla, Celica, Camry, and Avalon (see Photo 9.4). Each is different from the other and is priced and targeted to specific markets. **Price lining** means establishing different price points for the different products in a line. Each price is targeted to

skimming pricing Setting the price high for a unique or very desirable product to attract a selective segment of the market; when competition increases, the price is reduced.

penetration pricing Setting a low price to quickly penetrate the market, attract consumers, and build volume.

price level The price set in relation to similar products on the market.

flexible pricing Changing price according to changes in the environment.

stable pricing Strategy for maintaining price, regardless of changes in the environment.

price lining Setting different prices for the different products in a line.

Photo 9.4

The Toyota line of cars and trucks demonstrates price lining.

Our Company Line On Quality.

appeal to different market segments. Although most consumers cannot afford an Avalon, far more *can* afford a much lower-priced Paseo!

Decision 3: Tactics

As you learned in an earlier chapter, once a strategy is developed, specific tactics must be devised to serve it. Likewise, price tactics must serve the strategy (and objectives) set for price. This requires decisions that place a base price on a product. There are three types of tactics commonly used in pricing, based respectively on cost coverage, the competition's price, and consumer demand.

Cost coverage is commonly called *cost plus pricing.* This is an internally directed pricing tactic in that it gives primacy to recovering the costs of production plus an extra amount for profit. To effectively use cost plus pricing, it is essential to be able to determine all of the costs associated with a product in order to generate a profit. Remember,

$$Profit = Total \ Revenue - Total \ Cost$$

Costs usually considered are:

Total costs: All of the fixed and variable costs linked directly to the product.

$$TC = FC + VC$$

Fixed costs: All of the costs that remain unchanged, regardless of the number of units produced. Included are such things as insurance, rent, equipment, professionals' salaries, and so on.

Variable costs: All of the costs that change as the number of units produced changes. If it costs $5.00 to produce 1 unit, then producing 100 units costs $500 ($5.00 × 100 = $500); the variable cost of producing 1,000 units is $5,000 because $5.00 × 1,000 = $5,000.

Once total costs are calculated, a price is determined by identifying a profit target. For example, if the total cost is $7.00 per unit and the business establishes a profit target of $1.25 per unit, then the price per unit is set as

$$\text{Total cost (TC)} = \$7.00/\text{unit}$$
$$\text{Profit target} = \$1.25/\text{unit}$$
$$\text{Price per unit} = \$7.00 + \$1.25 = \$8.25$$
$$\text{List (base) price} = \$8.25$$

Resellers also price products to cover their costs and earn a profit. They take the producer's list price, in the above example $8.25, and add a markup. Many industries have standard markups: 1 percent, 5 percent, or even 100 percent. The retail selling price is calculated

$$\text{Retail selling price} = \text{List price} \times \text{Percent markup}$$

In order to begin making a profit, the business must pass beyond its **break-even point (BEP)** for the product, the point at which total revenue (TR) equals total costs (TC) at a particular price per unit. The break-even concept is shown in Figure 9.8. Beyond the point where TR = TC, profit is earned, because now only variable costs must be taken out of revenues. Unfortunately, there is no guarantee that the break-even point can be reached, let alone exceeded. The job of marketing is to stimulate demand so that the break-even point can be passed. However, break-even analysis can only indicate the point at which profits can be expected, if enough units are sold.

Competition-based pricing looks primarily at external forces for direction in setting price. This is risky, because there is no guarantee that the price charged by the competition or industry will cover your costs and return an acceptable profit. However, some businesses still use competition-based pricing through such tactics as leader pricing and customary pricing.

break-even point (BEP) The point at which total revenue equals total costs at a particular price per unit.

Figure 9.8

Break-Even Analysis

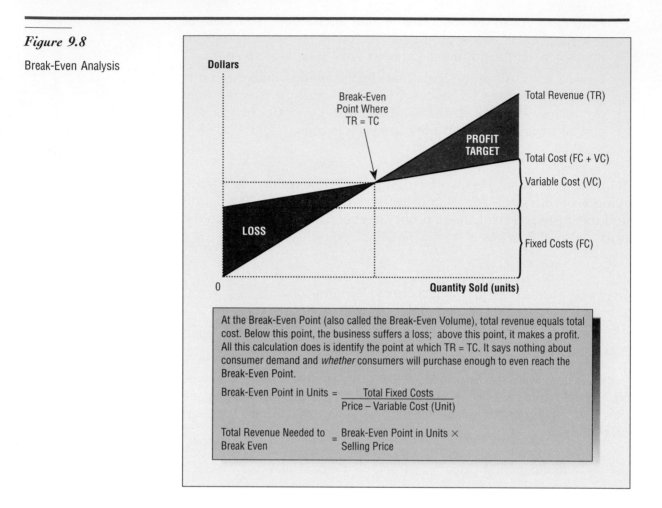

Dollars

Break-Even
Point Where
TR = TC

**PROFIT
TARGET**

Total Revenue (TR)

Total Cost (FC + VC)

Variable Cost (VC)

LOSS

Fixed Costs (FC)

0   **Quantity Sold (units)**

At the Break-Even Point (also called the Break-Even Volume), total revenue equals total cost. Below this point, the business suffers a loss; above this point, it makes a profit. All this calculation does is identify the point at which TR = TC. It says nothing about consumer demand and *whether* consumers will purchase enough to even reach the Break-Even Point.

$$\text{Break-Even Point in Units} = \frac{\text{Total Fixed Costs}}{\text{Price} - \text{Variable Cost (Unit)}}$$

$$\begin{array}{l}\text{Total Revenue Needed to} \\ \text{Break Even}\end{array} = \begin{array}{l}\text{Break-Even Point in Units} \times \\ \text{Selling Price}\end{array}$$

Leader pricing means following a price leader, typically a large, powerful competitor who dominates a market. If there is a mutual agreement on price it can be interpreted as price fixing, which is illegal. *Customary pricing* requires adhering to prices that consumers expect for similar products, typically over a long period of time; for example, soda from a vending machine has a customary price.

Demand-based pricing requires estimating consumer demand for different levels of price. Although **marginal pricing** is not used extensively because it requires sophisticated estimating procedures, it is a form of demand-based pricing that requires estimating consumer demand for a product and then identifying the profit-maximizing price. Profit is maximized when the marginal cost of production equals the marginal revenue. Demand can be estimated by surveying consumer intentions and using statistical analyses of previous sales data.

marginal pricing Demand-based pricing estimating consumer demand for a product, then identifying the profit-maximizing price.

Marketing Application 9.3

Have you seen signs at checkout counters or theater ticket windows that say "10% Discount for Senior Citizens 65 years or Older"? Age is a consumer segmentation variable often used as a base for a price discount. What kinds of discounts and preferential pricing are offered to infants, preteens, or college-age students? Try to identify as many age-related examples of preferential pricing as possible. Are these examples fair? How should price fairness be judged? Bring your list to class for discussion. ∎

Decision 4: Adjustments

Considering all the factors that influence price, it is no wonder that even after a price is set it often has to be changed to reflect a change in costs of production, the competition's price, the economy, consumer confidence, and demand, to induce channel members to move the product. Some frequently made adjustments are:

- *Discounts* awarded for large-quantity purchases, as when the buyer pays in cash or before the bill's due date, for preseason advance purchases, or to encourage the trade (channel members) to stock up or sell a greater volume. For example, when Eastman Kodak offers special discounts, often 10 percent to 20 percent, to dealers buying 10,000 or more rolls of film per month.[16]

- *Allowances* reduce the list price as an incentive. These include promotional allowances when a producer helps pay a retailer for local advertising, and automobile trade-in allowances given for trading in an old car for a new one. Rebates are often offered on automobiles in order to add value to the product and reduce the price.

- *Transportation terms* are often needed in order to spell out who pays to transport products from seller to buyer. Sometimes it is a uniform delivered price where the seller pays the freight. In zone pricing, a transportation charge is added to the price according to the location of the delivery zone. F-O-B pricing means free on board and indicates where the buyer is to pick up the product—at that point, the buyer pays the freight.

- *Preferential pricing* is used in many cases to legally discriminate between buyers. Examples include the use of peak use pricing on public transportation systems like the Washington, D.C., Metro subway, where fares are higher during rush hours and lower at other times to try to regulate usage. Seats at sports events and the theater often are priced by nearness to the action. Senior citizens receive age-related discounts on purchases, transportation, and entertainment tickets.

- *Product life cycle* affects price in that adjustments must often be made as the product begins to lose market share. In order to try to maintain, if not recapture, sales, price may be dropped.

- *Markdowns* are made on many products at the end of a season for a variety of reasons: to dispose of seasonal products, because of damage, or to move products in order to make way for new ones (sometimes the new ones are to be offered at a higher price). Markdowns also build store traffic and raise cash.

Check Your Understanding **9.3**	Describe the steps in making a price decision.

PRICING PRACTICES

Objective 5 Discuss popular pricing practices.

Most consumers consider price within a range, from the highest price they are willing to pay for a product to the lowest, below which the product's quality becomes suspect. Likewise, the marketer typically sets prices within a range, hopefully one that is congruent with the consumer's. You can relate the price range to a traffic signal. A red light shines "Stop" above the ceiling and below the floor, whereas the green light shines "Go" for the **acceptable prices** that fall within the price range, bounded by the ceiling at the top and the floor at the bottom.

acceptable price A price between the price ceiling and the price floor.

For the marketer, the ceiling is determined by demand in the marketplace. If prices rise above the ceiling, exceeding the acceptable range, then demand will drop or disappear entirely. For the bottom, however, the marketer's price floor is unlike the consumer's—it is established by the costs incurred in bringing the product to market. Obviously, a business can survive for only a limited period of time without covering its costs before it risks bankruptcy. Therefore, most prices fall within an acceptable range, clearing the floor but not hitting the ceiling.

Acceptable price ranges can change, along with their ceilings and floors. Take the case in which a business's production unit discovers a way to cut costs in making a product. This drops the cost floor so that price can be lowered, and the quantity sold and revenue will increase if the law of demand holds. Alternatively, the competition may start a price war that undercuts your product's price; this lowers your product's price ceiling and the range.

Marketing Application 9.4

When you go grocery shopping this week or read the grocery ads in your local paper, look for the loss leaders. What is being offered? Are several stores offering the same products? Do you think this might have something to do with their receiving favorable prices from the wholesalers or manufacturers that they are passing along to consumers? Bring your findings to class for discussion. ■

A price range can change as a function of the product's stage in the product life cycle, with a change in seasons (such as the summer clothing clearance sale in the chapter-opening story), or as a result of changes in the economy, inflation, or recession. In any case, the price of a product, whether it is a good or a service, must be high enough to cover costs yet low enough so that consumers will buy products and return enough profit for the business to survive and prosper.

A variety of pricing practices are shown in Figure 9.9.

• *Odd/even:* Used in the belief that consumers respond more favorably to a price just below an even number. For example, $5.95 is a price viewed more favorably than $6.00; $599 is a better price than $600. Common endings are 9, 5, 3, and 8.

• *Loss leader:* In order to build store traffic, grocery stores often will price some items at very low prices, often with quantity restrictions; for example, two-liter national brand colas priced at 59 cents each, limit two. These loss leaders represent a profit loss for the store, yet stores willingly take the loss because traffic is increased along with sales, because most consumers can rarely enter a grocery and leave with only the loss leader products. Products often used as loss leaders include soda, laundry detergents, paper towels, and milk (see Photo 9.5). Some states prohibit loss leader pricing because it places small retailers at a price disadvantage with large superstores.

• *Bundled:* Bundles are an entire package of items sold together to the consumer at one price. For example, a weekend getaway at a local hotel can be bundled with a continental breakfast; a season ticket to the ballet can be bundled with a preperformance dinner.

• *Prestige pricing:* This is above-market pricing used for luxury products and products whose image is associated with quality (see Photo 9.6).

Other popular pricing practices are shown in Figure 9.9.

Figure 9.9   A Creative Pricing Primer

CREATIVE PRICING PRIMER			
Pricing Approach	How It Works	Example	How Might It Apply to Your Business?
1. Time-period pricing	Adjust price up or down during specific times to spur or acknowledge changes in demand.	Off-season travel fares (to build demand); peak-period fees on bank ATMs (to shift demand).	
2. Trial pricing	Make it easy and lower the risk for a customer to try out what you sell.	Three-month health-club starter memberships; low, nonrefundable "preview fees" on training videos.	
3. Account-system pricing	Structure price to make it more salable within a business's buying systems.	Bill in phases so no single invoice exceeds an authorization threshold; classify elements so pieces get charged to other line items.	
4. Value-added price packages	Include free "value-added" services to appeal to bargain shoppers without lowering price.	A magazine's offering advertisers free merchandising tie-ins when they buy ad space at rate-card prices.	
5. Pay-one-price	Unlimited use or unlimited amount of a service or product for one set fee.	Amusement parks; office copier contracts; salad bars.	
6. Constant promotional pricing	Although a "regular" price exists, no one ever pays it.	Consumer-electronics retailers' always matching "lowest price" in town; always offering one pizza free when customer buys one at regular price.	
7. Price = performance	Amount customers pay is determined by the performance or value they receive.	Money managers' being paid profits; offering a career-transition guide for $80 and allowing buyers to ask for *any* amount refunded after use.	
8. Change the standard	Rather than adjust price, adjust the standard to make your price seem different (and better).	A magazine clearinghouse's selling a $20 subscription for "four payments of only $4.99."	

Source: M. D. Mondello, "Naming Your Price," *INC.* 14, p. 82. Reprinted with permission of *INC.* Magazine, July 1992. Copyright 1992 by Goldhirsch Group, Inc., 38 Commercial Wharf, Boston, MA 02110.

PRICE: ART OR SCIENCE?

Objective 6   Decide if price is an art or a science.

Some businesspeople think that pricing is an art, a talent that is developed through years of experience and a keen sense of what the market will tolerate. There is another school of thought that believes pricing should be a science, reflecting the application of mathematical models, statistical analysis, and computer technology. What is price then—art or science? In reality, it is both. Although the science

Figure 9.9 A Creative Pricing Primer *(continued)*

CREATIVE PRICING PRIMER			
Pricing Approach	**How It Works**	**Example**	**How Might It Apply to Your Business?**
9. Shift costs to your customer	Pass on ancillary costs directly to your customer and do not include those costs in your price.	A consulting firm's charging a fee and then rebilling all mail, phone, and travel costs directly to client.	
10. Variable pricing tied to a creative variable	Set up a "price per" pricing schedule tied to a related variable.	Children's haircuts at 10¢ per inch of the child's height; marina space billed at $25 per foot for a boat.	
11. Different names for different price segments	Sell essentially the same product, under different names, to appeal to different price segments.	Separate model numbers or variations of the same TV for discounters, department stores, and electronics stores.	
12. Captive pricing	Lock in your customer by selling the system cheap and then profit by selling high-margin consumables.	The classic example: selling razors at cost, with all the margin made on razor blade sales.	
13. Product-line pricing	Establish a range of price points within your line. Structure the prices to encourage customers to buy your highest-profit product or service.	Luxury car lines (high-end models enhance prestige of entire line but are priced to encourage sale of more profitable low-end models).	
14. Differential pricing	Charge each customer or each customer segment what each will pay.	In new-car sales, a deal for every buyer; Colorado lift tickets sold locally at a discount at full price for fly-ins.	
15. Quality discount	Set up a standard pricing practice, which can be done several ways.	Per-unit discount on *all* units, as with article reprints; discounts only on the units above a certain level, as with record clubs.	
16. Fixed, then variable	Institute a "just-to-get-started" charge, followed by a variable charge.	Taxi fares; phone services tied to usage.	
17. "Don't break that price point!"	Price just below important thresholds for the buyer to give a perception of lower price.	Charging $499 for a suit; $195,000 instead of $200,00 for a design project.	

Note: Once you've been creative, make sure you're covered. The most important aspect of any pricing approach is that it is legal and ethical. Check with counsel.

of pricing is evolving, the art of pricing will never die out. Even the most ardent science advocate will admit that information from salespeople, marketing managers, customer service representatives, and others who deal directly with consumers will always be needed for input into the mathematical models and statistical programs used to scientifically set prices.

Photo 9.5

Coupons may be used to advertise loss leaders.

Photo 9.6

Prestige pricing for luxury products is one strategy used to attract consumers who feel pride in being able to afford to spend more than most other people.

Career Watch

George Perrin is the chief executive of Paging Network, a small company located in Plano, Texas, that has big market clout. It is ranked the number one company in the paging industry and has outflanked much larger companies like Southwestern Bell. PageNet, as the company is called, is George Perrin's brainchild. He began the company in 1981 when he realized that there were opportunities to be had in the paging industry. Perrin's marketing plan called for aggressive price competition, which could be maintained because of low-cost production. PageNet's production costs are the lowest in the industry. Perrin's goal is a PageNet network that covers 75 percent of the U.S. population. Market penetration is his target; he sells his low-cost pagers through Kmart, Wal-Mart, and Home Depot. Perrin brought his expertise to this company from a previous post as president of a paging company that was a subsidiary of Communications Industries, Inc. Through pricing, PageNet has grown to be twice the size of its nearest competitor and it is still growing fast. ■

G. Morgenson, "A Pager in Every Pocket?" *Forbes* 150, no. 14 (December 21, 1992), pp. 210–11, 14; D. Foust and M. Lewyn, "These Airways Are Hotter Than Anyone Thought," *Business Week* August 15, 1994, p. 34;

L. Silberg, "PageNet Sets Nationwide Service," *HFD—The Weekly Home Furnishings Newspaper* 67, no. 46 (November 15, 1993), p. 104.

Photo 9.7

George Perrin, PageNet's chief executive, practices what he preaches.

PRICE AND THE OTHER MARKETING MIX VARIABLES

As the discussion in this chapter has indicated, price is a critical marketing mix variable and the only one that directly generates revenue. However, price cannot be considered apart from the other marketing mix variables because of their interdependence. For example, if consumers don't believe a *product* is worth its price, that it doesn't deliver good value, then the quantity sold will not meet expectations and revenue will be disappointing; if a product is not *distributed* efficiently and is rarely on the retailer's shelves when the consumer wants it, then sales volume and revenue will fall; and if *promotion* is not effective in informing consumers about a product, then the same volume and revenue outcomes may be expected. Some other ways in which the product, place/distribution, and promotion variables interact with price are shown in Figure 9.10.

Objective 7 Discuss the interrelationship among price and the other marketing mix variables (product, place, and promotion).

Figure 9.10 Some Examples of the Interactions of Price with the Other Marketing Mix Variables

PRODUCT	PLACE	PROMOTION
Value The consumer must perceive that the product gives good value for its price, and that it is worth the price or the price will not be paid.	**Store Format** Price is a signal to consumers informing them about store format, from low prices for products offered at Wal-Mart, to very high prices for image and status products offered at Saks Fifth Avenue.	**Advertising** While advertising adds to costs that are passed through to consumers in higher product prices, advertising also helps keep prices in line by informing consumers about competitive prices.
Product Life Cycle (PLC) Price typically changes over the PLC, for example, price is often higher at introduction, then it is lowered as competition intensifies and "me-too" versions appear on the market. In order to increase sales volume in the maturity stage, price is often lowered.	**Channel Members** For members of the channel of distribution, price can be a source of friction as members seek to mark up price to gain higher revenue or try to exert their power over other channel members.	**Sales Force** The industrial sales force generally has considerably more flexibility in changing price as they negotiate with organization buyers. This is less true in most retail sales.
Model Changes Different versions of the same product often have different prices. The base list price on a car with few options is going to be much lower than the price for a car that is filled with options, such as power brakes, air bags, a sunroof, and the like.		

Check Your Understanding 9.4

1. Discuss commonly used pricing practices.
2. Is price art or science?
3. Describe the interrelationship of price and the other marketing mix variables.

Review of Chapter Objectives

1. *Explain how different perspectives on price influence the pricing process.* Price is called by many different names, but its function remains the same as it generates revenues for the business and sets the terms of trade for the consumer. Price has grown in importance to marketers because of the rising costs of technology, competitive pressures, and lingering consumer lack of confidence in the economy. There are many different perspectives on price that the marketer must consider. In addition to the marketer's own view of price in its revenue-generation role, there is the perspective of consumers, government, others in the marketer's busi-

ness, the competition, and members of the channel of distribution. Influences on price include those whose perspectives were just mentioned, as well as the economy, seasons, special events, suppliers, and the weather.

2. *Describe how pricing decisions are made.* Information must be collected and evaluated before price is set and throughout the period that the product is offered. Information comes from internal sources such as salesperson reports and business documents, and from external sources such as government reports, trade journals, and reports from distributors. Steps in the pricing decision

process are set objectives, determine strategy, devise tactics, and make adjustments.

3. *Discuss further influences on price.* Price, of course, falls under many influences, both internal and external. Among these influences are total costs, business objectives and missions, sales, profit, and competitive factors, as well as consumer demand and outside regulation of commerce.

4. *Describe the four decisions made in pricing.* Pricing is based on determining a business's objectives, its overall strategy, the specific tactics it will use to carry out a strategy, and the ability to plan for adjustments to reflect changes in internal and external costs.

5. *Discuss popular pricing practices.* Pricing practices include setting price within an acceptable range for both the business and the consumers, as well as a variety of pricing customs like odd/even pricing, bundling, and prestige pricing.

6. *Decide if price is an art or a science.* Good pricing requires using the best scientific methods possible, along with good judgment and experience.

7. *Discuss the interrelationship among price and the other marketing mix variables (product, place, and promotion).* The marketing mix variables work together like a team; each depends on the others to be successful. Price contributes many things to the mix relationship. It is a signal to consumers, as well as the mechanism by which revenues are achieved and profit attained.

Key Terms

After studying Chapter 9, you should be able to define each of the following key terms and use them in describing marketing activities.

Barter, page 268
Consumer Confidence, page 269
Status Conscious, page 271
Price Comparison, page 272
Price Range, page 272
Price Floor, page 272
Price Ceiling, page 272
Law of Demand, page 273
Necessities, page 274
Inelastic Demand, page 274

Price War, page 280
Nonprice Competition, page 280
Markup, page 281
Cost Plus Pricing, page 282
Skimming Pricing, page 287
Penetration Pricing, page 287
Price Level, page 287
Flexible Pricing, page 287
Stable Pricing, page 287
Price Lining, page 287
Break-Even Point (BEP), page 289
Marginal Price, page 290
Acceptable Price, page 292

Discussion Questions

1. Why is it so difficult for marketers to arrive at the *right* price for a product?

2. Following are some of the names used for price—explain what the consumer gets for each price: rent, tuition, toll, charitable donation.

3. Discuss some of the reasons for the increasing importance of price to marketers and consumers.

4. What is consumer confidence? Why should marketers be concerned when consumers lack confidence?

5. Give an example of the purchase behavior of each of the following consumers: status conscious, price conscious, service conscious.

6. In your own words, explain the relationship between price and quantity sold as expressed in the law of demand.

7. Milk, gasoline, and urgent medical treatment are examples of inelastic products. What does this mean?

8. Why is the government concerned about the prices charged for products? *Should* the government be concerned about prices? What do you think?

9. What is a price war? Is it good for consumers?

10. Explain this statement: "Price and costs are inextricably linked."

11. What happens if the marketer's price range for a product and the consumer's range of acceptable prices are not similar?

What Do You Think?

FlashBake, a revolutionary new oven made by Quadlux, Inc., is turning heads in the restaurant industry. This oven cooks using visible light and infrared radiation, and 10 quartz-halogen lamps. It has a microwave's speed, yet food cooked in it tastes as good or better than food cooked in a conventional oven. Potentially it can increase production for pizzas and other foods from five- to tenfold while dropping cooking time substantially. Shrimp cook to perfection in 75 seconds; a steak takes 105 seconds; and a chicken breast is done in two minutes. The two models in production are list priced at $4,999 and $7,750, whereas regular restaurant ovens range from $2,500 to $7,500. FlashBake plans a home version in several years with an introductory list price of $1,000. Will consumers pay $1,000 for a home version of the FlashBake? Who is most likely to buy it? What do you think?

Sources: M. J. Ybarra, "Costly New Oven Challenges Microwave," *The Wall Street Journal*, July 13, 1993, pp. B1, 6; "Made to Order: Custom Blower Meets High-Tech Cooking Needs," *Appliance Manufacturer* 42, no. 6 (June 1994), pp. 48–49.

Photo 9.8

The Quadlux FlashBake 3000—are home consumers ready yet?

Mini-Case 9.1

The Price You See Is the Price You Pay—No Haggling

Dickering over the price of a new car is a high-risk, high-stress undertaking for most consumers. Few are skilled at negotiating price deals. There are two approaches to no-haggling car shopping. One involves going to a car dealer who operates under the no-dicker sticker plan; this includes General Motor's Saturn automobile dealers, who took the initiative and were the first to adopt a no-negotiating price strategy. The other approach is to pay a service to collect bids from several car dealers on the exact make and model you want. The service compiles a list of dealers and their prices for the car; then the consumer telephones the car dealers to fine-tune the offers. The use of "dial-a-deal shopping services" is growing, as consumers seek alternatives to the older and more risky pricing method.

While consumers and dealers may like no-haggling pricing, the U.S. Department of Justice may not. The Department is investi-gating this pricing strategy on the grounds that it may be anticonsumer and in violation of the Sherman Antitrust Act.

Case Questions

1. Do you think that a no-negotiating pricing policy will appeal to *all* consumers? What types of consumers might not like this price strategy?

2. What is the risk for the car dealer who adopts the no-haggling pricing strategy?

3. Do you think no-negotiating pricing is anticonsumer?

Sources: D. Lavin and K. Miller, "Goodbye to Haggling: Savvy Consumers Are Buying Their Cars Like Refrigerators," *The Wall Street Journal,* August 20, 1993, pp. B1, 3; V. Anderson, "The No-Dicker Car Sticker," *Lexington Herald-Leader,* May 24, 1992, p. E1; "No-Dicker Car Dealers Gaining Popularity," *Marketing News* 26, no. 20 (September 18, 1992), p. 19; K. M. Lundegaard, "Car Dealers Defend Pricing Strategy as Pro-Consumer," *Washington Business Journal* 13, no. 22 (October 14, 1994), pp. 17–18; W. Brown, "Justice Launches Probe of 'No-Haggle' Pricing," *The Washington Post,* October 11, 1994, p. C1.

Mini-Case 9.2

To Lease or Not to Lease: Is There a Question?

At one time, the majority of leasers of new automobiles in the United States were businesses, governments, and other organizations. For the most part, personal use consumers purchased automobiles using down payments and loans that took several years to repay. Car leasing became very popular beginning in the early 1990s. Instead of auto rebates (cash back for a purchase), automakers turned to leases. Many leases contain cash subsidies to buyers through reduced monthly payments. In 1994, 3 million vehicles, 25 percent of every automobile and truck sold in the United States, were leased.

For the moment, consumers seem happy; automakers and dealers *are* happy because they're moving large volumes of cars. But what happens when all these automobiles go off-lease? Some analysts believe the used car price of a Taurus, the largest-volume leased car, will be hard hit through rapid depreciation. Bargains should grow for used car shoppers. The economy may suffer as used car sales rise, new car sales stall, and automakers cut back on production. Used car leasing programs may help dealers move excess used car inventories. However, if a slowdown in new car sales hits at the same time there becomes a glut of used cars, the two trends could converge and prices for both new and used cars could plummet. On the other hand, automakers say that there are two distinct markets, one for new cars and the other for used cars. They believe new car sales won't suffer from a used car glut.

Case Questions

1. Do you think leasing rather than purchasing a new automobile is a good idea for all consumers?

2. Could automobile leasing be bad for the economy?

3. What are automakers and dealers going to do with all the cars coming back from being leased?

Sources: J. Knight, "Good News for Used-Car Buyers—Bad News for Sellers," *Washington Post National Weekly Edition* 11, no. 33 (June 13–19, 1994), pp. 21–22; R. L. Simison, "Leased-Car Glut May Lift Costs, Deflate Values," *The Wall Street Journal*, June 3, 1994, pp. B1, 4; D. Woodruff, L. Armstrong, J. Templeman, J. Flynn, C. Farrell, and J. Berry, "Leasing Fever," *Business Week*, February 7, 1994, pp. 92–96; N. Haas and F. Washington, "A New Lease on Life," *Newsweek*, April 4, 1994, pp. 42–43.

Chapter 9 Notes

1. P. S. Dempsey, "The Bitter Fruits of Airline Deregulation," *The Wall Street Journal*, April 8, 1993, p. A15.

2. N. Munk, "The Child Is Father of the Man," *Forbes* 152, no. 4 (August 16, 1993), pp. 88, 92.

3. W. Spindle, "Can't Get Enough of That Super-Yen," *Business Week*, October 4, 1993, p. 50.

4. B. Ortega, "Suit over Wal-Mart's Pricing Practices Goes to Trial Today in Arkansas Court," *The Wall Street Journal*, August 23, 1993, p. A3; J. Ramey, "Judge Finds Wal-Mart Guilty in Pricing Suit," *Supermarket News* 43, no. 42 (October 18, 1993), p. 4.

5. K. Fitzgerald, "Court Decision Stings Wal-Mart," *Advertising Age*, October 18, 1993, p. 8.

6. B. O'Brian, "Predatory Pricing Issue Is Due to Be Taken Up in American Air's Trial," *The Wall Street Journal*, July 12, 1993, pp. A1, 6.

7. J. Solomon, M. Hager, C. Friday, and S. Nayyar, "Drugs: Is the Price Right?" *Newsweek*, March 8, 1993, p. 38.

8. W. M. Bulkeley, "Tweeter's Customers Told: 'Your Check Is in the Mail,'" *The Wall Street Journal*, August 17, 1993, p. B8.

9. A. E. Serwer, "How to Escape a Price War," *Fortune* 129, no. 12 (June 13, 1994), pp. 82–90.

10. E. Shapiro, "Price Lure of Private-Label Products Fails to Hook Many Buyers of Baby Food, Beer," *The Wall Street Journal*, May 13, 1993, pp. B1, 8.

11. C. Palmeri, "Remodeling Your Business," *Forbes* 152, no. 4 (August 16, 1993), p. 43; L. Freeman, "Payless Cashways Rules Its Hometown," *Building Supply Home Centers* 167, no. 3 (September 1994), p. 64; "Payless Offers Customers More; New Store Combines Larger Inventory with Drive-Through Lumberyard," *Do-It-Yourself Retailing* 167, no. 2 (August 1994), p. 245.

12. C. Duff, "Single-Price Stores' Formula for Success: Cheap Merchandise and a Lot of Clutter," *The Wall Street Journal*, June 30, 1992, pp. B1, 6.

13. K. L. Miller, L. Armstrong, and D. Woodruff, "A Car Is Born," *Business Week*, September 13, 1993, pp. 64–72.

14. S. Greco, "Pricing Gets Easier (Sort Of)," *INC.* 15, no. 11 (November 1993), p. 124.

15. L. Nathans Spiro, "How AT&T Skimmed the Cream off the Credit-Card Market," *Newsweek*, December 16, 1991, p. 104.

16. J. E. Rigdon, "Kodak Quietly Offers Film Discounts of 10% to 20% to Some Big Customers," *The Wall Street Journal*, August 17, 1993, p. B8.

Place: The Role of Retailing

Chapter Objectives

After studying Chapter 10 you should be able to

1. Describe the evolution of retailing in the United States.

2. Explain the contribution of retailing to the U.S. economy.

3. Identify retailers' tasks and the decisions they make.

4. Recognize some of the common ways of classifying retailers.

5. Discuss the future of retailing.

*T*he technological advances of the Industrial Revolution allowed manufacturers to expand their operations and produce greater quantities and varieties of products. Most manufacturers also found that they had to rely on other businesses for some or all product distribution activities. The modern channel of distribution emerged from this need. A **channel of distribution** is a collection of businesses, often independently owned and operated, that cooperate in placing products where consumers need and want them. Some producers market directly to consumers through catalogs, telemarketing, direct mail, or interactive electronic systems. The majority of producers rely on other individuals and businesses to perform distribution functions and place their products on the market, mostly in traditional retail stores. As you learn about the retail placement of products in this chapter, consider this question: How will retailing change as more consumers gain the ability to shop from home through the electronic marriage of television, computers, and telephones?

channel of distribution   A collection of businesses that cooperate to place products where consumers need and want them.

Three mornings a week Erik and Fran Martin put on their athletic shoes to join other retirees for a brisk walk in a local mall. The Martins and their friends are senior striders—informal groups of older Americans who walk in the comfort of enclosed shopping malls for their physical health and to socialize.[1] Retailers like having retirees use the malls because they frequently end their brisk walks with a stroll through the stores, often stopping to make a purchase. Many mall stores and restaurants offer seniors discounts along with other buying enticements. Although seniors use the malls in the mornings, teens and young adults hang out at malls in the afternoons and early evenings, to meet friends, graze on fast food, and go to the movies or clubs, as well as to shop. On weekends and holidays, families with young children come to malls to see auto shows, flower exhibits, antique furniture displays, and, at Christmas, to have their children photographed with Santa. Many suburban shopping malls have evolved into central gathering places for people of all ages and interests, where shopping, socializing, and entertainment go hand in hand, much like they did in downtowns in small towns across America from the turn of the century to the late 1960s. Malls range in size from a few stores in a strip mall along a highway to supersized malls, such as The Mall of America complex in Minnesota that encloses 4.2 million square feet of floor space and houses four national retail anchors (Nordstrom, Sears, Macy's, Bloomingdale's) along with an indoor amusement park, Lego showplace, 350 specialty stores, nightclubs, and restaurants (see Photo 10.1).

THE EVOLUTION OF RETAILING

Objective 1 Describe the evolution of retailing in the United States

retailing Marketing activities designed to present products (goods and services) for purchase in stores, catalogs, vending machines, and by television, telephone, and computer.

retailer A business or organization primarily involved in retailing, providing products (merchandise) for sale to personal use consumers.

What do Wal-Mart, Lowe's, Saks Fifth Avenue, Waldenbooks, Mc-Donald's, Office Depot, The Home Shopping Network, Lands' End, a Coca-Cola vending machine, and a local dry cleaner/laundry have in common (Photo 10.2)? They are all part of **retailing,** marketing activities designed to present products (goods and services) to consumers for them to purchase both in stores as well as through nonstore mediums such as catalogs, vending machines, television, telephone, and now, on the Internet's World Wide Web. A **retailer** is a business or organization primarily or wholly involved in retailing, providing products (merchandise) for sale to personal use consumers. Because you are probably more familiar with retailers than other channel of distribution members, as a consumer and possibly as a retail employee, the discussion of place begins with the best-known channel of distribution member: the retailer.

In the early years when the United States was being settled, retailing spread across the country on the backs of peddlers who supplied an assortment of merchandise to customers on their routes. By the late 1700s and early 1800s, general stores appeared in cities and major settlements to serve large numbers of consumers and their diverse tastes. As the name *general* implies, general stores had a **scrambled merchandise** strategy, stocking an extensive merchandise assortment in many unrelated product lines. These all-purpose stores offered everything from crackers to cloth, guns to garden

scrambled merchandise An extensive merchandise assortment in many unrelated product lines.

Photo 10.1

The Mall of America in Minnesota offers shoppers acres of stores, as well as places to socialize, exercise, and be entertained.

Photo 10.2

Wal-Mart is the country's largest retailer.

seed, but rarely had more than a few alternatives of any item on hand. The lack of product depth limited the ability of general stores to regularly satisfy their customers.

The **specialty store** evolved as an alternative to the general store, and focused on offering a limited line of merchandise but a great number of choices within that line. Before long there were dressmakers, pharmacists, bakers, and other retailers whose offers focused on a particular specialty. What specialty stores lacked in product width (many different product lines), they more than made up for in product depth (the number of different alternatives offered within a product line). For example, the dressmaker's product width

specialty store A store that offers a limited line of merchandise with a great number of choices within that line.

was limited to product lines associated with dresses, but a substantial product depth was available through a vast array of different fabric colors and textures, as well as buttons, threads, laces, belts, and trims.

Contrast this with the contemporary retailing scene and you'll see how some large retailers have returned to the general store scrambled merchandise concept, but in enormous stores with great width and depth. For instance, Wal-Mart Supercenter stores are scaled-down **hypermarkets,** one-stop combination discount stores and supermarkets. The nation's number one retailer offers a vast width of products within almost 200,000 square feet of retail space.

Supermarkets have been at the forefront of the move back to the general store concept, expanding their food product lines to more scrambled merchandise assortments. In addition to flowers, videotapes, perfumes, jewelry, and home and auto gadgets, many supermarkets have on-site restaurants, dry cleaners, and in-store banking. In 1990, there were only about 900 supermarket bank branches; today, they number well over 2,000 nationwide.[2] Supermarket bankers seek out customers by cruising supermarket aisles, using store public address systems, and placing promotional signs on grocery shelves spouting such slogans as "Lettuce Be Your Banker." Because most supermarkets average 10,000 to 30,000 customer visits each week, banks understandably see this as a target market ripe for aggressive selling. Supermarkets rent space to the bank (usually about 400 square feet) and benefit from their customers' satisfaction with this additional service.

Many different types of retailers compete and coexist in the same town. Along with local, single-store, independent retailers you'll find national category killers such as Wal-Mart, Home Depot, and Toys 'Я' Us that can overwhelm local competitors with their deep price discounts and extensive inventories. You'll also find smaller national and regional specialty retailers, such as The Shoe Carnival, Great Harvest bakery, Midas automotive repair shops, Super Cuts beauty salons, and Pet Pantry stores (see Photo 10.3). Some specialty retailers are members of national chains, whereas others are locally or regionally owned and operated, often as franchises.

hypermarkets Very large stores, often 300,000 square feet or more, that offer discounted general merchandise and supermarket products under one roof.

Theories of Retail Change

Retailing is a highly dynamic marketing activity that continues to change because of intense competition, the volatility of consumer demands, and changes in the environment (particularly the development of new technologies like electronic scanning and computers). Several theories attempt to generally explain why changes occur

Marketing Application 10.1

Perform a retailer inventory of your city. Turn to the Yellow Pages Index in your local telephone directory. Select a product category, such as furniture, pet care, or automobiles. For the category you've selected, identify the different types of retailers listed. For example, an automobile category will typically list many different retailer types, from antique restorations and repair to automobile wrecking. What conclusions can you draw about the retailers serving the product category you've selected? Do they appear to specialize in offering product width or depth? Can you distinguish between retailers offering goods and services in the same product category? Bring your observations to class for comparison. ■

Photo 10.3

Shoe Carnival strives to make shopping a fun, carnival-like experience.

in retail organizations. One widely known theory of retail development, the **wheel of retailing,** suggests that as retailers become successful they decide to grow and enhance their image by trading up. This means that many businesses that begin as small, low-price, low-cost establishments will change as they become successful. As they grow larger, they improve the design and appearance of their stores, charge higher prices, offer more services, stock a better quality and greater assortment of products, and realize greater profits from fatter profit margins. As retailers move up the wheel to become higher-priced competitors, they leave an opportunity for new entrants to slip into the vacated low-cost, low-margin slot. Thus, the wheel continually spins and new retailers replace those who have traded up.

wheel of retailing   The theory that as retailers become successful they leave room for newer businesses at the lower end of the market.

Other theories explain retail change as a response to competitive pressure, an action–reaction type of response. In the process of responding, a retailer may develop into something new. Thus, retailers evolve because they reinvent themselves. This helps explain the evolution of the gasoline retailer. From a single product line (gasoline products), this type of retailer has evolved into various types of retail establishments that offer gasoline products and car repairs; or gasoline and convenience store products; or gasoline, convenience foods, and national franchise fast foods. Alternatively, another theory sees this evolution as being cyclical or accordionlike, with retailers moving from a general merchandise assortment to a specialty offering and back to a general assortment, as conditions demand and opportunities arise. By this theory, the gasoline station should eventually revert back to something close to its original form, perhaps selling only gasoline and performing minor car repairs.

What these different theories have in common is the recognition that retailing is constantly changing. Retailers must continually monitor their environments and, particularly, the competition and consumer demand, making changes as needed to survive and profit.

Check Your Understanding 10.1	1. Describe how retailing has evolved in the United States.
	2. Compare and contrast the retail strategies of scrambled merchandising and specialty merchandising.
	3. Explain the wheel of retailing theory.

New Retail Types

Retailing has changed dramatically from the heyday of the general store. Recent additions to the array of retail types include:

Outlet malls: These retailers offer brand-name products at discount prices. They began as cut-rate, low-overhead, no-frills warehouselike stores where manufacturers unloaded their excess, out-of-date, or damaged products. Many outlet malls have traded up, becoming dressier and higher priced, often offering first-quality products at prices comparable to those found in full-service department stores.[3]

Superstores, discounters, and supermarkets: These retailers offer everyday low pricing, convenience, large numbers of general merchandise lines, and frequently include in-store, freestanding specialty retailers like bank branches, dry cleaners, and restaurants that lease store space. A new entry is the pet supply superstore, 3 to 10 times the size of most traditional pet retail stores, offering an expanded line of goods and services, including pet physicals and photos.[4]

Warehouse clubs: These retailers offer their members discount-priced products, often packed in bulk, suitable both for personal use consumers and small businesses. Warehouse clubs in this $26 billion industry are very aggressive competitors and vie ruthlessly for members. In a recent shakeout, Kmart was worn down by the price competition and sold most of its PACE Membership Warehouse chain stores to Wal-Mart, which has over 400 Sam's Clubs. Price Co. and Costco Wholesale merged and now have 210 Price/Costco warehouse stores.[5]

Hypermarkets: Vast one-stop shopping centers with acres of floor space stocking groceries, furniture, sports equipment, toys, and other merchandise; these retailers are very popular in Europe, but until recently performed poorly in the United States.[6]

Television home shopping networks: Nonstore retailers where consumers select products shown on television and make their purchases by telephone. In the United States, this is a $2.5 billion industry dominated by QVC Network, Inc., and the Home Shopping Network.

Electronic retailers: On-line retailing offered by computer information networks like Prodigy and CompuServe. "Click" boxes are used to take customer orders, bill credit cards, and initiate purchase orders.[7]

Interactive kiosks: Commonly found outside banks, in malls, and at airports, kiosks are called "fancy vending machines" by some critics. The first interactive kiosks were automated teller machines (ATMs) provided in convenient locations by banks as an alternative to extending their lobby operating hours. Interactive kiosks are accessed through touch screens, often have both video and audio features, and accept credit card purchases. By the end of the decade, it is projected that there will be more than 500,000 nationwide, offering a variety of merchandise including wine, gourmet foods, clothing, compact discs, greeting cards, and postage stamps.[8] (See Photo 10.4.)

Resale shops: Once confined to low-price used merchandise sold through social welfare groups like Volunteers of America (VOA) or the Salvation Army, these retailers have gone upscale. Many now sell gently used designer clothing, children's clothing, or antiques. Some stores sell clothes on consignment, which means that the retailer gives the owner (consignee) a percentage of the sale when the merchandise is sold.

Marketing Application 10.2

Do you have any resale retailers in your area? Your telephone directory's Yellow Pages Index is a good place to find resellers. Select several product categories (e.g., clothing, automobiles, furniture) and see if there is a listing for retailers selling the product used. In what product categories are most of the resale retailers clustered? What product categories might present good retail opportunities? Bring your list to class for discussion. ■

Photo 10.4

Now consumers can get involved in creating their own custom products on the spot.

THE RETAIL TRADE: AN IMPORTANT PART OF THE U.S. ECONOMY

Objective 2 Explain the contribution of retailing to the U.S. economy.

It's extremely easy to become a retailer. All it takes is start-up capital (often a loan from friends or a bank), rented space in a strip mall along a well-traveled road, and products and supplies that can be purchased on credit. Internet retailing is also easy to initiate. Unfortunately, the ease of entry into retailing masks the difficulty of being successful at it. For example, more than 80 percent of all restaurant start-ups fail.[9] Retail success requires thoughtful planning, careful decision making, and the investment of considerable time and effort, as well as some good luck. The failure rate of small retailers is extremely high, and any local or national downturn in the economy,

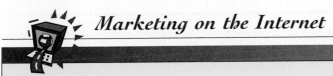

Marketing on the Internet

Smart retailers realize that, in order to survive and prosper, they must satisfy consumer needs and wants, and establish productive relationships with them over time. And time is exactly what many busy consumers don't have enough to spare.

Peapod Delivery System, Inc., has found a way to reduce the time consumers spend grocery shopping by offering its customers the convenience of on-line grocery shopping and doorstep delivery. Peapod's sophisticated software allows consumers to electronically browse 18,000 grocery items, viewing products as they are displayed in virtual grocery aisles using current prices. Each on-line consumer can make price comparisons, identify specials, use coupons, make shopping lists, and even leave special purchase instructions. Orders are made by E-mail, telephone, or fax and filled by Peapod

employees at one of seven Jewel Food Stores in the Chicago area or three Safeway Stores in San Francisco. Deliveries are made within 90-minute prearranged time slots throughout the day. The roughly 7,000 Peapod customers pay using a credit card, check, or from a computer account.

The service costs average around $30 per month. Consumers most likely to sign on with Peapod are busy professionals, the homebound, and busy families. ■

B. Marsh, "Peapod's On-Line Grocery Service Checks Out Success," *The Wall Street Journal,* June 30, 1994, p. B2; G. Moffat, "Future's in Peapod, Not Pork Bellies," *America's Network* 98, no. 22 (November 15, 1994), p.10; M. Garry, "Time for Home Delivery," *Progressive Grocer* 73, no. 11 (November 1994), p. 86; D. J. Wallace, "Logging On for a Loaf of Bread: Food Fight Looming as Grocery Stores Take Their Wares On-line," *Advertising Age* 65, no. 43 (October 10, 1994), p. 20.

change in consumer demand, or mistakes in product selection, pricing, or location can quickly prove fatal.

Retailing is big business in the United States: over 1.5 million retail establishments reported over $2 trillion in sales in 1993 and payrolls of over $247 billion.[10] About 21 percent of the U.S. labor force (19.6 million jobs) works in retailing. The distribution of sales by major retailer type is shown in Figure 10.1.

For record-keeping purposes, the U.S. government divides the retail trade into two segments: durable and nondurable goods. In 1993, nondurable goods sales of $1.3 trillion were almost twice that of durable goods sales. Personal use consumers spent about 32 percent of their money on nondurable goods; durables accounted for 12 percent, and services 56 percent.[11] Services, a broad category that includes everything from hair cuts to medical care, dominate the U.S. economy and provide almost 70 percent of the U.S. gross domestic product.

Retailing as a whole is expected to grow slowly but steadily throughout the 1990s, perhaps by about 5 percent per year.[12] This reflects the increased value consciousness of consumers (who are more careful about their purchases than they were in the 1980s), reduced consumer spending generally, and fewer new families being formed that need durables and housing.

Figure 10.1

Total Retail Sales in the
United States—1993

Kind of Business	1993 Sales and Inventories (in billions of dollars)
Retail trade, total	2,081.6
Durable goods stores, total	784.6
Automotive dealers	454.4
Building materials and garden supplies	115.9
Furniture and home furnishings stores	113.7
Sporting goods and bicycle shops	19.3
Bookstores	9.0
Jewelry stores	16.3
Nondurable goods stores, total	1,297.0
Apparel and accessory stores	106.1
Drugstores and proprietary stores	80.9
Eating and drinking establishments	211.0
Food stores	392.4
Gasoline service stations	133.5
General merchandise stores	267.0
Liquor stores	21.2
Nonstore retailers	50.5
Catalog and mail-order houses	29.3

U.S. Bureau of the Census, Current Business Reports, Combined Annual and Revised Monthly Retail Trade, January 1984–December 1993, Table No. 1281 Retail Trade—Sales, by Kind of Business, Department of Commerce, *Statistical Abstract of the United States*; @ gopher: // gopher.census.gov.

Check Your Understanding 10.2

1. Identify several new retail types.
2. What is a resale retailer?
3. Explain the importance of retailing to the U.S. economy.

RETAIL TASKS

Objective 3 Identify retailers' tasks and the decisions they make.

retail tasks Buying, selling, and leasing products; communicating information about the products, their prices, and where they can be obtained; and negotiating product exchanges with consumers.

Regardless of the type of retailer, **retail tasks** remain similar to those performed in the general store. The retailer performs marketing activities related to the exchange function. This includes buying, selling, and leasing products; communicating information about the products, their prices, and where they can be obtained; and negotiating product exchanges with consumers.

Retailers must *obtain a desirable assortment of products* to offer consumers. These products may be obtained directly from the manufacturer or through wholesalers. Many different producers and wholesalers may be used in order to assemble a consumer-pleasing product assortment. Alternatively, the retailer itself may make the products, in which case the channel of distribution is direct from the

International Marketing Report

Market saturation, overbuilding, and projected slow but steady growth in the United States have many retailers looking abroad, seeking new markets to conquer. Price/Costco Inc., an American deep-discount warehouse retailer, is invading Britain, along with category killers Toys 'Я' Us and Kmart. Analysts believe Europe is ready for U.S.–style discounters. Consumers there are tired of high prices (estimated at 30 percent higher than in the United States) and stores that close early. German stores must close from Saturday afternoon to Monday morning and are allowed only two in-store sales per year. Small retailers throughout Europe and many large retail chains are fighting hard against legalizing late-night and seven-day retailing in an effort to stop or slow the arrival of U.S.

discounters. European consumers are in the middle, eager for bargains and tired of government overregulation of retailers. There are several European category killers, but they tend to be found in only a few countries and often reflect local consumer tastes. Some have expanded continentwide and to the United States, such as IKEA, a discount furniture chain. ■

A. L. Stewart, "Category Killers Get Major Attention in EC," *Marketing News* 27, no. 23 (November 8, 1993), p. 9; P. Dwyer, K. Lowry Miller, S. Toy, and P. Oster, "Shop Till You Drop Hits Europe," *Business Week*, November 29, 1993, pp. 58–59; K. Helliker, "U.S. Discount Retailers Are Targeting Europe and Its Fat Margins," *The Wall Street Journal*, September 20, 1993, pp. A1, 4; "Europe's Discount Dogfight," *The Economist* 327, no. 7810 (May 8, 1993), pp. 69–70.

manufacturer to the consumer, with the manufacturer also acting as the retailer. Another variation is when the retailer provides used products. In this case, the used products are obtained either directly from the product owner or through a resale wholesaler.

The retailer must *inform consumers that the products are available.* This information typically is conveyed through advertising, sales promotions, direct marketing, or other marketing communication activities.

If the products are offered in a traditional store location, the retailer must *ensure that the location is appropriate, safe, and convenient,* with automobile parking facilities and, where available, public transportation access. Many shoppers have become fearful about shopping mall parking lots, which has led retailers and mall management companies to hire security patrols and guards for parking lots.[13]

The retailer must *make the products available at convenient times.* Although some retailers are moving toward operating 24 hours a day, a few have found that limited operating hours also can be profitable. Saturday Audio Exchange is open only 10½ hours a week, yet it is successful because consumers value its broad selection; bargains on new, used, and discontinued sound equipment; and record turntable repair service.[14] Tuesday Morning, a gift discounter, likewise has been successful opening on a limited schedule for certain weeks of the year, particularly around holidays and when seasons change.

Although many products carry a manufacturer's suggested list price, the retailer must *ensure that products are priced.* The retailer often adds a markup to the manufacturer's price, a higher amount to ensure that the retailer's costs are covered and to provide a profit.

Some food manufacturers have salespeople who stock their products on supermarket shelves. More commonly, the retailer must *take delivery of the products ordered, unpack, label, and display the products.* The label is a store identification and price tag. Product displays sometimes are provided by the manufacturer, particularly end-of-aisle and point-of-purchase displays. The retailer must provide shelves and design and display arrangements.

The retailer must *make payment arrangements and inform consumers about them.* This includes contracting with a credit business to offer card services. Alternatively, some retailers use a cash-only payment system or accept credit cards but give consumers a discount for using cash. Some retailers offer layaway arrangements, where consumers pay off their purchases over a period of time and take possession when all payments are completed.

Many consumers take their product purchases with them. In the case of bulky purchases (e.g., mattresses, building supplies) and large durables (e.g., washing machines, refrigerators), a retailer *may offer delivery service* free or for a nominal fee. Some retailers offer no delivery service.

Even in self-service retail stores, employees are needed to stock, maintain, and operate the store. The retailer must *hire, train, and supervise retail employees.* Retailers increasingly are using more automation and fewer employees. Some supermarkets are experimenting with self-scanning, where shoppers scan the bar codes on their groceries at a fully automated checkout counter. The customer bags the groceries and takes their computer-printed bill to a cashier to pay.[15]

Retailers also *offer additional services, as needed and/or desired.* Sometimes the retailer offers to assemble products for purchasers or teaches the purchaser how to use the product. Other services frequently offered are repairs, maintenance, and product upgrades.

Making Retail Decisions

The assumption throughout this book has been that good marketing requires making good decisions. This is certainly true in retailing, where there are many challenges to achieving success, not the least of which is overcoming the ferocious competition. Retailers are often forced to undergo rapid transformations just to survive, let alone prosper. Sears is certainly a case in point, as it struggles to redefine itself and combat the damage done to its sales by its loss of focus and the discounting success of Wal-Mart, Kmart, Target, and others (see Photo 10.5). Retailers like Kmart face decisions about

Photo 10.5

Sears, once the nation's largest retailer, now ranks number three.

whether or not to initiate expensive store upgrades in order to compete.

Just as with other marketing decisions, retailers must make both strategic, long-range decisions as well as tactical, short-range decisions. Some long-range decisions will include defining the market, deciding what assortment of products to sell, identifying product width and depth, and establishing the level of service to provide. One of the most critical short-term decisions for store retailers is that of *location*. Where a store is located determines what consumers will be drawn to it. A gasoline station located directly off an interstate highway draws from a different customer base than does a gasoline station situated near a suburban shopping center in the same city. A convenience store like a 7-Eleven must be located in a convenient place where consumers can enter and leave rapidly. Some alternative retail location decisions are whether to locate in a strip mall or shopping center, an enclosed mall or a megamall, or a central business district or a factory outlet mall near a highway or interstate.

---

1. Describe the types of tasks assumed by retailers.
2. Discuss the types of decisions made by retailers.
3. Explain the importance of retail location decisions.

Check Your Understanding
10.3

CLASSIFYING RETAILERS

Many different retailers usually operate in any particular geographical area. Some, like Wal-Mart and Kmart, compete directly, offering the same kinds of products at similar prices. Others are indirect

Objective 4   Recognize some of the common ways of classifying retailers.

competitors, such as Loew's movie theaters and Putt-Putt Miniature Golf. Some retailers do not compete at all, but instead complement one another, like Porter Paint and Custom Tile Co., both specialty retailers used by homeowners as well as home repair specialists for remodeling projects.

Retailers range in size from small, independent, owner-operated shops like the local florist, dry cleaner, or barber shop, to national (and often international) giant category killers like Toys 'Я' Us. Consumers patronize retailers for many reasons, most often to satisfy a specific need or want; for example, to purchase staples like bread and milk, a new car, a winter coat, or a set of tires. However, not all shopping is rational or objective in economic terms. Some consumers shop certain retailers because of loyalty to the owner who is a relative or friend, even though their prices may be higher than the large national discount chains. Others visit retailers to counteract loneliness, by seeking company through the shopping experience. Some consumers love to shop and find that browsing through an exclusive store like Neiman Marcus and looking at attractive displays and merchandise is entertaining. Research indicates that a growing number of consumers (nearly one shopper in five) buys some groceries at a large warehouse like Sam's Club, because it is fun to shop there and "they're bigger, brighter and have more surprises than supermarkets."[16]

By knowing different retailers' characteristics, consumers save time, effort, and money by matching their purchase needs to a retailer's attributes. One attribute is **store atmospherics,** the tangible and intangible elements, inside and out, that reflect what the store is all about, including its physical design, lighting, noise level, displays, and service personnel. Consumers perceive these signals and use them to form an opinion about the store and its products. For example, Barnes & Noble's superstores (book retailers with over 100,000 titles per store) have found that in-store cafes offering sandwiches and espresso, ample seating room for browsers, and good music (live and recorded) add a sense of entertainment to the stores that customers love.[17] Other consumers may prefer to shop

store atmospherics The tangible and intangible elements that give a store its identity.

Consumer Insight

A consumer may visit several retailers in a single shopping trip in order to accommodate a number of different shopping tasks, sorting out which retailers have the best prices, perform the right services, and have the needed products. A national survey of shoppers interviewed immediately after shopping in a cross-section of retailers reveals that time is a major factor that consumers use to evaluate and classify retailers. This includes the time spent finding products and the time needed to check out. Other important factors are treatment, efficiency, price,

atmosphere, and technology. These factors are addressed in Figure 10.2. Less money and time are primary reasons consumers recently gave for shopping less frequently at malls; other reasons include the crowds, congested parking lots, and high-priced merchandise.■

J. Peritz, "Retailers Who Keep Score Know What Their Shoppers Value," *Marketing News* 27, no. 11 (May 24, 1993), p. 9. Table used with permisson. D. Crispell, "Cost and Time Curtail Mall Shopping," *The Wall Street Journal*, April 25, 1994, p. B1.

Figure 10.2

Retail Factors That Consumers Value

Rank	Factor and Examples
1.	**Time** Check-out time Total time in store Time to pay
2.	**Treatment** Effort made by employees Ability to get help when needed Care employees take with your items Friendliness of employees
3.	**Efficiency** Number of open lanes or registers Quality of receipt Quality of signs Ease of finding items Knowledgeability of employees
4.	**Price** Displays offering specials Prices Clear marking of prices
5.	**Physicality** Atmosphere Roominess
6.	**Technology** Ease with which employees use cash registers Use of modern technology in the store

for books in a dusty, cluttered, owner-operated store that stocks out-of-print titles.

store image   The way in which consumers perceive a store.

Many things contribute to the formation of a **store image,** the way consumers perceive a store (their mental image of it). For example, a consumer shopping for a camera knows (or can easily find out) that cameras are sold in large national discounters like Wal-Mart, some upscale full-service department stores like Bloomingdale's, electronics stores like Circuit City, supermarkets like Kroger, and small specialty camera shops like Carol's Click Clinic. For an inexpensive, simple camera or even a disposable one, the consumer will consider one group of retailers; however, if instead the desired camera is quite expensive and very complicated, then another set of retailers will be selected. The most commonly used ways that retailers are classified is by product mix, pricing philosophy, service level, form of ownership, and site (see Figure 10.3).

product assortment   The variety of products collected and offered by a retailer.

Product mix refers to width and depth of the **product assortment** (the variety of products collected and offered by a retailer), which differs dramatically depending on retailer type. For example, a specialty retailer like Victoria's Secret offers a narrow but highly integrated line of related products that concentrate in depth on lingerie and sleepwear. At the other end of the product mix spectrum are large discounters that stock a wide assortment of lines,

---

Figure 10.3   Classifying Retailers

RETAILERS ARE OFTEN CLASSIFIED BY THEIR . . .

Product Mix
Width and depth of product assortment
  Mass merchandisers offer a wide but shallow assortment
  Specialty stores offer limited width but great depth
  General merchandisers, such as department stores, offer both
    width and depth

Pricing Philosophy
Range of prices, above, at, or below market
  Prestige, exclusive pricing as in a Saks Fifth Avenue or
    Tiffany store
  Full-price pricing as in a department or specialty store
  Discount pricing as in a Wal-Mart, Kmart, or T.J. Maxx

Service Level
Type of services offered, if any
  Full service as in a department store that offers credit,
    lay away, gift wrapping, alterations, delivery, and so on
  Limited service as in a Sears
  Self-service as in an outlet mall store or discount store

Ownership Form
Legal ownership
  Independently owned
  Franchise
  Chain
  Cooperatives
  Conglomerates

Site
Whether or not the retailer is based in a store
  Traditional store-based
  Nonstore through direct selling, telemarketing, direct mail,
    mail order, or vending machine

Marketing Application 10.4

As a class project, determine who in the class has had experience working in a retail establishment. Organize a class discussion of customer services offered by their retail employers. What conclusions can you draw about local trends in services? Do retailers appear to be moving toward offering more services or fewer? How do consumers feel about these service levels? ■

usually in shallow depths. A department store like Lazarus or Marshall Field's offers many different lines of merchandise in different depths—some lines are full of product variations while others are limited.

Pricing philosophy signals the consumer about the range of prices found at a retailer. Above-market prestige pricing is associated with products offered at Tiffany or Saks Fifth Avenue, exclusive retailers who stock high-quality, high-priced products. Far lower prices are expected from discounters like Target and Kmart. In the middle are traditional department stores (e.g., Dillard's) and specialty stores (e.g., The Limited) that charge full price but often hold sales.

Service level refers to the forms and extent of services offered. For example, full-service department stores like McAlpin's serve customers by providing gift wrapping, credit, alterations, knowledgeable salespeople, baby and wedding gift registry, seasonal fashion shows, layaways, delivery, and personal shopping assistance in decorating a home, buying a gift, or assembling a wardrobe. On the other hand, services offered by discounters are typically limited to credit, layaways, and (sometimes) delivery. Most discounters are self-service, which means that customers must serve themselves, select the products they want, and take them to a central location for payment. This is a common trade-off that many consumers actually prefer, trading a discounted price for the elimination of some or all services. In between are limited-service retailers, like Sears, that provide some sales assistance and service. Japanese retailers offer an extremely high level of service, which contributes to correspondingly high prices for the products they carry.[18]

Form of ownership is perhaps not as readily perceived by consumers, yet it is a well-known method for classifying retailers. The vast majority of U.S. retailers are independently owned; over 80 percent are single-outlet stores like the local barber shop, dry cleaner, furniture store, or florist. Independent retailers may operate several stores, but more commonly they are small and have limited sales and employees. At the other extreme are the retail giants, like Wal-Mart

retail chains Multiple stores having common ownership and some measure of centralized management.

and Sears, that operate as **retail chains** with multiple stores but a common ownership and some measure of centralized management. Often, these chains are publicly owned. Large national chains have considerable advantages over other retailers (particularly small independents) because they can buy in large quantities, often realizing economies of scale, and sell at lower prices because they are better able to keep their costs low.

An alternate ownership form is the retail franchise, like a McDonald's or KFC. McDonald's has over 9,000 stores, including more than 80 outlets in Wal-Marts.[19] **Franchising** exists when a business (the franchisor) agrees to allow another (the franchisee) to operate a business under the franchisor's name, offering the franchisor's products to consumers. Franchising is a $250 billion industry (excluding auto dealers and gasoline stations) that accounts for almost 13 percent of total retail sales and, in 1991 alone, created over 160,000 new jobs.[20]

franchising A form of ownership in which a business agrees to allow another business to operate under a franchisor's name, offering the franchisor's products to consumers.

A franchise agreement involves specific provisions for product mix, product quality, terms of operation, and even store architecture and construction. A franchisee typically becomes part of the franchisor's supplier network. Many franchises are independently owned but, as a term of the franchise association, must follow the rules set down by the franchisor. Rather than owning single outlets, franchisees tend to own and/or operate multiple units. McDonald's requires its franchisees to receive training in how to operate an outlet, and it establishes rules of operation, product mix, and service expectations. For the right to hold a franchise, the franchisee often pays an up-front fee to the franchisor and a percentage of profits as royalties. Different franchise arrangements reflect specific terms negotiated between the franchisor and franchisees. Retail franchises are growing both in the U.S. market as well as abroad. Perhaps one of the most widely publicized franchise openings was of the Moscow McDonald's in 1989, a joint venture between McDonald's of Canada and the Moscow Food Service.

cooperative A group of retailers who have voluntarily associated themselves for business purposes.

conglomerates Large groups of different types of retailers within a single corporate structure.

Another familiar ownership form is the **cooperative,** a group of retailers who have voluntarily associated themselves in order to take advantage of the types of economies available to chain stores. Western Auto and Ace Hardware, as well as many grocery cooperatives, represent this type of independent association. **Conglomerates** include some of the largest department store chains in the United States. Conglomerates are distinguished from chains in that they typically are larger and include different types of retailers within the corporate structure. Federated Department Stores and Allied Stores are chains within a larger conglomerate.

Site (store/nonstore/mixed) identifies whether the retailer is marketing solely through a store, by a nonstore mechanism, or using both. Using both is becoming a desirable alternative for traditional store retailers, because it expands their customer reach. Many full-service department stores (e.g., Nordstrom's) also use mail catalogs.

1. What are store atmospherics? Why are they important and to whom?
2. Describe the major ways of classifying retailers.
3. What advantages might a retailer achieve by offering products both in a store and through nonstore means?

THE FUTURE OF RETAILING

What will retailing be like in the next century? The size, diversity, competitiveness, and affluence of the U.S. market fuels retail diversity. Changes in technology will increase the retail choices facing consumers. Many types of store and nonstore retailers will flourish in the United States as long as they continue to satisfy consumers and strive to establish long-term relationships with them.

Objective 5 Discuss the future of retailing.

Is There a Future for Store Retailers?

Some of the many different contemporary types of store retailers are shown in Figure 10.4. The general merchandise group includes department stores, variety stores, and general stores. From the turn

Retailer Type	Example
The General Merchandise Group	
Department stores	Dillard's
Variety stores	Woolworth's
General stores	Dollar General
The Mass Merchandise Group	
Catalog stores	Service Merchandise
Members-only warehouse clubs	Sam's
Discount stores	Kmart, Target, Wal-Mart
Off-price retailers	T.J. Maxx, Loehmann's
Supermarkets	Kroger, Winn-Dixie
Superstores	Winn-Dixie Superstore
Hypermarkets	Wal-Mart's Hypermart USA
Home improvement centers	Lowe's
Convenience stores	Convenient, 7-Eleven
Combination stores	Wal-Mart grocery and discount store
The Specialty Merchandise Group	
Limited-line retailers	Pick 'n Save Shoes
Single-line retailers	Curry's Children's Shoes

Figure 10.4

Store Retailer Types

Photo 10.6

Macy's Thanksgiving Day parade is a world famous annual event that keeps the Macy's name and image fresh in the minds of consumers.

of the century to after World War II, full-service independent department stores dominated many town centers and were anchors for other downtown businesses. They offered a wide merchandise assortment by grouping together related product lines in departments—for example, toy departments, women's clothing departments, and shoe departments. They often had restaurants, coffee shops, and beauty salons, and offered many customer services. Products were usually offered at full price, with prices reduced during sales. Store image was important. In large cities like New York and Chicago, Macy's or Marshall Field's sponsored parades and civic events and were magnets for shoppers, drawing them into the city (see Photo 10.6).

Some grand old department stores still thrive in downtown locations (see Photo 10.7). Most contemporary department stores, however, lack the draw of their predecessors, as well as their merchandise mix. Many stores have abandoned downtown for shopping malls in the suburbs, and few offer as many amenities; most are now members of a chain. The changes they've undergone are the result of many factors. Discounters undercut the full-price strategies of most department stores, leaving the larger ones burdened with high operating costs that drove many into bankruptcy. As affluent consumers established themselves in suburbs, many department stores followed. Suburban shopping malls offer free parking and the safety that eludes many downtown areas. Department stores often anchor malls and still draw shoppers for their mix of products and amenities.

Photo 10.7

Strawbidge and Clothier's, in Philadelphia, is a downtown department store that is still thriving, bucking the trend to move to the shopping mall.

Photo 10.8

Woolworth's then and now. Clearly, Woolworth's has seen the need to diversify to give consumers what they want.

It would be a mistake, however, to assume that department stores are dead when they represent a $250 billion industry. To the contrary, traditional full-service department stores appear to be reviving and should survive well into the 21st century. Several department store chains have undertaken ambitious building and remodeling plans. One reason for optimism is the aging of the baby boomers and their preference for higher-quality products and more services. To capture greater market share, many stores are dropping such low-profit lines as major appliances and adding popular, high-profit lines in apparel. They are adopting discount pricing, computer inventory control, and streamlined management. Some department stores are even heading back downtown, where they can find reasonable rents and a growing customer base (office workers), as well as escape overcrowded suburban shopping malls.[21]

Very few general stores operate today; most were driven out of business by discounters and mass merchandisers. Variety stores like Woolworth still operate some five and dime stores, but their number has decreased from 1,306 in 1981 to 915 in 1992 (Photo 10.8). The Woolworthchain is rapidly changing to specialty retailing in its Foot Locker athletic shoe stores, Kinney family shoes stores, and Northern Reflections casual clothing boutiques.[22]

The mass merchandise group includes the workhorses of modern retailing that aim at the mass market, offer a more limited product assortment in breadth and depth, and typically compete on price. Generally, these retailers trade elegant stores for no-frills warehouse-type buildings with few aesthetic features—many use open metal shelves to stack and display merchandise, still in their original shipping boxes (see Photo 10.9). Mass merchandisers rely on volume and low prices to move products quickly off shelves. Few if any salespeople are available to assist customers, and checkout counters generally are located at the front of the store. Warehouse clubs are among the retailers that sell products both to personal use consumers and businesses. Up to 60 percent of their members are small local businesses that benefit from the clubs' low prices and bulk packaging.[23] Price-conscious consumers, in particular, will support these retailers into the next century.

Members of the specialty merchandise group restrict their merchandise assortment to a single or limited number of product lines but have a very deep assortment. Specialty retailers are the dominant form of independent owner stores. The two major types of specialty merchandisers are:

Photo 10.9

Office Depot is a superstore where personal use and business/organization consumers stock up on office products at discount prices.

1. *Single-line* retailers, which offer a narrow line of products, focusing on a particular consumer need, for example, a clothing store or an electronics retailer.

2. *Limited-line* retailers, which are even more narrowly defined, as in a children's clothing store or television store.

Many consumers prefer these retailers because of their product depth, services offered, and the personal relationships that specialty retailers often develop with their regular customers.

What Is the Future for Nonstore Retailers?

Growing numbers of consumers are turning to nonstore retailers because they are fast and accessible, offer many services, and can eliminate the need to leave home to shop. Nonstore retailing is a rapidly expanding, highly profitable form of retailing that includes a broad range of retail activities that occur apart from a traditional store. Advantages to engaging in nonstore retailing are that the retailer avoids the expenses typically associated with a store, including overhead, store personnel costs, and inventory storage. The retailer can save time and expense by eliminating other intermediaries, such as wholesalers, by performing these tasks "in-house." Nonstore retailers eliminate store-based shoplifting problems.

Direct Selling   There were nonstore retailers (peddlers) even in the early days of the United States. Contemporary examples of such **direct selling** activities (bringing products directly to the consumer's home) include Avon products, Amway, Mary Kay Cosmetics, Tupperware, and various insurance, vacuum cleaner, and encyclopedia sellers. Tupperware still holds demonstration house parties of their plastic storage products in consumers' homes, despite changing lifestyles and women's work schedules.[24] Avon, on the other hand, is changing its retailing strategy and now also sells its cosmetics, fragrances, and gifts in offices, via catalogs, through television advertising, and by 1-800 numbers.[25]

direct selling Nonstore retailing that brings products directly to the consumer's home.

Grocery-on-wheels, a recent entrepreneurial venture in Flint, Michigan, is successfully serving shoppers who find it difficult to get to traditional stores.[26] The concept of a mobile grocery is not new to the United States, although most other mobile food vendors specialize in one-commodity categories, such as fruits and vegetables, milk, ice cream, or soda. Mobile supermarkets are found throughout Europe, bringing a broad assortment of products (including meats and other refrigerated items) directly to consumers' homes on regularly scheduled visits. These and other home delivery services will flourish as the baby boom generation enters old age in the next century.

For over 100 years, Avon's retailing success relied on the efforts of its direct selling force. Today Avon is a $4 billion international business that still has an enormous number of salespeople, a cottage industry of women selling the company's products door to door. Its great success is based on the relationships that the "Ding-dong, Avon calling" ladies have with their customers. Consumers and salespeople become friends, and this personal relationship leads to high-value, lifetime customers. Until the mid-1990s, Avon's marketing budget went toward commissions, trips, trophies, and testimonial dinners for its salespeople. Avon's recent marketing strategy changes, diverting promotion support to catalogs and advertising, are criticized by some for undermining its salesforce and misreading customer relationships. ■

S. L. Hwang, "Updating Avon Means Respecting History Without Repeating It," *The Wall Street Journal*, April 4, 1994, pp. A1, 4.

direct response   Various nonstore approaches, such as mail order, catalogs, and electronic forms, that interact directly with the consumer.

Direct response uses various marketing approaches to interact directly with the consumer through mail orders, telemarketing (telephone sales), catalogs, and direct response advertising (television and print) and now, Internet shopping by computer. Retailers often use computer-based databases—computer-based lists of consumers who share characteristics that indicate they may be receptive to a retailer's offer. Often, these databases are used to generate personalized materials mailed to consumers with their names imprinted directly on the sales materials. For example, the Book-of-the-Month Club's (BOMC) database of over 3.5 million member names is used to offer books through BOMC's eight book clubs, targeting consumers by their reading preferences.[27] Medco Containment Systems Inc. is the industry leader in mail-order drugs, using sophisticated computer technology to process patients' pharmaceutical needs in an industry that is nearing annual sales of over $6 billion.[28] L.L. Bean mails millions of catalogs annually to over 15 million consumers, using one of the largest computer databases in the world. Lands' End, one of L.L. Bean's most aggressive direct competitors, has a mailing list of over 14 million names, who receive targeted catalogs each year selected from among the 33 different catalogs the company produces (see Photo 10.10).[29]

Although many department stores are increasing their direct-mail catalog operations, Sears, Roebuck & Co., the grandaddy of all catalogs with a nearly 100-year history, eliminated its catalog unit in 1993 in a restructuring effort designed to refocus the core business, respond to changing consumer shopping tastes, and restore profitability. Once the supreme mail-order retailer, Sears was known for its Big Book—the last one had 1,556 pages (see Photo 10.11). "Next to the Bible, the Sears catalogue was once the most popular home literature in America."[30]

Photo 10.10

Lands' End is a major player in the mail-order catalog products market.

Photo 10.11

The Sears catalog, known as the "Wish Book," evolved over the years.

Direct television advertising is a direct-response, nonstore retailing medium in which an advertisement for such products as exercise equipment or magazines encourages consumers to immediately telephone in their order using a credit card to pay. Alternatively, retailers may run **infomercials,** program-length commercials that present products in an entertainmentlike atmosphere. Even upscale department stores like Marshall Field's has had infomercials on CNBC; Nordstrom's, Bloomingdale's, and Williams Sonoma's infomercials have played on NBC Direct, a one-hour shopping infomercial from the Mall of America in Minneapolis.[31]

Infomercials Program-length commercials that present products in an entertainmentlike atmosphere.

Television home shopping on cable provides continuous selling programs offering low prices on a vast assortment of products, most of which are purchased in quantity directly from manufacturers, sometimes as closeouts. Consumers call in their orders by telephone and are guaranteed delivery, usually within several days. Home shopping is a $2 billion industry and growing; even upscale retailers offer their products on cable shopping networks.

Home shopping consumer demographics look very good. In a recent survey of 16,000 households keeping monthly television diaries, consumers who made apparel purchases by television were women in their peak earning years. Most (60 percent) were between the ages of 35 and 54, 59 percent worked full time, 21 percent had annual incomes greater than $60,000, and 92 percent were married.[32]

Research indicates that as many as 64 percent of consumers don't like to shop, the same as the number of people who dislike visiting dentists.[33] For consumers who are sophisticated users of electronic systems (computers, fax machines, and television), interactive shopping systems will be the retail wave of the future.[34] Shoppers will make their selections and pay for them simply by touching a button on a remote control that activates a converter box on their television set hooked into a telephone/computer-based modem.

Vending machines are an intensive form of product distribution offering mostly low-price convenience goods like soft drinks, cigarettes, candy, and newspapers in every location imaginable through approximately 4.5 million units in the United States.[35] Vending machine sales in 1993 totaled more than $1.5 billion. Drawbacks are that the machines require considerable maintenance, including frequent restocking, and sometimes they are vandalized. However, they are convenient and operate regardless of the time or weather. Products offered by vending machine are proliferating and include CDs, lottery tickets, panty hose, french fries, pocket sandwiches, pizza, and more. In Japan, vending machines are wildly popular and offer everything from beer and liquor to sirloin steaks. Vending machine sales should continue to grow because of their convenience and appeal to time-conscious consumers. If a $1 U.S. coin is issued, vending machines will become even more convenient.

Chapter 11, distribution processes, explores how products get to the retailers through a channel of distribution.

Check Your Understanding
10.5

1. Compare and contrast the major forms of store retailers.
2. Why do you think nonstore retailing is growing so fast?
3. Is vending machine shopping going to be popular with all consumers? Explain your answer.

Career Watch

Donald Jonas began his career in retailing in 1947, when he joined his two uncles in running Jonas Shoppes, which consisted of 40 dress shops located on the East Coast. Within five years, he had moved on to managing women's clothing departments for various regional discounters. With the experience gained from these jobs, he founded Barbara Lynn Stores, which eventually expanded to 19 of its own discount stores. He also managed over 140 women's clothing departments in various other stores. In 1977, Jonas and Albert Lechter opened their first housewares outlet in a New Jersey mall, hitting the market just right as department stores began eliminating products from their kitchen departments. Lechters, with over 600 stores, is expanding into outlet centers and superstores offering deep lines of dish towels, trivets, teapots, potato peelers, and other housewares. Lechters' aim is to meet customer needs and become a destination housewares store. Jonas is a retailing entrepreneur with a winning concept. ■

T. Gutner, "You Can't Say No to Opportunity," *Forbes* 150, no. 12 (November 23, 1992), pp. 158–60; "Lechter's 12% Sales Increase," *The Wall Street Journal,* November 3, 1994, p. A3; Paul, C.A., "The Thin Man," *HFD—The Weekly Home Furnishings Newspaper* 68, no. 40 (October 3, 1994), p. 121.

Photo 10.12 Donald Jonas, a retailing entreprenuer and leader of Lechters.

Review of Chapter Objectives

1. *Describe the evolution of retailing in the United States.* Retailing spread across the United States on the backs of peddlers, but soon included general and then specialty stores. Retailing is a dynamic marketing activity that continues to evolve because of intense competition, the volatility of consumer demands, and changes in the retail environment.

2. *Explain the contribution of retailing to the U.S. economy.* Retailing is the marketing activity that makes products available to consumers in stores as well as through nonstore outlets. Retailing in the United States is big business. It is expected to grow steadily through the 1990s.

3. *Identify retailers' tasks and the decisions they make.* Retailer activities relate to the exchange function. The tasks performed and the decisions made involve getting the right products, at the right price, to the right location, in order to satisfy the right target market. Location is one of the most critical retail decisions.

4. *Recognize some of the common ways of classifying retailers.* Retailers can be classified by their product mix, pricing philosophy, services offered, form of ownership, and site, whether they are store or nonstore.

5. *Discuss the future of retailing.* Retailing will flourish in many different forms into the 21st century. These include store and nonstore retailers.

Key Terms

After studying Chapter 10, you should be able to define each of the following key terms and use them in describing marketing activities.

Channel of Distribution, page 303
Retailing, page 304
Retailer, page 304
Scrambled Merchandise, page 304
Specialty Store, page 305
Hypermarkets, page 306
Wheel of Retailing, page 307
Retail Tasks, page 312

Store Atmospherics, page 316
Store Image, page 318
Product Assortment, page 318
Retail Chains, page 320
Franchising, page 320
Cooperative, page 320
Conglomerates, page 320
Direct Selling, page 325
Direct Response, page 326
Infomercials, page 327

Discussion Questions

1. What was retailing like in the early days of this country?

2. Describe some of the new retail types.

3. What is the significance of retailing for the U.S. economy?

4. Describe a retailer's tasks.

5. Compare and contrast a general and a specialty retailer.

6. What is a category killer? Explain the name, and give examples.

7. What factors are often used to classify retailers?

8. Explain what is meant by the term *product assortment.*

9. Compare and contrast the operations of store and nonstore retailers.

10. What kinds of retailers will be successful in the next century? Why?

What Do You Think?

Are supermarket shelves real estate? Supermarkets seem to think so, and consider them valuable real estate at that. Supermarkets are bulging with products, old and new, an average 26,000 different products per store. Shelf space is limited, yet the number of new products seems to be exploding. Most major supermarket chains demand a *slotting allowance* (a fee for renting grocery shelf space) from manufacturers, which helps cover the costs associated with new products, particularly new product failures. For a national distributor, slotting fees nationwide can run in the millions for a single item. Critics of slotting fees say they are keeping new goods off grocery shelves—cheating consumers out of innovative products because it costs so much to buy shelf space. Some supermarkets are trying to replace slotting allowances with fees based on performance. Others say that so many products are line extensions and copycats that consumers aren't missing anything. Are slotting fees harmful? If so, to whom? What do you think?

Sources: L. Therrien, "Want Shelf Space at the Supermarket? Ante Up," *Business Week*, August 7, 1989, pp. 60–61; E. Zwieback, "Four Vendors, Vons Work to End Slotting," *Supermarket News* 43, no. 11 (March 15, 1993), p. 1.

Mini-Case 10.1

Wal-Mart: Small Retailers' Nightmare?

Based in Bentonville, Arkansas, Wal-Mart is a public stand-alone company with over 2,000 stores, 1994 sales of over $67 billion, and profits of almost $2 billion. It is a giant among mass merchandise discounters, a category killer with whom very few small retailers can hope to compete. Wal-Mart has rolled through small- and medium-sized towns in the South and Midwest, changing the face of local retailing in the process, much like a scorched-earth policy. Until recently, Wal-Mart avoided New England, an area known for the solidarity of its small town retailers and the civic loyalty of its townspeople. When the company announced plans to build a 100,000-square-foot store outside Farmington, Maine, retailers in nearby Bath organized. Their goal was, if not to stop the giant, then to find strategies for staying alive once Wal-Mart opened its doors. By consulting with Iowa State University economics professor Kenneth Stone, who studied the Wal-Mart effect, the Bath retailers were advised to "niche around" Wal-Mart: Fill the voids in lines that a far larger company couldn't; compete on value because you can't compete with Wal-Mart on price. In addition, the Bath retailers extended their operating hours, jointly funded downtown shopping programs, and mounted a preemptive ad campaign before Wal-Mart opened. The jury is still out, but Wal-Mart is open and, so far, the downtown retailers are surviving.

Case Questions

1. Should Wal-Mart be admired as a well-run corporation or criticized for squeezing the life out of small town retailers?

2. What do you think of the "niche around" policy? Will it work?

3. Is there room enough for both a Wal-Mart and small retailers in the same town?

Sources: E. O. Welles, "When Wal-Mart Comes to Town," *INC.* 15, no. 7 (July 1993), pp. 76–88; "Living with a Giant," *The Economist* 327, no. 7808 (April 24, 1993), p. 31; T. Pack, "As Wal-Mart Grows, Is It a Predator or Friendly Giant?" *Lexington Herald-Leader* (Business Sunday), April 24, 1994, pp. 14–15; *Wal-Mart Stores, Inc., Annual Reports*, 1994.

Mini-Case 10.2

Saving Sears: A Retailing Challenge

To consumers and other retailers, Sears, Roebuck and Co. is a grand vision of a great American company, a giant company with a record 1993 profit of $2.4 billion on sales of over $50 billion. However, in the early 1990s, Sears faced declining profits and stock value. It had lost its focus and was losing sales and customers to aggressive discounters. The giant retailer was forced to lay off workers, abandon its decade-old acquisition and diversification strategy, and close its catalog operation. In order to raise capital, consolidate its efforts, and refocus its marketing strategy, Sears sold two major businesses, Dean Witter Reynolds Inc., the fifth largest stock broker, and Coldwell, Banker & Co, the largest real estate broker in the United States. Sears, the nation's third largest retailer, put aside $4 billion to revitalize its stores and closed over 100 unprofitable ones. It boosted its more than $1 billion annual marketing budget and increased the number of national brands carried in each store. The new, trendy merchandise strategy focuses on women's apparel and radically departs from Sears's old image as a dowdy place with unfashionable products. Sears has also established a strong retail position in Mexico, where sales have quintupled to $500 million in six years. Although Sears is busy reinventing itself, its competitors aren't sitting still. Rivals are snipping at all of Sears's product lines, from consumer electronics to home improvement and clothing items.

Case Questions

1. How important is image to Sears?

2. What part does store atmospherics play in establishing Sear's image?

3. JC Penney is challenging Sears's upscale image remake, in both the United States and Mexico. If these companies as well as other department stores like Dillard's, Saks Fifth Avenue, and Bloomingdale's are also entering the Mexican market, what do you think are the chances that this market will also become overbuilt?

Sources: G. A. Patterson, "Sears Raises Its Marketing Budget Amid a Shift into New Projects," *The Wall Street Journal,* February 16, 1994, p. B9; B. Ortega, "Penney Pushes Abroad in Unusually Big Way as It Pursues Growth," *The Wall Street Journal,* February 1, 1994, pp. A1, 7; S. W. Bhargava, S. Anderson Forest, and L. Therrien, "After the Big Book, the Big Race," *Business Week,* September 20, 1993, p. 106E-2; J. McCormick, "The Savior at Sears," *Business Week,* November 1, 1993, pp. 42–46; K. Kelly, "The Big Store May Be on a Big Roll," *Business Week,* August 30, 1993, pp. 82–86; J. E. Ellis, "Why Overseas? 'Cause That's Where the Sales Are," *Business Week,* January 10, 1993, pp. 62–63.

Chapter 10 Notes

1. W. Bounds, "Active Seniors Do Laps of the Mall—Then Cool Down by Eating Fast Food," *The Wall Street Journal,* December 9, 1993, pp. B1, 6.

2. G. B. Knecht, "Banks Bag Profits with Supermarket Branches," *The Wall Street Journal,* May 20, 1994, pp. B1, 8.

3. C. Duff, "Brighter Lights, Fewer Bargains: Outlets Go Upscale," *The Wall Street Journal,* April 11, 1994, p. B11; S. Gellers, "Outlet Shoppers Like the Values, Return for More," *Daily News Record* 24, no. 126 (July 1, 1994), p. 3.

4. T. Triplett, "Superstores Tap into Bond Between Owners and Pets," *Marketing News* 28, no. 9 (April 25, 1994), pp. 1–21; L. Eaton, "Hey, Big Spenders," *The New York Times,* September 11, 1994, Sec. 3, p. F1.

5. W. Zellner, "Learning to Survive the '90s," *Business Week,* January 10, 1994, p. 95; B. Ortega, "Warehouse-Club War Leaves Few Standing, and They Are Bruised," *The Wall Street Journal,* November 18, 1993, pp. A1, 6.

6. L. M. Grossman, "Hypermarkets: A Sure-Fire Hit Bombs," *The Wall Street Journal,* June 25, 1993, p. B1.

7. P. Hise, "Prodigy: Smart Sales Channel?" *INC.* 16, no. 2 (February 1994), p. 77.

8. J. A. Trachtenberg, "Interactive Kiosks May Be High-Tech, but They Underwhelm U.S. Consumers," *The Wall Street Journal,* March 14, 1994, pp. B1, 8; E. Ramstad, "Kiosk Craze Widening Interactive Networks," *Lexington Herald-Leader,* August 31, 1993, p. C7.

9. "The Inc. Network: Thought for Food," *INC.* 16, no. 2 (February 1994), p. 99.

10. Table No. 844 "Establishments, Employees, and Payroll, by Industry," Washington, D.C., *Country Business Patterns,* 1993 U.S. Department of Commerce, Economic and Statistics Administration, Bureau of Census.

11. *Standard & Poor's Industry Survey* (New York: McGraw-Hill, 1993), p. R78.

12. L. Zinn, "Steady Traffic at the Mall," *Business Week,* January 9, 1995, p. 86.

13. P. M. Reilly, "Retailers Fortify Security as Fear Deters Shoppers," *The Wall Street Journal,* May 26, 1994, pp. B1, 10.

14. B. Marsh, "Want to Be a Success? Try Opening Only Twice a Week," *The Wall Street Journal,* June 6, 1994, p. B2.

15. J. Pierson, "Do-It-Yourself Grocery Checkout," *The Wall Street Journal,* January 31, 1994, p. B1.

16. R. Gibson, "Warehouse Clubs Have Big Impact on Grocers," *The Wall Street Journal,* April 6, 1992, p. B1.

17. S. W. Bhargava, "Espresso, Sandwiches, and a Sea of Books," *Business Week,* July 26, 1993, p. 81.

18. T. R. Reid, "Savvy Shoppers Looking for a Bah-gahn," *The Washington Post National Weekly Edition* 11, no. 12 (January 17–23, 1994), p. 20.

19. B. J. Feder, "McDonald's Places Large Order for More Franchises," *Lexington Herald-Leader* (Business Sunday), January 16, 1994, p. 3.

20. M. Galen and L. Touby, "Franchise Fracas," *Business Week,* March 22, 1993, pp. 68–73; J. S. Stack and J. E. McKendrick, "Franchise Market Expands as Rest of Economy Slumps," *Marketing News* 26, no. 14 (July 6, 1992), p. 11.

21. G. A. Patterson, "Department Stores, Seemingly Outmoded, Are Perking Up Again," *The Wall Street Journal,* January 4, 1994, pp. A1, 4; G. A. Patterson, "All Decked Out, Department Stores Head Downtown," *The Wall Street Journal,* February 15, 1994, pp. B1, 7.

22. A. Miller, "A Dinosaur No More: Woolworth Corp. Leaves Dime Stores Far Behind," *Newsweek,* January 4, 1993, pp. 54–55; J. A. Trachtenberg, "Woolworth Hopes for a New Specialty-Store Winner," *The Wall Street Journal,* July 2, 1992, p. B3.

23. H. Schlossberg, "Warehouse Club Owners Hope to Sign Up Everybody Eventually," *Marketing News* 27, no. 19 (September 13, 1993), pp. 1, 10.

24. L. M. Grossman, "Families Have Changed but Tupperware Keeps Holding Its Parties," *The Wall Street Journal,* July 21, 1992, pp. A1, 13.

25. J. A. Trachtenberg, "Avon's New TV Campaign Says, 'Call Us,'" *The Wall Street Journal,* December 28, 1992, pp. B1, 4; R. Harris, "Avon Is Calling, and It's a Jungle Out There," *Los Angeles Times,* August 29, 1994, p. A1.

26. "Grocery-on-Wheels Finds Lucrative Niche That Traditional Supermarkets Can't Reach," *Marketing News* 26, no. 6 (March 16, 1992), p. 21.

27. D. Evans, "Too Late?" *Forbes* 151, no. 12 (June 7, 1993), pp. 106–7.

28. "Mail-Order Pharmacies Mushroom," *Marketing News* 27, no. 2 (January 18, 1993), p. 3.

29. P. Berman and A. Feldman, "Trouble in Bean Land," *Forbes* 150, no. 1 (July 6, 1992), pp. 42–44.

30. G. A. Patterson and C. Duff, "Sears Trims Operations, Ending an Era," *The Wall Street Journal,* January 26, 1993, pp. B1, 8; C. Miller, "It Was the Worst of Times: Sears Closes Book on Era; Competitors Hope to Improve Own Success Story," *Marketing News* 27, no. 6 (March 15, 1993), pp. 1, 7; T. D. Schellhardt, "Closing the Book on an American Tradition," *The Wall Street Journal,* January 26, 1993, p. B1.

31. L. Zinn, G. De George, R. Shoretz, D. J. Yang, and S. A. Forest, " 'Retailing Will Never Be the Same': With the Home Shopping Network–QVC Merger, the Stampede Is On," *Business Week,* July 26, 1993, pp. 54–60.

32. P. M. Reilly, "TV Shopping Hooks High-Toned Viewers," *The Wall Street Journal,* November 16, 1993, pp. B1, 10.

33. H. Schlossberg, "Pundits Tout Exceptionally Bright Future for Electronic Marketing," *Marketing News* 27, no. 22 (October 25, 1993), p. 7.

34. C. Roush, "Elbowing into Cable TV's Home-Shopping Slugfest," *Business Week,* May 10, 1993, p. 68.

35. S. Nordgren, "More Options for Our Loose Change," *Lexington Herald-Leader,* October 10, 1993, p. 11; R. L. Allen, "From Fresh Pizza to French Fries, Vending Enters New Era," *Nation's Restaurant News* 28, no. 37, p. 146.

Place: Distribution and Wholesaling

Chapter Objectives

After studying Chapter 11 you should be able to

1. Explain how distribution facilitates the flow of products from producer to consumer.

2. Identify the factors that influence the development of a channel structure.

3. Describe the different perspectives on channels of distribution.

4. Explain the role of wholesalers.

5. Characterize the logistics/physical distribution functions.

*T*he modern channel of distribution is a collection of individuals and businesses that cooperate in facilitating the movement of products from producers to consumers. Unless you work in some facet of distribution, it's unlikely that you're familiar with how products get from where they're produced to where they're sold. Evidence of distribution is all around us but, unlike other marketing activities, it does not call attention to itself. Yet, if you drive on most interstate highways in the United States, you can't miss seeing 18-wheel motor carriers transporting raw materials, supplies, parts, and finished products. Railroads, seaports, inland waterways, and airports are busy with commercial traffic bound across the nation or the world. Warehouses and distribution centers dot the landscape on the outskirts of cities in close proximity to rail spurs and motor highways, but remain hidden from most residential and retail shopping areas. Once you know what to look for you can't miss the signs of distribution networks operating in the United States and, from here, into foreign markets. As you learn about distribution in this chapter, consider this question: If distribution is so important a marketing function, why is it so invisible to most personal use consumers?

Where Are My Roses?

Mary Means is pacing her florist shop nervously, looking at the clock as she mentally counts off the minutes until the shop opens. There is a good reason for her anxiety. She is expecting a large shipment of fresh flowers that will go on sale this morning just in time for Valentine's Day. Flowers are sold at a premium in early February, and this shipment represents a significant investment and source of revenue for her business. The problem is caused by a flood on I-75 in Georgia that closed part of the highway, diverted traffic onto slower side roads, and delayed the refrigerated truck that is delivering Means's and other area florists' flowers. Just as she is about ready to print a sign explaining to her customers why the advertised flowers aren't available, she hears the back door delivery bell ring. With a sigh of relief, the florist opens the back door to accept delivery, just as her assistant opens the front door to customers.

DISTRIBUTION: MANAGING THE FLOW OF PRODUCTS

Objective 1 Explain how distribution facilitates the flow of products from producer to consumer.

The world's first truly multinational company, the English East India Company, was a global giant that controlled nearly half of the world's trade in the early 19th century. Its business interests spanned the world from London to India, Southeast Asia, and China. Company traders established elaborate networks to distribute Spice Islands pepper, English broadcloth, Japanese silver, and Indian cotton. Individuals associated with the company's channel of distribution included at one time the infamous pirate Captain Kidd along with gentlemen traders and adventurers.[1]

Modern channels of distribution may be less colorful than those established by the East India Company, but they are no less essential

Photo 11.1

Selling fresh flowers in the middle of winter is a distribution challenge.

to successfully placing products. As you know, the core job of marketing is to expedite the process of getting seller and buyer together so they can make mutually beneficial exchanges, trading items they value in order to satisfy needs and accomplish goals. The modern channel of distribution is the place variable in the marketing mix that facilitates and expedites marketing exchanges.

Even in today's complex consumer marketplace, many exchanges are still direct, from seller to buyer without go-betweens or intermediaries. A consumer making a purchase from a computer manufacturer is making a direct exchange with the producer. The manufacturer distributes its products with transportation assistance from independent businesses like Federal Express or UPS. The buyer typically pays for the product before it is shipped and pays a shipping and handling fee to have the product delivered. At the same time the computer producer is selling directly to consumers, it is also distributing through retailers, trying to reach the same target markets. This is **dual distribution,** using dual channels to distribute the same products to the same target markets. Others may use even more than two channels.

Around 80 percent of all product purchases involve **intermediaries,** members of a channel of distribution who cooperate and assist in completing the link between producer and consumer. In the case of Mary Means, a businessperson who owns and operates an independent local retail flower shop, she could buy roses directly from rose producers (growers). However, there are no commercial growers in her area, and she doesn't have the time to spend making contacts, negotiating contracts, complying with regulations, and making the many decisions needed to manage a distribution channel. Alternatively, she could become a member of a buying cooperative (independent businesses voluntarily acting together to make bulk purchases), negotiate lower prices, and manage distribution. However, like most retailers, her access to floral products is through a specialty merchant wholesaler that distributes flowers to many small retail florists like Mary Means. The wholesaler purchases its flower inventory from a number of specialty agents, including a rose broker who distributes roses produced by a farm cooperative in South America, an Israeli kibbutz, and an association of greenhouse growers in the Netherlands. The roses that eventually grace homes throughout Mary's town were sold, resold, and transported several times before reaching the retail florist who completes the link with the final consumer.

Marketing intermediaries can be any individual or business that, on a short- or long-term basis, facilitates product distribution and performs any marketing function associated with distribution. Intermediaries are paid for their efforts through fees, salaries, commissions, or product sales. Intermediaries or middlemen, the individuals

dual distribution The use of two channels to distribute the same products to the same target markets.

intermediaries Members of a channel of distribution who cooperate and assist in completing the link between producer and consumer.

Marketing Application 11.1

Imagine that you are a small independent retailer selling personal computers to individuals and businesses. You have a contractual arrangement to exclusively sell one major computer manufacturer's products in your area. You price the company's computers high enough so that you are able to cover your costs and make a reasonable but not excessive profit. You have just learned that the company has decided to also offer its computers through a mail catalog, a new channel of distribution for the manufacturer. The same computers that you sell in your store will be discounted in the catalog, sold below a price that you can match and still clear a profit. As a retailer who sells this manufacturer's product only, what are the likely effects on your business from the manufacturer's new channel of distribution? Could this action by the manufacturer result in friction and discord with you and the other retail members of its channel of distribution? Can you think of some alternative steps you might take to resolve this problem? Explain your answer. ∎

agents Intermediaries with legal authority to act in the name of a manufacturer.

brokers Middlemen who directly bring buyer and seller together to negotiate a sale.

wholesalers Intermediaries who sell to other intermediaries and, sometimes, to final users.

and businesses in the middle between producer and consumer, go by many different names: distributors, dealers, agents, brokers, wholesalers, and retailers. **Agents** are intermediaries with legal authority to act in the name of a manufacturer. Some are owned by manufacturers and are thus manufacturer's agents. **Brokers** are intermediaries who directly bring buyer and seller together, often face to face, to negotiate a sale. You may be familiar with real estate brokers who are the intermediaries facilitating the sale of real estate. A **wholesaler** is an intermediary who sells to other intermediaries, most often to retailers but also to other wholesalers, businesses, and less often to the final user. Retailers, the channel of distribution member most familiar to personal use consumers, are the last member in the distribution channel before products reach the final user.

Both goods and services must be distributed. It's easier to visualize the physical distribution of goods from producer to wholesaler to retailer; for example, the distribution path traditionally used for products sold in supermarkets. However, services are also distributed. Health care is distributed through diverse health care delivery systems. The health care channel structure includes individual clinicians, joint practices, clinics, and general and specialty hospitals. The film industry needs distributors to arrange theater bookings and get its entertainment products to the public. For example, the makers of *Howard's End,* a sophisticated British film, teamed with Walt Disney Studios to gain access to Disney's vast distribution network and advertising support to facilitate placement of their movie in theaters across the United States.[2] A retail chain like Fantastic Sam's needs a channel of distribution to deliver its hair cutting services in outlets in many locations nationally (see Photo 11.2). The Legal Research Network is a business that runs a distri-

Photo 11.2

Services, like haircuts from
Fantastic Sam's, are also
distributed.

bution system for legal research. It is the first of its kind of nationwide
network of lawyers linked by computer to perform legal research for
businesses and law firms on contract through the network.[3]

Distribution Utilities

Many different kinds of channels operate in the United States and
internationally—individuals and businesses working together to
smooth out supply–demand discrepancies and expedite marketing
exchanges. Intermediaries perform marketing functions that add
value to the products they move through a channel. Value is
measured by consumers and represents their increased utility. Intermediaries add value through their ability to perform distribution
activities better than a producer or consumer. Therefore, channel
intermediaries provide:

> *Place utility,* by making products available where they are
> wanted.
>
> *Time utility,* by making products available when consumers want
> them.
>
> *Form utility,* by making products available in the quantities,
> colors, sizes, and other shapes wanted.
>
> *Possession utility,* by providing mechanisms that allow consumers
> to exchange something of value (usually cash, check, or credit)
> for a product and then take possession of it.

Marketing Application 11.2

Education is a service that all Americans use. How is education delivered in your area? Using your own experience and observations, describe the education distribution system in your area. Begin with preschool at the top of your list. How is it delivered? Perhaps your list will include such channel members as Head Start, private for-profit schools, religious schools, and public preschools. Identify the delivery system alternatives for each level from preschool through elementary, middle school, high school, community (junior) college to public and private colleges and universities. What conclusions can you draw about the distribution of education in your area? Is it an efficient system? Are consumers satisfied with it? Bring your work to class for discussion. ■

Distribution Functions

Distribution marketing activities are often highly specialized, and economies can be achieved through specialization efficiencies. It would be costly in time and opportunity costs for Mary Means to become her own distributor; it is much more efficient and cost effective to have specialists do the job for her. Exchange, physical distribution, and servicing must be performed by some channel member when placing products, regardless of which channel member takes on a specific distribution task. The marketing functions associated with distribution are given in the following list:

Exchange functions: Purchasing products from manufacturers (producers), accumulating an inventory of products from which retailers can make their selections, communicating information about products to retailers, and negotiating product exchanges.

Physical distribution functions: Transporting products so that they will be available when and where needed, preferably by the most low-cost method available that still provides the level of service needed; storing products in order to smooth out imbalances between supply and demand, holding products until retailers need them (by carrying this inventory, the channel members assume the risk of storage including possible damage or theft); and sorting products to ensure that a desirable assortment is available to serve consumers (this includes the break bulk function, by which large bulk lots are broken into smaller assortments that can be sold more efficiently by retailers). (See Photo 11.3.)

Servicing functions: Promoting products through cooperative advertising and personal selling; communicating information about products to retailers; pricing products; performing market re-

Photo 11.3

The break bulk function of physical distribution.

search; and servicing other channel members by extending financing assistance, credit, or delivery.

1. What is a marketing intermediary?
2. Identify the utilities provided by distribution.
3. Describe the marketing functions associated with distribution.

CHANNEL STRUCTURE

Channel structure refers to the form a channel takes, its length, arrangement, and size. This reflects the types and numbers of intermediaries distributing a product. Product movement may be real, as in the physical transfer of a good from St. Louis to Chicago. It also refers to a legal transfer—changes in title and ownership of a product—that may move from one channel member to another with or without the accompanying physical movement of the product. Other movements within a channel involve payment transfers and risk transfer (when one channel member purchases—takes title to—products, it also accepts the risk of ownership).

Channel structure also exists for the distribution of services. For example, an automated teller machine is a retail outlet for the distribution of financial services to consumers. The distribution of credit can be traced through a channel that includes a major lending institution like Fannie Mae (which is a credit producer) through a bank wholesaler and retail bank lending office to a consumer.

An individual business may have little say in its channel structure, because the structure is characteristic of a particular industry, such as car dealers in the automobile industry. A business becomes part of an established contractual distribution channel when it

Objective 2 Identify the factors that influence the development of a channel structure.

channel structure The form of a distribution path—its length, arrangement, and size.

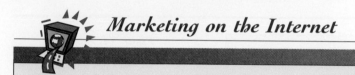

Marketing on the Internet

Marketers are exploring ways to use the Internet for product and information distribution particularly to their business customers, suppliers, and other channel members. The Internet is emerging as a most effective way to reach other business consumers; more effective than the commercial on-line services.

GE Plastics is one of the first Fortune 500 companies to establish a major Internet presence by seeking new and improved ways to use the Internet to establish closer relationships with business customers and suppliers. GE Plastics provides its customers and suppliers with immediate access to technical information, design guides, product information, and technical support. (The company's customers are scientists, designers, and engineers from businesses primarily in the computer and automotive industries.) GE Plastics uses a customized version of Spry's Internet-in-a-Box software that allows users to be automatically directed to the GE site. This software makes access fast and easy.

The Internet Shopping Network (ISN) keeps prices low for its 20,000 computer hardware and software products by eliminating many distribution-related selling expenses. Internet customer orders are handled electronically by computers that also automatically check inventory, debit the customer's account, and order the product electronically to be shipped directly from a distributor.

IBM is offering a new distribution method with its IBM NetView Distribution Manager and software that can be installed automatically from the IBM network. This purchasing and electronic delivery system is being pilot tested with a local area network service provider and Sears, Roebuck and Co. ■

T. C. Taylor, "Marketing: The Next Generation," *Sales & Marketing Management,* February 1995, pp. 43–44; S. D. Solomon, "Staking a Claim on the Internet," *INC. Technology Annual* 16, no. 3 (1994), pp. 87–88, 90, 92; "IBM Outlines Plans for Advanced Delivery System," *Purchasing* 117, no. 8 (November 24, 1994), p. 58.

becomes a franchisee of a McDonald's or KFC. Some businesses are bought by corporations and, therefore, become part of a corporation-owned distribution system. Others may have to shop around for a channel, seeking leads on wholesalers, suppliers, transport agents, and other intermediaries to establish relationships with and form into a distribution network. Names of potential channel members can be obtained through trade shows, manufacturer's directories, professional trade publications, and chambers of commerce.

A channel's structure is a function of a number of factors. These include *company attributes, product type, markets, competitors, custom,* and the *marketing environment.*

Company Attributes   Some businesses dominate their channels of distribution. For example, Toyota Motor Manufacturing U.S.A. and Wal-Mart have the resources to dictate the structure of their channels. Other businesses lack such resources and, from necessity, become part of an existing channel sometimes through a voluntary association, other times through an exclusive arrangement tied to a manufacturer or retailer. Independent businesses make distribution decisions that affect their channel structure based on how much they can spend on distribution. A business start-up strapped for cash may rent public storage space to store its inventory because it can't afford to enter into a longer-term agreement with a specialized warehouse facility. It may purchase office supplies and products for resale through Office Depot and Sam's Club rather than through a trade wholesaler. It may lease transport carriers instead of purchasing them, or use Federal Express or UPS for transportation services.

Product Type Product characteristics must be considered when deciding on the type and number of intermediaries to use. Because of their bulk and value, automobiles are generally shipped directly to dealers from the manufacturer without using other intermediaries. If you drive past the Toyota Motor Manufacturing U.S.A. plant in Kentucky, you'll see hundreds of new Toyota Camrys parked beside a railroad spur, waiting to be loaded and transported to Toyota dealers throughout the United States. Some of the automobiles will be transported by rail or motor carrier to seaports and then shipped to Japan, where they are sold door to door by automobile salespeople or through catalogs displayed at street-corner automobile stores. If, instead, the automobiles were transported to a warehouse and stored before being shipped to dealers, the additional intermediaries and transportation would add to their base cost and the final price paid by consumers.

On the other hand, most convenience and shopping goods are routinely sent from the manufacturer to a wholesaler who sorts, breaks bulk, prices, warehouses, and accumulates product lots before transporting them to retailers when and where, and in the form, size, and assortment, needed. Perishable products with a short shelf life, such as eggs, meats, and vegetables, are moved quickly through a

Photo 11.4

Quick movement through the channel of distribution will keep these grapes fresh.

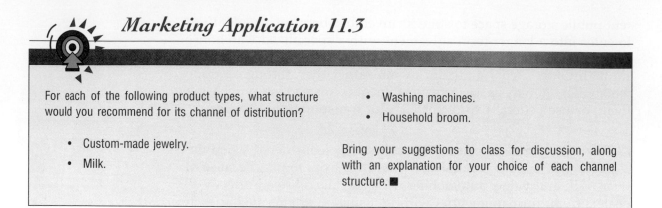

Marketing Application 11.3

For each of the following product types, what structure would you recommend for its channel of distribution?

- Custom-made jewelry.
- Milk.

- Washing machines.
- Household broom.

Bring your suggestions to class for discussion, along with an explanation for your choice of each channel structure. ∎

channel of distribution in order to reach market before they spoil. Nonperishable products, such as lumber, building tools, and washing machines, may spend considerable time in a warehouse before being transported to retailers. Seasonal products, such as Christmas ornaments or back-to-school supplies, are produced and then stored in warehouses or distribution centers until retailers are ready to stock and sell them. Custom-made or modified products call for a more direct distribution structure with few, if any, intermediaries.

Markets   Toyota Motor Manufacturing U.S.A. operates under a just-in-time (JIT) delivery system. This means that suppliers must be able to resupply Toyota within a day so that its assembly line never stops because of a raw materials or supply stockout. This relieves Toyota of the cost of maintaining a large inventory of raw materials and supplies on site. As a result of Toyota's JIT requirements, most Toyota suppliers are located within several hours' delivery time of the plant. The buyer (Toyota) dictated a very short channel structure, with no other intermediaries, located nearby. This type of short channel is common with products destined for business/organization consumers. Wholesalers and distribution centers often cluster around manufacturing centers, like the furniture producers in the Carolinas, computer software manufacturers in California, and tire makers in Akron, Ohio. An example of JIT delivery is shown in Photo 11.5. For more on JIT systems, see page 352.

The channel structure for most business/industrial products usually is very direct, with few (if any) intermediaries. A manufacturer takes in raw materials and supplies, produces products, and distributes them either directly or through agents. Manufacturers selling products to business/organization consumers often use inside and outside salespeople to negotiate product sales. Others use independent contractors such as manufacturer's representatives, who act on behalf of the producer by selling its products to other

Photo 11.5

Saturn has a just-in-time (JIT) delivery system in place for the delivery of raw materials and supplies for production and the transport of finished products to dealers.

businesses. Alternatively, the producer may sell title to its products and, therefore, product distribution is left to a wholesaler. When independent merchant wholesalers are used, they often are the only intermediary between the producer and business/organization consumer.

Market demand for many personal use consumer products calls for broad channel coverage. For example, vending machines are everywhere because consumers demand instant access to soft drinks and snack foods. The need to keep the machines supplied, as well as stock supermarkets, gasoline stations, convenience stores, movie theaters, restaurants, and other retailers, requires production close to the market and a large number of intermediaries to transport and store the products. As a result, there are many bottling plants and snack food production facilities nationwide that ensure uninterrupted product supply within their metropolitan area, state, or region. Consumer demand strongly influences channel structure. For example, Hospitality Franchise Systems Inc. has signed an agreement with McDonald's to test the delivery of McDonald's products to patrons of selected members of the Days Inn, Howard Johnson, Park Inn, Ramada Inn, and Super8 motel chains; McDonald's is also testing home delivery in Virginia.[4]

Channel structure in personal use consumer markets usually is more complicated than in business/organization channels. Figure 11.1 represents the most common forms of channels between producers and consumers in personal use markets. The simplest and most direct channel is example A; the most complex, least direct is example D. Direct channels account for about 20 percent of product distribution and are becoming increasingly popular as more consumers show their preference for shopping by mail, telephone, or computer.

Figure 11.1

Channels of Distribution
Structures for Personal Use
Consumers

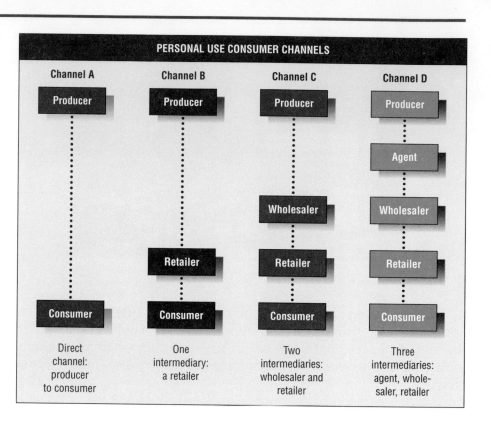

Let's take a closer look at Figure 11.1. *Channel A* is a *direct channel,* used by a producer like Dell Computers, without intermediaries between the manufacturer and consumer. Although salespeople are used to answer potential customer questions, demonstrate products, and take and deliver orders, they are not considered members of the channel. Instead, this channel presents an unbroken link between producer and consumer.

Channel B is a channel with one intermediary, usually a large national chain *retailer* with many stores, like a Wal-Mart, Toys 'Я' Us, Sears, or Kmart, that collects an assortment of products from many different manufacturers and offers them to consumers, sometimes with its own brand names on the products. A large retailer has buying power through the quantities it purchases and can negotiate attractive deals with producers that allow it to keep costs down and pass along savings to consumers in the form of price discounts.

Channel C is a two-intermediary channel. In addition to a retailer, this channel also has a *wholesaler,* a channel member who collects products from different producers and offers them to retailers that market directly to personal use and business/organization consumers. In order to offer an attractive assortment of clothing to consumers, a full-service department store's buyers work with one or more wholesalers (often manufacturer's representatives) to put together clothing from many different manufacturers.

Channel D is the most complex and involves even more intermediaries, perhaps three or more. In this type of channel, agents or brokers collect products from a number of producers, then distribute them to wholesalers and, finally, to retailers.

Some producers use multiple channels as a mechanism for maximizing their exposure to consumers. Personal computer producers often use multimember channel distribution systems. For example, personal computers may be distributed directly from the manufacturer as well as through small computer specialty stores; major computer dealers; discount stores; category killers; mail-order retailers; computer shows at colleges, universities, and other locations where large groups of users are found; and even by developing a distribution system for reconditioned used computers.[5]

Competitors The competition can influence channel structure. Computer makers who historically distributed their products through exclusive agreements with wholesalers and retailers have been forced by the pressure of competition to expand their distribution channels to include catalog and telephone sales as well as distribution through discount retailers. At one time, telephone service was tightly regulated and distribution was restricted. Deregulation and competition have changed distribution channels for both telephone services and telephones.

Custom For over a half century, automobiles in the United States have been distributed through dealers—manufacturer's representatives who sign exclusive contractual arrangements with one producer to sell only that producer's new products. Therefore, there is an exclusive dealer for Toyota products, another for Ford products, and others for Chrysler, Honda, or Mazda. It is also customary that although the Toyota dealer sells only new Toyota automobiles, vans, and trucks, it may also have many different used cars for sale on its lot, including Fords, Chryslers, Hondas, and Mazdas. Although customs generally are hard to change, some automobile dealerships now represent multiple manufacturers, selling new General Motors products along with new Volkswagens and new Hondas, as well as many different used cars. New automobiles are also sold to final consumers through warehouse clubs and independent discount businesses that consumers hire to help them get the best price on a new car.

International Marketing Report

Automobile distribution in Russia is far different than in the United States. Trinity Motors is a privately owned General Motors (GM) distributorship in Moscow. Private investors from the United States, Russia, and Great Britain set up the dealership in 1992, expecting to eventually expand to about 40 major cities in Russia. Trinity already has established dealerships to sell Chevrolets, Pontiacs, and Cadillacs in Moscow, St. Petersburg, and Kiev. All of the GM cars sold in Russia are made in the United States, transported by truck and rail to ocean ports, packed aboard cargo ships, and shipped to Finland. After arrival, the cars are taken to warehouses where they are stored, and then transported to one of the Russian dealerships on demand. It typically takes at least one month to transport a GM car from the United States to Russia. Sales are slow in Moscow, with an annual turnover running between 500 to 1,000 automobiles. Projections initially were for at least 5,000 units annually, but escalating import taxes (rising in two years from 25 percent to 166 percent per car), economic uncertainty, and a growing black market in smuggled automobiles is making it harder to sell GM cars legitimately. Each GM car costs the dealership about $30,000 in duties and taxes. A Chevrolet that sells for $24,000 in the United States is priced at two and a half times that amount in Russia. ■

A. Ignatius, "GM Dealer Hits Rough Road in Russia," *The Wall Street Journal*, June 28, 1994, p. A15;. J. Rossant, "Tackling Transport Problems: Obtaining Secure and Efficient Transport of Goods Is a Big Challenge for Companies with Business in the CIS," *Business Eastern Europe* 23, no. 31 (August 1, 1994), p. 1.

Marketing Environment   Many businesses' marketing environments are relatively stable and, therefore, so is their channel structure. On the other hand, other businesses experience highly volatile environments that can influence channel structure dramatically and rapidly. Changes in the economy and particularly an increase in interest rates, recession, or inflation can result in higher inventory holding costs. As a result, channel structure may shorten, often by eliminating storage to reduce inventory holding times and costs. General economic conditions affect consumer spending and shopping patterns; people working longer hours often turn to time- and labor-saving shopping alternatives. As a result, new distribution systems have evolved, many using computer-based home shopping services. This technology allows producers to experiment with new channel structures. For example, American Greetings Company is working with computer on-line service Prodigy and various multimedia companies to deliver its greeting cards electronically. Their system allows consumers to create and print greeting cards, posters, and even personalized books at home using interactive systems like those created by IBM and Sears Roebuck for Prodigy.[6]

Check Your Understanding
11.2

Identify some of the factors that influence channel structure.

Distribution Strategies

The distribution strategy for a product determines how broadly or narrowly a product is distributed and affects the number of intermediaries involved. Think about soft drinks and snack foods being constantly available just about everywhere. This distribution strategy means that the product distribution system must provide widespread product availability. The result is a complex distribution system designed to get the product from its many points of production to thousands of points of sale across the country and, often, into international markets as well. Regional production facilities, warehouses, and distribution centers shorten the distance from point of production to point of sale. This is the strategic alternative to a single or a few production facilities supported by a vast transportation system with carriers traveling long distances to reach widespread distribution points.

Intensive distribution makes convenience products readily available in as many places as possible. Products that are intensively distributed include groceries, laundry detergents, and low-cost products that can be purchased from vending machines, such as soft drinks and snack foods. PepsiCo is intensifying its already broad distribution of fast foods, moving into airports, supermarkets, and just about anywhere else consumers can be reached. The company is transferring the soft-drink mentality of "Be ubiquitous in distribution" to its fast foods in order to counteract slow growth in demand for its foods in restaurants.[7] However, when distribution is so broad, it becomes a considerable and critical task to ensure that products are kept stocked.

Other products are distributed more narrowly through far fewer outlets. **Selective distribution** decreases the number of distribution points compared to intensive distribution, but does not necessarily reduce the complexity of the distribution task. Selectively distributed products include shopping products, consumer durables, and many nondurables. (See Photo 11.6.) For example, a line of clothing may be sold only in several hundred exclusive retail outlets, but these outlets are located in major metropolitan areas and resorts spread across the United States. An industrial product may be sold to several hundred businesses, but they also are located in different parts of the country.

Finally, there is **exclusive distribution,** which restricts the coverage to a few or sometimes only one outlet in an area and, therefore, narrows the distribution system needed. Typically, exclusive distribution is used for prestige products, luxuries, and unique goods and services that are infrequently replaced or may be irreplaceable. Art galleries offering original paintings or bookstores with first editions

intensive distribution The strategy of making products readily available in as many places as possible.

selective distribution The strategy of limiting the number of distribution points.

exclusive distribution The strategy of restricting distribution, therefore narrowing the distribution system needed.

Photo 11.6

Tiffany & Company has expanded its channel of distribution to include a catalog and several retail stores outside its original New York City location.

are highly exclusive outlets for specialty products. The distribution of Porsche or Ferrari automobiles in the United States is highly exclusive, limited to a few dealers located in very high-income areas and a channel system to support them.

Channel Management

A channel of distribution is much like a marriage: some are happy and others are not. Ideally, all should be happy. A channel can be a smoothly operating, harmoniously interdependent, cooperative group of businesses and people working together, depending on one another for their mutual benefit. Conversely, it may be teeming with conflict and struggles for power and leadership. Most channels fall somewhere in between these extremes. Also, like marriages, some channels start out happy and eventually, over time, fall into discord and, finally, divorce.

The management of a channel is often left to a channel captain—a leader who directs channel activities, negotiates settlements in the case of channel conflicts, and establishes operating policies. By managing a smoothly operating, coordinated process, a channel captain can reduce costs and increase profits for all members. A harmonious channel also tends to be more stable over time.

For a long period of time, large manufacturers typically were the captains of their channels because of their concentrated power, size, and resources. Today, power is shifting to the large retailers like Wal-Mart, Kmart, Toys 'Я' Us, Home Depot, Circuit City, Dillard Department Stores, Target, and Costco.[8]

Wal-Mart has channel power because of its buying power and sophisticated information management systems that track consumer purchases and inventory resupply needs in real time, as they occur. Armed with real-time purchase information, Wal-Mart can dictate to its main suppliers such terms as what to produce, when it is to be delivered, at what price, and in what quantities.[9] This is not a unique example but appears to indicate a growing trend, by which powerful retailers dictate terms to suppliers, even when the suppliers are such manufacturing giants as Procter & Gamble. Other examples of a retailer's control over its channel include Servistar, a hardware company with over 4,500 stores nationwide, and Japan's Ito-Yokado, which owns over 4,000 7-Eleven stores.[10]

Often, in order to gain control over a channel, one member will purchase another member and **vertical integration** takes place. For example, a department store chain may purchase a trucking company or a warehouse operation in order to lower its channel costs and exert firmer control over its supply network. Often, there is greater harmony in a vertically integrated channel because all of the intermediaries are working for the same company and should have a united purpose and integrated management.

vertical integration Control gained over a channel of distribution often when one member purchases another.

Horizontal integration occurs when one channel member acquires others at the same level; for example, a buyout by one department store chain of another, similar chain. Often horizontal integration occurs when one chain wants to expand into a new market. Buying up established stores can be a better option than entering the market and encountering the established store's competition. Federated Department Stores, Inc., is an example of aggressive horizontal integration. Included among its holdings are such chains as A&S/Jordan Marsh (35 stores), Burdines (46 stores), Bloomingdale's (15 stores), Lazarus (40 stores), Rich's/Goldsmith's (23 stores), Bon Marche (39 stores), and Sterns (22 stores).[11]

horizontal integration Expansion and control resulting when one channel member buys out another at the same level.

Wal-Mart integrates horizontally each time it buys out a competitor; for example, it did so in its purchase of 122 Canadian Woolco units and 91 PACE stores from Kmart in the United States.[12] Wal-Mart closed many PACE outlets that were in direct competition with its own Sam's Clubs; noncompeting PACE stores were converted to Sam's.

just-in-time system An inventory tracking system that results in materials and supplies being delivered at the right time. This may be just in time for production, operations, or to restock shelves, thus eliminating storage time, warehousing costs, or idle production time.

Just-in-Time Systems   The first **just-in-time system** was developed by Marks & Spencer, an upscale British retailer, more than 50 years ago. Because of that chain's buying power and marketing information system, it was able to direct its suppliers' manufacturing schedules to accommodate the chain's needs, ensuring that products were delivered to the store *just in time* for them to restock shelves and be sold. Marks & Spencer spends about $55 million annually installing new information technology systems in its stores.[13] A JIT system, therefore, greatly reduces inventory holding costs by eliminating storage time and warehousing. Wal-Mart, 7-Eleven, Toyota, and many others use JIT systems to cut costs, increase efficiency, and manage their distribution system. By eliminating warehouses and storage time from a channel, the JIT system goes a long way toward eliminating the need for many wholesalers as well.

Supermarkets also are beginning to adopt JIT systems in an effort to stop the erosion of their profits to grocery sales at supercenters run by Wal-Mart, Kmart, and others. Although the grocery industry annually generates over $280 billion in revenues, stores operate on an average profit margin of only 1 percent. If supermarkets can reduce storage time for their products, they can also reduce costs and that can be passed along to consumers in lower, more competitive prices. For most supermarkets, JIT is tied to bar code scanning systems that allow stores to track their inventory in real time through electronic data interchange (EDI) systems. Reorders can be made based on store needs; thus, orders can be delivered directly to a store instead of a warehouse and **stockouts** (failing to have merchandise available when needed) can be avoided.[14]

stockouts Failures to have merchandise available when needed.

reverse channels Return of products to a producer in a recall or recycling of products.

Reverse Channels   Interest is growing in the distribution of products back to the producer. These backward distribution systems are often called **reverse channels,** by which products are returned to a producer in a recall or recycled by transporting them back to either the original producer or another business that separates usable from unusable materials, and then processes the usable and disposes of the unusable. The environmental movement has spurred interest in reverse channels, particularly over the past decade. When you return glass bottles or aluminum cans to a recycling center or a grocery store, you are involved with a reverse channel or backward distribution.

Another application of reverse channels is in product recalls. When a recall is announced, retailers pull products off their shelves and send them back through the channel (through a wholesaler if used) to the producer. Personal use consumers may also become involved in the process if they have the product in their homes. Their responsibility is to return the product to the retailer, who then sends it backward through the channel.

Check Your Understanding
11.3

1. Compare and contrast the three distribution coverage alternatives: intensive, selective, and exclusive distribution.
2. Are all channels managed smoothly? Explain your answer.
3. Discuss the use of reverse channels of distribution.

PERSPECTIVES ON CHANNELS OF DISTRIBUTION

Objective 3 Describe the different perspectives on channels of distribution.

A revolution is occurring in distribution, propelled by forces both inside and outside of marketing.[15] The computer has been a critical factor in information management, allowing the real-time assessment of stock needs that can be used to make just-in-time product deliveries. Computers also have automated many warehousing tasks formerly performed by people. Channels of distribution are experiencing consolidations and the emergence of larger organizations that tend to dominate their businesses. Distribution is seen as the last place where significant cost savings can be found; therefore, it is being pressed to remove inefficiencies and waste.

Another change in the overall perspective about channels of distribution is that roles are blurring. For example, what is Wal-Mart? The answer depends on the situation. A Wal-Mart discount store is a retailer that sells products to personal use consumers. A Sam's Club is both retailer and wholesaler. Before 11:00 A.M. each weekday the clubs are open only for business or organization customers; after 11:00 A.M. the clubs are open to both personal use and business/organization consumers. Wal-Mart also is a transport company, warehouser, wholesaler, creditor, advertiser, and so on. The lesson to be learned is that as businesses change so do the ways in which marketing distribution functions are performed.

There are many different perspectives on distribution. From the personal use consumer's perspective, distribution may seem like a waste of money, yet few consumers are willing to accept stockouts and time or place inconveniences. Most personal use as well as business/organization consumers in the United States expect products to be

Consumer Insight

Takuhaibin (home delivery) is extremely popular in Japan, transporting about 1.2 billion parcels annually, or 10 per each person. It has roots in the 17th century system of *hikyaku*, couriers who delivered items between Japanese feudal lords. In a mountainous, exceedingly congested country, *takuhaibin* is essential for getting deliveries anywhere, mostly overnight, for a reasonable price (about $7 for the smallest package). The largest *takuhaibin* company has annual revenues of slightly over $5 billion, about a third the revenue of the U.S. Postal Service. *Takuhaibin* is used to deliver thank-you gifts, suitcases to airports, dirty laundry to the cleaners, foods, and business products to companies using just-in-time delivery systems. Delivery trucks are high-tech, armed with refrigerators, two-way radios, printers, and satellite navigation systems. The only parcels that are not accepted are explosives and live animals; otherwise, *takuhaibin* delivers anything. ∎

J. Cody, "Ding-Dong, Here's a Thank-You Fish; Is There Any Reply?" *The Wall Street Journal*, July 12, 1994, pp. A1, 4.

available when and where they need and want them. Because there are so many ways to obtain most products, most consumers faced with a supply problem will shop around for a new channel delivery system to get what they want.

From the standpoint of the retailer, perspective depends to a great extent on the retailer's size and resources. For the largest, distribution is a key to cost savings; therefore, a channel is something to be dominated, its members forced to conform to the powerful retailer's expectations and demands. This often means squeezing smaller members to extract cost savings. For the small retailer, distribution costs can mean price disadvantages, yet the channel provides products that otherwise might be unavailable or only available in inappropriate sizes or assortments, and services they need to operate their businesses.

For the wholesaler, many of the advances in computer-derived efficiencies may either spell profit (if the wholesaler advances with the technology) or doom (if the wholesaler buries its head in the sand). Some observers believe that wholesaling will diminish in importance, replaced by computer technology that will allow production on demand and eliminate the need to break bulk, sort, store, and transport products to retailers. In the meantime, wholesalers are being squeezed by producers and retailers to eliminate waste, increase efficiency, and reduce costs.

Large manufacturers realize that their days of being able to dominate a channel without challenge have passed. Large retailers have the clout to make production demands on manufacturers that would have been unheard of at one time. All channel members should realize that only through cooperation and negotiation can they survive and prosper.

Government's perspective is that channels should be efficient, competitive, and benefit consumers and the economy. Government's role is to maintain competitiveness, monitor channel activities, and ensure that channel agreements do not undermine fair competition by tying up distributors in exclusive and binding agreements and restrict entry into distribution networks. In particular, the government wants to ensure that monopolies do not result. Laws that govern distribution practices include the Sherman Antitrust Act, the Clayton Act, and the Federal Trade Commission Act.

WHOLESALERS

A wholesaler is a channel of distribution member—an intermediary that provides retailers with products to stock and operate the retail business, expedites the distribution of manufacturers' products, and provides products for other businesses and organizations. Wholesalers don't make products and only rarely sell directly to the general public. They transport products, redirect them, and often transfer titles. Most goods and many services are handled by wholesalers.

Objective 4 Explain the role of wholesalers.

Wholesale Tasks

Independent wholesalers offer many useful services, to both retailers and manufacturers, to facilitate the efficient movement of products to consumers. Wholesalers achieve cost advantages by purchasing large quantities of products directly from manufacturers. The wholesaler breaks bulk—reduces large-quantity lots into smaller lots to sell to retailers. Take the case of the local florist who needs only 10 dozen long-stem red roses each week. The wholesaler purchases several *hundred* dozen that will be divided into lots of 10 dozen each and sold to many different local florists who don't need several hundred dozen roses but do need 10 dozen. By buying in bulk, the wholesaler gets quantity discounts that lower the price charged to the smaller retailer. Because retailer storage space often is quite limited, a wholesaler can offer temporary storage services and then prompt delivery of products when the retailer needs them. Wholesalers keep retailers informed about new products and market opportunities. They often allow retailers to delay payment and, through this credit, assist retailers in financing purchases. Some wholesalers offer seminars and various business assistance programs to retailers.[16] Some of the tasks commonly performed by wholesalers are identified in Figure 11.2.

Figure 11.2 Wholesaler Tasks

Purchasing
Identify sources of products for retailers and retailers that need products. Purchase products for retailers (often in large quantities) at lower costs, then break the bulky large purchase into smaller lots that are more usable and salable to retailers.

Sorting
Separate and group products into bunches of like characteristics (size, shape, color, form). Grade products and group by quality and uniformity.

Accumulating
Assemble sorted product bunches into larger parcels for transport to retailers in order to qualify for lower transport charges.

Storing
Temporarily hold products in a warehouse in order to smooth out imbalances between production and retailer demand.

Transporting
Deliver collections of products to retailers on demand while trying to obtain good transport rates.

Financing
Providing credit and other forms of financial assistance.

Some very large retailers, such as Wal-Mart, Kmart, and Circuit City, perform wholesale tasks themselves through retailer-owned wholesale facilities. Because of their buying power, they can make large-quantity purchases directly from manufacturers, achieve cost savings through bulk purchases, and then undertake wholesale tasks. Circuit City has one of the most efficient computerized inventory and distribution systems in the industry; it allows real-time tracking of products and just-in-time delivery to stores as the products are needed on the shelf.[17] Alternatively, some manufacturers often undertake wholesale functions because the products they offer require specialized handling that they alone can provide.

Distribution centers are among the fastest-growing part of wholesaling. These massive super warehouses (a quarter of a million to a million square feet) are highly efficient and built near highways to accommodate truck traffic. Since trucking deregulation in the early 1980s, truck haulers have become dominant shippers. Older warehouses are more often found near rail lines.[18]

The Economic Impact of Wholesaling

In 1991, there were almost 500,000 wholesale trade establishments in the United States. Almost 60 percent were durable goods wholesalers, and the remainder were nondurable goods wholesalers. Over 6.2 million Americans are employed in the wholesale trade with an

Marketing Application 11.4

With the help of your teacher, identify several retailers in your area who would be willing to discuss their channel of distribution. Develop several questions to ask these retailers about how they obtain products for their stores, from whom, and what wholesalers do for them. Contact the retailers and ask the questions, then report back to the class on your results. ■

Photo 11.7

Modern warehouses use computers to become more efficient, reduce costs, and serve customers more effectively.

annual payroll of about $183 billion.[19] Most wholesalers are small, often family-owned and -operated businesses that handle almost $2 trillion worth of products annually.

Classifying Wholesalers

There are three principal types of wholesalers: merchant wholesalers; brokers and agents; and manufacturer's representatives.

Merchant wholesalers are independent businesspeople who take title to the merchandise they handle and, thereby, assume all of the risks of ownership, including theft, damage, and the costs of merchandise that can't be sold. Merchants who distribute a broad array of products are general merchants. There also are specialty merchants that are highly specialized, just like the retailers to whom they supply limited lines of merchandise. Full-service merchants provide a full range of services such as offering credit, delivery, and assistance with other marketing activities such as advertising.

merchant wholesalers
Independent businesspeople who take title to the merchandise they handle and thereby assume all of the risks of ownership.

Limited-service merchants offer few if any services, something that some retailers actually prefer, because fewer or reduced services lower overall costs. Types of wholesalers are identified in Figure 11.3.

Brokers and agents are wholesalers that do not take title to the merchandise they handle (although they may take possession). Their role is to provide facilities for the transfer, for which they receive payment according to the quantity of goods sold. Manufacturer's agents sell products for a particular manufacturer. Brokers are not part of any manufacturer's network, and sell product lines rather than specific brands; for example, real estate brokers and vegetable brokers act as negotiators or mediators between buyer and seller. Brokers and agents may arrange for such services as credit and delivery, but don't offer this service themselves. Brokers and agents receive a commission for linking buyers and sellers.

manufacturer's representatives
Wholesalers employed by one or several producers and paid on commission according to quantity sold.

Manufacturer's representatives are employed by one or several producers; therefore, they are not independent businesses. These wholesalers are often a substitute field sales force for small manufacturers. For example, manufacturer's reps in clothing lines may

Figure 11.3   Major Types of Merchant Wholesalers

FULL-SERVICE MERCHANTS
These merchant wholesalers perform all of the services of wholesaling. They represent the largest number of all wholesalers. Their main clients are retailers.

LIMITED SERVICE MERCHANTS
These wholesalers perform only a limited number of wholesaling services. The major types are:

Truck Jobbers
Distribute a limited number of products that need immediate restocking, such as perishable staples, eggs, bread, and milk, to limited numbers of retailers. They trade off their fast delivery of products for higher price.

Drop Shippers
Are more facilitators than merchandise handlers. They take title to but not actual physical possession of merchandise, acting as intermediaries between buyers and sellers (retailers and producers) to arrange for the direct transfer of merchandise, often high-bulk, low-cost items like building supplies and coal. They are often called desk jobbers.

Cash and Carry Wholesalers
In exchange for lower cost goods, buyers pay cash and pick up goods themselves, thereby allowing the wholesaler to limit its costs and pass along the savings to the buyer. A restaurant may go to a produce wholesaler to buy fresh vegetables for the day's menu.

Rack Jobbers
These wholesalers provide the racks to shelves for such products as toys and housewares in supermarkets. They keep title for their products and sell on consignment to their customers, who pay only as products are sold.

represent a line of designer clothes that are taken to various retailers and offered for sale. Typically, reps are paid on commission according to quantity sold.

Check Your Understanding
11.4

1. What is the role of wholesaling in product distribution?
2. Describe the different wholesale tasks.
3. Identify the different types of wholesalers.

Making Wholesale Decisions

Wholesalers are facing many challenges as the marketplace evolves rapidly into one dominated by information. The major threat is that interactive retailing systems (television, computers, telephone) and just-in-time inventory control will eliminate many wholesaler tasks and wholesalers themselves. In addition, just as manufacturing and retailing are consolidating, many small independent wholesalers are being pressed to consolidate by the competition of larger wholesalers. In the face of these pressures, good wholesaling decisions are a matter of survival. Wholesalers must respond to the need for greater efficiency that requires decisions about computerized tracking of retailers' product needs and suppliers' production scheduling.

Overall, wholesalers must make marketing decisions about products, prices, promotions, and markets, as well as decisions specific to place. Such decisions include:

Products: What lines to carry, the assortment, width, and depth; what (if any) services to offer.

Prices: To a certain extent prices are industry standard; for example, a 1 percent profit margin in grocery categories. However, with the cost savings that accrue from better inventory control, prices may be lowered on some lines without reducing profit. Profit margins must be maintained in order to cover costs and preserve operations.

Promotions: These are not as immediate a concern to wholesalers as they are to most retailers. Personal selling is more of an issue, particularly in the case of manufacturer's representatives.

Markets: These are of concern to wholesalers, just as they are to retailers. Without a clear definition of the markets to be served, the other wholesaler decisions will miss their mark. In addition to identifying who is to be served, wholesalers must make location decisions that determine where wholesalers operate and what retailers they will serve.

LOGISTICS/PHYSICAL DISTRIBUTION FUNCTIONS

Objective 5   Characterize the logistics/physical distribution functions.

Some marketers make a distinction between logistics and physical distribution, whereas others don't. When the distinction is made, logistics is identified as an overall process that includes supply distribution and physical distribution. Supply distribution moves raw materials and parts into production; physical distribution moves products from producer to consumer (see Figure 11.4). Because the term **physical distribution** is most commonly used to describe the overall process, it will be used here. Physical distribution managers are the people responsible for ensuring that physical distribution activities are carried out effectively and efficiently from point of supply to point of production to point of sale.

physical distribution   The overall process of moving products from producer to consumer.

Most consumers give little if any thought to how products travel through a channel, yet physical distribution is actually far more than just transportation, although that is a large part. Physical distribution activities include:

Packing: Preparing goods for shipment, loading shipments on carriers, and packing goods for long-term or short-term storage.

Order processing: Ensuring that orders are received, processed, checked, and dispatched efficiently. Order tracking by computer-information system is increasingly common.

Inventory control: Managing the goods that are stored and ensuring that products are available so that stockouts do not occur requires smoothing supply and demand discrepancies. Goods are held in storage warehouses or distribution warehouses. Storage generally is for a longer period of time. Products may be held in a storage warehouse and then moved to a distribution warehouse, where they are prepared for shipment to retailers.

Figure 11.4

A Physical Distribution System

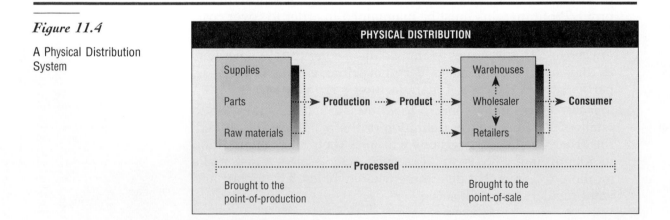

Transportation: Selecting the most cost-effective and time-efficient modes of transportation, whether by railroad, truck (motor carrier), waterway, pipeline, or airline, or through a use of multiple modes (called *multimodal transportation*). (See Photo 11.8.) Materials handling is the movement of goods while they are in a warehouse.

Service: Issuing customer credit, providing information about delivery schedules, and locating missing shipments.

Service Level Decisions

Physical distribution can be an expensive channel activity, particularly the storage, handling, and transportation of finished products. It is important to satisfy customers and ensure that their expectations are met; however, it is also important to determine what level of physical distribution service is really needed. Generally, more service means greater cost and, because accountability is emphasized by most businesses, service sometimes is sacrificed to lower costs. For example, overnight express delivery is very expensive; two-day deliveries are less expensive. As a result, Federal Express has seen slow growth in overnight deliveries while "deferred services" are becoming increasingly popular.[20]

Another issue is that not all businesses need all physical distribution services. Whereas a Wal-Mart has a great volume of products to transport over increasingly longer distances, a local mortgage

Photo 11.8

Transporting materials in the most efficient way is a key distribution function.

Doug Loewe is European Marketing Manager for CompuServe. His responsibilities include managing a sales staff of 15 in the company's London and Munich offices as they expand the distribution of network services into Europe. At the same time, he is also managing a salesforce in New York, keeping in constant contact by laptop computer, fax, modem, and cellular phone. Doug is dedicated to teamwork, as are the people working with him. They are all highly self-motivated self-starters who have the self-discipline to get the work done without constant supervision. Doug travels between New York and Europe several times a month, and maintains a travel plan that allows him to schedule sales visits on either continent. As befits the company he works for, Doug Loewe uses the product he sells, and does so efficiently.

As CompuServe and other on-line information services face increased competition, marketing managers like Doug Loewe will certainly seek more business users to expand CompuServe's commercial services. ■

A. Cohen, "Long-Distance Manager," *Sales and Marketing Management,* 146, no. 11 (October 1994), p. 25; L. Flynn, "In the On-Line Market, the Name of the Game Is the Internet," *New York Times,* September 25, 1994, Section 3, p. F7.

lender needs few if any transport or storage services. Understandably, it is important in controlling costs to determine exactly what physical distribution means to a business, and how much can be performed in-house or must be contracted.

Making Physical Distribution Decisions

Several factors influence physical distribution decisions. Company attributes and, particularly, resources determine how much can be spent on physical distribution. This affects choice of carrier mode. If resources are limited, expensive air transport should be avoided and cheaper ground transport, water, or rail used instead. Resources also influence storage decisions. Instead of using costly professional warehouses, some businesses substitute less expensive public storage facilities rented on a monthly basis.

Product characteristics influence physical distribution decisions. Bulky, heavy, and high-volume products are often transported by railroad, whereas highly valuable products are often transported by air freight. Perishable products frequently require swift transport and refrigeration. Storage decisions also reflect product characteristics, as do materials handling requirements.

Geography influences physical distribution. In transporting products to Europe or Asia, most American businesses select ocean cargo vessels as the most cost-effective alternative. The number of retailers to be serviced and their locations determine transport routes, storage points, and distribution center sites.

Photo 11.9

Doug Loewe, European marketing manager for CompuServe.

1. Describe the types of decisions wholesalers make.
2. What is the role of physical distribution?
3. Discuss the different tasks of physical distribution.

Review of Chapter Objectives

1. *Explain how distribution facilitates the flow of products from producer to consumer.* A channel of distribution links producer and consumer through marketing intermediaries—middlemen who use their expertise in various capacities to expedite the flow of products through a channel. Distribution provides place, time, form, and possession utilities. The marketing functions associated with distribution include those of exchange, physical distribution, and service.

2. *Identify the factors that influence the development of a channel structure.* A channel's structure is a function of a number of factors. These include company attributes, product type, markets, competitors, custom, and the marketing environment.

3. *Describe the different perspectives on channels of distribution.* There are many different perspectives on distribution. Personal use consumers often believe dis-

tribution expenses are a waste of money. Retailer perspectives depend to a great extent on the retailer's size. For wholesalers, computer efficiencies may spell either profit or doom. Large manufacturers realize that their days of being able to dominate a channel without challenge have passed. Government's perspective is that channels should be efficient, competitive, and of benefit to consumers and the economy.

4. *Explain the role of wholesalers.* Wholesalers provide retailers with stock, as well as assist producers in moving their products through the channel of distribution to consumers. Wholesalers provide many services to retailers, including purchasing, breaking bulk, storage, transportation, credit, and so on.

5. *Characterize the logistics/physical distribution functions.* Physical distribution involves packing, order processing, inventory control, transportation, and service.

Key Terms

After studying Chapter 11, you should be able to define each of the following key terms and use them in describing marketing activities.

Discussion Questions

1. What is the role of distribution in marketing?

2. Why are intermediaries also called *middlemen?*

3. Are retailers members of the channel of distribution?

4. Discuss the utilities provided by distribution.

5. How may the marketing environment affect channel structure?

6. Explain how intensive, selective, and exclusive distribution influence the number of middlemen needed in a channel.

7. What is JIT?

8. How does wholesaling serve retailing? How does it serve producers?

9. Describe the various perspectives on distribution.

10. What are the tasks of wholesaling? What are the tasks of physical distribution?

What Do You Think?

CompDesign began as a small retail business that custom designs computers for such corporate clients as the University of Kentucky and LexMark International (formerly an IBM typewriter and printer division). The retail business headquartered in Lexington, Kentucky, has been so successful that company owner Bryan McNee has opened a wholesale division. CompDesign purchases computer parts in bulk from domestic and international suppliers, and then resells them to retailers who make sales to final users. Wholesale clients for now are mostly regional, but the business has plans to expand nationally and achieve a production goal of 2,000 computers each month. A large demand is forecast for custom-designed computers by businesses and organizations that require systems specific to their needs. Is there a niche for a small wholesaler like CompDesign? What do you think?

Source: B. Bennett, "Business Expands into Wholesale," *Lexington-Herald Leader,* June 30, 1994, p. C8.

Photo 11.10

CompDesign's owner Bryan McNee began with retail sales and is now moving into wholesaling of custom-designed computer systems.

Mini-Case 11.1

A Tasty Case of Worldwide Distribution

Charles R. Shoemate became president of CPC International Inc. in 1988. Since then the food processor has spent almost $1 billion acquiring almost 50 companies worldwide, including Germany's Pfanni potatoes, Israel's Telma soups, Brazil's Vitamilho alimentary cereals, and Chile's JB sauces to add to its better-known U.S. brands of Knorr soups, Hellmann's mayonnaise, Best Foods, and Skippy peanut butter. CPC's goal is marketing synergy—buying a popular local product and then using its local distribution system to bring in other CPC brands while also distributing the new acquisition abroad in other CPC distribution systems. CPC, originally Corn Products Company, has become an international marketer of branded foods, with almost two-thirds of its profits generated abroad. CPC pays close attention to local tastes: for example, mayonnaise is lemony in Brazil and vinegary in Britain; glass jars are used in the United States and bags in other places. Knorr soups are the exception, crossing national and cultural boundaries virtually un-changed. Diversification, regional production, and worldwide distribution are keys to buffering the company against downturns in any single market.

Photo 11.11

CPC International's Hellman's is a U.S. brand distributed in many other countries, such as Chile.

Case Questions

1. What advantage is there for CPC in using the distribution channels of brands it acquires in other countries?

2. Why should food products in particular require adaptation to local tastes?

3. Could this strategy of worldwide marketing synergy in distribution be used by other businesses? What types of products might lend themselves to this strategy?

Sources: A. Feldman, "Have Distribution, Will Travel," *Forbes*, 153, no. 13 (June 20, 1994), pp. 44–45; A. Meyer, "Around the World with CPC," *Prepared Foods* 160, no. 8 (July 1991), p. 35; "CPC to Form Mexican Venture," *The Wall Street Journal*, October 31, 1994, p. A5.

Mini-Case 11.2

Ito-Yokado, Lojas Americanas SA, and Wal-Mart

What do Japan's Ito-Yokado and Brazil's Lojas Americanas SA have in common? They are both joint venture partners of the world's largest retailer, Wal-Mart. Ito-Yokado, a giant Japanese supermarket chain, is importing low-cost private-label goods from Wal-Mart's Sam's Club warehouse, including clothing, pet food, and glass tableware. While Ito-Yokado gets discounted products that appeal to Japanese consumers buffeted by an unsettled economy, Wal-Mart gains access to one of Japan's most sophisticated distribution systems, including state-of-the-art product ordering, inventory control, and delivery techniques. Ito-Yokado runs 143 general merchandise stores as well as the super-successful convenience store chain 7-Eleven Japan.

Lojas Americanas, Brazil's largest discount retailer, is opening three Sam's Clubs and one supercenter with its joint venture partner Wal-Mart. Because of high risks in the Brazilian market, Wal-Mart is concentrating on Sam's Clubs, which offer a narrower assortment of products than its Wal-Mart or supercenter stores. This minimizes supply and inventory control problems.

Case Questions

1. Wal-Mart is the first American retailer to open stores in Argentina and Brazil. It is also moving aggressively into Japan and Asia. What are the risks of extending its distribution system beyond North America?

2. How is Wal-Mart countering this risk?

3. Do you think Wal-Mart is on the way to becoming as widely distributed as Coca-Cola, McDonald's, and KFC? Explain your answer.

Sources: B. Ortega, "Wal-Mart Looks Beyond North America, Plans to Expand in Argentina, Brazil," *The Wall Street Journal*, June 6, 1994, p. A9; J. Cody, "Supermarket Giant Ito-Yokado Plans Venture to Import Goods of Wal-Mart," *The Wall Street Journal*, March 24, 1994, p. A13.

Chapter 11 Notes

1. K. Labich, "Risky Business," *Fortune* 130, no. 1 (July 11, 1994), p. 174.

2. C. Eller, "Merchant Ivory Links with Disney," *Variety* 348, no. 1 (June 27, 1992), p. 5; "Honey, I Sent the Kids to Oxford," *Time* 140, no. 6 (August 10, 1992), p. 22.

3. A. Stevens, "Law Firm Fat Threatened by a Lean Network," *The Wall Street Journal*, July 8, 1994, pp. B1, 7.

4. "For Some Motel Customers, McDonald's Will Deliver," *The Wall Street Journal*, June 24, 1994, p. B1.

5. S. Kichen, "Pick a Channel," *Forbes* 149, no. 5 (March 2, 1992), pp. 108–10.

6. "American Greetings Plans Cards Via Home Computer," *The Wall Street Journal*, June 24, 1994, p. A3; S. MacLachlan, "Greetings Made Easy: Card Goes Online," *The Christian Science Monitor* 86, no. 184 (August 16, 1994), p. 9.

7. A. Barrett, "Detergents, Aisle 2. Pizza Hut, Aisle 5." *Business Week*, June 7, 1993, pp. 82–83.

8. Z. Schiller, W. Zellner, R. Stodghill, and M. Maremont, "Clout! More and More, Retail Giants Rule the Marketplace," *Business Week*, December 21, 1992, pp. 66–73.

9. Z. Schiller and W. Zellner, "Making the Middleman an Endangered Species," *Business Week*, June 6, 1994, pp. 114–15.

10. P. F. Drucker, "The Economy's Power Shift," *The Wall Street Journal*, September 24, 1992, p. A16.

11. L. Zinn, D. Jones Yang, and W. Konrad, "Federated's Slow Ride on the Up Escalator," *Business Week*, September 7, 1992, pp. 70–71.

12. B. Ortega, "Wal-Mart Looks Beyond North America, Plans to Expand in Argentina, Brazil," *The Wall Street Journal*, June 6, 1994, p. A9.

13. "Retailing: No Frills, Please," *The Economist* 320, no. 7716 (July 20, 1991), pp. 73, 74.

14. M. J. McCarthy, "Supermarkets Reorganize Distribution to Help Fight K, Wal and Other Marts," *The Wall Street Journal*, January 19, 1993, p. B5.

15. R. Koselka, "Distribution Revolution," *Forbes* 149, no. 11 (May 25, 1992), pp. 54–62.

16. M. Selz, "Firms Innovate to Get It for You Wholesale," *The Wall Street Journal*, July 23, 1993, pp. B1, 2.

17. D. Foust, "Circuit City's Wires Are Sizzling," *Business Week*, April 27, 1992, p. 76.

18. S. Scherreik, "New Warehouses: Big, Bright, Efficient," *New York Times*, May 30, 1993, Section 10, pp. 1, 9.

19. United States Department of Commerce, Economics and Statistics Administration, Bureau of the Census, County Business Patterns, 1994, Table 844. Establishments, Employees, and Payroll, by Industry; @ gopher: //gopher. census. gov.

20. R. Frank, "Federal Express Grapples with Changes in U.S. Market," *The Wall Street Journal*, July 5, 1994, p. B3.

Understanding Promotion

Chapter Objectives

After studying Chapter 12 you should be able to

1. Explain how promotion works.
2. Discuss promotion decisions.
3. Identify the steps in a promotion plan.
4. Describe promotion budgeting practices.
5. Address criticisms of promotion.

*M*arketers wouldn't have to aggressively promote products if consumer demand exceeded product supply. Instead, many products must be heavily supported with promotions, because supply typically is greater than demand, parity (similar or identical) products glut most markets, competition is fierce, and there is a constant stream of new products. Marketers use promotion to inform, persuade, and remind consumers about products and to build and maintain brand image and goodwill. The average consumer must sift through an almost overwhelming promotion clutter in order to locate marketing communications that are personally meaningful and useful. As you learn about promotion in this chapter, consider these questions: How will marketers promote their products in the next century? Will promotion as we know it today via mass media (television, radio, newspapers, magazines) be as prominent?

Cutting through the
Promotion Clutter

Janelle Davis is awakened by her clock radio. Her sound sleep is punctured by a commercial for a television program being shown that evening on local television. She reads the morning newspaper over coffee, and clips cents-off coupons from the food section to take on her next trip to the grocery store. On the way to work, she notices that many other women are wearing brand-labeled athletic shoes with their professional clothes. In her office, she meets with sales representatives bearing product samples for her to consider purchasing for her company. She receives several faxes of messages with product offers, as well as many telephone sales calls and E-mail communications. After work she meets a friend for dinner and a movie, where coming attractions are shown along with reminders about the snacks available at the theater's refreshment counter. The theater's restrooms have movie advertisements posted on the back of the toilet stall doors. Janelle goes home in a cab that has advertisements for local restaurants in panels on the back of the front seat. At home, before retiring for the night, she turns on cable television for tomorrow's weather forecast and sits through commercials for tires, snow resorts, and Caribbean cruises before the local weather report appears. Janelle falls asleep to her clock radio playing light rock music between advertisements for scores of products, most of which don't interest her and are unconsciously screened out as background noise.

PROMOTION: PERSUASIVE MARKETING COMMUNICATION

Objective 1   Explain how promotion works.

Promotion is persuasive, purposive marketing communication about products. Some promotions inform consumers, build and maintain a brand's image, persuade consumers to make a purchase, remind them about a product's benefits, and even entertain them. Other promotions motivate employees to sell a product, channel members to carry it, investors to capitalize it through stock purchases, and various publics to support and accept it. A common goal of promotion is to make the ordinary appear extraordinary—to differentiate a product from its competition through effective advertising, personal selling, sales promotions, public relations, and/or direct marketing.

Janelle Davis experienced a day full of marketing promotions in the chapter's opening story. She awoke to promotions and fell asleep to them. Most of the promotions she received blended into a blur because there was so much **clutter,** the often excessive number of promotion contacts a consumer experiences in a period of time, during a single radio or television program, over an entire day, or other period. When clutter is high, as during the last hour of a televised movie or in magazines around the holidays, consumers usually screen most of them out—something marketers expect but work to avoid. Few promotions are received by consumers in isolation; few if any promotions have consumers' undivided attention.

clutter   An excessive number of promotion contacts that a consumer experiences in a period of time.

Marketing Application 12.1

Perform a personal clutter audit. Keep track of the promotions that you come in contact with in a typical work or school day. Begin tomorrow morning and, several times during the day, record the types of promotion messages you're receiving. For example, if you take a clutter audit during breakfast you might find that you are subject to marketing communications in print advertisements and coupons in the morning newspaper, television commercials while you watch a morning news program, or radio commercials in the car. At the end of your record-keeping day, analyze your list to identify the frequency of your exposure to the different promotion types (advertising, sales promotions, personal selling, publicity/public relations, and direct marketing). What can you conclude about promotion clutter in your life? How do you deal with it? Bring your list to class for discussion. ■

Cutting through the Clutter

In an ordinary day, the average consumer is bombarded by thousands of marketing messages. Some of these marketing communications are quite clearly goal-directed product promotions, as in the advertisements on Janelle's radio and in her newspaper and through sales calls in the office. Others are more subtle but also effective, such as brand labels displayed prominently on the outside of athletic shoes or other articles of clothing. Consumers self-protectively screen out most marketing communications that are not relevant to their needs, interests, and preferences, and those that are dull, overly repetitive, or copycat promotions. Promotion clutter is growing, which makes the marketer's job of cutting through the clutter all the more difficult, yet also more important. Being heard above the promotion clutter is the marketer's challenge of the 1990s.

Marketers use different strategies to capture consumers' attention. For example, during the early and middle parts of this century, most print advertisements and all early television commercials were black and white. The first color advertisements broke through the black and white clutter because they were visually distinct and novel. Today, most magazine and television advertisements are in brilliant color. Therefore, in order to stand out, some advertisers have gone back to black and white, resulting in a growing clutter of black and white advertisements.[1]

Magazines and television advertisements are breaking traditional typeface rules to cut through the clutter.[2] Many use reverse type (white lettering on a dark background), broken type, and jumbles of different typeface, which can strain the eye but also effectively call attention to the distinct visual image and the product's name (see Photo 12.1).

Photo 12.1

Some advertisers break typeface
and design rules to catch attention.

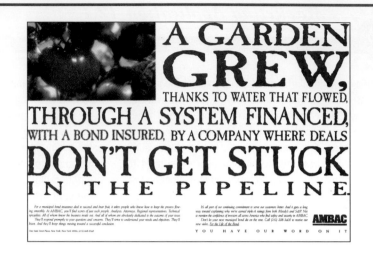

Other advertisers attempt to cut through the clutter by increasing the sound levels for their television or radio commercials in order to distinguish them from other commercials and programs. Role-reversal advertisements are appearing, in which females ogle males in eye-catching examples of reverse sexism.[3] Some direct-mail promotions come in envelopes that appear to be official U.S. government mailings, suggesting that they are important and should not be trashed unopened. Manufacturers try to break through the coupon clutter by making their coupons more valuable, by bundling them along with a sweepstakes offer, product sample, or charitable cause. Some automobile salespeople differentiate themselves by avoiding the hard sell and becoming sales counselors instead of price hagglers.

In an effort to escape the beer ad clutter on television. Coors Light brand beer became one of the first advertisers on electronic on-line services Prodigy and CompuServe.[4] Other promotions are appearing on the Internet, the international computer network. The Internet has been described as "the fastest growing telecommunications network ever, including the phone network."[5] It is a natural for marketing promotions.

Championing a Product through Promotion

A marketer promoting a product is acting as its champion, directing persuasive communications about it to various receptive target audiences in order to achieve specific marketing goals. The product often is portrayed as a hero, poised to solve the consumer's problems if given a chance. Advocacy communications on behalf of a product may also include negative comments about competitors' products.

Marketing on the Internet

When two attorneys placed an advertisement on the Internet offering their legal services in 1994, they suffered a barrage of criticism by E-mail from Internet users who maintain that advertising has no place on the net. The attorneys claimed, however, that they also received nearly 25,000 positive replies to their on-line advertisement, as well as $100,000 in new business. While the debate rages over Internet commercialization, advertising is rapidly finding its way into cyberspace.

A pioneering effort to stake out a commercial claim on the Internet is being made by the advertising agency Chiat/Day, known for producing the Big Brother ad during the 1984 Super Bowl for Apple Computer's MacIntosh. Chiat/Day is one of only a handful of advertising agencies that have made the move to the Net, specifically to the World Wide Web where multimedia presentations can be used to demonstrate agency assets. The Chiat/Day site has striking advertising campaign images and sound in a virtual gallery for prospective clients to browse along with statements of creative philosophy and descriptions of the work arrangements in their virtual advertising agency.

Another advertising agency on the World Wide Web is Minneapolis's Fallon McElligott, which offers text, audio, and photographs from current advertising campaigns. A spokesperson says their site is visited by around 3,000 visitors each week.

As advertisers look for more innovative ways to reach customers, they will pressure other advertising agencies to use the Internet and establish a presence there. ■

K. Goldman, "Ad Agencies Slowly Set Up Shop at New Addresses on the Internet," *The Wall Street Journal,* December 29, 1994, p. B3; L. Flynn, "Spamming' on the Internet," *The New York Times,* October 16, 1994, p. F9; C. Taylor and S. Garcia, "Emerging at Chiat: Research in Cyberspace," *ADWEEK Eastern Edition* 35, no. 50 (December 12, 1994), p. 9; K. Cleland, "Chiat Goes from Virtual to Interactive; Agency Taps BKG America Founder to Lead New Unit, Prepares to Open Internet Site," *Advertising Age* 65, no. 52 (December 12, 1994), p. 22.

Marketing promotion is used to establish relationships with consumers. **Relationship marketing** uses promotion as well as the other marketing mix variables to get close to consumers, make a connection with them, satisfy their wants and needs, inform them about a product and its benefits, and maintain their loyalty over a usage lifetime. For example, if you are marketing disposable diapers for newborns, you promote the product directly to expectant mothers, one of your prime target audiences. Your goal is to begin to establish a positive, long-term relationship with the mothers even before their babies are born. Your message describes how your disposable diapers for newborns are a sanitary, comfortable, reasonably priced product to keep babies dry and moms happy. Although promotion cannot create demand where no need or desire exists, it can channel demand in receptive consumers by using consistent and relevant image and benefit messages and incentives that communicate product value. Multiple delivery systems are often used. In this case, they may include magazine and radio advertisements, direct mail (messages) during the early months of the pregnancy, and cents-off coupons and free samples by mail (incentives) as delivery gets closer and after birth.

relationship marketing An approach that focuses on getting close to and connecting with consumers.

Marketing Application 12.2

What promotions successfully cut through the clutter for you? Over the next 24-hour period, pay close attention to the promotions that you receive. Identify two or three promotions (e.g., television commercials, print advertisements, direct-mail pieces, catalogs, telephone sales, etc.) that capture your attention. Describe these promotions and analyze what it is about them that made you pay closer-than-usual attention. For example, did you find a particular television commercial irritating? Was a print advertisement very creative? Did you receive a telephone sales call for a product that you are considering purchasing? From your observations, what ways would you suggest for a marketer to design future promotions that cut through the clutter? Bring your observations and analysis to class for discussion. ■

Personal selling is a highly effective vehicle in relationship marketing. Attentive service builds ties between individual consumers and a retail store. By joining personal selling and direct marketing, retailers can segment consumers by their spending patterns and target regular, loyal customers for future promotions.[6]

Perspectives on Promotion

Marketing communication can be thought of as holding conversations, often at a distance, with prospective customers. A simplified model of the marketing communication process is presented in Figure 12.1. In the communication process, a *source* constructs a message from interconnected words, visual images, and symbols through a process called *encoding.* The encoded *message* is transmitted through a communication *delivery system,* using such channels as radio, television, magazines, billboards, store displays, salespeople, computers, and so on. The *receiver,* the message's target audience, *decodes* the message into understandable patterns of thought. *Noise* may occur anywhere throughout the process and includes random physical disruptions such as radio static, interference from other

Figure 12.1

A Simplified Model of the Communication Process

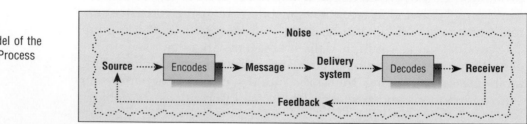

messages being transmitted, people interrupting the receiver's decoding process, messages from the competition about their products, and even the receiver's own psychological defenses. Finally, when the message has been received, the receiver communicates back to the source through *feedback* that may include a telephone call seeking product information, a consumer complaint, a product purchase, or a failure to make a purchase. Feedback is of growing importance as marketers seek to enter into relationships with consumers that require two-way communication: seller to buyer and buyer to seller.

Some promotion is personal, as in face-to-face personal selling; most is impersonal, through the mass media. Other types fall in between, as in direct mail that is mass produced but personalized to include a prospect's name and targeted based on information pulled from a database to certain segments of a list. (see Photo 12.2).

Some promotions are designed to stimulate word-of-mouth (WOM) communications—consumers communicating among themselves about products. Word of mouth is when you tell a friend about a great new movie you've just seen or a new place to eat. Word of mouth is not itself considered to be promotion, although a promotion goal may be to generate and direct it.

Target audiences for promotions include: consumers, employees, channel members, competitors, investors, the public, and the government. The content of promotion messages varies by audience. For example, a message to stockholders may focus on the strengths of the product's performance in the market, the revenue it's generating, and its profit potential. A message to consumers will focus on the

Photo 12.2

We've all received many pieces of personalized direct mail like this one.

benefits the product offers (particularly in comparison to competitors' products), its value, the gap it fills, or the opportunity it provides. To the competition, a message may be a challenge to do battle in the market for consumers' hearts and wallets. Messages to wholesalers and retailers encourage them to carry the product, and messages to salespeople encourage them to sell it. Messages directed toward the general public and government may focus on how the product and the company producing it are good corporate citizens.

Historically, a considerable amount of waste has always been associated with promotion. Waste is promotion received by nonreceptive audiences, often because targeting is inexact, not stressed, or misdirected. Because of the large amount spent on promotion, businesses are looking more critically at waste and demanding greater accountability, wanting to know what results they are getting for each promotion dollar spent.

Marketing promotion is performed by not-for-profit organizations, governments, causes, and individuals, as well as by businesses. Not-for-profit organizations use promotion to increase awareness about their activities, raise funds, and generate goodwill. State governments promote their public parks and economic development activities (see Photo 12.3). The U.S. government promotes many things, including the U.S. Army, which is seeking to get good volunteers to join.

Photo 12.3

A governor rolls up his sleeves in this advertisement that promotes a state as a good place to conduct business.

Marketing Application 12.3

Test this statement: "Most consumers don't distinguish among the various types of promotion; they call all promotion *advertising*." As a class project, each student should ask five other people (students and nonstudents) to explain what *marketing promotion* means to them. Bring the results to class to compare. What do you conclude about the statement? Do your class results dispute or support it? Is this a problem for marketers? ■

Most consumers don't distinguish among the various types of marketing promotion; they call all promotions *advertising*. Marketers must realize that although promotions are described by type (e.g., advertising, sales promotions, personal selling, public relations, direct marketing) *within* the marketing profession, to most target audiences promotion types are largely indistinguishable from one another.

Although consumers may not be interested in distinguishing among promotion types, they can tell the difference between a message and an incentive.[7] A **message** is a set of words, images, or symbols encoded by a sender and sent to a receiver, usually stored in a consumer's memory for use at a later time. An **incentive** is a cents-off coupon, trade discount, product sample, or other short-term tangible item designed to have an immediate effect by moving the consumer toward an exchange, typically a purchase (Photo 12.4). The **promotion delivery system** is any mechanism that delivers a message or incentive when it is most relevant to consumers—at the height of their receptivity—to stimulate consumer demand.

The key to effective promotion is to *focus on the consumer:* develop consumer insights, determine what is relevant (message or incentive) to the consumer when she is most receptive, and deliver it when this window of opportunity is open. The marketer must make the different types of promotion work together so that the overall effect is consistent and greater than if only one promotion type had been used. This approach lessens the risk of sending conflicting messages about a product that may confuse consumers. The goal of integrated marketing communications can be summed in one word, **synergy,** in which promotion types work together in an integrated way, communicating the same relevant message with such consistency that the whole effect is greater than the sum of the individual parts. An example of a coordinated set of promotions on the local level is shown in Photo 12.5.

Successful promotion must be built around consumer insight, that is, knowledge about the consumer—his needs, likes and dislikes, and purchase behaviors. The marketer uses this information to

message A set of words, images, and/or symbols encoded by a sender and sent to a receiver.

incentive A short-term tangible item designed to move the consumer toward purchase.

promotion delivery system Any mechanism that delivers a message and/or incentive when it is most relevant to consumers.

synergy The integration of resources toward sending out a consistent marketing message.

Photo 12.4

Coupons are incentives that encourage consumers to make a purchase by rebating a portion of a product's price.

Photo 12.5

This company is going whole hog with promotion.

construct and deliver relevant messages and incentives at the height of consumer receptivity. You might wonder how the marketer can get enough information about consumers to be able to identify relevant messages and receptive periods. Many marketers and communication specialists believe the answer lies in the use of databases and an integrated marketing communication approach to promotions.

Integrated Marketing Communication

Integrated marketing communication (IMC) is "outside-in" marketing communication that begins with knowledge of the consumer. Consumer knowledge is used to construct a promotion program with messages, incentives, and delivery systems that have been shown to be successful in the past.[8] For example, a considerable amount of information is collected from optical scanners that record personal use consumer purchases by reading Universal Product Codes (UPC) as purchases are made. Other data are collected from credit card purchases, catalog orders, consumer surveys, and panels or responses to telemarketing (telephone sales). This information is compiled in computer files, then accessed electronically to answer questions about who makes particular purchases (consumer demographics) and their lifestyles, activities, interests and opinions (psychographics), media preferences, and receptivity to various messages and incentives.

Data are collected, sorted, and offered for sale to marketers by marketing research companies. Certain industries, notably automobiles, have compiled extensive consumer databases about past purchasers. They use these data to develop marketing communication programs to encourage repurchases as well as to attract new purchasers. Data are used to establish consumer profiles by groups of individuals and households that show which promotions work, as reflected in actual purchase patterns.[9]

The integrated approach also works in business-to-business marketing. At Procase Corporation, a California software company, the 13-person sales force is supported by targeted direct mail. Rather than relying on hard-to-generate leads developed from trade shows, a database of potential buyers is sent direct mail designed to determine their initial interest in the company's software. Prospects respond by E-mail, fax, mail reply card, or telephone. Leads are qualified by telephone, then sent an information packet, followed by a personal contact from the technical sales force. In this case, the field sales force of engineers and technicians has been integrated with telephone sales and direct mail using a database to identify receptive consumers.[10]

Even in companies with traditional promotion programs, the idea of synergy and getting promotions to work together is attracting attention. The difference between IMC and traditional, single-promotion approaches is that IMC advocates that all promotion types be:

- Managed together.
- Developed "outside-in" from the consumer's perspective.

integrated marketing communication (IMC) A program based on knowledge of the consumer that uses messages, incentives, and delivery systems that have been successful in the past.

Marketing Application 12.4

Take the role of a marketer designing an integrated marketing communication program for three different small businesses. From your own knowledge of consumers, what advice would you give about promotions for the following situations? Be specific as to: (1) when you would time your promotions, (2) what delivery system(s) you would use, (3) what you would say (message), and (4) any incentive(s) you'd use for:

- A florist's Thanksgiving Day promotions.
- A candy store's Valentine's Day promotions.
- A diet center's promotions over one year. ■

- Finely targeted to receptive audiences using information obtained from databases.

- Unified so that all promotions speak with one voice and cut through the clutter of promotions in the marketplace.

Check Your Understanding
12.1

1. Describe the role of promotion in marketing.
2. What is relationship marketing? Why is it important?
3. Explain how integrated marketing communication differs from traditional promotion activities. How are they alike?

MAKING PROMOTION DECISIONS

Objective 2   Discuss promotion decisions.

Although the integrated marketing communication approach is gaining converts, most marketers still make promotion decisions from the "inside-out," following traditional historical approaches to produce promotions in quantities that their budget allows.

The Promotion Mix

promotion mix   The combination of promotion types used to reach a target audience and accomplish a promotion goal.

The **promotion mix** (shown in Figure 12.2) is advertising, personal selling, sales promotions, public relations/publicity, and direct marketing. Although these types are thought of as being distinct, the lines separating appear to be blurring as they are increasingly used together in integrated campaigns.

For the most part, how the promotion types are used is based on a marketer's judgment about the best way to reach a target audience and accomplish a promotion goal. A good product that delivers value to consumers should be the core around which good promo-

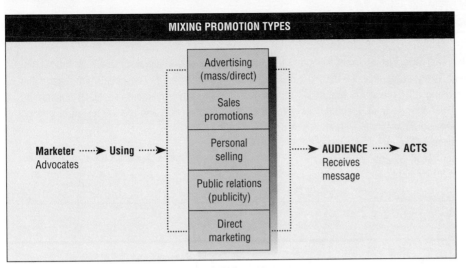

Figure 12.2

The Traditional Promotion Mix

tion is constructed. Good promotion should accomplish the marketing goals set for it and provide consumers with the information they need to make a purchase decision. Bad promotion can seriously harm if not kill a good but unknown product, by failing to catch consumers' attention, convince them of the product's unique benefits, and move them to trial. On the other hand, even the best promotion can't save a bad product: Although it may move consumers to make an initial purchase, consumers cannot be persuaded to repurchase a truly bad product.

The elements of the promotion mix will be discussed at length in the next chapter. A profile of each type is provided below, as preparation for the discussion of promotion decisions.

Advertising Mass advertising and direct response advertising are nonpersonal messages usually paid for by an identified sponsor using electronic (radio, television, computers), print (newspapers, magazines), and other types of media (billboards, kiosks). Because the advertiser pays for the message and media use, the advertiser also controls the message within the boundaries set by communication regulations, media contracts, and legal and ethical constraints. Direct response advertising solicits an immediate response from the target audience by using a 1-800 or 1-900 order number and/or mail order coupon (see Photo 12.6). Traditional mass advertising designed to create a brand image is passive and does not include a mechanism for an immediate consumer response. The advantage of mass advertising is that it's relatively inexpensive per contact. However, it can be very expensive to produce an advertisement (particularly a

Consumer Insight

What form of advertising is most effective at grabbing consumers' attention? A recent Gallup study revealed that, overall, more consumers are using ad circulars at home before going to the store. For shoppers at discount department stores and category-dominant retail stores, this means picking out purchases in the circulars *before* making a store visit. Consumer recall of product advertisements in circulars is over 80 percent. This exceeds

consumer recall of advertisements seen on television, newspapers, or other media. These data emphasize the importance of using advertisements to reach consumers when they need information and are interested in making a product purchase. ■

"Study: Ad Circulars Grab Consumers' Attention," *Marketing News* 28, no. 11 (May 23, 1994), p. 6.

Photo 12.6

Consumers can buy immediately or ask questions about a product through direct response ads like this one.

television commercial) and deliver it. It usually requires a somewhat lengthy lead time for preparation, execution, and placement, which limits flexibility and timeliness. The term *mass advertising* is somewhat misleading, because although many products may have a mass appeal, advertisers still target the media, the season, and the message to reach groups of receptive consumers.[11] Although advertising expenditures are high, total employment in advertising is low, around half a million people in the United States.

Sales Promotions This promotion type adds value to a product by offering purchase inducements on a temporary basis to stimulate consumer demand, build store traffic and sales, or encourage the trade to distribute or stock the product. Sales promotions come in many different types and include coupons, contests, rebates, and other incentives (see Photo 12.7). They are offered to both personal

International Marketing Report

Has the European Union given rise to the Euroconsumer? Some observers believe this is the case, at least for advertising. The chairman and chief executive of the advertising agency Lintas, Europe, Africa & Middle East, believes that advertising is becoming unified across Europe, even though the pace of creating a single Europe is slow. Because more international companies like Procter & Gamble, Nestlé, and Unilever regard Europe as one market, their advertising reflects this perspective. This affects advertising for clothing, supermarket products, and high-priced impulse purchases. General Motors Corporation has used pan-European advertising for its new car, Tigra. Language differences can easily be accommodated in television commercials by using dubbing and voice-overs on different sound tracks. Because there are so few really unique, effective advertising ideas, when one appears it should be used in more than one country if at all possible.■

J. Guyon, "One Ad Pitch May Fit All as Unified Europe Evolves," *The Wall Street Journal,* Journal Finder, AT&T World News Faxline Story #234, January 19, 1994; "Eurobrand not Eurobland," *Marketing,* November 17, 1994, p. XII; K. Robertson, "Strategies to Get Across Europe," *Marketing,* May 20, 1993, p. 19.

Photo 12.7

Sun Crunchers cereal is providing an immediate incentive to try a new product.

use and business/organization consumers as well as to the trade and the sales force, and can be personalized to match consumers' individual tastes and preferences. Incentives can quickly stimulate sales. Cents-off coupon distribution in the United States averages over 350 billion annually and is dominated by such product categories as prepared foods, household products, and cereals. [12] A drawback is that many sales promotions do not have immediate direct feedback that measures changes in sales and revenues. Even so, short-term promotions provide an effectiveness measure better than most mass advertising, which can take a much longer time to stimulate action.

Personal Selling   The most personal type of promotion is personal selling (see Photo 12.8). This can be face to face, door to door, by telephone, or selling at trade shows, events, and demonstrations. Advantages of personal selling are the ability to modify a sales presentation to suit the consumer and being able to counter consumer objections and resistance. Personal selling is a critical activity in industrial promotion. The cost per contact is very high and rising, making individual sales calls extremely expensive for many businesses. Retail selling is a popular career path in marketing and employs millions of Americans.

Public Relations/Publicity   The goal of public relations is to generate a favorable image and goodwill for a product, brand, business, organization, person, or cause through planned activities and information dissemination. Publicity provides information to the news media but is not paid for directly by an identified sponsor. This does not mean it comes cost-free: While the message may gain in credibility and believability if it is not directly paid for by a sponsor, the sponsor lacks control over the message, which can sometimes result in unsatisfactory outcomes. Most large and many medium and small businesses have a public relations department or person responsible for planning and implementing activities designed to promote the business and disseminate positive information about it.

Direct Marketing   At one time, most consumers identified direct marketing as junk mail and discarded it. Direct marketing has improved its reputation and is now used extensively by many kinds of retailers from discounters to exclusive department stores, and by a growing number of business-to-business marketers. Aided by computers and sophisticated databases that can store enormous amounts

Photo 12.8

Selling on the personal/retail level.

Consumer Insight

Direct marketing copy is designed to produce results fast. The goal is to get the reader to be so moved by the copy that, after reading it, he picks up the telephone and dials a 1-800 number to place an order. This applies to both personal use and business/organization targets. Some writing tips for effective direct marketing:

- *Show what's in it for me:* Hook the consumer with the product's benefit for the person or business: "Save up to 60 percent on our long-distance calls."

- *Use headline grabbers:* Grab the reader's attention with headlines: "Learn to use a computer in less than an hour."

- *Stress convenience:* Emphasize how having the product will save time: "Never stand in line for another ticket."

- *Ask provocative questions:* Questions about things that may be troubling the consumer: "When an employee gets sick, how long does it take your company to recover?"

- *Appeal to curiosity/greed:* People are curious, particularly about ways to earn more money: "If you thought we can't earn $100,000 with this new product, think again!"

- *Use bullets:* People are busy and they don't have the time to search through a long letter looking for the major points, so use bullets to emphasize key thoughts. For example, to sell driving glasses, write:
  - Beat headlight glare.
  - Drive through blinding rain.
  - Increase vision and safety. ■

P. Theibert, "They Laughed When I Sat Down to Write," *The Wall Street Journal*, April 11, 1994, p. A14.

of information, direct marketing targets consumers using compiled lists and provides rapid, sometimes immediate feedback about consumer responses to a promotion. This promotion type is evolving rapidly, which makes it difficult to identify all direct marketing activities. Traditional direct marketing includes catalog sales, direct-mail letters, telemarketing, product membership clubs, and others.

Promotion Tries to Get Consumers to Act

Many promotion decisions are based on the assumptions of a hierarchy of effects model first proposed in the 1960s. This model, shown in Figure 12.3, suggests that promotions, particularly mass advertising, help consumers move through a series of steps that climax in exchange, purchase, and repurchase. First, promotions help consumers become *aware* of a brand, then in stepwise progression consumers accumulate *knowledge,* and develop *liking,* a *preference,* and *conviction* that it is the best brand for them. The steps end in *purchase.* This model is often labeled "think-feel-do" to illustrate the rationality expected in high-involvement, deliberate consumer decision making. Messages high in informational content are effective in moving consumers to act through the think-feel-do process.

Figure 12.3

The Traditional Linear
Hierarchy of Effects Model

The assumption of the hierarchy
of effects model is that there is a
linear (straight-line) progression
as advertising influences
consumers to develop an attitude
about a brand. Advertising
repetitions move the consumer
through the steps in a straight
line to the point where the
advertising messages build up
and convince the consumer to
make a purchase.

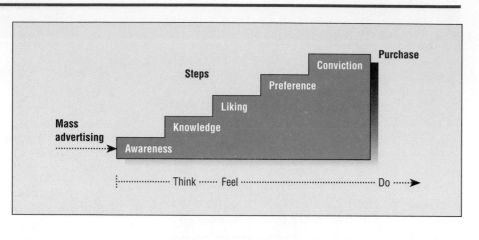

Needless to say, for any product promotion there will always be consumers who are not moved to act, regardless of the promotion effort. Many consumer decisions are not highly involving, do not require considerable information search, and often represent a casual choice between comparable products. Instead of think-feel-do, these consumer decisions are characterized as feel-do-think or even do-feel-think. The latter two cases reflect the importance of promoting a product by getting the consumer to try it first, perhaps through free samples or coupon incentives, in anticipation that she will develop a liking for the product and purchase it again. Incentives to do and feel also help persuade the consumer to select the marketer's brand over what may be an indistinguishable competitor.

Consumers Control Promotions

Consumers have always had the power to control whether or not they pay attention to marketing promotions. Now, more than ever before, they can also control whether or not they are even exposed to many types of marketing promotions. For example, when there were only three national networks, advertisers could set up roadblocks, showing the same commercial on all three networks at the same time to capture channel-changing consumers. Today, four major national and many cable networks make a roadblock very expensive and difficult to successfully implement. Television viewers can effortlessly use a remote control to channel surf and avoid commercials entirely. By taping television programs, viewers can fast forward through commercials to reach the next part of the program. Television sets with an avoidance mechanism that automatically screens out commercials as they are broadcast are being developed.

Consumers can have their names taken off direct marketing lists by notifying the business concerned or the Direct Marketing Association, the national trade association of direct marketers. Consumers can control telephone sales calls by using caller identification technology to screen out unknown or unwanted callers. Consumers can ask the U.S. Postal Service to stop delivery of unwanted third-class mail.

Consumers control promotions in another way. Because good promotion communicates effectively with consumers, it is important to determine the best way to make the communication connection. For example, consumers who are deeply offended or irritated by a promotion usually are less likely to buy the product being promoted. Marketers seeking to make positive communication connections with consumers should avoid promotions that consumers reject. In this respect, consumers exert the ultimate control over promotions.

Check Your Understanding 12.2

1. Can good promotion save a bad product? Can bad promotion kill a good product? Explain.

2. What is the hierarchy of effects model? Does it always accurately describe consumer responses to promotions?

3. Explain some of the ways that consumers control promotions.

THE PROMOTION PLAN

The promotion plan is an important element in the marketing of a product and in the development of a marketing plan (see Chapters 2 and 15). Although most large companies may construct written promotion plans, the plan may be unwritten in small to medium-sized firms. A **promotion plan** is a blueprint for action that sets specific objectives for the promotion program to achieve over a designated time period. It represents a series of promotion decisions. Objectives may be expressed in terms of awareness, sales, market share, store traffic, or other desired ends. The promotion plan must be coordinated with the other marketing mix elements and reflect the goals of the marketing plan and business plan. Factors affecting promotion decisions are the promotion goal, product category, life cycle stage, target market, competition, channels, company situations, time frame, and economic conditions.

Promotion planners must clearly identify the product benefit to consumers, for this is the core insight on which promotions should be developed. The promotion plan must take into consideration the complexity and newness of product features as well as the product's life cycle stage. As shown in Figure 12.4, different promotion goals can be identified in the life cycle, suggesting what promotion types might be used and appropriate delivery systems. At about the time a

Objective 3 Identify the steps in a promotion plan.

promotion plan A blueprint for promotion action that sets specific objectives to achieve over a designated time period.

Figure 12.4

Relating Promotion Goals to
Product Life Cycle (PLC)
Stage

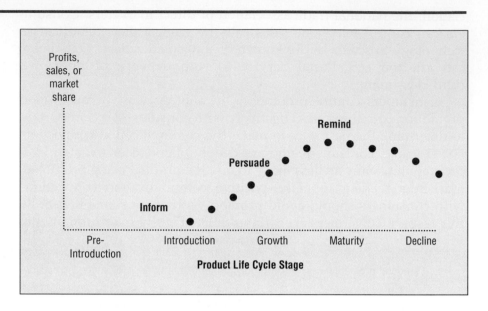

new product is introduced, the promotion task is to inform consumers and build awareness, mainly using mass advertising and sales promotions. During the growth stage, the promotion task is to remind consumers about the advantages of the product (compared to competitors' products) and persuade them to buy. At maturity, sales promotions become prominent as competition intensifies and price becomes a key factor. During the decline period, promotional intensity decreases. At some point, a decision will be made to end promotion and eventually take the product off the market.

Price and place also influence promotion planning. Because price conveys messages about a product's value, particularly in the absence of other cues, it is often an integral element in planning a message or incentive and deciding on a delivery system. Price influences media selection, because the demographic and psychographic characteristics of consumers reached through various media alternatives must be compatible with the product's price. For example, a luxury automobile must be promoted through media commonly used by an affluent target audience with a promotion message designed to build awareness about the automobile or even change attitudes about it. Price affects choice of delivery system; for example, knowing that an affluent target audience is likely to own videocassette players opens the way to mailing a videotape about the car to a select target audience. Likewise, where a product is sold (e.g., a fine department store like Saks Fifth Avenue, a discounter like Wal-Mart, or a convenience store) conveys product information to consumers.

Promotion planning must consider the competitions' promotions, because it is often necessary to counter negative claims or aggressive discounting. Likewise, promotion planning is also influenced by what is happening in product delivery channels and the economy.

Steps in Promotion Planning

Promotion planning generally proceeds through several steps.

Identifying Promotion Goals   It is important to clearly state what the promotion is expected to accomplish and what opportunity it is designed to capitalize on. By defining promotion goals, it becomes possible to measure outcomes against the goals to evaluate the promotion's success. For example, a promotion goal may be to have 50 percent of the target audience *aware* of a new product within three months after launch. Another goal could be to increase product purchase by 20 percent or store traffic by 15 percent. These quantitative goals provide benchmarks against which results can be measured. Like all goals, promotion goals must be measurable, realistic, supportive of the marketing plan, and flexible if the need for change becomes evident. A common broad promotion goal is to use promotions to differentiate a brand from its competition and achieve a sustainable competitive advantage for it in the marketplace. However, in order to be meaningful and actionable, the broad goal must be made more specific, detailed, time bounded, and quantified.

Making Promotion Assignments   Promotions can be planned and implemented internally, externally, or by using a combination of the two alternatives. Many businesses prefer doing promotions in-house because they have competent staff and may save money and time— in-house personnel typically have greater product and company knowledge than do external professionals. A disadvantage of going solely in-house, particularly with advertising, is that you may sacrifice some creativity and objectivity. External agencies and professionals may be able to realize cost savings because they have wider experience or more contacts within their profession. Some businesses use a combination of assignments, managing personal selling in-house while advertising, public relations, and sales promotions are contracted out. Others may have an inside sales staff that works in conjunction with a contracted outside sales force.

Formulating Promotion Strategy   Strategy involves making decisions about *how* to achieve promotion goals. At this stage, it is important to integrate promotion planning with channel strategy. Promotion delivery systems and targets vary according to whether the distribution channel strategy is push, pull, or mixed (see Figure 12.5). A push

Figure 12.5

Promotion Strategies
Coordinated with Channel
Strategies

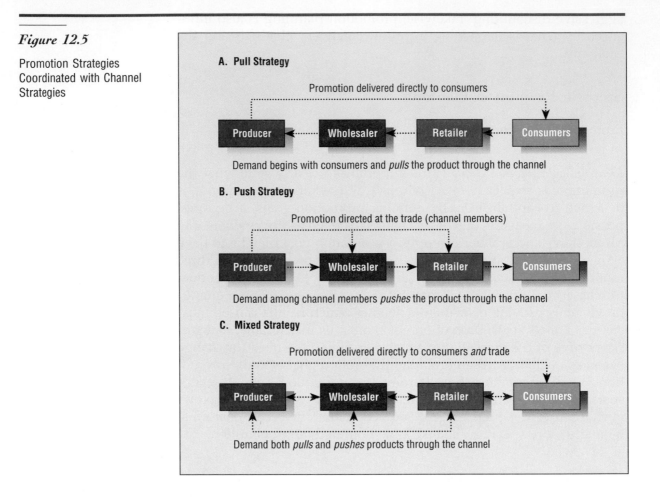

A. Pull Strategy

Promotion delivered directly to consumers

| Producer | Wholesaler | Retailer | Consumers |

Demand begins with consumers and *pulls* the product through the channel

B. Push Strategy

Promotion directed at the trade (channel members)

| Producer | Wholesaler | Retailer | Consumers |

Demand among channel members *pushes* the product through the channel

C. Mixed Strategy

Promotion delivered directly to consumers *and* trade

| Producer | Wholesaler | Retailer | Consumers |

Demand both *pulls* and *pushes* products through the channel

strategy is often heavily weighted toward personal selling; a pull strategy tends to use more advertising and sales promotions. A mixed strategy uses both.

In the pure pull strategy, promotions are directed straight to consumers, using advertisements and coupons, samples, and other incentives. The goal is to build demand for the product and have consumers pressure retailers to order the product from wholesalers. Demand, therefore, *pulls* the product through the channel of distribution.

In the pure push strategy, promotions are targeted at members of the distribution channel to encourage them to *push* the product to consumers. Push strategies include personal selling, business-to-business advertising, and trade deals, including discounts and rebates. Sometimes businesses will join forces and co-promote a product. Therefore, a joint promotion strategy will be devised.

Identifying Target Audience(s)   Effective promotion must be built on consumer insight. This requires identifying your targets in order to learn about their likes and dislikes, what they want in product benefits and value, how they make purchases, how often, and for whom. Demographic and psychographic characteristics identify personal use consumer target(s) of the promotion delivery system. For example, marketers use databases compiled from UPC scanner records to identify who is purchasing their products, when, and in what quantities. This can be integrated with information about purchasers obtained from credit card sales, consumer surveys, customer service contacts, or sales force reports. The speed and flexibility of computers allows consumer information to be combined with promotion data. These data identify both the message and incentive sent to specific targets by communication delivery system and the target audience(s) that are most receptive to a particular promotion (as well as those that are not receptive). It also facilitates consumer testing, which can be used to develop product positioning and repositioning strategies. Similar processes are used in developing promotions for channel members or business consumers.

Developing the Message(s)   Consumer insight must be used in designing a relevant, meaningful message to capture the target audience's attention. This includes deciding *what* to say and how best to say it. The choice of delivery system will affect message structure. A salesperson is usually more effective in delivering a complicated, highly informative message. A television advertisement is best at delivering an **emotional appeal** (e.g., humor, love, fear, desire, guilt, etc.), like the emotional appeal in the Taster's Choice television commercials (see Photo 12.9). A **rational appeal** is highly informative and objective. It often lists product benefits, as shown in Photo 12.10. Along with an appropriate message, the best message sender must be selected. Many shoe companies rely on star athletes to deliver their promotion message to target audiences because the athletes are credible product endorsers, particularly of sports and leisure products.

emotional appeal   A message designed to use feeling to arouse a response.

rational appeal   A message designed to use logic to elicit a response.

Selecting the Promotion Type(s)   One of the principal advantages of using consumer insight to guide promotion planning is that it helps indicate the most effective promotion type for reaching the consumer. Message and promotion type decisions go hand in hand, along with those of delivery systems. Computers are blurring some of the distinctions between promotion types. Before the computer, the only way to deliver messages personally was through face-to-face or telephone sales. Now, however, many previously impersonal media types are becoming personalized.

Allocating the Budget   Marketers with promotion responsibilities are typically handed a promotion budget set by higher-level managers.

Photo 12.9

Can an emotional appeal help sell coffee?

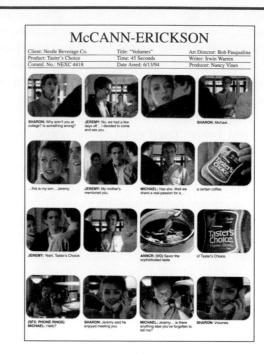

Photo 12.10

Getting rational about a luxury community.

How to allocate the promotion budget means determining how much to spend on advertising (television, radio, magazines, newspapers, computers), sales promotions (coupons, contests, other incentives), the sales force (salaries, expenses), public relations (events, sponsorships, press conferences, meetings), and direct marketing (direct mail). These decisions may become contentious, for example,

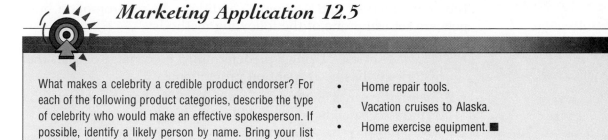

Marketing Application 12.5

What makes a celebrity a credible product endorser? For each of the following product categories, describe the type of celebrity who would make an effective spokesperson. If possible, identify a likely person by name. Bring your list to class for comparison.

- Expensive diamond jewelry.
- Caffeine-free herbal teas.

- Home repair tools.
- Vacation cruises to Alaska.
- Home exercise equipment. ∎

when advertising managers compete with other marketing managers (e.g., sales force, sales promotions, public relations, or direct marketing managers) for scarce resources.

Implementing, Evaluating, and Making Modifications   Finally, it's time to implement the promotion plan. Before launch, it must be established how the promotion will be evaluated; for example, a television commercial may be evaluated through a combination of audience awareness measures (advertising recall) along with scanner sales data and consumer telephone surveys. The feedback should indicate whether or not it is necessary to modify the plan. If a television advertisement is shown and recall tests indicate that consumers can't remember having seen the ad, even though it was on a saturation schedule with multiple repetitions, it may be necessary to modify the media plan. Some options are to increase the number of times the advertisement is aired, change the ad itself, or pull the ad.

THE PROMOTION BUDGET

The promotion **budget** specifies how much money can be spent on promotion and its related expenses. **Allocations** are the amounts set aside from the budget for specific promotion activities. For example, money is allocated from the budget for messages, incentives, and delivery systems such as mass advertising on television, in print, and through outdoor billboards. Good budget decisions estimate what it will cost to achieve the promotion goals as well as consider other factors, including the product category, life cycle stage, target(s), competition, channels, company situation, time frame to accomplish

Objective 4   Describe promotion budgeting practices.

budget   A plan that specifies how much money can be spent on promotion and its related expenses.

allocations   The amounts set aside from the budget for specific promotion activities.

the goals, market, and economic conditions. Most promotion budgets are set using one of the following methods:

- *Percentage of sales:* Using a predetermined percentage of sales that historically has been spent on promotions.
- *Competitive parity:* Setting aside a match for what the competition or industry spends on promotion.
- *All that's left:* Using everything that can be spent after all other marketing costs have been covered.
- *Seat of the pants:* Relies on judgments of people who have good insights into a businesses' promotion needs, particularly for sales force and advertising expenses.
- *Objective and task:* The marketer must identify and cost the promotion needed to accomplish goals, then build a budget based on those justified needs.
- *Models:* Use of computer-based models to analyze large batches of relevant data, identify specific promotion needs, and determine budgetary requirements to accomplish goals. Relies on sophisticated quantitative methods.

Check Your Understanding 12.3	1. Why is planning an important part of promotions?
	2. Describe the steps in promotion planning.
	3. Compare and contrast several promotion budgeting methods.

CRITICISMS OF PROMOTION

Objective 5 Address criticisms of promotion.

Promotion is the one marketing mix variable that deliberately, blatantly calls attention to itself. Because of this exposure and the hundreds of millions of dollars spent on it annually, promotion is also the most highly criticized marketing mix element. Some critics believe that the intensity of promotion and its pervasiveness encourage consumer materialism and result in **conspicuous consumption,** where purchases are exhibited as social signals of a person's financial worth and/or social status. In addition, because of its costliness and excessiveness, promotion is blamed for resulting in higher product prices because promotion costs are passed along to consumers.

conspicuous consumption The use of purchases to indicate a person's financial worth.

Others censure promotion, particularly advertising and personal selling, for being devious and untruthful. Advertising is criticized because of the widespread use of **puffery,** making obviously exaggerated but generally harmless statements in advertisements. Critics

puffery Obviously exaggerated, generally harmless statements made in advertising.

censure advertising of unsafe products like alcohol and tobacco, advertising to children, and violence in advertising.

Other criticisms of promotion focus on:

- *Scams:* Telemarketing and direct marketing are cited for various scams (deceptions). For example, when consumers are told they have won a prize or sweepstakes but must send in a promotion fee to collect the prize—the fee is sent, but the prize either is not as valuable as claimed or is never sent. An estimated 29 percent of all U.S. adults have received at least one fraudulent telephone or direct marketing promotion. Telemarketing scams are estimated to cost consumers from $10 to $40 billion annually. Complaints about mail scams are handled by the U.S. Postal Service; about telephone scams, the Federal Communications Commission.[13]

- *Hostile competitive advertising:* Often, competitive advertisements dissolve into harsh bickering where the competition is named and maligned. The long distance telephone wars illustrate this criticism. The telephone carriers' aggressive comparative advertising about one another has been called the "Reach out and choke someone" model. They are often criticized for telling half-truths and being overly negative.[14]

- *Visual blight:* Many consumers and environmental groups believe that outdoor advertisements deface the landscape. Four states have completely banned highway billboards, and others may follow.[15]

- *Misleading advertisements:* Misleading advertisements often are designed to stimulate product use among those whose decision-making ability may be impaired.[16] Misleading advertisements may contain deceptive price comparisons or product disclaimers that are too small to read.

- *Tasteless advertising:* Many consumer complaints are registered about repetitive, irritating, and tasteless advertisements,[17] including those that use negative stereotypes or sex and nudity.[18]

- *Toxic advertising:* Fragrance strips in advertisements and direct mail pieces can cause illness among sensitive consumers who are unwilling recipients.[19]

- *Privacy issues:* As technology permits the collection of greater amounts of information about individuals, concern about privacy increases. There is a collision of interests between collecting information about individuals that is needed to better serve their needs and not invading their privacy. Many consumers fear that marketers have far too much information collected about their private lives.[20]

The defense of promotion centers on its role in providing information that increases competition in the free market by giving consumers knowledge about a wider choice of products. This benefits consumers, because competition exerts a downward pressure on prices. Advertising revenues for television, radio, newspapers, and magazines subsidize these media and keep consumer costs down while providing nongovernmental support for a free press. Promotion provides a public service by executing and placing free public service announcements (see Photo 12.11), through community event sponsorships, and via similar activities. Promotion provides employment for many millions of people in the United States and worldwide.

Although critics may complain that promotion is uncontrolled, like all business activities, promotion is monitored and regulated by government at the federal, state, and local levels. Laws such as the Sherman Antitrust Act, the Clayton Act, the Robinson–Patman Act, and others that prohibit anticompetitive practices, price discrimination, and disparate treatment also control promotion. Consumer protection laws extend to the prohibition of unfair advertising practices.

Promotion is regulated by government agencies like the Federal Trade Commission (FTC), Federal Communications Commission

Photo 12.11

A public service announcement (PSA) paid for by the Ad Council.

Career Watch

Over three decades ago, Ronald G. Shaw, president of Japan-based Pilot Pen Corporation of America, was Ronnie Shaw, stand-up comedian. Facing life in a succession of smoke-filled nightclubs, the uncertainties of that profession led him to a more traditional one, as a Bic Pen Company salesman. Leaving Bic for Pilot Pen in 1975, he rose through the ranks from national sales manager up to president of the company's American subsidiary in 1986, while helping the business grow from $1 million in sales and 9 employees to $92 million and 200 employees. In 1993, he was made a director of Pilot Pen's parent company. Shaw is one of only six Americans to sit on a Japanese board of directors. Using humor in marketing promotions was a Shaw innovation. His goal was to make consumers laugh along with Pilot Pen advertisements so they would remember the brand when it came time to make a purchase. One of his biggest successes was a radio and print campaign built around the humor of Rodney Dangerfield. In the campaign, everywhere the comedian went, people would take his Pilot Pen, "Pens You Have To Hold On To." Naturally, Dangerfield deadpanned his way through situations in which he got no respect, but his Pilot Pen did! Sales during this two-year campaign rose $9 million. Shaw's marketing promotions philosophy is to grab customers' attention, maybe make them chuckle, listen to what they want, and give it to them. ■

G. Brewer, "Take My Pen—Please!" *Sales and Marketing Management,* 146, no. 2 (February 1994), p. 11; S. Feldman, "An American Plants a Culture in a Japanese Company," *Personnel* 68, no. 7 (July 1991), p. 24; J. E. Rosenberger, "Japanese Firm Opens Door to Executive at U.S. Unit with Board Appointment," *The Wall Street Journal,* March 27, 1992, pp. B7, 9.

Photo 12.12

Ronald Shaw, president of the Pilot Pen Corporation of America.

(FCC), U.S. Postal Service, and state attorneys general, as well as by trade associations, self-regulation by the American Association of Advertising Agencies (4 As) and the Direct Marketing Association (DMA), the activities of local Better Business Bureaus (BBB) nationwide, and so on. These controls help keep promotion honest and punish those who deviate from established rules, regulations, and norms. For example, the FCC has recently adopted rules to control telemarketing practices and is considering rules to control infomercials. Marketers must be aware of and adhere to the self-, government, and trade regulations designed to control promotion. Marketers found guilty of violations may be fined, forced to issue retractions and apologies, or both.

Check Your Understanding
12.4

1. What are some of the criticisms of promotion?
2. What are some of the positive things associated with promotion?
3. Describe some of the controls on promotion.

Review of Chapter Objectives

1. *Explain how promotion works.* Promotion is an important element in the marketing mix. Although there are many different types of promotions, for the most part promotion works by informing consumers about products, persuading them to make a purchase, reminding them about the product, and even entertaining them as part of the process of building product awareness and brand image. The ultimate promotion goal is to get consumers to act. A serious problem facing marketers is the communication clutter in the marketplace. Integrated marketing communication (IMC) breaks through the clutter by coordinating a unified, consistent message and incentive promotion effort. IMC relies on synergy to get a greater effect from the integrated promotion than could be achieved from the individual parts.

2. *Discuss promotion decisions.* The promotion mix types are advertising (mass and direct response), personal selling, sales promotions, public relations/publicity, and direct marketing. Promotion decisions focus on selecting the most effective, efficient promotion types to achieve promotion goals.

3. *Identify the steps in a promotion plan.* The promotion plan is a blueprint for action. It sets specific promotion objectives, identifies strategies and tactics, sets timetables, and identifies how promotion is to be evaluated. An important part of the planning process is making decisions about which promotion type(s) to use and their delivery system(s). Good promotion must be built around consumer insight. Other considerations are organizational strengths and weaknesses, competition, and general economic conditions.

4. *Describe promotion budgeting practices.* Promotion budgeting (how much of the marketing budget is designated for promotion) is often a top management decision. Allocating the budget to particular promotion types, delivery system expenses, and administrative costs is a tactical set of decisions.

5. *Address criticisms of promotion.* Promotion is often criticized for the hundreds of millions of dollars it costs, because it may encourage conspicuous consumption, it may mislead and deceive consumers, and it increases prices so that advertisers can cover promotion costs. Other criticisms center around issues of privacy, tastelessness, visual blight, and causing consumers harm. Promotion is defended because it supports a free press, is a major employer, and is an important part of the economy and social fabric of the United States.

Key Terms

After studying Chapter 12, you should be able to define each of the following key terms and use them in describing marketing activities.

Clutter, page 370
Relationship Marketing, page 373
Message, page 377
Incentive, page 377
Promotion Delivery System, page 377
Synergy, page 377

Integrated Marketing Communication (IMC), page 379
Promotion Mix, page 380
Promotion Plan, page 387
Emotional Appeal, page 391
Rational Appeal, page 391
Budget, page 393
Allocations, page 393
Conspicuous Consumption, page 394
Puffery, page 394

Discussion Questions

1. If consumer demand exceeded product supply, would there still be a need for promotion? Explain your answer.

2. What is promotion clutter? Identify some sources and explain why it is a problem.

3. Discuss the simple model of the communication process. Explain the importance of this model to promotion.

4. Why is relationship marketing of concern to marketers? Can it benefit consumers?

5. Compare and contrast integrated marketing communication (IMC) and traditional promotion.

6. How is consumer insight important to promotions?

7. What are some of the promotion decisions that marketers must make?

8. Identify the promotion mix types.

9. What are the steps in promotion planning?

10. Discuss some of the criticisms and defenses of promotion.

What Do You Think?

The Quebec Court of Appeal has upheld the Canadian ban on all tobacco advertising. This means that display advertisements for tobacco products must be removed from stores, bigger health warnings will be required on all tobacco packages, and each package must contain printed materials describing the hazards of smoking. Canada has some of the world's toughest antismoking laws, including very high taxes and bans on tobacco advertising in newspapers and magazines and on billboards. The tobacco industry voluntarily stopped advertising on television and radio in 1972. Canadian antismoking groups are lobbying to get tobacco sponsorships of sports and cultural events banned as well. Could this happen in the United States? What do you think?

Sources: R. Tamburri and C. J. Chipello, "Court Upholds Canadian Ban on Tobacco Ads," *The Wall Street Journal*, January 18, 1993, p. B5; "Canadian Court Upholds Tobacco Ad Ban," *Advertising Age* 64, no. 3 (January 18, 1993), p. 8.

Mini-Case 12.1

Promoting through Sports Sponsorships

Does it pay for businesses to promote themselves and their products through sports sponsorships? Some businesses believe the answer is a resounding *yes*. Their spending on sports sponsorships rose 16 percent in 1993 to almost $3 billion. In addition to well-known athletic shoe and equipment makers, other recent sports sponsors include John Hancock Mutual Life Insurance Company, a cosponsor of the Olympic games; Snickers, Philips Electronics, Sprint, and MasterCard International, cosponsors of the World Cup; and AT&T, Miller Brewing Co., and Hiram Walker & Sons, corporate sponsors of the Gay Games IV.

Although some critics scorn the value of sports sponsorships as being ineffective and driven by the egos of company executives, others believe that if they're done right, they can bring in new customers, motivate a sales force, recruit new employees, and raise employee moral. Their advice is to either go for the supersize events like the Olympics or stick with local sports, like youth soccer or little league baseball. Philips Electronics has a Ten Commandments of Sponsorship that provides useful guidelines for businesses thinking about this form of marketing promotion:

1. There shall be a natural relationship to products.
2. The event shall fit the marketing game plan.
3. There shall be a mass audience.
4. There shall be direct exposure.
5. The project shall not be risky.
6. Results shall not depend on an athlete or team.
7. There shall be a major role for the company.
8. There shall be no legal, environmental, or other hazards.
9. The event shall be well organized.
10. There shall be continuity with past sponsorships.

Case Questions

1. Is sports sponsorship a good idea for every business?

2. The Gay Games IV, which were held in New York City, involved 11,000 athletes, had over a half million out-of-town spectators, and pumped over $100 million into the New York City economy. In the United States, there are estimated to be 13 to 14 million adults who identify themselves as gay or lesbian. As a group, they are well-educated with higher disposable incomes than straight consumers; gay consumers are five times more likely to earn over $100,000 a year. The next Gay Games will be held in Amsterdam in 1998. What are the benefits/costs of being a business sponsor for the Gay Games?

3. Was 1994 World Cup sponsorship a good promotion idea?

Sources: P. Oster, "Philips: Playing by Its Own Rules at the World Cup," *Business Week,* June 20, 1994, p. 80; W. M. Bulkeley, "Sponsoring Sports Gains in Popularity: John Hancock Learns How to Play to Win," *The Wall Street Journal,* June 24, 1994, pp. B1, 7; J.Tilsner, "Gold in the Gay Games," *Business Week,* July 4, 1994, p. 38; T. Triplett, "World Cup Winners," *Marketing News* 28, no. 13 (June 20, 1994), pp. 1, 9.

Mini-Case 12.2

Wilma! A Blowout of Promotions

The Flintsones is a movie based on an animated network situation comedy that appeared on ABC Television from 1960 to 1966. Wilma and Fred Flintstone, their friends Betty and Barney Rubble, and an assortment of Stone Age characters (both human and dinosaur) stimulated a blowout of promotions designed to hype the movie and sell everything from hamburgers to toys to cereals to boxer shorts. McDonald's committed over $40 to its first-ever global promotion that included Flintstone's "Grand Poobah" value meals, Bedrock mugs, and Happy Meals at franchises worldwide.

Businesses spend more on consumer promotions than on media advertising. Instead of being just short-term incentives, sales promotions are becoming long-term strategies that companies tie to special themes (e.g., *The Flintstones* or the World Cup) or a steady stream of new offers like apparel, vacations, contests, and sponsorships wrapped around a brand (e.g., Marlboro's). Sales promotions are being used like media advertising—to brand build—which is dimming the distinction between the goals of the two promotion types. Companies look for sales promotions ideas to pop up. Barq's Inc., a niche soft drink marketer, had a "Soviet Union Going Out of Business" promotion. After the breakup of the Soviet Union, Barq's bought two tons of Soviet memorabilia, buttons, pins, and other items for company promotions.

In another movie, *Demolition Man*, Pepsi-Co launched what is considered the most extensive global promotion yet with its domestic Taco Bell and international Pizza Hut chains and Time Warner, Inc., the movie's maker. Taco Bell's product was placed throughout the U.S. version of the film. Because there are more Pizza Huts abroad than Taco Bells (outlets in 78 countries, more than McDonald's), for the international version of the film the studio edited out references to Taco Bell and inserted Pizza Hut. In several scenes, star Sylvester Stallone's mouth says "Taco Bell" but his dubbed-in voice says "Pizza Hut." In the U.S. version, Stallone refers to being rewarded for saving a man's life by being taken to dinner at Taco Bell, the only fast-food chain left on Planet Earth in the year 2032. In the international version, the line is rerecorded to refer to Pizza Hut.

Case Questions

1. Some members of the film industry are very critical of movies being reedited for marketing promotion purposes. How do you feel about it?

2. Have movie sales promotions and product placements become intrusive or are they effective ways to sell products?

3. Can sales promotions like Barq's and Marlboro's build the brand?

Sources: K. Goldman, "Mammoth Marketers and Merchandisers Are Leaving No Flintstone Unturned," *The Wall Street Journal*, February 22, 1994, pp. B1, 8; J. Berry and L. Bongiorno, "Wilma! What Happened to the Plain Old Ad?" *Business Week*, June 6, 1994, pp. 54, 58; T. R. King, "'Demolition Man' Trades Tacos for Pizza Abroad," *The Wall Street Journal*, December 2, 1993, pp. B1, 8; B. Lippert, "Yabba-Dabba-Don't: As a Movie, 'The Flintstones' are Instantly Forgettable, but Its Massive Merchandising Push Will Show Off Stone Age Endurance," *ADWEEK Eastern Edition* 35, no. 24 (June 13, 1994), p. 24.

Chapter 12 Notes

1. K. Goldman, "Black and White Ads Are Everywhere Now," *The Wall Street Journal*, July 5, 1994, p. B6.

2. J. Levine, "Gutenberg's Revenge," *Forbes* 153, no. 10 (May 9, 1994), pp. 166–67.

3. M. Ingrassia, "Going One Step Ogle the Line," *Newsweek*, March 14, 1994, p. 66.

4. K. Goldman, "Coors Tries PC Ads to Key Up Viewers," *The Wall Street Journal*, September 21, 1993, p. B6.

5. M. W. Miller, "Internet to Get Hit with Ad Clutter," *The Wall Street Journal*, August 27, 1993, p. B1.

6. E. de Lisser, "Retailers Are Trying Harder to Please Regular Customers," *The Wall Street Journal*, May 5, 1994, pp. B1, 8.

7. D. E. Schultz, "Integration and the Media: Maybe Your Approach Is Wrong," *Marketing News* 27, no. 13 (June 21, 1993), p. 15.

8. D. E. Schultz, "Integration Helps You Plan Communications from Outside-In," *Marketing News* 27, no. 6 (March 15, 1993), pp. 12.

9. D. E. Schultz, S. I. Tannenbaum, and R. F. Lauterborn, *Integrated Marketing Communications: Pulling It Together and Making It Work* (Chicago: NTC Business Books, 1993).

10. M. Everett, "Integrated Marketing: Making It Work," *Sales & Marketing Management* 146, no. 8 (August 1994), pp. 85–86.

11. R. A. Sims, "Advertising Has Mass Appeal, but It's Not Mass Advertising," *Marketing News* 27, no. 18 (August 30, 1993), pp. 4, 13.

12. T. Triplett, "Marketing Briefs," *Marketing News* 28, no. 11 (May 23, 1994), p. 15.

13. T. L. O'Brien, "Direct-Mail Scams Surge as Tele-Schemes Grow Stale," *The Wall Street Journal*, December 17, 1992, p. B5; M. L. Carnevale, "Fighting Fraud," *The Wall Street Journal*, May 18, 1992, p. R13; T. Triplett, "Telemarketing Law Aims at Big-Money Fraud," *Marketing News* 28, no. 21 (October 10, 1994), p. 5.

14. K. Goldman, "Long Distance Risks of AT&T–MCI War," *The Wall Street Journal*, April 14, 1993, p. B3; K. Goldman, "MCI Ad Rebukes AT&T Tactics in Bid for Market Share," *The Wall Street Journal*, December 20, 1994, p. B5; K. Goldman, "AT&T–MCI Negative Ad Volleys Are

Long-Distance Risk for Both," *The Wall Street Journal,* April 14, 1993, p. B8.

15. C. Miller, "Outdoor Advertising Weathers Repeated Attempts to Kill It," *Marketing News* 26, no. 6 (March 16, 1992), pp. 1, 9; A. S. Hayes, "Signs of Battles over Billboards Are Easy to See," *The Wall Street Journal,* March 23, 1993, p. B1.

16. E. Tanouye, "Critics See Self-Interest in Lilly's Funding of Ads Telling the Depressed to Get Help," *The Wall Street Journal,* April 15, 1993, pp. B1, 6; M. Fitzgerald, "Postal Service Takes Action against Bogus Ad Invoicing Scheme," *Editor and Publisher* 127, no. 44 (October 24, 1994), p. 25; "North Dakota Ad Laws Made Clear to Retailers," *Jewelers Circular Keystone* 165, no. 7 (July 1994), p. 200.

17. K. Goldman, "Repetitive Ads Keep Viewer Recall Going," *The Wall Street Journal,* April 7, 1993, p. B7.

18. K. Goldman, "Seniors Get Little Respect on Madison Ave.," *The Wall Street Journal,* September 20, 1993, p. B6.

19. L. M. Grossman, "The Smell of Chanel May Be No. 2 Issue after Cigarettes," *The Wall Street Journal,* May 13, 1993, pp. A1, 4.

20. K. Dentino, "Taking Privacy into Our Own Hands," *Direct Marketing* 57, no. 5 (September 1994), p. 38; J. Waldrop and M. J. Culnan, "The Business of Privacy," *American Demographics* 16, no. 10 (October 1994), p. 46.

The Promotion Mix: Advertising, Sales Promotions, Personal Selling, Public Relations, and Direct Marketing

Chapter Objectives

After studying Chapter 13 you should be able to

1. Describe the role of advertising in product promotion.
2. Explain how sales promotions are used.
3. Explain the promotion advantages of personal selling.
4. Characterize public relations/publicity activities.
5. Identify the advantages of direct marketing.

*I*nform, persuade, remind, and sometimes entertain: These are the tasks of promotion as it is used to achieve marketing goals. *Advertising, sales promotions, personal selling, public relations/publicity, and direct marketing:* These are the promotion mix variables, the tools used to achieve promotion objectives. Promotion is highly visible to the public, volatile, controversial, yet critical to marketing success. As you learn about each of the promotion mix variables in this chapter, consider this question: Do most consumers think *marketing* and *promotion* are synonymous?

Alicia Hernandez is faced with a marketing dilemma. It's February and in only two months she'll open her fresh fruit, vegetable, and flower shops for the season; for the first time she's going to have strong direct competition. In the past she hasn't put much effort into marketing promotions; satisfied customer word of mouth was enough to get her started and successfully grow her business so that she now has five stores open from April until October. However, this year she feels it's particularly important to run preseason promotions designed to build awareness and, when the stores open, store traffic. She believes that if she can get people to visit her stores they will realize that she offers top-quality products and service at reasonable prices. Value is what will differentiate her stores from the competition along with the relationships that she and her sales force establish with customers.

What promotions should she use to accomplish her marketing goals? Faced with a limited budget and only two months until opening, she puzzles over the respective benefits and costs of several promotion alternatives. On paper she lists some options:

- *Direct mail:* Hernandez has a mailing list of last year's customers that she assembled from addresses on personal checks, special orders, and deliveries. She could send these people personalized letters with a 10-percent-off coupon for their first purchase of the new season. By tracking coupon redemption from the letters, she can determine whether or not a mailing is worth the cost.

- *Print:* Hernandez could place freestanding inserts (FSIs) and/or display advertisements in the local newspaper, which has a 70 percent area readership. The FSIs (on bright green heavy paper stock) and display advertisements with 10-percent-off coupons could be placed in the paper's Food & Home Section. Coupon redemption can be tracked to learn if the newspaper is an effective promotion medium.

- *Radio:* Using radio station–provided demographic and psychographic listener profiles, Hernandez could match her customers to appropriate stations and programs. Each station produces radio spots for local retailers and runs them at the best times to capture the attention of a receptive audience. Listeners will be told to mention the station's name at a store cash register and get a free gift. Alicia can track the effectiveness of the radio commercials through the number of referrals.

- *Door hangers:* She could send flyers directly to targeted homes. A commercial direct-delivery service has started offering local businesses the service of having their promotional flyers delivered door to door in plastic bags hung on front doorknobs. At only pennies per house, Hernandez can target neighborhoods where her current customers live, using addresses from her mailing list. She assumes that her customers' neighbors will also appreciate her products.

- *Sponsorship:* The area arts and crafts fair will be held just before her stores open for the season. This is a very popular event, drawing people from miles around. She could become a fair co-sponsor, rent booth space, and have product samples on display along with free recipes, flower arranging demonstrations, and 10-percent-off coupons.

- *Contest:* Last year one of Alicia's artist friends designed a brilliantly colorful, highly abstract T-shirt for Alicia's employees to wear as a store uniform with jeans or shorts. Customers kept asking to buy them. She could have a T-shirt giveaway in each store. Each redeemed 10-percent-off coupon would also serve as a contest entry form. This way she could build a more extensive in-house mailing list of old and new customers. After the contest, T-shirts could be sold at a profit.

Hernandez needs to find out more about each of these promotions, particularly their costs, deadlines, advantages, and disadvantages. She can make an informed decision about which promotions to use only after she has studied this information. If you were a marketing consultant advising Hernandez, what promotions would you suggest?

ADVERTISING

Advertising is nonpersonal persuasive marketing communication, mostly conveyed in the mass media and paid for by an identified sponsor who controls the message. It is the one promotion that all consumers can identify, although most often they do so inaccurately by labeling *all* promotion advertising! This results in advertising being censured for the daily glut of promotions that inform, persuade, remind, and entertain consumers about products from the frivolous to the noble.

Objective 1 Describe the role of advertising in product promotion.

advertising Nonpersonal marketing communication mostly conveyed in the mass media and paid for by an identified sponsor who controls the message.

Types of Advertising

There are many different types of advertising. Some advertising builds a brand image; other advertising establishes goodwill for a company, as shown in the television storyboards in Photo 13.1. Some is national or even global in coverage; other advertising is local or regional. Some advertising is directed at personal use consumers; other advertising is directed at businesses, government, and other organizations, as well as distributors and employees. The most frequently used advertising classifications are:

By Coverage
- *Local (retail):* Local in scope, advertising products offered in a city, town, urban area, or region.
- *National (brand):* Nationwide advertising typically used to build brand image.
- *International:* Products advertised in two or more countries, often customized to the local culture.
- *Global:* Standardized advertising used in different countries worldwide with a unified image and message.

By Task
- *Commercial:* Advertising designed to persuade consumers to purchase products in order to generate revenues and profit.
- *Noncommercial:* Advertising by not-for-profit organizations and government that is not specifically profit oriented.
- *Corporate (institutional):* Advertising designed to build goodwill for a company among stockholders, employees, distributors, the public, and the government.
- *Public service:* Advertising donated by agencies, the media, and advertisers that supports causes and social welfare activities.

By Media Type
- *Indirect response:* Advertisements that use the indirect mass media of electronic (radio, television, computers), print (newspapers, magazines), or outdoor (billboards, transit) delivery systems.

Photo 13.1

Promoting goodwill is the top priority here.

(Music under)

ANNCR: When Bill Demby was in Vietnam, he dreamed of coming home and playing a little basketball.

MAN: Hey, Bill!

ANNCR: A dream that all but died when he lost both legs to a Vietcong rocket. But then researchers discovered that a Du Pont plastic could help make truly lifelike artificial limbs.

(SFX: sounds of game in progress)

ANNCR: Now Bill's back, and some say he hasn't lost a step. At Du Pont, we make things that make a difference.

MAN: Hey, Bill, you've been practicing!

ANNCR: Better things for better living.

- *Direct response:* Advertising that provides a mechanism for direct consumer action via a toll-free telephone number, mail-in coupon, fax number, or similar device.

By Consumer Target

- *Personal use consumers:* Advertising directed at individuals, households, and families buying for themselves or others.

- *Business and organization consumers:* Advertising directed at other businesses, government, professions, and agricultural consumers.

Although indirect response mass media advertising has been the dominant form of advertising throughout most of the 20th century, direct response advertising is gaining in popularity. **Direct response advertising** is more personalized than mass advertising in that it attempts to establish a relationship with the consumer by encouraging interaction; it is measurable in that it can capture a consumer response almost immediately. Direct response television advertisements for such things as records, investments, and household

direct response advertising
A form more personalized than mass advertising that attempts to establish a dialogue with the consumer by encouraging interaction.

Marketing Applications 13.1

Advertising is a promotion familiar to most consumers. To reinforce your ability to distinguish among different types of advertising, make a collection of print advertisements from magazines and newspapers. Find one example of each of the following advertising types: national brand, local retail, corporate institutional (goodwill), public service announce-ment, and business to business. For each type, explain its characteristics and the promotion goal. Critique the adver-tisement for its consumer insight—does it show insight about what consumers need and want; will it get consum-ers to act? ■

products employ a 1-800 or 1-900 telephone number to allow an immediate purchase. They generally run 60 to 120 seconds, long enough to persuade the consumer to make a purchase, call to ask for more information, or write a check. A coupon, mailing address, or telephone number is the interactive element in a direct response print advertisement.

A new type of advertising is often confused with entertainment programming. An *infomercial* is an extended direct response televi-sion advertisement that runs as long as a 30- or 60-minute television program. The Federal Communications Commission opened the door to this type of advertising in 1984 when it revoked a rule that limited a commercial to two minutes and a total of 14 minutes of commercials per hour.[1] These extended, long-form advertisements are designed to entertain as well as sell, and may compete with programming for a viewer's attention. Often hosted by a celebrity spokesperson, infomercials are used by the Juiceman, Jay Kordich, to sell juice-making machines (see Photo 13.2);[2] General Motors to launch its Saturn line of automobiles; Revlon Consumer Products Corporation to introduce its Dolly Cosmetics with a 30-minute infomercial hosted by Dolly Parton;[3] and Norelco to introduce a new product, Satinelle, a hair-removing epilator for women.[4] K-tel International was one of the first marketers to use mini-infomercials in the early 1980s. You've probably seen a K-tel direct response advertisement for the Veg-O-Matic slice-and-dice machine, "great hit retrospective" music compact discs, or exercise videos. K-tel has expanded its format to infomercial length and is taking them to Europe.[5]

One advantage of mass advertising is its relative low cost in reaching a large number of consumers. Mass advertising is a good promotion choice for products aimed at the mass market, but there are also disadvantages. Because mass advertising does not provide

Photo 13.2

A famous infomercial—juice anyone?

direct feedback, it is often difficult to evaluate its effectiveness. It's particularly difficult to prove a direct relationship between advertising and sales, because there may be a long delay between when the advertisement appears and when sales respond. It can be very expensive to execute and place mass advertisements, particularly on national television. Finally, mass advertising is wasteful—many disinterested consumers are reached by advertisements they consider clutter and, therefore, ignore.

Advertising provides information and image signals that help consumers position products. Positioning refers to how a consumer mentally perceives products and, in particular, compares brands. A consumer may evaluate several brands using information from advertisements, and then position the brands in her mind. For example, how does the consumer perceive a Saturn automobile? Is it comparable to a Toyota Corolla or a Lexus? General Motors would like advertising to create a high value brand image for Saturn, perhaps so consumers perceive it to offer Lexus-type quality at a Corolla-type price.

The Importance of Advertising

Annual advertising spending in the United States is over $147 billion; worldwide, advertising spending, in U.S. dollars, is over $317 billion.[6] Procter & Gamble (P&G), the Ohio-based consumer products giant, has been the top U.S. advertiser for many years. By the early 1990s, P&G was spending over $2.39 billion annually advertising its products in the United States, and several billion more

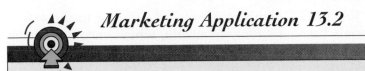

Marketing Application 13.2

Some consumers are fooled by the entertainmentlike format of infomercials and don't distinguish between regular programming and this extended form of commercial. Infomercials are often shown at night, when air time is cheaper and talk shows are popular. How do consumers feel about infomercials? Are they effective promotion tools? As a class project, construct a short survey about infomercials designed to determine consumer attitudes toward them. Have consumers seen them? Do they like them? Have they bought any of the advertised products because of an infomercial? Each class member should question several consumers. Bring the results to class for discussion. ■

advertising worldwide.[7] P&G also advertises extensively in many emerging foreign markets, where advertising's contribution to local economies is growing. It recently launched the largest single advertising campaign in Thailand—$5 million to advertise its Vidal Sassoon hair-care products. Western shampoo and conditioner makers are flooding the Thai market, seizing an opportunity to reach Thailand's 57 million compulsively clean consumers who often take several showers each day.[8] P&G and other Western companies are moving into mainland China, where one national television advertisement can reach 600 million consumers. Chinese consumers, unlike many Americans, believe what they see on television; thus, state-run TV, at $20,000 for a prime-time minute, is a great bargain.[9]

The top U.S. advertising agency by brand is Leo Burnett, Co., with almost 2,000 employees and gross income of over $304 million on annual U.S. billings of over $2 billion.[10] Advertising is a significant social and economic force in the United States and abroad, as well as a major employer. There are 1,700 recognized advertising agencies in the United States that employ over 225,000 people. The U.S. advertising industry is the largest in the world. When it comes to the amount of money advertisers will spend to reach consumers in a particular location, New York City ranks first, with $28,460 million spent in total advertising dollars in 1994. Next were Los Angeles ($18,535 million), Chicago ($13,124 million), and San Francisco ($10,683 million).[11]

A Short History of Advertising

Advertising has been around since ancient times. Posted notices, signs carved into wood or stone, and tacked-up flyers were among the earliest forms. The invention of the printing press in the mid-1400s by Johannes Gutenberg simplified printing to the extent that text materials became widely available, which encouraged the spread of literacy. This helped advertising, because print advertisements could be made quickly, cheaply, and in great quantities for wide distribution in newspapers, magazines, and as freestanding posters. A literate population could read printed advertising messages, which increased the messages' effectiveness and desirability.

Benjamin Franklin sold advertising space to help support the publication of his many newspapers. Advertising flourished as businesses grew, and the United States reaped the benefits of technological advances made during the industrial revolution. Modern advertising began to develop beginning in the mid-1800s. Changes in transportation, communication, and the American way of life contributed to the growth of advertising, including:

- *Railroads:* The transcontinental railroad moved products coast to coast and accelerated the need for advertising to promote product availability in communities across the country.

- *Communication inventions:* The teletype, telephone, and other communication inventions contributed to the proliferation of media delivery systems and the development of the mass media.

- *Mail delivery:* Universal rural mail delivery ensured that everyone could receive promotions, including direct-mail catalogs as pioneered by giant retailers like Sears, Roebuck & Co.

- *Growth of the mass market:* Population growth accelerated during the late 1800s, and an expanding labor force meant greater consumer demand, more competition, and an increased need for mass advertising.

Advertising has become increasingly more sophisticated and widely used throughout the 20th century. Even during World War II, when the country's production capacity focused on the military, advertising was used extensively to sell war bonds and promote national security and patriotic causes. The war's end brought a major transformation to a peace economy in which consumer products proliferated, supply rapidly overtook demand, and mass advertising became the primary means of reaching the new mass market, particularly through the electronic media (first radio, then television. In the waning years of the 20th century, advertising seems to pop up everywhere. For example:

- Channel One, a daily television news program for schools, includes 30-second advertisements along with its programs.[12]

- *Forbes* magazine placed a 5.25-inch computer disk containing advertisements for 10 products in its June 22, 1992, issue, between pages 64 and 65.[13] This is believed to be the first example of computer disk advertising in a national magazine.

- Eveready's Energizer Bunny appears on a screen saver program designed to prevent permanent images from burning into computer screens. In addition to the pink bunny screen saver, there are also screens featuring *Jurassic Park* and popular television characters.[14]

- Muzak Limited Partnership has added radio advertisements to its 12 music channels received by more than 200,000 businesses nationwide. It is connecting over 1,800 supermarkets into a satellite system that beams music along with national brand advertising to subscribing supermarkets nationwide.[15]

- Advertisements are shown on television screens located in shopping malls, airports, and doctor's offices.

It is no wonder that the average U.S. adult is the target of as many as 3,000 advertising messages each day.[16]

The Advertising Triad

In a small or medium-sized business, one or two employees may be responsible for making advertising decisions. This often means contacting the local newspaper to arrange for print advertisements to be placed on a regular basis or to announce special events, such as end-of-season clearance sales. Most newspaper advertising departments assist businesses in making design and placement decisions. Local radio stations help businesses by cutting radio commercials, using copy supplied by the business, that are read on the air by a station announcer. Local television spot announcements can be prepared and aired by the staff of a local television station. Some businesses hire specialists to perform advertising tasks, such as a marketing consulting to write advertising copy, a photographer to take product pictures, and a print shop to set up print advertisements and produce camera-ready copy. Another alternative is to perform advertising tasks in-house, through a department staffed with your own business's advertising professionals. Some businesses use a combination approach that assigns both in-house marketing staff and outside agencies to the same or different products.

Larger businesses frequently hire an outside, full-service advertising agency to perform all advertising tasks, including designing an entire advertising campaign, creating the advertisements, producing the finished advertisements, placing them in appropriate media, and evaluating the results. Advertising agencies—the businesses that create, execute, and place advertisements—make up an impor-

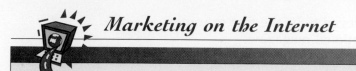

Marketing on the Internet

Numerous World Wide Web (WWW) home pages are under construction as marketers hop on the Internet and explore how this new commercial medium can be used to promote products. Many marketers are patterning their advertising on what they already offer in print and on television; some marketers even use sales promotions. For example, Club Med offers a $50 gift certificate to visitors to the Club Med home page site who complete an on-line survey. One of the most creative home page sites belongs to MCI Communications Corporation, where Net browsers are invited to tour a fictional publishing house, Gramercy Press. By clicking on icons, visitors can tour staff offices, read E-mail, provide feedback, and learn about networkMCI. What makes this promotion unique is that it is supported by network television commercials that spin a story about the people working for MCI's fictional company. MCA/Universal allows visitors to download and sample photographs from studio movies as well as audio and video clips. Playboy Enterprises, Inc., offers subscriptions, merchandise, and two bulletin boards to its home page visitors. Company executives read messages posted by visitors on the bulletin boards as part of their informal market research effort.

Promoting on a World Wide Web home page is different than sending unwanted on-line advertising messages via E-mail to unwilling recipients. Visitors to home pages seek out the sites by directing their computers to take them to a particular WWW address. Most on-line interactive forums (also called bulletin boards, newsgroups, lists, and message boards) forbid unsolicited advertising and many forum managers (called the list manager or majordomo) screen out blatant advertisements before they can be relayed to the entire mailing list. When unsolicited advertisements slip through, they are often met with flames (rude messages that list subscribers send back to advertisers telling them, in no uncertain terms, that their message wasn't wanted or appreciated!). Like the other forms of marketing promotions, to a certain extent, Internet users can control the clutter by filtering out unwanted promotions and attending only to those that are interesting and entertaining. ■

J. Sandberg, "Net Working: Corporate America Is Falling in Love with the Internet (The Wall Street Journal Reports: Technology)," *The Wall Street Journal*, November 14, 1994, p. R14; "Interactive: Making Moves on the Internet, Who's on the 'Net," *Advertising Age* 66, no. 2 (January 9, 1995), pp. 22–24; P. Hise, "The Flameproof On-Line Marketing Pitch," *INC.* 17, no. 3 (March 1995), pp. 87–89.

---

advertising triad The three main participants in advertising when outside resources are used: the advertising agency, the advertiser, and the media.

tant part of the **advertising triad,** which also includes advertisers and the media. The advertising triad is shown in Figure 13.1.

Full-service advertising agencies provide broad services to their clients, including advertising planning, execution, placement, and evaluation of results. Their organization includes account management, creative and media services, business support services, and, often, research. Many small agencies specialize in one or more facets of the advertising process. For example, creative boutiques specialize in creative work, photography, animation, and/or computer graphics. With modern computer technology, all it takes is creativity, computer hardware, draw and print software, and a laser printer to make camera-ready advertisements.

A trend of the 1980s was the creation of mega-agencies, extremely large worldwide agencies formed by the merger or buyout

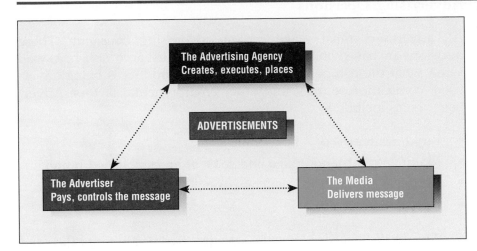

Figure 13.1

Members of the Advertising Triad

of many smaller groups. The largest mega-agencies are WPP Group with 1993 worldwide billings of $18,485 million followed by Interpublic Group of Companies, Omnicom Group, Dentsu, Inc., and Saatchi & Saatchi.[17]

Advertisers are businesses, organizations, individuals, or other sponsors who pay for the advertisement, control its contents, and are identified. An advertiser may be a politician purchasing advertising services from an agency to create and place political advertisements for an upcoming election, or it may be a very large company, like General Motors. Large advertisers may hire several advertising agencies, one to handle each of its many different product lines. The advertiser may be a small or mid-size business, an organization, a cause, an individual, or any paid sponsor.

Media are the delivery systems by which advertisements are conveyed to an audience. The major mass media delivery systems are newspapers and magazines (print media), radio and television (electronic media), and outdoor (billboards, transit). Advertising volume in the United States by medium in millions of dollars are newspapers $31,840; magazines $7,420; radio $9,390; television $30,030; direct mail $27,425, and outdoor $696. Top advertised categories are retail, automotive, business and consumer services, entertainment, food, toiletries, and cosmetics.[18] Major media companies include Time Warner (magazines and Cable television), Capital Cities/ABC (newspapers, magazines, television), and Gannett Co. (newspapers, broadcast, and other media). Advertising delivery systems also include many emerging systems, such as fax machines, video and computer disks, interactive computer-telephone-television systems, and the Internet's World Wide Web.

advertiser The business, organization, person, or other sponsor who pays for the advertisement.

media Delivery systems for sending a message to an audience.

Advertising Decisions

All advertisers must make certain advertising decisions. These decisions are based on the *goals* advertising must accomplish, as well as on what the competition is doing, what product is being advertised, company resources, and other environmental factors. Advertising goals include to:

- Build awareness of a new brand.
- Maintain the brand image and sales of an established brand.
- Establish goodwill for the company.
- Increase store traffic.

AIDA *A*wareness, *i*nterest, *d*esire, and *a*ction: a model for the tasks set for advertising as it moves the consumer toward a purchase.

An *advertising budget* must be set with specific amounts allocated for producing advertisements, buying media time and space, conducting research to evaluate consumer responses, and paying the administrative costs of the agencies and staff. A *message* must be developed to attract attention, create interest, stimulate desire, and get the consumer to act. The **AIDA** (*a*wareness, *i*nterest, *d*esire, *a*ction) model identifies the tasks set for advertising to accomplish as it moves the consumer toward action (a purchase). *Media* must be selected, and the advertisement must be executed, placed, and then evaluated for its effectiveness. Often, these decisions will be organized into an **advertising campaign,** a coordinated series of advertisements using one or many media designed to convey a unified message and image about a product. Some campaigns run for years, using variations on a creative theme. Examples are the television and print campaigns built around the Energizer Bunny and the art poster print advertisements for Absolut Vodka (see Photo 13.3).

advertising campaign A coordinated series of advertisements using one or many media designed to convey a unified message and image about a product.

copy platform Statement of how verbal elements are to be used in an advertisement and outlines the creative plan; provides direction for using creative alternatives.

Creative Strategy   The creative strategy identifies the creative elements to be used for an advertisement. The **copy platform** is a statement of how verbal elements are to be used; it outlines the creative plan and provides direction for using creative alternatives. Many different creative alternatives exist. A television advertisement may use an emotional or rational appeal, provide facts and information, demonstrate how to use a product, show a slice-of-life story that relates the benefits of using a product, show humor, or use a celebrity spokesperson endorsing the product or a testimonial from real people. The **creative mix** is the integration of the verbal message (copy) and visual images (art) that gives an advertisement its consistency and impact.

creative mix The integration of the verbal message (copy) and visual images (art) that give an advertisement its consistency and impact.

Creativity is an elusive concept. Most people recognize when something is creative; usually, they can't explain how it happens. Yet creativity is not just "Eureka!" experiences where inspiration sud-

Photo 13.3

Absolut Vodka's art advertising contributes to its marketing success.

denly strikes; people can be trained to be more creative by systematically developing the innate creativity that everyone harbors and learning to express it. A frequent problem with advertising creativity, however, is that the advertisement is celebrated for its creativity but not because it achieves its marketing goal. Many highly creative advertisements don't sell the product, which is the basis for the creativity versus selling controversy that periodically erupts in advertising and marketing. Most marketers agree that a highly creative advertisement is a failure if it doesn't achieve its marketing goal.

Media Strategy   There also must be a strategy for the selection of media in which to deliver the advertisement. A **media plan** states what media are to be used, how often, and when. **Reach** refers to the total number of consumers in a target audience who are contacted once in a fixed period of time using a particular delivery system. **Frequency** is the number of repetitions, or the total number of times consumers in a target audience are contacted in a fixed period of time using a particular delivery system. **Waste,** media contacts with consumers who are disinterested, can be high in mass advertising.

Another media decision is about scheduling, when and for how long an advertisement should appear. A **flighting** or bursting schedule places advertisements in heavy bursts, not on a regular schedule, often with periods of no advertising; a **pulsing** schedule runs at least some advertisements all the time, interspersed with periods of heavy advertising; and a **continuous** schedule maintains the same base level of advertising over time.

media plan Statement of what media are to be used, how often, and when.

reach The total number of consumers in a target audience who are contacted once in a fixed period of time using a particular delivery system.

frequency The number of repetitions consumers in a target audience are contacted in a fixed period of time.

waste Media contacts with consumers who are disinterested.

flighting A way of scheduling the placement of advertisements in heavy bursts integrated with periods of no advertising.

pulsing An advertising schedule that runs some advertisements all the time interspersed with periods of heavy advertising.

continuous An advertising schedule that maintains the same base level of advertising over time.

Consumer Insight

A frequently heard criticism of advertising relates to what seem like endless, mindless repetitions of the same commercial, particularly on network and cable television. However, this advertisement, selected as the advertisement of the decade, appeared only once! It aired during the 1984 Super Bowl and introduced Apple's Macintosh with a slap at Big Brother IBM. In the commercial, a young woman runs down the center aisle of a theater where dronelike people are fixedly viewing a man's head speaking from a large movie screen (see Photo 13.4). She pivots and slings a sledgehammer at the screen, which breaks with a rush and the printed words scroll across the television, "On January 24th Apple Computer will introduce Macintosh, and you'll see why 1984 won't be like '1984.'" This take-off on George Orwell's book *1984*, with its memorable visual and verbal images, provoked considerable controversy among Apple's board members, who voted against showing it. However, airtime had already been purchased and another buyer couldn't be found for 60 seconds of it. Faced with dead airtime, the Apple board let the commercial show once. It made such an immediate impression that television news programs picked up on the story and the resulting widespread publicity was a promotions windfall. What began as an advertisement that almost didn't get aired turned into a promotions triumph and a great marketing success. ■

M. Potts, "Putting the Apple in Their Eye," *Washington Post National Weekly Edition*, 11, no. 13 (January 31–February 6, 1994), p. 21.

Photo 13.4

This ad aired only once, but the controversy surrounding it created shock waves.

Commonly used media delivery systems are:

- *Electronic media:* Television and radio are the primary electronic mass media, although other forms are growing more popular, including computer-based systems. There are slightly over 1,140 commercial television stations and almost 10,000 commercial radio stations in the United States. Cable offers selective programming that helps advertisers decide where to place advertisements by comparing consumer demographics and psychographics to audience profiles. Radio is also demographically selective, with stations programming country, rock, classical, all-talk, or other formats to satisfy listeners' tastes. Each has an audience that an advertiser may find very attractive.

• *Print media:* Newspapers and magazines are widely read in the United States and abroad. Consumers believe newspapers are credible sources of information; thus, they are a popular media choice for advertisers. Newspapers are timely, often have important retail information for consumers, and are a primary source of local advertising. Over 1,500 newspapers are published everyday in the United States. Magazines are demographically selective and give consumers and advertisers a wide choice of topics. There are over 11,000 magazine titles published in the United States. Newspapers and magazines were among the first media choices at the beginning of U.S. advertising and remain very popular today.

• *Direct advertising:* Although direct advertising takes many forms, its principal advantage is the ability to provide rapid consumer feedback. Direct television and radio advertisement offer consumers a 1-800 or 1-900 telephone number. Direct advertisements in newspapers and magazines may use a combination of telephone numbers, coupons, and mail-in forms. Although costs for some of these alternatives may be relatively high, advantages are interactivity, accountability, and, usually, less waste.

• *Catalogs:* Catalogs are a form of direct-mail marketing that share the advantages of other direct, targeted approaches. Mail catalogs are sent by firms to their business/organization customers, by store-based retailers like Bloomingdale's, Dillard's, and Gump's, and predominately nonstore retailers like Lands' End and L.L. Bean to personal use consumers. Specialty catalogs number in the thousands, and once a consumer gets on a specialty mailing list through an expression of interest or purchase, his name is often sold to other catalogers. Most catalogs are free; some charge a small fee for postage and handling.

• *Outdoor advertising:* Outdoor advertising includes billboards (see Photo 13.5), the sides of trucks and buses, hot air balloons (Photo 13.6), and other types that are stationed outdoors. Often, there are legal controls over where they can be used.

• *Yellow pages directories:* Yellow pages and other directories are used extensively in the United States and abroad. The word *directory* explains its advantage, that directories direct consumers who are already aware of their need for a product. Directories help consumers locate products and retailers. Display advertisements in yellow pages directories come in many different colors and for national as well as local and regional products. There are directories for businesses and products serving highly targeted audiences, such as

Photo 13.5

Some people consider billboards an eyesore, but others see them as the best advertising medium.

Photo 13.6

Marketers can become quite creative when it comes to outdoor advertising.

senior citizens, Hispanic-Americans, Asian-Americans, orchid growers, environmentalists, and car enthusiasts. Some directories are offered on-line. Nynex Corp., a Baby Bell, has allied with Prodigy to offer on-line directory assistance and display advertisements for almost 2 million businesses in New York and New England.[19] The immediacy of on-line directories gives advertisers the ability to make timely changes and corrections. This eliminates a big problem, because hard-copy directories are issued only once a year, which means mistakes cannot be corrected and new businesses can't be listed until the next printing.

- *Other advertising media:* The only boundary on other media appears to be the limits of the human imagination. New media include advertising by fax machine, computer screen, movie theater, videocassette, computer disk, and the Internet.

1. Compare and contrast indirect mass advertising and direct action advertising. 2. Describe some advertising types. 3. Discuss some of the advertising decisions that must be made.	**Check Your Understanding** *13.1*

SALES PROMOTIONS

Sales promotions are a type of marketing promotion that adds value through short-term inducements to take action, make a product purchase, move products through a distribution channel, and ultimately increase sales. There are many different types of sales promotions directed to personal use consumers, business/ organization consumers, employees, and distributors (see Figure 13.2).

Sales promotions designed to stimulate demand are very popular. A recent study of promotion practices nationwide found that almost half of a typical business's promotion budget is spent on sales promotions. Advertisers have shifted many advertising dollars into sales promotions, and in 1992 spent about $52.2 billion on trade promotions and $62.4 billion on promotions aimed at personal use consumers.[20] A recent survey of personal use consumer attitudes and practices in coupon redemptions found that they like and use coupons, with 99 percent of the responding households saying they had used coupons in the past year.[21] Sales promotion use is growing, because of its effectiveness with consumers and the pressure of competition. Some businesses that might like to get out of couponing are afraid to because they know the competition will capitalize on their departure. When the economy is unsettled, the rational economic appeal of a sales promotion can be highly effective to all targets.

One important reason for sales promotions' popularity is that they can generate rapid revenue increases by quickly increasing store traffic, product purchase, and movement of products through the distribution channel. However, there are problems. Some critics contend that sales promotions undermine brand loyalty by increasing consumers' sensitivity to and demand for added incentives. Sales promotions by one company can lead to counterpromotions by

Objective 2 Explain how sales promotions are used.

sales promotions Short-term marketing techniques that add value and stimulate demand.

Figure 13.2 Types of Sales Promotions
Sales promotions may be directed specifically at one of the principal groups of targets or they may include several or all targets.

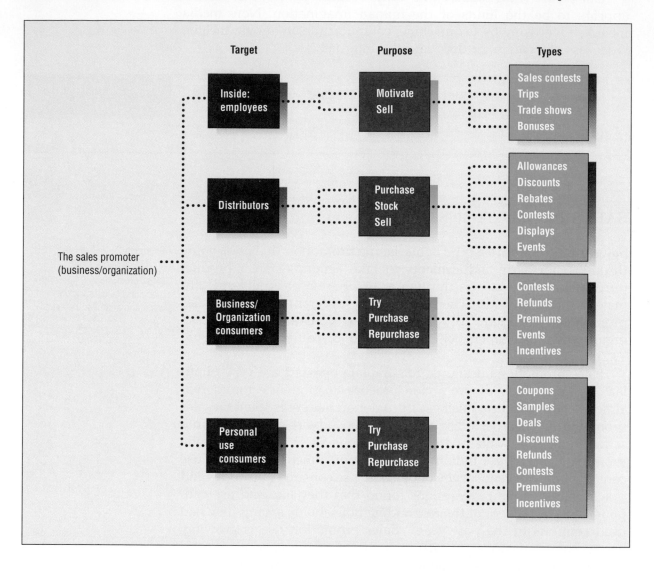

the competition, which may benefit consumers in the short term but can bring on damaging promotion wars. More sales promotions also mean more clutter, which can be costly to all promotion types.

Even not-for-profit organizations and governments use sales promotions. For example, Clifton Middle School students in Houston, Texas, participated in a video contest organized by K-Swiss athletic shoes and Foot Locker stores. Students were awarded shoes for producing a winning stay-in-school video.[22] Sales promotion contests are used by religious groups, social clubs, and civic organizations to raise funds for their activities and causes.

Marketing Application 13.3

For what products are coupons used most? Conduct a coupon check. For the next week, track the cents-off coupons that you come across in Sunday newspaper freestanding inserts, in the daily newspaper, in magazines, via direct mail, and in stores. At the end of the week evaluate your list and identify coupon sources and product categories. What can you conclude from your observations? Bring your results to class for discussion. ■

Sales Promotion Strategy

Effective sales promotion requires planning and a clear statement of objectives. Sales promotion strategy must be defined as carefully as other marketing and promotions strategies. After evaluating the environment in which the sales promotion will be offered, the target audience must be identified and objectives set. Objectives typically are quantitative, a distinct advantage over mass advertising. Some frequently used objectives are to:

- Build traffic.
- Create awareness.
- Increase sales (initial and repurchase).
- Stimulate a product's movement through a channel of distribution.
- Combat the competition.
- Build goodwill.

Because sales promotions run for a short period of time (e.g., a coupon may have a 90-day expiration date), it presents a good opportunity to track results and establish accountability. This means that by the end of the sales promotion, results should indicate whether or not objectives were met. For example, if the objective is to raise traffic by 10 percent and the beginning traffic count is an average of 1,500 customers per day, an increase on average of 150 customers per day suggests that the sales promotion was effective and the objective was met. However, it is critical to determine if anything else occurred during the time of the sales promotion to influence the results. Another concern is what happens to sales at the conclusion of the sales promotion. If the promotion encouraged already-loyal consumers to stock up, sales will fall when the special offer is withdrawn because these consumers won't repurchase until their inventory is drawn down. If sales promotions are run on regular cycles, consumers often play along, buying only when promotions are run.

The next step is to decide which sales promotions to use. The list of alternatives is lengthy, including, among others, cents-off coupons, samples, prizes, rebates, contests, and premiums. Sales promotions should coordinate with and complement other promotions, such as advertising or public relations. Often, a sales promotion strategy calls for one product to be bundled or tied to another. For example, soft drink promotions in the summer are often bundled with reduced admission tickets to local amusement parks or recreation areas.

With the objectives set and alternatives selected, the timing for the promotion is established with a beginning and an end date. An evaluation plan should identify benchmark times for evaluating the promotion's progress. Then the promotion is implemented and progress is monitored.

Despite good planning, sales promotions sometimes go wrong. For example, Pepsi ran a bottle-cap promotion called "Number Fever" in the Philippines, where a few winning numbers of "349" printed in selected caps would win grand prizes of about $36,000. Because of a computer error, "349" was printed in over 500,000 bottle caps. The company paid out over $10 million, $19 to each winner, to defuse the situation. However, public discontent was so great that Pepsi became the target of lawsuits, rallies, terrorist attacks, and at least four killings.[23]

In another case, Maytag's Hoover vacuum cleaner division offered a free international airfare travel promotion to consumers purchasing the vacuum cleaners in Great Britain and Ireland. When consumers realized that the vacuum cleaners cost less than the tickets, there was a rush to purchase and over 200,000 cleaners were sold. Hoover has made good on the sales promotion, at a cost of almost $49 million. Three Hoover executives also lost their jobs in this disaster.[24]

Sales Promotion Targets

Sales promotions can be targeted to personal use consumers, business/organization consumers, members of the channel of distribution, and the business's employees, particularly the sales force. Promotions often have multiple targets. For example, an event sponsorship may be experienced by many different people, including employees, business associates, and the general public (see Photo 13.7). A coupon may be used by personal use and business/organization consumers.

The mass market often receives sales promotions, as in national mass media cereal couponing and regional soft drink/theme park bundled purchase offers. Promotions also include small-scale, local activities such as distributing fliers, coupons, or posters by hand in a

Photo 13.7

Toyota Motor Manufacturing sponsors an annual event to celebrate the Kentucky Woman of the Year.

promotional effort sometimes called "street marketing."[25] Promotional flyers can be slipped under a car's windshield wipers, distributed by hand to shoppers, or attached to posters tacked to community bulletin boards.

Sales promotions often are categorized by whether they are targeted to personal use consumers, business/organization consumers, channel of distribution members, or the sales force.

Personal Use Consumers The sales promotion most familiar to personal use consumers is probably the cents-off coupon found in newspapers, particularly Sunday freestanding inserts; in magazines; in mailers; via shelf vending machines in stores; and on or in product packages. Coupons lower the price on the product when it is purchased in a store or by mail. Some coupons bundle products together; for example, buy a gallon of ice cream at the regular price and get a small can of chocolate syrup free. The leading product categories for couponing are cereals, prepared foods, and health and beauty aids.

Coupons come in many different denominations and expiration dates. The amount of the price savings depends on the product, promotion goal, and competition. Expiration dates are getting shorter, which forces a timely consumer purchase decision and faster results. Coupons are very effective in getting consumers to try a product.

Coupons are often redeemed by mistake or by fraud. A coupon may be mistakenly redeemed after it has expired, if the consumer buys the wrong product, or if the consumer makes no purchase. Negligent or criminal store employees may be at fault.

Other familiar sales promotions are contests, free samples, rebates, discounts, bonuses, refunds, premium incentives, and event sponsorships. Premium incentives can include key chains, toys, coffee mugs, and various trinkets adorned with a company's logo given to salespeople, consumers, and even employees by giant companies, such as AT&T, Apple Computer, and Kraft General Foods, as well as by local retailers, politicians, and even college bookstores. One advantage of these gizmos is that they keep the company's name and logo in front of the recipient as the product is used, serving as a constant reminder.[26]

Approach Software used a different sort of sales promotion to speed the introduction of a new program. This small software company made a special introductory low-price offer to a select group of influential users in order to stimulate positive word of mouth about the product. The company reports that "The number of people who purchased the product on the advice of friends or associates tripled in the six months following the original shipment of the product."[27]

Business/Organization Consumers Sales promotions targeted to business/organization consumers often involve a form of discount or rebate to purchase or stock up; materials distributed through trade shows; and sales meetings, events, and contests. Some of the incentive systems used for personal use consumers are also used for business/organization consumers.

Channel Members The incentive with distributors is to get them to move products through the channel of distribution to the final consumer. These include allowances, contests, bonus products, rebates, and other discounts and deals. Assistance often is provided in making product and point-of-purchase displays, as well as in sponsoring cooperative advertising in which part or all of the cost of advertising in a local newspaper or local electronic media is contributed by the manufacturer.

The Sales Force Motivation is a prime goal of many sales promotions targeted to the inside or outside sales force. These often take the form of contests, events, sales meetings, bonuses, and deals designed to increase sales force productivity, improve work outcomes, increase sales volumes, and improve morale. One problem with these incentive systems is that in their zeal to reap the rewards, some salespeople engage in questionable if not illegal practices designed to stimulate sales.

Check Your Understanding 13.2

1. Who are the targets of sales promotions?
2. What are some sales promotion types?
3. Describe what is meant by *sales promotion strategy*.

PERSONAL SELLING

Unlike other promotion forms, personal selling establishes a personal link with consumers. **Personal selling** is promotion that is direct, personal, and often a face-to-face interchange between a business's salesperson and a consumer. Personal selling is important in retail as well as in business/organization markets, where the industrial sales force is essential. Personal selling is an accepted part of marketing promotion in the United States and many other countries. In some parts of the world, however, American-style direct selling can cause trouble. Direct sales by door-to-door distributors for American businesses like Avon and Nu Skin have drawn fire for cutting into traditional department store sales and changing shopping patterns. Many women homemakers become product distributors and earn their own money for the first time, which is seen as a threat to traditional societies in some East Asian countries.

The salesperson is a **boundary spanner,** bridging the gap between company and consumer (often with a foot in each camp), employed by the company to promote its products while also bound to deliver the best possible deal for the consumer so that he will become a loyal customer. Salesperson and customer form a personal selling **dyad,** the connection by which seller and buyer interact in a personal contact to make a marketing exchange. This key role in establishing relationships often places the salesperson in a conflicting role, caught between the sometimes contradictory demands of company and consumer.

Objective 3 Explain the promotion advantages of personal selling.

personal selling Promotion that is direct and personal.

boundary spanner The salesperson who is employed by the company to promote its products while building customer loyalty.

dyad The connection between buyer and seller in a marketing exchange.

Advantages and Disadvantages of Personal Selling

Perhaps the greatest advantage of personal selling is the immediacy and personal contact with the buyer, which allows the seller to counter objections, negotiate terms, solve problems, and establish a long-term personal relationship. Salespeople can provide feedback to their company by collecting and analyzing information from the environment, including information about the competition, that can be used to make marketing decisions.

A downside of personal selling is that it requires costly human resources. It is expensive to pay for the maintenance of a sales force in the field (e.g., travel costs, hotels, food). Likewise, the costs are high for such sales force activities as recruiting, hiring, training, and compensating. Personal selling is indispensable in many industries where face-to-face contact is expected and required. However, it is highly cost ineffective in trying to reach a mass audience. Even in many retail settings, companies are trying to shift more and more selling responsibilities onto consumers, through self-service and even self-billing.

Selling Contributes to the Economy   Over 20 million people are employed in some facet of personal selling in the United States. Salespeople sell products in grocery, department, and drug stores; they are stockbrokers, bankers, real estate and insurance agents, clerks, and stockpeople; and they sell retail, wholesale, and industrial products. Some salespeople receive little if any job training; industrial salespeople, on the other hand, may receive months if not several years of training before they are trusted to begin the more complicated business-to-business selling. The cost of training new salespeople averages about $6,000 and takes about four months.[28]

Personal selling is particularly effective in counteracting negative feedback and sales resistance. It is not effective in reaching large numbers of consumers, a task better left to mass advertising and sales promotions. Personal or hand selling is growing in importance in many industries, some not previously identified with extensive personal selling. For example, in publishing, where the competition is intense, publishers' salespeople make personal pitches to bookstores to get special attention for promising new books.[29]

New Selling Technologies

telemarketing Sales technique using computer-managed dialing systems and telephones to make sales.

Because of the costs involved in training and supporting a sales force in the field, sales force managers have been quick to adopt new technologies to increase efficiency and cut costs. **Telemarketing** overlaps both personal selling and direct marketing; it involves salespeople using computer-managed dialing systems and telephones to make sales. Computer software programs can identify the most efficient itinerary for a salesperson to take when making sales calls. Other computer programs can place and track orders electronically, create customer databases, manage contacts and leads, and determine which sales contacts actually make money.[30]

Another computer-based change in personal selling is the growing use of home-based sales representatives. In April 1993, Compaq Computer Corporation moved its sales force into home offices; the result has been gains in productivity and revenues.[31] From their homes they are linked by telephone and computer to headquarters and their territories. They focus on developing leads and servicing existing accounts, and they avoid commutes to work. Automation has freed these salespeople from the traditional office-based routine and allowed them to concentrate on what they do best. The downside is that many miss the relationships nurtured in a group work environment and, because they are based at home, there is a tendency to put in excess hours.

Consumer Insight

Could you do telemarketing? Telemarketing is highly stressful; large telemarketing businesses have dozens of people working together and against the clock in large table-lined rooms. Tethered by telephone headsets attached by cords to their computers, telemarketers typically make at least a hundred calls in a shift, working from scripted sales pitches and talking with prospects whose telephone numbers are dialed by computer. On average, they reach 50 percent and land about 15 percent of the people called. Most telemarketers are paid by commission based on sales. Telemarketers are closely monitored by supervisors who often listen in to monitor their performance. Telemarketers and telephone-based data processors make up a surprisingly large segment of the American workforce: 45 percent of all workers born since 1945. Tens of thousands make their calls from the industry hub in Omaha, Nebraska. Although it is a high-turnover profession, it attracts students, retirees, homemakers, people between jobs, and part-timers. Of the 3 to 4 million telephone sales representatives in the United States, about 70 percent are women.■

D. Milbank, "Telephone Sales Reps Do Unrewarding Jobs That Few Can Abide," *The Wall Street Journal*, September 9, 1993, pp. A1, 8.

The Sales Force as a Strategic Tool

Because of the close link between salesperson and consumer, salespeople are an excellent source of information about customers, the competition, and other environment factors. Smart companies use information gained by their sales force in formulating marketing strategy. Customer orders can provide insight into demand trends in the general economy; customer complaints can guide product improvements and new product development; customer contacts often can expand the selling network.

Salespeople add value to the products they sell by providing service to their customers. This can mean providing services that help reduce the customer's workload, organizing the selling effort around what the customer needs, and delivering products when and where they are needed. For example, Fletcher Music Centers in Clearwater, Florida, serve primarily older, often retired Floridians. They don't just sell organs; they provide music lessons, music books with large type-faces, large organ controls, social gatherings, and free group lessons. They meet the musical, physical, and social needs of their customers.[32]

Sales Tasks and Steps

Salespeople perform many different tasks. Some only take orders, as in retail selling; others prospect for new orders, a task associated particularly with business and industrial selling. Some business selling involves both prospecting and order taking. The selling process is outlined in Figure 13.3. Other salespeople stock shelves,

Figure 13.3

The Selling Process

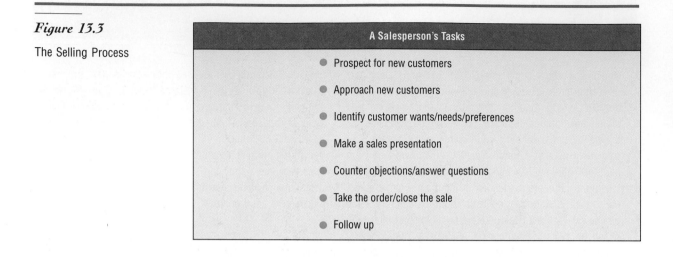

A Salesperson's Tasks
● Prospect for new customers
● Approach new customers
● Identify customer wants/needs/preferences
● Make a sales presentation
● Counter objections/answer questions
● Take the order/close the sale
● Follow up

traveling between retail locations, delivering their products, display-ing them, and taking orders. Some industrial salespeople act as consultants to their customers and help solve their problems, as in the case of computer salespeople advising clients on the best com-puter systems for their business needs and how to network them.

Sales Force Management

Human resources management is a business field that studies sales force recruiting, selection, hiring, training, motivation, evaluation, and related personnel topics. Businesses are paying greater attention to these issues because the costs of making a mistake are so high. Businesses are advised to clearly define sales force tasks before recruiting, so that prospects can be informed of the job requirements during the process. Selection should be based on relevant job criteria—determining whether or not prospects have the ability and motivation to do the job. Training is needed in all selling jobs, including retail. It is essential in industrial selling and, for complex selling tasks, training may be a multiyear process. Salespeople must learn about the product, the business, the competition, customers, and the marketing environment. They must be familiarized with the business's presentation materials and how sales calls are made. As more selling tasks are computerized, new recruits must be trained to use the business's software and hardware.

Every sales force, even if it's only one person, must be managed. (See Figure 13.4.) Sales force management requires planning, imple-mentation, and control activities. Members of the sales force must be recruited, hired, trained, motivated, compensated, evaluated, and, sometimes, fired. One of the first requirements in managing a sales

Figure 13.4   Sales Force Management Decisions

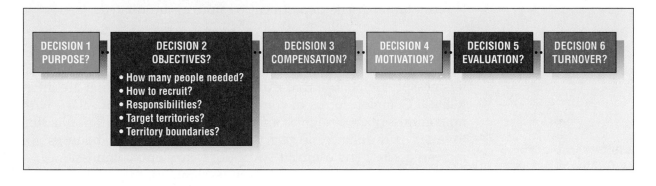

force is determining its purpose. For example, in industrial selling the inside sales force may be used exclusively to follow up leads developed by the outside sales force. In other cases, the sales force may divide its time between leads and performing customer service. Often, salespeople are asked to do many things concurrently, such as prospecting, tracking orders, fielding customer service calls, and preparing sales materials and presentations. In retail selling, the sales force may be required to service customers, tally sales, change prices, track inventory, restock shelves, and take inventory.

Subsequent decisions are made based on the objectives. These include the determination of how many salespeople are needed, how they will be obtained, their responsibilities, and their territories. If an industrial sales force must cover a large geographical territory, making calls on many different present and potential customers, it may be more cost effective to hire outside salespeople employed by an independent contractor. Small and mid-size businesses frequently make this decision because they lack the resources to develop and deploy their own sales force. An outside sales force made up of sales agents, brokers, or manufacturer's representatives may work for many businesses at the same time, selling noncompeting, complementary product lines. Although they can provide greater coverage, sharing an outside sales force can be less satisfactory because their time and loyalties are divided and not dedicated to one company. In retail selling, the choice is between hiring full-time permanent employees and temporary employees. The last recession and slow recovery convinced many retailers to pare down their numbers of permanent employees, whose fringe benefits (e.g., insurance, retirement, and vacations) are high, and, instead, use more temporary employees hired from an agency, whose fringe benefits are minimal and terms of employment are more flexible.

Another decision involves targets and territory: who the industrial sales force calls on and where. For the retail sales force, this is a decision about placement—whether salespeople are assigned for lengthy terms in one department or store or are rotated.

Sales Force Compensation   Often, one of the most difficult management tasks is to decide on a sales force compensation method. Most businesspeople believe that compensation and motivation are interrelated. Common forms of compensation are a straight salary with no commission; a straight commission, where compensation is tied to sales performance; a salary or commission plus bonuses for increased sales; and a mixed system of salary and commission.

Some criticize the commission system, saying that it forces salespeople to hard sell their products in order to make a living. The dilemma is how to still motivate salespeople while not making them too aggressive. This was a particular problem for Sears, Roebuck's auto service centers in California, where salespeople were so anxious to get their commission that they recommended auto repairs that were not needed. Sears has since abandoned its commission compensation plan and returned its automobile service employees to an hourly pay plus bonus system.[33]

Sales Force Motivation   Sales force motivation is less of a concern in some companies because their recruitment process has carefully weeded out potential hires who are not a good match with the company's goals and organizational climate. Many salespeople go into sales because they are highly self-motivated, aggressive, and outgoing. However, even good salespeople must be able to accept rejection, realize it isn't a personal affront, and move on to the next contact. Personal selling can sometimes be frustrating and physically exhausting; therefore, companies often establish internal programs to motivate their sales force, stimulate their enthusiasm, and promote sales. Motivational programs include sales contests tied to sales goals, where top sellers win prizes and recognition; retreats and special meetings, often held in resort-type environments with dinners and motivational speakers; forming sales teams, where members can discuss methods for improving performance as well as build rapport; and promoting a positive organizational climate that supports and encourages desirable sales performances.

The subject of motivation has generated endless books and research papers, yet there are no certainties in motivating a sales force. Some motivators that appear to work include:

- *Work climate:* Establishing a positive organizational environment for the workforce so that they have an internal motivation to

Marketing Application 13.4

Personal selling is one of the largest areas of marketing employment. The odds are high that some members of your class are or have been part of a sales force. As a class project, determine the proportion of your classmates who have selling experience. Categorize their backgrounds by retail, industrial, or other selling. Determine how they learned about job opportunities, how they were selected, the kind of training they experienced, how they were compensated, how they were evaluated, and their job tasks. What insights can you draw about personal selling from your analysis? ■

succeed and providing them with a supportive staff to help them with training, feedback, and encouragement.

- *Goal setting:* Including salespeople in the process of establishing hard but attainable goals, like sales quotas, that can be reached through effort. Feedback is critical so that salespeople are informed of their progress toward goal achievement.

- *Sales promotions:* You've learned how sales promotions are used as motivators through sales contests, bonus plans, and other incentives. These short-term stimulants are effective with at least some salespeople. However, cutthroat competition for sales prizes can backfire and result in conflict and discouragement. There also is a risk that if a salesperson receives a monetary reward for achievement, it undermines the internal satisfaction that may be a more powerful motivator.

Sales Force Evaluation   How do you know if your sales force is effective? One method is to compare outcomes with goals such as annual sales, new customers, or signed contracts. Most businesses have personnel evaluation processes. These can be informal meetings with a supervisor to get feedback on monthly, quarterly, semiannual, or annual performance. Often, this includes a formal, written performance evaluation. Some businesses post sales figures, which often sets up a competition between salespeople.

Sales Force Turnover   Because it is costly to train salespeople and, when they leave, there often is a delay before a replacement fills the slack, companies increasingly are looking for ways to manage turnover. Concern about turnover often lessens when the economy falters, typically because job opportunities grow scarce. However, when opportunities are more plentiful, turnover can rise. Companies seek to manage turnover through such practices as profit sharing and stock option plans, by which employees hold a stake in the company's long-term success. A positive organizational climate that encourages, rewards, and supports employees can lessen the urge to move. Likewise, clear career paths, opportunities for advancement, and help with self-improvement have proven beneficial.

Check Your Understanding *13.3*	
	1. Explain the meaning of the term *dyad*.
	2. How are new technologies affecting personal selling?
	3. Identify some of the activities associated with sales force management.

PUBLIC RELATIONS/PUBLICITY

Objective 4   Characterize public relations/publicity activities.

public relations   Establishes communication links between businesses and potential clients and customers.

Public relations is the promotion type that establishes a communication link between a business/organization and various public(s)—groups of people who have some interest or involvement in what the business does. Public relations works to build and maintain goodwill and a positive image through such activities as:

- *Holding press conferences* to disseminate information that can be used by the news media.
- *Producing printed and electronic materials* that can be sent to interested groups and individuals, employees, distributors, and others outside the company.
- *Lobbying* on behalf of a business or organization.
- *Organizing events or sponsorships* that show how a business or organization contributes to society.
- *Advising businesses and organizations* about how to handle unexpected situations and respond in emergencies.

Sometimes a business is presented with an unexpected promotion opportunity that public relations can develop. For example, singer Diana Ross appeared in a recent ABC television movie about a mother's struggles with mental illness. After 18 years, the woman was freed from her torment by a Swiss pharmaceutical company's newly released drug. Sandoz, who makes the antipsychotic drug, used public relations to navigate a tricky balancing act, supporting related mental health causes while avoiding the appearance of being self-serving and cynical about promoting drug sales.[34]

Confusion exists about the relationship between public relations and publicity. Some believe they are the same; others consider publicity as one set of activities within broader public relations

Marketing Application 13.5

Public relations specialists often work with the news media to convey accurate information about their business or organization. The news media is oriented toward short, concise news briefs. Therefore, a goal of public relations is to communicate enough information in a news release within strict time and space limits. Try your hand at writing short, concise, complete news statements. Compose a one- or two-paragraph news release for one of the following scenarios (use your imagination to fill in the details):

A.   A pharmaceutical company has just received FDA approval to market a pill that completely eliminates all symptoms of the common cold—runny nose, headache, congestion, fever, and body ache. The prescription medicine, whose brand name is Kold-Stop, will cost $1.25 per tablet. Your task: Announce this medical advance to the public.

B.   An oil business has experienced a storage tank rupture. Oil is seeping toward a popular local fishing spot, Blueye Run. Your task: Inform the public that your company is doing everything possible to get the situation under control and is an environmentally responsible business. ■

promotions. Although their goals are the same, one difference is that public relations is paid for by a sponsor, whereas publicity is typically not paid for at all.

Targets of Public Relations/Publicity

You are already familiar with the promotion clutter in our society. This clutter greatly complicates the job of the marketing public relations specialist, who is trying to communicate positive information about a business, organization, or other client. In addition, there are many different targets that often require different messages. These include communications with people such as *employees,* to build morale and motivate productivity; *stockholders,* to reassure them about the business's condition; *potential investors,* to convince them to buy into the business; *government,* to demonstrate that the business is a good contributor to the betterment of society; *distributors,* to motivate them and build loyalty; and *consumers,* to inform them about new products, communicate important messages about existing products, and present the business in a good light. The public relations goal is to convey information, influence attitudes and opinions, and prompt positive responses.

Criticisms of Public Relations/Publicity

This type of marketing promotion is under increasing scrutiny and criticism as public relations professionals visibly and aggressively attempt to put a positive spin on everything from political candidates' offhand statements to oil spills. Critics contend it is undemocratic, because public relations uncritically presents clients' interests in a positive light whether it is deserved or not. By clogging the media with press releases, news conferences, televised events, and photo opportunities, sophisticated public relations can alter public opinion through media manipulation.

Public relations can also be highly beneficial to consumers. Johnson & Johnson effectively used public relations to allay consumer fears when one of their products was tampered with and several consumers died as a result. The company's president used public relations to establish communication links through television, radio, and print to let consumers know that the company was responding immediately by removing its products from store shelves, inspecting all production facilities, and cooperating completely with authorities to find the guilty person(s).

Public Relations/Publicity Processes

Publicity appears in the mass media encoded by an intermediary sender such as an editor, reporter, commentator, or other third party. Publicity could begin as a press release about a store opening, new product release, company event, sponsorship, philanthropy, or other activity. The problem with publicity is that there often is little control over the message that is finally delivered; sometimes the outcome may be negative rather than positive.

Publicity is often disseminated through written news releases, live press conferences, open meetings, photographic (photo) opportunities, and the distribution of press kits and company video programs. Although time and space are cost-free, there are costs associated with arranging for the creation and distribution of publicity materials.

Public relations (PR) is practiced by nonprofit and government units, perhaps even more so than by many small to medium-size businesses. Often, the job of a public relations department is to plan events and sponsorships for a company. This is a continuous process, in contrast to publicity, which often is episodic, being used for special events or crises.

Public Relations/Publicity Decisions

Before deciding what to do, a complete analysis must be conducted to become knowledgeable about the company and its environment. This requires studying the business, its products, the competition, consumers, and the marketing environment. It is important to know what people already know and think of the business and its products. Information can be obtained from a marketing research business that conducts company, product, and consumer surveys.

The collected information is a starting point for assessing public relations opportunities. For example, if the analysis indicates that the business is positively associated with sports sponsorships, then future sponsorships are reasonable. Many businesses sponsor local soccer clubs or Little League baseball, purchasing team uniforms that also display its name. Considerable goodwill can be generated through local sponsorships and the support of charitable, social, and cultural organizations.

Toyota Motor Manufacturing U.S.A. (TMM) has been highly effective in demonstrating to the citizens of communities near its manufacturing plants that it is a good citizen. In addition to contributing $1 million to a local university library building fund, TMM has provided new Camry sedans for the Georgetown, Kentucky, mayor's office and the Scott County, Kentucky, judge executive's office; contributes to cultural groups; sponsors an annual statewide conference on opportunities for women as shown earlier in Photo 13.7; and hosts plant visits for school groups and the general public that include a guided tour of the plant by motorized tram.

An opportunity analysis may indicate that a business faces a problem—perhaps a change in its marketing environment, like the appearance of a new competitor; a regulatory change; a downturn in the economy; or the loss of public confidence in the company's products. The problem could unexpectedly arise from a disaster, crisis, or bad news. Public relations can stem the damage through effective communications. Knowing what to do depends on what situation the business faces.

Once the situation is assessed, objectives are stated for the goal of the public relations effort. Common goals are to build goodwill, raise awareness, reinforce an image or develop a new one, inform the public, or demonstrate societal responsibility.

Target audiences must be identified. For public relations to be effective, it must be carefully developed to reach a target audience. What is said or done, and how it is said and done will vary according to the target. Public relations techniques are selected and their respective implementation costs assessed. Once implemented, results are monitored in a continuing process to ensure that the public relations effort is having the desired effect.

Check Your Understanding
13.4

1. Identify some public relations/publicity tasks.
2. Describe some criticisms of public relations/publicity.
3. Contrast public relations/publicity and advertising.

DIRECT MARKETING

Objective 5 Identify the advantages of direct marketing.

direct marketing The promotion mix element that uses computer databases and lists to direct mail and telephone offers to consumer targets.

It is not easy to define direct marketing, because there is so much controversy surrounding what it is. Likewise, not everyone agrees that it is part of the promotion mix. **Direct marketing** is the promotion mix element that makes extensive use of computer databases and lists to direct mail and telephone offers to consumer targets; gives immediate response measurement capacity to the mass media through direct print and electronic advertising; and can personalize messages and offers, refine targeting, and reduce the waste of contacting nonreceptive audiences. It is more measurable than are other promotion types and, therefore, promises greater accountability. The tools of direct marketing are catalogs, letters, telemarketing, brochures, direct advertising, direct mail, and other forms moving through the channels shown in Figure 13.5.

Direct marketing is both a victim and a cause of clutter. In addition, because of the amount of information accumulating in databases, concern is rising about privacy issues and the rights of businesses to sell versus the rights of personal use consumers to privacy. This is not as much an issue among business/organization consumers.

Figure 13.5 Channels of Direct Marketing

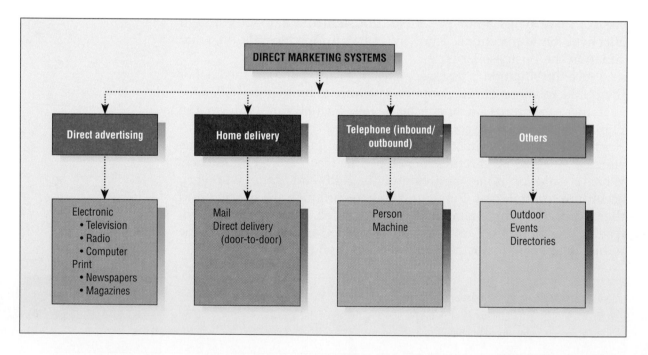

Consumer Insight

Businesses often make a mistake that is common to first-time direct marketers: They launch overly ambitious direct marketing campaigns with an extensive mailing list, then find they haven't the time or staff to follow up on the leads generated. Anatomical Chart Co., a 100-employee company, avoided this problem by launching its first direct marketing attempt with a highly targeted direct-mail special poster offer sent to 9,000 bookstores. Follow-up telemarketing calls to attractive niches like college book-

stores were made in-house by the business's existing employees. Within three months, the campaign had generated hundreds of qualified leads, landed almost 100 bookstore orders, paid for the promotional costs, and made a profit. ■

S. Greco, "First-Pass Telemarketing," *INC.* 15, no. 10 (October 1993), p. 29; F. Brookman, "Them Bones, Them Profitable Bones," *Stores* 74, no. 1 (January 1992), p. 146.

The Database

The computer database of consumer information is the backbone of contemporary direct mail and telemarketing. Scanner data provide sales information in real time. Data captured at the moment of sale can identify who made the purchase and what was bought. This can be coded and filed in a database; matched with archival data like credit history, past purchases, and home and automobile ownership; and then compiled and selected to compose mailing and telephone lists of prospects for specific offers. High-speed computers with vast memory storage capacity provide tremendous potential for compiling lists based on highly personal consumer information.

The benefits of computer databases to businesses using direct marketing are appreciable. An accurate, timely database can eliminate considerable waste in a mailing or telephone list. A **list** is a prime set of names and addresses identified by specific characteristics in a database, set into order, and compiled into a mail or telephone contact list. For catalog sales, a good list means saving money by ensuring that catalogs are mailed to targets who have made similar purchases in the past and have the resources to buy the products. For telemarketing, a good list means eliminating nonreceptive targets and saving time and salesperson effort. A good database is constantly changing, with addresses being updated and names eliminated to avoid misdirected mailings. All databases experience **churn,** where people's circumstances change (e.g., they move, change their names, die, etc.) and having their name on a particular list is no longer desirable.

list A prime set of names and addresses identified by specific characteristics in a database.

churn A change in people's circumstances resulting in their names no longer being desirable on a particular list.

Generating Lists

The best list is the in-house list compiled from the names of current or past customers. Alicia Hernandez from the chapter-opening story was planning to mail a sales promotion flyer to a list of last year's customers. In-house lists outsell any other form of list.

Lists are available from list brokers who purchase them from list owners. These businesses purchase subscription lists, contributor lists, mail-order buyer lists, inquiry lists, and lists compiled by record-keeping agencies like universities and motor vehicle departments. Lists can be generated from responses to print and television advertisements, such as calls to 1-800 and 1-900 telephone numbers. They can be formed from names of people who enter contests, send away for product information, or return a product registration form. List brokers work with the mailer to develop a profile of the mailer's customers that forms the descriptors for the contact list.

A list's value is determined by several factors. It must provide a reasonable quantity of names, sufficient so that it is profitable to initiate contact with these prospects; selections should be accurate; and the information must be current. There should be room for growth so that new names can be generated and added, and nonproductive names can be eliminated.

Direct Mail

The first form of direct marketing was direct mail. You'll remember previous references to the early Sears, Roebuck catalog, one of the first direct mail efforts. Direct mail uses letters, postcards, catalogs, brochures, videocassettes, computer disks, and product samples. Although most direct mail specifies the name of the occupant, which indicates a targeting effort, some direct mail is still very broad and often addressed to *occupant* or *resident*. This is still targeting, because the mail may be sent only to specified ZIP codes. Direct mail is not without its problems, however. As the costs of using the U.S. Postal Service escalate, direct mail marketers are seeking cheaper alternative delivery systems. The explosion of direct mail volume is a source of growing concern about environmental impact through paper use and disposal. Along with the ability to target consumers, there is a concern that the thin line between a marketer's right to do business and a consumer's right to privacy may result in increased government regulations that will further restrict the direct mail industry.

Career Watch

Selling the Japanese on Chrysler's four-wheel drive Jeep Cherokees calls for a master salesperson. Mitsuru Sato, manager of Honda Motor Company's joint venture with Chrysler Corporation, is a master salesperson in a company where American automobiles are not an easy sell. Sato has a long career of selling—Honda motorcycles in Brazil, power generators in the Middle East and India, and as president of Honda in Thailand. He keeps a close eye on consumer reactions to his products and is not afraid to transmit this information back to either Chrysler or Honda

so that it can be used in making product improvements. His greatest assets are his powers of persuasion and his ability to "talk straight!" However, a price cut to offset the appreciated yen, like one made for the 1994 model, will certainly help Sato sell the product in Japan. ■

K. Lowry Miller and D. Woodruff, "The Man Who's Selling Japan on Jeeps," *Business Week,* July 19, 1993, pp. 56–57; R. Johnson, "Cherokee Price Cut in Japan Expected," *Automotive News* no. 5521 (October 11, 1993), p. 6.

Telemarketing

Often called the most irritating form of direct marketing, telemarketing involves telephone sales calls to homes and businesses by both human salespeople and machines. Inbound calls are those made by consumers to telephone banks operated by the telemarketer, frequently using the telemarketer's 1-800 or 1-900 number; outbound calls are made by telemarketers to consumers. Computers often guide random access and sequential dialing. Telemarketers use scripts to make their sales pitch.

Direct Marketing Decisions

Direct marketing decisions differ slightly from other promotion types. Although the process begins with environmental analysis and objective setting, the selection of the target market is a critical early step. Once the target has been selected, appropriate direct marketing types and media are identified. Direct mail and telemarketing require the selection of databases and lists. Like the other promotion types, the message is developed, the promotion is implemented, and then it is monitored for effectiveness in achieving the goals set for it.

Check Your Understanding
13.5

1. Why is it difficult to define direct marketing?
2. How is a database used in direct marketing?
3. How are direct marketing lists generated?

Review of Chapter Objectives

1. *Describe the role of advertising in product promotion.* Like all marketing promotion, advertising is designed to inform, persuade, remind, and, often, entertain. There are many different types of advertising. Direct response advertising is interactive and more measurable than is traditional mass advertising.

2. *Explain how sales promotions are used.* Sales promotions are directed toward consumers, employees, and distributors. They are short-term incentives designed to stimulate an immediate response. Commonly used sales promotions include coupons, rebates, refunds, bonuses, contests, samples, and discounts.

3. *Explain the promotion advantages of personal selling.* Although personal selling can be highly expensive, it is also highly effective in those situations where the sales pitch must be tailored to specific client needs. Advantages are that the salesperson can make relevant counters to a consumer's objections, establish a positive and lasting relationship with consumers, and develop and follow up leads.

4. *Characterize public relations/publicity activities.* Public relations and publicity are used to communicate with the individuals and groups who compose a business's publics. Unlike advertising, this form of promotion is not always directly identified with a paid sponsor, although the goal is to develop and maintain goodwill for the sponsor. Public relations activities include preparing and distributing printed and electronic information, organizing press conferences and events, lobbying, and advising businesses on how to respond in emergencies and other unexpected situations.

5. *Identify the advantages of direct marketing.* Direct marketing comes in many different forms. It makes extensive use of computer databases that generate lists of consumers who are potential customers. It is measurable and interactive. Direct marketing systems include direct advertising, direct mail, and telemarketing.

Key Terms

After studying Chapter 13, you should be able to define each of the following key terms and use them in describing marketing activities.

Advertising, page 405
Direct Response Advertising, page 407
Advertising Triad, page 412
Advertiser, page 413
Media, page 413
AIDA, page 414
Advertising Campaign, page 414
Copy Platform, page 414
Creative Mix, page 414
Media Plan, page 415
Reach, page 415

Frequency, page 415
Waste, page 415
Flighting, page 415
Pulsing, page 415
Continuous, page 415
Sales Promotions, page 419
Personal Selling, page 425
Boundary Spanner, page 425
Dyad, page 425
Telemarketing, page 426
Public Relations, page 432
Direct Marketing, page 436
List, page 437
Churn, page 437

Discussion Questions

1. What are the tasks of promotion?

2. How did railroads, communication inventions, and mail delivery contribute to the need for national mass advertising?

3. What is an infomercial? How does it differ from traditional television commercials?

4. Compare and contrast advertising and sales promotions.

5. What groups may be sales promotion targets?

6. Explain the advantages and disadvantages of using:
   a. advertising.
   b. sales promotions.
   c. personal selling.
   d. public relations/publicity.
   e. direct marketing.

What Do You Think?

Promotions clutter is getting so bad that some advertisers are resorting to tactics that pay consumers to pay attention. One tactic being tested by a telephone company delivers a 30-second sales pitch to pay phone users. When a pay phone receiver is picked up, the user hears the offer. If they agree to listen to the commercial, their call is free; if they refuse, the call costs 25 cents. The rationale is that because consumers tune out most of the advertising they hear, in the future they will have to be paid to give up some of their privacy and pay attention to advertisements.

TBWA Advertising is taking a different approach. The advertising agency that produces the highly successful Absolut Vodka print advertisements is selling an interactive floppy diskette that tours a virtual reality museum containing 216 pieces of Absolut Vodka art, photography, and fashion designs. The viewer pushes a computer mouse to wander in and out of museum rooms where still and video exhibits are accompanied by music, text, and sound. The advertising diskette costs $30 and can be ordered electronically on CompuServe. Profits will benefit the American Foundation for AIDS Research. Will these two approaches work? What do you think?

Sources: K. Goldman, "Paying People to Listen to Ads, Spread the Word May Be Coming," *The Wall Street Journal*, May 12, 1994, p. B3; N. Hutheesing, "This Ad Costs $30 to See," *Forbes* 153, no. 8 (April 11, 1994), p. 127; J. Valente, "Absolut 'Museum,'" *The Wall Street Journal*, March 11, 1994, p. B2.

Mini-Case 13.1

"Mattress Mack's" Winning Ads

James "Mattress Mack" McIngvale annually sells about $44 million of furniture at his one store in Houston, Texas, that stocks mostly middle-of-the-line, discounted furniture. McIngvale turns over his inventory 15 times each year in an industry where the

Photo 13.8

Mattress Mack's low budget ads have always grabbed attention.

average is 2.5! In a typical Mattress Mack ad, McIngvale jumps up and down, grasps bundles of cash in each hand, talks at an almost unintelligible speed, and always ends his ads with "Gallery Furniture will save you money!"

Professor Keith Cox's marketing students at the University of Houston vote on the worst local television advertisements each year. Mattress Mack's advertisements always win for being obnoxious, poorly executed, and just plain bad! The advertisements are even designed to look like home videos, consistent with the store's low-price image. Along with his bad advertisements, McIngvale also has a highly efficient distribution system, a same-day delivery guarantee (within 100 miles), and salaried salespeople who don't hard sell customers.

Case Questions

1. Can irritating advertisements be effective? Explain your answer.

2. Which media seems to have more irritating advertisements than the others? What is irritating about these advertisements?

3. Would most consumers sit through an irritating infomercial?

Sources: W. P. Barrett, "Real Life Marketing 101," *Forbes* 149, no. 11 (May 25, 1992), pp. 146–47; P. Schancupp, "Mattress Infomercial to Debut," *HFD—The Weekly Home Furnishings Newspaper* 67, no. 45 (November 8, 1993), p. 18.

Mini-Case 13.2

Is There a Free Lunch?

Have you ever eaten your way through a grocery store? Food shopping is becoming an in-your-mouth experience, particularly on weekends. Consumers are in supermarkets to shop, and have their checkbook, credit card, or cash in hand. Almost 70 percent of all purchase decisions are made when the consumer gets in the store, so what better place to influence them? Marketers are capitalizing on consumer readiness to buy at the point of sale by increasing their free sampling. Much of sampling is directed toward children, because they influence many food decisions. There is a downside to sampling, primarily through spills, garbage generated, blocked aisles, samplers who dislike the product and show it, and sample hogs who eat and eat but never buy. A typical result is that over 60 percent of consumers will try a sample and, of these, almost 40 percent will buy the product. Product demonstrators are often older, retired women. These demo women must put up with cold aisles, rude shoppers, and people who pick through the food, which means the rest must be discarded.

Case Questions

1. Describe some reasons why consumers like free samples.

2. Is sampling a good idea?

3. Do any retailers other than supermarkets give away free samples?

Sources: G. Stern, "With Sampling, There Is Too a Free Lunch," *The Wall Street Journal,* March 11, 1994, p. B1; "Grocers Say Best Place to Influence Consumers Is in Store," *Marketing News* 27, no. 18 (August 30, 1993), p. 7.

Chapter 13 Notes

1. R. L. Cosby, "Surf's Up! Infomercials Making Waves in Advertising Industry," *Link* 5, no. 6 (June 1993), pp. 10–14, 24; C. R. Hartman, "Infomercial Power," *D&B Reports* 41, no. 5 (September–October 1992), p. 52.

2. G. Slutsker, "The Power of Juicing," *Forbes* 149, no. 5 (March 2, 1992), pp. 82–83; D. Oldenburg, "Getting Juiced," *The Washington Post,* August 30, 1991, p. C5.

3. S. Strom, "With Help from Dolly Parton, Revlon Will Be the First Big Cosmetics Maker to Try TV Marketing," *New York Times,* September 20, 1993, p. C8; P. Sloan, "Revlon Set to Jump into Home Shopping," *Advertising Age* 64, no. 10 (March 8, 1993), p. 1.

4. L. Bird, "Norelco Creates Infomercial for New Device," *The Wall Street Journal,* July 15, 1993, p. B8.

5. G. G. Marcial, "K-Tel Tunes in to Infomercials," *Business Week,* October 18, 1993, p. 90.

6. "Advertising: Strong Growth Ahead in Foreign Markets," *Standard and Poor's Industry Surveys* 162, no. 19 (May 12, 1994), Sec. 1, p. MEDIA/M15.

7. "The Advertising Fact Book," *Advertising Age* 66, no. 1 (January 2, 1995), p. 11.

8. C. Owens, "Thailand's Market for Hair Products Launches Ad War," *The Wall Street Journal,* January 4, 1994, p. B5.

9. S. Strasser, "Where the Admen Are," *Newsweek,* March 14, 1994, p. 39.

10. "The Advertising Fact Book," p. 11; M. Wells and R. C. Endicott, "Big Agencies Still Gripped by Contractions," *Advertising Age* 65, no. 51 (December 5, 1994), p. S8.

11. M. Campanelli, "Where the Ads Are," *Sales and Marketing Management,* October 1994, p. 63; *Industry and Trade Summary: U.S. Industrial Outlook 1994—Professional Services* (Washington, DC: U.S. Department of Commerce, 1994) pp. 51–54.

12. C. Miller, "Teachers Fight Channel One; Two Advertisers Drop Out," *Marketing News* 26, no. 17 (August 17, 1992), pp. 1, 2; K. J. Kelly, "Whittle Dream Fades in Hard-Nosed '90s," *Advertising Age* 65, no. 33 (August 8, 1994), p. 44.

13. "*Forbes* Issues Has Floppy Disk with Ads from 10 Firms," *Marketing News* 26, no. 14 (July 6, 1992), p. 11; S. Elliott, "*Forbes* to Include Ads on Floppy Disk," *New York Times,* June 8, 1992, p. C8.

14. K. Goldman, "Computer Screen Saver Is Latest Medium," *The Wall Street Journal,* May 12, 1993, p. B10; B. Horovitz, "Don't Touch that Mouse! Advertisers Want to Fill Your Computer's Idle Time," *Los Angeles Times,* July 27, 1993, p. D1.

15. D. J. Yang and J. Warner, "Hear the Muzak, Buy the Ketchup," *Business Week,* June 28, 1993, pp. 70, 72.

16. "Advertising Everywhere!" *Consumer Reports* 57, no. 12 (December 1992), pp. 752–55.

17. "Advertising: Strong Growth Ahead," p. MEDIA/M16.

18. *Ibid.,* p. MEDIA/M17; "The Advertising Fact Book," p. 11.

19. L. Cauley, "Nynex and Prodigy Team Up on Yellow Pages That Will Provide On-Line Listings and Ads," *The Wall Street Journal,* December 10, 1993, p. B1.

20. S. Hume, "Trade Promos Devour Half of All Marketing $," *Advertising Age,* 63, no. 15 (April 13, 1992), pp. 3, 53; "Advertising: Strong Growth Ahead," p. MEDIA/M16.

21. H. Schlossberg, "Coupons Likely to Remain Popular," *Marketing News* 27, no. 7 (March 29, 1993), pp. 1, 7.

22. A. de Rouffignac, "School Contests Help Concerns Promote Brands," *The Wall Street Journal,* July 3, 1992, pp. B1, 2.

23. M. J. McCarthy, "PepsiCo Is Facing Mounting Lawsuits from Botched Promotion in Philippines," *The Wall Street Journal,* July 28, 1993, p. B2; "Prize Fiasco Has Filipinos Angry at Pepsi," *Lexington Herald-Leader,* July 29, 1993, p. A3.

24. "Hoover Isn't Cleaning Up on Promotion for Travelers," *Lexington Herald-Leader,* April 28, 1993, p. B4.

25. V. Gibbons, "Street Marketing," *INC.* 15, no. 2 (February 1993), p. 27.

26. K. Goldman, "Gizmos Get Fancier as Trade Show Opens," *The Wall Street Journal,* May 4, 1993, p. B8.

27. S. Greco, "Smart Use of 'Special Offers,' " *INC.* 15, no. 2 (February 1993), p. 23.

28. S. Greco, "The Cost of Training New Salespeople," *INC.* 15, no. 4 (April 1993), p. 28.

29. M. Cox, "Crown Tries 'Hand Sell' for a Hard Sell," *The Wall Street Journal,* May 5, 1993, pp. B1, 6.

30. "News of Note: Open a Window," *Personal Selling Power* 13, no. 7 (October 1993), p. 12.

31. R. L. Sullivan, "The Office That Never Closes," *Forbes* 153, no. 11 (May 23, 1994), pp. 212–13.

32. S. Greco, "The Art of Selling," *INC.* 15, no. 6 (June 1993), pp. 72–80; C. Clancy, "It's No Mirage: Area Retailers Find Market in the Desert," *Tampa Bay Business Journal* 14, no. 44 (November 4, 1994), p. 1.

33. G. A. Patterson, "Distressed Shoppers, Disaffected Workers Prompt Stores to Alter Sales Commissions," *The Wall Street Journal,* July 1, 1992, pp. B1, 5; R. Halverson, "Sears Nixes Commission Pay in Light of Fraud Charges," *Discount Store News* 31, no. 13 (July 6, 1992), p. 7.

34. M. W. Miller, "Sandoz Gets PR Windfall from TV Movie," *The Wall Street Journal,* January 10, 1994, p. B1.

Extending Marketing

Extending Marketing: Marketing of Services and Not-for-Profit Marketing

Chapter Objectives

After studying Chapter 14 you should be able to

1. Explain the differences and similarities between goods and services.
2. Describe the Four Ps in services and the service advantage.
3. Recognize the characteristics of not-for-profit marketing.
4. Discuss some other for-profit extensions of marketing.
5. Characterize the marketing concept in services and not-for-profits.

*F*arming was the primary economic activity during the colonial period of American history, although merchants, small-scale producers, and some service providers were important parts of the emerging business community. The emphasis shifted during the 19th century as the industrial revolution gained steam and agrarian dominance gave way to manufacturing power. The economy has experienced another shift in the 20th century as manufacturing has been succeeded by services that now employ more people and make a greater contribution to the U.S. gross domestic product (GDP) than either agriculture or manufacturing. With the shift to a predominately service economy, marketing has broadened to also include services and the not-for-profit sector. The myopic concentration on goods that dominated marketing since its inception has been broken.

There's also been a shift from a narrow brand management tactics perspective to a broader view of marketing as an operating philosophy. Marketing is a long-term strategic orientation practiced by businesses, individuals, and organizations. It's also a set of tools designed to achieve organizational and individual goals. Marketing has evolved into a highly diverse and sophisticated field, making it difficult to discuss all its facets in an introductory marketing book. As you learn about some newer applications of marketing in this chapter, consider this question: Is there anything that *cannot* be marketed?

Services: An Indispensable Part of Daily Life	Denise Dunbar turns her car into the McDonald's® drive-through lane and orders an Egg McMuffin® and coffee. As she pulls up to the first window to pay for her breakfast, she buys a morning paper from a vending machine positioned beside her car window. After eating, she drives down the street to her bank, where a friendly teller at the drive-through window quickly deposits her check and gives change in the denominations requested. Arriving at work, she turns her car over to the parking lot attendant, who carefully parks it in her assigned space. At her desk, she examines a pile of mail that collected while she was out of town on business last week. Along with the other mail are letters from the American Red Cross, the United Negro College Fund, and the Sierra Club requesting support for their activities, and a brochure from the U.S. government with high-quality pictures of their latest postal stamps and an order form; they know Dunbar is an avid stamp collector.

THE MARKETING OF SERVICES

Objective 1 Explain the differences and similarities between goods and services.

Like most consumers, Denise Dunbar is busy, rushing from one task to another, juggling home responsibilities, work, community, and social activities. She depends on other people to provide needed services throughout a typical day. They prepare her breakfast, expedite her financial transactions, park and guard her car, launder her clothes, fly her to distant business meetings, provide hotel accommodations, take care of her when she is sick, and tend her children while she and her husband are at work. Dunbar's life would be considerably more difficult if she didn't have access to services.

service An intangible, perishable product.

A **service** is an intangible, perishable product of variable quality whose production and consumption are inseparable. A service may or may not be associated with a good. Service ownership does not transfer to the consumer during a marketing exchange; for example, the customer doesn't take possession of the bank when the teller

Photo 14.1

McDonald's® is well known for its quality, service, cleanliness, and value in the United States and abroad.

cashes her check. Services are offered by businesses, individuals, and not-for-profit organizations, including government. Service consumers include personal use consumers, businesses, and organizations (including government).

Unique Characteristics of Services

Unlike goods that are tangible and can be stored and inventoried, whose quality can be standardized, and whose production and consumption are separate, services are characterized by their intangibility, perishability, inseparability, and variability.[1]

Intangibility A refrigerator is a product—a good with the quality of **tangibility.** A consumer can touch it, see it, feel the coolness inside, smell the clean freezer air, hear the door slam, and generally assess its quality by the many cues given by its palpable properties. Contrast the refrigerator with a haircut. The consumer may have heard about a beauty shop from a friend who got a good haircut there. However, the consumer won't know for sure about the quality of the haircut until *after* it has been delivered, when he looks in the mirror and is either pleased or horrified.

To compensate for service intangibility, many businesses try to give substance to what is not obvious. As shown in Photo 14.2, financial services often associate their product with a tangible

tangibility A product quality that can be perceived by the senses (e.g., touch, sight, smell, hearing, and taste).

Photo 14.2

The Traveler's red umbrella is a tangible symbol of protection.

symbol to provide consumers with a visual anchor around which they can develop a product evaluation. Prudential Insurance associates its product with the stability and durability of "the rock"; The Travelers uses a red umbrella that shields its customers from harm; while Visa, MasterCard, American Express (Photo 14.3), and other credit card companies use a picture of their cards in advertisements, displays, and company materials in order to provide consumers with a visual anchor. Hospitals often use reassuring photographs of smiling employees to convey the message that they are caring service providers.

perishability   A service cannot be stored, inventoried, or stockpiled.

Perishability   A service is fleeting: it is a perishable product that cannot be stored, inventoried, or stockpiled. For example, on a Saturday, a barber shop is typically extremely busy, and customers must often wait before being served. On a Monday the same shop will be practically empty, with the barbers sitting in the chairs talking to each other, waiting for a customer to arrive, and collecting their salaries even if they are idle. It's too bad that all the barbers' free time on Monday can't be stored and stockpiled for the Saturday rush.

demand fluctuation   Demand that shifts between various levels.

The same situation exists for banks, airlines, transit systems, and other services. **Demand fluctuation,** demand that shifts between various levels from high to low or vice versa, is a problem facing most service providers. The challenge is to identify efficient methods for accommodating peak demand periods while not wasting resources during low demand periods. Many transit systems and airlines use **peak period pricing** to level out demand peaks and valleys by charging more for the service during peak demand periods and less during off periods. Metro subway riders in Washington, D.C., pay more for tickets during peak rush hours; tourists or

peak period pricing   Increasing prices during peak demand periods and lowering them during off periods.

Photo 14.3

A visual anchor helps consumers create an image of a product's benefits.

mid-day shoppers pay less, because they are traveling during demand lulls. Airlines offer special reduced fares to encourage flyers to travel when planes are almost empty, often at undesirable times like on late night red-eye specials. Lower fares during nonpeak flying times help airlines build their load factors. Thanksgiving or Christmas travelers, however, usually pay full fare because when the planes are traditionally full there is no need for the companies to encourage demand by offering consumer incentives.

Other approaches also attack the problem of demand variability. A trend in the American workplace is for businesses and organizations to use temporary employees, people who are available to work for short periods of time only as needed. Many service businesses hire temporary workers only for peak demand periods, which keeps payroll expenses down during nonpeak times. Theme park recruiters visit college campuses each spring to hire temporary workers for peak summer month work; a tax service hires extra accountants for tax season; and fast-food restaurants put "help wanted" signs out as the end of the school year approaches and demand begins to rise. Although temporary workers may help keep operating costs down, turnover can affect service quality and, ultimately, profitability, because each new batch of employees has to be trained to be efficient workers and service providers.

Automation has helped some businesses smooth out demand fluctuations. Most banks use automated teller machines (ATMs) so that they can serve customers even when the lobby is closed (see Photo 14.4). Vending machines dispense tickets (Photo 14.5) to serve baseball fans at all hours of the day and night. Hotels offer patrons

Photo 14.4

Twenty-four-hour banking is now commonplace, thanks to ATMs.

Photo 14.5   Tickets at the touch of a button.

advance check-out services via computer in order to avoid delays at the front desk when cashiers are busy. Some universities register students by telephone, so that they can sign up for classes without having to physically stand in long registration lines.

Inseparability   When a good is produced, its consumption typically does not occur until a later time, usually without contact between producer and consumer. Automobile assembly line workers typically don't make contact with the consumers who purchase the cars they've made; therefore, production and consumption are separate. Contrast this with a **service encounter,** in which the business or organizational representative makes personal contact with the customer and a marketing interaction occurs. Service encounters are noteworthy for their **inseparability.** They occur when a plumber unclogs a drain, a dentist fills a cavity, a lawyer writes a will, an accountant files a tax return, and a stockbroker fills a buy order—production and consumption are inseparable. A service is consumed at the same time it is performed (see Photo 14.6).

The closeness of producer and consumer is a source of considerable marketing concern. The service provider *is* the business, as far as the consumer is concerned. Therefore, it is critically important for the business or organization to ensure that the service encounter, as much as possible, is a positive experience for the consumer. For example, fear of an encounter with the dentist is blunted by a cheerful atmosphere in the dentist's office, soft music, pretty pic-

service encounter The personal contact made between the business representative and the customer.

inseparability Consumption of the service at the same time that it is performed.

Marketing Application 14.1

From your own experience, consider a service encounter situation that has the potential to be unpleasant; for example, an annual physical checkup or a car repair where the consumer must wait for the job to be finished and is apprehensive about the results and cost of the outcome. What could be done to improve the service encounter environment? Make a list of your suggestions and bring it to class for discussion. ■

Photo 14.6

Instant production and consumption

tures, friendly staff, and even funny sayings taped to the ceiling over the dentist's chair—all efforts to improve the service encounter environment.

Training service providers to interact effectively with service customers is as important as the skills they bring to the job. A hairdresser may give a good haircut, but if he or she is unpleasant, customers won't return; a rude bank teller or a surly hotel front-desk clerk can make the service encounter a disaster, leaving the customer with a bad impression of the business and a vow not to return. Even the government is waking up to the realization that service providers trained to be both competent in their jobs *and* effective organization representatives will be more productive in the long run, because their customers or clients will be more cooperative and the service will be delivered more effectively.

International Marketing Report

Good service relationships were not the rule in the former Soviet Union, where customer contact employees were more apt to snarl at a customer than smile. Imagine the service challenge McDonald's® of Canada faced in becoming the first Western fast-food franchise in Moscow. It took 14 years of negotiations and extensive planning for McDonald's® to make this service breakthrough. Many obstacles had to be overcome, from teaching Russian farmers how to use sophisticated potato harvesting equipment to the careful instruction of customer contact service personnel. Order takers had to be trained to smile and be courteous, patient, and considerate. This represented a

complete change from the Soviet norm but is the hallmark of McDonald's,® where quality, *service,* cleanliness, and value are company principles. The Moscow McDonald's® is a miracle in Pushkin Square, defying many problems to become the busiest McDonald's in the world. ■

C. Goldberg, "Perestroika Pioneer Makes 'Beeg Meks' Work in Moscow," *Los Angeles Times,* August 6, 1991, p. H6; L. Feldman, "Muscovites Have Fallen in Love with a Pair of Golden Arches," *The Christian Science Monitor* 82, no. 189 (August 24, 1990), p. 11; "Soviet McDonald's Serves 30,000 Daily," *New York Times,* March 1, 1990, p. D5; C. Bernstein, "Miracle at Pushkin Square: McD Defies the Odds," *Nation's Restaurant News* 24, no. 8 (February 19, 1990), p. 23.

Photo 14.7
Anticipation outside the Moscow McDonald's®
in Pushkin Square.

Variability   On a typical day, John can tune 27 automobile engines. Today, however, he has a cold and barely gets through 18 tune-ups. John is a top mechanic, but Tony is just learning the trade and can do only 16 tune-ups on a good day. This example gets at the problem of service quality **variability.** Because of inseparability and perishability, there are many opportunities for quality variations. As the engine tune-up example shows, variation can occur because of differences in the quality of service provided by the same person at different times and with different people performing the same task. There also are differences in service performance as a result of interaction dynamics between service provider and consumer. Sometimes a customer is difficult to work with and, even if the service provider is extremely competent, the encounter is a disaster. Even when the fault lies with the customer, however, the business's

variability   Differences in quality of service performance.

reputation may suffer through a dissatisfied customer's negative word of mouth.

The quality of a good is often based on the number of defects per product, with zero defects meaning extremely high quality. Quality is evident in design, aesthetics, reliability, and other tangible attributes. Ultimately, however, the most important definition of quality is furnished by the consumer. **Service quality** lics in the consumer's evaluation of service performance. Any gap between service expected and service delivered lowers the perception of service quality. This leaves room for disagreement between what the service provider and consumer deem to be high quality. The problem may arise because the consumer's expectations are too high or the quality of the service is actually low. Either way, the marketer must determine consumer expectations about quality and use this consumer insight in developing service delivery strategies. A commonly used method for determining customer satisfaction is the written survey card left in a hotel room or on a restaurant table for the customer to complete (see Photo 14.8). An analysis of consumer feedback can be useful in assessing perceptions of quality.

service quality   The customer's evaluation of service performance.

Check Your Understanding
14.1

1. What is a service? Is a service a product?
2. Describe the unique characteristics of services.
3. Discuss why a marketer's and a consumer's perception of service quality may differ.

Photo 14.8

Have you ever filled out a comment card?

Services Classified

Marketers increase their understanding of services through the process of identifying their similarities and differences. However, it's not always easy to classify services because of their variety and great flexibility. Services can be more easily modified than can goods, and a new service can be developed quickly to suit consumer needs. Although there are difficulties in classifying services, the value of doing so is not in question. Through classification and the grouping of services by their commonalities, marketing strategies and tactics can be developed and, if successful, can be applied broadly to similar services. The most common service classifications are discussed in the following sections.

Product Attributes Most consumers don't spend much time distinguishing between goods and services, although the topic interests marketers. Goods and services often are inseparable, and the marketer must develop a marketing strategy that considers both. For example, in the purchase of a new automobile, the consumer is interested in the automobile *and* the service that comes with it (see Photo 14.9). If a company offers an extended warranty lasting seven years (or 100,000 miles) for less than $600, the consumer feels reassured about product quality and protected by the extended

Photo 14.9

Toyota offers a total product, including service that goes beyond the expected.

service agreement. The marketer uses the insight that many consumers want the security of an extended service contract as a key part of the total product offer: good and service combined. Contrast new car buying with purchasing a used car without service. The absence of service and the accompanying higher risk, along with the car's accumulated mileage, account for the used car's having a lower price than does a new car. Many consumers are willing to take the risk in return for a lower price.

Not all consumers want a full range of services, and this consumer insight has led some businesses to capitalize on profitable windows of opportunity. Hampton Inns (see Photo 14.10) is a limited-service, high-quality lodging alternative for the business traveler. Typically found adjacent to interstate highways in over 40 states in secondary markets (not large urban centers), Hamptons offer a clean, comfortable room in a good location—and free breakfast. They do *not* offer room service, expensive decorations, gourmet restaurants, glass cage elevators, and fancy multistory atriums. Hampton Inns extends a 100 percent satisfaction guarantee to its guests that can be enacted by *any* employee, from the maid to the desk clerk.[2] This practice empowers service providers to act on behalf of the company and impresses guests with the company's dedication to customer satisfaction.

Marketers must recognize a product's tangibility attribute, whether it is a pure good, a pure service, or somewhere in between—a mixed good and service. A continuum of goods and services is illustrated in Figure 14.1, along with examples. There are far more mixed goods and services, like an automobile tune-up or a restaurant meal, than there are either pure goods or pure services. Some services are not associated with a good; for example, teaching or psychological counseling. Some goods are not associated with a

Photo 14.10

At Hampton Inns, limited service is a key selling point.

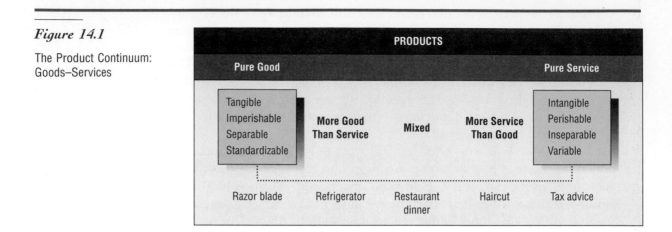

service; for example, a hammer, loaf of bread, or pencil. Yet even pure goods may involve service at some point. A to Z Rental Center rents just about everything from punch bowls to tools, Mr. Tuxedo rents eveningwear for men, U-Haul rents trucks—all goods that are sometimes associated with a rental service. In Tokyo, where people often live in cramped apartments or have pet-hating landlords, consumers who yearn for canine companionship can even rent a dog for between $10 to $20 an hour (depending on the dog's size).[3] Nintendo of America, Inc., provides service to the computer-illiterate, frustrated consumers who purchase its electronic games and can't figure out how to play them. Telephone lines run 20 hours each day, 360 days a year, with "game-playing consultants" answering an average of 170,000 calls a year. Nintendo spends between $15 to $20 million each year on its game counseling service.[4]

Consumer Targets   Services may be targeted to personal use consumers or business/organization consumers. Often, it is difficult to separate the targets or differentiate the services because many services are used by all of them, adapted for their needs, and frequently delivered by different units of the same company. Real estate companies often have retail and commercial divisions; telephone services are offered to personal use consumers as well as businesses, organizations, and the government. All these consumer types use legal services, delivery services, cleaning services, and travel services.

Despite the universality of some services, there are others that are directed solely to personal use consumers; for example, personal hair care services, golf or swimming lessons, aerobics classes, and house repairs. Other services are targeted solely at other businesses.

Some services are offered nationally, like Hertz or Avis rental cars; others are regional or purely local. Trendata, for example, offers a radio ratings service to Phoenix stations that measures what stations are playing on car radios in the city's largest intersections.[5] A. C. Nielsen is the only company offering television viewership monitoring services nationwide.[6]

Many business services are traditional, such as advertising, financial services and management consulting. Other business services are uncommon, as in Flyaway Avian Averting Systems, which offers businesses and organizations a harmless pigeon removal service,[7] and Odor Science and Engineering Inc., which relies on the olfactory skills of its founder to track bad smells to their source. This 16-employee company has provided service to General Motors, refineries, and cities to smell out the source of bad odors so that solutions can be found.[8]

Provider Training   A **service provider** is the individual or organization that delivers a service to consumers. Some services require highly skilled, professionally trained and accredited service providers, as is the case with physicians, lawyers, accountants, teachers, nurses, and dentists. Often called *white-collar professions,* they require an advanced education, professional credentials, and certification. A relatively new professional service is the nurse-call telephone line. When a consumer needs advice about a medication, rash, fever, treatment options, or some other medical problem, instead of rushing to a doctor many opt to first call a nurse on one of the many toll-free lines staffed by local hospitals or clinics.[9]

service provider The individual and/or organization that delivers a service to a consumer.

Blue-collar services are manually oriented and delivered by people who, for example, mow lawns, drive public transportation vehicles, repair plumbing, and paint houses. Skill level may be very high, but training is not linked to completion of a higher education degree or professional credentials.

All service providers should be trained both for professional competency and how to successfully interact with consumers. Service providers involved in face-to-face consumer relationships represent the company to its target markets, and their job performance is the benchmark against which the business's reputation is evaluated.

Delivery System   The service delivery system identifies whether the service is provided primarily by people, equipment, or a combination of the two. A psychiatrist provides an almost purely people-based service typically using no tangible objects other than a tape recorder or writing instruments. An automated teller machine is a machine that takes customers' orders and acts on them with only a limited range of options; this is an equipment-based service.

Marketing Application 14.2

Perform your own personal service inventory. When you wake up tomorrow morning and for the next 12 hours, identify all the services you encounter. Evaluate these services to determine if they are people- or equipment-based (or mixed), targeted solely to personal use consumers or also to businesses/organizations, white collar or blue collar, and if they require close personal contact. What can you conclude about the types and quality of services you encounter in your typical day? ■

Contact Closeness   The closeness of consumer contact indicates the level of personal interaction between service provider and consumer in the service encounter. For example, a psychiatrist delivers a people-based service and has close personal contact with the consumer/patient. Contrast this personal service delivery system with the automated teller machine, with which there is physical contact (the consumer interacts with a machine) but no personal contact. Schools are high contact and mostly people-based, yet increasingly courses are taught on television, where a live teacher is not in personal contact with students and equipment plays a very large part in the delivery of the service.

The Shift to Services

Denise Dunbar from the chapter-opening story illustrates two of the primary reasons why services have grown in importance during the latter part of the 20th century. Growing numbers of women in the out-of-home workforce and the time demands and complexities of modern life have presented windows of opportunity for service marketers to offer everything from home cleaning, child care, fast food, laundry, and dry cleaning to lawn care service and more. Studies indicate that consumers are stressed out and looking for ways to cope, often through time-saving personalized services.[10]

Other trends have contributed to the shift to service. Changing demographics in the United States and other industrialized countries indicate that people are living longer and often need assistance with many daily living tasks; hence, the growing need for home health, residential care, transportation, physical therapy, and similar services. Having two incomes lets many middle-class families hire others to perform tasks they dislike, such as mowing the lawn, washing windows, changing the oil in the car, and preparing dinner. Another factor magnifying the shift to services is the loss of many manufacturing jobs to other countries where labor is cheaper. At the same time the manufacturing labor force was shrinking, service labor was increasing through expansion and new job creation. Manufacturing labor in the United States has become cheaper in the past decade while United States productivity has risen. Because of this some of the manufacturing jobs that left the country are returning, but any major shift back toward manufacturing has not yet been noted.

Service Providers

Every service employee who makes contact with a consumer represents the business. The performance of service that puts employees in close contact with consumers can make or break a business's or organization's reputation. Effective relationships are critical, because employee performance is a key factor in the consumer's evaluation of service quality. Because businesses are increasingly concerned about the **lifetime value** of customers (their loyalty and patronage over their consuming life), greater attention is being given to ensure that the right people are hired for customer contact positions. Although good hiring decisions are very important, other areas also require attention because they affect the service employee's performance. Such areas that affect an employee's service performance are his or her:

lifetime value Customers' loyalty and patronage over their consuming life.

Capacity to perform: Are the employee's job knowledge, skills, education level, energy level, and general ability and job training sufficient to support his or her providing good service?

Willingness to perform: Is the employee's attitude about the job and company, job status, personality, and feelings of job equity positive and sufficient enough to support his or her providing good service?

Opportunity to perform: Does the employee have access to needed tools and equipment, materials, and supplies to deliver good service? This includes working conditions, actions of co-workers, budgetary support, organization rules and procedures, information, and the time to do a good job.[11] Of the three variables, this is the one that is most often overlooked.

capacity to perform The combined total of an employee's experience, training, and general ability that affects the ability to provide good service.

willingness to perform An employee's attitude and feelings that affect the ability to provide good service.

opportunity to perform Physical, organizational, and environmental resources affecting an employee's service abilities.

Figure 14.2 presents a visual display of this concept.

Service businesses often undertake comprehensive **internal marketing** programs designed to market the business to its employees, in order to develop their understanding of the importance of their role as service provider. This should help them develop strategies for becoming more effective in their customer contacts.

internal marketing Promotion of a business or organization to its employees in order to increase their understanding and make them more effective.

Consumer Insight

Total customer service is not an empty phrase at the Phelps County Bank (PCB), a community bank with headquarters in Rolla, Missouri. Unlike its two main competitors, PCB is not affiliated with a large bank holding company. The bank's service area includes about 35,000 people. Most of the bank's 55 employees work at the downtown bank, while the remainder are at three other locations including a branch, a drive-in bank, and a small office at the University of Missouri. Customer service representatives are trained to be courteous, letting customers know that PCB's employees are there to help them. Customers aren't kept waiting in lines, lending officers are trained to carefully explain everything on complicated loan applications, and newspaper advertisements include the telephone numbers of the bank's lending officers and administrators. On occasion, lending officers go to customers' homes after hours to provide bank services when a customer can't get to the bank. Customers are regularly asked to evaluate the bank's services and employees. Service is part of the bank's culture; an everyday part of

the employee's performance that reflects people going out of their way to help other people.

Citicorp follows the same customer service philosophy as PCB, but it does so in Germany, where it serves 2.3 million Germans with over 300 branch banks. It has 85 more branches in Germany than it has in New York, its headquarters. In only three years, the bank has achieved a 50 percent name recognition rate among Germans, mainly because its concept of service is far ahead of its German competitors, which include the mighty Deutsche Bank. Citibank's customer service tactics are to stay open six days a week, even during lunchtime; locate 24-hour automated teller machines (ATMs) in convenient locations; offer telephone banking 24 hours a day; give their customers access to Citibank services worldwide; and train employees to be good service providers. ■

J. Case, "Total Customer Service," *INC.* 16, no. 1 (January 1994), pp. 52–61; R. C. Morais, "Citi Über Alles," *Forbes* 153, no. 2 (January 17, 1994), p. 50.

Figure 14.2

Service Performance Dimensions

These dimensions affect the performance of the service provider as he or she interacts with the consumer in the service encounter. Deficiencies in any of the dimensions can negatively affect the service outcome.

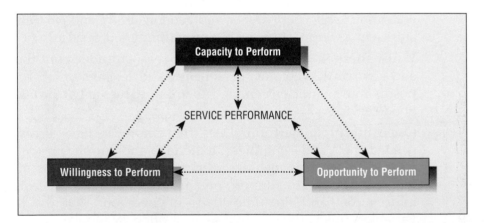

Service Consumers

In close contact services, the service consumer both contributes to the encounter and evaluates the quality of the service provided. For example, if a customer approaches a bank teller with a deposit slip correctly filled out, there is a greater chance that the teller can do his

Marketing Application 14.3

From your own experience with services, identify one experience that is an example of a high-quality service performance and a second that is an example of a low-quality performance. Compare and contrast the two on the basis of the particular service provider performing the service, including as much as you can tell about their capacity, willingness, and opportunity to provide you with high-quality service. What do you recommend for improving service provider performance in the low-quality service example? ■

job efficiently without delay. However, if the customer doesn't know how to fill out the form, neglects to do so, or demands that the teller do it for her, a delay results and the customer may become annoyed. If other people are standing in line, tempers may flare. Marketers must evaluate the role of the consumer in the service encounter and eliminate potential problem sources. Often, this can be accomplished by educating the consumer to be a better service recipient and service encounter participant. As supermarkets become more automated, customers will have to be taught how to use handheld scanners to check out their purchases because store employees will no longer provide this service. Service providers can be trained to work with consumers to help them become better at participating in the service encounter. For example, bank tellers can help customers fill out forms correctly so that next time the customer can do so without assistance.

Check Your Understanding
14.2

1. Explain why services have become so important to consumers and the U.S. economy.
2. What is the role of the consumer in the service encounter?
3. Discuss the importance of employee capacity, willingness, and opportunity in the effective delivery of services.

THE FOUR Ps OF SERVICES

Marketers help make product attribute decisions for both goods and services. The marketing mix variables of price, place, and promotion also are as important in marketing services as they are in marketing goods. In some cases, they are used similarly; in others cases they differ.

Objective 2 Describe the Four Ps in services and the service advantage.

Consumer Insight

For both goods and services, product decisions *must* be built on consumer insight. For example, an Iowa State University student observed how bored people were in laundromats and, from that consumer insight, founded Duds 'n' Suds, which has bars adjacent to its laundry facilities. Duds 'n' Suds is now in 70 locations in the United States and abroad (see Photo 14.11). Likewise, The Brainwash laundromat offers a 49-seat cafe, live music, and happy hours next to their washing facilities. The challenge is to determine what service consumers want and then deliver it consistently in order to achieve customer retention. It's usually far more cost effective to work hard at retaining customers than trying to find new ones. This is particularly true in saturated markets where gaining new customers usually means snatching them from the competition. ∎

M. Lee, "Service Providers Try to Make the Mundane Bearable," *The Wall Street Journal,* July 13, 1993, p. B2; P. Holley, "Taking the Coin Out of Coin-Operated," *The Business Journal–Milwaukee* 11, no. 15 (January 15, 1994), p. 1.

Photo 14.11

Duds 'n' Suds successfully combines two worlds.

Product

Like tangible goods, a service is a product whose characteristics must be determined before it can be offered to consumers. A category or brand manager of laundry detergents must decide on such features as size (e.g., giant economy, single wash), packaging (e.g., box, plastic bottle), ingredients (e.g., with or without bleach), and so on. A service marketer makes product attribute decisions about how much service is offered and its characteristics.

Frequently, a product decision involves a tangible good and its associated services. For example, decisions must be made about the level of service to provide personal computer purchasers. Some businesses offer free 1-800 customer service numbers and unlimited time to solve consumer problems. Other businesses offer 1-900 telephone numbers, where the consumer must pay for the time spent with a company service representative. PC manufacturers say that because of the overwhelming volume of help calls (as many as 70 percent are from computer illiterate beginners) they have been forced to begin charging help-line users.[12] On the other hand, sellers of older rebuilt personal computers may not offer any service at all.

Just as with goods, services can also be repackaged as new and improved. Retail banks are particularly adept at inventing variations on the services they offer. This occurs mainly because often the only point of differentiation between banks is their service, because the prices they can charge (and interest offered) are regulated and tend not to vary greatly between institutions.

Price

Pricing a service calls for a careful analysis of what is being priced (an equipment- and/or people-based service) and its value to consumers. For a service that relies on equipment, cost-based pricing may be used. For a service provided by people, pricing is often based on competitive prices as well as demand and the image of the service provider. Price sometimes reflects the service provider's training and experience, as is the case with physicians and lawyers. Other times, it reflects uniqueness or artistic accomplishment. Service pricing can be used to skim or penetrate a market.

Service pricing is frequently determined by following a price leader. For example, uncomplicated hair cuts in the beauty shops in a particular area may all hover around $15 a cut, which follows the lead of the most influential service provider in the area, typically the market share leader. Alternatively, a service price or price guidelines may be set by a union, professional organization, or the government.

Pricing a service is just as or even more difficult than pricing a good. The added uncertainty comes from the variability of service quality and demand. Peak demand pricing is common, as cited earlier in the example of the Metro in Washington, D.C., where fares rise during peak demand hours and fall during slack hours. Because it is not always easy to project what a service will actually cost, it is not easy to determine what price will be needed to cover costs.

Place

Although many services are not thought of as having a channel of distribution, place is important in services. People-based personal services like beauty salons require retail location decisions, including decisions about store aesthetics, convenience, operating hours, and safety. A channel of distribution exists for financial services.

When a credit card is activated at a retailer's, the charge information is delivered backward through a channel to a clearing house and on to the lending agency that finally bills the consumer. Service channels are most likely to be short and, often, electronically based.

Some short service channels are traditional and involve the physical transfer of goods to undergo repair services. This is the case of computer repairs where the tangible good is conveyed backward through a channel of distribution, often to the manufacturer.

Promotion

Service promotion often involves personal selling and extensive advertising designed to make the product tangible and establish a positive product image. The Mecklenburg Community Church in Charlotte, North Carolina, uses advertising and direct mail to build its image as the place for baby boomers to meet their spiritual needs.[13] Episcopal congregations are running television commercials targeting women between 25 and 45 years old to encourage them to return to the church and bring their families along with them.[14] The Lifetime cable television network promotes its image as the "woman's network."[15] Personal services are even advertised for dogs (see Photo 14.12).

Service Strategy and Tactics

Like the marketing of goods, the marketing of services also requires the formulation of strategy and the development of tactics to achieve the goals set for service products by the business. This means that

Photo 14.12

A very specialized personal service.

Your Dog's Hearing Is 17 Times Better Than Your's.

So How Come He Doesn't Listen.

Luis Gomez · Master Dog Trainer · 212 866-7836

service marketers must conduct marketing research, plan, segment their markets, target attractive segments, and position their product in the minds of potential consumers. Service marketers conduct marketing research to determine market characteristics, develop consumer insights, and evaluate market offers in much the same way that goods are researched.

The Service Advantage

Marketers strive to create and sustain a competitive advantage for their products. Giving good service can provide that advantage. This is the advantage enjoyed by Phelps County Bank in Rolla, Missouri, and by many other large and small businesses that seek to deliver total customer satisfaction. A service advantage is often the only way that a business or organization can differentiate itself from the competition. This is a result of the availability of many product copies, powerful price competition, and the clutter of promotions that create such a din that many consumers tune most of them out.

Achieving a service advantage requires three things. First, that marketers develop consumer insight into what consumers value and want, and then determine how quality service can be delivered. Second, it requires training employees to be good service providers who consistently provide peak service performance. Third, it requires constant monitoring to seek opportunities where services can be offered successfully.

Check Your Understanding
14.3

1. Explain some of the ways that services are priced.
2. Can services be promoted? Explain your answer.
3. Can a service provide a sustainable competitive advantage for a business?

NOT-FOR-PROFIT (NFP) MARKETING

The designation **not-for-profit (NFP)** indicates that earning a profit is not a primary organizational goal. It describes a sector of the U.S. economy that is diverse, large, and for years wanted little to do with marketing because of the belief that marketing didn't fit an NFP's image. Times have changed, however, and not-for-profit marketing has been increasing since the early 1980s. One reason is that funding support for many NFPs has diminished just as competition has increased, and many NFPs must now work very hard to find resources to maintain their operations.

Marketing in the NFP sector involves public and private organizations as diverse as governments, charities, hospitals, politicians,

Objective 3   Recognize the characteristics of not-for-profit marketing.

not-for-profit (NFP) marketing
Marketing for organizations in which earning a profit is not a primary goal.

Photo 14.13

Marketing the Toronto Zoo.

unions, religious groups, zoos (see Photo 14.13), social causes, and activist groups, such as Mothers Against Drunk Driving (MADD) and Amnesty International. Not-for-profits, unlike for-profit businesses, do not have the goal of increasing owner's or stockholders' equity. A not-for-profit hospital must operate efficiently in order to collect enough revenue to cover its costs, but it is not pricing its services to benefit investors, whereas a for-profit hospital's patient service decisions may be influenced by its need to satisfy current investors and attract new ones. A not-for-profit organization that markets its cause may seek to profit from various activities, but the proceeds are not used to enhance shareholder wealth.

fund raising Using marketing strategies and tools to develop and harvest revenue sources.

Many NFPs, including charities, engage in **fund raising,** using marketing strategies and tools to develop and harvest revenue sources in order to run a positive cash flow, cover operating expenses, and support benevolent activities. An emerging not-for-profit sector problem, however, is the misuse of fund-raising marketing. Some charities are criticized for excessive operating costs: Contributions that should go to the benefit of the charity's clients are used to support ever-more-intense marketing efforts and costly administrator salaries. The public is advised to check out a charity in order to ensure that contributions actually reach those for whom they were raised.

Increasingly, NFPs are using business strategies and methods to achieve their goals. They use marketing to obtain revenue from their operations in order to support their social mission. Often, a not-for-profit will hire a for-profit business to direct its marketing operations. Three relief organizations and two not-for-profit medical foundations employ Aria Communications Corporation in St. Cloud, Minnesota, to conduct their direct mail operations using highly successful professionally handwritten letters.[16] The U.S. Postal Service uses marketing extensively to encourage consumers to collect and use stamps and to counter the services offered by such competitors as United Parcel Service (UPS) and Federal Express. The Postal Service's goal is to raise revenues sufficient to cover costs and deliver an important public service without incurring further debt.

Not-for-profit marketers include:

• *Organizations:* The U.S. government markets its publications through the Government Printing Office, its business consulting services through Small Business Administration offices, and even military service (see Photo 14.14). Many state governments market their lotteries, and many state development offices use marketing to attract business investments. Small, local organizations also use marketing. For example, the Los Angeles Mission was faced with closing after 30 years of serving the poor because its building was not up to county earthquake codes. The Mission successfully used marketing to raise funds to repair its building and place its operations on a long-term, secure financial foundation.[17] Universities use marketing in order to recruit students, faculty, and donors. Volunteer agencies use marketing to recruit unpaid workers. McDonald's

Photo 14.14

The National Guard knows the value of good marketing.

promotes its Ronald McDonald Houses for families of hospitalized children, an example of a for-profit business engaged in cause marketing.

Public television and public radio have become aggressive marketers. As government support has diminished, these organizations have been forced to seek new funding sources. This has led to comprehensive marketing research, the development of marketing plans, and the implementation of promotional programs on a regular basis. They seek subscribers, both individual and corporate sponsors, to support programming, and they sell station-related goods through catalogs and on-air sales. This includes sales of compact discs played on public radio stations, where a portion of the revenue from each disc sale benefits the station in the buyer's area.

- *Causes:* The Red Cross is one of the largest volunteer agencies in the United States. Faced with two great disasters in one year (Hurricane Hugo and the San Francisco earthquake), the Red Cross used marketing to raise funds to support its disaster activities.[18] Mothers Against Drunk Driving (MADD) has successfully marketed the idea of not drinking and driving; various groups are marketing the idea of safe sex to slow the spread of AIDS. The U.S. Surgeon Generals have been highly effective in promoting smoking cessation.

- *People:* Perhaps one of the most widely known forms of not-for-profit people marketing is that of political candidates and parties. Although one might challenge the notion of this being a not-for-profit example, because some politicians profit from their election, typically it is considered an NFP. Marketing strategies and methods were used extensively by both candidates in the last U.S. presidential election.

- *Events:* Events are marketed by either organizations or foundations set up specifically for the event. A not-for-profit foundation was established and successfully marketed the U.S. bicentennial celebration. Likewise, extensive marketing was associated with the renovation of the Statue of Liberty in New York Harbor. The City of Atlanta used marketing to develop its winning bid for the 1996 Summer Olympics.

- *Places:* States use marketing to attract visitors to their parks. In this case, the profit motive is combined with public service, raising revenues to cover park maintenance and expansion. State and local economic development agencies use marketing to attract business investments. Extensive marketing by the Commonwealth of Kentucky helped convince Toyota Motor Manufacturing to invest $2 billion to build an automobile manufacturing plant in the central part of the state. Alabama engaged in aggressive marketing of the state in order to land a Mercedes-Benz assembly plant there.[19] The

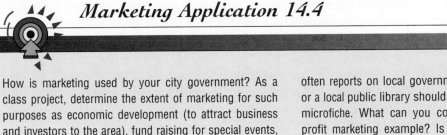

Marketing Application 14.4

How is marketing used by your city government? As a class project, determine the extent of marketing for such purposes as economic development (to attract business and investors to the area), fund raising for special events, promotion of parks and recreation areas, and so on. A good source of information is the local newspaper, which often reports on local government activities. Your school or a local public library should have newspapers on file or microfiche. What can you conclude about this not-for-profit marketing example? Is your city using marketing effectively? ■

City of Chicago engaged in a vigorous marketing effort to attract *both* the Democratic and Republican national conventions to the city in 1996.[20]

Check Your Understanding
14.4

1. Explain how profit and not-for-profit marketing differ.
2. Identify some types of not-for-profit marketing.
3. Are there any not-for-profits that shouldn't market?

OTHER FOR-PROFIT EXTENSIONS OF MARKETING

As you have learned, marketing has been extended to services and NFPs, as well as to organizations, people, causes, and ideas that are business ventures designed to profit. Many contemporary marketing applications are notable for their magnitude and the effective use they make of marketing strategies and tactics. The following examples highlight some of the newer for-profit applications of marketing. All present interesting insights into how marketing is being used extensively throughout our contemporary society.

Objective 4   Discuss some other for-profit extensions of marketing.

Health Care Marketing

For-profit hospitals market niche services, like women's pavilions that provide birthing centers as well as areas set aside for handling medical problems unique to women. For-profit hospitals are marketing their services south to Mexico, where they are enticing wealthier Mexican consumers to U.S. clinics set up north of the border. Many hospitals are marketing the idea of wellness, setting up special classes to teach their patients about nutrition and exercise and, in the process, improve their health and lower medical costs.[21]

Despite turmoil in health care as reforms are debated, marketing opportunities flourish. For Costal Healthcare Group, it's meant recruiting medical residents and doctors to staff hospitals and clinics on contract. Costal concentrates on signing up obstetrics/gynecology and emergency room physicians for the over 500 medical facilities nationwide that it serves.[22]

Health care organizations increasingly are showing greater concern about customer service and satisfaction. This reflects the competitiveness of modern medicine as well as the realization that the best customers are also the ones who can select from among many health care alternatives, including hospitals, clinics, and insurers.[23]

People Marketing

Some people are their own product, actively marketing themselves for profit. This includes the rich and famous, the noble and notorious, as well as the average person. Michael Jordan has been called basketball's greatest player. For years, he has been the most valuable endorser in professional sports. Along with marketing others' products, including Nike, McDonald's, Gatorade, Wheaties cereal, and Ball Park Franks, Michael Jordan also is marketed by a professional agent in order to match his awesome basketball talent with his engaging personality and product endorsement skills.[24]

The marketing of Shaquille O'Neal differs from the marketing of Michael Jordan. O'Neal is being marketed to a small group of businesses that have agreed to coordinate their efforts in order to develop a coherent image of the young basketball player. The O'Neal brand image is being supported by a logo and a copyrighted phrase "Shaq Attaq."[25]

Professional athletes aren't the only people who market their talent. More lawyers are finding that they must market themselves in order to be competitive. The legal profession remains divided about whether or not lawyers should engage in marketing activities. Some lawyers believe it may be unprofessional and encourage litigation.[26] Other lawyers believe they have no choice but to market themselves because the competition for clients is so fierce. The U.S. Supreme Court has affirmed that lawyers have the right to advertise under the First Amendment guarantee of freedom of speech.

Dentists and physicians are involved in much the same type of professional soul searching over the propriety of marketing themselves. Although their professional societies have eased the total ban on advertising, the debate over the marketing of professionals continues.

Entertainment Marketing

Marketing is used extensively by professional athletic franchises as well as by university athletic departments to encourage fan participation. Symphony orchestras market, as do popular music companies and stars. Mercury Records's skillful marketing of Billy Ray Cyrus and "Achy Breaky Heart" resulted in a hit record along with a dance craze.[27] Frito-Lay Inc. and Bantam Books are copromoting country singer Reba McEntire's hardcover book *Reba: My Story* by offering $3 book rebates in specially marked bags of Fritos corn chips.[28]

Many movies would never be noticed in the entertainment clutter were it not for far-reaching marketing efforts. However, even good marketing cannot save a bad movie. The movie *Last Action Hero* was a box office disappointment despite a massive $25 million marketing effort by Columbia Pictures that included a soundtrack album, toys, general merchandise, and a tie-in with Burger King.[29] More is spent on television advertising than other forms of movie promotions, with an average movie promotion easily costing $8 million for television commercials alone.[30]

Leisure Activities and Places Marketing

Just as not-for-profit state parks are marketed, businesses also market leisure activities and places. The resort industry aggressively markets package vacations for families. Premier Cruise Lines has Caribbean cruises packaged with Universal Studios and Sea World, as well as with Walt Disney World.[31] Feeling the effects of the Japanese economic recession of the early 1990s, many Japanese companies force their *sararimen* (salarymen) to take vacation time. This has resulted in a bloom of leisure service marketing, from "Dad's Outdoor School," where Japanese fathers are taught how to take their offspring camping, to canoeing and fishing lessons.[32]

Event Marketing

Event marketing has become a big business. The classification of events is not well defined. Events consist of a broad range of activities including for-profit trade shows, conventions, seminars, retreats, holiday celebrations, trade missions, and extravaganzas like the Olympics and World Cup Soccer.

Educational Marketing

Private educational institutions engage in marketing activities. This includes private day care facilities that offer educational activities along with child care. There are for-profit business and professional schools: These educational businesses aggressively use marketing to attract students and investors. Many public, state-supported institutions of higher education also have private for-profit foundations that market technology, particularly by finding businesses to commercialize the inventions and discoveries made by university faculty.[33]

Information Services Marketing

The information age has ushered in the marketing of many different kinds of information services. You're familiar with customer assistance services offered to purchasers of personal computers, video games, and other electronic equipment. In addition, individuals and organizations market classes that teach people how to get on the Internet, use E-mail, access information retrieval systems, and use software. Consultants market their ability to reconfigure a business's computer network or troubleshoot computer systems to remove the bugs. Impartial consumer advisers offer information services to personal use consumers to help them make informed decisions when buying a new home, an automobile, financial investments, and even insurance.[34]

On-line computer services like Prodigy and CompuServe offer subscribers access to the information highway. This is an electronic interactivity service that opens up worldwide opportunities to retrieve information, shop, be entertained, and communicate with others electronically.[35]

The competition between the telecommunications giants (AT&T, the seven Baby Bells, MCI, and Sprint) domestically and internationally is heating up as they vie for increasing shares of the markets being created by new technologies and loosening government regulations. These include cellular and mobile data networks, residential telephone service, cable television, and satellite transmission services. The telecommunications service market in Europe by itself is $160 billion.[36] Marketing plans and marketing activities are critical to their success.

THE MARKETING CONCEPT IN SERVICES AND NOT-FOR-PROFITS

Objective 5 Characterize the marketing concept in services and not-for-profits.

Do you remember the definition of the marketing concept from Chapter 1? The *marketing concept* is an operating philosophy that has customer satisfaction at its core. It requires the integration of all organizational operations in a business. This means that not only marketing but also production, management, finance, accounting,

As you have learned in this chapter, marketing is no longer only a for-profit business activity designed to sell tangible goods. Marketing on the Internet, particularly on the Net's multimedia World Wide Web, embodies the widespread extension of marketing applications to services, not-for-profits, and other types of businesses. Marketing on the Internet is highly volatile, since new commercial and noncommercial sites appear daily. Therefore, the following list of examples of extended marketing on the Internet is subject to change.

- *Services Marketing* Among the many services offered to browsers of the Inter-Active Yellow Pages™ are business planning services, tax assistance, communication and long distance services, educational services, and real estate and financial services. At another site, Interdex offers many pages of goods and services for sale on the Internet. DealerNet is a World Wide Web site offering automobile-related services. Some businesses, such as Hewlett-Packard, maintain customer support sites on the Internet.

- *Government Marketing* The United States government markets U.S. Government Publication Office products on its Internet site at The Federal Bulletin Board. The U.S. Small Business Administration home page (SBAONLINE) lists its services along with a file of Small Business Success Stories. Many states and communities have home pages, gopher servers, and/or bulletin boards where information and services are listed, usually by site addresses that end in "gov".

- *Cause and Charitable Organization Marketing* A search program such as Veronica or Jughead can identify causes and charities by name, often by site addresses that end in "org". These include state and local sites, such as the United Way in Nevada and the American Cancer Society in New York, as well as national and international sites, such as a bone marrow transplant fund in the United Kingdom.

- *Health Marketing* Hospitals are showing up on the Internet in growing numbers. It is estimated that almost 50 percent of all hospitals access the Internet but not all have their own sites. Some health insurance companies have sites, including a local listing for Blue Cross and Blue Shield. Many medical home pages are sponsored by universities.

- *Political Marketing* Political candidates, the U.S. Congress, and many state governments have established their presence on the Internet. A recent candidate for lieutenant governor in Massachusetts used an America Online bulletin board to introduce himself to voters. Massachusetts Governor William Weld held a "Governor's Forum" on America Online. Campaign bulletin boards are listed for all 50 states. Some U.S. senators have set up Net sites through the Senate to keep in touch with their constituents.

- *Religious Marketing* Many religious groups have Internet sites. Some only list the times of their religious services; others have more elaborate interactive sites.

- *Entertainment Marketing* Already a large and rapidly growing marketing presence on the Internet, entertainment marketing is as diverse as the industry itself. Entertainment marketing includes film studios, music, video games, magazines, books, and travel. There is a home page devoted to *Star Trek: Generations.* Walt Disney World Company has a multiplex cinema that offers film clips of current movies. Amp is MCA Record's on-line magazine that includes Noise (album information and concert tour dates) and Loot (monthly promotions and giveways). A November 1994 Texas concert by the Rolling Stones is believed to be the first to be broadcast live on both video and the Internet. Playboy Enterprises Inc.'s World Wide Web home page offers merchandise, subscriptions, and two bulletin boards.

- *Event Marketing* You can browse a 1996 Summer Olympics World Wide Web home page as well as sites for the Kentucky Derby, trade shows, and other events.

- *Place Marketing* States have Internet sites that are particularly rich in travel information. Many travel sites offer cybertours as well as booking and reservation information. Outrigger Hotels Hawaii offers Hawaii InfoWeb with information, color pictures, and booking directions.

- *Educational Marketing* The Internet lends itself to language lessons, tutorials related to software and hardware use, and communications. Many universities, colleges, and other educational institutions are on-line, offering information and other products. ■

J. Jensen, "Tinseltown Is Tangled in the Web," *Advertising Age* 66, no. 10 (March 16, 1995), p. 16; B. Kantrowitz and D. Rosenberg, "Ready, Teddy? You're Online," *Newsweek,* September 12, 1994, pp. 60–61; "Outrigger Hotels Introduces Data Base for Users of Internet," *Travel Weekly* 53, no. 98 (December 12, 1994), p. 79; C. Waltner, "Kicking the Cybertires: DealerNet Links Car Buyers, Sellers Online," *Advertising Age* 66, no. 7 (February 13, 1995), p. 18; J. H. Ellsworth, "Businesses on a Virtual Rush to the Virtual Mall," *PC Magazine* 14, no. 3 (February 7, 1995), p. 190; M. A. Gillen, "Internet Gets Its First Live Concert," *Billboard* 106, no. 48 (November 26, 1994), p. 1; P. H. Lewis, "Exploring New Political Soapboxes: Politicians and Voters Using the Information Superhighway to Publicize Their Messages," *New York Times,* January 10, 1995, p. B8; D. C. Churbuck, "Is There a Doctor On-Line?", *Forbes* 154, no. 11 (November 7, 1994), p. 311; R. Bergman, "The World at Their Fingertips; Rural Providers Turn to Internet," *Hospitals & Health Networks* 68, no. 14 (July 20, 1994), p. 52; "The Bunneynet," *PC Week* 11, no. 36 (September 12, 1994), p. A3.

and other operational areas cooperate to satisfy the customer. Consumer research is conducted on a regular, ongoing basis to keep the firm informed about consumers and changes in the marketplace. Customer service activities are important. As a guide to strategic planning, the marketing concept philosophy requires a long-term perspective. The organization also tries to achieve its own goals, whether for profit, efficiency, survival, or nonprofit service delivery.

This definition and the contemporary extensions of marketing demonstrate that the marketing concept is being applied successfully in both the service and not-for-profit sectors of the U.S. economy. Although the operational environments and the names for various departments may differ, at the core is the concept that the consumer must be satisfied and the organization's goals achieved. However, in marketing situations where close personal customer contact is required, employee satisfaction is also important and should be a top organizational concern. Some business scholars have even suggested that, particularly in personal services, the first people to be satisfied must be employees, for only when they are motivated, well trained, and have the opportunity to satisfy consumers *can and will* they do so.

Finally, when it comes to the societal marketing concept, not-for-profits practice what many for-profits are still debating. The *societal marketing concept* is a broadened concept that includes the good of society as a business goal and requires that the business satisfy customers and society as well as realize its own goals. The societal marketing concept follows the basic form of the marketing concept, but in an expanded framework.

One of the particular cruelties of capitalism is that inequities develop between "haves" and "have nots"; while some people become wealthy, others barely survive. The challenge for businesses in adopting the societal marketing concept is to recognize business's obligation to work with the not-for-profit sector in moderating societal inequities and ensuring the common good.

This book concludes with a discussion of managing marketing, in Chapter 15.

Check Your Understanding
14.5

1. Identify some of the newer applications of marketing.
2. Do all lawyers agree that the marketing of legal services is desirable?
3. Are the marketing concept and societal marketing concept applicable to service businesses and not-for-profit organizations that engage in marketing?

Career Watch

Jody Samson is a mile-high marketer, offering free in-flight trials of seatback air telephones to passengers on selected flights of Alaska Air, Northwest, American, Southwest Airlines, and other carriers. In-flight airline marketing of airphone service is brand new, although airlines have offered catalog sales for years, including merchandise information in flight magazines tucked in seatback pockets. Jody talks to as many as 50 fliers each day as she offers free promotional calls. In addition to in-flight marketing, she also audits the system to ensure its smooth operation, and shows flight attendants how to use it. Claircom Communications, marketers of AirOne seatback airphones, wants to give free trials to as many passengers as possible, both business travelers and vacationers. Jody Samson is marketing this service with a smile. Marketers like Jody may soon be marketing this service in foreign markets as Claircom Communications extends their product to Europe and Asia. ■

"Mile-High Marketing," *Sales and Marketing Management* 146, no. 9 (September 1994), p. 172; E. Nelson, "Air-Phone Market Spreads Its Wings," *Business Marketing* 79, no. 8 (August 1994), p. 3.

Photo 14.15 Jody Samson of Claircom Communications.

Review of Chapter Objectives

1. *Explain the differences and similarities between goods and services.* As the U.S. economy has become dominated by services, service marketing has become an increasingly important activity. A service is differentiated from a good by its intangibility, perishability, variability, and inseparability. Services are classified by such characteristics as their product attributes, consumer targets, provider training, delivery system used, and closeness of the contact between service provider and consumer.

2. *Describe the Four Ps in services and the service advantage.* Services are products and, like tangible goods, they also must be priced, promoted, and placed. Because of the abundance of me-too products and strong price competition, businesses are finding that service can be the way to differentiate themselves from the competition and achieve a sustainable competitive advantage.

3. *Recognize the characteristics of not-for-profit marketing.* Not-for-profit marketing is growing in importance. This sector is large, diverse, and has only recently been drawn to marketing because of increasing competition.

4. *Discuss some other for-profit extensions of marketing.* Notable contemporary marketing extensions include marketing by for-profit hospitals and health care organizations, people, entertainment, leisure activities, events, education, and information services.

5. *Characterize the marketing concept in services and not-for-profits.* At the core of the marketing concept is consumer satisfaction and the achievement of the business's or organization's goals. Numerous examples throughout this chapter indicate that the marketing concept is being successfully applied in services and not-for-profits.

Key Terms

After studying Chapter 14, you should be able to define each of the following key terms and use them in describing marketing activities.

Discussion Questions

1. In your own words, discuss the characteristics that make services unique.

2. In the continuum of goods and services, where would an automobile tune-up be placed? A skating lesson? Five-pound bags of flour? Explain your answers.

3. What might a college do to combat demand fluctuation problems during the summer for classes and housing?

4. Explain how a consumer may affect the outcome of the service encounter.

5. Compare and contrast the evaluation of quality in a good and a service.

6. Discuss the reasons behind the economy's shift to services.

7. What dimensions affect a service provider's performance?

8. Why did not-for-profits avoid marketing for many years? Why are so many using marketing now?

9. What are some forms of people marketing? Give both for-profit and not-for-profit examples.

10. Discuss whether or not the marketing concept applies to services.

What Do You Think?

What are two services that most consumers probably would most like to avoid? The Internal Revenue Service and burial services. When it comes to the latter, Lloyd Mandel is a specialist in providing gravesite services. Mandel uses low prices, new products, and mass advertising as marketing tools. Many families are willing to reject costly, elaborate funeral home services in favor of simplicity and a lower cost at graveside. Changing demographics and increased longevity indicate that Mandel may be on the brink of a highly successful approach to burial services. Others in the burial business are using marketing to attract new customers, often through prepaid burial plans. What do you think about this type of service marketing?

Sources: J. Levine and S. Luboves, "Cash and Bury," *Forbes* 149, no. 10 (May 11, 1993), pp. 162–64, 166; E. Klein, "The Maverick Mortician," *Crain's Chicago Business* 14, no. 41 (October 14, 1991), p. 1; K. Shermach, "Pay Now, Die Later: Consumers Urged Not to Delay that Final Decision," *Marketing News* 28, no. 22 (October 24, 1994), p. 1.

Mini-Case 14.1

Mail Room Outsourcing: A Big Service Business

Mail rooms are known for sorting, folding, stamping, moving out, receiving, and delivering mail. It is estimated that this service is worth about $15 billion annually to the 95 percent of all businesses who perform the service in-house and the 5 percent who employ such giants as Pitney Bowes and Xerox to do it for them. Burns International, however, is a small business that wants to crack this market. By targeting businesses that already use Burns's security services, they seek small mail rooms of two to five people, for whom they offer to select the necessary equipment, hire, and train the staff. They plan to charge cost plus for the operation, including staff salaries. The rationale for a security service taking over a mail room is that this is where revenues and expenses

pass and where information is transmitted through the letters, packages, and materials intersecting in and out. The banking industry is one of the largest generators of mail in the United States, churning out over 5 billion pieces annually.

Case Questions

1. What do you think of the rationale behind Burns's service proposition?

2. Do you agree with it?

3. Where else might Burns target its service? Explain your answer.

Sources: H. Canaday "Selling a New Service," *Personal Selling Power* 13, no. 7 (October 1993), pp. 36–37; M. Barthel, "Mail Room Operators Signing Up Bigger Banks," *American Banker* 157, no. 113 (June 12, 1992), p. 3.

Mini-Case 14.2

Turmoil and Opportunity in Health Care Marketing

Managed care is a hot topic in health care these days. Health service insurers, the government, and various organizations are developing plans to provide broader consumer coverage at a lower cost, mainly by getting consumers to join health maintenance organizations (HMOs) and health service purchasing alliances. There are three key players in the health care services pay-

ment triangle: the consumer, the employer, and the payors (mainly insurance companies and health maintenance organizations). The consumer is a payee for health care services, along with her employer, who contributes to paying for the employee's health care services. The amount of paying going on is enormous. Health care services in the United States cost about $1 trillion annually.

This amount is expected to escalate as the population ages and the demand for health services increases. However, health care costs are dropping, so the rate of escalation is expected to slow.

Health service payors are for-profit insurance companies and HMOs as well as the not-for-profit Blue Cross/Blue Shields. However, the characterization of the Blues as strictly not-for-profit is changing as their national association has dropped its 60-year-old nonprofit stipulation and is offering its regional members the option of becoming for-profits. This move is designed to allow them to compete more effectively. One thing seems clear: No matter how changes in health services are made in the United States, organizations such as insurance companies, HMOs, not-for-profits, and hospitals will continue marketing their services and seeking new opportunities to serve consumers more efficiently and cost effectively.

Case Question

In the highly competitive health care market, insurers like Prudential of America, Aetna Life & Casualty, and the various Blue Cross/Blue Shields are rivals that seek to sign up consumers, either through self-purchased health insurance or employer-purchased insurance. Do you think that marketing differs between the for-profit and not-for-profit payors?

Sources: C. J. Loomis, "The Real Action in Health Care," *Fortune* 130, no. 1 (July 11, 1994), pp. 149–57; C. Roush, "Reality Plays Matchmaker," *Business Week*, June 27, 1994, p. 32; "Blue Cross–Blue Shield Offers Members a For-Profit Option," *Lexington Herald-Leader*, July 1, 1994, p. C8.

Chapter 14 Notes

1. V. A. Zeithaml, A. Parasuraman, and L. L. Berry, "Problems and Strategies in Services Marketing," *Journal of Marketing* 49 (Spring 1985), pp. 33–46.

2. P. Yoshihashi, "Limited-Service Chains Offer Enough to Thrive," *The Wall Street Journal*, July 27, 1992, p. B1; R. T. Rust, B. Subramanian, and M. Wells, "Making Complaints a Management Tool," *Marketing Management* 1, no. 3 (1991), pp. 41–45.

3. V. Reitman, "Hi, Rover! Fetch the Ball, Rover! Now Beg, Rover! Bye-Bye, Rover!" *The Wall Street Journal*, June 23, 1994, p. B1.

4. B. Richards, "A Prisoner of Zelda and Two Lost Pilots Are on the Line," *The Wall Street Journal*, December 30, 1992, pp. A1, 8.

5. H. Schlossberg, "New Radio Ratings Services Zero In on Moving Cars and Smaller Markets," *Marketing News* 27, no. 9 (April 26, 1993), pp. 1, 7.

6. C. Miller, "Networks Rally around Study That Shows Strong out-of-Home Ratings," *Marketing News* 27, no. 9 (April 26, 1993), pp. 1, 6; M. Hudis, "Nielsen Stands Alone," *MEDIAWEEK* 3, no. 43 (October 25, 1993), p. 10.

7. R. M. Selzer, "A Business Takes Wing Despite Customers' Doubts," *Nation's Business* 80, no. 1 (January 1992), p. 8.

8. R. Tomsho, "This Nose for Hire: He Is Always on Call at the Olfactory," *The Wall Street Journal*, June 11, 1992, pp. A1, 14.

9. F. L. Kritz and J. Novack, "Patient, Educate Thyself," *Forbes* 150, no. 6 (September 14, 1992), pp. 504, 506.

10. E. H. Fram, "Stressed-Out Consumers Need Timesaving Innovations," *Marketing News* 26, no. 5 (March 2, 1992), p. 10.

11. M. Blumberg and C. D. Pringle, "The Missing Opportunity in Organizational Research: Some Implications for a Theory of Work Performance," *Academy of Management Review* 7, no. 4 (1982) , pp. 560–69.

12. J. Carlton, "Befuddled PC Users Flood Help Lines, and No Question Seems to Be Too Basic," *The Wall Street Journal*, March 1, 1994, p. B1.

13. "New Church Uses Marketing to Appeal to Baby Boomers," *Marketing News* 27, no. 8 (April 12, 1993), p. 11.

14. L. Bird, "And They're Very Good at Praying for Success," *The Wall Street Journal*, October 15, 1993, p. B1.

15. M. Robichaux, "Lifetime Aim: Be All Things to All Women," *The Wall Street Journal*, April 5, 1993, pp. B1, 2.

16. J. P. Sterba, "Old-Fashioned Letter Is Fund Raising's Cutting Edge," *The Wall Street Journal,* August 18, 1992, p. B2.

17. G. Claiborne, "How Marketing Rescued an L.A. Rescue Mission," *Marketing News* 23, no. 26 (December 18, 1989), p. 13; B. Streisand, "Gimme Shelter," *U.S. News & World Report* 112, no. 4 (February 3, 1992), p. 17.

18. H. Schlossberg, "Surviving in a Cause-Related World," *Marketing News* 23, no. 26 (December 18, 1989), pp. 1, 12; P. Sebastian, "Tough Times," *The Wall Street Journal,* September 15, 1992, p. A1.

19. D. Woodruff and J. Templeman, "Why Mercedes Is Alabama Bound," *Business Week,* October 11, 1993, pp. 138–39; J. S. DeMott, "States Scramble for Fewer Prizes," *Nation's Business* 82, no. 9 (September 1994), p. 56.

20. P. Merrion, "Convention Hopes Shot: Dems or GOP, but Not Both," *Crain's Chicago Business* 17, no. 2 (January 10, 1994), p. 1.

21. R. Tomsho, "U.S. Hospitals See Opportunity in Mexico," *The Wall Street Journal,* August 13, 1993, pp. B1, 5; H. Cooper, "Offering Aerobics, Karate, Aquatics, Hospitals Stress Business of 'Wellness,'" *The Wall Street Journal,* August 9, 1993, pp. B1, 3.

22. K. Bohner, "Doctors on Demand," *Forbes* 152, no. 10 (October 25, 1993), pp. 124–26.

23. E. Tobin, "Market Cancer Care from the Patient's Perspective," *Marketing News* 25, no. 18 (September 2, 1991), pp. 21–23.

24. K. Goldman, "Jordan & Co. Play Ball on Madison Avenue," *The Wall Street Journal,* June 1, 1993, p. B5; K. Goldman, "Is There Life After Basketball? Companies That Use Jordan Are About to Find Out," *The Wall Street Journal,* October 7, 1993, pp. B1, 12; J. Jensen, "A Year Off Court, MJ Still Big in Ads," *Crain's Chicago Business* 17, no. 43 (October 24, 1994), p. 10.

25. R. Lane, "Prepackaged Celebrity," *Forbes* 152, no. 14 (December 20, 1993), pp. 86, 87–90.

26. T. Triplett, "Lawyers Face Pressure to Become Marketers," *Marketing News* 28, no. 6 (March 14, 1994), p. 9.

27. T. Pack, "Hit Depends on Who Pushes It, Not Just Who Plays It," *Lexington Herald-Leader,* July 6, 1992, p. A12.

28. "Bantam Books, Frito-Lay Market Country Singer," *Marketing News* 28, no. 13 (June 20, 1994), p. 14.

29. L. Landro and T. R. King, "'Last Action Hero,' Critically Wounded, Takes Some Marketers Down with Him," *The Wall Street Journal,* July 16, 1993, p. B1.

30. T. R. King, "Studios Battle Clutter of TV Movie Spots," *The Wall Street Journal,* June 25, 1993, pp. B1, 8.

31. L. Lincoln, "Premier Expands Its Family Niche: Line Adds Universal Studios and Sea World Packages to Its Itineraries," *Travel Weekly* 53, no. 18 (March 17, 1994), p. C3.

32. "Chirpy Logic," *The Economist* 325, no. 7791 (December 26–January 8, 1993), p. 89.

33. U. Gupta, "Hungry for Funds, Universities Embrace Technology Transfer," *The Wall Street Journal,* July 1, 1994, pp. A1, 5.

34. B. Marsh, "Entrepreneurs Provide Advice to Help the Buyer Beware," *The Wall Street Journal,* October 1, 1993, p. B2.

35. J. Sandberg, "Prodigy Transforms Olympics Viewers into Couch Critics," *The Wall Street Journal,* February 15, 1994, p. B12.

36. G. Edmondson, J. Rossant, and J. Flynn, "AT&T Is No Smooth Operator in Europe," *Business Week,* April 11, 1994, p. 48.

Managing Marketing

Chapter Objectives

After studying Chapter 15 you should be able to

1. Explain the role of the marketing manager.
2. Explain the role of the marketing plan.
3. Describe implementation activities.
4. Explain the function of marketing control.
5. Discuss how control results may be applied in marketing.

*T*he primary focus of this book is to examine how marketing works in business, be it a small business, a business unit of a large corporation, or a global giant with worldwide marketing operations. Marketing doesn't occur spontaneously; people make marketing happen, and marketing managers in particular bear much of the responsibility for ensuring the success of marketing efforts. Obviously, it is difficult to generalize about how individual marketing managers make marketing work, because of enormous variations in company size, mission, complexity, organizational structure, industry, and location. Despite these differences, basic marketing management activities are strikingly similar whether practiced in a business, not-for-profit organization, or government, by one or several thousand marketers. This chapter focuses on marketing management—how people in businesses, organizations, and government manage marketing. As you learn about marketing management in this chapter, consider these questions: What does it take to manage marketing successfully? Why is it sometimes so difficult to do?

Marketing Managers Oversee Marketing Activities

The day didn't begin particularly well for Josh Bagby. First, the company's chief executive officer (CEO) called a meeting and told the company's vice presidents that because of rising costs and threats to their market share positions she was calling for each operational area to streamline its operations and cut costs. She assigned goals for the cuts and deadlines for making them. The CEO told Bagby, the company's chief marketing officer, that his people would have to both make cuts *and* increase revenues. Bagby left the CEO's meeting and called one of his own, bringing together his marketing managers for sales promotions, advertising, product development, distribution, and sales. He explained the nature of the CEO's remarks, noting the deadlines and targets. Bagby listened carefully to his managers' initial responses, then told them he would work with them to iron out the details, but needed their input for planning cuts and reaching revenue targets. Bagby was pleased with the support he got from his managers. Although they weren't happy about the cuts, Bagby knew they would cooperate. He was confident that the marketing department could achieve the CEO's goals.

MARKETING MANAGERS

Objective 1 Explain the role of the marketing manager.

The people who market products in small and mid-size businesses, large corporations, not-for-profit organizations, and government perform a key role. You will recall that marketing is the operational area that establishes the most intimate link between the company and its outside environments and, in particular, with consumers, competitors, and channel of distribution members. Marketers act as information conduits—bringing information from outside the business into the company and transmitting information about the company and its products to the outside. The business marketer is also a revenue collection agent—providing products when and where consumers want them, generating revenue from product sales, and transmitting it back to the business. Consequently, marketers are boundary spanners who connect the internal business with its external environments, and facilitators who expedite marketing exchanges (see Figure 15.1).

Figure 15.1

Marketing Is a Boundary-Spanning Activity

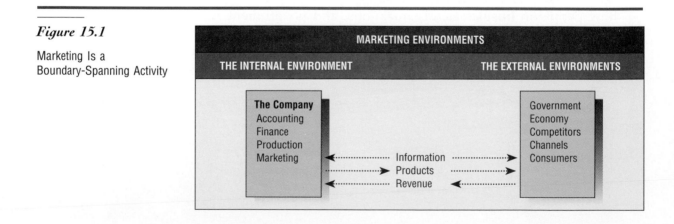

Marketing managers guide marketing programs and people in the diverse activities associated with offering products to markets. In corporations (large, multibusiness companies), marketing managers with varying amounts of responsibility are located at different management levels in the organization.

There is no single best marketing organization structure; rather, it is a decision that must be tailored to a business's individual characteristics, particularly its size, mission, operations, technology, environments, and philosophy of doing business. Organizational structures differ considerably, even within the same industry. Some organization structures are rigid, formed vertically around a traditional hierarchial pyramid structure that often slows decisions, fosters turf conflicts (resource battles between departments), and fails to encourage flexibility and cooperation.

A recent trend is to reengineer the business and adopt the flattened hierarchy of the horizontal corporation, where the corporation is organized around core processes instead of functions or departments (e.g., marketing, finance, or production), with far fewer management layers. This is designed to eliminate barriers between employees, improve processes that add value to products, and ultimately better serve consumers. Processes are the tasks that must be accomplished in order to add value.[1] In a flattened corporation, multidisciplinary teams manage themselves, contact between employees and customers and suppliers is increased, employees are trained to use raw data to make informed decisions, and the focus stays trained on the customer. Corporations moving toward horizontal management include units of AT&T, Du Pont, General Electric, and Motorola.[2]

In Corporations

In multibusiness corporations with traditional organizational structures, the top marketing manager usually is a vice president who reports directly to the CEO, the corporation's general manager. The marketing vice president is a top-level executive who oversees the corporation's entire marketing program, encompassing many different businesses, hundreds of products, and, often, thousands of marketing plans. The marketing manager of each strategic business unit reports to the marketing vice president. These mid-level managers hold different job titles and operational responsibilities. Some are *category managers,* responsible for marketing a business unit's related product lines. There are over 30 category managers at Procter & Gamble (P&G) who manage such product lines as laundry detergents, diapers, or deodorants. Each category manager is the chief operating officer of a fairly independent business that operates under the P&G corporate umbrella. At other companies, a category manager might be in charge of marketing a line of home electronic products or even an unrelated group of products managed together because they are targeted to the same markets.

Category management is a relatively new marketing management design, first seen in the late 1980s and heralded by some as a move toward streamlining marketing organizations.[3] It provides a more integrated approach to managing related brands within a product line. Category management should cut costs, promote efficiencies, and, ultimately, benefit consumers, because it coordinates brand marketing activities in such areas as advertising, distribution, and sales promotions, as well as moderates resource conflicts between brand managers.[4] Critics say category management only adds another management level to already top-heavy organization structures, and any advantages are more imagined than real.[5]

At a lower management level, a *brand manager* manages the marketing of a single brand. At P&G, for example, one brand manager markets Tide, another markets Dreft, and all laundry detergent brand managers report to the laundry detergent category manager. Procter & Gamble is credited with inventing the brand management form in 1931; therefore, the company's restructuring to a category management form in the 1980s represents a significant change.

Other businesses appoint separate marketing managers for different operational areas like sales force, promotion, advertising, marketing research, or distribution. Sometimes management is structured by customer group, with marketing managers responsible for products targeted to personal use consumers, businesses, or government. Another form assigns marketing managers to different geographical regions where customers are concentrated or, as in the case of Campbell Soup Co., where manufacturing plants are located. Some commonly used traditional marketing organization structures are shown in Figure 15.2.

Mini-General Managers A company's general managers are responsible for accomplishing broad organizational goals through planning, organizing, directing, and controlling organizational resources.[6] Their domain is the entire organization. Although marketing managers focus on only one part of the entire organization—marketing—they are regarded as mini-general managers because they undertake the same basic tasks as do general managers, although in a smaller, more concentrated, focused operational area.

The management methods of marketing managers and general managers are under considerable pressure to change. Rather than bossing people around in the kind of autocratic management style found in the military, contemporary managers are more apt to coach

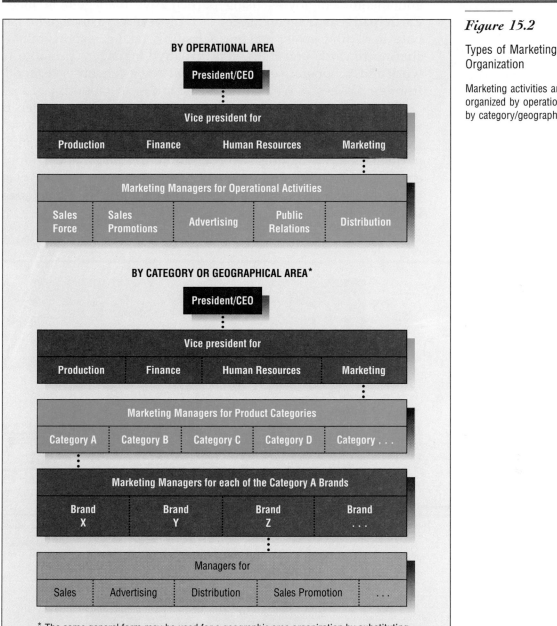

BY OPERATIONAL AREA

President/CEO

Vice president for

| Production | Finance | Human Resources | Marketing |

Marketing Managers for Operational Activities

| Sales Force | Sales Promotions | Advertising | Public Relations | Distribution |

BY CATEGORY OR GEOGRAPHICAL AREA*

President/CEO

Vice president for

| Production | Finance | Human Resources | Marketing |

Marketing Managers for Product Categories

| Category A | Category B | Category C | Category D | Category . . . |

Marketing Managers for each of the Category A Brands

| Brand X | Brand Y | Brand Z | Brand . . . |

Managers for

| Sales | Advertising | Distribution | Sales Promotion | . . . |

* The same general form may be used for a geographic area organization by substituting a geographical "Region" for "Category." For example, instead of "Category A" substitute "Region A" with a marketing manager responsible for Region A, which could perhaps include the southeastern United States and the states of Kentucky, Tennessee, Georgia, and Florida. For "Category B," substitute "Region B," and so forth.

Figure 15.2

Types of Marketing Organization

Marketing activities are usually organized by operational area or by category/geographical area.

participative management A management method in which employees participate in setting goals, making decisions, taking responsibility, and sharing rewards and risks.

and mentor employees using participative management methods. **Participative management** views employees as partners who participate in setting goals, making decisions, taking responsibility, and sharing rewards and risks.[7] Participative managers promote teamwork and a cooperative environment. They listen, observe, and learn from employees as well as from customers. In modern jargon, they "talk the talk and walk the walk," which means that managers don't isolate themselves in their offices but instead are part of the action, talking with people in all aspects of the business, encouraging participation, facilitating two-way communication, and supporting employee involvement. In some businesses, employees control many of the decisions while managers tend to administrative chores. (See Photos 15.1 and 15.2.)

Photo 15.1

Contemporary managers are encouraged to get involved, listen, and observe.

Photo 15.2

With participative management, employees are encouraged to work in teams, share responsibility, and share in decision making.

Consumer Insight

Many Americans will work in a small business at some point in their careers. Currently over 50 percent of the U.S. workforce is employed by a small business; by the year 2000 that number is projected to rise to over 70 percent. Of the 17 million businesses in the United States, about 98 percent are small, most employing 20 or fewer people. Half of all small businesses have fewer than 10 employees and sales less than $0.5 million. Because they are labor intensive, small businesses account for a disproportionate number of recently created new jobs, 75 percent of those created in 1987 alone. Small businesses produce almost 40 percent of the U.S. Gross Domestic Product. New small business incorporations in 1993 jumped 6 percent to just over 700,000 in number. The importance of small businesses to the U.S. economy cannot be overstated. ■

T. Pouschine and M. Kripalani, " 'I Got Tired of Forcing Myself to Go to the Office,' " *Forbes* 149, no. 11 (May 25, 1992), pp. 104–141; W. G. Nickels, J. M. McHugh, and S. M. McHugh, *Understanding Business*, 2nd ed. (Homewood, IL: Richard D. Irwin, 1990), pp. 163–64; H. Banks, "Business Startups: on the Rise Again," *Forbes* 153, no. 12 (June 6, 1994), p. 37.

In Small and Mid-Size Businesses

There is no single definition of small business. According to the Small Business Administration Act of 1953, a small business is one that is "independently owned and operated and not dominant in its field of operation."[8] If a business fits the definition of *small*, it becomes eligible for assistance (e.g., monetary and technical, educational and advisory services) from the U.S. Small Business Administration (SBA). The SBA also sets guidelines for size limits on revenues and numbers of employees within Standard Industrial Classification (SIC) codes. For example:

- *Wholesale trade:* Annual revenues no greater than $9.5 million to $22 million, depending on specific industry.

Photo 15.3

Small businesses are significant contributors to the U.S. economy.

Marketing Application 15.1

As a class project, test the observation that small businesses account for much of the recent job creation. Have each student identify several friends or relatives who currently or recently worked for a small business. Ask these people about the employment situation at the business. Have there been any new hirings? Bring your results to class for discussion. ■

- *Services:* Annual revenues no greater than $2.5 million to $14.5 million, depending on specific industry.
- *Retail trade:* Annual revenues no greater than $3.5 million to $13.5 million, depending on specific industry.

Whatever the size of the business or organization, marketing activities must be managed, whether by one person or hundreds. In many small businesses, marketing management is predominately sales force management because the sales force often represents the largest part of the workforce. The sales manager's responsibilities are primarily associated with hiring, firing, training, supervising, motivating, and evaluating the sales force. Marketing management responsibilities may be assumed by the business's owner-operator, with various employees performing different marketing tasks as needed. If you work in a small business you may be asked to assume marketing management responsibilities and make both day-to-day and long-term marketing decisions.

Obviously marketing management is more complex and formal in a very large business than it is in a smaller one. Small business marketing managers may have greater flexibility in getting the job done, because they don't have to fight through multiple management layers to get their plans approved and funded or changed. What a small business marketer lacks in resources (e.g., people, money, technology, materials) can be overcome through creativity and quick responses to changes in the environment (both opportunities and threats).

Although small businesses have been widely cited for their employment and economic contributions, mid-size businesses tend to be ignored. Many analysts believe the decade of the 1990s will see greater job growth and marketing activity in mid-size (annual sales of $5 million to $150 million) businesses than in either small businesses or corporate giants. Many of these mid-size businesses are small businesses that have grown larger. Often, they are among the most aggressive entrants into international marketing.[9]

International Marketing Report

Most people assume that only large corporations like General Motors or IBM can successfully penetrate the Japanese market. Tell that to DSP Group Inc., Avid Technology Inc., or Dexter Shoe Company—all small to mid-size U.S. businesses that have tried hard and succeeded in marketing their products in Japan. Their stories reflect a similar theme—a long-term commitment to success, modest beginnings, dedication to learning the market, patience in laying the groundwork (particularly in establishing distribution channels), and flexibility in responding to increased Japanese consumer demand for Western products and decreased trade barriers. These businesses did their homework. They offer products with the quality in design, packaging, function, and service that Japanese consumers demand. As an added benefit, the lessons these businesses are learning in the highly demanding Japanese market will make them even better competitors in the United States and elsewhere worldwide. ∎

C. J. Chipello, "Small United States Companies Take the Plunge into Japan's Market," *The Wall Street Journal*, July 7, 1992, pp. B1, 2.

Marketing Management

Marketing management is what marketing managers do: Manage marketing, making decisions about people, money, technology, and materials through the interlinked processes of planning, implementing, and control. Decisions often must be made quickly, frequently under serious time constraints and rarely with complete information. Some marketing decisions are routine, whereas others are intermittent or unique. Most decisions have relatively minor consequences; some have major ramifications and long-term effects on product profitability and cash value.

Regardless of specific organizational characteristics, structure, and size, marketing management generally involves:

marketing management The set of marketing activities related to formulating strategies, planning activities, implementing programs, supervising personnel, allocating resources, and evaluating outcomes.

- Formulating marketing strategies.
- Planning marketing activities.
- Implementing marketing programs.
- Supervising and leading marketing personnel.
- Allocating resources.
- Evaluating marketing outcomes.

The steps in accomplishing marketing management tasks are:

1. Set goals for marketing to accomplish.
2. Perform a situation analysis: identify opportunities and threats.
3. Select target markets.

Marketing Application 15.2

With the help of your teacher, identify several marketing managers in your community. If possible, assemble a panel of managers from several different businesses and marketing areas to discuss their jobs during one of your classes. Try to get a sales force manager, advertising or promotion manager, distribution manager, and a product development manager. Prepare a list of questions to give to each panelist prior to the discussion. You might focus on questions comparing their job tasks; describing how they develop, implement, and control marketing plans; and discussing the style of management encouraged in their business. ■

4. Develop a marketing strategy.
5. Write a marketing plan.
6. Develop marketing mix tactics.
7. Implement and control the marketing program.

The tasks described in the first six steps are presented in the preceding chapters of this book. In particular, review Chapter 2 for the discussion of marketing decision making and planning, the marketing plan, and marketing mix tactics.

marketing program All the operating marketing plans and activities that represent the total marketing effort at a particular time.

The Marketing Program A **marketing program** is all the various operating marketing plans and activities that represent the total marketing effort at a particular time. A very large business may have an extensive marketing program with hundreds of different marketing plans operating simultaneously. On the other hand, a single product or brand may require many different marketing plans, each directed at a distinct target audience, geographic region, competitor, or season of the year. For example, a personal computer business needs a different marketing plan for each of its customer groups, as differentiated by:

- Size of the customer's business.
- Customer's geographic location (a different marketing plan for each region of the United States).
- End user (individual, business, or government).
- Domestic and/or international site.

A small business may have very few or even a single marketing plan operating at one time; thus, its marketing program *is* its operating marketing plan.

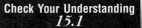

1. What is the role of the marketing manager?
2. Why are marketers called *mini-general managers?*
3. What tasks are performed by marketing managers?

DEVELOPING A MARKETING PLAN

As you learned in Chapter 2, the marketing plan is the blueprint for what marketing is to accomplish. In a company where there are many strategic business units operating under the corporate umbrella, a vice president for marketing (like Josh Bagby in the chapter-opening story) helps develop a strategic business plan that establishes what marketing will accomplish overall for the entire company and how each individual strategic business unit will contribute. The category manager at the strategic business unit level develops a marketing plan specifically for the category of products marketed by her strategic business unit. This is equivalent to a marketing plan developed for an independent business that is not part of a corporation. At the brand level, a marketing plan identifies target markets for the brand, as well as specifies how the marketing mix elements (product, price, place, and promotion) will tactically respond to facilitate exchange with the markets. At both the business and brand levels, the marketing plan typically covers a minimum of one year but usually no more than two years. The plans must be compatible with and complement plans from the other operational areas, as well as integrate with the overall business and corporate plans. They specify:

Objective 2 Explain the role of the marketing plan.

*   Product–market matches.
*   Marketing mix tactics.
*   Evaluation and control mechanisms.
*   Resource allocations.

Because many different marketing plans may be operating simultaneously at any time, considerable coordination is needed to ensure that all marketing plans are managed efficiently and effectively without having one plan undermine another. A detailed outline of a typical marketing plan is presented in Figure 15.3. However, marketing plans follow many different forms. The outline in Figure 15.3 identifies *in general* the types of information needed, but each business must decide if all of the sections are necessary for each

Figure 15.3   A Marketing Plan Outline

Company Name
Product or Brand Name
Date

I. Executive Summary

A one to two page summary that includes key points from each section designed to give an overview of the high points of the plan. The executive summary is the last part of the plan to be written as it relies on completion of the other sections for its contents.

II. Situation Analysis

A detailed analysis of the factors that will influence the marketing of the product. Much of the information can be obtained from company records, annual reports, sales records, and anecdotal and judgmental contributions from company personnel associated with and knowledgeable about the product. Other information can be found in government documents, industry and trade journals, reports and articles in the current popular business press, as well as SEC Form 10-K reports and publications by Moody's, Standard and Poor's, and Dun & Bradstreet that are available in most public and university business libraries.

a. Industry analysis including history, trends, growth forecasts, demand patterns, general characteristics, and regulatory environment.
b. Company analysis including history, mission, current situation, projected growth, core competencies, and strengths and weaknesses.
c. Product analysis including development background, history, life cycle stage, features, benefits, value, classification, packaging (goods and service), pricing, consumer positioning characteristics, diffusion history, and market share.
d. Market analysis including specific identification and market particulars, potential, demand, present customers, potential customers, customer retention patterns, responses to promotions, and receptivity to messages and incentives.
e. Competitive analysis including characteristics of competitive environment, identification of direct and indirect competitors, trends among competitors, relative strengths and weaknesses, and marketing mix activities—product characteristics and policies, pricing, promotion strategies, and distribution.
f. Analysis of other environmental factors including industry trends, economic forecasts, political outlook, technological advances, and relevant social forces.

III. Marketing Objectives

A statement of the objectives set for marketing to accomplish, how marketing is integrated with corporate and business objectives, and a definition of specific goals for marketing to achieve. Goals should be clearly stated, quantifiable, measurable, achievable, and related to time allocated for their achievement.

a. Identification of priority objectives to be satisfied, whether defined by the corporation, customers, public, government, or another group.
b. Specification of goals on basis of sales volume, market share, units, awareness, or other quantifiable measures.
c. Specification of other objectives, such as social or corporate goodwill goals.

IV. Marketing Strategies

A statement of how marketing will achieve the objectives and goals set for it within each target market.

a. Statement of general marketing strategies for positioning, product quality and value, and competitive advantage.
b. Statement of specific marketing strategies for each target market including strategies for each marketing mix element (product, price, place, promotion).

V. Tactics

A statement of how the strategies will be implemented. This includes organization for implementation and staffing, and detailed plans for each of the marketing mix elements.

a. Identification of tactical responsibilities and how personnel will be organized to carry out the action plans.
b. Product tactics including product features, benefits, associated services, and packaging.
c. Price tactics including price points, introductory pricing, and price adjustment policies.
d. Place tactics including where the product will be sold and what channels will be used.
e. Promotion tactics including plans for sales force support to promote the product, use of mass and direct response advertising, direct-mail tactics, and sales promotions and public relations/publicity plans.

VI. Budget

A statement of how the budget is to be allocated with associated costs.

a. Detailed analysis of costs including those associated with product development, research, sales, and promotion.
b. Detailed breakout of allocations for how the budget will be spent to cover costs and market the product.

VII. Control

A detailed description of how the marketing plan will be evaluated by outcome measures designed to compare expected and delivered results. Benchmarks and time frames should be provided. Provisions for a marketing audit may be included along with an explanation of whether it will be an internal or external audit.

a. Statement of expected outcomes quantified with target dates.
b. Explanation of methods that will be used to collect data and statistically analyze results.
c. Identification of benchmarks when specific objectives are to be met and various parts of the plan are to be implemented.

VIII. Appendixes

At the end of the document, addition of materials that support various parts of the plan, may include forecasting results, research studies, detailed cost estimates, and other information.

marketing plan. Other decisions concern the level of formality required: if the marketing plan should be written and presented in report form or evolve informally out of consensual decisions. Although the typical time frame is one year, different time frames may be more useful in particular marketing situations. A maximum of two years is about the longest period for which tactics can be reasonably suggested, because of the volatility of most businesses' environments. Given the fundamental importance of a marketing plan to all types of businesses, it is important that you familiarize yourself with the sections and the types of information required in each.

Large businesses have extensive resources that can be used in developing formal written marketing plans that often utilize computer-derived demand forecasts, simulations that approximate effects of price changes on consumer demand, cost projections for achievement of additional market share points, economic trend analysis, and similar elaborate quantitative inputs (see Photo 15.4). Small businesses are less likely to have access to such sophisticated computer-derived information sources. However, this must not stop a small business from developing a marketing plan.

The Small Business Marketing Plan

Although small businesses may lack the resources and, particularly, the time to write an extremely detailed, highly sophisticated formal marketing plan, such extensive planning is not always necessary. It is not desirable or productive to become consumed by the planning

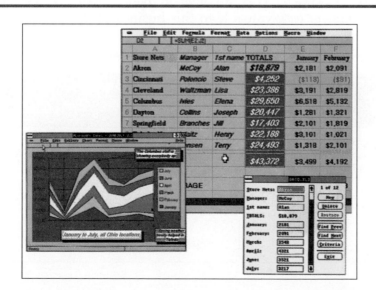

Photo 15.4

Business computers can generate many kinds of analytical materials.

process. Although the value of the marketing plan and the planning process is not disputed, marketers must maintain a realistic attitude toward planning, realizing that it is an important marketing management activity, but not the only one.

Some small businesspeople claim they haven't time to develop a marketing plan, so if planning is done at all it is on an ad hoc basis, only when time permits or when there is a crisis. They fail to realize the inherent value of systematically developing the information required in a marketing plan. By addressing each of the plan's sections, the business is forced to confront issues that are key to its future success, if not survival. Writing the plan forces the business to adopt some degree of organization. If a small business can't put its plan into writing, it may mean that it really has no plan at all![10] For more on creating a small business marketing plan, see Appendix A.

The value of the process of developing a marketing plan is shown by a small industrial products business that gained valuable customer insights by writing the marketing plan section on customers. In the process of evaluating the consumer environment, the business's owners constructed a customer matrix and ranked each of their customers on several criteria important to the company. By making these direct comparisons, the company found that the majority of their revenue was generated by relatively few customers. This is popularly known as the 80–20 rule. A matrix of the type of criteria by which the company evaluated its customers is shown in Figure 15.4. Each customer is ranked on all criteria. The number in each box shows how each customer is evaluated against one another, with a value of 1 at the top and 5 at the bottom. In Figure 15.4, the customers are evaluated on sales volume, potential sales, central purchasing, company contacts, and loyalty. Other criteria can be added as needed. The rankings in Figure 15.4 suggest that two customers are *very* valuable to this business. Who are they?

Figure 15.4

A Simplified Customer Comparison Matrix

CRITERIA	CUSTOMERS				
	A	B	C	D	E
Sales volume	5	1	2	4	3
Potential sales	4	3	2	5	1
Central purchasing	3	1	2	5	4
Company contacts	3	2	1	4	5
Loyalty	2	1	3	5	4

Small businesses have several advantages over large businesses when it comes to developing a marketing plan. For one thing, small business customer-contact employees often are the same people who often help write and execute the marketing plan. This personal, hands-on contact means that the small business marketing plan frequently reflects very current information, first-hand knowledge of customers, and timely insights into competitors' actions. When employees help formulate the marketing plans that establish marketing goals, they are more likely to accept the goals because they took part in defining them. Because the small business has fewer management levels, marketing plans can be more responsive to sudden changes in the environment. Plans can be revised quickly, and new plans developed without costly bureaucratic delays. Finally, small size is sometimes an advantage when it comes to disputes over resource allocations identified in the marketing plan. There are fewer people to become embroiled in turf conflicts, and greater personal contact in small businesses can facilitate both formal and informal negotiations to resolve conflicts. The advantages can be summed up as up-to-date, first-hand information; greater goal acceptance; heightened responsiveness; and simplified conflict resolution. ■

The **80–20 rule,** that 80 percent of the business's revenue is generated by 20 percent of its customers, is an observation that businesses often miss because they don't bother to systematically evaluate their target markets and customers. The rule does not mean that a business should ignore the less-productive majority of its customers, for within this group there are bound to be light purchasers who can be developed into heavier ones. However, the 80–20 rule does have implications for how effective the marketing is, because *excessive* marketing allocations targeted to the low-purchasing 80 percent indicate a probable misdirection of marketing resources.

80–20 rule The observation that 80 percent of a business's revenue is generated by 20 percent of its customers.

IMPLEMENTATION: ACTIVATING THE MARKETING PLAN

Ideally, the immediate outcome of the planning process is a marketing plan, one that:

Objective 3 Describe implementation activities.

- Is developed systematically.
- Is based on sound information from multiple sources.
- States clear, measurable goals.
- Provides a feasible blueprint for action.
- Reflects how value is supplied through the product offer.

implementation The activation of a marketing plan.

Marketing plans by themselves are meaningless, unless and until they are activated. **Implementation** is the activation of a marketing plan, when people, money, technology, and materials are brought together in an organized way to execute marketing mix tactics and achieve marketing objectives. Planning and implementation, followed by control, are the three interrelated, unified marketing management processes that marketing managers manage. These linked processes are shown in Figure 15.5.

Implementation requires organizing people to get marketing work done, as well as filling in the details of the work they are to perform and providing sufficient money, materials, technology, and leadership so that they can do their jobs well. The emphasis on implementation has implications for the importance of human capital to the business and, most critically, to marketing. Marketing is a people-intensive activity, and often the people who market products are the business's defining differential advantage over the competition.

Obviously, the goal is to have good implementation when activating a good marketing plan. However, this doesn't always happen. Coca-Cola found that good implementation couldn't save a flawed plan when they launched the new Coke.[11] On the other hand, Kmart learned that although a good plan is important, execution is perhaps more so. Its recent failure to improve profitability despite impressive plans to refurbish and renovate stores has

Figure 15.5

The Interrelated Processes of Planning–Implementation–Control

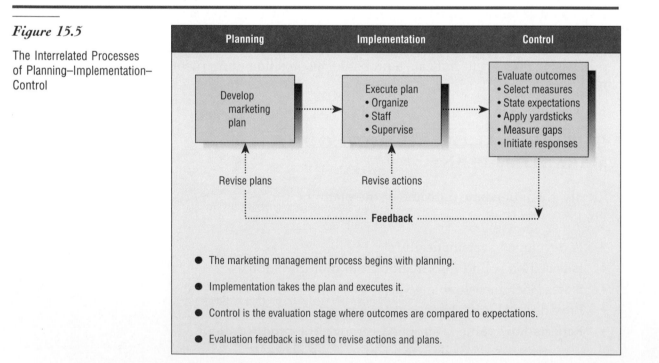

been blamed on poor execution.[12] Likewise, Compaq Computer Corporation's comeback plan to regain lost market share by introducing a new line of low-cost, workhorse ProLinea computers was frustrated when they seriously underestimated consumer demand. The resulting product shortages left once-eager consumers angry and disappointed.[13]

Organizing, Staffing, and Supervising

Implementation requires that various individuals perform marketing activities working collectively or individually. You will recall that performance is a function of the interrelationship of *capacity to perform, willingness to perform,* and *opportunity to perform.* Three key activities associated with implementation performance are:

1. **Organizing:** Determining what organizational form is needed to accomplish the tasks, structuring jobs, assigning responsibilities, dividing up sales territories, making work assignments and schedules, and ensuring that there is the *opportunity to perform.*

2. **Staffing:** Identifying people who have the capacity to perform the tasks, hiring and training them, firing them if necessary, and ensuring that the people involved in implementation have the *capacity to perform.*

3. **Supervising:** Developing a work environment where people's *willingness to perform* is enhanced, directing their performance, delegating authority, encouraging cooperation and teamwork, establishing good lines of communication, and providing needed resources.

organizing Determining the organizational form needed to implement the marketing plan.

staffing Ongoing hiring, training, and supervising of personnel required for implementation.

supervising Overseeing, directing, and optimizing physical and organizational environments and personnel performance of marketing activities.

Leadership is an important ingredient in successful implementation, because it has a direct impact on performance. Many contemporary marketing managers have embraced the practice of employee empowerment (providing information and authority for employees to make decisions and take responsibility for their work) and teamwork (where individual accomplishment and reward are deemphasized and working cooperatively to achieve team goals and benefits are emphasized). Others have found better results by empowering employees while still rewarding individual effort and improvement.

Implementation Problems

Implementation is not always easy. It requires knowledgeable marketers with good interpersonal skills. It often means making a change in what people do and how they do it. Because people tend

downsizing Personnel reductions designed to increase company productivity and decrease costs.

to resist change, implementation may be resisted and sometimes sabotaged by those who feel most threatened by change. Recently, change has come to be equated with **downsizing,** personnel reductions designed to increase company productivity and decrease costs. Fear of downsizing (losing one's job) often has the opposite effect from that intended, leading to productivity losses and high workforce anxiety—both threats to implementation success. Some economists fear that continuous downsizing will lead to corporate anorexia—businesses will get so thin that they'll lose energy and economic health.[14] So far, the effect of corporate downsizings on product improvements in many organizations has been disappointing.[15]

Other implementation problems are associated with inadequate or blocked communication, where marketing personnel don't receive clear messages and haven't the information to carry out their jobs. If goals are not clearly communicated, understood, and accepted, they can rarely motivate people to achieve them. Turf conflicts can undermine successful implementation as internal disputes over resources distract attention from implementation activities.

Managers must identify threats to implementation before they can begin to resolve them. Conflict resolution, negotiation, and brainstorming sessions can be helpful in identifying problem areas and developing solutions. Sometimes solutions may not be readily apparent or easily achieved and, as a result, the alternative is to reevaluate and revise the marketing plan or implementation strategies.

Check Your Understanding
15.2

1. How do marketing plans differ in large and small businesses?
2. Explain how implementation activates the marketing plan.
3. What are some implementation problems that marketing managers may experience?

CONTROL

Objective 4 Explain the function of marketing control.

control Evaluation of marketing performance and outcomes in order to learn whether or not marketing goals have been met and, if not, why not.

A teacher uses control systems to determine if students are achieving their learning goals. The teacher has expectations of what students *should* have mastered by certain points in a semester. Tests are yardsticks used to measure what students *have* learned, identify deficiencies, and suggest places for improvement. Marketing managers use control systems to track the progress of marketing plan implementation. **Control** is the evaluation of marketing performance and outcomes in order to learn whether or not marketing goals have been met and, if not, why not. Control is applied at the corporate, business, and product levels. At each level, control methods evaluate performances and outcomes and identify problems so that they can be corrected. Controls can provide useful information that can lead to changes in marketing plans and implementation activities, as well as the elimination of poor-performing products and positions and the divestment of money-losing businesses from the corporation's business portfolio.

Control is particularly important where a business faces intense competition, because an effective control system can be a way to achieve competitive advantage. For example, cost control is important in distribution, where just-in-time delivery systems and computer-managed inventories can cut costs and improve competitiveness. Cost control is also important in advertising, where skyrocketing costs and a lack of accountability are forcing agencies to stringently evaluate advertising expenditures and find better ways to demonstrate effectiveness.

Control, like planning and implementation, must be systematic. A haphazard control system gives untrustworthy, unusable results. Accurate, consistent, and timely tracking of what actually is happening can provide invaluable information for the marketer, particularly if it indicates where corrective responses are needed. A control system tracking model has five steps:

1. Select measures that state what is to be evaluated.
2. State quantitative expectations for each measure (how much of a response will be considered significant).
3. Evaluate outcomes for each measure.
4. Measure gaps between expected and delivered measures.
5. Provide feedback to plans and implementation designed to initiate a response.

Control Tracks Performance and Outcomes

In order to have an effective control system, the marketing manager must first establish what is to be tracked. This includes deciding where the measures are to be taken, when, and what or who is to be measured. The most common measures are:

- *Sales measures:* Sales volumes or dollar amounts.
- *Market share measures:* The product's share of the total market.
- *Cost measures:* Direct costs associated only with the product, or full costs, both direct and indirect.
- *Customer satisfaction measures:* Consumer attitudes measured by evaluating customer service contacts through customer surveys and observations.

The next step is to determine what is expected from the measure(s): an optimum amount or one that is acceptable when compared either with previous performance or the competition. Yardsticks are applied in the sense that the measures are taken and a gap analysis is performed to determine the difference between what was expected and what was delivered. If the results are disappointing, this feedback is used to initiate a response. The response may be to modify an existing marketing plan or implementation strategy as input into the development of a new plan or strategy, or to discontinue an implementation activity. The control system may run continually, providing information on a daily basis or for summary statements reported on a weekly, monthly, quarterly, or even annual basis. Managers must decide when and how much control information is needed in order to control marketing activities without causing *information overload,* where the sheer volume of information generated and distributed overwhelms the marketer's ability to analyze and use it.

The Marketing Audit

marketing audit An unbiased, comprehensive examination of the business's marketing activities conducted by impartial auditors.

Just as many businesses require an extensive audit of their financial operations, many also require a marketing operations audit. A **marketing audit** is an unbiased, comprehensive examination of the business's marketing activities that is conducted periodically by impartial internal or external auditors. Marketing audits may be conducted at all organizational levels from corporate to product. A checklist of questions often is prepared to systematically evaluate the marketing environment, target markets, marketing mix elements, the competition, and other relevant factors.

APPLYING CONTROL RESULTS

Objective 5   Discuss how control results may be applied in marketing.

Just as a marketing plan is unproductive unless it is implemented, control results are meaningless unless they activate a response. If they are good, the response may be to maintain the status quo. But even that requires planning and implementation to respond to environmental changes (particularly competitors' actions) in order to maintain stability. Bad results may require a more vigorous response. At top executive levels, bad results may lead to a reevaluation of corporate or business marketing plans and strategies. At the product level, where the spotlight is on brand productivity, bad control results should provide a warning signal that something has gone amiss and improvement is needed. Control results can point to the need for quality improvements, as well as changes in products and markets.

Quality Improvement: *Kaizen*

Many U.S. businesses have adopted the Japanese philosophy of *kaizen*, a commitment to continual improvement that seeks to make products and processes better and, thereby, enhance quality.[16] *Kaizen* can be seen as part of an unbroken cycle of evaluation and response that uses control systems to provide input for improving plans, implementation, and quality on a continuous basis. By adopting the principle of *kaizen*, a business and its marketing managers confirm their commitment to quality as well as to flexibility, because continuous improvement means that everything is constantly subject to change. As a result, plans must be dynamic, action-oriented instruments. Implementation must be responsive and people-adaptable. The advantage of the philosophy and practice of *kaizen* is that improvements are made continuously, often before they are needed. This reduces the chance of being caught in a crisis-inspired response to sudden, unexpected bad control results. *Kaizen* is a considerable challenge, yet it is quickly becoming a competitive necessity.

kaizen A Japanese principle that is a commitment to continual improvement in products and processes and enhancement of quality.

At the Toyota Motor Manufacturing U.S.A. plant in Georgetown, Kentucky, there are almost 300 quality improvement circles involving about 36 percent of the plant's workforce. Each circle is a team, made up of 10 to 20 workers from the same process area of the plant trained to analyze and solve quality-control problems. Recently, members of the "Quick-Reliable-Accurate" team devised a solution to a persistent door scratch problem on Toyota Camrys assembled at the plant. The scratch resulted from an electric screwdriver slipping in a worker's hand while installing the door lock. The team eliminated the problem by devising a plastic plate that was slipped onto the doors to protect them from scratching during installation of the locks. If this improvement is adopted by Toyota assembly plants worldwide, it could save the company $6 million annually.[17]

Product Decisions

Sometimes regular control system or marketing audit results indicate that, for a product to become profitable or return to profitability, it must be significantly changed. Marketers must evaluate the situation and decide whether or not the costs of change are justified when compared to the potential benefits. If they are not, a sometimes painful product withdrawal decision may be required.

In a business with many different products and lines, control results may be used to make choices between products, particularly when it comes to budget support. Products that can support a business's growth goals may be awarded significantly greater resources than are less profitable products. This can also have business-level implications, affecting decisions about which businesses should make up the corporate portfolio.

Product Portfolio Decisions   Just as individuals have investment portfolios in stocks, bonds, and other monetary instruments that comprise their financial holdings, large corporations have business portfolios made up of their **strategic business units (SBUs)**, businesses that operate with greater or lesser degrees of autonomy under the corporate umbrella. SBUs are the company's business holdings. Individuals make decisions about what investments to buy, sell, or hold in order to achieve their financial goals. Corporations make similar buy, sell, and hold decisions about their SBUs, along with strategic decisions about resource support for each SBU.

Because there is no single best formula for determining how many products a business (strategic business unit or independent business) should have in order to achieve its goals and how each product should be managed, SBU portfolio model techniques have been adapted for use in making product decisions. **Product portfolio models** provide insight into individual product or product line cash contributions to the business and their potential by comparing them along such dimensions as their market share compared to the market growth rate. A popular portfolio approach, shown in Figure 15.6, is The Boston Consulting Group (BCG) model.[18] This model is a simplified version of reality that can be helpful only in developing descriptive insights about the relative productivity of products.

The BCG model is well-liked, perhaps partially as a reflection of its colorful designation of products in the cells of the four-quadrant matrix. Products are labeled as either stars, cash cows, question marks, or dogs. A product's location in the matrix depends on its relative productivity (market share) and the growth potential of the market in which it competes (growth rate). In bottom-line terms, products or product lines are compared by their relative cash value to the business.

For example, if a business has five products, using the BCG approach each would be analyzed (often using data collected from control systems or a marketing audit) and located within a cell of the matrix based on an analysis of its share-growth profile. The cell space each product occupies reflects the actual size of that product's cash contribution in relation to the others with which it is compared. Although market growth rate is largely uncontrollable, market share will respond to marketers' actions. Some typical responses *suggested* by a product's location in the BCG matrix include:

- Hold and milk cash cow products in order to support other business operations and to build question marks, because cash cows generate excess cash over their costs.

strategic business units (SBU)
Businesses that operate with varying degrees of independence under the same corporate umbrella.

product portfolio models
A technique for gaining insight into product cash contributions and their potential.

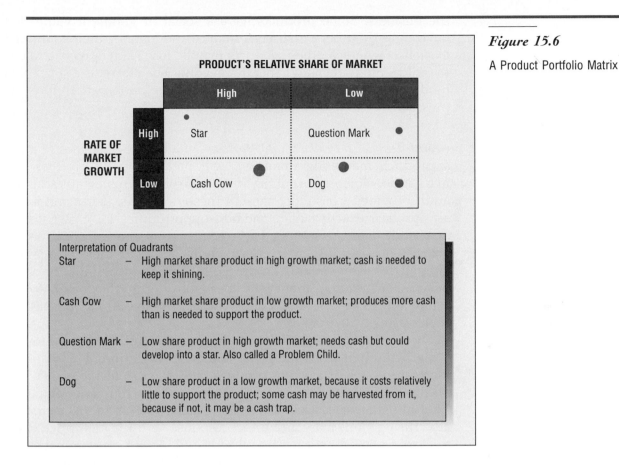

Figure 15.6

A Product Portfolio Matrix

- Build market share by feeding cash to the question mark products, nurturing them so they can develop into cash cows or stars.
- Harvest question mark products—sell them off, because it will cost too much to get them to become stars.
- Divest dog products in order to raise cash to feed the stars to get them to shine more brightly.
- Leave the stars alone as long as they shine, polishing them when necessary by adding cash.

Portfolio analysis methods, on both the product and business levels, have descriptive value but often result in dubious prescriptions. Although they can provide insights into relative product or business productivity, they should not be used as the sole justification for making product or business decisions, for several reasons. In many cases, it is difficult to determine exactly where the separation occurs between the categories: At what point does a cash cow cross a matrix line to become a dog or even a star? In addition, there are reasons other than cash value for judging a product's contribution to the business: Some products have a social or goodwill value that outweighs their poor cash performance and justifies their continued existence, whereas other products may be loss leaders whose role is to build store traffic and generate revenue. The matrix is a simplified model of what is in reality a complex situation; therefore, its prescriptive value is minimal.

Growth Decisions: Products and Markets   If a business decides to grow a product, marketing managers will have to make product and market decisions. Information from control systems or a marketing audit provides a base for many of these decisions. Because it is not always clear exactly where the best opportunities for growth exist, marketing managers often use such tools as the product/market growth opportunity matrix (see Figure 15.7) to identify feasible alternatives. This organizing device may be used by large or small business marketing managers to identify growth potential and actionable strategies, and assess the relative costs and benefits of each strategic alternative.

Box 1 in Figure 15.7 identifies an opportunity for achieving growth through the strategy of **market penetration.** This requires increasing sales of existing products among current target markets without changing the products or markets. Growth may be achieved by stimulating sales and market share using such tactics as increased advertising, both mass and direct response, and through price deals and couponing in freestanding inserts and instant coupon machines. Because no brand, no matter how good, is purchased by all the people within its target market, marketing efforts may be directed toward encouraging nonpurchasers in the target market to switch brands.

Campbell Soup Company has developed a **contraseasonal marketing** strategy of market penetration designed to get current users

market penetration Increasing sales of existing products among current target markets without changing the products or markets.

contraseasonal marketing A strategy of market penetration designed to get current users to use the unchanged product at nontraditional times.

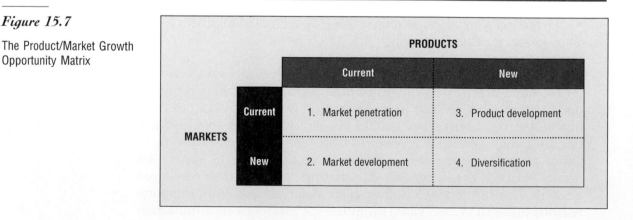

Figure 15.7

The Product/Market Growth Opportunity Matrix

Marketing Application 15.3

Can you think of other ways contraseasonal marketing could be used other than by Campbell Soup Company? Form two- to three-person teams to brainstorm ways that other national brands could use this strategy. Compare team lists and identify the most interesting and feasible ideas.■

to use the unchanged product at nontraditional times. Instead of heavy advertising just in the coldest winter months, when about 50 percent of sales occur, Campbell is increasing advertising spending in the off months and deemphasizing soup as just a cold weather food.[19]

Alternatively, marketing managers may be able to identify growth opportunities in new markets without changing the product. These markets may be in geographic areas other than those currently being served, other cities, other states, and even other countries. The **market development** growth strategy (Box 2 in Figure 15.7) also suggests identifying new markets by demographic or psychographic characteristics or industry. Thus, a baby shampoo was repositioned for adults who were encouraged to baby their hair; various jeans makers widened their markets by targeting denims to a trendier, stylishly relaxed lifestyle; and many of the largest U.S. fast-food businesses are expanding into institutional settings such as universities, factories, and airports in their search for new markets.

market development
Identifying new markets by demographic and/or psychographic characteristics.

By adopting a **product development** strategy (Box 3 in Figure 15.7), products are changed or new ones developed but the market remains the same. Thus, a product line may be extended to include different product formulations or quantities as well as new products.

product development The strategy of changing products or developing new ones while the market remains the same.

Finally, there are growth opportunities in **diversifying** (Box 4 in Figure 15.7), offering new products to new markets, outside existing product and market lines. Diversification is risky for businesses expanding into products beyond their core competencies. Alternatively, instead of buying new products and markets, the decision could be to develop new products in-house. However, developing new products and markets not related to the core business can be very costly, requiring a considerable investment in people, time, money, and materials.

diversifying Offering new products to new markets outside of existing products and market lines.

Other Product Decisions Growth decisions are not the only ones that follow from control system outcomes. Good control outcomes may result in a decision to maintain the status quo. Maintenance decisions often reflect satisfaction with the product as well as the market.

Marketing on the Internet

In his 1959 book, Peter Drucker introduced the term "knowledge worker." People perform many different kinds of knowledge work, from market research to neurosurgery. However, in general, knowledge workers have advanced formal educations, can apply theoretical and analytical knowledge to problem solving activities, and learn continuously. While the industrial labor force is shrinking dramatically in most industrialized countries, the number of knowledge workers is growing. Many processes that are credited with increasing productivity, particularly computer-assisted management, multifunctional teams, and just-in-time delivery systems, rely on knowledge skillfully applied. Sustainable competitive advantage depends on how well knowledge is acquired and used.

Marketers are knowledge workers and, as such, are well suited to collaborate in the commercialization of the Internet. Marketers can use their consumer insight, facility in managing the Four Ps (product, price, place, and promotion), skill in developing long-term relationships, and adeptness in boundary spanning to develop the potential of cyberspace marketing. The Internet can revolutionize the way products are developed, promoted, placed, and priced. In this textbook, we have examined Internet commercialization almost from its inception. As knowledge accumulates about successful Internet marketing efforts, marketing on the Internet will accelerate. As technology makes Internet access as easy as turning on a television set, marketers will use their knowledge to facilitate growing numbers of mutually satisfying exchanges in cyberspace in ways that we cannot even dream of today. ■

P. F. Drucker, "The Age of Social Transformation," *The Atlantic Monthly* 274, no. 5 (November 1994), pp. 53–59, 62, 64, 66–68, 74–78, 90; G. Moody, "How Do You Do Business over the Internet?" *Computer Weekly*, September 29, 1994, p. 47; J. Sandberg, "Net Working: Corporate America Is Falling in Love with the Internet," *The Wall Street Journal Reports: Technology, The Wall Street Journal*, November 14, 1994, p. R14.

The decision may be to harvest the product: milk the cash cow of its excess cash while not investing in product support. Another choice is divestment: selling off a business or part of a business, or discontinuing a brand, product, or product line. Even products that were once revolutionary may be discontinued if control results are unsatisfactory. The last product in the Apple II line, the Apple IIe, which sold 5.5 million units in its 16-year history, was discontinued by Apple because it represented only 2 percent of 1993 sales.[20] P&G has eliminated several low-productivity brands, including Puritan cooking oil and White Cloud bathroom tissue.[21]

Check Your Understanding 15.3

1. Explain the use of marketing control systems.
2. What is a marketing audit?
3. How may control system results be used?

A FINAL WORD ABOUT MARKETING

Although this chapter concludes our discussion of marketing in this textbook, it should not end your association with marketing. Marketing is deeply ingrained in our lives and society. Because market-

Career Watch

George J. Bull is the CEO of Grand Metropolitan PLC, a British-owned international corporation with third-quarter 1993 sales of $11.3 billion and operating profits of $1.4 billion. Grand Met currently operates three main groups that offer products familiar to most Americans: retailing (Burger King, Pearle Vision), liquor (J&B, Smirnoff, Bailey's), and food (Pillsbury, Green Giant). Since 1987 it has divested a hotels group, betting shops, and a pub chain. Bull vows to focus the company on its core branded foods and drinks and has pledged to maintain or expand its $1.3 billion market-ing budget to do so. In his over 30 years at International Distillers & Vitners Ltd. (IDV), he played a significant role in taking a small business and turning it into the world's largest spirit company. He is called a "tough but inspiring manager." Bull's marketing management expertise is needed at Grand Met to improve its profitability and provide strategic direction. ◼

J. Flynn, L. Therrien, and G. DeGeorge, "A Grand Design for Grand Met," *Business Week,* December 20, 1993, pp. 58–59; J. Valente, "Grand Met's New CEO Emphasizes Premium Brands," *The Wall Street Journal,* October 7, 1993, p. B4.

Photo 15.5

George Bull, CEO of Grand Metropolitan PLC in London.

ing is such a powerful economic force and societal change agent, marketing activities must be constantly monitored—not just by government regulators, but also by private citizens and consumer groups. Marketers who claim to adhere to the marketing concept must be held to the highest scrutiny to ensure that abuses do not occur and, if they do, that the abusers are caught and punished. The power of marketing to change society should be harnessed to serve the public good as well as deliver business profit. Marketing delivers a standard of living and should be a living standard for ethical practices and ethical people.

Review of Chapter Objectives

1. *Explain the role of the marketing manager.* Marketing managers are found at many different levels in large organizations. Regardless of organization size, market-ing managers are responsible for the planning, imple-mentation, and control of marketing activities and people. Contemporary marketing managers are more apt to use management styles that call for involving employ-ees in making decisions, taking responsibility, and shar-ing risks and rewards. This is often identified as *partici-pative management.*

2. *Explain the role of the marketing plan.* The marketing plan is the blueprint for marketing actions. Marketing plans specify product—market matches, marketing mix tactics, evaluation and control mechanisms, and resource allocations. The marketing plan typically covers a one-year period, although some plans may be written for two years.

3. *Describe implementation activities.* Implementation is the activation of marketing plans. Implementation involves organizing, staffing, and supervising marketing employees, who are performing marketing activities.

4. *Explain the function of marketing control.* Control is the system used to evaluate marketing performance and outcomes. Gaps between expected and delivered results may call for various types of responses.

5. *Discuss how control results may be applied in marketing.* Control results are used in making various marketing decisions, many of which involve products and markets. Often, a business will use a product portfolio model to provide insight into the comparative productivity of products.

Key Terms

After studying Chapter 15, you should be able to define each of the following key terms and use them in describing marketing activities.

Marketing Managers, 487
Participative Management, 490
Marketing Management, 493
Marketing Program, 494
80–20 Rule, 499
Implementation, 500
Organizing, 501
Staffing, 501
Supervising, 501

Downsizing, 502
Control, 502
Marketing Audit, 504
Kaizen, 505
Strategic Business Units (SBUs), 506
Product Portfolio Models, 506
Market Penetration, 508
Contraseasonal Marketing, 508
Market Development, 509
Product Development, 509
Diversifying, 509

Discussion Questions

1. Why are marketers called *boundary spanners*? Do you think this is an appropriate designation?

2. Contrast the jobs of category manager and brand manager.

3. How are the jobs of general manager and marketing manager alike?

4. Why are small businesses important to the economy and marketing?

5. What is the marketing program? Why does it require careful coordination?

6. Discuss the interrelationship and interdependence of planning, implementation, and control.

7. Explain why ignoring the 80–20 rule can be a serious mistake for the marketing manager.

8. Compare and contrast authoritarian and participative management styles.

9. Could a business exist for long without some controls? Explain your answer.

10. What role does marketing play in the consumer's life? In society?

What Do You Think?

Small businesses are finding that they must become more efficient in order to survive in the highly competitive 1990s. Rather than just struggling to survive, many small businesses are improving their productivity, cutting costs, and running leaner operations. They also are finding that teaming up with other small businesses in co-ops and alliances can give them breaks on manufacturing and marketing costs. Other ways they are tuning up is by upgrading workers' skills, outsourcing jobs (hiring temporary workers or consultants), forming buying alliances, and improving their telecommunications and computer systems, finding a

way to market on the Internet, and adopting efficient consumer response systems. Improvements in technology and company restructuring are expensive, and many of the productivity-enhancing activities also have reduced profit margins. However, many small businesses also say the expense is worth it. They have to become more efficient to survive. What do you think?

Sources: L. Touby, "The Big Squeeze on Small Business," *Business Week,* July 19, 1993, pp. 66–67; D. Merrefield, "Does ECR Mean Much for Independents?" *Supermarket News* 45, no. 5 (January 30, 1995), p. 2; R. Peterson, "Strategic Alliances Also Can Aid Small Businesses," *Marketing News* 27, no. 11 (May 24, 1993), p. 2.

Mini-Case 15.1

China Coast Restaurants—Coast to Coast

There are over 28,000 Chinese restaurants in the United States, but not one nationwide sit-down chain. General Mills Inc. is trying to change that. In Florida, the company has been testing a Chinese restaurant concept called China Coast, and will soon add other locations to the chain. With so many Chinese restaurants already in most cities, the question is whether or not General Mills can make a go of this new venture. The company is no stranger to chains: It has 670 Red Lobster and 458 Olive Garden restaurants already responsible for almost a third of the company's revenues (almost $8 billion annually). The key to good Chinese food is always the chef, and having enough good Chinese cooks for a nationwide chain will pose a considerable challenge. Considering that the U.S. Oriental restaurant market is

$6.5 billion, General Mills obviously believes the risk is worth taking.

Case Questions

1. Explain how marketing managers may use planning, implementation, and control in determining whether or not to expand the China Coast chain nationwide.

2. General Mills is trying to grow a new business. Where would this fit in the product/market growth opportunity matrix shown in Figure 15.7 (i.e., what strategy is it)? Explain your answer.

Sources: R. Gibson, "General Mills Tries to Cook Up Fix for Restaurant Unit," *The Wall Street Journal,* November 16, 1994, p. B4; J. Whalen, "General Mills Turns East for Inspiration," *Advertising Age* 65, no. 33 (August 8, 1994), p. 4; R. Gibson, "China Coast Restaurants May Mushroom," *The Wall Street Journal,* April 18, 1993, pp. B1, 5.

Mini-Case 15.2

Managing Marketing and the Information Revolution

Businesses worldwide are spending billions of dollars annually to wire their companies for the information revolution. Computer networking is changing the ways in which businesses and marketing are managed. Computer networks instantaneously connect people around the world. Meetings can be held and teams formed without regard to where employees are physically located. People are directly connected to other people and data. Because of the freedom and power of electronic networking, the nature of management and work is changing. Planning, budgeting, supervising, and controlling are vastly different when everyone has access to the same information at the same time.

Because personal computers are now cheap enough for almost everyone to have one on their desk, a technological network is replacing the hierarchial networks that used to dominate management in many businesses. Processes such as trading stocks, stocking inventory, routing orders, and developing new products can be done by computer, involving employees at multiple locations simultaneously. Management is becoming less formal and more interactive.

Information overload is a looming problem, and E-mail messages in particular can overwhelm recipients. For example, in a typical month Hewlett-Packard's 97,000 employees exchange 20 million E-mail messages inside and 70,000 outside the company. Electronic systems designed to speed customer service instead become clogged. Too much information is coming in, circulating, and being trashed. By 1994, Americans had over 148 million E-mail addresses, a 365 percent increase from 1987. Since 1983, the number of personal computers in offices in the United States has increased by 25 million; since 1987, the number of fax machines in offices and homes has increased by 10 million. It is estimated that almost 120 trillion messages were left on voice mailboxes in 1993.

Case Questions

1. How can the information revolution help marketing management?

2. How can the information revolution frustrate marketing management?

Sources: T. A. Stewart, "Managing in a Wired Company," *Fortune*, 130, no. 1 (July 11, 1994), pp. 44–56; R. Tetzeli, "Surviving Information Overload," *Fortune* 130, no. 1 (July 11, 1994), pp. 60–64; J. A. Byrne, R. Brandt, and O. Port, "The Virtual Corporation," *Business Week*, February 8, 1993, pp. 98–102.

Chapter 15 Notes

1. M. Hammer and J. Champy, "Avoiding the Hottest New Management Cure," *INC.* 16, no. 4 (April 1994), pp. 25–26.

2. J. A. Byrne, "The Horizontal Corporation," *Business Week*, December 20, 1993, pp. 76–81.

3. Nielsen Marketing Research, "Category Management: Marketing for the '90s," *Marketing News* 26, no. 19 (September 14, 1992), pp. 12–13.

4. K. T. Higgins, "Category Management: New Tool Changing Life for Manufacturers, Retailers," *Marketing News* 23, no. 20 (September 25, 1989), pp. 1, 19.

5. K. T. Higgins, "Firms Tune-Up Their Management," *Marketing News* 23, no. 20 (September 25, 1989), pp. 1, 26.

6. W. G. Nickels, J. M. McHugh, and S. M. McHugh, *Understanding Business,* 2nd ed. (Homewood, IL: Richard D. Irwin, 1990), p. 331.

7. J. Case, "A Company of Businesspeople," *INC.* 15, no. 4 (April 1993), pp. 79–93.

8. T. W. Zimmerer and N. M. Scarborough, *Small Business Fundamentals* (Columbus, OH: Merrill, 1988), pp. 15–16.

9. S. Pearlstein, "Riding into the '90s on the 'Gazelle,'" *Washington Post National Weekly Edition* 10, no. 20 (March 15–21, 1993), p. 22.

10. H. Goetsch, "Integrated Marketing Plans Help Small Businesses Stay Ahead," *Marketing News* 27, no. 23 (November 8, 1993), p. 14.

11. J. B. Clark, *Marketing Today: Successes, Failures and Turnarounds,* 2nd ed. (Englewood Cliffs, NJ: Prentice Hall, 1990), pp. 203–21.

12. S. N. Chakravarty, "The Best-Laid Plans . . .," *Forbes* 153, no. 1 (January 3, 1994), pp. 44–45; J. B. Treece, "Kmart: Slick Moves—Or Running in Place," *Business Week,* January 17, 1994, p. 28.

13. K. Pope, "Compaq Can't Cope with Demand for Pro-Linea PCs," *The Wall Street Journal,* July 10, 1992, pp. B1, 12.

14. S. Pearlstein, "The Downsizing Trap," *Washington Post National Weekly Edition* 11, no. 11 (January 10–16, 1994), pp. 8–9.

15. F. Rose, "Job-Cutting Medicine Fails to Remedy Productivity Ills at Many Companies," *The Wall Street Journal,* June 7, 1994, p. A2.

16. C. Miller, "TQM Out; 'Continuous Process Improvement' In," *Marketing News* 28, no. 10 (May 9, 1994), pp. 5, 20; P. R. Cateora, *International Marketing,* 8th ed. (Homewood, IL: Richard D. Irwin, 1993), pp. 310–11.

17. S. Togo, "American Workers, Getting Up to Scratch," *Washington Post National Weekly Edition* 11, no. 16 (February 14–20, 1994), p. 22.

18. G. S. Day, "Diagnosing the Product Portfolio," *Journal of Marketing* 41, no. 2 (April 1977), pp. 29–38.

19. E. Shapiro, "Food Firms Seek a Plan for All Seasons," *The Wall Street Journal,* July 29, 1993, pp. B1, 6.

20. J. Schwartz, "Goodbye to an Old Friend: The Apple II, 1977–1993," *Washington Post National Weekly Edition* 11, no. 9 (December 27–January 2, 1994), p. 22.

21. C. Hymowitz and G. Stern, "Taking Flak: At Procter & Gamble, Brands Face Pressure and So Do Executives," *The Wall Street Journal,* May 5, 1993, pp. A1, 8.

Writing a Small Business Marketing Plan

As you learned in Chapters 2 and 15, a marketing plan is a blueprint that describes how the marketing mix variables will be used to satisfy consumers and achieve organizational goals. Although marketing plans take many different forms, *in general* they follow an outline like that shown in Figure 15.3 (see page 496) but at varying levels of detail. As you will see in the following example, sections that are appropriate to a large corporation marketing plan may not be useful in a small business marketing plan, and vice versa.

Why should a marketer take the time to write a marketing plan? Although no plan can ever guarantee success, it is generally accepted that writing a good marketing plan, and effectively implementing and controlling it, can help the marketer cope with volatile environments, risk, and uncertainty. The discipline required to carefully work through each section of a marketing plan can be highly beneficial in itself, since the business is forced to systematically address issues that are sometimes considered only superficially if at all.

How do you write a marketing plan? The best way to learn is by doing one yourself. For that reason, an opportunity for you to *learn by doing* is presented in the Student Study Guide that accompanies this textbook. Before you try writing a marketing plan, however, you should read through the following example of a marketing plan for a small business to get an idea of what is involved.

GETTING STARTED

Do you remember the Chapter 13 opening story about Alicia Hernandez, the owner-operator of several fresh fruit, vegetable, and flower shops? Hernandez must write a marketing plan to accompany her request for a small business loan to weatherize one of the stores so it can stay open year-round. She is seeking help from a marketing specialist in the Small Business Development Center (SBDC) at the local state university. The SBDC is part of the U.S. government's Small Business Administration (SBA). Hernandez got the local SBDC's address and telephone number from the government listing in her city's telephone book. If she had looked them up in the Small Business administration listing on the Internet, at address http://www.sbaon-line.gov, she could have read about SBA services and small business success stories, as well as found the local SBA number to call.

At their first meeting, the SBA marketing specialist, Salah Rudel, asked Hernandez to describe her business. She told Rudel that she opened her first store in the early 1980s. Because she operates from March to October (closing during the coldest winter months), the stores are designed to give the appearance of a roofed-over open-air market. Fruits and vegetables are inside the store, attractively stacked in woven baskets on long, rough wood tables. Store fronts are wide open and filled with large displays of seasonal flowers, ceramic fountains, and hanging ferns. In the fall, summer flowers are replaced by piles of pumpkins, gourds, and potted chrysanthemums. Hernandez contracts with a local herb farm to supply fresh herbs in pots and a basket weaver to supply handwoven baskets. A friend, who is a caterer, operates a small in-store kitchen, making fruit salads to go or on order. Hernandez's store employees are all high school and college students, with the exception of the company's full-time bookkeeper.

Competition includes area chain and independent grocery stores, a local farmer's market (open seasonally three days each week), and several health food stores and owner-operated fruit and vegetable stores. Her target market includes students, faculty, and staff from three nearby universities, lawyers, doctors, and other professionals, vegetarians, and anyone who enjoys high quality, fresh products, at fair prices, seven days a week, 8 AM to 8 PM. For the first time, she faces strong direct competition from a store much like her own, one that offers consumers similar goods in convenient locations.

Hernandez and Rudel met several times over the next three weeks. They evaluated the information Hernandez provided, talked through her goals for her business, and systematically developed the sections of her marketing plan. When they were finished, Hernandez had a marketing plan that could help her increase her businesses' profitability, even in the face of new competition, *if* she is successful at implementing the plan and controlling the outcomes. Hernandez has spent a considerable amount of time working with Rudel to develop the marketing plan. At each step, she also consulted her key employees, having them provide information and suggestions that she brought to her meetings with the SBA marketing specialist. Hernandez is confident that, with the help and encouragement of her loyal employees, Alicia's soon will be acknowledged as the best produce value in the city and exceed estimated profit projections.

An abbreviated copy of Hernandez's marketing plan is provided on the following pages. As you read through this plan, consider the issues that Alicia Hernandez, as the owner of a small business, must face. How are these similar to and how are they different from the issues covered in the general marketing plan outlined in Figure 15.3?

A Small Business Marketing Plan
ALICIA'S
Fresh Fruits, Flowers, and Vegetables

I. **Executive Summary**

Alicia's follows the marketing concept philosophy of doing business. Alicia's employees are committed to satisfying customers and building long-term relationships with them. Alicia's will build on the loyalty of its customers using service, top-quality products, and fair prices, to sustain its competitive advantage.

II. **Situation Analysis**

A. **Industry**—Small, owner-operated retail produce stores have always done well in locations where products can be delivered quickly from the farmer or wholesaler to the store. Area farmers like these stores because they can deliver their products directly to the retailer and cut out the wholesaler, which increases their profit. Strong growth is forecast for these specialty stores, mainly because of the growing numbers of consumers who are concerned about their health and believe in the value of eating nutritious food. Recent reports linking diets low in fruits and vegetables with cancer and heart disease have helped stimulate interest in eating fresh produce. Alicia's also offers an organic produce section for consumers who want their fruits and vegetables free from pesticides and other chemicals that can harm the environment.

B. **Company**—Alicia's has shown steady revenue growth from the opening of the first store. There has not been a year without profit, although several years in the late 1980s had lower than expected profit. Costs also have shown a steady rise, particularly those related to rents, taxes, and salaries. Produce costs have remained relatively steady, with cost peaks in years with droughts, floods, or cold spring months.

C. **Product**—Alicia's has become known throughout the area for high-quality products, friendly employees, fair prices, and excellent service. All fruits and vegetables are top grade, fresh, and ripe. Prices are only slightly higher than those found in national chain grocery stores and slightly lower than other grocery stores and produce stores. Alicia's offers a home delivery service for homebound senior citizens and others who cannot or prefer not to shop for themselves. For a small charge (10 percent of the total bill), a phoned-in order will be filled and delivered directly to the customer's home or office within a prearranged time period. All store orders are carried to the customer's car. Employees are trained to help customers pick out the ripest produce. Alicia's assembles and delivers fruit gift baskets and special order fruit salads. In 1995, Alicia's had a 19 percent market share, annual sales of $2.1 million, and a net income of $224,000.

D. **Market**—Most of Alicia's customers live in the city or adjacent small towns. The combined area population is just under 300,000. The city's largest employer is the state's major land grant university. Other large employers are the two other universities, seven for-profit hospitals, a university hospital, a major automobile plant 20 minutes north of the city, an international computer printer facility, and various financial institutions. Alicia's customers are college educated (64 percent) with annual household incomes above national averages: singles' incomes average over $28,000 and couples' incomes average over $47,000. More than 60 percent of Alicia's customers own computers or use them at work; over 30 percent are linked to the Internet. Customer loyalty is high, and the same core group comes back year after year. Their positive word-of-mouth advertising is an important asset and responsible for Alicia's strong community image. The internationalization of area businesses has brought a large number of foreign nationals to the city. Many have become steady customers at Alicia's, where they find high-quality produce and a product line that has been expanded to satisfy their tastes. The city is becoming a retirement center. Many retirees take advantage of the state university's Senior Scholars program that extends free enrollment in any university class to anyone of retirement age or older.

E. **Competition**—Strong competition comes from Treadley's, a national chain whose stores blanket the city. They have the highest market share and heavily promote their fresh produce sections. Two recently opened Treadley superstores have extensive fruit and vegetable sections, in-store floral departments, and garden flowers for sale in season. Other competitors are several independent groceries that have limited fresh produce sections, a warehouse club that offers fresh produce in bulk packages, other owner-operated fruit and vegetable stores that are smaller than Alicia's and have higher prices, and the Farmer's Market, where local farmers sell products from the back of their trucks. The newest competitor, Malcolm's, poses a serious threat to Alicia's. It is owned and operated by a local family that also runs a highly successful plant nursery and greenhouse operation, along with a landscaping service. Malcolm's has been in the area since 1966 and has a loyal customer base. They have opened two farm stores in prime locations and plan to open at least two more within the next three years. Their product line is broader than Alicia's and includes fresh milk, farm fresh eggs, and local fresh cheeses. They are using their greenhouses to grow herbs for the farm stores. They plan to be open year-round. They do not deliver.

F. **Other environmental factors**—The local economy is strong and has been less vulnerable to national economic downturns than any other city in the state or region. This means that demand for Alicia's products should remain steady (and growing), cushioned against recessions. City unemployment is averaging 3.4 percent annually.

III. **Marketing Objectives**

A. **Objectives**—Alicia's has a loyal customer base. These customers and new ones like them are the targets of Alicia's marketing efforts. The top priority is to satisfy these customers and build long-term relationships with them. Service is Alicia's competitive advantage, supported by high-quality products and fair prices.

B. **Measures**—Alicia's seeks to raise its market share to 24 percent within two to three years and increase sales revenues $250,000 within one year. The small business loan will be used to winterize the highest profit store so it can be open year-round. Alicia's will become more involved in community affairs and particularly in the support of environmental issues locally. Alicia's will extend its services and product lines to better satisfy its customers.

IV. **Marketing Strategies**

A. **General marketing strategies**—Alicia's seeks to be positioned as the best service provider in the area, offering top-quality, fair-priced, high-value products. It will continue to target its present target markets and extend its service area to other communities whose residents come to the city for their shopping.

B. **Specific marketing strategies:**

Product—Alicia's will determine what products and services customers want using a customer survey. Fruits, vegetables, flowers, and herbs that are not currently available at Alicia's will be offered on special order. If sufficient demand is identified, these products will be stocked regularly. Alicia's will continue to offer only fresh, top-quality products.

Price—Alicia's will offer competitive prices, even on specialty products. When prices must be higher, Alicia's will make sure that customers know they are paying more for a reason, whether it is a drought, flood, or being out-of-season. Alicia's pricing plan aims at prices set between 15 to 20 percent above cost.

Place (Distribution)—Alicia's will extend its free delivery area to include all local universities, nursing homes, senior citizen retirement complexes, and government offices. Because so many customers and other city residents have computers and links to the Internet, Alicia's will rent home page space on the local CityNet service. This is a directory of local businesses that provides information about such things as operating hours, location, and product mix. Visitors to Alicia's home page will be able to make fruit, vegetable, flower, and herb orders by E-mail. Alicia's will deliver the order within a prearranged time period. In addition to taking orders, Alicia's home page will offer fruit and vegetable recipes, give tips on growing herbs, and have an announcement section where local environmental groups can leave messages and list meetings.

Promotion—Alicia's will undertake promotion strategies outlined in Chapter 13 for direct mail, sponsorships, radio, and print.

V.   **Tactics**

Responsibilities—Ned Hernandez, Alicia's husband and a computer programmer, will design the CityNet home page and make all arrangements required to get it up and running. Erik Hernandez, Alicia's son, a senior majoring in marketing at the local state university and a long-time store employee, will develop the print and radio advertisements with the help of in-house advertising professionals at the city newspaper and local radio stations. Patrice McGuire, the company's bookkeeper, will help develop sponsorships. An outside agency or consultant will implement the direct-mail campaign and conduct customer surveys.

VI.   **Budget**

A budget of $75,000 has been set to carry out the activities outlined in previous sections. The cost of weatherizing the one store is in the loan amortization budget in the appendix section.

VII. **Control**

Alicia Hernandez will supervise all activities and work with Patrice McGuire to monitor costs and revenues on a weekly and monthly basis. Store counts will be taken on a daily basis to track customer arrivals and departures. Ned Hernandez will implement all computer activities and monitor results. Erik Hernandez will track sales from radio and print advertising. The outside consultants will monitor direct mail results and analyze all customer surveys. Profit and loss statements will be prepared at the end of each quarter and figures will be tracked to determine if the objectives are being accomplished.

VIII. **Appendixes**

Attached to the end of the marketing plan are various materials that support sections of the plan. These include résumés of key personnel and additional financial statements.

Using Mathematics in Marketing Decisions

Many marketing decisions involve mathematical measures, their calculation, interpretation, and application. These measures provide information that is essential to making good marketing decisions about the effective and efficient use of the Four Ps (product, price, place [distribution], and promotion). Mathematics is fundamental to marketing.

A REVIEW OF SOME BASICS

Place

The place value system based on numerals and their relation to a decimal point allows us great precision when we are making mathematical calculations and communicating the result of these calculations to others.

Figure B.1 illustrates the precision with which even a large number can be communicated. The decimal separates the whole numbers (also called integers, natural numbers, and counting numbers) from the number parts to the right of the decimal point. Marketers must be able to read place values, express them, and use them in making comparisons and identifying relationships. Even a small mistake in reading a number's place in relation to a decimal can have unfortunate results.

Percent

Many of the mathematical expressions used in marketing are in percentage form. A percent expresses what part one thing is of something else on a base of hundredths. News commentators talk about percent changes in Gross Domestic Product; manufacturers complain about percent increases in raw materials prices; and advertising agencies worry about percent decreases in network television viewing.

Many marketing decisions rely on establishing numerical relationships. Therefore, it is important to be able to convert whole numbers, decimals, and fractions to percentages.

Figure B.1

Place Values

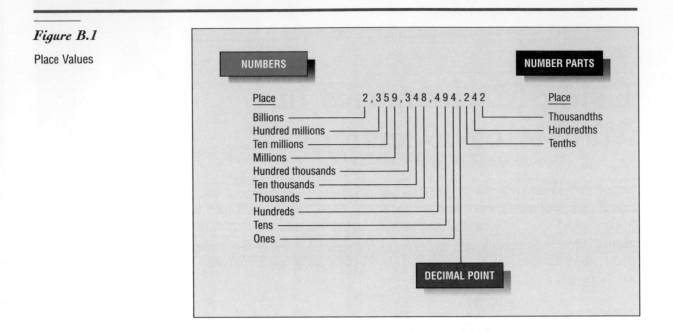

The expression 25% can be expressed as a decimal, a common fraction, and a reduced fraction. The decimal is formed by taking 25% (which is also 25.0%), moving the decimal two places to the left, and dropping the % sign. The fraction is formed by placing the numerator (in this case, 25) over the hundredths denominator. The reduced fraction is formed by finding the greatest common factor and dividing by it. For some numbers, there is no common factor and further reduction of the fraction is not possible. The conversion process is illustrated below:

Percent *to* Decimal *to* Fraction *to* Reduced Fraction

$$25\% = 25.0\% = 25.0\% = 0.25 \quad = \quad {}^{25}/_{100} \quad = \quad \frac{1}{4}$$

Move decimal two places to the left

Ratios

A ratio is another way of comparing numbers. For example, we often hear of advertising to sales ratios, written as A/S. This is a comparison of advertising expenditures to sales. It can be used to compare a company's A/S ratio to an industry, to a competitor, or even to its own A/S ratios over a period of several years. For example, if a company spends $2M on advertising and their sales for 1996 are $80M, their A/S ratio is 2/80 which can be reduced to 1/40. This gives a ratio of 1:40 which is read, one to forty. The colon means that we are to compare 1 and 40. Therefore, the company spends $1 on advertising for every $40 in sales. On a percentage basis, 2.5% of their sales is allocated to advertising. This is calculated as follows:

$$A/S = \frac{\text{Advertising } \$}{\text{Sales } \$} = \frac{1}{40} = 0.025 = 2.5\%$$

MARKET SHARE

Marketers must often determine what part of a market is held by a brand, product, or company compared to its competition in a particular market. Market share expresses your sales in relation to total sales. Most marketers, particularly those following a growth strategy, want to have a larger and growing market share; other marketers are content to just not lose market share.

Market share can be calculated by units sold as well as for revenue dollars. For example, if total category sales for all brands of peanut butter sold in the southeastern United States in 1996 is 16.0 million units and Crunch brand peanut butter sells 0.6 million units, the market share (MS) for Crunch brand is calculated:

$$MS = \frac{\text{Brand Sales}}{\text{Total Category Sales}} = \frac{0.6 \text{ Million Units}}{16.0 \text{ Million Units}} = 3.75\%$$

Market share also can be calculated for services, on a dollar sales amount or for other comparative units, such as clients served.

ADVERTISING AGENCY COMMISSIONS

For years, the standard media commission received by recognized, full-service advertising agencies was 15%. This practice goes back to the last century when advertising agencies were space brokers, buying blocks of space in magazines and newspapers and then reselling the space to advertisers.

The standard 15% commission works as follows: The media bills the advertising agency the full price for placing the advertisement for its client, the advertiser. The agency charges the client the full price and keeps 15% of this amount as their media commission. In other words, the media rebates 15% to the agency placing the advertisement as payment for the media purchase. The 15% commission is still used by slightly under 50% of American advertising agencies, although it is being replaced by various negotiated fee structures, cost-plus arrangements, sliding scales, and other payment forms. See Figure B.2 for the payment flow in the commission system.

Figure B.2   Payment Flow for a 15 Percent Agency Commission

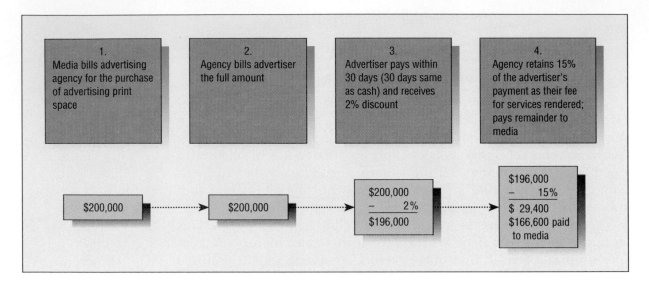

INCOME STATEMENTS/PROFIT AND LOSS STATEMENTS

Income statements are summaries of profits and losses compiled for a prespecified period of time, typically as a record of financial transactions over a tax year. These statements also are used in reports made to the government, stockholders, and the public.

While there are some differences in the exact format used, the simplified income statement shown in Figure B.3 is representative of standard profit and loss statements, identifying categories of revenues and expenses, and providing the summary information needed to calculate important performance ratios.

The first number on the income statement is **gross sales,** the total amount of money that came into the business from product sales over the recording period. **Returns and allowances** are reductions made against gross sales for such items as returned goods that had to be marked down, stolen goods, and employee discounts. After returns and allowances are taken out of gross sales, the remainder is **net sales.** The **cost of goods sold (COGS)** records how much it actually cost the business to make its products available for sale to consumers. It represents the cost of manufacturing and obtaining the finished goods to sell. The categories that combine to make the COGS are the inventory at the beginning of the reporting period, the ending inventory, and purchases made during the period. The **gross margin (gross profit on sales)** is the difference between net sales and

Figure B.3   A Simplified Income Statement

A&S COMPUTERS
Income Statement
for the year ending
December 31, 1996

Gross Sales		$1,620,000
Less returns and allowances		120,000
Net Sales		$1,500,000
Sales Revenues		
Beginning inventory at cost	$ 53,800	
Net purchases.	1,024,900	
Goods available for sale	1,078,700	
Less ending inventory at cost	46,600	
Cost of Goods Sold (COGS).		1,032,100
Gross Margin (Gross Profit on Sales)		$ 467,900
Less Operating Expenses		
Salaries.	$ 169,600	
Travel	18,400	
Depreciation	4,100	
Miscellaneous office expenses	2,000	
Marketing	119,700	
Insurance	30,000	
Utilities	4,700	
Payroll taxes.	23,100	
Total Operating Expenses		$ 371,600
Less Nonoperating Expenses		
Bad debts	$ 1,200	
Loan interest.	16,000	
Total Nonoperating Expenses		$ 17,200
Total Expenses		$ 388,800
Net Income (Profit or loss before taxes)		$ 79,100

the COGS. It represents the profit on merchandise sales revenues before expenses are deducted and is the amount available to operate the business.

Expenses may be listed in one category or divided into two broad categories, **operating expenses** and **nonoperating expenses.** Expenses are totaled and subtracted from the gross margin to derive the **net income,** which is profit (or loss) before taxes.

PERFORMANCE RATIOS AND MARKETING ANALYSIS CALCULATIONS

Performance ratios are used to compare a business's performance to an industry average, a group of competitors, a market leader, or the business itself over a previous period. These ratios communicate information about a business's relative financial health. Some frequently used performance ratios are described in the following sections.

The **gross margin ratio** indicates the amount (by percent) of each sales dollar that can be used to cover operating expenses and taxes and be applied toward achieving the profit target.

$$\text{Gross Margin Ratio} = \frac{\text{Gross Margin}}{\text{Net Sales}} = \frac{\$467,900}{\$1,500,000} = 31.19\%$$

The **net income ratio** is net income divided by net sales, which indicates how much of each dollar in sales can be identified as before-tax profits.

$$\text{Net Income Ratio} = \frac{\text{Net Income}}{\text{Net Sales}} = \frac{\$79,100}{\$1,500,000} = 5.27\%$$

The **cost of goods sold ratio** is COGS divided by net sales.

$$\text{Cost of Goods Sold Ratio} = \frac{\text{COGS}}{\text{Net Sales}} = \frac{\$1,032,100}{\$1,500,000} = 68.8\%$$

The **operating expense ratio** is a measure of how much of each dollar is needed to be applied toward operating expenses. It is a measure of operating efficiency. Expenses may include such categories as salaries and benefits, marketing costs, administrative expenses, rents, and utility charges. Taxes are deducted from net income (profit).

$$\text{Operating Expense Ratio} = \frac{\text{Total Expenses}}{\text{Net Sales}} = \frac{\$388,800}{\$1,500,000} = 25.92\%$$

The **inventory turnover ratio** (or stockturn rate) indicates how many times in a year the average inventory is "turned over" or sold. If the number is lower than the industry average, it indicates that too much inventory is being held "on hand"; if the number is higher than the industry average, then the firm is turning over their stock faster than the industry average, which indicates that it has high demand for its products. It can be calculated in several ways, including:

$$\text{(a) Inventory Turnover in Dollars} = \frac{\text{Cost of Goods Sold}}{\text{Average Inventory at Cost}}$$

$$\text{Average Inventory at Cost} = \frac{\text{Beginning} + \text{Ending Inventory}}{2}$$

$$\text{(b) Inventory Turnover in Units} = \frac{\text{Net Units Sold}}{\text{Average Inventory in Units}}$$

$$\text{Average Inventory in Units} = \frac{\text{Beginning} + \text{Ending Inventory}}{2}$$

PRICING: MARKUPS/MARKDOWNS

You are probably familiar with price markdowns from your experiences as a personal use consumer. Price markdowns are the price changes most consumers like. They are often taken at the end of a season, when merchandise isn't selling fast enough, or when it has been damaged.

A markdown is an adjustment made in the selling price, reducing the price to a level that will encourage a consumer to purchase the product. For example, if a sweater from the markup example that follows is left at the end of the season and it is marked down to $45, that markdown is a change of $15.

$$\text{Markdown percent on Original Selling Price} = \frac{\text{Change in Selling Price}}{\text{Original Selling Price}}$$

$$25\% \text{ Markdown} = \frac{\$15}{\$60}$$

A markdown can also be calculated based on the sale price, which provides a greater incentive for the consumer to make a purchase.

$$\text{Markdown Percent on Sale Price} = \frac{\text{Change in Selling Price}}{\text{Sale price}}$$

$$33\% \text{ Markdown} = \frac{\$15}{\$45}$$

What consumers don't see are markups, the amount that each channel of distribution member adds in order to cover that channel member's costs and make a profit. The markup is added before the product is sent to the next member of the channel and it (the markup) plus the cost are the selling price.

Some marketers use a fixed (also called standard) markup for all of their products. This is often true in specialty retail stores where the retailer knows that a particular markup percentage is needed in order to cover costs and make a target profit. For example, a standard industry markup in jewelry stores is around 50 percent; it is often several hundred percent in furniture stores.

To illustrate how markups work, consider the following example:

Manufacturer's cost to produce a sweater	$20.00
Adds a 25% markup	+ 5.00
Selling price to wholesaler	$25.00
Wholesaler's cost to purchase the sweater	$25.00
Adds a 50% markup	+ 12.50
Selling price to retailer	$37.50

Retailer's cost to purchase the sweater $37.50
  Adds a 60% markup   + 22.50
  Selling price to personal use consumer $60.00

$$\text{Markup Percent on Cost} = \frac{\text{Amount Added to Cost}}{\text{Cost}}$$

If, instead, the markup is calculated on the selling price, it will be less than the markup percentage calculated on cost, as long as selling price is greater than cost. This assumes the same dollar markup is used.

$$\text{Markup Percent on Selling Price} = \frac{\text{Amount Added to Cost}}{\text{Selling Price}}$$

Introduction to Marketing Careers

As society changes and we continue into the information age, jobs in marketing will change and new opportunities will develop. Jobs will appear that are not even imaginable today. Consider that people 50 years of age or older who are alive today did not have color or cable television, microwave ovens, personal computers, cellular telephones, compact discs, or telephone answering machines when they were children! These products have led to the creation of jobs that didn't exist before the products were developed and commercialized. We don't know where the information highway will take business, but we do know that we are entering an exciting time that holds considerable promise for marketers and the development of new marketing jobs.

A career begins with a first job. Whether you are a traditional student seeking your first, entry-level marketing job or a nontraditional student seeking a first job after a career change, you must take responsibility for your job search, organize and direct your job search efforts, and be determined to stick with the process until you find the marketing job that is right for you. Set goals for yourself at each step of the search process and give yourself sufficient time to accomplish them. Use all available job search resources, especially the career planning and development office at your school.

From reading this textbook, you can begin to grasp the differing marketing activities. Understandably, the many different marketing activities result in a corresponding diversity of marketing career paths and marketing job types. When you think that millions of Americans work directly or indirectly in marketing, you can understand why any attempt to describe each and every type of marketing job would soon become overwhelming. Therefore, this appendix is about marketing employment *in general*, and you must expect that there will be many differences in specific job definitions and responsibilities.

COMPLETE A SELF-INVENTORY AND PERSONAL MARKETING PLAN

It is important to begin any job search by evaluating your personal job-related strengths and weaknesses and the value that you bring to a job. You should also clearly understand what you are seeking in a job. If you aspire to enter or advance in marketing, you should think of the process in terms of marketing yourself: developing a marketing plan for finding a good match between your skills, abilities, experiences, and interests and an appropriate marketing job that leads to a rewarding marketing career in the long term. You are encouraged to work through the exercises in the "Marketing Yourself" section in the Student Study Guide that accompanies this textbook. In "Marketing Yourself," you will find such job search aids as a matrix for identifying your job-related strengths and weaknesses, tips on writing a résumé and developing interviewing skills, and a marketing career resource reference list. These exercises and resources will help you create a personal marketing plan as shown on page C–3.

DEVELOP THE SKILLS THAT EMPLOYERS VALUE

Although it is impossible to identify the skills valued by each and every marketing employer, some skills are generally highly valued, regardless of marketing job type. These include:

- **Communication skills**—Writing and speaking fluently, expressing your thoughts accurately and concisely, and listening carefully.

- **Learning skills**—Pursuing lifetime and job-specific learning and educational attainment.

- **Information skills**—Skillfully using modern tools and technologies to identify information needs and resources, retrieve information, and use it in making sound marketing decisions.

- **People skills**—Knowing how to interact effectively with customers, work productively on teams, negotiate, and be flexible in developing collaborative solutions to marketing problems.

- **Creativity skills**—Seeking new ways to solve old problems and seeking unexpected paths to achieve organizational success, avoiding habitual responses to situations that demand unique reactions.

- **Motivation skills**—Willingly taking the initiative and encouraging others to do so, accepting leadership responsibilities, and sticking with a task until it is successfully completed.

A Marketing Plan Outline for Marketing Yourself to Prospective Employers
Your Name
Date

I.   Executive Summary

A one- to two-page summary that includes key points from each section designed to provide an overview of the high points of the plan.

II.   Situation Analysis

A detailed analysis of the factors that will influence your success in marketing yourself to prospective employers. Information can be obtained from your personal records; from academic records; and, for external information, from government documents, industry and trade journals, industry and company reports and articles in the current popular business press, and many sources on the Internet.

A.   Industry analysis including employment trends, growth forecasts, demand patterns, and job types in the industries where you are most interested in working, for example, in retail, wholesale, agriculture, health care, or government.

B.   Company analysis for the businesses where you would most like to work, including their history, mission, current employment situation, projected growth, core competencies, strengths and weaknesses, hiring practices, names and addresses for obtaining employment forms, and contacts.

C.   Product analysis including a summary of your academic background, relevant courses completed, job experiences, professional interests, organizational memberships, job location preferences, value you can bring to a job, and a thoughtful analysis of what you want and expect from a job.

D.   Market analysis of occupational forecasts from such sources as the U.S. Department of Labor and U.S. Department of Commerce.

E.   Competitive analysis including characteristics of others who may be competing for the same jobs, both entry-level applicants and applicants with experience, their relative strengths and weaknesses, and distribution.

F.   Analysis of other environmental factors that may affect your job search including economic forecasts, political outlook, technological advances, and relevant social forces.

III. Marketing Objectives

A statement of the objectives set for marketing to accomplish in your job search.

A.   Identification of priority objectives to be satisfied, time frames for achieving objectives, time limits by which specific job search activities are to be completed.

B.   Objective specification of goals on the basis of résumés mailed, job contacts made, interviews completed, job offers received, or other quantifiable measures.

C.   Specification of other objectives, for example, establishing a network of contacts and learning about job opportunities or how to conduct a job search.

IV. Marketing Strategies

A statement of how marketing will achieve the objectives and goals.

A.   Statement of general marketing strategies for positioning (making a prospective employer aware of your value compared to other job applicants), and your competitive advantage.

B.   Statement of specific marketing strategies, particularly for gathering needed information, obtaining necessary assistance from others, obtaining employment forms, making contacts, and arranging interviews.

V.   Tactics

A statement of how the strategies will be implemented. This includes plans for each of the marketing mix elements.

A.   Identification of tactical responsibilities, how others may assist in your job search including employment contacts, job and character references, your school's career office personnel who can help you develop job search and interview skills, professional employment agencies, and resources for conducting Internet job searches.

B.   Product tactics including improving necessary job and interview skills and selection of appropriate clothing to wear to a job interview.

C.   Price tactics including statements of price points from introductory pricing (lowest beginning salary) to mid- and top salary expectations, price adjustments (when you would reasonably expect to receive increases), and benefits including vacations, medical, dental, retirement, and profit-sharing.

D.   Place tactics including if and where you are willing to relocate, and whether or not you are willing to travel some, moderately, or extensively on the job.

E.   Promotion tactics including plans for producing hardcopy and electronic résumés, development of employer mailing lists, identification of employment bulletin board addresses on the Internet, and newspaper classified advertisement sections.

VI.   Budget

A statement of how the budget is to be allocated with associated costs.

A.   Detailed analysis of costs including those associated with résumé production and distribution, interviewing, travel and clothing costs, postage, telephone, and electronic expenses.

B.   Detailed breakout of allocations for how budget will be spent to cover costs and market the product.

VII.   Control

A detailed description of how the marketing plan will be evaluated by outcome measures; benchmarks and time frames should be provided along with the construction of a time line that identifies key time periods when objectives should be accomplished.

VIII.   Appendixes

At the end of the marketing plan, additional materials that support various parts of the plan, including transcripts, letters of recommendation from teachers or previous employers, samples of best work including class reports and analyses, industry reports, articles on job search skills, and lists of contact names and addresses.

In addition, there are job-specific skills associated with the major categories of marketing jobs. It is important for entry-level job seekers to identify the job skills needed in the marketing employment areas that interest them, then take the initiative and obtain the skills they currently lack.

IDENTIFY TRENDS IN THE EMPLOYMENT ENVIRONMENT

As you have learned in this textbook, marketing activities take place in volatile environments that can affect marketing decisions and change even the most carefully planned outcomes. These same environments affect marketing jobs. As a job seeker, you should stay informed about environmental factors that affect employment including job demand, availability, and changing occupational requirements. Look for employment trends, because they often present rewarding employment opportunities. An excellent source of information about the occupational outlook is the U.S. Department of Labor, Bureau of Labor Statistics, which issues labor force projections and identifies emerging employment trends biannually for 10 to 15 years in the future.

The Information Revolution

In all industrialized societies, work is changing as businesses, governments, individuals, and organizations rely on increasingly more sophisticated information technologies to accomplish their objectives. The information revolution is transforming jobs and the way people do them. Marketing, like the other business professions, is feeling the effects. Marketers with the ability to use computers and sophisticated information search technologies should find rewarding jobs in the next century.

Demographic Changes

Population changes also affect employment opportunities, and changes in the composition and size of the population will influence demand for products as well as for the people who produce and market them. Geographic shifts in population will strongly affect local job markets; therefore, information about job prospects on a national level may be far less accurate for a particular local job market.

Employers have rising expectations about the educational attainment of entry-level employees. This is associated with the dramatic rise in the numbers of college graduates over the last two decades. Job growth rates are expected to be higher for careers that require greater educational training.

Changes in lifestyles and consumer values affect marketing jobs. For example, consumers with less spare time demand more services and convenience products. This is particularly true for working parents with home and family responsibilities. Likewise, growing international competition will result in greater numbers of international marketing jobs.

COLLECT JOB-SPECIFIC EMPLOYMENT INFORMATION

Many traditional sources provide information about marketing jobs and career paths, including:

- Your college or university placement center.
- Professional organizations and trade associations.
- Career guidance books and periodicals, library career databases.
- Career or job fairs.
- People employed in the type of job you'd like to have.
- Business magazines and newspapers.
- Industry and company information.
- State employment offices.

There is also a new and exciting way to locate employment information—on the Internet. Students who can reach the Internet can access a large and constantly growing collection of employment information. Since the Internet changes rapidly, often daily, addresses also may change; however, standard search methods should continue to deliver useful employment information, if properly used. Always use caution on the Internet, assume that privacy is not assured, and investigate employment offers carefully before you pursue them.

OPPORTUNITIES IN MARKETING

One of the first questions most entry-level job seekers ask is "How much salary can I expect to earn?" No single answer can be accurate because many different factors affect compensation packages, including such considerations as educational attainment, previous experience, company size, company location, job requirements, and benefits. Generally, entry level marketing majors can expect beginning salaries somewhere in the $20,000s. Beginning advertising account executives often start at around $20,000; market research analysts often start around $25,000; sales representatives can begin in the mid- to high $20,000s, particularly if they work on part or whole commission. Although marketing skills come into play in many, many careers, most marketing-related jobs fall into the broad job areas described as follows.

Marketing on the Internet

There are many different ways to locate employment information on the Internet. The following suggestions represent only a small subset of what is available. Employment information searches can be made with a text-only or a graphics browser. Graphics browsers often differ in how address instructions are accepted; therefore, text-only browse instructions are provided, with the understanding that they can also be used by graphics interfaces.

Locate a search engine such as jughead or veronica. Activate the search by typing in the word JOBS and then press the enter key. This sends for a list of directories that is 20 computer screens long. This comprehensive list is filled with informative directories and files that can be used to refine job search skills and locate job openings. For example, the list provides access to job resource directories that include multiple files on job-related business and marketing topics. Directories provide hypertext links to such information sources as America's Job Bank, FedJobs, International Jobs, and Jobnet. Different directories have information on careers, employment services, and employers. Employment information links can be made to Career Magazine, Career Taxi, the U.S. Department of Labor's *Occupational Outlook Handbook*, the Catapult, and various other career resource directories.

Job seekers searching the JOBS and its hypertext links can find their way to such resources as:

- **CareerMosaic**—A service that lists jobs from throughout North America, primarily in high technology fields, but also in business. Includes employer lists, college connections, and college and university home pages with links to career resource centers.
- **The Monster Board**—Lists job openings primarily in the northeastern United States; can be searched by key descriptors; accepts résumés; lists on-line virtual career fairs.
- **Online Career Center**—A nonprofit association of employers in the United States and abroad that posts job opportunities and résumés; can be searched by job title, company, or other key descriptors; provides on-line career resources, employment events, résumé assistance.
- **Federal Jobs**—Job postings for agencies of the United States government; also can be accessed through fedworld.gov.
- **Career Magazine**—A net magazine that compiles articles, résumés, job listings and career resource links. ■

Sales

Entry-level jobs in marketing are often found in **sales.** The many different types of sales jobs include retail selling as well as business-to-business and direct sales. Many job seekers enter the marketing professions through sales and jobs with such titles as sales and service representative, sales associate, inside sales representative, real estate broker, insurance agent, sales trainee, claims representative, purchasing agent associate, and telemarketer. Marketers sell both goods and services, to personal use consumers as well as to other businesses, governments, and organizations.

Retail

It is estimated that as many as 20 to 30 percent of civilian jobs in the United States are in **retail.** These jobs have titles such as sales associate, assistant buyer, retail associate, customer relations associate, regional marketing associate, merchandise assistant manager, and store buyer. Retailers conduct marketing activities designed to facilitate exchanges with personal use consumers. There are store and nonstore retailers. Store retailers may work in department stores, warehouse clubs, discount centers, specialty shops, or countless other facilities. This is primarily a sales activity, but marketers also work as merchandise purchasers, obtaining the stock needed to supply a store or chain.

Advertising/Promotions/Public Relations

Many other job seekers find positions in **advertising** or **promotions.** They hold such job titles as advertising account associate, advertising sales representative, media planner, media buyer, advertising account executive, marketing communications assistant, account services representative, and advertising researcher. They may work in a full-service advertising agency, a creative boutique, a media buying service, a television or radio station, a newspaper or magazine, a Yellow Pages directory, a promotions company, or a marketing communications business. Some work in the creative part of marketing promotions; others work strictly in customer service and account management. Other jobs are in **public relations,** as a public relations assistant, event planner, project coordinator, or promotions/special events manager. Many jobs involve customer service activities designed to build long-term relationships with customers.

Research

Jobs in **marketing research** often have such titles as marketing research assistant, assistant analyst, sales analyst, interviewer, field research assistant, or research analyst. In addition to gathering information about consumers, buying habits, and what is happening in the marketplace, marketing researchers also monitor the competition, identify target markets, and work with new product development teams to test consumer acceptance of new products. Research is conducted by various channel members as well as by marketing research businesses. Marketing research can be about consumers, markets, products, pricing, distribution, and promotion.

Product Development/Distribution

Jobs in **product development/distribution** often require the ability to work in new product development teams, or as part of a team managing the sales of a brand or product line. Among the job titles are marketing management trainee, product coordinator, assistant brand manager, assistant category manager, and product planning assistant. These people are involved in all aspects of product, from new product idea generation through commercialization and product management. Their work involves packaging products, pricing, distributing, and selling them.

International Marketing

As the volume of international business increases, demand for marketers will grow within both American and foreign-owned businesses. Jobs in **international marketing** are found in exporting and importing businesses, joint ventures, licensed manufacturing, and foreign subsidiaries. Marketing activities are similar to those in domestic markets, but with the added dimension of marketing in foreign markets with their different laws, customs, languages, practices, and expectations. International marketing jobs often require travel, language expertise, and heightened cultural sensitivity. Jobs are found in international product development, pricing, distribution, and promotion. International selling and promotion activities are often more complex than similar activities conducted solely in domestic markets mainly because they are so culturally bound. When products are marketed across country borders and ethnic groups, great care must be taken not to give offense or to violate cultural taboos that can cause negative consumer reactions.

Small Business Marketing

The majority of new jobs in the past decade were generated in small businesses, often by entrepreneurs who left corporations to start their own business. Small business marketing opportunities are in retail, wholesale, consulting, franchising, and many types of in-home business enterprises. Small business entry-level positions most often are in personal selling; however, a salesperson may also write company brochures, place advertisements in local newspapers and electronic media, participate in developing a marketing plan, assist in product development, and place products through distribution channels. A small business is often one of the best places to learn how to perform all marketing activities.

Not-for-Profit Marketing and Services

Many job opportunities are in **not-for-profit** and **services marketing.** Many colleges and universities, as well as private elementary and secondary schools, must market their services and offer interesting and challenging job opportunities, particularly in the area of promotions. Professional groups, religious organizations, special interest groups, and trade associations hire marketers to promote their activities. For-profit and not-for-profit services dominate the American economy and are the source of the majority of American jobs. These include marketing jobs in retail services, health care services, financial services, personal care services, and customer services. Generally, service jobs are highly people-intensive and require strong communication and interpersonal skills.

Glossary

80–20 Rule The observation that 80 percent of a business's revenue is generated by 20 percent of its customers.

Acceptable Price A price between the price ceiling and the price floor.

Advertiser The business, organization, person, or other sponsor who pays for the advertisement.

Advertising Nonpersonal marketing communication mostly conveyed in the mass media and paid for by an identified sponsor who controls the message.

Advertising Campaign A coordinated series of advertisements using one or many media designed to convey a unified message and image about a product.

Advertising Research Research on advertising and copy effectiveness, recall, and media choice.

Advertising Triad The three main participants in advertising when outside resources are used: The advertising agency, the advertiser, and the media.

Agents Distribution intermediaries with legal authority to act in the name of a manufacturer.

AIDA *A*wareness, *I*nterest, *D*esire, *A*ction: A model for the tasks set for advertisingas it moves the consumer toward a purchase.

Allocations The amounts set aside from the budget for specific marketing activities.

Annual Plans Plans based on decisions made for an entire year, most often beginning January 1 or the first day of a federal or state fiscal year.

Augmented Product What the consumer expects beyond the core product and the seller adds to make the offer more attractive.

Baby Boomers People born from 1946 to 1964.

Barter A nonmonetary exchange, involving the trading of products, labor, or other things of value for possession or use of something else.

Boundary Spanner The salesperson who is employed by the company to promote its products while building customer loyalty.

Brand A name, symbol, design, or other element that identifies one seller's product and differentiates it from all others.

Brand Equity The added financial value of owning a popular brand with a valuable image.

Brand Extension Inclusion of additional products usually in the same product category under the original brand's name (e.g., Dial bath soap extended to Dial deodorant).

Brand Loyalty Repeated purchases made by consumers on the basis of brand name.

Brand Manager Marketing professional having overall responsibility for a brand, including monitoring sales, planning changes in the brand's marketing mix, developing responses to competition, allocating resources, and deploying people to ensure the brand's profitability.

Brand Mark   A visual brand identification, like the NBC peacock, Apple Computer's apple, or Quaker Oats's Quaker.

Brand Name   The spoken version of the brand identification (e.g., Coke, Tide, MasterCard).

Break-Even Point (BEP)   The point at which total revenue equals total costs at a particular price per unit.

Brokers   Distribution intermediaries who directly bring buyer and seller together to negotiate a sale.

Budget   A plan that specifies how much money can be spent on a marketing activity, like promotion.

Business   A for-profit organization under a single management.

Business and Organization Consumers   People making purchases on behalf of their companies, to use in production processes, for resale, or to operate a business.

Business Group   A multifunctional team of professionals from marketing, production, and other areas who manage a group of products and concentrate on such activities as product development.

Buying Center   A more-or-less formal group of people who work together to make a purchase decision.

Cannibalizing   Stealing market share from one or more of a company's own brands by another in the same category.

Capacity to Perform   The combined total of an employee's experience, training, and general ability that affects the ability to provide good work performance.

Category Manager   A mid-level marketing manager responsible for all the products in a category, usually with many brands.

Channel of Distribution   A collection of businesses that cooperate to place products where consumers need and want them.

Channel Structure   The form of a distribution path—its length, arrangement, and size.

Churn   A change in people's circumstances resulting in their names no longer being desirable on a particular direct marketing list.

Clutter   An excessive number of promotion contacts that a consumer experiences in a period of time.

Cobranding   Doublebranding or piggybacking of one distinctive brand onto another.

Cognitive Dissonance   Postpurchase consumer dissatisfaction.

Conglomerates   Large groups of different types of businesses within a single corporate structure.

Conspicuous Consumption   The use of purchases to indicate a person's financial worth.

Consumer Behavior   All the activities involved in selecting, purchasing, evaluating, and disposing of products.

Consumer Behavior Research   Research about consumers and their behavior and preferences in the marketplace.

Consumer Bill of Rights   The right to have safe products, to be informed about products, to choose from among a variety of products, and to be heard and have complaints resolved.

Consumer Confidence   The positive or negative feelings consumers have about the present, the future, their job security, and their spending ability.

Consumer Gap Analysis   Determining the difference between what consumers need (or want) and what is currently available to them.

Consumer Insight   Understanding the consumer's perspective about marketplace activities.

Consumer Satisfaction   Correspondence between what the consumer expects and what the marketer delivers.

Consumerism   Activities undertaken to defend and protect consumer interests.

Continuous   An advertising schedule that maintains the same base level of advertising overtime.

Continuous Product Innovations Products that differ only slightly from existing ones and require little if any effort by the consumer to learn their use.

Contraseasonal Marketing A strategy of market penetration designed to get current users to use the unchanged product at nontraditional times.

Control Evaluation of marketing performance and outcomes in order to learn whether or not marketing goals have been met and, if not, why not.

Cooperative A group of retailers who have voluntarily associated themselves for business purposes.

Copy Platform Statement of how verbal elements are to be used in an advertisement; outlines the creative plan; provides direction for using creative alternatives.

Cost Plus Pricing Price setting that covers costs plus an extra increment to deliver profit.

Creative Mix The integration of the verbal message (copy) and visual images (art) that give an advertisement its consistency and impact.

Cultural Blinders A preferential view of one's own culture that blinds the observer to the value of the ways of another, different culture.

Cultural Borrowing Adopting elements from another culture.

Cultural Change Changes resulting from cultural borrowing.

Cultural Sensitivity Viewing people from other cultures objectively, respectfully, and non-judgmentally.

Culture The social institutions, values, beliefs, attitudes, customs, languages, and preferences that a group uses to solve problems and keep order.

Culture Clash Failure of people to understand and accommodate patterns of behavior and attitudes of people from a different culture.

Data The raw materials that make up usable information, such as facts, figures, observations, and reports.

Decisions Choices between sets of alternatives.

Demand Fluctuation Demand that shifts between various levels.

Demarketing A situation in which consumer demand is greater than product supply and the marketer must act to temporarily or permanently dampen demand.

Demographics Statistics describing a particular population in terms of age, income, birth and death rates, and education level.

Depth The number of items within a product line.

Derived Demand Demand for one product increases the demand for other products.

Descriptive Information Information describing what consumers do, buy, and say.

Design Product attributes developed to solve a consumer problem.

Deviant Consumer Behavior A variety of actions in the marketplace that are different from norms expressed by other consumers, marketers, and society.

Diffusion of Innovations The process of product acceptance within society.

Direct Exporting Keeping international marketing tasks within a parent company.

Direct Marketing The promotion mix element that uses computer databases and lists to direct mail and telephone offers to consumer targets.

Direct Ownership A company owns production facilities and manufactures and markets products abroad without partners.

Direct Response Various nonstore approaches, such as mail order, catalogs, and electronic forms that interact directly with the consumer.

Direct Response Advertising A form more personalized than mass advertising that attempts to establish a relationship with the consumer by encouraging interaction.

Direct Selling Nonstore retailing that brings products directly to the consumer.

Discontinuous Product Innovations Revolutionary new products that are unique or extremely different from existing products and require a considerable effort to learn their use.

Distinctive Competencies What the company and its businesses do best.

Diversifying Offering new products to new markets outside of existing products and market lines.

Domestic Marketing Marketing within a business's home country.

Downsizing Personnel reductions designed to increase company productivity and decrease costs.

Dual Distribution The use of two channels to distribute the same products to the same target markets.

Dumping The selling of a product abroad at price lower than it is sold for in the company's home market or lower than the cost of production.

Durable Goods Long-lasting goods that are replaced infrequently, such as washing machines, lawn mowers, and home freezers.

Dyad The connection between buyer and seller in a marketing exchange.

Dynamically Continuous Product Innovations Products that are different from existing products but not unique.

Elastic Demand Demand changes when price does, and the two change in opposite directions, for example, when price rises, demand falls.

Emotional Appeal An advertising message designed to use feelings to arouse a response.

Ethical Dilemmas Difficult situations in which there are valid but conflicting alternatives and it may not be clear which action or decision is right.

Ethics The moral principles and values that both establish expectations for people's behavior and determine standards that set limits and define the boundaries of good and bad.

Exchange A voluntary trading of items of value between parties.

Exclusive Distribution The strategy of restricting or limiting distribution, therefore narrowing the distribution system needed.

Exploratory Research Research conducted to collect information to help redefine or clarify a problem.

Export To offer finished products, supplies, and materials to markets in other nations.

External Marketing Environment All the external factors that directly affect or indirectly impact on marketing success.

Flexible pricing Changing price in response to changes in the environment.

Flighting A way of scheduling the placement of advertisements in heavy bursts integrated with periods of no advertising.

Fluctuating Demand Demand rises and falls, usually responding to the state of the economy.

Franchising A form of ownership in which a business agrees to allow another business to operate under a franchisor's name, offering the franchisor's products to consumers.

Frequency The number of advertisement repetitions consumers in a target audience experience in a fixed period of time.

Fund Raising Using marketing strategies and tools to develop and harvest revenue sources.

GATT The General Agreement on Tariffs and Trade, an association of 103 nations representing 80 percent of the world's trade, which is attempting to eliminate trade restrictions and encourage open markets.

Generalizability Occurs when data come from a representative, randomly selected sample population and the results can be projected from the sample to the greater population that the research was designed to test.

Global Marketing The use of a standardized marketing approach in all countries, based on the principle that the world is really just one market.

Goals Long-range, general, and relatively unbounded ends to be achieved.

Goods Physical products that can be felt, stored, inventoried, mass produced, transported, tested in advance of purchase, and controlled for quality.

Green Marketing Marketing activities that are environmentally friendly rather than environmentally harmful.

Gross Domestic Product (GDP) A composite figure indicating the total value of the products produced annually by a country.

Hardware Electronic equipment, such as computers, printers, and scanners.

Heterogeneous Dissimilar.

Homogeneous Alike.

Horizontal Integration Expansion and control resulting when one channel member buys out another at the same level.

Hypermarkets Very large stores, often 300,000 square feet or more that offer discounted general merchandise and supermarket products under one roof.

Image How the brand appears to the customer through such details as colors, use of symbols, packaging, displays, price, and how and where it is sold and advertised.

Implementation The activation of a marketing plan.

Import To bring finished products, supplies, and raw materials into the domestic market.

Impulse Purchase Something bought on a whim.

Incentive A short-term tangible item designed to move the consumer toward purchase.

Indirect Exporting Assigning products to an agent who markets the products abroad.

Industrial Products Goods and services used by businesses and organizations.

Inelastic Demand When demand remains the same, regardless of changes in price, as with essential products.

Infomercials Program-length, direct-response commercials that present products in an entertainmentlike atmosphere.

Information Knowledge that can be used to solve a problem.

Information Overload A situation that exists when the quantity and/or disorganization of information overwhelms and jeopardizes good decision making and the marketer's ability to analyze and use it.

Inseparability Consumption of the service at the same time that it is performed.

Integrated Marketing Communication (IMC) A coordinated promotion program based on consumer knowledge using messages, incentives, and delivery systems successfully used in the past.

Intensive Distribution The strategy of making products readily available in as many places as possible.

Intermediaries Members of a channel of distribution who cooperate and assist in completing the link between producer and consumer.

Internal Marketing Promotion of a business or organization to its employees in order to increase their understanding and make them more effective.

Internal Marketing Environment The departments and functions that affect marketing activities within the business.

International Marketing Marketing across national borders.

Joint Venture Companies working together to market products.

Just-in-Time Systems An inventory tracking system that results in materials and supplies being delivered at the right time. This may be just in time for production, operations, or to restock shelves, thus reducing or eliminating storage time, warehousing costs, or idle production time.

Kaizen A Japanese principle that is a commitment to continual improvement in products and processes and enhancement of quality.

Law of Demand The hypothesis that when prices rise, consumer demand falls, and vice versa.

Laws Formal statements that guide actions and set limits and penalties for infractions.

Lifetime Value Customers' loyalty and patronage over their consuming life.

List A prime set of names and addresses identified by specific characteristics in a database.

Long-Range Plans Plans that reach ahead for 5, 10, 25, 50, or more years.

Macroculture An entire society's culture.

Macromarketing The way marketing contributes to our economic system and overall societal welfare by balancing supply and demand.

Manufacturer's Representatives Wholesalers employed by one or several producers and paid on commission according to quantity sold.

Marginal Pricing Demand-based pricing estimating consumer demand for a product, then identifying the profit-maximizing price.

Market Buyers and sellers.

Market Development Introducing existing products to new target markets.

Market Penetration Increasing sales of existing products among current target markets without changing the products or markets.

Market Research Research performed to answer questions about market potential, share, targets, sales, and other issues related to specific markets.

Market Segmentation The process of grouping consumers by shared characteristics; the sorting of large groups of consumers into segments—smaller groups of consumers who are similar to one another and different from other consumer groups.

Marketers The people and organizations that perform the various marketing functions that connect a business and target customers in exchanges.

Marketing The process of planning and executing the conception, pricing, promotion, and distribution of ideas, goods, and services to create exchanges that satisfy individual and organizational objectives.

Marketing Audit An unbiased, comprehensive examination of the business's marketing activities conducted by impartial auditors.

Marketing Concept An operating philosophy that has customer satisfaction at its core and requires that not only marketing, but all business operational areas, cooperate to satisfy consumers and achieve business goals.

Marketing Concept Period The latter half of the 20th century.

Marketing Information System (MIS) A process for making marketing decisions using computers, in which information is collected, analyzed, and disseminated or distributed.

Marketing Management The set of marketing activities related to formulating strategies, planning activities, implementing programs, supervising personnel, allocating resources, and evaluating outcomes.

Marketing Managers People who guide marketing programs and people in the activities associated with offering products to markets.

Marketing Mix Variables The Four Ps: product, price, place, and promotion.

Marketing Plan A blueprint for using the marketing mix variables to satisfy consumers and achieve organizational goals.

Marketing Program All the operating marketing plans and activities that represent the total marketing effort at a particular time.

Marketplace Where exchanges are negotiated and made.

Markup Price increase.

Materialism A preference for material possessions over spiritual and intellectual pleasures.

Media Delivery systems for sending a message to an audience.

Media Plan Statement of what media are to be used, how often, and when.

Merchant Wholesalers Independent businesspeople who take title to the merchandise they handle and thereby assume all of the risks of ownership.

Message A set of words, images, and/or symbols encoded by a sender and sent to a receiver.

Microculture A small, distinguishable group within a macroculture.

Micromarketing The way marketing connects a business and its suppliers, distributors, and consumers in activities designed to deliver satisfaction.

Mid-Range Plans Plans based on decisions made for two to five years into the future.

Mission Statement A written definition of the present state of a business, indicating what the company should be at a specified time in the future.

Mixed Branding Manufacturers offer their products under their own national brand name and through store brands.

Modified Rebuys Rebuys of alternative products resulting from dissatisfaction with some aspect of the existing product.

Multicultural Society A society made up of cultures representing different backgrounds, preferences, and lifestyles.

National Brand Branded products distributed and known nationally.

Necessities Products that consumers consider indispensable, such as milk or gasoline.

Need A state of tension caused by a deprivation.

New Task Buy A purchase made for the first time that requires gathering additional information and selecting among alternatives.

Nondurable Goods Goods that are replaced frequently, such as laundry detergent, clothes, and perishable food.

Nonprice Competition A rivalry that deemphasizes or ignores price differences and emphasizes nonprice factors.

Not-for-Profit (NFP) Marketing Marketing in organizations in which earning a profit is not a primary goal.

Objectives Bounded, shorter-range, specific intermediate stages on the way to achieving goals.

Opportunity to Perform Physical, organizational, and environmental resources affecting an employee's work performance.

Organization A not-for-profit entity or an educational institution, or cultural or religious association.

Organizing Determining the organizational form needed to implement the marketing plan.

Participative Management A management method in which employees participate in setting goals, making decisions, taking responsibility, and sharing rewards and risks.

Peak Period Pricing Increasing prices during peak demand periods and lowering them during off periods.

Penetration Pricing Setting a low price to quickly penetrate the market, attract consumers, and build volume.

Perceptual Maps Plots of how consumers perceive different products or brands in relation to one another along several key measures.

Perishability A service or product cannot be stored, inventoried, or stockpiled.

Personal Selling Promotion that is direct and personal.

Personal Use Consumers People purchasing products for their own or family use, or to give as gifts.

Physical Distribution The overall process of moving products from producer to consumer.

Place Refers to where, when, and how the product is made available to consumers.

Planning A process for preparing to make quick, efficient, and effective decisions.

Planning Horizons Time frames indicating how far into the future the plan will reach and the time allotted to achieve the plan's goals.

Plans Coordinated, integrated, systematic sets of decisions that act as blueprints to guide future actions during a specified time period.

Positioning Consumer perception of a product in relation to others.

Potential Product What might be added to increase the value of the offer for the consumer; often what is called the "new and improved" version.

Prescriptive Information Information that marketers use to make decisions and solve marketing problems.

Price The amount charged for the product that generates revenues to cover costs and return a profit.

Price Ceiling The highest price that a consumer is willing or able to pay.

Price Comparison Evaluation of the value of a product according to its price in comparison to similar or even alternative products.

Price Floor The lowest price acceptable to a consumer.

Price Level The price set in relation to similar products on the market.

Price Lining Setting different prices for the different products in a line.

Price Range The span of prices that a consumer is willing or able to pay.

Price War Aggressive price cutting among competitors.

Primary Data Data collected specifically for the immediate task or problem.

Product Anything offered to buyers to satisfy their wants and needs in exchange for something of value; for goods, this includes packaging, warranties and guarantees, associated services, installations, and maintenance.

Product Adoption Process Stages from becoming aware of a product to adopting it.

Product Assortment The variety of products collected and offered to consumers.

Product Category Items in a different but related product line, or in the same product line but having different features.

Product Development The strategy of changing products or developing new ones while the market remains the same.

Product Differentiation Using the marketing mix variables to make a unique product offer.

Product Line A group of several related products that accommodate different levels of consumer need.

Product Mix All of the business's offerings, product lines, and product items.

Product Portfolio Models A technique for gaining insight into product cash contributions and their potential.

Product Strategy The planning efforts designed to bring products from the idea stage to commercialization.

Production Life Cycle (PLC) Cycle in which products are introduced, grow and accrue profits, reach maturity, and decline.

Production Period The late 1870s through the late 1920s.

Products   The items of value that the seller brings to the exchange and the buyer needs or wants.

Promotion   Activities—including advertising, personal selling, sales promotions, public relations, and direct marketing—used by marketers to communicate with consumers; persuasive, purposive marketing communication.

Promotion Delivery System   Any mechanism that delivers a message and/or incentive when it is most relevant to consumers.

Promotion Mix   The combination of promotion types used to reach a target audience and accomplish a promotion goal.

Promotion Plan   A blueprint for action that sets specific objectives to achieve over a designated time period.

Protectionism   Protecting domestic business at the expense of foreign business.

Public Relations   Promotions designed to establish goodwill between a business and others.

Puffery   Obviously exaggerated, generally harmless statements made in advertising.

Pulsing   An advertising schedule that runs some advertisements all the time interspersed with periods of heavy advertising.

Qualitative   Subjective information, such as observations and anecdotal reports.

Quantitative   Numerical facts and figures.

Rational Appeal   An advertising message designed to use logic to elicit a response.

Reach   The total number of consumers in a target audience who are contacted once in a fixed period of time using a particular delivery system.

Regulations   The rules, standards, and guidelines used by government agencies to implement laws.

Relationship Marketing   An approach that focuses on getting close to and connecting with consumers.

Reliability   Accuracy and consistency, characterized by lack of bias and freedom from random error.

Repositioning   Altering a brand's position in consumers' minds in response to changes in consumer demands and events in the environment.

Retail Chains   Multiple stores having common ownership and some measure of centralized management.

Retail Tasks   Buying, selling, and leasing products; communicating information about the products, their prices, and where they can be obtained; and negotiating product exchanges with consumers.

Retailer   A business or organization primarily involved in retailing, providing products (merchandise) for sale to personal use consumers.

Retailing   Marketing activities designed to present products (goods and services) for purchase in stores, catalogs, vending machines, and by television, telephone, and computer.

Reverse Channels   Return of products to a producer in a recall or recycling of products.

Sales Promotions   Short-term marketing techniques that add value through temporary sales incentives.

Scrambled Merchandise   An extensive merchandise assortment in many unrelated product lines.

Secondary Data   Data collected for purposes other than the immediate task or problem.

Selective Distribution   The strategy of limiting the number of product distribution points.

Self-Reference Criterion   A reaction to one's personal and cultural background.

Selling Period   The Great Depression to the mid-20th century.

Service Encounter The personal contact made between the business representative and the customer.

Service Mark Brand identification for services.

Service Provider The individual and/or organization that delivers a service to a consumer.

Service Quality The customer's evaluation of service performance.

Services Intangible, persihable products; activities that are performed for a customer, such as cutting hair, counseling, or entertaining.

Short-Range Plans Specific decisions made to run a business, business area, or marketing activity in the near future.

Situation Analysis An evaluation of a business's internal and external environments.

Skimming Pricing Setting the price high for a unique or very desirable product to attract a selective segment of the market; when competition increases, the price is usually reduced.

Socialization A learning process through which people learn acceptable ways to think and behave.

Societal Marketing Concept The marketing concept that includes the good of society as a business goal and requires that the business satisfy both consumers and society.

Society A political, geographic, and social entity defined by the rules, regulations, values, and behavior its people accept and by which they live.

Software Computer programs that perform such functions as spreadsheet, word processing, and database management.

Specialty Store A store that offers a limited line of merchandise with a great number of choices within that line.

Stable Pricing Strategy for maintaining price, regardless of changes in the environment.

Staffing Ongoing hiring, training, and supervising of personnel for marketing activities.

Standard of Living A measure of a country's economic health reflecting the kinds of products consumed, their quality, and quantities.

Status Conscious This describes consumers who use price as a surrogate for prestige or social prominence, flaunting the price they have paid as a measure of their social status.

Stockouts Failure to have merchandise available when needed.

Store Atmospherics The tangible and intangible elements that give a store its identity.

Store Brand Products sold by national manufacturers to distributors who put their own name on the product.

Store Image The way in which consumers perceive a store.

Straight Rebuys Repeat purchases of products that are bought and consumed on a regular basis; sometimes called *standing orders.*

Strategic Business Units (SBUs) Businesses that operate with varying degrees of independence under the same corporate umbrella.

Strategy A plan or method that establishes broad directions for future actions.

Supervising Overseeing, directing, and optimizing physical and organizational environments and personnel performance of marketing activities.

SWOT A systematic situation analysis of a business's strengths, weaknesses, opportunities, and threats.

Synergy In promotions, the integration and coordination of efforts designed to increase message impact.

Tactics The specific details on actions needed to advance a strategy.

Tangibility A product quality that can be perceived by the senses (e.g., touch, sight, smell, hearing, and taste).

Target Market Groups of consumers who are current or potential customers.

Target Marketing Selecting well-defined groups of potential customers and tailoring a marketing mix to their needs and preferences.

Tariff A tax on selected imports, designed to protect native industries.

Telemarketing Sales technique using computer-managed dialing systems and telephones to make sales.

Test Market A group of consumers in one or several cities who determine purchase responses by trying a new or improved product or the idea of a product.

Trade Deficit The imbalance occurring when the value of imports is greater than the value of exports.

Utility The benefit or value that buyers receive from an exchange.

Validity Measuring what you are trying to measure by asking the right questions and collecting the right information for the problem.

Value The consumer's definition of the worth added to products through marketing activities; consumers' evaluation of the relationship between the product's relative price, quality, and image.

Values What a society holds in high esteem.

Variability Differences in quality of service performance.

Vertical Integration When one member purchases another member at a different channel level.

Want A desire or preference that represents a socially molded need.

Waste Promotion contacts with consumers who are disinterested.

Wheel of Retailing The theory that as retailers become successful they leave room for newer businesses at the lower end of the market.

Wholesalers Intermediaries who sell to other distribution intermediaries and, sometimes, to final users.

Width The number of different product lines in a mix.

Willingness to Perform An employee's attitude and feelings that affect the ability to provide good work performance.

Window of Opportunity A chance for a business to meet a need or gap in the marketplace.

Workflow Automation A system using computers and software to distribute information.

Photo Credits

Number	Description	Credit
1.1	Instant coupon machine	Courtesy of Actmedia
1.2	Chinese open-air market	J. P. Laffont/Sygma
1.3	Audi advertisement	Courtesy of Audi of America, Inc.
1.4	Dolphin-safe tuna label	Richard Hutchings/PhotoEdit
1.5	International Coke labels	Courtesy of The Coca-Cola Company
1.6	SGD ad	Courtesy of SGD Corporation
1.7	Sprint ad (swimming pool)	Reprinted by permission of Sprint Communications Company L.P. Photo © Alan Krosnick.
1.8	Elvis stamp	Reuters/Bettmann
1.9A	Mazda ad	Copyright (1994) Mazda Motor of America, Inc. Used by permission.
1.9B	Jan Thompson	Robert Burroughs
2.1	AT&T ad	Courtesy of AT&T
2.2	Hotel lobbies	Courtesy of Kimco Hotel & Restaurant Management Co.
2.3	Amati luxury car	AP/Wide World Photos
2.4	Mel Weitz	Edward Santalone
3.1	Saturn ad	Used with permission of Saturn Corporation.
3.2	Fujitsu ad	Courtesy of Fujitsu Business Communications Systems
3.3	Clairol ad	Courtesy of Clairol
3.4	Michelin ad	Used with permission of Michelin Tire Corporation. All rights reserved.
3.5	Texas Instruments ad (printer)	© Texas Instruments, used with permission.
3.6	Texas Instruments ad (kids)	© Texas Instruments, used with permission.

Number	Description	Credit
3.7	IBM ad (balancing act)	Reprinted by permission from International Business Machines Corporation.
3.8	Wheaties box	Used with permission of Wheaties cereal.
3.9	Merrill Lynch ad	Reprinted by permission of Merrill Lynch, Pierce, Fenner & Smith Incorporated. Copyright 1992.
4.1	Ben & Jerry	E. J. Camp/Outline
4.2	Newman's Own label	Newman's Own, Inc.
4.3	MacGregor's Tomatoes	Courtesy of Calgene, Inc.
4.4	Health Jolting Chair	n/a
4.5	Recycled paper products	Tony Freeman/PhotoEdit
4.6	Susie Tompkins of Esprit	Larry Ford
5.1A	Family buying pumpkin	Alan Goldstein/Folio
5.1B	Elderly couple	Courtesy of Pepsi-Cola Company
5.2	KFC and Coke	Copyright © Al Guiteras/Nawrocki Stock Photo, Inc. All Right Reserved.
5.3	McDonald's billboard	Tony Freeman/PhotoEdit
5.4	Shani ad	© 1994 Mattel, Inc. Used with permission. All Rights Reserved.
5.5	Coke delivery in China	Ron McMillan/Liaison International
5.6	Port of Miami	Photo: Port of Miami/Dan Cowan
5.7	Chunnel	AP/Wide World Photos
5.8	Scott and Joe Montgomery	Scott Goldsmith
5.9	London Pier 1	Martyn Goddard
6.1	IBM ad (P.S. Value)	Reprinted by permission from International Business Machines Corporation.
6.2	Dow Jones ad	Courtesy of Dow Jones & Company, Inc.
6.3A	Ashcraft Research ad	Courtesy of Ashcraft Research
6.3B	M.O.R. ad	Market Opinion Research
6.4	Infiniti ad	Courtesy of Nissan
6.5	Bar code	n/a
6.6	Sprint ad (fax)	Reprinted by permission of Sprint Communications Company L.P. Photo © Lawrence Fried/The Image Bank
7.1	T-shirts	Photographs © 1992 by Jonathan Atkin
7.2	White Diamonds	Lee Salem/Shooting Star

Number	Description	Credit
7.3	Ford ad	Courtesy of Ford Motor Company
7.4	Gillette ad	Courtesy of The Gillette Company
7.5	Quaker Oats box	Courtesy of The Quaker Oats Company
7.6	Ziploc ad	Photo courtesy of Ziploc® brand sandwich bags
7.7	Betty Crocker ad	Reproduced with permission—Betty Crocker Supreme Dessert Bars
7.8	Energizer ad	© 1993, Eveready Battery Company, Inc.
8.1	Naturistics ad	Naturistics, Div. Del Laboratories, Inc.
8.2	Campbell's products	Campbell Soup
8.3	Ben & Jerry's ad	Courtesy of Ben & Jerry's
8.4	Hugs	Courtesy of Hershey Foods
8.5	Mattell Top Speed team	Alan Levenson
8.6	Mary Rodas, Catco	Catco Inc.
8.7	Jill Shurtleff, Gillette	Damian Strohmeyer
9.1	Waterford ad	Waterford Wedgewood USA, Inc.
9.2	Waldorf-Astoria	Courtesy of The Waldorf-Astoria
9.3A	Buick Le Sabre ad	Used with permission from GM Corp.
9.3B	NEC ad	Used with permission of NEC Corporation
9.4	Toyota ad (company line)	Courtesy of Toyota Motor Sales
9.5	Newspaper coupons	Courtesy of Giant Food, Inc.
9.6	Bentley ad	Reprinted by Permission of Rolls-Royce Motor Cars Inc.
9.7	George Perrin, Page Net	Mark Graham
9.8	Flashbake oven	Courtesy of Quadlux, Inc.
10.1	Mall of America	Courtesy of Mall of America. Photo by Bob Perzel
10.2	Wal-Mart	Steve Starr/Stock, Boston
10.3	Shoe Carnival	Brenda Black/Lewis Toby
10.4	Machine shopping	Courtesy of CreataCard, Inc.
10.5	Sears store	Sears
10.6	Macy's Parade	Lisa Quinones/Black Star
10.7	Strawbridge's	© 1994 John McGrail
10.8A	Old-fashioned Woolworth's	Archive Photos
10.8B	World Foot Locker	Steve Winter/Black Star
10.9	Office Depot interior	Courtesy of Office Depot

Number	Description	Credit
10.10	Lands' End	Courtesy of Lands' End
10.11	Sears' catalogs	Sears
10.12	Donald Jonas, Lechters	Sherrie Nickol/CRAIN'S NEW YORK BUSINESS
11.1	Kroger flowers	Courtesy of Kroger
11.2	Fantastic Sam's	Courtesy of Fantastic Sam's International, Inc.
11.3	Wholesaler	The Southland Corporation
11.4	Perishable products	Courtesy of SUPERVALU, Inc. Photo by James Schnepf.
11.5	JIT system	Ryder Dedicated Logistics
11.6	Tiffany ad	Courtesy of Tiffany & Co.
11.7	Warehouse computer	Ira Wexler/Folio
11.8	Loading containers on ship	Greg Pease/Tony Stone Images
11.9	Doug Loewe, CompuServe	Don Kushnick
11.10	Bryan McNee, CompDesign	Ron Garrison/*Lexington Herald-Leader*
11.11	Hellmann's ad	Hellmann's is a Registered Trademark of CPC International.
12.1	Ambac ad	Courtesy Mullen Advertising and Ambac. Photo © George Simhoni.
12.2	Fingerhut offer	Fingerhut Corporation
12.3	North Carolina ad	North Carolina Department of Commerce
12.4	Looking at coupons	Myrleen Ferguson/PhotoEdit
12.5	Hogan's Market campaign	Graphic Design Firm: Hornall Anderson Design Works. Project Photographer: Tom McMackin. Illustrator: Larry Jost. Calligrapher: Nancy Stentz
12.6	Apple Catalog ad	Courtesy of Apple Computer, Inc.
12.7	Sun Crunchers coupon	Used with permission from Sun Crunchers cereal
12.8	Personal selling	Rhoda Baer/Folio
12.9	Taster's Choice storyboard	Courtesy The Nestlé Beverage Company and McCann-Erickson San Francisco
12.10	Fisher Island ad	Advertisement by McGuire Company, Coral Gables, FL.
12.11	Crash dummies ad	Courtesy of U.S. Department of Transportation
12.12	Ron Shaw, Pilot Pen	Don Kushnick
13.1	DuPont storyboard	Courtesy of DuPont
13.2	Juiceman	Ann Summa
13.3	Absolut ad	Courtesy of TBWA Advertising

Number	Description	Credit
13.4	MacIntosh TV still	Courtesy of Apple Computer, Inc.
13.5	Outdoor Network ad	Gannett Outdoor Group
13.6A	Truck panel ad	Brent Jones/Stock Boston
13.6B	Pepsi sailboat ad	Courtesy of Pepsi-Cola Company
13.6C	Hot-air balloon ad	Vince Streano/Tony Stone Images
13.7	Toyota Women's Conference	Courtesy of Toyota Motor Manufacturing
13.8	Mattress Mack	Doug Milner
14.1	McDonald's drive-thru	McDonald's Corporation
14.2	Traveler's ad	The Travelers Insurance Co. and its Affiliates, Hartford, CT 06183
14.3	American Express sign	Larry Mulvehill/Photo Researchers
14.4	ATM	Robert Rathe/Folio
14.5	Baseball vending machine	Photos by Alvis Upitis
14.6	Service encounter	Jim Pickerell/Tony Stone Images
14.7	Moscow McDonald's	AP/Wide World Photos
14.8	Customer satisfaction card	Mary Ellen Zang
14.9	Toyota ad (Part & Service)	Courtesy of Toyota Motor Sales
14.10	Hampton Inn	Courtesy of Hampton Inns
14.11	Duds 'N' Suds	Courtesy of Duds 'N' Suds
14.12	Dog trainer ad	Todd Godwin and Luis Gomez
14.13	Toronto Zoo ad	Courtesy Chiat/Day Inc. Advertising, Toronto
14.14	National Guard ad	n/a
14.15	Jody Samson	Don Kushnick
15.1	Manager walking around	PhotoEdit
15.2	Participative management	Jeff Zaruba/Folio
15.3	Small business owner	Dan Ham/Tony Stone Images
15.4	Computer graphics	Reprinted from PC MAGAZINE, December 22, 1987. Copyright © 1987 Ziff-Davis Publishing, L.P.
15.5	George Bull	David Levenson

Name Index

Aaker, David A., 134 n
Alexander, K. L., 133, 266 n
Alexander, S., 134 n
Allen, R. L., 333 n
Ames, K., 101 n
Anderson, C., 198 n
Anderson, Hornall, PC–1
Anderson, V., 301
Annin, P., 101 n
Applegate, J., 233 n
Aragon, L., 265 n
Armstrong, G., 168 n
Armstrong, L., 31, 67 n, 302
Arthur, C., 101 n
Atchinson, S. D., 134 n
Atkin, Jonathan, PC–2

Baer, Rhoda, PC–4
Bagozzi, R. P., 35 n
Baker, Jaye, 106
Banks, H., 491
Barad, Jill, 230
Barnathan, J., 169 n
Barrett, A., 265 n, 367 n
Barrett, W. P., 442
Barthel, M. 481
Beall, P., 199 n
Beaver, W., 33
Bennett, B., 364
Bergman, R., 477
Berkwitz, D. N., 147
Berman, P., 333 n
Bernstein, C., 482 n
Berry, J., 401
Berry, L. L., 482 n
Berss, M., 266 n
Bhargava, S. Wadekar, 100, 168 n, 332, 333 n
Biagiotti, Laura, 263
Bianchi, A., 47
Bingaman, R., 65
Bird, L., 134 n, 135 n, 175, 265 n, 443 n, 483 n
Black, Brenda, PC–3
Blackwell, R. D., 127, 134 n

Bleakley, F. R., 134 n
Blumberg, M., 482 n
Blustein, P., 233n
Bohner, K., 483 n
Bollier, D., 130
Bongiorno, L. 401
Bounds, W., 332 n
Bowen, T. S., 1776
Bradburn, E., 266 n
Braichli, M. W., 233
Brandt, R., 514
Bremner, B., 168 n, 169 n
Brenner, J. G., 265 n
Brewer, G., 397
Brockman, F., 437
Brott, A. A., 115
Brown, F., 240
Brown, W., 301
Bruni, F., 109
Bryant, Barbara E., 194
Bulkcley, W. M., 101, 151, 199 n, 231, 302 n, 400
Bull, George J., 511, PC–5
Burgi, M., 199 n
Burke, S., 135 n
Buroughs, D. L., 164
Burroughs, Robert, PC–1
Burton, T. M., 135 n
Byrne, J. A., 20, 514, 514 n

Caggiano, C., 134 n
Caminiti, S., 199 n
Camp, E. J., PC–2
Campanelli, M., 35 n, 443 n
Canaday, H., 481
Carey, J., 199 n, 234 n
Carlson, J., 35 n
Carlton, J., 482 n
Carnevale, M. L., 401 n
Carney, K., 208
Carroll, A. B., 130
Carroll, P. B., 67 n
Carson, Rachel, 125–126
Carver, Barbara, 261
Case, J., 482 n, 515 n

Castro, Fidel, 269
Cateora, P. R., 90, 168 n, 515 n
Cauley, L., 443 n
Chakravarty, S. N., 515 n
Champy, J., 514 n
Chideya, F., 101 n
Chin, Ted, 106
Chipello, C. J., 399, 493
Cho, N. J., 168 n
Chonko, L. B., 107
Choo, A. L., 167
Churbuck, D. C., 199 n, 477
Claiborne, G., 483 n
Clancy, C., 444 n
Clancy, K. J., 233 n
Clark, J., 168 n
Clark, J. B., 515 n
Classe, A., 198 n
Cleland, K., 373
Clift, V., 23
Clinton, Bill, 28
Cody, J., 354, 366
Cohen, A., 261, 362
Cohen, Ben, 112–113
Coleman, L. G., 199 n
Contreras, J., 115
Cooper, H., 483 n
Copeland, Melvin T., 207, 233 n
Corey, E. R., 134 n
Cosby, R. L., 443 n
Cowan, Dan, PC–2
Cox, A. D., 101 n
Cox, D., 101 n
Cox, Keith, 442
Cox, M., 444 n
Crispell, D., 198 n, 317
Cronin, M. P., 65, 134 n
Culnan, M. J., 402
Cuneo, A. Z., 35 n
Curry, L., 169 n
Cyrus, Billy Ray, 475
Czepiel, J. A., 67 n, 233 n
Czinkota, M., 196

Dangerfield, Rodney, 397
David, K., 168 n

Company Index

Subject Index